4,5

ACCOUNTING CONCEPTS
OF PROFIT

By

STEPHEN GILMAN

CERTIFIED PUBLIC ACCOUNTANT. VICE PRESIDENT AND EDUCATIONAL
DIRECTOR, INTERNATIONAL ACCOUNTANTS SOCIETY, INC.

THE RONALD PRESS COMPANY
NEW YORK

6

Library of Congress catalog card number 39-12150

PRINTED IN THE UNITED STATES OF AMERICA

PUBLISHERS' FOREWORD

Published in 1939, this book was written to summarize and interpret the basic accounting principles affecting income determination which had developed over the years but had not hitherto been organized and presented in book form. Many of its concepts have since been accepted as standard by the consensus of accounting opinion and practice, while others have inevitably been superseded by later developments. But the book as a whole remains today a classic treatment of accounting theory.

The book was widely reviewed and discussed in the years following publication, and its influence has since made itself felt in ever broadening circles. Encouraged by the continued interest, the Publishers are pleased to reissue this volume in its original form in the belief that it has a contribution to make to a rising generation, often working in different circumstances, but concerned as always with the same fundamental problems.

THE RONALD PRESS COMPANY
PUBLISHERS

January 1956

PREFACE

The justification for this book is to be found in the history of the past half-dozen years which have witnessed a shift in accounting emphasis from the balance sheet to the profit and loss viewpoint.

Some to whom this volume is addressed may not be aware of the far-reaching effects of this changed emphasis. I refer, of course, to those having some general knowledge of accounting together with a collateral interest in accounting problems, particularly lawyers, engineers, economists, statisticians, credit men, investors, and business managers. Accountants, professionally and privately engaged, for whom this book is more directly intended, know of the present dominant importance of the profit and loss statement and are informed of some of the accounting confusions resulting therefrom. Because of the pressure of daily work many accountants have found it impossible to keep in touch with the numerous current discussions, arguments, and viewpoints referring to income determinations, particularly so since no small amount of research is required even to locate and assemble the various significant materials from a great variety of books, booklets, periodicals, releases, bulletins, and other scattered technical and business sources published in the past half-dozen years. Such assembly, together with critical comparison and attempted interpretation, was a necessary prerequisite to the preparation of this book. To the accountant in search of accounting "principles" articulating with present-day practice, this work primarily has been directed.

Is it possible to discuss profits without extravagant repetition and restatement of the scholarly treatments of the same subject by such undoubted authorities as Hatfield, Paton, Littleton, Canning, Kester, and others? What can be added to their views? What new materials are available? What new influences must be considered? These are questions of primary importance to any author attempting to write in this field.

There is, perhaps, little that is novel in connection with income accounting. Nevertheless, the events of recent years have indicated concepts demanding reinvestigation and have disclosed certain conflicts and inconsistencies.

While the basic problems of profit determination are nearly as old as accounting itself, it is hoped that a somewhat different approach may justify this present study. In this there may be some similarity to the problem of the artist who, with standard implements, familiar materials and an often-posed subject, must create something different by selection and emphasis.

Exercising the same liberty I have attempted to present in an organized pattern the more important conventions, doctrines, and rules which influence the determination of accounting profits, while at the same time avoiding certain areas which have been discussed voluminously and adequately by others and in which coercive legal influence is most marked. One of these areas refers to income taxation. It is well recognized that the computation of taxable income is controlled by special considerations which do not necessarily influence the procedure of ascertaining accounting profits. Another area is also highly legalistic. I refer to corporation accounting in relation to profits, surplus, and reserves and the numerous problems bearing upon distributions to stockholders. For somewhat similar reasons little reference has been made to the net profit problems of utilities, railroads, or other industries the accounting for which is specified by governmental authority.

Rather than attempt an encyclopedic treatment, it has seemed preferable to emphasize two common types of accounts which are particularly important in their relation to accounting profits. Accordingly, a substantial number of chapters have been devoted to net profit problems arising from inventories and fixed assets, these two categories representing vehicles for the discussion of profit determination and profit distortion, in the belief that the conclusions reached will be applicable generally to other categories.

I recognize that the phrase "accounting profits" is not in general use. Occasionally the term has been found helpful by economists for the same reason that it has been adopted here, i.e., to distinguish the final result of the strictly accounting computation from those other concepts known variously as "pure profits," "taxable profits," and "distributable profits."

If I have inadvertently misquoted or misinterpreted the writings of others, or if I have failed to give credit where credit was due, I can only hope for charitable forbearance since the responsibility for errors is wholly mine. On the other hand, credit for much that is good in this volume must go to those who have helped me.

A debt of gratitude is acknowledged to John T. Madden and to his associates, Clarence W. Fackler, Gould L. Harris, Herbert B. Dorau, and Frederick Dannenberg, not only for help and counsel in the preparation of this manuscript but for invaluable research work in connection with certain phases of the subject matter. Special mention must be made of the contribution of Lawrence W. Robson of London, England, who provided original material on the English history of inventory valuation, with particular reference to the rule of cost or market.

Last in order of mention, but first in their claims upon my gratitude, are the two men who assumed the burdensome and difficult task of reading and criticizing this manuscript. With great patience and at a considerable sacrifice of their time, W. A. Paton and Paul W. Pinkerton furnished me such a wealth of critical and constructive suggestions as to put me deeply in their debt.

STEPHEN GILMAN

Chicago, Ill.
March 1939

CONTENTS

CHAPTER I

vii

realization—trading merchandise for fixed assets, dividends received in property, dividends received in merchandise, dividends received in securities, donations, buildings of lessee reverting to lessor, accretion, construction contracts, sale of services. Provision for doubtful accounts—correction of income, reporting correction of income, doubtful installment accounts. Inventories and income realization—anticipation of profits, production theory of income, inventory overstatement and the entity. Conclusion.

CHAPTER 9

Cost accounting. General accounting. Time and amount uncertainties. Practical difficulties of matching. Averaging of costs. Inventory revaluation. Conservatism.

CHAPTER 10

Entity losses and gains. The allocation of unusual items. Need for mutually exclusive classification. A fourfold classification illustrated. Surplus adjustments. Reconstruction of prior statements. Distortion of operating results. Income from correction of understated assets. Comparison of three common methods. Commonly accepted practice.

CHAPTER 11

Important corporate characteristics—legal entity, continuous life, limited liability, delegated management. Types of corporate ownership. Corporate profit determination. Control of the corporation. Secret reserves. Disclosure to stockholders. Corporate complexity—affiliated corporations, unrealized profits, consolidated statements. Initial valuation of corporate assets. Treasury stock—profit and loss on sale, analysis by entity convention, opinions of authorities, balance sheet classification, dividends on treasury stock, retired stock. Conclusion.

CHAPTER 12

Elaboration of accounting—increasing complexity of business, increasing problems of business. Accounting precedents. Principles of accounting. New form of certificate. Disagreement as to principles. Attempts to formulate principles. Difficulties in formulating principles—the accounting period

—current vs. non-current, current subclassification, valuation accounts, special receivables, supplies, non-current subclassification, land, deferred charges. Liability classification—current liabilities, non-current liabilities, reserves, details of current liabilities, non-current subdivision, proprietorship classification.

CHAPTER 18

Primary classification of proprietorship. Corporate proprietorship. Types of surplus—revaluation surplus, the problem of surplus accounts, earned surplus, availability for dividends. Profit and loss classification—primary subdivision, American Institute classification, income, costs and expenses, incidental operations, functional classification, significance of profit and loss divisions, allocation, distortion and consistency, final net profit. The profit and loss statement. Accounting history and disclosure.

CHAPTER 19

Expenditures and income. Costs, expenses, and losses—cost valuation, entity valuation, elements of cost, difficulties of cost valuation, barter, trade-ins. Assets as deferred charges—the deferred charge concept, tests for classification, rearrangement of balance sheet. Nature of inventories—inventories and fixed assets, inventory revaluation, inventory characteristics. Intent as a test of classification. Apportionments and transfers—convention of transferred values, modification of convention. Recovery of deferred charges.

CHAPTER 20

Expenditures of the insurance type—kinds of insurance, nature of insurance costs, insurance and valuation, charitable donations, taxes, legal expenditures, graft, bribery, and espionage. Organization expense—balance sheet viewpoint, profit and loss viewpoint. Special cost problems. Imputed costs—economic recognition of imputed costs, accounting for imputed costs, imputed costs in manufacturing, imputed depreciation, imputed interest in manufacturing, premium on retired bonds, other imputed costs. Reabsorbed costs—coal mining, farming, institutions, reabsorption and accounting theory. Joint costs—economic recognition of joint costs, accounting recognition of joint costs, joint costs and profits. Expenditures and time lags—small enterprises, large enterprises, convention of transferred values, non-manufacturing time lags, sales promotion costs, future service and guarantee costs.

and net sales—allowances and returns, incidence of allowances
and returns, provision for doubtful accounts, erroneous provisions, price and volume in sales, seasonal fluctuations.   Inventories—errors of bias, errors of compensation, the cost
basis.   Cost of sales—matching cost and income, matching
and dollar valuation, historical limitations of accounting, fixed
and variable costs.   Gross profit on sales—departmental gross
profits, departmental profit interpretation, comparability of
gross profits, accounting doctrines and gross profit, significance of gross profit components, sales volume, apportionments, final costs.

CHAPTER 33

Selling, general, and administrative expense.   The break-even
point—fixed, semi-fixed, and variable, historical method, weaknesses of historical method, current analysis method, use by
financial analysts, use by management.   Percentage analyses—
common report practice, comparative statements, other examples, deceptive comparisons.   Distortion—lack of matching, changed business policies, profits and salaries.   Significance of net operating profit.

CHAPTER 34

Components of other income.   Components of other charges.
Summary of viewpoints.   Surplus and reserves—surplus as
a liability, contingency reserves, disposition of reserve balances, intent in the creation of reserve, disclosure of reserve
changes.   Net profit and the investor.   Net profit and business management.

CHAPTER 35

The ingredients of accounting.   Specialized profit concepts.
Accounting profit and accounting conventions.   Entity vs.
proprietary viewpoint.   Viewpoints toward asset values—distributions to stockholders, income and profits, realization,
other influences.   A concept of accounting profit.   Opinions
of authorities.   Distortion and inconsistency.   Conclusion.

ACCOUNTING
CONCEPTS OF PROFIT

CHAPTER 1

INTRODUCTION

Established institutions and traditional viewpoints in numerous areas have been and are being criticized. Accordingly it causes no surprise that long-established accounting doctrines, conventions, and rules are being challenged; that accounting practices are being scrutinized; that the limitations imposed by accounting precedent are being investigated.

Current criticisms of accounting originate to some extent within the profession itself, but more often they are heard from those who use or rely upon accounting figures.

Three Groups of Critics.—In general, accounting is undergoing examination and criticism by three groups: (1) those who misunderstand the accounting mechanism itself, (2) those who misunderstand accounting terminology, and (3) those who understand both the accounting mechanism and accounting terminology but who wish to improve accounting by adding to its functions.

MISUNDERSTANDING OF THE ACCOUNTING MECHANISM. There can be little doubt that many, to their sorrow, have failed to understand the conventional limitations of accounting.

Losses have been suffered by investors who believed that asset valuations appearing on balance sheets were realizable amounts. Serious consequences have occasionally befallen creditors who have failed to understand the relationship between the elements constituting current assets and the effect thereof on the comparison of current assets and current liabilities. Mistakes have been made by business men whose decisions and policies were based upon misinterpretation of conventional accounting for income and cost.

These investors, creditors, and business men have at times

3

felt free to criticize accounting and accountants. Often these criticisms are based not only upon a misunderstanding of the accounting mechanism but also upon overly narrow viewpoints. Failure to understand that balance sheets and profit and loss statements are usually general-purpose statements intended for the enlightenment not merely of the creditor or the investor or the business manager, but all of them, has been responsible for some of the criticisms heard.

These viewpoints have perhaps been responsible for certain published comments of which a few samples may be of some interest.

One author expresses his belief that profit and loss statements might as well never be made unless the management can determine from them the things that are necessary to "steer the ship." Another suggests that accounting "is no good and it should not exist" unless it offers some real aid to management in the making of profit. Such overemphasis of one viewpoint is echoed by the quotation "accounting to be scientific must prescribe what to do in order to make a business profitable."

There is, to be sure, an important management aspect to accounting reports. Many decisions, policies, and programs made by business men in their search for greater profits are based upon the analysis and interpretation of accounting records.

ACCOUNTING TERMINOLOGY.   Accounting can be greatly misunderstood by those who are unfamiliar with accounting terminology. Such words and phrases as "current assets," "net worth," "surplus," "value," "capital," "revenue," "fund," and "reserve" are commonly employed by accountants, to whom their meanings usually are clear. Laymen, however, sometimes fail to understand those meanings and as a result may be led into confused thinking.

DISSATISFACTION WITH ACCOUNTING LIMITATIONS.   The third group of critics, while recognizing the limitations of accounting, express dissatisfaction with them.

Generally such dissatisfaction refers to the conventions, doctrines, and rules underlying (1) the determination of net profit, and (2) the valuation of assets. Among criticisms of the first group is one written by an accountant who asserts that "the accepted method of making up profit and loss statements is remarkable for its obscuring of its essential facts." An economist speaks of "the distorting influence of business accounting practices." Another commentator suggests that the public "cannot know what any company's profit really is."

These and similar criticisms will be regarded by many as trivial. It is, however, none too easy for the accounting traditionalist to be amused at the decision made by a financial analyst connected with a well-known investment service to adopt dividends paid as a more satisfactory measuring rod than reported profits. In explaining his decision he said, "This involves no 'accounting practice,' no 'adjustments,' no 'bookkeeping.'"

Criticisms of accounting valuation are even more numerous. One author compares the traditional methods of valuation to "measuring a field with a rubber tape line." Another comments, "One could as well say, 'I bought a cat yesterday and a dog today. I now own two dogs.' The dollar spent two years ago is a different measure from the dollar spent today." A third, concerned with the valuation of total assets, has observed that "measures with instruments of precision should not be added to measures made with instruments of approximation or estimate."

Thoughtful men have long been aware of the dangers in using money as a unit of measurement, this unit not being a common denominator when values originating in different periods are compared.

Henry W. Sweeney in his various writings, and particularly in his book *Stabilized Accounting,* has discussed this problem at length. Sweeney is concerned with the investor's real income in terms of purchasing power as compared with his fictitious income in terms of the dollar as a unit. When an individual makes an investment, he surrenders a certain measure of purchasing power. Instead of buying $1,000 worth of groceries, meat, rent, or transportation, he saves the money and entrusts it to another in the hope of ultimate gain. Some years later, after the general price level has increased, he may have received from his investment a profit in terms of dollars but have suffered a loss in terms of groceries, meats, rent, and transportation. Sweeney proposes a plan of stabilized accounting for the purpose of reporting asset values and profits in dollars adjusted to a purchasing power basis. The plan is somewhat elaborate, involving adjustments based upon an established system of index numbers.

His proposal has been given serious consideration by accounting thinkers. During severe inflationary periods his plan, or a variation of it, may be almost a necessity.

It is, however, rather unlikely that stabilized accounting will win much acceptance until an actual inflation sets in, since there is no powerful group behind it and no tax-saving advantage inherent in it.

There are, perhaps, two possible objections to stabilized accounting.

One of them refers to viewpoint. Accounting, as will be seen, is founded upon the viewpoint of an entity separate and distinct from its owners or other sources of capital. Sweeney's plan is in reality not a suggestion for improving accounting but rather a method of interpreting accounting statements and reports in terms of the individual investor.

Furthermore, the use of a general price index for the purpose of modifying dollar values and dollar results assumes that all investors are alike, having the same purchasing habits. This assumption is probably a necessary one because of the utter impossibility of constructing a special price index for each individual investor. In a given case, had his money not been invested it might have been spent for luxuries, automobiles, yachts, pleasure trips, pedigreed cattle, or night clubs instead of food, clothing, and rent.

Until price indexes have been constructed for luxury items, the investor who refrains from buying luxuries in order to put his money into Steel common is not going to be interested in the same index adjustment as the investor who actually sacrifices food, clothing, and shelter.

Methods of Examining Accounting Propositions.—The proposal to scrutinize the so-called inadequacies of accounting in relation to profit determination implies some methodology. Accounting, unfortunately, is not a field in which technique of controlled experimentation may be used. There are, however, certain devices commonly used for testing accounting propositions. While overliberality in the application of these methods may be considered academic, they do on occasion serve useful purposes, as has been well recognized by nearly all accounting writers. These methods are of three general types.

THE REVERSAL TEST. An accounting proposition may often be examined by the reversal test in which one transaction or one situation is examined from two different aspects, i.e., the viewpoints of a buying company and of a selling company, and the consistency or inconsistency of decisions which might be made by an accountant serving both.

THE EXAGGERATION TEST. Another common method of examining an accounting proposition is by exaggerating it in some of its terms, thus reducing it to absurdity.

Extravagant amounts may be substituted for immaterial ones or long accounting periods may be substituted for annual or monthly periods. This method is often used by those who are opposed to surplus adjustments when they point out that the profit shown by one profit and loss statement for a ten-year period would not be the same as the aggregate of the profits reported by ten annual statements.

IDENTICAL COMPANY TEST. A third method of examining an accounting proposition is by the identical company test or, more accurately, the identical entity test. In its customary form this involves the assumption that two or more different business entities can be absolutely identical in every respect save one. This provides an imaginary controlled experiment and results in a comparison which is often helpful in dramatizing or clarifying some moot point or in showing deviations from some assumed standard. Illustrative of this test is the assumption of two hypothetical business organizations identical in every way except that one uses, for example, the last-in, first-out method of inventory while the other uses the first-in, first-out method.

These tests are often valuable and where appropriate will be used from time to time in this book as helpful aids in the examination of problems having to do with accounting profit.

Inherent Limitations of Accounting.—While references earlier in this chapter could have been expanded considerably, probably enough have been noted to indicate that there exists a body of opinion which is critical of orthodox theory and practice.

Since criticisms may be based in part upon improper conceptions of accounting conventions, it is one purpose of this volume to examine these conventions in an attempt to determine the natural limitations of the accounting mechanism.

Approach to Accounting Profits.—Fundamental to this study of accounting profits is the assumption that accounting itself represents not one area but rather the overlapping of three areas: (1) statistics, (2) economics, and (3) law.

The statistical phase of accounting consists of simple enumeration and classification. Historical in nature and employing monetary measures exclusively, this statistical phase is conventionalized in harmony with a certain basic formula which provides a simple partial proof of clerical accuracy by balancing.

This conventionalized statistical plan generally refers to economic phenomena, primarily to the movements of money, or of property translated into terms of money, or the exchange of one for the other, in relation to individuals and groups of individuals having possession of, or having claims of one sort or another against, such money or property.

Because economic phenomena often affect the public interest, generally from the investor's, creditor's, consumer's, employee's, or tax collector's viewpoint, the overlapping effect of law must also be considered.

Sometimes it has been found helpful to think of statistics, economics, and law from another viewpoint. In some respects they may be considered as ingredients, in varying proportions, of a mechanical mixture. The properties or characteristics of a batch of concrete, for example, cannot be understood without first knowing the relative proportions of water, cement, and gravel. Similarly, the characteristics of accounting in any given situation can only be described in terms of the statistical, economic, and legal ingredients.[1]

It is, of course, true that there are many elements of similarity in the accounting for an automobile repair shop and for the United States Steel Corporation; for a hospital and a book store; for a railroad and a meat packing establishment. These similarities, however, are often of less importance than the dissimilarities. Dissimilarities may often be accounted for by the varying proportions and characteristics of the statistical, economic, and legal ingredients. To discuss accounting, and particularly accounting profits, without giving consideration to these ingredients must result in confusion.

In so far as it is practicably feasible to do so, this present study will attempt identification and isolation of these ingredients. Particularly it will attempt to eliminate the various effects of the legal element. The legal element in modern accounting is not only arbitrary and coercive but often capricious. To eliminate this influence seems to be the first step in an attempt to establish a general concept of accounting profit.

If accounting profit can be found to result from certain conventions, doctrines, and rules, then it seems that a norm which is practically independent of the legal influence and which should be helpful in gauging the extent of such influence in any individual situation can be established.

Obviously, this method of stating the problem does not deny but rather emphasizes the almost overwhelming influence of law as an essential ingredient in modern accounting and particularly in the computation of accounting profits.

Sequence of Presentation.—Some of the more important characteristics of accounting are the natural result of the conventions upon which it is based. Because the influence of these conventions upon the computation of accounting profits is con-

---

1 There are probably other ingredients of modern accounting but their recognition and isolation do not seem important to this study. The one exception to this statement refers to reporting, i.e., occasionally it has been necessary to conceive of reporting as a field separate and distinct from accounting. The conception can probably be justified since the methods and technique of reporting are not confined to accounting but are the same or nearly the same in such unrelated fields as engineering, law, economics, sociology, or the experimental sciences. The distinction between reporting and accounting can, however, be ignored in connection with most of the topics in this book.

trolling, it is these conventions which must receive first consideration in the present study.

The first eleven chapters of this volume are devoted to a consideration of the basic accounting conventions, their historical development, and their profit and loss incidence.

While the conventions are of primary importance because they control the design of accounting, there are also certain doctrines, rules, and principles[2] which exercise even greater effects upon the profit calculation. These doctrines, rules, and principles are given consideration in Chapters 12 through 16.

Account classification in general and profit and loss classification in particular are the topics for discussion in Chapters 17 and 18, while the relation of expenditures to income represents the subject matter of Chapters 19 through 21.

Chapters 22 through 27 refer to what is often the most important single asset category, namely, inventories. The relation of inventories to accounting profits is direct and of first significance.

Sometimes equal or greater in importance are fixed assets. The relationship between fixed assets and accounting profits is the subject matter of the next four chapters, 28 through 31.

The next three chapters of the book deal with the three primary classifications of the profit and loss statement. In these three chapters an attempt is made to reach tentative conclusions as to the nature of accounting profit and the more important factors which predetermine its characteristics. The final chapter is, of course, a summary.

Briefly, this sequence appears as follows:

Accounting Conventions (Chapters 1-11)
Doctrines, Rules, and Principles (Chapters 12-16)
Classification (Chapters 17-18)
Expenditures and Income (Chapters 19-21)
Inventories (Chapters 22-27)
Fixed Assets (Chapters 28-31)
Profit and Loss Statement (Chapters 32-34)
Summary (Chapter 35)

---

[2] This and any other reference to "principles of accounting" should be considered only in relationship to the discussion in Chapters 12 to 16, inclusive. While the phrase is one in common use, its propriety is questionable.

CHAPTER 2

EXTERNAL INFLUENCES ON ACCOUNTING

Accounting differs from some other specialized fields because of the large number of laymen who are somewhat familiar with its basic mechanism, its fundamental conventions, and its general characteristics.

More than one profession has found its cloak of mystery rather advantageous. Notably this is true of law and medicine. That such mystery is an accidental by-product of historical development can hardly be doubted but if anyone had deliberately set out to create a technical atmosphere for the purpose of puzzling laymen he would have done well to include in his program the invention of a terminology which would inspire awe and wonderment and discourage any attempt to make suggestions for the improvement of professional technique.

The impressive use of Latin phrases by both lawyers and doctors, the convention of special technical meanings for common words as in law, the complex system of reference which makes effective use of a legal library impossible to the unenlightened, the strangeness of the hieroglyphics used by physicians in writing prescriptions; all these help to build up an atmosphere which can hardly fail to have some relationship to professional fees. Few of the uninitiated ever attempt to penetrate these technical mysteries.

The value of an accountant's work, however, depends so completely upon his ability to make others understand it that a far different situation prevails in accounting. Someone has said that every man thinks of himself as competent to manage a newspaper, a farm, or a hotel. Similarly, many apparently feel themselves competent to discuss, criticize, and improve accounting. The economist, who would resent having any accountant venture into his own technical specialty, often discusses accounting problems with the conviction of authority. The engineer suggests improvements in industrial accounting, cost analysis, the treatment of depreciation, or the recording of factory inventories. Often statisticians, bankers, business men, lawyers, and legislators offer critical and sometimes constructive comments regarding accounting matters.

This lay conviction of expertness has created a situation which is none too happy. The willingness of experts in other fields to contribute to the accounting fraternity has often tended to create confusion. It therefore seems desirable briefly to consider the relation of accounting to some of these other fields of activity.

Groups Served by Accounting.—Accounting serves many different purposes and groups.

The original accounting mechanism probably was designed to serve chiefly the proprietors of business—those men who were both owners and managers. Because of the growth of the corporate form of organization, the separation of business ownership and business management, the great increase in the number of corporate shareholders, the development of large-scale operations, and more recently the adoption of income taxes, the simple mechanism of accounting was expanded to serve not only proprietors and their appointed managers but also bondholders, bank creditors, merchandise creditors, taxing bodies, regulatory bodies, lawyers, and engineers, and later financial statisticians, investment counselors, economists, legislators, investigating committees, and consumer groups.

Reflecting the resulting difficulties Kester,[1] in his review of *A Statement of Accounting Principles,* says:

> Government bureaus and regulatory bodies and self-appointed bodies, such as security exchanges, have given impetus to the formulation of accounting principles and have even taken the lead in the statement of them. Such statements have in general theory been set forth as "accepted accounting principles," although unfortunately in some instances they have been arbitrary assumptions or determinations of what such accepted principles are, or what they should be in order best to serve the purpose of the one formulating them.

[1] Roy B. Kester, *The Journal of Accountancy,* March 1938, p. 265.

In the June 1938 issue of *The Journal of Accountancy,* Montgomery[2] speaks "of the conflicting views of economists, courts and accountants which are deemed to be irreconcilable within the lives of accountants now living and 21 years thereafter."

A strong opinion was reflected by Carman[3] in his assertion that "accountancy has been shaped almost entirely by outward circumstances. Accounting thought has lain dormant for generations at a time, arousing itself sluggishly for self-improvement only after it has been kicked awake."

Barr[4] believes that: "accountants seem too willing to be ruled by law rather than economics."

Referring specifically to the inventory rule of cost or market, Husband[5] asserts that it is "a concession to the viewpoint of management, creditors, prospective investors, etc., and is inconsistent with the ownership procedure of presenting historical costs."

It is common knowledge among accountants that when lawyers, economists, and business men discuss accounting, they often misunderstand its most elementary concepts.

All in all, it is a matter for considerable dismay that laymen should consider themselves competent to influence accounting while keeping a respectful distance from the ceremonials and technical areas of other professions.

To one who looks upon accounting as a conventional mechanism for recording financial history, some of the proposals which have been made to distort that history seem to resemble the efforts of a former Chicago mayor to eliminate from the public library certain volumes of English history which contradicted him in his red-herring campaign against the English king. History is history whether palatable or not, and while it may be improperly recorded or conventionally distorted, the

2 Robert H. Montgomery, "Dealings in Treasury Stock," *The Journal of Accountancy,* June 1938, p. 478.

3 Lewis A. Carman, "Primary Accounting Concepts," *The Journal of Accountancy,* May 1936, p. 348.

4 Andrew Barr, in his comments on "A Statement of Accounting Principles," by Paton, *The Journal of Accountancy,* April 1938, p. 323.

5 George R. Husband, "Accounting Postulates: An Analysis of the Tentative Statement of Accounting Principles," *The Accounting Review,* December 1937, p. 390.

accountant knows that there is no justification for deliberate misrepresentation.

Legal Influence on Accounting.—Adequate portrayal of the extent of legal incidence upon accounting would require not a few pages but an entire volume. It is, however, generally conceded that this influence has had profound and far-reaching effects, some good, some bad, some based upon clear thinking, some based upon confusion and misunderstanding. Much of it has been irritating to accountants, as indicated by the criticism of May[6] that "lawyers apparently seek to atone for the bewildering complexities they have introduced into their own sphere of activity by insisting on the utmost simplicity in other spheres." Stewart[7] asserts that "the legal concepts of accounting and its terminology, unfortunately, do not conform, in many instances, to accepted principles of accounting."

More vigorous is this statement by Montgomery:[8]

The aphorism "A little learning is a dangerous thing" has its exemplification in the treatment given by many lawyers to questions of accounting. They often have the temerity to settle matters of the greatest importance, involving complicated accounts, without any evidence that anyone who understands accounts has been consulted in the settlement.

Fisher[9] told the American Institute of Accountants that:

The existence of federal and state penal statutes, of corporation laws, of state statutes imposing civil liabilities, of state and federal regulatory and administrative bodies, as well as the presence of numerous court decisions, establishes extensive control of the practices and concepts of the accounting profession.

Cochrane[10] warned the Dominion Association of Chartered Accountants that "professions, like accounting, must of necessity fall in line with any edict issued by the government. There is no redress for business or the professions."

6 George O. May, *Twenty-Five Years of Accounting Responsibility 1911-1936* (New York, American Institute Publishing Co., Inc., 1936), p. 275.
7 Andrew Stewart, "Accountancy and Regulatory Bodies in the United States," *The Journal of Accountancy*, January 1938, p. 56.
8 Robert H. Montgomery, *Auditing Theory and Practice* (New York, The Ronald Press Company, 1934), p. 470.
9 Editorial, *The Journal of Accountancy*, November 1938, p. 281.
10 George Cochrane, in an address before the Dominion Association of Chartered Accountants, *The Canadian Chartered Accountant*, October 1938, p. 265.

An editorial in *The Journal of Accountancy*[9] said:

The statutory law, which by its very nature must be controlling, is written by lawyers, with a lawyer's concept of duty. When it treats of accounting matters, it frequently conflicts with what accountants have come to look upon as "accepted practices."

The general classification of lawyers includes, in addition to practicing attorneys, national and state legislators, taxing bodies, and the personnel of various regulatory groups such as the Interstate Commerce Commission, the Securities and Exchange Commission, the Federal Trade Commission, various state public utility commissions, and last but not least, the courts.

CORPORATION LAWS AND DECISIONS. An important incidence of law upon accounting is noted in connection with corporation statutes which contain requirements which may definitely affect accounting practice.

The general purpose of such statutes is praiseworthy, since few will deny the importance of protecting creditors and stockholders. The phrasing of such laws or their interpretation by the courts may not be so acceptable to accountants who may find themselves somewhat baffled thereby.

For years many accountants winked at obvious overvaluations in new corporations because of legal restrictions against selling original stock issues at less than par. Promoters were forced to pay for the stock of a newly created corporation in overvalued property. Part of the stock thus received was then donated back to the corporation, legally becoming treasury stock which could be sold to the public at any price. Had not this method of evasion been invented, the formation of needed enterprises would have been impossible and yet the final result was to put fixed assets upon the books of corporations at inflated valuations.

In their attempts to devise laws referring to such accounting matters as profits and surplus, legislators frequently have been ill advised.

Legal misunderstanding of surplus has long been a sore point with accountants. Many have lived in hope that lawyers would finally take the trouble to find out what accounting surplus and other proprietorial accounts really signify, but no longer ago than April 1938, Paton[11] noted that "the primary encouragement for a breaking down of a simple and useful classification of net worth is found in our lax and confusing legal situation."

During the worst of the 1929 depression, at a time when all security values were tumbling, great fear was felt for life insurance companies. It was proposed that market values of insurance company investments be disregarded and another method of valuation adopted which would present not so disastrous a showing. With reference to this proposal Stewart[12] commented: "Perhaps this novel method of valuation of investment securities was justified from the viewpoint of public policy and because of the existing emergency; however, the principle of valuation of assets by governmental fiat in a published balance-sheet finds no sanction in the tenets of sound accounting principles."

INCOME TAX LAWS. It is in relation to taxation that the greatest amount of confusion is found.

Using accounting data, forms, and terminology, taxing authorities, because of their special requirements and special interpretations, have put taxpayers in the uncomfortable position of (a) changing their accounting systems to conform to tax requirements, (b) maintaining parallel accounting records, one for tax purposes and the other for business purposes, or (c) making numerous adjustments and reconciliations of accounting records in order to obtain figures appropriate for tax reports.

Differences are noted in the treatment of depreciation not only of operating assets but of idle and excess facilities. Different methods of depreciation may be used. Different treatment is required for certain types of expense deductions such as bad debts, capital losses, charitable contributions, officers' salaries, and the cost of lobbying or other protection

---

11 W. A. Paton, "Is It Desirable to Distinguish between Various Kinds of Surplus," *The Journal of Accountancy*, April 1938, p. 286.
12 Andrew Stewart, "Accountancy and Regulatory Bodies in the United States," *The Journal of Accountancy*, January 1938, p. 59.

against punitive legislation. Different viewpoints are maintained toward gross income, particularly as to its allocation to accounting periods or its recognition as in the cases of donated property, interest on government bonds, and capital gains.

Some of these differences are due to special tax considerations and are necessary even if in conflict with sound accounting usages. Others are designed to protect the government against tricks of tax avoidance and hence appear to be justified.

As will be seen in subsequent chapters, inventory practices have long been affected by tax considerations. The illogical rule of cost or market, while not originating in this country, became popular here upon the advent of the Federal income tax program. Paton[13] says that: "The early American enthusiasm for the device—among trade associations, business managements, and corporate accountants—was not a tribute to the merits of the scheme as a worthwhile accounting mechanism—but as an immediate method of reducing taxable income." He adds that the cost or market rule is not time-honored and that "it waxed on account of considerations far removed from the development of sound accounting."

ACCOUNTING INDEPENDENCE.   Some have feared the effect upon accounting practice due to resentment of accountants against tax inequities.

Accountants as professional men have long been jealous of their reputations for fairness and independence. As a matter of professional ethics they have consistently refused to take the position of advocates. Despite the fact that the client pays the fee, the public accountant is bound to occupy an independent position between the client and the government.

There is, however, a new trend in the philosophy of taxation, as has been pointed out by Hugh Johnson[14] as follows:

It had already been decided that the taxing power need not be restricted to the object of raising revenue. It is the power to destroy.

---

13 W. A. Paton, "Comments on 'A Statement of Accounting Principles,'" *The Journal of Accountancy*, March 1938, p. 202.
14 General Hugh Johnson, "Vested Interests in Government Spending," *Proceedings of the Academy of Political Science* (New York, The Academy of Political Science, January 1938), p. 481.

If it can be used to destroy, it can probably be used for any lesser purpose—such as to punish, prevent, restrict and regulate anything within the now infinitely broadened scope of the taxing power.

If taxation is to be used as a punitive instrument, accountants with their essential ideas of fairness may find it difficult to retain their professional independence. They may, like the lawyers, become advocates. The effect of such a change would be far-reaching and disastrous in its effect upon accounting.

To the layman who believes that income taxes have proved highly profitable to accountants, it may seem strange that accountants have complained, often so bitterly, about tax inequities.

Thus Canning[15] speaks of "ill-considered and changing statistical determinations of taxable income," while Byerly[16] writes: "the income-tax point of view has, I think, affected the ideas as to sound accounting which have insinuated themselves into many of us." Stempf,[17] Chairman of the American Institute Committee on Federal Taxation, refers to the "ever-widening breach between 'tax accounting' and 'business accounting.'" He thinks[18] also that "too many managements, and likewise accountants, permit tax attitudes to color their reasoning and distort the application of sound principles of accounting." Even the fair and conservative *Journal of Accountancy*[19] commented editorially upon one income tax ruling in these words: "General counsel's memorandum 20021, promulgated in May, 1938, again exemplifies the needlessly irritating and futile variance between commercial practice and the highly legalistic concept of income held by the Bureau of Internal Revenue."

Some reference should also be made to conflicts between accounting and governmental bodies and controls such as the late NRA, the Robinson-Patman Act, the Federal Trade Com-

15 John B. Canning, *The Economics of Accountancy* (New York, The Ronald Press Company, 1929), p. 195.
16 F. P. Byerly, "Formulation of Accounting Principles or Conventions," *The Journal of Accountancy*, August 1937, p. 96.
17 Victor H. Stempf, "Recommendations for Amendment of Federal Revenue Act," *The Journal of Accountancy*, May 1938, p. 380.
18 Victor H. Stempf, "Accounting for Fixed Assets," *N.A.C.A. Bulletin*, April 15, 1938, p. 939.
19 Editorial, *The Journal of Accountancy*, July 1938, p. 5.

mission, the Securities and Exchange Commission, and the Interstate Commerce Commission. Haskell,[20] referring to two great industries, asserted that the grief they were suffering might be due to the "fact that in perhaps no other fields of business activity have accounting and reporting methods been subject to such variegated and detailed regulation by nonprofessional and nonbusiness regulatory agencies."

Economic Influence on Accounting.—Next, a brief view of the relationship between economics and accounting may be taken.

Fortunately, the economists, unlike the lawyers, do not have the power to make their opinions coercive. Also, it is probable that a greater proportion of economists understand the accounting mechanism.

John B. Canning, who is not only an economist but also an accountant, wrote a book in 1929 entitled *The Economics of Accountancy,* which is thoroughly recommended to those interested in the relationship between these two fields.

It is a common belief that accounting is derived from economics, but Canning[21] points out that they had independent origins. He asserts that:

Not only are the professional origins different, but also, from the beginning the two groups have had important diverse interests. At no time can either's field of learning be looked upon as including the other's; nor is either calling an offshoot of the other.

Echoing this same opinion, May[22] says that "where accounting and economic thought run along parallel lines, they do so because both are running parallel to business practice."

A brief but clear discussion of some of the more important differences between accounting and economics was furnished by Kohler and Morrison.[23] Pointing out that the economist has a social point of view, they say: "The accountant, employed

20 John Haskell, "The Securities and Exchange Commission, the Accountant, and the Stock Exchange," *The Journal of Accountancy,* April 1938, p. 297.
21 John B. Canning, *The Economics of Accountancy* (New York, The Ronald Press Company, 1929), p. 310.
22 George O. May, *Twenty-Five Years of Accounting Responsibility,* 1911-1936 (New York, American Institute Publishing Co., Inc., 1936), pp. 406, 407.
23 Kohler and Morrison, *Principles of Accounting* (New York, McGraw-Hill Book Company, Inc., 1931), p. 7.

by the management of a business enterprise or its creditors, analyzes business transactions with the express object of interpreting their effect on that enterprise." These authors note the difficulties encountered by the instructor in economics when members of his class have had courses in accounting and ascribe this difficulty to the fact that "while the phenomena being studied are largely the same, the approach is quite different."

This is confirmed by Lawrence[24] who suggests that differences in opinion between accountants and economists "are irreconcilable because they have no common meeting point."

Canning[25] thinks that very few economists "really have learned much about accounting procedure and that very few have any realizing sense of how difficult it is to acquire a serviceable familiarity with the subject."

Business Influence on Accounting.—A less abstract economic influence is that exerted by business men.

To management, accounting offers but one of many important groups of business problems. The task of directing a corporation in such a manner as to obtain profitable results is complicated by varied and serious difficulties. Occasionally these difficulties can be solved by revision of the accounting.

For example, an income tax difficulty seriously threatening the very existence of certain industries often can be solved in either one of two ways—by changing the tax law or by changing the accounting procedure. Since the latter alternative is easier, the practical business manager with little or no knowledge of or regard for the traditions of accounting naturally adopts the easier method and is impatient of "theoretical" arguments in opposition.

When the department store industry finds itself criticized by employee or consumer groups for the wide margin between cost prices and selling prices, it seems expedient to change the accounting methods in such a way as to close the gap. The department store manager is likely to brand as "academic" the

24 W. B. Lawrence, *Cost Accounting* (New York, Prentice-Hall, Inc., 1937), p. 415.
25 John B. Canning, *The Economics of Accountancy* (New York, The Ronald Press Company, 1929), p. 313.

suggestion that his proper remedy lies in a program of public relations and educational publicity.

Public accountants are often in conflict with clients who find it difficult to understand why some change in accounting is not preferable to a longer and more difficult, yet more direct, solution.

Often the business executive, if untrained in accounting, fails to see all of the probable consequences of a simple change in accounting method.

As a matter of fact, business management is often right in its attitude. The manager's contention that accounting should be a servant and not a master is in full accord with sound common sense. Few of those who argue strenuously with a client against some accounting expedient would not be equally tempted if the positions were reversed.

Only when tampering with the accounting mechanism results in harmful deception, tax evasion, or even worse, from one viewpoint, in misleading managers as to the meanings of their controlling indexes, does it become necessary for the accountant to take a firm stand.

RIGHT OF BUSINESS CONTROL OVER ACCOUNTING. If the master of a ship owns and controls his own instruments of navigation, it may be said that such ownership and control give him the right, disregarding navigation laws, to manipulate or distort them.

If, for example, he deliberately modifies his compass so that the needle no longer points to the magnetic north, he may argue that it is his compass and let the matter drop there. If the master's craft carries no passengers, if the owner and the crew are acquiescent, and if there is no matter of public interest involved, then his subsequent disastrous crash upon a rocky coast may be considered his own private affair.

Similarly, to obtain some advantage through a changed accounting method the mechanism of accounting may be so altered that figures commonly used for purposes of management control are distorted. When the distortion is recognized and fully considered in managerial interpretation and where there is no public interest affected, it is not easy for the business man to see why accountants should stand upon academic objections.

It is difficult, for example, to find any real fault with such a proposal as that involved in the Clark plan of retail accounting which shifts certain expenses from the selling, general, and administrative classification into the cost of sales. These shifted costs of buying, receiving, and marking have a tendency to reduce a gross profit spread of perhaps 35% to a lower figure, perhaps around 20%. If superficial consumer, labor, or political trouble-makers are thereby quieted, the mere fact that the change is unorthodox is a trivial objection.

The plan is illogical in that the expenses in question are shifted into the cost of sales classification without at the same time affecting inventory values, but this inconsistency is in fact a saving factor, since no accountant could permit his department store client to pad inventory values by any such expedient.

Unorthodox and often supported by false analogy are the plans of inventory valuation commonly referred to as the base-stock method or the last-in, first-out method but their adoption remedies an inequitable and evil tax discrimination. If neither management nor others at interest are deceived by the consequent distortion of profit and loss figures and if the Treasury Department recognizes the maneuver as a practical method of side-stepping the awkward if not impossible task of educating congressmen in accounting, it is difficult to see how great harm results.

It is only when proponents of such plans attempt to sanctify them by unsound arguments and false analogy that there may be cause to fear deceptive distortion of controlling business figures.

MOTIVES FOR REQUIRING ACCOUNTING CHANGES. Often it is difficult for the accounting practitioner to draw the line between managerial pressure for accounting changes which are harmless and pressure which is inspired by such improper motives as tax evasion, window-dressing for credit purposes, or so-called conservative undervaluations which have for their purpose overstatement of subsequent profits or inducement of stockholders to part with their shares for the selfish profit of the management. Because of difficulties in determining motives and in foreseeing secondary effects of changes in accounting policy, public accountants rightly adopt the general policy of opposing changes which seem to be tinged even slightly with a deceptive motive.

The burned child quite properly dreads the fire. Many accountants have seen only too clearly the distorting effects which have followed upon such accounting practices as the inventory rule of valuation at cost or market which, while considered conservative from the balance sheet viewpoint, during some period or another has an inflationary effect upon profits.

THE PUBLIC ACCOUNTANT AND HIS CLIENT.   Modern accounting has become highly complicated despite the fact that it is rooted in a simple logical mechanism.

Many of these complications result from conflicts between the managerial viewpoint and the accounting viewpoint. It has often become necessary for accountants to compromise between strict application of accounting theory and practical expediency. Professional accountants constantly must pass upon schemes, proposals, and shortcuts pushed upon their attention by lawyers, economists, bankers, analysts, and above all by business men who are their clients, upon whose goodwill they must depend, and to whom their sympathies naturally extend.

As will be seen, this is perhaps the most complicating of all factors in connection with various attempts that have been made to codify and standardize accounting principles. It is the practicing accountants, having clearly in mind the problems and necessities of their clients, who insist that inviolable accounting rules must not officially be adopted.

While the accounting practitioner is expected to be independent, it is only human for him, at times, to become unconsciously an advocate for his client. If he has an important client in the tanning business, he automatically reacts against any rigid rule which would forbid the last-in, first-out method of inventory valuation. If he has a corporate client which buys and sells its own capital stock, he is inclined to take exception to certain rules governing the treatment of profit or loss on the sale of treasury stock. If his client is a department store, he naturally objects to the adoption of any accounting principle which will prevent the inclusion of buying, receiving, and marking costs in the calculation of gross profit.

All of this was recognized by May[26] when he expressed doubt whether the auditor is "always as independent in fact as in theory."

Mathews[27] voiced a similar opinion as follows:

Despite encouraging developments, persistent qualities and factors of the active professional environment operate to handicap both independent growth and development of accounting principle and wholly independent reporting. Servitudes, less tangible and influential than earlier servitudes, though no less real, still exist.

Successful business men are not always right nor are selfish clients a rarity and there can be little doubt that part of the present pattern of accounting practice is the result of business expediency. No adequate survey of modern accounting can ignore this factor.

If there is any conflict between accounting teaching and accounting practice, as there seems to be, it may be somewhat due to the aloofness of the teacher from clients' troubles. This aloofness permits him to view accounting as a simple and logical mechanism, a viewpoint too often stigmatized by the harassed practitioner as "theoretical" and "academic."

[26] George O. May, "Improvement in Financial Accounts," *The Journal of Accountancy*, May 1937, p. 358.

[27] George C. Mathews, "Accounting in the Regulation of Security Sales," *The Accounting Review*, September 1938, p. 230.

CHAPTER 3

THE NEW EMPHASIS ON PROFITS

Not only has accounting development been greatly influenced by law and economics, both theoretical and applied, but also in recent years it has been profoundly influenced by a fundamental change in accounting viewpoint.

Since double entry accounting became the accepted method of recording the financial history of business, the balance sheet viewpoint has dominated.

Within the last few years accounting emphasis has shifted somewhat to the profit and loss viewpoint with numerous effects, some not yet evaluated. Accounting is in a period of transition marked by conflicts of opinion and those inevitable confusions which naturally result from the clash between old and new. In any attempt to study these conflicts and confusions, it is necessary first to consider the assumptions upon which accounting is based.

Three Basic Accounting Conventions.—The basic accounting assumptions or conventions are three in number. There are, of course, many others which are derivative. In fact, it may be doubted whether upon sudden demand anyone could prepare an inclusive list of all accounting conventions some of which are such natural and inevitable assumptions that they have long been taken for granted. There are, however, three conventions which are so fundamental that they should be helpful in any attempt to present a plausible, satisfying explanation of the probable development of accounting.

These three conventions are: (1) the entity convention, (2) the valuation convention, and (3) the accounting period convention.

THE ENTITY CONVENTION. The entity convention asserts that the unit for which double entry records are kept is an artificial person having possession of or "owning" certain assets contributed, in one form or another, to it by others who are, therefore, its creditors.

Disregarding legal objections—and this is most important for proper understanding of the entity convention—those who advance funds or the equivalent of funds to an accounting entity are its creditors and, in so far as double entry bookkeeping is concerned, it is unimportant whether, as in the case of lenders or vendors, they consider themselves as outsiders or, as in the case of proprietors, consider themselves as identified with the accounting entity.

THE VALUATION CONVENTION. The second convention is that of dollar valuation.

By this convention non-homogeneous assets and claims to assets are translated into financial equivalents or money values. Thus, the man who owns a sheep, a cow, and a horse may translate these possessions into $5, $50, and $100, and will say that he has assets of $155.

THE ACCOUNTING PERIOD CONVENTION. The third convention is that of the annual accounting period.

It is this convention which is responsible for most of the difficult accounting problems. Without this convention, accounting would be a simple matter of recording completed and fully realized transactions: an art of primitive simplicity.

Original Accounting Viewpoint.—Based originally on the first two conventions, and later on the three, the accounting mechanism has long been adequate to serve simple commerce. Because there was seldom any distinction between proprietorship and management, the development of a complex profit and loss classification was relatively unimportant.

Littleton[1] has pointed out that the balance sheet viewpoint prevailed even in the early days because the primary interest was in obtaining information about capital. He says:

. . . this was the center of the interest of partners, shareholders, lenders, and the basis of the calculation of early property taxes. Thus

[1] A. C. Littleton, *Accounting Evolutions to 1900* (New York, American Institute Publishing Co., Inc., 1933), p. 153.

balance-sheet data were stressed and refined in various ways, while expense and income data were incidental—in fact, the latter in the seventeenth century were presented merely as a "proof of estate"—to demonstrate by another route the correctness of the balance-sheet.

It seems reasonably safe to reconstruct early accounting as a simple sort of conventionalized statistical scheme derived from the entity concept in conjunction with that convenient expedient which translated non-homogeneous into homogeneous expressions, subsequently followed and considerably modified by the further convention of accounting periods. It naturally developed as a mechanism having an asset and liability, rather than an income and expense viewpoint.

Four influences have so profoundly affected this simple accounting mechanism as to require brief consideration. These four are: (1) the introduction and growth of the corporate form of organization, (2) the development of large-scale manufacturing, (3) taxation of income, and (4) the balance sheet audit.

The Corporation.—Fascinating to the historian, but of no immediate practical value, is a study of the various roots of the modern corporate form of organization.

Originating in the middle ages and largely influenced by the organization of speculative ventures such as the East India Company in the fifteenth century, the corporate form of organization has influenced accounting in various ways. It has reinforced the entity convention since the corporation, by definition and general understanding, is an artificial person. The corporate form has influenced accounting by introducing the concept of permanent capital.

Finally, the corporate form has influenced accounting because of its limited liability feature which introduced an important problem of credit granting. Until recently the creditor's interest in accounting matters, and his demands for accounting information, were regarded as more important than the enlightenment of the permanent investor.

While the creditor's rights are still considered of great importance, the stockholder, who was previously the forgotten man of finance, has found champions who insist that accounting owes an obligation not only to him who supplies temporary capital but also to him who supplies permanent capital.

The adoption of the corporate form also focussed attention on the distinction between ownership and management. In small corporations this distinction may be unimportant, but in the larger corporations, and particularly those listed upon stock exchanges, much less than a majority interest in the capital stock is needed to insure control over the corporation. As a result the real owners of the business, because they are scattered and frequently because they consider themselves not so much a part of their corporation as speculators dealing with stock certificates, are treated as though they were outsiders.

All of this seemed quite satisfactory to those concerned until the spectacular crash of 1929, when enormous losses were suffered by investors. This excited the attention of reformers, with the result that the years 1933 and 1934 saw the establishment of governmental controls culminating in the creation of the Securities and Exchange Commission. Emphasis upon this development should not, however, obscure the interest in protecting investors which was shown by the accountants themselves and by the New York Stock Exchange. It was in 1930 that a representative of the New York Stock Exchange made an appeal for cooperation addressed to the American Institute of Accountants.

The awakened interest in the investor's viewpoint has constituted a most important force, tending to shift accounting emphasis from the balance sheet to the profit and loss statement.

Investors are, of course, interested in balance sheets and necessarily give consideration to such items as current assets in connection with current liabilities, inventory methods, and the bases of valuing fixed assets. But the investor is even more interested in earnings. Recognition of an obligation to protect the investor is also recognition of the profit and loss statement as a report at least equal in rank with the balance sheet, and probably of more importance.

Cost Accounting.—Accompanying the rapid growth of corporations was the development of cost accounting.

The assembly of large amounts of capital was seldom feasible for individuals or partnerships but the corporation, with its limited liability feature and its continuity, contributed greatly to the formation of large manufacturing units. With the change from small to large manufacturing establishments came the need for a specialized kind of accounting for production costs.

THE COST CONVENTION. This new subdivision of accounting, as Paton has pointed out, was based upon a convention that costs could be transferred from one object to another, from one classification to another, and from one activity to another. Thus, the depreciation of a building operates as a transfer of value from the building itself to the materials in progress of manufacture, simultaneously lessening one value and increasing another.

This convention enables the cost accountant to visualize a flow of values springing from expenditures of various types, through classified channels, finally attaching themselves to, and increasing the valuation of, the materials in process of manufacture. Direct labor and various other factory costs, such as rent, heat, light, property taxes, insurance, and supervision, came to be regarded as assets because they attach themselves to materials in process.

THE PERPETUAL INVENTORY. Prior to the development of cost accounting, the common method of determining inventory was to count and value whatever merchandise, materials, and supplies remained on hand at the end of any period.

When a periodic inventory was taken in this way, it was necessary to assign a value to each item, this value often being based on recent purchase transactions or on current market quotations.

Such methods of valuing called for no comparison with any actual or average cost such as can be provided by a perpetual inventory. The accountant, therefore, gave but little thought to the effect of his valuation procedure upon comparative profits.

The adoption of the perpetual inventory, however, introduced a conflict between the valuations of the periodic inventory and those representing actual cost. As a result it became necessary to reconcile these values. This reconciliation often resulted in periodic adjustments of the perpetual inventories, which adjustments naturally had their effect upon current profits.

From this conflict of practice there were developed two opposing schools of thought. Auditors clung to the older method of determining inventory values at the end of an accounting period, while the cost accountants believed that their new mechanism produced true costs currently and saw no reason why they should be adjusted to any other basis. This conflict has been responsible for numerous misunderstandings and controversies.

Clearly there is little common ground when one group is thinking in terms of realizable values on a balance sheet and the other is thinking in terms of actual cost on a profit and loss statement.

EXPENSE RATES. The cost accounting problem of overhead, burden, or manufacturing expense has long been serious.

Traditionalists have believed that all factory expense should be apportioned to work in progress. Others, less attached to original concepts, could not fail to note the great cost disparity caused by varying rates of manufacturing activity in relation to the inflexible character of some of the expense items. To these men who were thinking of accounting as an index of efficiency it seemed unreasonable that great variations in cost should be reported when the causes of such variations lay outside of their control. They argued, if other departments, whose duty it was to obtain orders for goods, were unable to keep the factory scheduled at full capacity, should not excess costs due to inflexible expenses in combination with lessened operating activity receive a different treatment from other costs over which they had full control and which measured their efficiency?

It was perhaps natural for factory men to think of accounting in terms of efficiency reports. Many of them had no substantial background of accounting training and perhaps failed to realize that accounting might not be the best of all mechanisms for recording relative efficiencies. These men were faced with a very practical problem. They were being held responsible for production costs and were being blamed or rewarded based upon cost accounting reports. It is small wonder, then, that they refused to be held responsible for cost increases due to subnormal operations. Thus was born the idea of burden rates based upon normal operating capacity. This in turn led to another modern phenomenon, standard cost accounting, in which cost variations of different kinds receive special treatment.

As the result of such treatment, values finally appearing in the finished goods inventory are often lower than they would otherwise be. Accordingly, a portion of the total costs is often applied to diminish net profit in the period when goods are manufactured rather than in the period when they are sold.

All of these cost accounting developments represented forces tending to shift emphasis from the balance sheet to the profit and loss viewpoint.

Income Taxation.—The effect of income taxation in influencing a shift from the balance sheet to the profit and loss viewpoint is obvious.

While there were three prior attempts to tax incomes in the United States, it was not until 1913 that the influence of this legislation upon accounting practice was noticeable. Income taxation is, perhaps, the most powerful of all the forces which have influenced accounting practice. When business men realized that incomplete or inadequate records were likely to prove costly, accounting departments were spot-lighted and great executive interest was manifested in records previously ignored or neglected. Furthermore, since the tax was based upon income rather than property values, it was only natural that greater attention should be given to proper determination of earnings, costs, expenses, and losses.

The Balance Sheet Audit.—The balance sheet audit, which was first heard of in 1910 or thereabouts, had a powerful and rather extraordinary influence upon accounting and, accordingly, justifies somewhat extended treatment.

THE PERIOD PRIOR TO 1910. The origin of the balance sheet audit has been indicated as about 1910 but this is probably closer to the date of its christening than to the date of its birth.

The technical features and limitations of the balance sheet audit seem to have had their roots in the previous century and in English soil. There is some slight evidence of this in Dicksee's *Auditing,* second edition, published in 1895.

In the United States, D. A. Keister's *Corporation Accounting and Auditing,* published in 1899, carried no warning of the forthcoming event which was to influence accounting so greatly. Beach and Thorne, in their *The Science and Practice of Auditing,* published in 1903, discussed "a condensed method of auditing" for which a client would be willing to pay as a substitute for the complete audit.

In 1903 there was another author, Macpherson,[2] who mentioned the importance of "verifying the balance sheet put forward as presenting the condition of affairs of the business under review," although rather sensibly he added,

> I cannot well see how an accountant can accept and prepare a report from any balance sheet without satisfying himself by a sufficient analysis of the regularity of the accounts and of the methods followed to produce the various items which enter into the assets of a concern, and which go to make up revenue and expenditure accounts.

FIRST MENTION OF BALANCE SHEET AUDIT. Montgomery's American edition of Dicksee's *Auditing,* published in 1909, did not specifically name and describe the balance sheet audit which was so soon to dominate the practice of accounting in the United States. But in 1911, P. F. Collier & Son published *The American Business Manual* in which Montgomery[3] specifically mentioned the balance sheet audit by name.

He referred to "an audit which very largely takes for granted the integrity of the current operations and in which the chief interest devolves upon the assets and liabilities—do they correctly represent the true financial position at a certain date?" This he describes as "a balance sheet audit so called." He goes on to explain that "where there is an auditing department properly conducted, or where the purpose of the examination is to

---

2 F. H. Macpherson, "Duties of Auditors," *The Science and Practice of Accounting,* compiled by Beach and Thorne (Detroit, Mich., The Book-Keeper Publishing Co., Ltd., 1903), pp. 14, 15.

3 Robert H. Montgomery, *The American Business Manual* (P. F. Collier & Son, 1911), p. 1095.

determine the net worth of the concern, the auditor will usually confine himself entirely to the items of the balance sheet."

The following year Montgomery[4] published his *Auditing Theory and Practice* in which he specifically described the balance sheet audit in the following words:

GENERAL PRINCIPLES. The underlying principles of a balance-sheet audit may be reduced to writing and are not subject to change to fit particular businesses or special systems of account. They are few in number and can be applied generally.

The principles upon which all balance-sheet audits are based are as follows:

(1) The auditor must ascertain that all of the assets shown by the books to have been on hand at a certain date were actually on hand.

(2) He must ascertain whether any other assets, not on the books, *should* be on hand.

(3) He must ascertain that the liabilities shown by the books to be owing at a certain date were *actual* liabilities.

(4) He must ascertain whether or not all liabilities were in fact shown by the books.

(5) He must ascertain whether or not the liabilities so shown were *properly* incurred.

It appears fairly safe to give credit to Montgomery for the invention of this name, since Bentley's *Bibliography of Works on Accounting by American Authors* (Boston, 1934) lists only eleven titles on auditing which were published for general circulation from 1892 to 1910 and none of the volumes found mentions a balance sheet audit.

DEVELOPMENT OF BALANCE SHEET AUDIT. In 1912 news of the balance sheet audit crossed the border to Canada. In April of that year, *The Canadian Chartered Accountant* said of it, "We have heard this expression used several times of late, and our inquiries have not elicited anything definite or authoritative as to its meaning."

In 1913 J. C. Scobie, connected with the public accounting firm of Price, Waterhouse & Co., prepared for private distribu-

[4] Robert H. Montgomery, *Auditing Theory and Practice* (New York, The Ronald Press Company, 1912), pp. 82, 87.

tion a memorandum entitled "General Remarks on a Balance
Sheet Audit." In April 1917, the *Federal Reserve Bulletin*
(Vol. III, No. 4) stated that the Federal Trade Commission
had been impressed by the lack of uniformity in financial
statements and had enlisted the aid of the American Institute
of Accountants with a view to remedying the condition. The
bulletin added the significant statement that "probably more
than 90% of the statements certified by public accountants are
what are called balance-sheet audits." This provides an interesting revelation of the general acceptance of the balance sheet
audit within about six or seven years from the date of its first
mention.

The auditing suggestions which appeared in the April 1917
issue of the *Federal Reserve Bulletin* and which were reprinted
for general distribution in 1918 under the title, *Approved
Methods for the Preparation of Balance-Sheet Statements,*
contain some phrases, passages, and paragraphs which had previously appeared in the Scobie memorandum above referred to.
It appears, therefore, that the procedures described in the Federal Reserve document were derived to some extent from the
Scobie memorandum.

The balance sheet audit did not penetrate to England. On
November 23, 1918, a letter from G. Seymour Thompson, written to the editor of *The Accountant,* suggested that the profession in England would do well to consider the more general
adoption of the balance sheet audit, to which the leading article
in the December 28 issue replied: "The term 'Balance Sheet
Audit' is not generally used in this country; indeed, it might,
we think, be said to be practically unknown."

From 1918 on, references to the balance sheet audit became
increasingly numerous and it became firmly established among
professional accountants in the United States. Indicative of
this the Federal Reserve Board published, in May 1929, a
revision of its *Approved Methods for the Preparation of
Balance-Sheet Statements* under the new title of *Verification of
Financial Statements.*

THE AMERICAN INSTITUTE AND THE NEW YORK STOCK
EXCHANGE. As has been said, the depression which started in

1929 profoundly disturbed the business world in general and accountants in particular. On September 22, 1932, the American Institute's Special Committee on Cooperation with Stock Exchanges wrote to the Committee on Stock List[5] of the New York Stock Exchange asserting that "the earning capacity is the fact of crucial importance in the valuation of an industrial enterprise, and that therefore the income account is usually far more important than the balance-sheet."

Elsewhere the letter says,

As a rule, the first objective has been to secure a proper charge or credit to the income account for the year, and in general the presumption has been that once this is achieved the residual amount of the expenditure or the receipt could properly find its place in the balance-sheet.

In 1935 Andersen[6] told the American Institute of Accountants that if the investor

buys a $1,000 mortgage bond which, according to the balance-sheet, is backed by $3,000 of plant assets, he blames the accountant if, some years later, he realizes only $300 in liquidation. He believes the original statement of asset values must have been in error. He cannot credit the fact that there are different bases for valuation in a going business and in a liquidated business or in the same going business under different economic cycles.

In January 1936, the American Institute of Accountants published *Examination of Financial Statements by Independent Public Accountants*, which was a revision of the 1929 bulletin and in which great care was taken to eliminate references to the balance sheet audit, the term "examination of financial statements" being substituted therefor.

From this brief review it is apparent that the life span of the balance sheet audit has been short. First introduced under that specific title in 1911, it had achieved widespread popularity by 1917. This popularity continued until the publication by the American Institute of the interchange of correspondence between the Institute Committee and the Stock Exchange Com-

5 *Audits of Corporate Accounts* (New York, American Institute of Accountants, 1934), p. 10.
6 Arthur Andersen, "Present-day Problems Affecting the Presentation and Interpretation of Financial Statements," *The Journal of Accountancy,* November 1935, p. 333.

mittee. In January 1936, the name "balance sheet audit," by strong implication at least, received official disapproval.

It is, of course, too early to say that January 1936 marked the demise of the balance sheet audit. That it persists to some extent, in fact if not in name, in smaller communities or in the practice of accounting firms unconnected with large-scale financing, is a tribute to its former popularity and vitality.

By May 1937, May[7] was able to announce that the determination of income "is now generally recognized as the most important single problem in the field of financial accounting." The period of mourning for the balance sheet audit was over and accountants began seriously to question some of the resulting problems.

These problems were concerned with such matters as inventory valuation, depreciation, the profit and loss treatment of plant write-downs, and the correction of prior period errors. The doctrine of consistency which was so much emphasized in the *Examination of Financial Statements by Independent Public Accountants* was found to conflict with some previous practices appropriate to the balance sheet audit.

Even such a sacred rule as the valuation of inventories at cost or market was examined and voices were heard protesting that application of this rule distorted profit and loss statements, that the rule itself was not conservative from the profit and loss viewpoint, and that it contradicted the doctrine of consistency.

POPULARITY OF BALANCE SHEET AUDIT. In looking back upon the short, very active, life of the balance sheet audit, one may perhaps wonder what caused its enthusiastic adoption.

The obvious but probably inaccurate explanation is to be found in the threefold relationship between banker, public accountant, and client. The argument runs somewhat as follows: Bankers wanted audited statements from their borrowers. The borrowers wanted to spend as little money as possible on audit fees. The balance sheet audit provided necessary credit information at a minimum cost to the client.

One might also add that in their demands for audited state-

---

[7] George O. May, "Improvement in Financial Accounts," *The Journal of Accountancy*, May 1937, p. 346.

ments bankers helped to create public accounting work and it was only natural for public accountants to cater to the bankers.

In examining this plausible explanation, slight evidence is found in its support. Undoubtedly, some public accountants did attempt to curry favor with bankers in the hope of gaining new clients thereby. Undoubtedly, a certain amount of this is still going on. It is doubtful, however, whether this practice was ever widespread. Public accountants have always been professionally minded and have jealously safeguarded their reputations for integrity and independence. In some isolated instances alliances may have been arranged between public accountants and bank officials but this was far from a general practice.

A more probable explanation is to be found in the relation between the public accountant and his client and the legitimate and perfectly proper desire of the public accountant to favor his client by reasonable audit fees.

In looking back upon the balance sheet audit, it is mere hindsight to note that it was inadequate and that its emphasis was wrongly placed. It required the sharp lesson of 1929 to reveal the deficiencies of this audit. The legitimate desire on the part of clients to save expenses, coupled with the fact that the balance sheet audit was authoritatively sponsored and because of its specialized conservatism was acceptable to bankers, appear to have been the factors primarily responsible for its brilliant, if brief, popularity.

That popularity was very important since it temporarily counteracted those forces which normally would have shifted accounting emphasis to the profit and loss statement much sooner. It has already been mentioned that the growth in the corporate form of organization, the development of modern cost accounting, and the passage of income tax laws were all factors which tended to emphasize the profit and loss viewpoint. It was the balance sheet audit, with its almost 100% acceptance by public accountants and clients, which temporarily nullified these strong forces.

CHAPTER 4

THE PERSONAL ACCOUNTING ENTITY

The entity convention has already been mentioned as one of the three basic assumptions of accounting. Since it has predetermined the design of the accounting mechanism and since it provides the most logical explanation of what the accountant means by net profit, adequate consideration of its origin and development is justified.

The origin of double entry accounting is not definitely known. Peragallo found little evidence of its existence prior to the development of medieval commerce. Some, however, hold the opinion that double entry accounting may have originated from the relationship between the Roman slave and his master. Peragallo[1] suggests no more than that double entry "may have been present in embryonic form in the Roman bookkeeping system."

Whether this is true seems immaterial. As an explanation it is completely logical and satisfying since only through the personal viewpoint of a slave does the entity convention of accounting become vivid and plausible.

The story told by Littleton in *Accounting Evolution to 1900* explains that it was beneath the dignity of a Roman patrician to engage in trade. Buying, selling, and other practical matters of business were considered unfitting for the free citizen, who found it necessary to engage in commerce by proxy. Since many Roman slaves were men of education and ability, citizens advanced money to them which the slaves in turn would loan at interest. The slave himself could own no property. Money advanced to him by his master merely changed hands but not ownership.

---

[1] Edward Peragallo, *Origin and Evolution of Double Entry Bookkeeping* (New York, American Institute Publishing Co., Inc., 1938), p. 3.

When the business transactions were at all complex, it was necessary for the slave to keep records. This relationship of master and slave as represented by records introduced a certain pattern of accounting which has persisted to the present day.

Effect of Separate Personalities.—Because the slave was a person separate and distinct from the master, the record he kept was his own personal record. It reflected the slave's viewpoint toward his master and toward the world in general. Despite the personal viewpoint of his record keeping, the slave was owned and controlled by the master.

These two characteristics of (1) ownership and control, and (2) separate personality and viewpoint, represent so logical and satisfying an explanation of the accounting mechanism as to justify the adoption of the entity convention regardless of positive historical proof.

OWNERSHIP AND CONTROL. By virtue of his ownership of the slave, the master could direct and control all the slave's various financial transactions.

It is convenient to think that the slave had no power of initiative, no opportunity to exercise independent business judgment; that he merely followed directions. By command he received and disbursed money, made loans, collected interest and principal, and repaid the interest and principal to his master.

Because he was a slave, he was merely an extension of his master's personality.

SEPARATE PERSONALITY. Because the slave was a human being with a personality and a viewpoint of his own, he could not fail to regard his master as a person separate and distinct from himself. His records, therefore, were the kind of records any man might make in dealing with another.

When the master advanced him a certain sum of money, it was natural for the slave to adopt the record keeping viewpoint that he personally owed that amount to his master. When the master demanded the return of money, it was natural for the slave to consider that he was paying his debt to the master.

Any increase in the amount of funds held by him as agent for his master represented an increase in the amount of his debt to the master. Any decrease, on the other hand, represented a decrease in the amount of his debt to his master.

Losses and Gains.—Illustrating in terms of dollars instead of Roman currency, a typical transaction might occur as follows:

The master advances $1,000 to his slave; from the slave's viewpoint he has possession of $1,000 and he owes $1,000 to his master. At the master's direction, the slave loans $1,000 at 6% interest. He has replaced the actual currency with a receivable, i.e., a claim to currency. If the borrower is unable to repay the loan a loss is suffered, but it is not a loss to the slave. He was commanded to make the loan and the loss is the master's.

From the slave's own viewpoint this reduction in the amount of funds in his possession operates as a release of his liability to the master. His personal indebtedness of $1,000, therefore, is extinguished.

A different situation would result had the investment proved to be good rather than bad. Upon command the slave loans the same amount of money as before, but this time with more fortunate results, since the borrower not only repays the $1,000 but also adds $60 for interest. Upon completion of the transaction, therefore, the slave is in possession of $1,060, whereas he started with but $1,000.

Bearing in mind that he can own no property and that he is merely acting as an agent, it is clear that the increase of $60 in the amount of funds also represents an increase of $60 in the slave's liability to his master.

The Charge and Discharge Record.—This elementary illustration would hardly justify extended discussion were it not that the institution of slavery during Roman times provides so convincing a background for examining the basic elements of the accounting mechanism. Any other illustration is less vivid in picturing the agency relationship between a business and its proprietor and the absolute right of control over the business by the proprietor.

The relationship between a Roman slave and his master suggests that charge and discharge concept upon which all double entry accounting rests. The slave is charged with certain funds advanced to him by his master and also with any increase of those funds due to fortunate investments. He is discharged of his responsibilities by repaying funds to his master. He is also discharged of his responsibility by losses incurred. The slave himself neither benefits nor suffers because of increases or decreases in the funds transferred to him.

In this master-slave relationship are two basic accounting concepts: (1) that of record keeping in terms of money rather than physical things, and (2) that of an entity as separate and distinct from proprietorship.

The familiar accounting equation is derived, of course, from the slave's viewpoint since he must regard his master as a separate personality. It is inconceivable that any plan of record keeping could have developed other than one which would show his master as his creditor. To the slave the accounting equation was natural, logical, and necessary since his assets always and necessarily equalled his liabilities.

By the same simple logic, increases in total assets automatically resulted in increases in total liabilities, while decreases in total assets automatically resulted in decreases in total liabilities. This logic, from the slave's viewpoint, is inescapable.

The Valuation Convention.—Just how or when it happened that money valuations came to be used as accounting symbols is somewhat obscure. Imagination, however, may supplement historical inadequacy. A series of transactions between master and slave following the simple lines already described would naturally start a habit of thinking about commercial transactions in terms of money.

If a hundred money transactions took place, it would be only natural to follow the same method of record keeping for the hundred and first transaction in which, for the first time, the slave must account for property instead of money.

Consider some of the problems involved, employing for convenience modern rather than ancient measures of value. The master advances $100 which the slave properly shows as a liability. On instruction the slave invests it in 100 bushels of wheat. Immediately he is confronted by a new record keeping problem. No longer is he dealing in money and yet his record is a money record. He has already entered his personal liability of $100 to his master but he has on hand neither $100 nor a claim against a borrower for $100. He has something new in so far as his record keeping is concerned, namely, 100 bushels of wheat.

His equation really shows that 100 bushels of wheat equals $100 owing to the master but the terms are not homogeneous. Just as the farmer who owns three sheep and owes his neighbor two hogs must use a medium of exchange, so was the slave forced to express his agency property and his agency liability in common terms. When there was an actual substitution of one kind of property for another, namely, 100 bushels of wheat for $100, it became essential for record keeping purposes for the slave to call the wheat $100.

That physical bushels of wheat are not currency is unimportant from the viewpoint of the equation record. For the purpose of that record the wheat is translated into dollars and the transaction is reflected by a change from the original equation "$100 (of cash) equals liability to the master $100," to an equation which reads "$100 (of wheat) equals liability to the master $100."

The convenience of this translation is evidenced when the wheat is sold for $120, whereupon an increase in the total funds held by the slave is necessarily equalled by an increase in his debt to the master, so that the equation then becomes "$120 (of cash) equals liabilities to the master $120."

This matter of translation or valuation has been a cause of much concern to those who have overlooked the simple necessities of record keeping derived from the master-slave relationship.

Meaning of Valuation.—In the transaction as outlined there is no real problem. One hundred bushels of wheat have merely replaced $100.

Economic theories of valuation seem unrealistic when considered in terms of this elementary problem. Such a substitution is an even trade for record keeping purposes, regardless of whether the slave spent too much or too little for the wheat.

By sharp bargaining he might have obtained the 100 bushels of wheat for $90. Through carelessness he might have spent $110. These are mere suppositions. As a matter of actual fact, he substituted 100 bushels of wheat for $100 and from his viewpoint no other valuation is conceivable.

It is, of course, true that his master can interfere in this matter. The master, because of his control, can insist that the wheat is worth $200 and can require the slave to prepare the record accordingly. When the slave exchanges $100 for 100 bushels of wheat, he may be forced to translate the wheat into $200, but since he cannot hold any more or less than he owes, his bookkeeping equation must show the following: "$200 (of wheat) equals liability to the master $200."

So far as the slave's chargeability is concerned, this record is just as satisfactory as if the $100 valuation had been used. His responsibilities and obligations are just as clearly defined by one valuation as the other.

The fact that his master, by an arbitrary decision, may have insisted upon a higher than cost valuation of the wheat is of no concern to the slave. Later, when the wheat is sold for $120, there follows an $80 reduction in the amount which he owes his master, representing a loss upon the inflated valuation.

From the master's viewpoint, too, the final outcome is the same under either valuation since he is actually $20 ahead either way.

The matter of initial valuation is, therefore, unimportant but its unimportance refers to these two viewpoints only. If, for example, the master merely supplied the funds but employed some other person to manage those funds and to give instructions to the slave, then a different situation is presented, since the go-between, or manager, may properly attach a great deal of importance to the profitability or unprofitability of the various transactions. From the viewpoint of such a go-between, initial valuation at other than cost may appear to distort the record with reference to managerial efficiency.

This general observation is perhaps a step ahead of the present subject matter but because of its importance in all except small unincorporated business organizations it deserves brief mention here merely to avoid misunderstanding.

Only when there are two and only two parties—namely, the slave as the entity on the one hand and the master, also exercising the function of a manager, on the other—can it be said that the amount of initial valuation is of no significance save from the viewpoint of charge and discharge and that, therefore, there is no sensible reason for the master to require any initial valuation of the wheat other than the $100 of cost.

Non-Cash Transactions.—It seems desirable to carry the master-slave illustration one step further.

Heretofore, it has been assumed that the relation between master and slave involved only money. The slave, as a proxy for his master, engages in transactions with outsiders involving conversions from money to commodities and back again into money, but by assumption the dealings between the master and slave have been restricted to actual money. It is on this assumption that the equation is founded and difficulties are introduced when the master transfers property, rather than cash, to his slave.

THE NON-CASH INVESTMENT.   Suppose that the master gives his slave ten sheep to sell.

It is necessary for the slave to make a record of the property entrusted to him and of his corresponding indebtedness to the master. But this immediately prompts the question, "What valuation shall be used?"

As the slave is without power to set the valuation, the master must do so. Assume that he names an arbitrary figure of $5 per head. This decision enables the slave to prepare his record, charging himself with $50 worth of sheep and showing a liability of $50 to his master.

From the slave's viewpoint it does not make the slightest difference whether the valuation of $50 is high or low. He is intent only upon reflecting his responsibilities in financial terms.

From the master's viewpoint the matter may be of greater importance. His profit or loss on the subsequent sale of the sheep will inevitably be influenced by the valuation. If the sheep actually cost the master only $4 per head and he turns them over to the slave at $5 per head and the slave sells them at $6 per head, then the master has made a total profit of $2 per head, or $20, half of which is not apparent from the slave's record, which, perforce, merely shows $50 worth of sheep sold for $60.

THE NON-CASH WITHDRAWAL. To complicate the picture, assume that before selling the sheep the master demands that one of them be killed and dressed for his table.

The sheep stands on the slave's books at $5 and when he returns it he extinguishes his liability to the master by the same amount, namely, $5.

From the master's viewpoint, however, he is consuming a $4 sheep upon which he took a preliminary "profit," now cancelled, of $1 when he turned it over to the slave at the arbitrary $5 valuation.

Advantages of Roman Slave Theory.—This master-slave relationship is so adequate a vehicle for discussion of fundamental accounting problems that it must be abandoned with reluctance. There is no method of explaining the basic accounting mechanism which is so helpful. The slave is a separate personality and yet under the absolute domination and control of a master. It is from the interplay of these two concepts that modern accounting theory and practice has developed.

THE SLAVE'S VIEWPOINT. From the slave's viewpoint an increase in his indebtedness to his master represents the simple fact of increased chargeability regardless of whether the increase was due to an additional advance by the master or whether it was due to a gain realized from some profitable transaction. The slave treated funds advanced to him in the same way as gains because he was interested in recording his liabilities to his master regardless of how those liabilities originated. His responsibility is neither greater nor less whether the increase in his liabilities is due to a profit or to an additional advance by the master.

THE MASTER'S VIEWPOINT. From the master's viewpoint the distinction is vital and the master can be imagined as giving his slave instructions to maintain two records, one reflecting the slave's liability for funds advanced and the other his liability for gains. Both may be thought of as liability accounts but from the slave's viewpoint they are as one.

The distinction, however, provides a comparison between investment and the results achieved from that investment— between capital and income. Here is the imagined origin of those investment and surplus accounts which have become so important in corporation accounting.

CHAPTER 5

THE IMPERSONAL ACCOUNTING ENTITY

In modern times the accounting entity lacks the element of human personality which characterized Roman record keeping. Instead, the accounting entity is invested with an imaginary or artificial personality.

Many will recall Chief Justice Marshall's definition of a corporation as "an artificial person." Sole proprietorships and partnerships may also be regarded in the same manner. The separate entity was a fact in the master-slave relationship. Accounting records are still written from the viewpoint of an entity until it has now become an accounting convention.

Terminology.—Of all the names that have been applied to this artificial person, the word "entity" seems to be the most appropriate. Possible substitutes are such phrases as "economic entity," "economic unit," "accounting unit," "enterprise," and "the business."

The last phrase is probably the one most often employed. A man commonly speaks of his business as something separate and distinct from himself. His bookkeeping records reflect the activity of his business. If he is engaged in three or four different enterprises, even though they are unincorporated, he thinks of each as a separate entity. Such enterprises, even though entirely owned by one man, may have dealings with another, as where merchandise is transferred from one store to another.

The phrase "the business" is, however, unfortunate, not only because it is too general in its application but also because it implies economic activity, trading, money-making.

This disregards various non-commercial activities which also require accounting records. Wherever accounting records are maintained there is found the fiction of an artificial person. The phrase "the business" is, therefore, not sufficiently broad to apply to a municipality, a hospital, or a club. The same objection can be raised against the terms "economic unit" and "economic entity."

Various authors have given consideration to this problem of naming the artificial person, and the term "entity" seems to be their choice. Preferably it should be modified by "accounting." The phrase "accounting entity" clearly indicates that the artificial person is conceived in relation to accounting records. While resembling somewhat the improper practice of defining a word in terms of itself, the practical advantage of "accounting entity" as compared with "entity" seems to justify the phrase.

"Entity" is preferable to "unit" because the word "unit" is commonly employed in other meanings in such phrases as "unit costs," "unit posting media," and "unit" as a descriptive title for a subdivision of a department.

Entity and Proprietary Concepts.—It should not be assumed that all authorities agree with the entity convention.

There are two common methods of viewing the fundamental accounting structure. One is the entity theory and the other is often called the "proprietary theory." The difference between the two is a difference in viewpoint.

In the entity theory the proprietor, regardless of how closely he may be identified with the business, regards himself as a person separate and apart from the business.

In the proprietary theory this is not true. It becomes necessary, therefore, to adopt another explanation of the proprietor's account. This is done by assuming that bookkeeping represents an accounting by the proprietor for his own property.

In the one case the entity, and in the other the proprietor, is the central figure.

According to the entity theory, profit is an increase in the amount the entity owes to the proprietor, disregarding capital advances and withdrawals. According to the proprietary theory, profit is the excess of proceeds over outlays during the business process.

That the ancient writers used the entity convention in the same way as the moderns is suggested by Paciolo's explanation quoted by Peragallo,[1] that "a branch of a store is in effect the debtor of the proprietor, so that the latter may debit the store for all he puts in it and credit it for all he takes out of it, just as he would do in the case of a debtor who contracted a debt and subsequently paid it."

Littleton[2] stated the essentials of the entity convention in the following words:

Thus to the reporting (record-keeping) person the account with a "proprietor" was not different in principle from an account with a lender; in fact, a lender often took the form of a proprietor to avoid the appearance of being a lender. To the active manager (in contrast to the silent partner) of the trading ventures so common in the fifteenth century, there were two elements present: (a) kinds of property for which he was accountable and (b) sources of property to which he was accountable; profit was but an additional "indebtedness" to the sources of the property in use.

Porter and Fiske[3] define profit from the entity viewpoint as "a proprietary claim to an excess of values received over values given up in exchange." Their use of the word "claim" in this connection clearly intimates the adoption of the entity viewpoint.

MacFarland and Ayars[4] take a more definite stand, saying that: "The concept of an enterprise as a unit or undertaking for which financial records should be classified and kept, summarized, and interpreted is absolutely essential in accounting."

In discussing the two theories, Husband and Thomas[5] assert: "Accountants may be divided into two groups: (1) those who claim that the proprietor owns all of the assets but owes certain amounts to creditors, and (2) those who hold that both liabilities and proprietorship are merely claims against the assets. The former point of view, which is the older of the two, is held by the greater number."

1 Edward Peragallo, *Origin and Evolution of Double Entry Bookkeeping* (New York, American Institute Publishing Co., Inc., 1938), p. 99.
2 A. C. Littleton, *Accounting Evolution to 1900* (New York, American Institute Publishing Co., Inc., 1933), p. 194.
3 Porter and Fiske, *Accounting* (New York, Henry Holt & Company, 1935), p. 37.
4 MacFarland and Ayars, *Accounting Fundamentals* (New York, McGraw-Hill Book Company, Inc., 1936), p. 1.
5 Husband and Thomas, *Principles of Accounting* (New York, Houghton Mifflin Company, 1935), p. 18.

Both the entity and proprietary conventions have value. Like all conventions, each contains an element of artificiality. Either is valuable so long as it is consistently maintained. It is only when an unconscious shift in viewpoint from one to the other occurs that there is danger of false reasoning.

The entity convention, as a basis for the study of accounting profits, is appealing because of its simplicity and because actual bookkeeping procedure does, in fact, treat the proprietor just as though he were a creditor; that is to say, the elementary plus and minus entries which constitute the bare mechanics of double entry are similar with respect to all sources of capital.

Authorities Opposing Entity Concept.—To those who have received their accounting training from the proprietary approach, the invention of an artificial person to replace the Roman slave seems an arbitrary fiction.

An early authority, Sprague[6] took a decided stand against the entity theory. While recognizing certain of its advantages, he failed to see that "it justifies the inclusion of proprietorship among the liabilities." He thought that the entity did "not stand in the same relation to its proprietors or its capitalists as to its 'other' liabilities. It would seem more appropriate to say that it is 'owned by' than 'owes' the proprietors." Elsewhere[6] he said:

> Thus the right-hand side of the balance sheet is entirely composed of claims against or rights over the left-hand side. "Is it not then true," it will be askt, "that the right-hand side is entirely composed of liabilities?" The answer to this is that the rights of others, or the liabilities, differ materially from the rights of the proprietor.

Henry Rand Hatfield has consistently used the proprietary rather than the entity approach in his writings.

Legal dislike of overextension of the entity concept is reflected by such comments as this one of Judge Oliver B. Dickinson's,[7] "The relation of corporation and shareholder is not the relation of debtor and creditor otherwise, perhaps, than in a secondary and remote sense."

---

[6] Charles E. Sprague, *The Philosophy of Accounts* (New York, The Ronald Press Company, 1913), pp. 49, 46.

[7] Quoted by Robert H. Montgomery in "Dealings in Treasury Stock," *The Journal of Accountancy*, August 1938, p. 112.

Canning[8] discussed the entity theory as follows:

The accounts, it is said, constitute an accounting by this entity to all who have commercial and financial relations with it. Some writers even profess that, in the case of corporate enterprise, the entity may be more than a figure of speech. This they do by making the blunder of identifying the shareholders as the proprietor and making the corporation correspond to this entity.

The point involved here seems somewhat obscure. If any form of business organization is entitled to be considered an entity, it is the corporation which is recognized as such by law, whereas the so-called blunder of identifying the shareholder group as the proprietor appears to be no blunder at all but merely the extension of a useful, albeit somewhat artificial convention.

Legal Contradiction of Entity Concept.—Many discussions of the entity theory as contrasted with the proprietary theory have been influenced by legal considerations.

Legal considerations, important as they are, have no bearing upon the merits of these two conventions. For this purpose only, it is of no importance that the law regards the proprietor of any enterprise as different from an ordinary creditor. While an artificial person, strictly speaking, can have no viewpoint, nevertheless for clarity it seems permissible to say that from the viewpoint of the entity there is no distinction between the proprietor and other creditors.

Canning[9] has mentioned that accountancy writings are full of "the notion that the distinction between liabilities and net proprietorship is in some way or other dependent on the relative legal priority of claims."

In some forms of business organizations it is true that a proprietor cannot withdraw his investment or his profits at will. That this is a restriction imposed by law, not by accounting, is evidenced by the fact that if the proprietor disregards the law and does make such withdrawals there is nothing in the entity theory to prevent recording them just like any other liability.

8 John B. Canning, *The Economics of Accountancy* (New York, The Ronald Press Company, 1929), p. 55.
9 *Ibid.*, p. 63.

The entity convention insists that the proprietor is a person, or group, separate and distinct from the accounting entity; that the proprietor lends money to the accounting entity; that the accounting entity may or may not pay the money back to the proprietor, this being a matter determined by the proprietor's own wish and by any legal restrictions.

Description of Entity.—Disregarding for the moment non-proprietorship liabilities, increases in entity property automatically become additional liabilities to the proprietor and decreases in property automatically reduce the liability to the proprietor.

The entity is as soulless and automatic as a slot machine. Its activities are in response to the demands of proprietorship either direct or through appointed managers. An intangible and usually a complicated mechanism, the entity is operated by human beings for their own benefit. In and of itself the entity makes no profits, suffers no losses, is incapable of enjoyment, sorrow, greed, or other human emotions which influence those who direct it.

There are, of course, various types of accounting entities but their essential characteristics are the same. There is no fundamental accounting difference between the entity implied by some small unincorporated society, association, or club, and the accounting entity for which records are kept in a steel corporation, a railroad, a bank, or a municipality.

How, then, shall one distinguish an accounting entity? It exists only in relation to a double entry accounting record. If a social club maintains no double entry record, then no accounting entity exists although the association may conceivably be visualized as some other type of entity.

The double entry record implies an accounting entity. Conversely, an accounting entity implies a double entry record. If a department or branch of a business maintains its own double entry record, inevitably there exists an accounting entity. Each group of fund accounts in a municipality relates to a separate accounting entity. An accounting entity exists even in the case of a single milk wagon, if a double entry record is maintained for that milk wagon.

In certain business organizations having isolated plants, warehouses, or similar units there will be as many accounting entities as there are sets of double entry books maintained. In New York savings banks it is not uncommon to find several departments of one bank each with its own set of double entry records. In such a case there would be as many accounting entities as there were departmental bookkeeping systems.

Entity Concept in Relation to Size.—Some authorities are willing to adopt the entity convention for corporations but not for partnerships or sole proprietorships; or are willing to adopt the entity convention for large or moderate-sized business units but not for small ones, or for enterprises where proprietorship and management are so merged that it seems ridiculous to think of the business as having an artificial personality.

Paton[10] has pointed out that: "A blind insistence on the independence of the business entity in such situations is bound to lead to unreasonable conclusions." Elsewhere he insisted that: "To conceive of the business of the pop vendor at a football game as having any distinct existence, to take an extreme example, would obviously be quite fantastic."

Fantastic or not, and regardless of whether it is accepted or rejected, it remains true that if the pop vendor at the football game maintains a double entry accounting record, the viewpoint it expresses is that of an entity separate and apart from himself. Even the housewife cannot keep her household accounts in double entry without unconsciously accepting the entity convention.

Admittedly this is carrying the entity convention rather far, but it either has general application[11] or is valueless and it seems preferable to think of it as general in order to determine whether it can stand the test of unusual application.

The objection to the entity convention in such a situation as that of the pop vendor may be due to an assumption that the pop vendor must himself recognize the entity convention. This,

10 W. A. Paton, *Accounting Theory* (New York, The Ronald Press Company, 1922), pp. 476, 477.
11 It is, of course, recognized that any reference to general or universal application of this or any other convention is somewhat dogmatic. No one could argue for universality in the application of any proposition.

of course, is not true. The entity exists only in relation to double entry bookkeeping the rules and practices of which many have learned without ever having considered the artificial person whose viewpoint determines the accounting equation.

Here it is intended to adopt this entity conception and pursue it to its logical conclusions. To do so may be helpful in an attempt to survey the nature of accounting profits.

In any event, either the proprietary or the entity viewpoint must be adopted in order to reason intelligently regarding accounting matters. Of the two the entity theory appears more logical and more helpful. The one real danger to be feared is that of a shifting viewpoint which, as will presently appear, causes many accounting misunderstandings.

Valuation Convention.—The first convention is that of the entity itself, but there is another convention which is equal in importance. This second convention is of money valuation involving various translations of physical or other assets held by the entity as agent for the owner.

This convention of money valuation adopted as a convenient aid to record keeping has caused much difficulty in the understanding and interpretation of accounting records. This is due in part to confusion with the economist's viewpoint. Thus Canning,[12] in his discussion of the subject, says:

> To show the importance of the income expected from any existing controlled source, a money valuation is placed upon it. If for any set of assets, e.g., those dedicated by the proprietor to the uses of an enterprise, correct money valuations are found, the sum of these asset valuations is not only the measure of the services running from the designated items, but is also the measure of the benefits running to their recipient.

This conception of the valuation of wealth in terms of rendered services represents a broader viewpoint than that of the accountant who uses money valuations merely as symbols.

To insist that accountants always regard valuation from this limited viewpoint would be a serious error. Many authorities are both accountants and economists, and while they rec-

12 John B. Canning, *The Economics of Accountancy* (New York, The Ronald Press Company, 1929), p. 48.

ognize the simple purpose of the valuation convention, they also attempt to reconcile it with the economic viewpoint. Many difficult problems of present-day accounting practice result from this attempted reconciliation.

In any examination of the fundamental accounting structure, only confusion can result from combining the two viewpoints.

The entity, as such, is not concerned with economic measures of valuation but rather symbolizes in terms of money various transactions reflecting a charge and discharge relationship between entity and proprietor.

Some have been concerned about the improper statistical basis of accounting valuation. Canning[13] refers to the fact that "the measurements in accountants' reports are of diverse statistical orders." It appears, however, that this comment, like many others, is based upon a shifted viewpoint. The recognition of dollar valuation as mere symbolism appears to be essential in order to avoid such confusion.

Some authorities, among them Henry Rand Hatfield, refer to valuation at cost as "a rule." Hatfield[14] says that it "clearly rests upon an assumption and is not an expression of a fundamental principle. It obviously does not apply where the asset is found or received as a gift."

It is true that the accounting mechanism is not designed to take care of such situations without arbitrary valuation. On the other hand, such arbitrary valuation is assigned by the proprietor and thereafter represents the basis for the charge and discharge relationship.

Valuation at Cost.—From the entity viewpoint valuation at cost is natural, but the accounting equation is not affected by valuations at other than cost. If, in the sheep illustration previously cited, another sheep had been found and added to the flock, it would, of course, have been necessary for the accounting mechanism to show entity responsibility for eleven rather than ten sheep, but the value assigned to the newly found sheep would not be significant save as a symbol.

---

13 *Ibid.*, p. 320.
14 Henry Rand Hatfield, *Accounting* (New York, D. Appleton-Century Company, Inc., 1927), p. 66.

The concept that valuation is no more than a convenient method of symbolizing is helpful in simplifying accounting problems. The explanations frequently offered by accounting writers that cost valuation should be used because it is "the easiest of objective verification," or that cost valuation has merit because of "its certainty, rather than its exactness as a measure of value," may be true. The entity, however, adopts cost for initial valuation because it is the natural valuation when cost figures are obtainable. It is not a matter of entity concern when other initial valuations necessarily must be used.

Only when this question of valuation is approached from the ownership, credit, or legal viewpoints does a non-cost basis become of serious import. It is only when the task of interpreting accounting figures is faced that the convention of dollar valuation causes trouble. Such interpretation is always from the ownership, legal, or credit viewpoint, never from that of the entity. From the entity viewpoint valuation offers no problem of "diverse statistical orders."

He would indeed be a poor analyst who failed to consider the effects of such symbolizing. Spahr and Swenson[15] insist that it is only the careless and untrained who are deceived by money units.

One of the most commonly used and misused accounting words is "value." It is impossible to write on accounting matters without employing it frequently, and yet it has confusing connotations. Thus, value may be interpreted by one as cost value, by another as economic value, and by a third as realizable value. It therefore seems desirable to assert that, unless otherwise indicated, the word "value" as used here refers to accounting value based upon the monetary unit as a symbol for recording accountability and responsibility of the entity.

Both the entity concept and the valuation concept possess those qualities of artificiality and general acceptance which justify their being called conventions. There is a third basic accounting convention, namely, that of the accounting period, which will be examined shortly.

15 Spahr and Swenson, *Methods and Status of Scientific Research* (New York, Harper & Brothers, 1930).

Since it is impossible to conceive of accounting save as it is expressed in writing, similarly it is impossible to conceive of the accounting entity save in relation to double entry accounting records.

This need involve no elementary discussion of journals, the general ledger, and subsidiary ledgers. The actual mechanism of compiling the historical record of accounting transactions and then redistributing the items so listed is essentially simple. The collection of facts in one order and their subsequent redistribution in another order is an elementary statistical operation.

Classification.—The nature of the final classification is a matter of importance. The classification is, of course, derived from the equation "assets equal liabilities."

The process of elaborating this equation is in complete harmony with the charge and discharge concept of accounting. The responsibility of the entity as an agent is well served by classifying assets according to their obvious natural characteristics. The one asset upon which accounting rests is money. All other assets are translated into terms of money and it is inevitable that they are classified descriptively for identification.

CLASSIFICATION OF ASSETS. The natural classification of assets may be indicated somewhat as follows:

Cash . . . . $..............
Sheep . . . . $..............
Cloth . . . . $..............
Olive Oil . . . . . . $..............
Grain . . . . $..............
etc.

The adoption of this natural scheme of classification has the advantage of showing the dollar valuation and also of describing the different kinds of physical property which the dollar valuations symbolize.

From the entity viewpoint the classification of the liabilities is equally appropriate. The entity must keep a record of the people to whom it owes money and the amount owing to each one.

CLASSIFICATION OF LIABILITIES. The elementary classification of liabilities might be somewhat as follows:

John Jones	$. . . . .
George Brown	$. . . . .
Will Cass.	$. . . . .

USE OF CLASSIFICATION.   This asset and liability classification is perfect from the limited entity viewpoint.

On the one hand are described the various kinds of assets held by the entity together with their monetary translation. On the other hand are listed the names of the various persons who are creditors of the entity. One of these persons may be the proprietor. The others may have no rights of control or direction over the entity.

Cass may be assumed to be the proprietor, having full direction and control over the entity. To his account must be applied the gains and losses which result. This simply means that a gain is reflected as an increase in the entity's indebtedness to Cass, while a loss is shown as a decrease of the entity's indebtedness to Cass.

Smith and Brown, not having control over the entity, may be considered merely as non-proprietary creditors. The indebtedness to them is not influenced by the success or non-success of the entity's trading transactions.

NATURE OF LIABILITIES. The liabilities to Smith and Brown are generally described as "fixed and contractual" as compared with the liability to Cass which is "elastic and residual." This is the distinction made by Paton in his *Accounting Theory*.

As early as 1917, Paton suggested replacing the word "liabilities" with the word "equities." The preference for the word "equities" seems a somewhat euphemistic attempt to avoid legalistic reproach, particularly in those cases where the total liabilities exceed the total assets. In some such instances a deficit might conceivably be considered equivalent to an asset, in that it represents a claim of the entity against proprietorship. This is a rather roundabout justification for such treatment but contains a germ of truth in the case of sole proprietorships, partnerships, and municipalities.

By all commercial standards a municipality may appear hopelessly insolvent as judged by comparison of its actual assets with its liabilities, but the municipality does not rely upon its assets to meet its liabilities. Rather, it relies upon its power to obtain assets through taxation. If the citizens of that municipality be regarded as the proprietorship, then any deficiency of assets as compared to liabilities may be considered as an enforceable claim of the accounting entity against these citizens.

A deficit in corporation accounting is, if the same fiction be adopted, an asset representing a claim against proprietorship. This is rather meaningless in view of the fact that it is usually uncollectible because of the limited liability feature of corporations. In a corporation, therefore, no true net worth deficit can exist. A deficit may take the place of a surplus but not of surplus and capital. The going corporation generally shows some net liability to stockholders.

When a corporation is winding up its affairs, the statement of asset values may not be prepared on a going concern basis but on a realizable basis. A sizable discrepancy between such realizable assets and a greater amount of creditors' claims is fictitious, since all of the creditors will not be paid in full if any deficit exists after corporate capital and surplus have been extinguished.

Liquidation must proceed according to a proper sequence and it is more than a matter of convenience to schedule liabilities at their full amounts even though it may be known that some of the liabilities ranking low in the priority scale may never be paid in full, if at all. In such instances the deficit is equivalent to deduction from all of the liabilities without being specifically apportioned to them.

None of these situations refutes the entity convention. The entity convention itself is certainly not violated by showing a deficit as an asset even though such a showing would be highly improper from other viewpoints. Such a deficit may, therefore, be regarded as a bookkeeping claim against proprietorship regardless of its legal collectibility or uncollectibility.

Modifications of Classification.—The effect of original entity classification upon modern accounting is of greater importance. The natural and elementary classification of assets according to kind has, of course, been greatly modified. The division of assets into current and non-current assets has resulted in grouping from a non-entity viewpoint. Also some of the items must be subdivided. Thus, an inventory of merchandise may be shown in part among the current assets and in part among non-current assets.

For convenience such an item as cash itself may be subdivided according to its custodianship. In ancient accounting the slave was the custodian of all cash, but in modern accounting the entity deposits cash with various custodians, resulting in such a classification as Cash in the First National Bank, Cash in the Marine Midland Trust Company, Cash in the Chase National Bank, and Petty Cash in the possession of an employee.

It is interesting to note retention of the fiction that the entity is still in possession of the funds, although it has really parted with them and actually possesses only certain receivables in lieu of cash. Nevertheless, the traditional viewpoint still persists and these various claims against banks, cashiers, etc., are generally classified as though they were cash in possession of the entity. Even where such cash is described as "cash in bank," it still retains its character as currency.

The segregation of current assets also called for a similar grouping of liabilities with the result that the amount owed by the entity to one individual may be subdivided. This introduces a subordinate accounting convention, namely, that of treating various relations with one individual as though they were separate relations with two or more individuals. Frequently the proprietor of a business may also be a short-term creditor and also a long-term creditor with the result that the accounting mechanism, although not necessarily the accounting report, treats him as though he were several people instead of one.

Some of the practical necessities causing modification of the basic entity classification will be examined in later chapters. It is sufficient at this time to realize that modern accounting with all of its complexities and its elaboration of classification is still influenced by some of the natural descriptions for establishing charges and discharges in primitive accounting.

Relation of Assets and Liabilities.—An inevitable result of classifying assets according to their obvious physical characteristics and liabilities by persons is the difficulty experienced by some laymen when they attempt to relate asset items to liability items.

Since a different scheme of classification is used for each, there can be no direct relationship between an item on one side and an item on the other except where such a relationship is deliberately specified as in the case of liens.

Numerous difficulties of accounting interpretation have resulted from attempts to imagine such relationships.

Entity and Proprietor.—It is important to note the essential nature of the accounting record as it is built around the entity convention.

First of all, the accounting record is a specialized mechanism derived from an equation which reflects the viewpoint of an entity. In other words, it is conventionalized statistical history expressed only in terms of money. The specifications of this mechanism, then, are: (1) entity viewpoint, (2) derivation from an equation, (3) historical nature, and (4) expression in financial terms.

Of particular interest is the relationship between the accounting entity and the proprietor or owner. In fact, it seems safe to say that originally this was the only relationship for which the accounting mechanism was designed. While insisting that the investment of an owner in a business together with accumulated undistributed profits represent a liability of the entity, it must be admitted from the proprietor's viewpoint that a fundamental distinction must be made between amounts owing him by the entity for money invested and amounts owing him by the entity for accumulated undistributed profits. It has already been explained that this subdivision is not important from the entity viewpoint, but the proprietor advances money to the entity in hope of its ultimate return with accretions and he must have some simple method of distinguishing between his capital investment and the subsequent profit thereon.

From this necessity is derived the present distinction between investment and surplus.

Many accountants will disagree with this viewpoint since they conceive of investment and surplus as corporate phenomena only. The use of investment and surplus accounts in sole proprietorships and partnerships is practically unheard of. There seems to be a well settled legal principle to the effect that profit in the case of the sole proprietor rests immediately in him. Similarly, profits in the case of a partnership rest immediately in the partners according to some predetermined ratio. These are, however, legal viewpoints of no present concern.

The distinction between capital invested and the income return on that capital is a natural one which is independent of legal consideration and there is probably no sole proprietor who does not attempt to distinguish, in his own mind at least, between the actual capital which he has invested and the return thereon, even though he may not do so by the bookkeeping device of separate accounts. Furthermore, the whole philosophy of accounting profit rests upon this distinction between invested capital and the net income return thereon. Accordingly, for convenience it may be assumed that the total amount owing by an entity to its proprietor may, instead of appearing as a single liability, be divided into two liabilities represented by two accounts, one reflecting the entity liability for investment and the other representing the entity liability for accumulated profits.

Investment and Profits.—The liability of the entity for a proprietor's investment does not change except to record additional investments or withdrawals of investment. The entity's liability to the proprietor for accumulated undistributed profits is subject to various changes.

Every transaction which does not involve an even exchange of some kind must increase or decrease the entity's indebtedness to the proprietor.

Theoretically such increases and decreases are recorded in the surplus or undivided profits account. The liability of the entity represented by this account is not only increased by profits made and decreased by losses, but is also decreased by actual payments by the entity to the proprietor.

Assuming the existence of a surplus, or undivided profits, account and thinking of it as a certain kind of liability owing by the entity to the proprietor, subsequent classification becomes simplified, since all of the various profit or loss accounts may be regarded as a break-down of the undivided profits account.

With only two proprietorship accounts it would be possible to operate the accounting mechanism and to provide the principal accounting information needed by the proprietor. This, it must be insisted, represents the real test of the accounting mechanism.

This realization that the entity itself makes neither a profit nor a loss is useful in attempting to reconcile the accounting for ordinary business activities and the accounting for so-called non-profit organizations. Basically there is no accounting difference between an organization for profit and a non-profit organization. The same essential accounting mechanism, the same essential entity convention, apply regardless of whether there is a proprietorship intent to make a profit and regardless of any legal rules.

Indefinite Proprietorship.—It should be noted that liabilities may at times be indefinite. The liability for bearer bonds outstanding is a true liability even though the creditors are not identified by name. Similarly, actual proprietors and the reported proprietors may not be the same in large corporations whose stock is actively traded on exchanges or in unincorporated clubs and societies whose membership is constantly changing. In such instances a subordinate convention is evident, namely, that the entire proprietorship group is treated for equation purposes as a single proprietor. In corporation accounting one balance sheet item of capital stock outstanding may refer to thousands of stockholders of subsidiary record.

The treatment thus far has completely disregarded certain legal and economic viewpoints. Their importance practically and theoretically cannot be denied but they had little or no part in shaping the original design of the accounting mechanism. It is only by understanding the original design that a starting point for subsequent explorations can be established.

Advantages of Entity Convention.—There is undoubtedly just as much authority in favor of the proprietary viewpoint as there is in favor of the entity viewpoint.

To many it seems unnecessary to consider accounting problems from the viewpoint of an artificial person, particularly when such a concept involves the treatment of proprietorship investment as a liability in the face of express denial of this relationship by law. No one can quarrel with Montgomery's[16] statement that: "In the case of general partnerships there can be no liability to any partner." Of course this is true, but it is a legal truth rather than an accounting truth.

It is believed that simplification results from taking a firm stand that such an accounting liability does exist, completely disregarding the conflict with the legal viewpoint.

Entity Concept and the Accountant.—The accountant who bases his reasoning upon the entity convention may, and frequently does, conceal that element of his working philosophy which baldly asserts that an artificial entity owes money to a proprietor for his investment and accumulated profits. But this may be due to no lack of faith. Rather, it may be prompted by the desire to avoid legal arguments.

One thing seems relatively certain, regardless of whether the accountant openly adopts the entity convention, and whether he is willing to follow it to its logical conclusion, nevertheless the various procedures he employs assert his faith. The old saying that "actions speak louder than words" is strictly appropriate here because the accountant's actions in making debits and credits to liability, capital, and surplus accounts bear silent witness to his adoption of the entity viewpoint.

Additional evidence that this viewpoint is fundamental to accounting is found in the popularity of the caption "liabilities" in corporate balance sheets as a substitute for such captions as

---

16 Robert H. Montgomery, *Auditing Theory and Practice* (New York, The Ronald Press Company, 1934), p. 328.

"liabilities and capital," "liabilities and net worth," and other variations thereof. Over 86% of the balance sheets inspected by Fjeld[17] used "liabilities" alone as the caption of the right-hand side.

17 E. I. Fjeld, *Balance Sheet Classification and Terminology* (New York, 1936), p. 14.

CHAPTER 6

PROFIT DETERMINATION IN TRADING VENTURES

That type of business activity known as the venture demanded a broadened accounting and contributed greatly to the development of present-day concepts of accounting profit. From Littleton[1] comes this short but comprehensive description of the typical venture:

The silent capitalist (*commendator*) entrusted his goods, and occasionally a ship of his own, to the active trader (*tractator*) upon a partnership basis. Naturally, in these circumstances the latter would have to make a careful and detailed report upon his return; especially if he had been trading with goods belonging to several silent partners. Here was a definite need for capital accounts comparable to the master's account kept by the Roman slave, and here too was a need for goods accounts, whereas the Roman needed only personal accounts for loans made.

The Liquidated Venture.—As a basis for discussing the influence of the venture upon the development of accounting, a special situation, probably uncommon in the early days, may be assumed.

To avoid certain problems of valuation of no immediate concern, assume that a capitalist makes a cash investment in a trading venture and that his employed manager uses the money to buy a ship and to stock it with merchandise for a long voyage. During the voyage he stops at a number of ports, sells merchandise, buys other merchandise, and finally at the termination of the voyage he returns home, all the merchandise having been sold for cash. He then sells the ship and deducts from the cash then on hand his own salary or share of the proceeds and returns the remainder to the owner.

[1] A. C. Littleton, *Accounting Evolution to 1900* (New York, American Institute Publishing Co., Inc., 1933), p. 37.

66

This situation differs from the master-slave illustration in two important ways. First, the business venture was limited to one voyage of indeterminate length. Second, a new type of asset, namely, the ship itself, was involved.

NECESSITY FOR REPORTING. The single venture calls imperatively for a final report.

There is no reason to assume any formal reporting in the master-slave relationship—the master had full access to the accounting record maintained by his slave. When he desired any information regarding the state of his affairs, he could obtain it by inspection. The business venture, on the other hand, is characterized by geographical separation which makes it impossible for the owner to obtain information from time to time. He must wait until the venture has been completed, at which time it is natural for him to require a full report summarizing all of the transactions from the inception to the termination of the voyage.

CAPITAL ASSETS. The introduction of a new type of asset also is interesting.

This asset was not acquired for purpose of resale at a profit but rather as a secondary but essential instrument serving the major trading purpose of the venture. Nevertheless, the final profit for the expedition cannot be determined until after the ship has been sold. The ship may, of course, be sold for a price either higher or lower than the cost, but since physical property ordinarily deteriorates due to wear and tear and the passage of time, it may be assumed that the selling price is less than the cost of the ship, thus offsetting to some extent gains made from merchandise trading.

This cost, represented by the difference between the cost of the ship and the price for which it is later sold, may be referred to as depreciation. Since trading operations could not be conducted without the ship and since the ship cannot be owned without depreciation, it is clear that depreciation represents an essential element in the determination of final net profit.

In this illustration there is a complete cycle from cash to cash. The venture starts with the investment of cash by the owner or proprietor. The cash is then converted into merchandise and into a ship. The merchandise is then reconverted again into cash, the cash again into merchandise, and this merchandise again converted to cash. At the end of the voyage the ship itself is converted into cash, the trader is compensated, and the amount of profit is determined by subtracting the amount of cash first invested from the amount of cash then on hand. It is this latter amount which represents the debt of the accounting entity to the capitalist. Note that this proprietorship debt may be classified in two ways, i.e., the debt representing the original investment and the debt representing the net profit.

In this situation there are two important elements: (1) complete termination of the enterprise, and (2) complete realization of all assets in cash. Accordingly, there can be no uncertainty as to the amount of profit.

The Partially Liquidated Venture.—Obviously, a successful trader would soon accumulate capital of his own.

Perhaps he himself might purchase a ship and rely upon others to finance the merchandise. At the conclusion of one voyage he might embark immediately upon another, each voyage being financed by a different backer. Immediately a new accounting problem is presented involving two separate ventures and but one capital asset.

Just what procedure can be adopted in order to make an acceptable statement of profits for each of the two voyages separately? The difficulty refers only to the depreciation of the ship. At the end of the first voyage it is not sold. The amount of depreciation is not determinable by the sale of the asset. Accordingly, it is necessary to make an estimate. At the end of the first voyage the trader must estimate the amount of depreciation his ship has suffered, must include that as an element of cost in determining the profits from the first voyage, and should carry the depreciated value of the ship as an asset in the new set of accounting records prepared for the second voyage.

The situation becomes further complicated if the trader has some merchandise left on hand at the end of the first voyage which he carries over as the beginning inventory of the second voyage. Since the value of the merchandise left on hand has not been put to the test of actual realization by sale, another problem of estimation is presented. Accordingly, this situation provides the background for considering certain modern problems of inventory.

INVENTORIES. Unquestionably, the inventory in ancient times was a physical inventory, taken by actually counting and valuing whatever asset values were left on hand at report time.

There is no reason to believe that such inventories, whether of fixed assets or of merchandise, were valued on the basis of actual initial cost. Generally, it must have been the trader's purpose to establish inventory values as close as possible to what could have been realized if they had been sold instead of retained on hand.

The trader returning from the Orient with bales of silk, rugs, perfume, and similar commodities would naturally desire to avoid unpleasant altercations at settlement time. Theoretically, the proper course for him to follow would be to dispose of such merchandise and render his accounting on a cash basis. The next best thing would be for him to estimate as closely as possible the current selling price for such merchandise.

Reasonably assured that he could, if he so desired, make a sale and receive such prices, he was then fairly safe in using current market prices of inventory in rendering his report. He may have adopted the same method in valuing his vessel, although its larger cost complicated determination of a market price.

The need for valuing remaining assets on a basis equivalent to that of actual realization created a precedent which has caused numerous accounting difficulties in later years.

INVENTORIES AND MIXED ACCOUNTS. The inventory idea was long applied, not only to inventories but to other assets. Often but one account was used for each asset, income resulting therefrom and costs referring thereto, the mixed balance of the account being corrected, periodically, by revaluation of the asset.

This early inventory procedure persisted for many years.

Littleton[2] quotes several authors on this point and concludes that: "The inclusion of the cost of the building on the debit side and periodically, in the inventory, on the credit side was quite in harmony with the long established usage which brought an earning asset into account with its own expenses and incomes."

In 1854 one writer recommended that a steamboat account "be debited with costs and charges and credited with what was produced either by sale, freight or passage." In 1863 an accounting text showed taxes charged to real estate account, this same account being credited with rent received.

Even in the present century, a somewhat similar practice has persisted with respect to merchandise. The so-called old-fashioned merchandise account is a mixed account which includes among its elements the beginning inventory, subsequent purchases, merchandise sales, and the inventory on hand at a later time.

This method of relating an asset to its corresponding expense and income doubtless appealed to the earlier accountants as representing a logical association of ideas.

The former popularity of these mixed accounts may help to explain the persistence of certain related practices such as market price valuation and irregular depreciation. This primitive plan of "taking inventory" of all assets was necessary to achieve the equivalent of actual realization.

Also, the figure resulting from mingling in one account an asset and its related expense and income could only be adjusted by an actual inventory.

PROFIT DETERMINATION BY BALANCE SHEETS. Perhaps these circumstances provide a possible explanation of the popularity of the balance sheet viewpoint.

About the only way that the trader could render a final accounting was by a balance sheet. It was only by comparing the balance sheet at the beginning of a venture and the end of a venture that the profit could be determined. This, of course, was true because of the estimates of value which had to be made.

Littleton[3] refers to this use of balance sheets as indicating

2 A. C. Littleton, *Accounting Evolution to 1900* (New York, American Institute Publishing Co., Inc., 1933), p. 356.
3 *Ibid.*, p. 216.

"a conception of profit which is associated with the final liquidation and winding up of a company: the profit consisting of whatever property was left after using the assets to discharge the liabilities and reimburse the shareholders for their capital contributions."

Canning[4] emphasizes this viewpoint when he says: "the determination of profit not distributed in dividends and of loss is really made by successive valuations of assets and of liabilities."

ACCURATE PROFIT DETERMINATION. There are still many who believe that termination of a business venture and complete realization represent the only basis for profit determination.

Those holding this belief might find consolation in the views of Byerly[5] who says that, disregarding arbitrary accounting periods, "it might be logical to say that we have no profit until the money expended on the plant has been recovered."

Canning[6] asserts that the gross income of any person arising out of his relation to an enterprise is never determined until that relation has ceased to exist and he adopts the sound view that: "All measures of income for periods less than the total lapse of time during a relationship or less than the duration of an enterprise are approximate indexes only."

It is in termination and complete realization that accuracy is attained in calculating the profits of a single venture.

It is the estimated valuations involved when one venture follows upon the heels of another which cause uncertainty as to the profits of the two ventures.

The trader engaging in successive ventures will, at some time, reach the point where his merchandise is completely exhausted and his ship has been disposed of. At that time, and at that time only, can he accurately determine the realized profit for the series of ventures, but he still will find himself unable to verify the accuracy of profit estimation for *each* of the voyages made during the entire cycle from cash to cash.

4 John B. Canning, *The Economics of Accountancy* (New York, The Ronald Press Company, 1929), p. 65.
5 F. P. Byerly, "Formulation of Accounting Principles or Conventions," *The Journal of Accountancy*, August 1937, p. 96.
6 John B. Canning, *The Economics of Accountancy* (New York, The Ronald Press Company, 1929), p. 124.

The Venture in Modern Times.—The venture is not an extinct phenomenon. The man whose cash savings permit him to buy a plot of ground, erect a house, hold it for a period of time, and then sell it at a profit, is engaged in a single venture not different fundamentally from the early trading voyages. Such an investor knows full well that his profit can be determined only upon the termination of his venture by complete realization in cash.

It is in this manner that he thinks of his investment regardless of the fact that annual tax returns or other legal requirements may make it necessary for him to report annually.

The salesman who buys a second-hand automobile and starts on a trip throughout the western states selling magazine subscriptions is engaged in a single venture which is terminated when he returns home and sells the car.

Successive Ventures in Modern Times.—As an illustration of successive ventures there is the typical case of a small building contractor constructing a succession of houses.

His various tools, his truck or tractor, his concrete mixer, and other items are equivalent to the trader's ship mentioned in the previous illustration. Until this contractor winds up his affairs and sells all of his equipment, he cannot know his total profit. Even then he cannot tell how much should be ascribed to one job and how much to another.

Even in some business organizations usually thought of as continuous there are elements of the business venture. An excellent example of this is to be noted in the case of a retail book store where every purchase of newly published books represents a new and untried venture. The book store manager would indeed be guilty of folly if he viewed his commitments in any other way. One purchase of ten books may be very popular and all be sold. Another lot of ten books may move slowly and the bookseller may be left with several copies on hand. It is an axiom in this trade that the profit lies in the last books sold, and this is indeed literally true. The usual discount in the book business is 40%. Thus, the bookseller may acquire ten books for $1.20 each, or a total cost of $12, which he marks to sell for $2 each, or $20. When he has sold six of the books he has recovered his purchase cost, and if the four remaining books are never sold he has made no profit.

This method of reasoning applies with much less force where standard merchandise is handled, but the book business actually does consist of a series of separate business ventures although conducted under one roof and under one management.

The persistence of the single venture even into modern times has caused considerable accounting difficulty in certain industries which have been forced to adopt the year as a basis for tax or other reporting purposes. The shipyard which undertakes a two- or three-year task of building a large boat cannot determine the profit on this venture until the boat is completed, delivered, and the cash received. Modern reporting methods require annual estimates of profit and the attempt to reconcile a venture, such as building a ship, with the calendar has been the cause of accounting conflict and the assertion that even so well-founded a convention as that of income realization cannot always apply.

Overlapping Ventures.—The next step in the development of modern accounting practice is to be found in overlapping ventures.

Many modern business enterprises consist in reality of a series of overlapping ventures, particularly if the viewpoint is adopted that each acquisition of merchandise is equivalent to a separate venture. This change from separate ventures to a continuous stream of transactions, such as may be noticed in many manufacturing plants or retail stores, introduces the all-important convention of accounting periods. Where business ventures were isolated phenomena extending over lengthy periods a report was expected at the termination of each venture. Where the ventures overlapped in such a way as to provide continuity, the older procedure of reporting was inapplicable.

Accordingly, there was introduced the third major convention of accounting and one which has proved most troublesome, namely, the convention of the fiscal year or other accounting period.

CHAPTER 7

ACCOUNTING PERIOD CONVENTION

The development and rapid growth of business created certain accounting problems which were unknown in the days of trading ventures. Most present-day trading is in the form of a continuous stream of transactions.

Business Continuity.—This transition from successive to overlapping ventures has been more noticeable in certain industries than in others.

In the early days of automobiles their manufacturing and marketing conformed somewhat to the successive venture type. As automotive manufacturing practice became standardized and as effective distribution channels were developed, individuality as between one car and another was practically lost. With the introduction of the modern production line, automobile manufacturing now resembles a continuous stream like the manufacture of soap, breakfast foods, matches, or razor blades.

It is conceivable that the automobile business might have developed along the same lines as boat building. While many attempts, some moderately successful, have been made to standardize boat building, thus permitting continuous production, the boat builder generally must regard the manufacture of each boat as a separate venture.

Where a product must be adapted specifically to its environment, installation costs may be so high as to give each order some of the aspects of a venture. Thus, the venture idea persists in certain phases of such manufacturing as that of structural steel or boilers and in many applications of air conditioning and heating. The manufacturing of airplanes is even now undergoing the transition from a series of separate ventures to continuous production.

In many other fields of business endeavor it has become

almost impossible to trace separate ventures. Transactions differ from one another in various respects but industry in general is characterized by so much standardization and uniformity that the traditional profit tests of termination and realization have been considerably modified.

Generally, the modern corporation has permanent life which effectively prevents any final casting up of money profits such as would result from liquidation of all the assets leaving only cash on hand for distribution.

Termination and Liquidation as Tests of Profit.—In practice a business may be liquidated by legal action. In such instances the traditional profit tests of termination and realization are applied, although it must be observed that such liquidation generally shows losses rather than profits.

In small business units voluntary liquidation is not uncommon. The confectionery store, tobacco store, or other modest establishment is often terminated and liquidated with the result that profits, if any, can accurately be determined over the period between the birth and the death of such an enterprise. Temporary ventures such as rooming houses and restaurants, that always spring up in the neighborhood of construction work, are in this same class. This is true also of concessionaires at world's fairs.

It is somewhat ironic that true accounting profits may be determined for such evanescent ventures while the same simple and accurate determination of profit is utterly impossible for the large, well-managed corporation with an indefinite life tenure. This point of view has been recognized by numerous authorities.

Kester,[1] for example, says that: "Profits are accurately and definitely determinable only when a business ceases and is liquidated. Profits of a going concern are always estimates."

Canning[2] also touches upon this same matter from the viewpoint of both accounting and economics in the following statement:

[1] Roy B. Kester, *Advanced Accounting* (New York, The Ronald Press Company, 1933), p. 494.
[2] John B. Canning, *The Economics of Accountancy* (New York, The Ronald Press Company, 1929), pp. 123, 124.

1. No measure of gross income made before an enterprise is wound up either is, or purports to be, a precisely determined matter of fact about the history of the enterprise.

2. The gross income of any person, arising out of any of his relations to an enterprise, is never determined as a matter of fact until that relation has ceased to exist. This is true no matter whether that person be proprietor, shareholder, creditor, or what not.

3. But a final measure of gross income that is a fact and that describes a state of affairs in the real world does inevitably result from the accountant's procedure both (a) when the relation of any person to an enterprise ceases in reality, and (b) when any enterprise is wound up.

4. All measures of income for periods less than the total lapse of time during a relationship or less than the duration of an enterprise are approximate indexes only.

Interim Profit Estimation.—For numerous excellent and practical reasons the computation of profits cannot await the termination of a business enterprise. There is a demand from all sides for frequent profit determination. The owners of a business require periodic reports. The managers of an enterprise must receive regular financial information as a basis for administration. Last, but not least, taxing authorities will not wait indefinitely to learn accounting profits.

These demands for regular accounting reports may be considered responsible for the third basic convention of accounting, namely, the accounting period.

Along with the entity convention and the valuation convention, the convention of accounting periods must take equal rank even though of later development in point of time.

Length of the Accounting Period.—In the past, accounting periods were not necessarily of same length. Hatfield[3] reports:

. . . of the old account books which have come down to us, one was not balanced until the end of nine years, another not until twenty-seven years had elapsed. The British East-India Company prepared a general balance sheet in 1665—but not again until 1685. But during the seventeenth century the custom of business men changed and a marked step was taken by the French Ordinance of 1673 requiring a balance sheet each two years.

[3] Henry Rand Hatfield, *Accounting* (New York, D. Appleton-Century Company, Inc., 1927), p. 3.

THE ANNUAL PERIOD. The now accepted and generally recognized accounting period is the year, usually the calendar year.

Commenting on the yearly period, Littleton[4] points out that "man is strangely agricultural in his traditions, even though society has become industrial." He also sets forth in some detail the importance of the recurring cycle of the year and the significance of seed time and harvest and suggests that the year, as representing the common accounting period, is little more than an inheritance from astronomy through agriculture.

MONTHLY AND QUARTERLY PERIODS. Seasonal characteristics rule out any formal accounting period shorter than a year. Thus, Sanders[5] has pointed out that: "The seasonal nature of many businesses renders short term reports of little or no significance." It is, of course, true that most business organizations do prepare monthly or at least quarterly reports, but these are generally regarded as operating reports for the guidance of operating men and are seldom considered sufficiently reliable in certain respects for general publication.

The demand by the New York Stock Exchange for quarterly reports to stockholders ran into this seasonal objection. Various accounting authorities expressed their belief that quarterly reports might prove deceptive rather than enlightening, with the result that the Exchange agreed to a compromise whereby a full year's report was rendered at the end of each quarter, thus eliminating the influence of seasonal variations.

LONGER PERIODS THAN THE YEAR. Business men who have been seriously and unfairly affected by taxes on yearly profits have at times expressed the belief that the annual accounting period may be too short. The opinion of Graham[6] bears upon this problem. He asserts that: "Even a casual review of price ranges and production statistics in most industries

4 A. C. Littleton, *Accounting Evolution to 1900* (New York, American Institute Publishing Co., Inc., 1933), p. 10.
5 T. H. Sanders, "Reports to Stockholders," *The Accounting Review*, September 1934, p. 206.
6 E. W. Graham, "Current Practices in Inventory Valuation," *N.A.C.A. Bulletin*, March 1, 1937, p. 753.

indicates that the business cycle extends over a longer period than a year—in some instances five or more years."

The same thought is expressed by Woodward[7] as follows: "The meaning of most figures is limited by the fact that they are available at twelve-month intervals; a year does not, in most businesses, represent the normal operation cycle."

ADVANTAGES AND DISADVANTAGES OF THE ANNUAL PERIOD. It appears that a period of twelve months represents the least objectionable of any of the various accounting periods which have been suggested. A longer period, such as five years, for example, would furnish needed information too infrequently. A shorter period, such as the calendar month, is so greatly affected by seasonal variations as to affect comparative accuracy in reported profits.

While many corporations do prepare monthly accounting reports, it is doubtful whether operating executives place complete confidence in the determination of monthly net profits. They are more concerned with some of the detail figures on such monthly reports. Such items as sales, purchases, and certain of the costs have value from the viewpoint of management control even though the final figure of monthly net profit to which these contribute is admittedly erroneous.

Accountants and business men are disturbed because calendar years themselves are not comparable and also because the months of which calendar years are composed show substantial differences in the number of working days. The natural variation of the length of months, coupled with the distorting influence of Sundays and holidays, has frequently been noted. In an attempt to obtain greater comparability, certain establishments have adopted four-week periods rather than monthly periods for operating reports. This, of course, is bound to cause some variation at the year end, necessitating adjustments which the majority of authorities consider undesirable.

NATURAL BUSINESS YEAR. The general acceptance of the year as the accounting period does not necessarily involve acceptance of the *calendar* year.

7 Donald B. Woodward, "Changes in Capital Financing," *Journal of the American Statistical Association*, March 1938, p. 13.

The natural business year generally does not end on December 31, but rather on the last day of some other month depending upon the seasonal characteristics of each particular business, i.e., when business activity is at its lowest seasonal point and inventories are at a minimum.

The desirability of adopting the natural business year has long been recognized as evidenced by an editorial in *The Journal of Accountancy* (March 1937) relating that one Isaac Preston Cory wrote in 1839:

It is customary with every merchant once or twice a year to make what is called a "rest," when he balances his books, and examines all his stock in hand, in order to ascertain the amount of this stock and the profits and losses of his business. To this operation he usually devotes that time of the year when business is most flat, and when most of the personal accounts are made up, and real accounts exhausted by the sale of the articles in which he deals.

The adoption of the natural business year probably results in more accurate profit reporting than the use of an arbitrary closing date. Professional accountants have been persistent in urging the adoption of the natural business year not only because it is logical, not only because it provides more accurate results, but also because professional accountants prefer to distribute rather than concentrate their efforts. The public accountant all of whose clients use the calendar year finds that they demand his services at about the same time. Such an accounting firm faces a serious seasonal problem. The auditing staff may be largely augmented for a few months, after which only a skeleton staff may be maintained. By persuading clients to adopt the natural business year the firm can render better service to the clients and can maintain a stronger staff of employees.

Disregarding the natural business year for convenience of discussion, it may be assumed that the customary accounting period is the calendar year which ends at midnight December 31, and begins immediately following midnight on the morning of January 1. Theoretically, this leaves an infinitesimal fraction of time interval between the end of one accounting period and the beginning of the other, so that one of the old writers, reported by Charles E. Sprague in his *The Philosophy of Accounts,* referred to the opening date of an accounting period as January o instead of January 1. Modern practice, however, uses January 1 as the opening date of a new accounting period.

Periodic Asset Valuations.—The accounting period convention introduces the problem of annual asset valuations.

A problem of valuation was met in the case where merchandise or fixed assets remained unrealized at the end of a venture. Profits were then determined by estimating what such assets would have realized had they been disposed of. In other words, the price for which the merchandise could have been sold or the figure at which the ship might have been disposed of, represented the logical substitutes for actual realization through sale.

This method of figuring is not entirely unknown in periodic accounting reports, but complete revaluation on a realizable basis is generally impossible under modern conditions of large-scale operation, nor is there the same necessity for it as where successive ventures involved substantial changes in proprietorship.

Completely to reappraise a mammoth manufacturing plant each year would be an expensive task and one of little practical value even were the determination of its market value feasible.

The problem of appraising a ship, for example, at its realizable value and the problem of appraising even one plant of the United States Steel Corporation at realizable value are entirely different. A ship, particularly a small ship, generally possesses a sales value in that a number of prospective buyers are existent, but where is a prospective buyer for an entire manufacturing plant? There is no active trading market for large aggregates of fixed assets which have been put together into a specialized production design for specialized use. Any attempt to assign a market value to the aggregate of land, buildings, machinery, equipment, and motive power constituting the average industrial plant is obviously impossible.[8]

8 This matter of estimating realizable market value should not, of course, be confused with the type of service rendered by appraisal companies. The values they assign do not purport to be realizable values which can be used as a substitute for actual realization in a profit calculation.

Convention of the Going Business.—The adoption of the accounting period convention resulted in still another convention, namely, that of the "going business."

Based upon this "going business" convention, no attempt is made on December 31 of each year to value all the assets of a company on a realizable basis. Rather the emphasis is shifted to the amortizing of initial costs.

Clearly this shift represents an important change of viewpoint, since the resulting asset figures are not influenced by market price fluctuations ascribable to the law of supply and demand. The convention of the going business assumes that the owners of the business do not cease being owners on December 31 of each year but rather that there is a continuity of proprietorship.

Since December 31 represents a fictitious rather than an actual termination, the necessity for appraisal at realizable values as a substitute for actual realization no longer exists. It therefore becomes necessary to apportion the original cost of the assets over the various accounting periods benefiting from their use, as business practice does not contemplate a complete distribution on December 31 either of total assets or of total profits.

Accrued and Deferred Items.—The adoption of the accounting period convention introduced further problems referring to the expenditures of one period the benefit of which is enjoyed in another or the receipts of one period which represent the income of some other period. Thus, in 1938 rent may be paid for the use of property in 1939 or the property may be used in 1938 but the rent not be payable until 1939. Customers may pay in advance for merchandise in 1938 although the actual shipment and the charge against the customer are not made until 1939. Interest may be paid in advance. Payroll liabilities may extend over the end of an accounting period. These are a few examples of the various adjustments which are required in order to assign income and expenses to the proper periods. These adjustments result in certain asset accounts commonly known as accrued assets and deferred charges, and certain liability accounts termed accrued liabilities and deferred income.

These assets and liabilities are calculated on what may be considered equivalent to an inventory basis not only for balance sheet purposes, but more important, to distribute to the proper accounting periods their fair shares of cost and income.

Accrued assets are commonly considered as receivables payable in cash, while accrued liabilities will be liquidated in cash. Deferred charges, on the other hand, represent the asset portion of expenditures already made which must be carried over when they apply in part to a subsequent period. They are, therefore, not assets in the sense that they have a cash value but rather because they take the place of cash in so far as being available to meet a cost properly chargeable to a future accounting period. Deferred income, which usually represents a payment in advance by a customer, is equivalent to a deposit. While a liability, it is not a liability which is generally paid in cash. Rather it is to be paid by the rendering of service in some form or another.

The various adjustments creating these four types of accounts are necessary in order that the net liability of the entity to the proprietor at the end of each accounting period may be wholly expressed. That liability cannot be wholly expressed on December 31 of any year unless all of the income and all of the costs, expenses, and losses, no more and no less, properly applicable to that year have been taken into consideration.

The common method of expressing an equivalent thought is to say that accounting periods should be charged with costs in accordance with the benefits received by those accounting periods and should be credited with income on a similar basis, i.e., in proportion to corresponding services rendered.

PREPAID EXPENSES AND DEFERRED CHARGES. Many accountants make a distinction between prepaid expenses and deferred charges. For example, Miller[9] suggests that prepaid expenses differ from deferred charges in that they "represent a lessened demand for one of the most important of current assets—cash. This is probably the best reason which may be

[9] Hermann C. Miller, "Prepaid Expenses and Deferred Charges," *The Ohio Certified Public Accountant,* August 1938, p. 2.

advanced for including prepaid expenses in the current asset group." This suggestion for current asset grouping would, it is suspected, meet with little favor from credit men or accountants.

Sanders, Hatfield, and Moore[10] call attention to the fact that the common and most important element in both deferred charges and prepaid expenses "is that they are all amounts held in suspense, to be charged as expenses in subsequent fiscal periods; in the meantime, they are carried as assets in the balance-sheet." The same authors attempt to differentiate between deferred charges and prepaid expenses by reciting the broad characteristics of each: "Prepaid expenses are mostly of short duration, are for services not yet received, but to be received in the near future, and are usually parts of ordinary recurring expenses." "Deferred charges, on the other hand, generally are of longer duration, and are for services already received though the benefits from them may accrue in the future; often they do not constitute parts of regular expenses, and sometimes are abnormal losses which it is not yet convenient to write off."

Many accountants would quarrel with the latter part of this quotation since they would not consider abnormal losses as assets. To them the loss of an asset by flood, fire, or windstorm represents a disappearance of entity property which operates as a discharge to the entity and should be applied in reduction of the entity's liability to the proprietor.

It is, of course, easy to understand the occasional reluctance of management to authorize any such treatment. As a result such a loss is sometimes carried as though the destroyed asset still existed although under a different caption. A portion of that loss is then absorbed in each of a number of succeeding accounting periods. This, however, seems to be a case where expediency should not be the controlling factor and there appears to be no justification whatever for showing "abnormal losses which it is not yet convenient to write off" as an asset under any caption.

10 Sanders, Hatfield, and Moore, *A Statement of Accounting Principles* (New York, American Institute of Accountants, 1938), p. 75.

THE PROBLEM OF DEFERRED INCOME. Deferred income
has already been explained as a liability; however, it should be
repeated that it is a liability which ordinarily will not be settled
in money but rather in goods or services and that it therefore
may involve an element of profit. This element of profit has
been discussed by Sanders, Hatfield, and Moore[11] in the following words:

> Amounts received from customers in advance in the regular course
> of business are, strictly speaking, a mixture of liabilities and profit.
> In so far as they call for merchandise or services to be rendered in
> the future, the cost of such merchandise or services represents a liability.

The same authors also express the opinion that if cost is the
predominant element, then the whole amount may appear as a
current liability in the balance sheet, but if the cost is only a
small part of the amount, then the whole of that amount "may
properly be shown as a deferred credit to income rather than as
a current liability. In other words, such amounts received in
advance are deferred credits not to net income but to gross
income."

The balance sheet classification of deferred income seems to
be a problem of reporting rather than of accounting, i.e., it
results only from the attempt to segregate current liabilities
from other liabilities. Even from this viewpoint it seems that
the total amount should be shown in the current classification.
If by any chance the service or merchandise for which payment
was made in advance should not be rendered or delivered, then
the whole amount would be returnable to the customer. In
other words, the liability is for a deposit which has been made
and no profit element of any kind can be recognized until service
has been rendered or goods parted with. Only at that time is
the profit realized. Any other treatment gives undue consideration to intent, and intent surely affords no test of profit
recognition even in connection with such a comparatively unimportant matter as current or non-current classification on a
balance sheet.

In general, the adoption of accrual and deferment accounts
made necessary by the accounting period convention has had

11 *Ibid.*, p. 83.

an important effect upon the balance sheet. Its original character as an actual physical inventory offset by claims is somewhat altered, i.e., the inventory concept has been broadened to include accrued assets and deferred charges, and claims against the assets are increased by the inclusion of accrued liabilities and deferred income. The basic concept, however, remains unchanged, since the introduction of the new assets and liabilities merely provides a more accurate record of entity liability to the proprietor at each closing date.

Retained Profits.—The liability for profits as determined for each accounting period may be partially paid by the accounting entity. The remaining retained profits are commonly reflected in a liability account known as surplus account or undivided profits account.

From one viewpoint profits retained at the end of one year become permanent capital at the beginning of the subsequent year.

It is this viewpoint which prompted Husband[12] to ask: "Is it not true that from the standpoint of the later fiscal periods any success which is attained is due to the capital with which each fiscal year begins, or the paid-in capital minus the earlier deficits?"

There is a certain amount of logic underlying this viewpoint which is reflected in the attitude of some authorities toward testing the legality of dividend distributions. To those who agree with this line of reasoning, a corporation which starts a fiscal year with a deficit instead of a surplus but makes profits during the year should be permitted to declare dividends from such profits regardless of the fact that the profit for the year is insufficient to extinguish the prior deficit. These, however, are legal matters not of present concern.

Capital and Revenue.—Because the terms "capital" and "revenue" commonly appear in accounting writings, they must be adopted and used even though they are none too clear. Broadly speaking, problems of capital and revenue have to do

---

12 George R. Husband, "Accounting Postulates: An Analysis of the Tentative Statement of Accounting Principles," *The Accounting Review,* December 1937, p. 399.

with the allocation of expenditures to accounting periods. That portion of an expenditure appearing as an asset at the end of an accounting period represents the capital element in the phrase "capital and revenue," whereas that portion which, by the process of year-end valuation or in accordance with some predetermined plan, has disappeared and become an expense or loss refers to the revenue element.

Since revenue conveys the idea of an income or earning, the phrase is commonly understood to mean "capital and expired capital deducted from revenue." Thus, depreciation or other decrease in asset value is a deduction from gross earnings required in order to compute the net profit for an accounting period.

The Problem of Fixed Assets.—In reviewing the development of accounting it was seen that a true profit report of a single venture could not be made until the ship or other property was actually sold.

A difficulty arose when the ship was not sold but was retained for use in a subsequent venture financed by a different capitalist.

This difficulty was solved by preparing a report as though the ship had been sold; by assigning to it the value at which it could have been disposed of. The difference between the purchase cost of the ship and its salable, but unrealized, value at the end of the venture represented an element to be considered in estimating the net profit of the venture. To the extent that the realizable value was over- or underestimated, the net profit for the first and second ventures was over- or understated and either the first or the second capitalist received more or less than was properly due him.

In the case of overlapping ventures, i.e., in a continuing business, no attempt is made to determine the realizable value of a fixed asset in use at the end of an accounting period. Rather, a certain portion of the initial cost of the asset is considered as a loss of the period, that portion being predetermined by estimate.

To forecast how much of the cost of a fixed asset should be assigned to each period requires the formulation of a depreciation plan based on an estimate of the length of the asset's life. If it is decided that a ship, for example, will have a useful life of ten years and that its realizable value at the end of the ten years will be nil, then one-tenth of the ship's cost may be considered a deduction from earnings of each annual accounting period.

There were, therefore, three stages in the development of fixed asset accounting, the first involving actual realization, followed by the second involving fictitious realization by valuation, and third a recovery of original cost based upon a preliminary estimate of the length of the asset's life. Unlike the first two, the third is not influenced by varying market prices and attempts merely to distribute the cost of the asset over the years which benefit from its use.

Balance Sheet Method of Calculating Profit.—If there have been no additional proprietary investments or withdrawals, it is possible to calculate periodic profits by comparing the balance sheet at the end of one accounting period with the one at the end of the subsequent period.

The total of all of the values in the possession of an accounting entity must, of course, equal the entity's total liabilities to all creditors, including the proprietor, and this equilibrium is evidenced by the balance sheet. An earlier balance sheet as compared with a later balance sheet will usually show a change in the entity's debt to the proprietor because of transactions during the interim. Assuming that there have been no additional investments or withdrawals, this difference equals the profit or loss.

The balance sheet method of profit determination has an obvious disadvantage since it gives no indication as to how a net profit was made, a fact often of preeminent importance from the managerial viewpoint.

Analytical Method of Calculating Profit.—In Chapter 5 profit and loss classification was presented as a break-down of an account reflecting the entity liability to proprietorship for undivided profits.

If it is assumed that the gross income on each trading transaction appears as an addition to the entity debt to the proprietor and that the cost of each such sale together with the variety of other costs, expenses, and losses incurred appear as deductions from the entity liability to the proprietor, then the undivided profits account or surplus account contains all of the data necessary to construct a detailed statement of how the final liability to the proprietor, as shown by the balance of that account, occurred.

To prepare such a profit and loss statement it is only necessary to analyze the surplus account or undivided profits account and classify, assemble, and summarize the debits and credits shown therein according to some logical plan.

CURRENT ANALYSIS. Analysis of the various increases and decreases in this particular entity liability to the proprietor is not practically feasible because of the large number of trading transactions occurring in even a small business. It has, therefore, become almost universal practice to make an equivalent analysis currently.

This current analysis results from establishing several accounts with the proprietor in addition to the two already suggested, namely, investment and surplus. These additional accounts furnish classified information regarding the profit and loss elements during any one accounting period. At the end of that period balances appearing in those accounts are transferred to surplus account (or some equivalent account).

PROFIT AND LOSS ACCOUNTS. Following in a general way the American Institute classification as shown in *Examination of Financial Statements by Independent Public Accountants,* the temporary analytical accounts with the proprietor may consist of the following:

> Sales Account
> Cost of Sales Account
> Selling, General, and Administrative Expense Account
> Other Income Account
> Other Charges Account

When separate accounts with these titles are used, it is

sometimes convenient to think that the first and fourth accounts, since they commonly show credit balances, may be considered as equivalent to liability accounts reflecting certain phases of entity liability to the proprietor. Since the remainder of the accounts normally show debit balances, it is convenient to think of them as reflecting special types of liabilities of the proprietor to the entity.

When the sum of the credit balances is greater than the sum of the debit balances, then their combination represents a net credit which reflects the net increase in the total entity liability to the proprietor resulting from transactions not related to changes in the proprietor's actual investment. If the consolidation of these five accounts shows a net debit, then that figure, of course, represents a decrease in the entity liability to the proprietor.

RELATION OF PROFIT AND LOSS ACCOUNTS TO BALANCE SHEET. The development of proprietorship accounts can be illustrated diagrammatically by the following balance sheet form. This form, of course, is one which would practically never be suitable for a report and yet it has a certain graphic value for explanatory purposes.

This diagrammatic balance sheet is intended to emphasize the entity-proprietor relationship as being one of debtor and creditor, the various profit and loss accounts being temporary accounts representing classified additions to or deductions from the entity indebtedness to the proprietor.

Forms somewhat resembling this were in use, according to Peragallo,[13] as long ago as 1836. More recently Carman[14] commented: "It would be perfectly feasible to incorporate an entire income statement in a balance-sheet—all one need do in the conventional arrangement is to indent sufficiently under the caption of 'surplus' and write in the items."

The Separate Financial Statements.—In general practice, of course, the information appearing in such a diagrammatic

13 Edward Peragallo, *Origin and Evolution of Double Entry Bookkeeping*, (New York, American Institute Publishing Co., Inc., 1938), p. 140.
14 Lewis A. Carman, "Primary Accounting Concepts," *The Journal of Accountancy*, May 1936, p. 371.

DIAGRAMMATIC FORM OF ENTITY BALANCE SHEET

December 31, 1938

Assets

Cash	$ 880
Merchandise	2,100
Fixed Assets	1,000
Other Assets	70
Total Assets	$4,050

Liabilities

John Jones, owed to for merchandise			$ 300
George Brown, owed to for loan			700
Will Cass (proprietor):			
Investment, owed for			2,000
Surplus, owed for:			
Surplus, January 1			$600
Additions to liability for year:			
Sales . . .	$5,000		
Other Income . . .	100	$5,100	
Deductions from liability for year:			
Cost of Sales . . .	$3,000		
Expense . . .	1,500		
Other Charges . . .	150	4,650	
Net Profit for Year		450	
Surplus, December 31			1,050
Total Liabilities			$4,050

form would be reflected in two separate statements. Thus the balance sheet, still in diagrammatic form of course, might appear as follows:

ENTITY BALANCE SHEET

December 31, 1938

Assets		*Liabilities*	
Cash	$ 880	John Jones, owed to for mer-	
Merchandise	2,100	chandise	$ 300
Fixed Assets	1,000	George Brown, owed to for	
Other Assets	70	loan	700
		Will Cass (proprietor):	
		Investment, owed for	2,000
		Surplus, owed for	1,050
Total Assets	$4,050	Total Liabilities	$4,050

It will be noted that the amount of entity indebtedness to the proprietor shown as surplus is the indebtedness at the end of an accounting period after having taken into consideration the various classified gains and losses which increased the surplus from $600 at the beginning of the period to $1,050 at the end of the period. The profit and loss statement must, therefore, represent a break-down of the $1,050 surplus balance. Such a profit and loss statement might appear as follows:

ENTITY PROFIT AND LOSS STATEMENT

For the year 1938

Net Sales	$5,000
Cost of Sales	3,000
Gross Profit on Sales	$2,000
Selling, General, and Administrative Expense	1,500
Net Profit before Other Income and Charges	$ 500
Other Income	100
	$ 600
Other Charges	150
Net Profit for period, carried to Surplus	$ 450
Surplus, January 1	600
Surplus, December 31	$1,050

This particular arrangement of balance sheet and profit and loss statement is only one of several permissible combinations. Some accountants prefer to show the surplus at the beginning of the year in the balance sheet and also the net profit for the year added thereto in order to indicate how the final surplus resulted. When this plan is followed, the profit and loss statement will end with the net profit of $450.

Other accountants prefer to show $1,050 surplus on the balance sheet and still present the profit and loss statement ending with the net profit of $450. When this is done it is necessary to prepare a third statement which links the profit and loss statement with the balance sheet. This third statement is often referred to as the "surplus reconciliation." These variations are a matter of no importance at this particular stage in the development of a profit theory. It is merely important that there should be some definite link between the two statements.

The form presented is favored by many accountants since it tells the complete story of surplus changes between the beginning and end of an accounting period. Also it is a form which is helpful in developing a theory of profit and loss, since the profit and loss statement appears as no more and no less than the break-down of one balance sheet liability account.

Interest in Relation to Profit.—Mention should be made of a difference of opinion among accountants as to the treatment of interest on indebtedness. In the diagrammatic balance sheet just presented a liability of $700 appeared. Assuming that this liability resulted from a loan made by George Brown to the entity and assuming further that the interest on the loan was 6%, or $42, per year payable on December 31 of each year, then the question arises as to whether the $42 of interest should be treated as an expense or whether it represents George Brown's share of net income.

A number of accountants would hold the latter view, pointing out that Brown just as truly as Cass was providing capital to the entity. Opposing accountants hold that the interest on the $700 loan is an entity expense rather than a share of net income. It is on this latter theory that the profit and loss statement just presented was prepared, the $42 being one of the items making up the total of $150 of "other charges."

REVISED PROFIT AND LOSS STATEMENT. Those who consider that the $42 interest is a share of net income would prefer to see the profit and loss statement presented as follows:

ENTITY PROFIT AND LOSS STATEMENT
For the year 1938

Net Sales	$5,000
Cost of Sales	3,000
Gross Profit on Sales	$2,000
Selling, General, and Administrative Expense	1,500
Net Profit before Other Income and Charges	$ 500
Other Income	100
	$ 600
Other Charges	108
Total Net Income	$ 492
Interest Charges	42
Net Profit to Proprietor, carried to Surplus	$ 450
Surplus, January 1	600
Surplus, December 31	$1,050

The only important difference between this form and the one previously shown is found in the treatment of the interest. Even sturdy proponents of this method would probably not insist upon its use save where the entity has a large indebtedness.

ARGUMENTS FOR REVISED STATEMENT. The arguments in favor of this second method are two in number: first, comparisons between different enterprises otherwise may tend to be misleading, and second, any other method of arranging the profit and loss statement obscures the entity's earning power from the economic viewpoint.

The first argument is well founded, as will be seen by imagining two companies identical in every way save in their method of capitalization, one of them being financed to the extent of $1,000,000 by a group of proprietors and the other being financed to the same extent but with $500,000 contributed by proprietors and another $500,000 contributed by creditors in the form of interest-bearing loans, i.e., bonds, mortgages, or long-term notes. It is suggested that each of these companies has $1,000,000 of capital invested and that the whole return on such invested capital should be displayed instead of showing interest as an expense.

The second argument is of little importance from the single viewpoints of the entity and of the proprietor. To the proprietor, particularly, an expenditure for interest influences the amount of net profit finally accruing to him. It makes little difference whether it is shown as a cost, expense, or as a special deduction from an intermediate figure called "net income."

OPINIONS OF AUTHORITIES. It is probable that the majority of accountants consider interest cost as an item of non-operating expense and would in the foregoing classification include it under the caption of "other charges." Such treatment is suggested in *Examination of Financial Statements by Independent Public Accountants*.

The Executive Committee of the American Accounting Association[15] disagrees, suggesting that "the amount of interest incurred on borrowed money, including debt discount and expense properly amortized during the year" should be included in the operations section of the income statement.

Sanders, Hatfield, and Moore[16] mention the matter of interest under the general heading of "non-operating section" in the following words: "it is desirable to show the division of the earnings of the business as an economic enterprise between those who furnish capital on loan at fixed interest rates and the stockholders who take the residuary gain or loss. Interest will thus be a separate charge against earnings."

Berle and Means[17] state that: "Though the law still maintains the conception of a sharp dividing line recognizing the

---

15 Executive Committee of the American Accounting Association, "A Tentative Statement of Accounting Principles Affecting Corporate Reports," *The Accounting Review*, June 1936, p. 189.

16 Sanders, Hatfield, and Moore, *A Statement of Accounting Principles* (New York, American Institute of Accountants, 1938), p. 38.

17 Quoted by George R. Husband in "The Corporate-Entity Fiction and Accounting Theory," *The Accounting Review*, September 1938, p. 244.

bondholder as a lender of capital and the stockholder as a *quasi*-partner in the enterprise, economically the positions of the two have drawn together. Consequently, security holders may be regarded as a hierarchy of individuals all of whom have supplied capital to the enterprise, and all of whom expect a return from it."

Commenting on this matter from the management viewpoint which looks upon the business enterprise as an operating and financial unit regardless of the sources of the capital employed, Paton[18] asserts that "it is quite unreasonable to treat interest on bonds or any other contractual or preferred income charge as an operating expense similar to the cost of labor and materials. To the manager, that is, the amount of operating expense does not vary with the type of capitalization employed."

For purposes of intercompany comparison, Kester[19] seems to agree with Paton but from the strictly theoretical standpoint he thinks that "these items [interest income and expense, cash discount items, bad debts, collection losses, etc.] are as much elements of normal operation as the selling and administrative item."

As will be seen, the treatment of interest cost is controversial. It does, however, appear to be more a matter of reporting practice than of accounting theory and does not, it is believed, have any significant relationship to the development of a profit and loss classification, since the bookkeeper under all circumstances treats the interest cost as a deduction from the amount owed by the entity to the proprietor. Accordingly, it always represents one of the elements to be considered in computing the amount of increase in the entity indebtedness to the proprietor regardless of whether it is thought of as an expense or as an income deduction.

Influence of Accounting Period Convention.—Because the profit and loss statement is frequently referred to as a revenue statement and because the assets of a company are, from the viewpoint of economists, its capital, the entire problem of differ-

18 W. A. Paton, *Essentials of Accounting* (New York, The Macmillan Company, 1938), p. 103.
19 Roy B. Kester, *Advanced Accounting* (New York, The Ronald Press Company, 1933), p. 73.

entiating between balance sheet items and profit and loss items is called the problem of capital and revenue. It is safe to say that this is the central problem of accounting and, since it springs from the convention of accounting periods, it follows that the convention itself is dominant in accounting.

Prior to the adoption of accounting periods there was no real consideration of capital and revenue; the early accountants were never troubled with such matters.

Since periodic revaluations of fixed assets have become unnecessary, few informed people attach much importance to the figures representing unexpired fixed assets.

Such figures obviously do not represent realizable values. In fact, they result only from a convention and are themselves conventional. They indicate merely the amount of unexpired expenditure to be deducted from the earnings of future periods.

In practice, problems of capital and revenue are complicated; so much so that Stewart[20] described some of the past difficulties of determining income as due "to the absence, in many cases, of a clear distinction between revenue and capital expenditures."

Sanders[21] briefly explained the complexity of the problem by saying that: "The manner in which capital and income intermingle with each other, the income stream emerging from the capital funds only in large part to rejoin them, creates a situation where nobody can make positive assertions with complete assurance."

Acceptance of the accounting period convention, and its subordinate convention of the going business, introduced a new accounting concept, namely, that inventorying at realizable values was not appropriate for periodical reports, there being at the end of each period a fictitious rather than an actual termination of the business unaccompanied by substantial change of proprietorships.

While the convention of accounting periods may be consid-

20 Andrew Stewart, "Accountancy and Regulatory Bodies in the United States," *The Journal of Accountancy,* January 1938, p. 40.

21 T. H. Sanders, "Is It Desirable to Distinguish between Various Kinds of Surplus?" *The Journal of Accountancy,* April 1938, p. 284.

ered a development subsequent to the two primary accounting conventions, it is nevertheless equal in importance.

In fact, it is probably safe to say that many who deal regularly with accounts take for granted the entity and valuation conventions but are always conscious of the accounting period convention because of the serious and difficult problems which result from it.

Paton[22] emphasizes that accounting "might almost be defined as the art which attempts to break up the financial history of a business into specific units, a year or less in length."

The introduction of income tax laws focussed the attention of every business man on this particular problem. If income tax laws and rates were uniform from year to year, taxing authorities might not be so greatly concerned with correct annual reports. They might figure that collection of the full tax was inevitable in one period or another. With the laws and the rates changing every year or so, however, it is possible to evade taxation by allocations of costs and income to improper fiscal periods. The Treasury Department is, therefore, most insistent upon regarding each taxable year as a unit, scrutinizing with great care the accounting treatment which allocates profits to particular periods. Since the tax viewpoint more and more dominates accounting and business thought, the importance of the accounting period convention may readily be understood.

One may fairly conclude that the convention of financial periods is responsible for the numerous problems of capital and revenue and is also responsible for that most important accounting report, the periodic profit and loss statement.

22 W. A. Paton, *Accounting Theory* (New York, The Ronald Press Company, 1922), p. 469.

CHAPTER 8

THE REALIZATION OF PERIODIC INCOME

Modern accounting offers a difficult problem of periodic income recognition. Various viewpoints toward this problem have been expressed.

Some people intimate that the mere act of producing salable goods results in income which should be reflected in the accounting records. Others suggest that the exchange of property or services for cash only furnishes the test for recognition of income. The third, and larger, group asserts that the exchange of property or services for cash, or cash equivalent in the form of a legal claim to cash, offers the only proper basis for recognition of income. This latter viewpoint, with a few notable exceptions, is now commonly accepted and accordingly justifies a brief examination of its origin.

Realization in Cash.—In the earlier simpler days of accounting when it was relatively easy to conceive of profit as an increase in entity debt to the proprietor, the calculation of profit and its payment to the proprietor were often simultaneous.

Because of the early insistence upon termination and complete realization as the test for profits, there is indirect precedent for the view that income from which profits are derived should be recognized only at the time cash is received in return for merchandise parted with. Thus it is difficult to disagree with Paton[1] in this suggestion:

To credit revenue with the amount of closed, i.e., cash sales, allocating thereto the cost of these sales and considering net income to be disclosed by the balance, is an accounting scheme not wholly devoid of reasonableness.

[1] W. A. Paton, *Accounting Theory* (New York, The Ronald Press Company, 1922), p. 447.

Realization by Transfer of Title.—Strictly from the accounting viewpoint Paton's position is sound. Legally, however, any sale involves a contract. As a result of that contract the title to property changes hands. In exchange for his surrender of merchandise the vendor may receive in lieu of cash a legally enforceable claim to cash. At the instant when title to merchandise passes, the vendor has parted with an asset value and it is reasonable and logical to conclude that the transaction is closed and income realized at that time. This is a substitute for true cash realization; the passing of title to merchandise being strictly a legal concept.

In a business conducted solely on a cash basis, the passing of title and the receiving of cash occur simultaneously. Modern trading transactions, however, are generally conducted on a credit basis, with the result that the vendor parts with actual merchandise and receives in return, not cash, but only a claim to future payment of cash. Nevertheless, this surrender of merchandise for a receivable when it coincides with the legal passing of title marks recognition of income realization.

Legal claims to cash, while contractual, are not always the result of formal contracts. Many individuals trading at retail establishments probably are unaware of the contractual aspect of their casual purchases.

When such a sale is made to a credit customer, the claim then originating against that customer is commonly referred to as an account receivable.

Two of the most important legal tests referring to the transfer of titles to merchandise, to the creation of such a receivable, and hence to income recognition are: (1) will the seller or the purchaser suffer the loss if merchandise delivered is lost or destroyed, and (2) will the merchandise delivered be subject to attachment by creditors of the seller or by creditors of the purchaser? Despite its legal basis, as reflected by these tests, the credit sale, as Paton[2] has pointed out, is often but a kind of gentlemen's agreement. As he says, "Frequently no definite date for payment is set and the terms are in some other respects

[2] W. A. Paton, *Accounting Theory* (New York, The Ronald Press Company, 1922), p. 451.

vague." From the practical accounting viewpoint the important factor is that of intent. This is somewhat supported by the legal doctrine that a contract results only from a meeting of the minds of the parties involved.

Realization by Shipment or Delivery.—Because most business men are not lawyers and hence are ill equipped to determine in each instance just when the title to merchandise passes, it has become a matter of business custom to assume that title passes, a receivable is created and income is realized when shipment or delivery of merchandise is made and when there is an intent to pass title (thus excluding consignments or approval sales). This is not always true but it is true often enough to be justified as a practical expedient.

In résumé it is sufficient to note that accounting recognition of income has passed through three historical stages: first, on the basis of cash realization; second, on the basis of practical realization through legal passing of title and the consequent creation of an account receivable; and third, on the basis of actual shipment or delivery of the goods with intent to pass title and consequent creation of an account receivable.

By the reversal test recognition of an account receivable as an asset also implies the recognition of an account payable as a liability. If one company buys from another on a credit basis, the vendor's account receivable results from the same transaction as the buyer's account payable. The accounting test for a sale, therefore, is the same as the accounting test for a purchase, and the account receivable of one entity necessarily implies a corresponding account payable of another entity.

Tests for Realization.—There is probably no phase of accounting upon which so many accountants are in such complete harmony as the modern realization test for income.

Practically all agree with Sanders[3] in his statement which reads: "that profit is considered to be realized when a sale is effected, unless collection of the sale price is in doubt, and that unrealized profit, or profit not properly includable on an accrual

---

3 T. H. Sanders, "Reports to Stockholders," *The Accounting Review*, September 1934, pp. 216, 217.

basis, should not be credited to income either directly or indirectly."

The Board of Tax Appeals touched upon this matter in the Kansas City Structural Steel Company[4] case in the following words:

> In fact, however, each sale or exchange of the individual items of the inventory is a realization of taxable profit or deductible loss in the year in which it occurs and a method of accounting which disregards such realization does not truly reflect income.

Dohr[5] has offered four propositions relating to the income concept, of which the following three are appropriate at this time:

> 1. Income is an *increase in wealth* provided it be understood that it does not include an increase in wealth resulting from gift, appreciation (meaning thereby an increase in the market value of an asset or an increase in its cost of reproduction or replacement), or investment (as in the case of a stockholder's contribution to the capital of a corporation).
>
> 2. Income is a *summation* of increases (increments) and decreases (decrements) in wealth over a period of time.
>
> 3. In the periodic summation an increment in wealth is to be recognized only as and when the business in question has become legally entitled thereto, without substantial restriction, in a reasonably determinable or measurable amount.

Canning[6] suggests that income is realized when the following three conditions are fulfilled: "(1) the future receipt of money within one year has become highly probable; (2) the amount to be received can be estimated with a high degree of reliability; (3) the expenses incurred or to be incurred in the cycle can be estimated with a high degree of accuracy."

THE TIME FACTOR. While the time factor referred to by Canning is also mentioned by other accounting writers, it must be regarded more as a practical rule than as an essential element

---

4 Ross G. Walker, "Income Accounting and the Base-Stock Inventory," *Credit and Financial Management*, June 1938, p. 14.

5 James L. Dohr, "Income Divorced from Reality," *The Journal of Accountancy*, December 1938, pp. 362, 363.

6 John B. Canning, *The Economics of Accountancy* (New York, The Ronald Press Company, 1929), p. 103.

in the recognition of income, since it probably is derived from the credit viewpoint toward current assets and current liabilities.

It is the cash aspect of the exchange that represents the primary test of realization, whereas the period of time elapsing between the receipt of a good claim to cash and the actual receipt of the cash itself really has no theoretical significance although admittedly important from the practical financial viewpoint.

THE MONEY FACTOR. Adopting the theory that the true realization refers to money, immediate or deferred, then in any specific instance the test for realization is found in the question: Will the relinquishment of merchandise result in cash or in the creation of an asset which, in the normal course of events, will be converted into cash, i.e., does any further selling have to take place in order to obtain cash?[7]

In analyzing the significance of this question strictly from the accounting rather than the tax viewpoint, the exaggeration test may be applied to some of the interesting problems which suggest themselves. A used-car dealer, for example, has on hand two identical Ford cars each carrying a price tag of $250. He sells one to a customer and receives in exchange therefor a ten-year interest-bearing note for $250. The other car is sold to a customer in exchange for five shares of General Motors common stock which has an instant and ready market.

Assuming that the dealer retains both the note and the stock, certain questions then present themselves. Is there a realized income on both sales? On either sale? Or on neither sale?

Disregarding the intentionally exaggerated and unnatural character of these transactions, the sale of the first car for a ten-year note clearly results in realized income. In spite of the unusual time lag a note represents a claim to cash. The exchange of the automobile for five shares of General Motors

---

[7] This test has been adopted in the present volume because it represents the end-result of certain logical steps of development and also is one acceptable to accountants in connection with the normal transactions of business. In connection with uncommon transactions many accountants would, illogically it seems, broaden this test to give effect to liquidity, i.e., the current status of the asset received in exchange, or to the fair market value of the asset received in exchange. The adoption of these related concepts would permit the realization of income merely by the passing of title unaccompanied by the creation of a claim to cash. Practical as these additional tests admittedly are, they appear to be expedients having no place in the development of a theory of accounting profit.

stock, on the other hand, cannot result in true realized income, nor as a matter of theoretical accuracy is income ever realized on this particular kind of a transaction.

EXCHANGE OF MERCHANDISE FOR SHARES. Capital stock of General Motors or of any other company is not a legal claim to cash. When and if the General Motors stock is sold, realized income may result but it should be noted that this income is from the sale of the stock and not from the sale of the automobile. In the hands of the automobile dealer this General Motors stock is an asset which merely replaces the used car and which takes the same value. If, on the books of the dealer, the used car stood at a value of $200, then regardless of market quotations the five shares of General Motors stock received in exchange therefor should also be valued at $200, or $40 per share. If subsequently the dealer sells this stock at $46 net per share, he has realized income of $230 and a gross profit of $30 on the sale of the stock, not on the sale of the automobile.

This illustration emphasizes what appears to be the important concept of realization; when an entity exchanges one asset for another asset, no income is realized unless the new asset is a claim to cash which, in the normal course of events, will be converted into actual cash without the necessity of any subsequent sales transaction. The time element, practically of great importance, has no theoretical significance in this connection.

SIGNIFICANCE OF INTENT. A further question presents itself—Is this test dependent upon intent? It may be the intent of the used-car dealer to hold the ten-year note until maturity. Subsequently, being in need of funds, he may sell that note without recourse.

The reverse situation may be true. At the time of the transaction it may be the dealer's intent promptly to sell the note without recourse but, as a matter of fact, he may subsequently decide to hold it until maturity.

Do these intentions of the dealer have any relation to the realization of income on the transaction?

It seems clear that they do not. If he enters into the transaction with the intent of holding the note until maturity, he has realized income on the sale of the car when the title thereto passes in exchange for the note. This realization cannot be altered by subsequent transactions. If the cost of the Ford to the dealer is $200 and he accepts in exchange a ten-year interest-bearing note for $250, he has at the moment of transfer realized a gross profit of $50. Later, desiring cash, he sells the note for $240. Because he has disposed of what is then a $250 asset for $240, he has suffered a loss of $10. This loss has no relation to the former $50 gross profit but rather is the result of a separate and different transaction, the two transactions having no theoretical relationship to one another.

The test of realization, therefore, demands an actual immediate or deferred effect upon cash, the time lag involved in any deferment being no element of the test. If, employing a greater exaggeration, the $250 interest-bearing note received by the dealer ran for a hundred years instead of ten years the income would still be a realized income at the time of the transfer of title.

OTHER EXCHANGES. The exaggeration test may be applied to the concept of income realization in other ways. Thus, instead of exchanging the $200 car for a long-term interest-bearing note, the dealer might have exchanged it for five $50 interest-bearing bonds due in twenty years. Would such a transaction result in realized income? The bonds undoubtedly represent claims to cash and, disregarding the time element, they may be thought of as the equivalent of cash, since in the normal course of events they will become converted into cash without the necessity of any further sales transaction. The same conclusion might be reached in the case of an exchange of the car for a $250 mortgage. If, on the other hand, the automobile dealer had exchanged the car for office equipment or for gasoline or for shop tools, there would be no realization of income, and these new assets, regardless of their market value and regardless of how quickly they might be disposed of, would take the same value on the dealer's books as the automobile which they replaced, namely, $200.

OFFSETTING CLAIMS. An immediate or subsequent cash account entry is not necessarily the result of a sales transaction upon which income is truly realized. Income may be realized under such assumed conditions as the following, which uses the same illustration as before. The automobile dealer may owe his customer $300 and may offer to settle that indebtedness by turning over to him the Ford car. The question then arises as to whether income has been realized by the transaction, since the cash account is not affected. As a matter of fact, the cash position is affected if the $300 debt is a bona fide liability, since the dealer's cash account, if this arrangement was split into its elements, would eventually be $300 smaller because of the required payment of the liability and would be $250 greater because of the sale of the car, this diminution and addition representing the normal expectancy resulting from the fruition of claim and counter-claim were they not offset against each other.

In this illustration the dealer enjoys two different kinds of gains: one of $50 upon the sale of the car, and one of $50 from liquidation of the liability at a discount.

It is, of course, true as a practical matter that this distinction probably would not be recognized by either party, with the result that one gain of $100 would be recorded, no part of that amount being separately assigned to the car sale and to the liability compromise. This, however, does not affect the theoretical analysis of such a transaction.

There are many other examples of offsets in business. It is not unusual for two companies to buy from and sell to each other, with the result that either's books will show at the same time an account receivable from and an account payable to the other. Often cash settlements are made in terms of the net difference between such claims. No one would contend that this practice of offsetting affects the realization of income, since the significant test of realization is that a legal claim to cash has been established. The manner of final settlement of such a claim, whether by offset or otherwise, does not affect the income realization which occurred when that claim originated.

IMPORTANCE OF REALIZATION TEST. These exaggerated illustrations deliberately emphasize the basic test of income realization. The day by day transactions of normal business offer few such problems. In fact, they are so rare that when confronted by one the business man might easily reach the wrong conclusion. He might, through improper analogy or some other form of false reasoning, think of income realization in terms of the liquidity of the asset received in an exchange. He might easily convince himself in one of the automobile illustrations just cited that the receipt of General Motors common, because the shares are readily marketable, represented a realization of income, while the receipt of the interest-bearing note having no ready market did not. These conclusions would, of course, be the exact reverse of the truth.

Unusual Problems of Realization.—Much more interesting problems of income realization and income anticipation are noted in connection with certain rather uncommon business transactions.

Admittedly, business men seldom acquire property by donation or accretion. Infrequently do they exchange merchandise for fixed assets. It is rare that they are able to settle their liabilities at less than the full amount claimed, and it is unusual for them to receive dividends in merchandise or securities rather than in cash. Somewhat more common, but still outside of the experience of the majority of business organizations, is the problem of income realization in connection with long-term construction contracts.

Merely because these situations are relatively uncommon does not mean that they may lightly be dismissed. The very foundation of routine accounting is based upon certain concepts and conventions, a clear comprehension of which may depend upon proper analysis of these more unusual problems.

TRADING MERCHANDISE FOR FIXED ASSETS. If a business man sells merchandise for cash and then invests the cash in a fixed asset, he has clearly engaged in two separate and unrelated transactions and his recognition of realized income in the first transaction is proper.

By analogy does this justify similar income recognition if the two transactions are combined into one, i.e., if the merchandise is exchanged directly for a fixed asset? Such a situation occurs so seldom that it has not received adequate consideration. One statement was made by Kester[8] as follows:

Profit received in assets which must from their nature become a part of fixed plant is usually to be treated as an invested profit, although it is none the less earned and realized. Such a profit is not available for distribution to stockholders, for it has been reinvested in fixed form in the business; it has been appropriated to a special purpose for the use of the company. It does not differ in this regard from cash profits which by suitable action are authorized for investment in the company's fixed plant instead of being distributed to stockholders.

The reasoning here does not seem convincing. It is, of course, true that the final effect is the same regardless of whether income has or has not been realized in cash. Under either method the entity finally possesses fixed assets which cannot be disbursed as dividends. The fact that the fixed assets cannot represent the basis for dividend declarations is not important to the problem.

The existence of a true earned surplus representing accumulated and undistributed profits represents only one of the requirements for dividend declaration. The other refers to available cash and it is well recognized that there is no specific relation between undistributed profits on the one hand and any particular asset or assets on the other. The reasoning can be demonstrated by reversal, i.e., the case where a corporation has a substantial cash balance but shows a deficit instead of a surplus.

The final availability of assets for distribution is not the test to be applied in this problem. Rather it is the interim availability, i.e., has the transaction at any time resulted in cash proceeds or a claim to cash proceeds which if not reinvested in fixed assets could have been distributed?

The sharp significance of this question must not be dulled by improper analogy. When merchandise is sold for cash and that cash is then reinvested in a fixed asset, even though the two transactions are practically simultaneous they are nevertheless

8 Roy B. Kester, *Advanced Accounting* (New York, The Ronald Press Company, 1933), p. 506.

two transactions. Upon the consummation of the first income has been realized. When merchandise is exchanged directly for a fixed asset, there is only one transaction, not two, and at no time from the beginning to the completion of that transaction has there been any practical or actual realization in cash and hence there has been no realization of income.

DIVIDENDS RECEIVED IN PROPERTY. One occasionally hears of a dividend distribution made in property other than cash, i.e., usually merchandise or securities.

Montgomery,[9] in discussing this situation from the viewpoint of a recipient, agrees with the Treasury Department: "Dividends in kind, that is, dividends paid in some other form of property than cash, should be included in income at the fair value of the property at the time of its distribution."

Such situations are not extremely common, yet as a problem in accounting theory they deserve further analysis.

DIVIDENDS RECEIVED IN MERCHANDISE. One thing seems to be reasonably certain, i.e., there has been no realization of income by the stockholder if, at the time the dividend was declared, it was specifically limited to the distribution of merchandise. If it was not so limited, the stockholder would be justified in setting up in his books an item of dividends receivable, i.e., a legal claim to cash. If subsequently the stockholder accepted merchandise in lieu of cash, he would be merely trading one asset, dividends receivable, for another asset, merchandise. Under these circumstances the realization of income occurred at the time the dividend was declared, the subsequent substitution of merchandise for cash being a separate transaction and having no relation to such realization.

If at the time of declaring the dividend it was specified that it would be payable only in merchandise, then no receivable representing a legal claim to cash is created on the stockholder's books. True, a special receivable may be created and offset by a credit to some unrealized income account, but as this receivable is one which asserts a legal claim to merchandise rather than cash, it can involve no element of realization. When the mer-

9 Robert H. Montgomery, *Auditing Theory and Practice* (New York, The Ronald Press Company, 1934), p. 496.

chandise is received, the special receivable may be credited and the inventory account may be debited. When the merchandise is sold, the full amount received therefor becomes realized income. It is only at this point that any actual realization takes place. The valuation at fair market value referred to by Montgomery is a valuation for convenience in establishing a book record in harmony with the income tax return and has no real relation to the dividend transaction.

DIVIDENDS RECEIVED IN SECURITIES. Dividends payable in securities may or may not represent realized income to the recipient, depending upon a number of different factors.

In the case of a dividend in the declaring company's own bonds, for example, the *Accountants' Handbook*[10] notes that: "Logically such a transaction also requires some adjustment of the investment value of the stock with respect to which the bond dividend is issued, on the ground that the issue of the bonds as a dividend absorbs part of the value of the stock on the corporation's books and thus also affects the fair market value of the stock."

In view of the decision of the Supreme Court to the effect that such dividends are income measurable by the fair market value of the bonds received, the *Handbook* continues: "it is expedient to ignore the logic of the case, and credit the full amount to income."

Since any dividend, no matter how payable, absorbs part of the value of the stock on the corporation's books, there would seem to be no more necessity for the recipient of the dividend to make an adjustment of the book value of his stock than if the dividend had been received in cash.

This matter is, however, of less present importance than the treatment of the dividend itself. It is in this respect that theory and acceptable practice often diverge. In theory, on the assumption that the dividend is received in the form of sound interest-bearing bonds or interest-bearing notes whether issues of the declaring corporation or not, income to the recipient has been realized to the extent of the face value thereof, i.e., the amount

[10] *Accountants' Handbook* (New York, The Ronald Press Company, 1934), p. 358.

which will ultimately be paid upon the due date. If the instruments are non-interest bearing and if the period between their receipt and their due date is of material significance, then many would contend that the income should be recognized at the discounted value.

Theoretically and practically the receipt of such instruments must be regarded as income both from the accounting viewpoint and from the Treasury viewpoint. Where these two diverge is on the basis of valuation, the Treasury Department holding quite properly that only the fair market value at time of receipt should be recognized as income. This tax viewpoint is, of course, thoroughly defensible since the taxpayer should not be put into a position where his shortage of cash may make it impossible for him to pay his tax. Under the fair market rule of valuation the taxpayer can, if his bank account is low, make an immediate sale of the bonds, notes, or similar instruments received as dividends and theoretically at least will suffer no loss and make no profit merely because the Treasury Department insists that the receipt of such instruments constitutes income upon which tax must be paid.

When the stockholder of a corporation receives a dividend in stock, the problem assumes a different complexion. In this connection it should be noted that this does not refer to the usual stock dividend paid in the shares of the declaring company. Rather it refers to the distribution by a corporation of shares of some other company held in its treasury. To the recipient such a dividend does not represent realized income. This statement is, of course, based upon identically the same theory as has previously been set forth, namely, that shares in a corporation are not legal claims to cash but merely represent property which cannot be converted into cash without being sold. Properly, therefore, such shares should be recorded on the books of the recipient at the same figure as their book cost to the issuing corporation. Here, of course, is found a sharp divergence from tax practice since the Treasury Department applies the same rule to stocks as to bonds, i.e., the receipt of such stock must appear as income to the recipient on the basis of the fair market value of the shares themselves.

Practically, the Treasury Department rule is fair. Theoretically, it denies the basic theory of income realization, since there is no true realization of income to the stockholder until the shares have been sold regardless of whether such sale occurs the day after the shares are received or ten years later.

DONATIONS. When property is donated to a business as an outright rather than a conditional gift, it should theoretically not give rise to any entry. The value parted with having been zero, the value received is also zero.

On the other hand, this treatment is undesirable, since it results in the entity's possession of an asset with which it is not formally charged. It therefore becomes necessary to assign some arbitrary value to the donated asset. Such value may be the nominal amount of $1 merely for the purpose of establishing a record, or it may be on some estimated basis of market value.

Under any of these conditions there is no realization. Regardless of any assigned valuation, accountants generally agree that a donated asset, while it does result in an increase in the indebtedness of the entity to the proprietor, does not result in realized income. Accordingly, the credit should be made to a restricted surplus account such as Donated Surplus. If the property subsequently is sold, then income is realized, requiring adjustment of the donated surplus.

When title to the donated property does not pass, i.e., where the donation is a conditional one, then no entry whatever is required until the conditions have been satisfied. For purpose of adequate disclosure, Kester[11] suggests that on such a conditional gift subject to reversion before the expiration of five years, "the pro-rata portion of the gift may be shown periodically by a charge to Donated Land or Equity in Land, offset by an equal credit to some suitable reserve such as Donated Land Reserve or Unrealized Profit on Land. On the balance sheet, the reserve should be treated as a valuation item, no value being extended among the assets."

11 Roy B. Kester, *Advanced Accounting* (New York, The Ronald Press Company, 1933), p. 361.

This method of providing offsetting accounts for statistical purposes only seems entirely proper.

BUILDINGS OF LESSEE REVERTING TO LESSOR. Bona fide donations to business entities are rare, since they involve the surrender of value without receiving any equivalent, a procedure which is repugnant to man's economic nature, but a situation somewhat similar to a donation arises when buildings are erected by a lessee upon leased ground and where for one reason or another the lessor comes into possession of the ground and the buildings prior to the expiration of their useful life. Such an acquisition somewhat resembles a donation in that the lessor receives property without surrendering other property in exchange therefor.

The question of whether any value assignable to such a building is income to the lessor is one which has assumed some importance in tax discussions. This matter was reported on in a special supplement to the Alexander Tax News Letter, dated February 18, 1938, in the following words:

> In the case where a building is put up on leased ground and the lessee is forced to give up the entire property because of non-payment of rent or for any other reasons, the tax board has held that the acquisition of the building does not represent taxable income but merely appreciation of realty without realization of gain by sale.

If the lessor reported the value of the building as a gain, then he would, of course, show a corresponding amount as the cost of the property on his books and would have to depreciate that value against future income. This, according to the Tax News Letter, "would be the same as reporting income in one period and deducting it later. Hence the problem balances itself either way."

ACCRETION. An unusual and puzzling accounting problem arises in connection with accretion.

Accretion usually occurs in farming, the natural increase of flocks and herds representing increases in economic value. The question involved is whether the birth of calf, colt, or lamb gives rise to income. Such accretion is sometimes treated as income, an arbitrary value being assigned to these animals.

Husband and Thomas[12] regard such increase in value as being "in the nature of a capital gain and may be recorded by debiting the asset involved and crediting an account entitled 'Income from Accretion.'"

Elsewhere comparing appreciation and accretion these same authors say, "Appreciation differs from the usual accounting income, however, in that the latter, like accretion, usually has a physical basis. Whether this difference is sufficient to permit the application of the term income to the one while denying it to the other is open to question."

The *Accountants' Handbook* (second edition, pages 514 and 1087) also discusses accretion observing that there is no general income tax necessity for recognizing accretion after March 1, 1913, and suggesting the convenience of omitting such adjustments from the accounts. If they are to be made, however, the account, Surplus from Accretion, is suggested as the resting place of the unrealized profit, this surplus being transferred to income as the accretion is actually realized upon.

Hatfield[13] expresses the opinion that it is not obviously objectionable to treat as income the accretion due to the growth of standing timber. In support of this he uses the following analogy: "The increased value, if unquestioned, is akin to the increasing value of a discounted note which by most authorities is counted as income available for dividend even though it has not as yet been converted into cash." It is noted, however, that Hatfield[13] takes a somewhat different position in connection with the growth of orchards, the trees being "more valuable primarily because the larger trees yield a larger supply of fruit. The increasing yield is a cause of larger income. It in itself constitutes the larger income and this income can be distributed or divided or consumed by the owner."

The practical accounting difficulties of farmers and nurserymen have been recognized by the Treasury Department, which does not require, but permits, accretion to be reported as income. This practical necessity arises from the impossibility of keeping

---

[12] Husband and Thomas, *Principles of Accounting* (New York, Houghton Mifflin Company, 1935), pp. 552, 553.
[13] Henry Rand Hatfield, *Accounting* (New York, D. Appleton-Century Company, 1927), pp. 253, 252.

accurate farm accounts. As a result farmers usually determine periodic income by the traditional method of taking annual inventories of assets and from a comparison of the resulting balance sheets determining the amount of gain. This is, however, a practical procedure having little justification in accounting theory.

It would indeed be difficult to argue that accretion represents realized income on the commonly accepted accounting theory of realization. Realization does not result from valuing a found asset at what it could be sold for in cash. Such valuation, as Canning has pointed out with reference to the money value of a yearling colt, must be a matter of opinion.

Unlike some other cases of unrealized income, accretion is usually the result of a deliberate plan, i.e., money and effort being spent in promotion thereof. If income from accretion should not be recognized, then of course the costs and expenses incurred for the purpose of encouraging accretion should theoretically at least be set up as deferred charges to be applied against realized income when the animals, timber, or other property has been sold.

CONSTRUCTION CONTRACTS. An interesting income problem is noted in connection with large construction contracts. Montgomery[14] has described the problem in the following words:

. . . a contractor might be engaged for a period of three years on a single large project to the exclusion of all other work. If his books were kept on a completed contract basis, he would show losses in the first two years, and the third year would reflect the profits of three years' operations.

Referring to the same type of situation, Kester[15] intimates that: "To withhold profits, if earned, until the completion of the contract might work a real injustice." The injustice mentioned must refer to injustice to stockholders, particularly in the case of those companies whose shares are actively traded. A practical

14 Robert H. Montgomery, *Auditing Theory and Practice* (New York, The Ronald Press Company, 1934), p. 490.
15 Roy B. Kester, *Advanced Accounting* (New York, The Ronald Press Company, 1933), p. 499.

income tax problem also is involved which may well be one of the factors of injustice.

Sweeney, in his *Stabilized Accounting,* clearly recognizes that the treatment of unfinished long-term contracts is an exception to the general rule and asserts that this exception is for the sake of expediency.

Practically all accountants argue in favor of allocating the profits on such long-term contracts to the several periods involved. Few, however, attempt to justify this procedure and many have observed that it is illogical and that it represents an important exception to the general convention of realization. It is, however, probable that few would go as far as Montgomery[16] in his conception of "the true earnings of each fiscal year" suggested in the following words:

Concerns engaged on long-term contracts at fixed prices frequently make no accounting for profits on a job until it is completed, keeping their books on what is known as the "completed contract" basis. While this method does not have the advantage of reflecting the true earnings of each fiscal year, it does avoid the necessity of estimating the profits accrued on each uncompleted job at the end of the fiscal year.

It is difficult indeed to see how Montgomery's phrase "true earnings" can be justified. The type of contract usually discussed is in the nature of a venture. Like the venture, the final profit or loss on the contract can be determined only upon its completion. Interim profit estimates are mere approximations.

While it may be impossible to disagree with the many voices raised in favor of such allocation of estimated profit, it does not seem necessary to dignify these estimates as "true earnings."

Where a construction job requires two or more years for its completion, where title does not pass and where no contractual provisions justify setting up periodically an actual claim to cash, no income and hence no profit is actually realized during any interim period.

Partial payments usually made at various designated stages of work completion may represent no more than advances to the contractor as an aid to him in financing the work and should

16 Robert H. Montgomery, *Auditing Theory and Practice* (New York, The Ronald Press Company, 1934), p. 531.

theoretically appear on the contractor's books as liabilities just like any other deposit by a customer.

It is in connection with such long-term contracts that one of the most awkward features of the accounting period convention develops. Just as in the case of the isolated venture of the older trading days, the true business cycle involved is not one of twelve months but is a natural one extending from the beginning of the work until its completion, whether that be one month, fifteen months, or fifty months. Until the work is completed, until title has passed, until a legal claim to cash results, there is no realized profit. Only an exception to the convention of realization made in order to harmonize a venture of this type with the convention of accounting periods justifies the customary procedure of interim income recognition.

It is true that it is a necessary expedient. It may be admitted that it is fully justified on practical grounds, but it should be recognized as an exception to a common convention of accounting and should not be rationalized by fallacious arguments.

The common recognition of interim income on long-term contracts is undoubtedly fair to all concerned, stockholders, management, creditors, and government. Any change to a more rigorous basis might result in burdensome tax inequity. None the less, it must be insisted that such interim profit estimates under the bare conditions set forth are not only not "true earnings" but are not, as a matter of fact, realized earnings at all.

As will be seen, there is a similarity between the problems of uncompleted contracts and of installment sales where title does not pass until the last payment has been made. The logic applying to the one is also applicable to the other. The same accounting expedient, i.e., that of recognizing income as being realized before it actually is so realized, is generally applied in both instances, cash collections, percentage of completion based upon engineering reports, or some other indirect basis being employed to measure such periodic income. Neither plan can be justified on the basis of accounting theory. Both are abundantly justified by practical necessity.

SALE OF SERVICES. It is usual for accounting writers to illustrate income realization by reference to the sale of merchandise or other tangible assets and to ignore consideration of the sale of services.

To be sure services, having no tangible aspect, cannot change hands in the same manner as physical goods. In performing service there is no question of transfer of title. Nevertheless, by analogy and common consent the rendering of service is assumed to result in a contractual relationship somewhat similar to the delivery of goods. The doctor, dentist, lawyer, or public account-ant follows much the same procedure as the merchant in estab-lishing an account receivable against his customer or client and simultaneously recognizing realized income.

Legally the claim for services rendered may be just as enforce-able as the claim for goods delivered, in spite of the fact that the technical requirement of transferred title cannot be applied as a test.

Provision for Doubtful Accounts.—While an account re-ceivable or other claim is often considered the equivalent of money, in actual practice such equivalence may not exist.

Not all customers pay their accounts willingly. Not all cus-tomers have the financial means to pay them at all. One of the most serious problems in many business organizations is the problem of collections. Accordingly, while the account receiv-able may be a legal claim to cash, there is no certainty that all the cash claimed will be forthcoming.

CORRECTION OF INCOME. To the extent that accounts re-ceivable are not paid an error has been made in recognizing income as realized, i.e., the cash equivalence presumed to have characterized the receivables did not, in fact, exist. Had this been known at the time of sale, the amount of realized income recorded would have been modified accordingly, since the test of realization requires the receipt of cash or a legal claim to cash which will be paid. If subsequent events proved that the seller was deceived as to ultimate full collectibility, it follows that he was correspondingly deceived as to the amount of real-ized income. The loss on accounts receivable is technically, therefore, a correction of or deduction from the same income which was recognized at the time of sale.

To recognize income at one time and to cancel or correct it at another time is a logical procedure and would be satisfactory were it not for the fact that two different accounting periods may be involved.

A sale made the latter part of 1938 would involve the recognition of 1938 income and the creation of a receivable appearing on the balance sheet December 31, 1938. In January 1939, it may be determined that the customer cannot pay. The correction of the original entry must be made in 1939 because the 1938 accounts are closed with the result that there is a distortion between the two fiscal years, the 1938 income being overstated and the 1939 income being understated by the same amount.

Recognition of this possibility of distortion is responsible for the common practice of estimating probable losses from bad debts and recording such estimates as losses of the period during which the corresponding sales were made, and by the same entry setting up a valuation account the effect of which is to reduce the face value of the accounts receivable to an amount which it is estimated will actually be collected in cash.

REPORTING CORRECTION OF INCOME. A strong argument can be advanced in favor of reporting the amount of this estimated loss as a direct deduction from gross income, contradicting the common practice which treats the amount as an expense or cost. In fact, the provision of a reserve for doubtful accounts, if accurately estimated, places all sales transactions on a cash realization basis in so far as amounts are concerned, even though there is a difference in the time element between a cash and a credit sale.

If one can imagine two companies identical in every way except that one sells invariably for cash and the other sells invariably on the credit basis and if those two companies each have a sales volume of $1,000,000 for the same year, it will be apparent that the realized income for the first company is, of course, $1,000,000. The realized income for the second company is perhaps $980,000 if the estimated provision for doubtful accounts should be 2% of sales. To deduct the 2%, or $20,000, from the $1,000,000 of sales in order prominently to set forth the estimated realized net income of $980,000 seems to be a procedure which is justifiable and in fact almost mandatory. The mere fact that the 2%, or $20,000, estimate may later prove to have been either inadequate or excessive seems to have little bearing on the procedure if the provision has been predetermined thoughtfully and intelligently.

DOUBTFUL INSTALLMENT ACCOUNTS. Recognition of income presents an important problem in installment selling. Ideally the recognition of income from installment sales, like all other sales, depends upon the point of time when title is passed. One of two situations generally prevails. The title to merchandise may pass at the time the sales contract is made or it may pass when payments are completed.

The first results in the establishment of a legal claim to cash and the immediate realization of income in spite of the fact that the actual payments applying to the receivable may be spread out over a number of months. The fact that the receivable may have dubious credit value does not affect the realizatior of income but does have a direct reference to the amount of income so realized. The problem of providing reserves or allowances for doubtful accounts is thereby intensified without affecting the realization convention.

Because installment receivables created during a period of prosperity may have to be collected in a period of depression, or vice versa, estimates of uncollectibility made at the time of sale may be stained with serious error and the reserves or allowances may accordingly require correction from time to time. Such corrections, like the original uncollectibility provisions, do theoretically affect the amount of the realized income but, because of the time lag and the periodic profit and loss closings, it is seldom possible to reflect such adjustments in the income of the period when it was first recognized.

It is commonly held that such correcting adjustments are properly to be made through surplus account, that account being the resting place of the error at the time of its discovery. The modern distaste for the correction of prior period errors through surplus would appear to justify the reflection of such adjustments in the non-operating section of the profit and loss statement for the period in which they are discovered even though they may refer to prior periods.

In the more common type of installment selling, title does not actually pass until the final payment is made and income is not actually realized until that final date, all of the interim payments being theoretically in the nature of customers' deposits. Practically, this viewpoint is seldom if ever adopted, the income being measured and allocated by the cash payments actually received. This problem closely resembles that of profits on long-term construction contracts already discussed.

Inventories and Income Realization.—Attempts have been made to justify valuation of inventories at selling price. These attempts have, however, been notably unconvincing since they disregard the transfer of title to the merchandise which must take place as prerequisite to the creation of the account receivable.

This, of course, does not mean that inventories are never valued on a selling price basis. In certain accounting situations it is impossible to determine true costs. This is true in farm accounting and it is also true in accounting for certain types of by-products. Some authorities have held it to be true in gold mining. Finally, there is a substantial body of opinion which holds that it is not illogical to value goods or merchandise on a selling price basis if a binding and enforceable sales agreement exists and the goods represented are merely awaiting delivery.

Referring to this last point, Paton[17] considers that "there is some force in the contention," while Montgomery[18] asks this question: "Why should good accounting practice blindly accept delivery of goods and transfer of title as equivalent to realization, and refuse to sanction as good accounting practice the taking up of profits on orders which in some businesses will be converted into cash long before many of the accounts receivable in other businesses will be collected?"

As long ago as 1915, Dicksee,[19] commenting on firm orders

[17] W. A. Paton, *Accounting Theory* (New York, The Ronald Press Company, 1922), p. 454.

[18] Robert H. Montgomery, *Auditing Theory and Practice* (New York, The Ronald Press Company, 1934), p. 224.

[19] Lawrence R. Dicksee, *Auditing: A Practical Manual for Auditors* (London, Gee and Company, 1915), p. 201.

for future delivery, said: "The general rule which has been laid down in this work is, it is thought, unquestionably the safe one to adhere to in all cases, namely, that the profit on the sale of goods should be taken credit for at the time when the sale actually occurs." He added that "the actual sale would certainly appear to be at the date of delivery."

ANTICIPATION OF PROFITS. In those cases where it is impossible to determine inventory costs there may be some practical justification for valuing inventories on a selling price basis (the actual selling price less costs necessarily involved in effecting the delivery and sale of such merchandise).

That this procedure anticipates profits will be strongly affirmed by those who regard the transfer of title as the only proper test for recognition of income. Unfortunately, they have no acceptable substitute to offer in those instances where costs are actually unobtainable. Such situations are not at all upon the same plane as those others where actual inventory costs are known but because firm contracts exist for future delivery of merchandise a less conservative mode of valuation is desired.

There is so little practical advantage to be gained by anticipating income and there is so much real danger in attempting to substitute some other test for that of title transfer that it is difficult to see why this should ever be a matter of more than academic interest.

Every business man is aware of the fact that merchandise which he holds for future delivery on a so-called firm contract may, during a period of rapidly falling prices, never be delivered, thus leaving him with an expensive and often unsatisfactory lawsuit as his only remedy. Often his relations with the buyer are such that he must gracefully accept cancellation in order not to jeopardize future trading relations.

PRODUCTION THEORY OF INCOME. Some accountants and economists express the opinion that income is the result of production rather than of sale, and advance certain arguments accordingly.

Often such arguments seem unrealistic when applied to practical business situations. It is easy for any man not engaged in business affairs to minimize the difficulty and importance of selling. For this practical reason alone, even disregarding accounting conventions, the consummation of a sale would normally be considered the significant signal for income recognition.

There are, of course, certain types of commodities which are almost equivalent to money. Marketing such products may be no more than a simple matter of delivery to buyers. Thus, the gold miner has no practical sales problem in disposing of his product, nor is the farmer forced to employ sales managers, advertising men, or sales representatives in order to market his wheat, corn, or oats. In dealing with standard commodities for which there is ready demand, price and transportation rather than selling become the important factors.

In most business situations, however, the problem of selling overshadows other business problems. This is clearly evident in such specialized fields as the manufacture of refrigerators, automobiles, radios, or bookkeeping machines. For such products there is no existing demand, and a demand must be created by skilled salesmanship and by substantial expenditures for sales promotion, advertising, and other forms of customer enticement. The history of specialty enterprises clearly indicates that companies manufacturing excellent products are often unsuccessful and have suffered large losses through inability to sell them.

Recognition of income on the basis of production could hardly fail to result in a most fantastic situation in the case of a new company organized to produce cash registers in competition with the National Cash Register Company, or adding machines in competition with Burroughs, or automobiles in competition with Ford. Because recognition of income on the production basis appears reasonable for companies to which ready markets are available, scarcely seems a valid argument for their adoption of a different accounting convention. This seems particularly true since the production theory generally applied to all economic units would be ridiculous for many of them, while the realization test, if applied to all, would result in no practical disadvantage to any.

INVENTORY OVERSTATEMENT AND THE ENTITY. Recognition of the practical difficulties of selling specialized products is admittedly no adequate argument against the production theory of profits.

A more basic viewpoint is perhaps found in the nature of the simple conventionalized accounting mechanism in which recognition of income on the basis of production, although entirely permissible, would result merely in an increase in entity indebtedness to the proprietor, an increase which would be meaningless in view of the charge and discharge relationship existing.

Since the entity is an artificial person controlled by the proprietor, there is nothing in accounting to prevent that proprietor from insisting upon inflated inventory valuation. The substitution, however, of any figure greater than cost of acquisition results only in a meaningless increase in the entity's debt to the proprietor. It is like some father's insisting that his small child has a million dollars when the child actually has only a dime. The two of them may pretend that the dime is a million dollars but it still remains a dime, no more and no less.

Similarly in accounting, the proprietor may pretend that the entity owes him some imaginary amount based upon an inflation of inventory value but what the entity will finally and actually owe to the proprietor will be determined by actual realization as the result of trading transactions with outsiders. The money actually or constructively received on such trading transactions represents the one and only factor which substitutes reality for imagination, fantasy, and pretense. This is well set forth by Porter and Fiske[20] as follows: "The sales transaction confirms the existence and amount of profit by the willingness of an outsider, the buyer, to commit himself to pay the agreed price. The opinion of the owner as to the value of his own assets is eliminated as a basis for profit determination."

Conclusion.—Regardless of the reasoning involved, it appears true that most accountants and business men do subscribe to the recognition of regular income only upon the exchange of goods or services for cash or cash equivalent. Whether this is

---

[20] Porter and Fiske, *Accounting* (New York, Henry Holt & Company, 1935), p. 339.

done on the basis of conservatism, or because it is not practical to recognize income until it has been more or less definitely crystallized, is unimportant.

The repeated insistence that liquidity is not a proper test of income realization seems fully justified in spite of the fact that the great majority of business men and accountants would properly regard it as an essential element. As a practical matter, no one can or should flout the importance of liquidity, i.e., it would be sheer folly in the automobile illustration previously noted for the dealer to recognize income realization based upon his receipt of a ten-year promissory note.

It may well be asked, therefore, why some of these problems of realization have been discussed from such a technical viewpoint.

The recognition of a sound general theory of income realization is, it appears, a most important element bearing upon the subject of accounting profits. That the strict application of such a theory may be and should be modified in the rare case may be thoroughly justified. It can be justified, however, only on the basis of practical business necessity, not because of misunderstanding of the fundamental concept.

CHAPTER 9

MATCHING COSTS AND PERIODIC INCOME

Prior to adoption of the accounting period convention, the matching of costs, expenses, and losses with income offered no serious problem.

The determination of profits in terms of accounting periods introduced a new problem, that of matching realized income with related costs (including expenses and other deductions). While nearly all accounting writers recognize the desirability of matching costs, expenses, and losses with specific items of realized income, most of them insist that such a relationship should be established in accounting only in so far as this may be practicable. Thus Kester[1] says that "expenses, so far as possible, should be related to the income produced by the expenditure." Elsewhere[1] he says that: "All costs in connection with a sale should, therefore, be charged to the same period."

Paton[2] insists that "expense should always be defined as an adjunct of revenue, the controlling classification."

This problem of matching income with related costs may be considered from two viewpoints—cost accounting and general accounting.

Cost Accounting.—The cost accountant makes an attempt to establish a specific relation between all costs of manufacture and individual classifications or items of product in order to determine the manufactured cost of each unit of product sold.

Littleton[3] has referred to cost accounting as "that field in which greatest stress is laid upon refinements in the classification of expenses and allocation of costs to units of products. It is

[1] Roy B. Kester, *Advanced Accounting* (New York, The Ronald Press Company, 1933), pp. 509, 502.
[2] W. A. Paton, *Accounting Theory* (New York, The Ronald Press Company, 1922), p. 445.
[3] A. C. Littleton, *Accounting Evolution to 1900* (New York, American Institute Publishing Co., Inc., 1933), p. 322.

here that attention is centered upon the correct association of units of income with units of the cost-outlays made to produce that income."

Sanders, Hatfield, and Moore[4] express the same general thought in somewhat different words: "In principle the costs charged should be the specific costs of the specific goods and services sold, and this principle should be followed as far as may be practicable. There should be no material discrepancy between the physical quantities on which the sales revenues are based and those included in the computations of cost of goods sold."

The cost accountant's method of matching units of income with units of cost-outlay is based directly upon an accounting convention, namely, "that the value of any commodity, service, or condition, utilized in production, *passes over into* the object or product for which the original item was expended and *attaches to* the result, giving it its value. This postulate is the essential basis for the work of the cost accountant; without it, there could be no costing."[5]

Adoption of this convention has provided a fictitious appearance of accuracy in matching costs and income which tends to ignore the time relation of the original expenditures to the sale of manufactured items. The cost accountant makes an assumption that depreciation of a factory building, in itself an estimate, passes over, partially, into the cost of producing power, for example, which cost in turn passes over into and is divided among producing and non-producing departments, these latter costs ultimately and through roundabout channels passing over into the product itself. By means of this assumption or convention the cost accountant establishes an artificial relationship between the depreciation of a factory unit and a specific item of final product such as one washing machine, one baby carriage, or one barrel of flour.

Failure to recognize the artificial nature of this convention is responsible for a number of loose statements about the accuracy of cost accounting and about the close relationship thus estab-

4 Sanders, Hatfield, and Moore, *A Statement of Accounting Principles* (New York, American Institute of Accountants, 1938), p. 30.
5 W. A. Paton, *Accounting Theory* (New York, The Ronald Press Company, 1922), pp. 490, 491.

lished between specific items of income and the associated items of cost-outlay.

Only occasionally have the cost accountants attempted to establish relationships between the selling price of the product and those non-factory expenditures which are frequently referred to as selling, general, and administrative expense.

The Robinson-Patman Act encouraged cost accountants to experiment in this field but it was soon discovered that many important differences existed between manufacturing expenses and other expenses, the latter being less controllable and less recurring, originating, as many of them do, from the necessities of varied and shifting competition.

General Accounting.—When the general accountant, as distinguished from the cost accountant, speaks of matching costs and income, he usually refers to their inclusion in the same accounting period, not to the direct relation of specific items of income to specific items of cost-outlay. This is a different problem from that of the cost accountant. While it is probably no more accurate, at least it does not present any fictitious appearance of accuracy.

May[6] speaks of "charges and credits which cannot be allocated to the years to which they strictly apply because not then ascertained or ascertainable." He also mentions charges and credits "arising from changes in conditions or policies."

Referring to the ordinary mercantile or manufacturing enterprises, Canning[7] says: "It is wholly impossible, except by purely arbitrary methods, to disengage the elementary operations, complete from cash to cash, from one another. Expenses are incurred that cannot be allocated to particular sale contracts except by methods of which one can say nothing more favorable than that the arithmetical calculations may be correct."

Time and Amount Uncertainties.—Assigning costs and expenses to the same accounting period in which so-called related income is recognized is often impossible due to two

---

[6] George O. May, "Improvement in Financial Accounts," *The Journal of Accountancy*, May 1937, p. 347.

[7] John B. Canning, *The Economics of Accountancy* (New York, The Ronald Press Company, 1929), p. 98.

uncertainties, i.e., uncertainty as to time and uncertainty as to amount.

Expenditures made for purposes of research illustrate uncertainty as to time. There may be a general conviction on the part of a business man that $10,000 spent upon research in the year 1938 will have a favorable effect upon earnings of subsequent years, but it may never be possible to determine just how much of that $10,000 is properly assignable to 1939, how much to 1940, and how much to 1941. There is no uncertainty here as to amount; $10,000 is the definitely established cost. All of the uncertainty has to do with the allocation of this cost to subsequent accounting periods. Various types of sales promotion costs and nearly all expenditures for fixed assets fall into this same category.

Uncertainty as to amount may be illustrated by the guarantee of product not extending past the current fiscal period. Here the time element is not left in doubt but the extent to which customers may demand costly service under this guarantee is indeterminate.

Many cases of uncertainty refer both to time and to amount. Thus, a product guarantee covering a five-year period refers to an item of cost which is uncertain as to total amount and uncertain as to periodic incidence.

Practical Difficulties of Matching.—Often practical considerations make it unwise to attempt a close matching of costs with income. This is noted in connection with executive salaries where part of an executive's time may be devoted to planning for the future and part to current problems. Conceivably such an executive might be required to keep a time report to show just how much of his salary should be charged against future periods and how much should be absorbed as a current cost. But seldom would any business man be willing to keep the records necessary for such an allocation.

Averaging of Costs.—Some of the averaging methods employed in cost accounting may interfere with the theoretical matching of costs and income. Thus, one lot of goods undergoing manufacture may actually cost twice as much as another due to various causes such as temporary labor inefficiency, operating at less than capacity, or the substitution of new and unfamiliar materials. The cost accountant, however, either averages his costs so that the excess actual cost of one particular lot is spread over other similar lots, or absorbs the excess costs in variance accounts in such a way that when a high cost inventory item is actually disposed of, no attempt is made to relate that particular high cost with the particular income resulting from the sale. Even with the greatest amount of ingenuity nonrecurring, non-operating losses due to fire, flood, or other catastrophes cannot be related to specific items of income.

These various problems are practical and few accountants would give a moment's consideration to hair-splitting treatment of them. Nevertheless, they illustrate to what extent practical necessities, arbitrary assumptions, and general conventions do modify the ideal of matching costs with income.

Inventory Revaluation.—Accounting practice generally recognizes unrealized declines in the value of inventories although the logic underlying this treatment is not convincing.

It is one thing to recognize the actual diminution of assets as a loss; it is another but a related thing to recognize as a loss diminution in the cost of fixed assets due to depreciation; but it is difficult to justify the recognition of losses due to decrease in price levels where there has been no diminution or deterioration of the asset. Such revaluation is perhaps the most illogical of accepted accounting practices.

To illustrate the effect of inventory revaluation, assume that a specific item of merchandise was purchased for $10 early in 1938. At the end of 1938 it could have been purchased for $9, in spite of the fact that its condition remained unchanged. In 1939 the merchandise is sold for $11. Relating the original cost of the item to its sales price in 1939 reveals a gross profit of $1. But this is not in accord with the viewpoint which insists that the value of the item be reduced from $10 to $9 on December 31, thus showing a $1 loss in 1938. In 1939 the item, then showing a book value of $9, is sold for $11 with the result that a gross profit of $2 is indicated in 1939.

This illustration, while simplified, suggests that the ideal of matching costs and income is disregarded by this common practice of recognizing unrealized losses due to decrease in replacement price.

Conservatism.—Conservatism has a tendency which is opposed to the ideal of matching costs with income. Ruled by the doctrine of conservatism, the accountant declines to recognize income until such recognition is clearly warranted but, on the other hand, has a tendency to be generous in recognizing costs, expenses, and losses and including them in the profit and loss statement of one period even though there may be some doubt as to the fairness of such inclusion.

The general accounting viewpoint in this connection has been set forth by Dohr[8] in the following proposition which is the last of four propositions relating to the income concept, the first three of which were mentioned in Chapter 8.

4. In the periodic summation a decrement in wealth is to be recognized whenever the business in question (a) becomes legally obligated without offsetting assets or (b) has utilized or consumed assets (depreciation, depletion, etc.), or (c) has lost, or *probably will lose,* assets by any one of a variety of causes, in each instance in an amount which can be measured or determined with reasonable accuracy.

Dohr's emphasis of the phrase "probably will lose" in the above is reinforced by his subsequent comment: "In the matter of losses the accountant recognizes those which have actually occurred and attempts to anticipate those which are *probable.*" Briefly stated, the conservative accounting rule requires that in case of doubt income should be excluded from a periodic profit and loss statement while in case of doubt costs, expenses, or losses should be included. That the adoption of diverse viewpoints toward income and expense may often interfere with the accounting ideal of matching is, of course, clearly indicated.

To summarize, it appears to be general accounting procedure to recognize only realized income of a period and to deduct from that income all costs, expenses, and losses, realized or unrealized,

8 James L. Dohr, "Income Divorced from Reality," *The Journal of Accountancy,* December 1938, p. 363.

in so far as they can practically be related to that same accounting period, despite the facts that (1) such relationships are often
arbitrary because of the convention of transferred values, (2)
many costs, expenses, and losses are uncertain as to time or as
to amount, or both, and (3) the recognition of unrealized losses
due to decreasing market prices deliberately contradicts the general policy of matching.

CHAPTER 10

UNUSUAL GAINS AND LOSSES

It is sufficiently difficult to match costs and income even when the various items thereof are normal and recurring, but matching is often impossible in the case of abnormal, extraordinary, or non-recurring costs and income.

The sale of a fixed asset such as a building or machine, or the destruction of property by fire or flood, may represent items of income or loss requiring special treatment. The correction of material errors in the accounting of former periods also provides an accounting problem as to the treatment of which accountants do not yet agree.

Entity Losses and Gains.—From the entity viewpoint, disregarding the convention of accounting periods, the treatment of such losses and gains is simple.

The entity is relieved or discharged of responsibility just as surely by a fire loss as by the sale of merchandise for less than cost. The chargeability of the entity is increased just as surely by the sale of a building at a profit as by the sale of merchandise at a profit. The liability of the entity to the proprietor is affected in the same manner by one kind of loss as another or by one kind of gain as another.

It is only when the accounting is modified by the adoption of accounting periods and of profit and loss classification that the treatment of extraordinary items of income or loss becomes puzzling. The problem, therefore, is entirely one of allocation as between accounting periods or between profit and loss classifications.

The Allocation of Unusual Items.—The essential profit and loss structure derived somewhat from the American Institute bulletin, *Examination of Financial Statements by Independent*

Public Accountants, has been illustrated in Chapter 7 but for ready reference is repeated here.

Net Sales . . . . $. . . . . .
Cost of Sales . . . .

Gross Profit on Sales . . . . $. . . . . .
Selling, General, and Administrative Expense . . . .

Net Profit before Other Income and Charges . . . . . $. . . . . .
Other Income . . . .

$. . . . . .
Other Charges . . . .

Net Profit for the Period, carried to Surplus . . . . . $. . . . . .
Surplus, beginning of period . . . .

Surplus, end of period . . . . $. . . . . .

When a decision must be made as to the accounting treatment of some unusual item of income, the problem resolves itself into choosing whether such income shall be credited to Sales Account or to Other Income Account, or whether it should be refused recognition as an item of the current period income and therefore be credited to Surplus Account.

The first question to be decided in connection with any such item of income is whether it is applicable to the current accounting period. If it is considered as being applicable to the current accounting period, a decision must be made between crediting it to Sales or to Other Income.

A similar type of decision must be made in the case of an unusual cost, expense, or loss, although here there is an additional option since the item may be charged to Cost of Sales, to Selling, General, and Administrative Expense, or to Other Charges if it is one properly to be reflected in the current period; otherwise to Surplus Account.

To the layman it may seem somewhat strange that such decisions should still cause serious disagreement among accountants. Nevertheless, it is true that the practice of accounting with respect to unusual costs, losses, and gains is not yet crystallized.

Whatever treatment is adopted in any instance may prove deceptive to those who rely upon accounting reports.

Need for Mutually Exclusive Classification.—It is elementary that classifications should, in so far as possible, be mutually exclusive. The classification of a group of people into males and females is mutually exclusive. The classification of a group into children and adults is mutually exclusive, but the classification of a group into males and adults is not mutually exclusive since a male adult may appear in either subdivision.

Of this same type is the common error which attempts to classify expenses as operating and non-recurring, or operating and extraordinary. If the operating viewpoint is adopted, then expenses must be classified as operating and non-operating. If the recurrence of the expense is important, then the classification to be mutually exclusive must be in terms of recurring and non-recurring.[1]

From the viewpoint of a business manager, the classification of losses and gains into operating and non-operating is particularly important because he uses the operating data as an index of business efficiency and progress. The prospective investor, on the other hand, is generally interested in the distinction between recurring and non-recurring losses and gains. He would not wish to purchase common stock of a company which in one year, due to some unusual circumstances, had earned a profit so substantial as to more than counter-balance the losses of several other years. Satisfied that this particular profit was due to some special circumstance not likely to be repeated, he would prefer to invest his money elsewhere.

Accordingly, the discussion may be approached on the basis of a fourfold classification as follows:

> Operating recurring losses or gains.
> Operating non-recurring losses or gains.
> Non-operating recurring losses or gains.
> Non-operating non-recurring losses or gains.

1 The words "recurring" and "non-recurring" have been adopted here because they are in common use rather than because they are particularly suitable. It is probably improper to speak of an assuredly non-recurring item. Possibly the words "normal" and "abnormal" should be substituted for "recurring" and "non-recurring."

A Fourfold Classification Illustrated.—There are numerous available examples of operating recurring losses and gains. Such items as the expense or cost of the rent of a plant or of lighting it belong in this group. A common example of operating recurring income is represented by sales made in the normal course of business.

Typical items of operating non-recurring cost or expense are to be found in the extra cost of overtime work needed to complete some rush order, or the cost of a special sales convention or special sales promotion plan. Where certain materials immediately needed for production cannot be obtained through normal sources owing to strikes or weather conditions, it may be necessary to have them brought by airplane from a considerable distance. The extra costs involved are operating costs but in the non-recurring group.

An illustration of operating non-recurring income is noted where sales are booked at an abnormally high price due to some dislocation of commerce. Shortly before the United States entered the World War, for example, one of the German raiders, hunted by a British cruiser, put into Mobile for coaling and offered an unusually high price for the immediate delivery of fuel. To the coal yard fortunate enough to obtain this order the resulting income was operating and non-recurring.

Commonly, although not unanimously, suggested as examples of non-operating recurring costs and gains are purchase and sales discounts, interest expense and interest earnings, and income received by manufacturing corporations from rentals of homes to its employees.

Uninsured fire loss, flood damage or loss from other types of destruction are examples of non-operating, non-recurring losses, while the sale of a fixed asset at a profit represents a non-operating, non-recurring gain.

Surplus Adjustments.—If it is decided that any item of expense or income belongs in any one of these four classifications, then that item will appear in the profit and loss computation of the current period. But if it is decided that the item should not be shown as a loss or gain of the current period, it has been customary to debit or credit it direct to Surplus Account.

The logic underlying this treatment is clear. Assume that an item is erroneously entered as a loss during 1938. At the end of 1938 this item reduces the 1938 profit by the same amount. This unduly low profit is transferred to Surplus. In 1939 Surplus remains understated by the amount of this error. When the error is discovered in 1939, it is regarded as too late to correct the profit and loss of 1938 and the correction must be made to that account which reflects the error at the time of its discovery, namely, Surplus Account. In so far as the mechanics of bookkeeping are concerned, this method of correcting errors of prior periods is unassailable, but abandoning the narrow viewpoint of bookkeeping mechanics and considering the problem more broadly, it is seen that this logical treatment may prove deceptive.

As George O. May and others have clearly explained, correction of prior errors by charging them to Surplus Account for a succession of ten years, for example, would result in a substantial discrepancy between the aggregate of the figures on the ten separate profit and loss statements and the figure which would have appeared if one profit and loss statement had been made for the entire ten-year period.

Based upon this viewpoint, the Executive Committee of the American Accounting Association[2] formulated its Postulate 8, as follows:

The income statement for any given period should reflect all revenues properly given accounting recognition and all costs written off during the period, regardless of whether or not they are the results of operations in that period: to the end that for any period of years in the history of the enterprise the assembled income statements will express completely all gains and losses.

Littleton[3] agrees with this general idea when he suggests that the earned surplus at the beginning of an accounting period

2 Executive Committee of the American Accounting Association, "A Tentative Statement of Accounting Principles Affecting Corporate Reports," *The Accounting Review,* June 1936, p. 189.

3 A. C. Littleton, "High Standards of Accounting," *The Journal of Accountancy,* August, 1938, p. 102.

is in the nature of a capital equity which may be affected by financial activities but not by operating activities. This view "justifies the exclusion from the income statement of cash or stock dividends, as well as the results of transactions in the corporation's own shares. The same view of the distinction between earnings and surplus also directs the inclusion of all income and expense, and all losses and gains of whatever kind, in the income statement in some way."

Considering surplus as an equity of this kind enables Littleton[4] to set forth the rule that:

. . . the only diminutions of assets to be charged directly against any equity would be those coming from—

1. A withdrawal of assets to discharge a debt to a creditor, to pay a dividend declared, or to mark the withdrawal of an investor's interest, with an accompanying cancellation of his shares.

2. A net loss from the administration of the assets for the period, after including corrections due to losses just now recognized, losses from unpredictable destruction, confiscation, theft, and the like.

3. A reorganization of financial structure placing the company substantially in the position of a new corporation without a previously accumulated earned surplus.

Such proposals have been the cause of dispute among accountants and various significant opinions have been rendered. May[5] regards it as impossible "to lay down any rule to be universally applied." He calls attention to the loss upon disposal of an asset due to insufficient depreciation in prior years and indicates the logical treatment, namely, that it should be charged "against the income over the years of the useful life which has now come to an end. Since the accounts of those years are closed and done with, the loss must be dealt with in some other way; and the question arises, shall its character as a charge against income control, and the loss be charged against income account even though it is in the wrong year, or shall its relationship to the past determine the treatment, and the loss be charged against the accumulated undistributed income?"

This question discloses the two horns of a serious dilemma.

[4] *Ibid.*, p. 103.
[5] George O. May, "Improvement in Financial Accounts," *The Journal of Accountancy*, May 1937. p. 354.

Adoption of the first suggestion is opposed to the desirable practice of matching costs with income. Adoption of the second alternative results in failure of the assembled income statements for a period of years to express completely all gains and losses.

Reconstruction of Prior Statements.—The Executive Committee of the American Accounting Association[6] was not unmindful of this predicament and their Postulate 13 suggested a procedure to be followed:

> When the income for any period or series of periods is found to have been inaccurately stated to such a degree that it is desirable completely to recast the accounts, at least one published report after such revision should include a corrected income statement for each prior period for which adjustments have been made.

Obviously this is the one and only logical treatment to correct inaccurately stated profits. It does, however, offer certain practical difficulties in that corporation managers may not care to have their past errors so signally publicized. Also the reconstruction of these corrected profit and loss statements may require an unjustifiably large expenditure of accounting effort.

Stempf[7] asserts that he is "loath to insist that the corporation should also assume the expense and somewhat futile effort of determining an allocation against each of the prior years affected." While the expense would necessarily be a factor of some importance, it appears that the strength of Stempf's case really rests upon the futility of the procedure.

Obviously, the doctrine of materiality must be reconsidered and a new conception thereof must be adopted if Postulate 13 is to become a standard alternative practice in accounting. It may be assumed that materiality, in so far as profit and loss statements are concerned, is determined by the size of amounts in relation to their effect upon the comparability of the statements. It is anybody's guess in any given instance as to how large an item must be to affect the comparability of statements.

6 Executive Committee of the American Accounting Association, "A Tentative Statement of Accounting Principles Affecting Corporate Reports," *The Accounting Review*, June 1936, p. 190.

7 Victor H. Stempf, "A Critique of the Tentative Statement of Accounting Principles," *The Accounting Review*. March 1938, p. 60.

If a given item of expense in one year is $20,000 and in the succeeding year it is $25,000, then the increase is 25%. If there was an error of $1,000 made in allocation and if the expense of the first year should have been $21,000 and of the second year should have been $24,000, then the percentage increase would be only 14%.

Is this an error sufficiently material to justify recasting the statements? Being only $1,000, a small item in relation to, perhaps, a half-million dollar sales volume, it might be regarded as immaterial. Because it changed the percentage of increase from 25% to 14%, this error might be regarded as particularly material.

What, then, is the test of materiality in a case of this kind? Is it the size of one amount as compared with other amounts involved or does it refer to the change in the percentage of increase or decrease?

If comparability is the essential factor, then the latter test would appear to be the valid one, and yet how many accountants would demand a recasting of the accounts for such an error?

Before Postulate 13 can receive serious consideration, it must be supplemented by a more definite statement as to when it should be applied and by provision of some test for materiality. If this is not done, one can envision a constant program of recasting accounts and a constant succession of corrected prior period profit and loss statements.

It can be asserted that materiality in this connection must refer to comparability and that comparability must be tested not by absolute amounts of increase or decrease but by percentages of increase or decrease. If this is true, then a relatively small percentage error in some of the larger constituents of a profit and loss statement may easily result in a magnified percentage error in the final figure of net profit—an error so substantial as greatly to change the net profit comparison as between one period and another. Accordingly, while Postulate 13 may be accepted as a logical compromise between the pro-surplus and anti-surplus advocates, it does not appear acceptable as presently defined and explained.

Distortion of Operating Results.—To those who regard as most important the distinction between operating and non-operating losses and gains, Postulate 8, previously quoted, may appear somewhat illogical, particularly as modified by Postulates 9, 10, and 11 which provide that the profit and loss statement shall be divided into two sections, one for operating items and the other showing "realized capital gains and losses and extraordinary credits and charges resulting from income realization and cost amortization not connected with the operations of that period."[8]

This latter or non-operating section of the profit and loss statement should include, according to the American Accounting Association, "extraordinary charges and credits to income, including substantial adjustments applicable to but not recognized in prior years."[8]

Just what does this mean? It means that an error made in reporting an operating item in one period must be corrected by an adjustment in the non-operating section of the profit and loss statement in a subsequent period. Accordingly, the integrity of the operating figures, regarded as so important to management, is destroyed and the aggregate of the operating profits as reflected by a series of profit and loss statements for ten years will not be the same as the operating profit shown by one profit and loss statement for that same ten-year period.

Of course, this can be cured by adopting the previously mentioned suggestion of preparing corrected profit and loss statements for the prior periods.

Adopting a somewhat different viewpoint, Pinkerton[9] asks:

Should substantial prior-period adjustments, when made to current income, be included in the section of the profit and loss statement in which they would have been included had they been entered in a prior period, or should they be shown separately as income charges or credits even when they pertain to operating results?

He continues:

8 Executive Committee of the American Accounting Association, "A Tentative Statement of Accounting Principles Affecting Corporate Reports," *The Accounting Review*, June 1936, pp. 189, 190. (For other postulates of the American Accounting Association see Chapter 14.)
9 Paul W. Pinkerton, in a personal letter of October 9, 1937.

The former treatment is followed in the case of non-substantial amounts, and I favor it in all cases, believing that the justification for including the items in current income at all is found in the assumption that the net income of the prior year was determined as accurately as was then possible, and that the items are proper charges against income of the year in which determined. And since it is argued that the item should be included in income rather than in surplus so that the income statements of a number of years will show the results of those years without referring to the surplus account, isn't it also to be argued that the item should be included under its proper caption rather than somewhere else, so that the statements of a number of years will show in respect to each caption the results of those years without reference to other captions?

This viewpoint seems soundly based. If the prior period error was reflected in the operating section of the profit and loss statement for that period, then it should be corrected in the operating section of the profit and loss statement for the period when discovered. When such corrections are substantial in amount, Pinkerton insists upon their parenthetical disclosure.

Correction of prior period errors generally involves the current recognition sometimes of income but much more often of some expense, cost, or loss which was previously understated or omitted. Since the realization convention does not apply to such debit items, any objection to reflecting such adjustments in a profit and loss statement is based only on grounds of profit distortion and lack of matching.

Income from Correction of Understated Assets.—Occasionally the prior period error is one of cost overstatement. Often this results from overdepreciation. The traditional policy of correction is illustrated by the treatment of overdepreciation suggested in the *Accountants' Handbook*.[10]

Where depreciation charges in the past have been excessive the earning power of the concern has been correspondingly understated and the so-called depreciation reserve, in principle an offset to gross book value of property, includes an element of surplus. When this fact becomes apparent an adjustment of the reserve account (involving a debit to the reserve and a credit to earned surplus) is in order.

[10] *Accountants' Handbook* (New York, The Ronald Press Company, 1934), p. 626.

Disregarding, for the moment, its Postulate 4, the American Accounting Association would show this correction in the non-operating section of the profit and loss statement. This is clearly set forth in Postulate 11, just quoted.

This recognition of non-operating income must, of course, be accompanied by the increase in an asset but to any such increase Postulate 4 applies. It reads: "Costs charged off in accordance with these principles should not be reinstated as assets subject to reamortization, except as required corrections are reflected in revised income statements for each period affected."[11]

Here is a clear contradiction. Correction of prior over-depreciation should be shown as an item of non-operating income in one profit and loss statement according to Postulate 11. If the adjustment is too large, Postulate 13 suggests re-casting the prior statements affected, but, large or small, Postulate 4 demands such recasting at least for the asset element.

This is not mere quibbling since an important issue is involved, that of income realization. Postulate 11 permits correcting an understated asset by a credit to current non-operating income. Does such a credit represent realized income? Many who would answer "yes" believe that depreciation represents realization of asset cost in installments and accordingly the correction of overrealization of cost would represent realization of income.

The point is, however, arguable and some accountants, logically or conservatively, would object to such flexibility of the realization convention which is based on actual, rather than hypothetical, cash incidence.

It is easy enough to argue that past realized profits would have been larger had the overdepreciation never been taken, hence the correction of understated past profits also represents income realization. It is, however, doubtful whether it represents realization referring to one accounting period. It is this doubt which may have been responsible for Postulate 4 and its contradiction of Postulate 11.

11 Executive Committee of the American Accounting Association, "A Tentative Statement of Accounting Principles Affecting Corporate Reports," *The Accounting Review*, June 1936, p. 190.

The problems involved in this entire discussion are serious from the viewpoint not only of management but more particularly from that of investors who buy or sell securities on the basis of reported annual profits.

Comparison of Three Common Methods.—It may perhaps simplify this discussion to include here a highly simplified diagrammatic form of comparison showing the effects of the various methods discussed.

Assume that three corporations absolutely identical in every respect started in business on January 1 of the same year, and for the first year and for the second year each reported net sales of $100,000 and costs and expenses of $90,000, leaving a net profit of $10,000.

In the third year each of these corporations would show exactly the same profit and loss statement as for the two previous years except for the fact that a $6,000 loss, properly chargeable equally to all three years, requires adjustment. It is assumed that none of the companies follows the plan of including the surplus reconciliation as part of the profit and loss statement.

The first company follows the surplus adjustment plan, as a result of which the $6,000 is divided into two amounts, $2,000 being included among the costs and expenses of the third year, thus increasing the $90,000 to $92,000, while $4,000 is debited directly to surplus. After this adjustment the profit and loss statement for this company for the three years will appear as follows:

CORPORATION A

	1st Year	2nd Year	3rd Year
Net Sales	$100,000	$100,000	$100,000
All Costs and Expenses	90,000	90,000	92,000
Net Profit for Period	$ 10,000	$ 10,000	$ 8,000

Assuming that there were no dividends paid nor any other entries to surplus, the balance of the surplus account at the end of the third year will be $24,000, while the aggregate of the reported annual profits is $28,000.

The second corporation follows the American Accounting Association plan as set forth in Postulate 11, and therefore includes the entire $6,000 item as part of the costs and expenses of the third year, with the following results:

CORPORATION B

	1st Year	2nd Year	3rd Year
Net Sales	$100,000	$100,000	$100,000
All Costs and Expenses	90,000	90,000	96,000
Net Profit for Period	$ 10,000	$ 10,000	$ 4,000

At the end of the third year the surplus of the company will be $24,000, agreeing with the aggregate of the reported annual profits.

The third company, believing it desirable to recast the accounts because of the size of the adjustment, distributes the $6,000 equally to the three years, thus increasing the costs and expenses for each year from $90,000 to $92,000, with the following results:

CORPORATION C

	1st Year	2nd Year	3rd Year
Net Sales	$100,000	$100,000	$100,000
All Costs and Expenses	92,000	92,000	92,000
Net Profit for Period	$ 8,000	$ 8,000	$ 8,000

At the end of the third year the surplus of this company is $24,000, agreeing with the aggregate of the reported annual profits.

It seems that the method followed by the third company is preferable to the other two in so far as a comparable historical record of profits is concerned. This conclusion, however, is based upon the assumption that the three companies do not include surplus reconciliations as an integral part of their profit and loss statements. Had they done so, many accountants would believe that the method followed by Corporation A is generally preferable. The profit and loss statements of Corporation A with the surplus reconciliations appended would appear as follows:

CORPORATION A

	1st Year	2nd Year	3rd Year
Net Sales	$100,000	$100,000	$100,000
All Costs and Expenses	90,000	90,000	92,000
Net Profit for Period	$ 10,000	$ 10,000	$ 8,000
Surplus — January 1	. . . . . .	10,000	20,000
	$ 10,000	$ 20,000	$ 28,000
Surplus Adjustment	. . . . . .	. . . . . .	4,000
Surplus — December 31	$ 10,000	$ 20,000	$ 24,000

This form of report directs the reader's attention to the surplus adjustment in such a way as to remove many of the criticisms which have been leveled at other methods.

Commonly Accepted Practice.—It is probably true that the majority of accountants believe in using the Surplus Account, regardless of whether it is made a part of the profit and loss statement, as the means of correcting prior period errors when the amounts involved are material. When the amounts involved are immaterial, the majority of accountants treat the items as though they belonged to the current period.

The test of materiality in this instance involves consideration of the comparability of successive profit and loss statements. Where the amounts involved are so small as not to affect the comparative value of the statements, then it is believed unnecessary to pass corrections through the Surplus Account. Accordingly, an immaterial error in the operating section of a 1938 profit and loss statement may be corrected by an off-setting error in the operating section of the 1939 profit and loss statement. This is the treatment suggested by Sanders, Hatfield, and Moore[12] in the following comment: "Since by assumption such corrections in the income statement are small in amount, they may properly be combined with the items to which the corrections apply." If this treatment does not destroy the comparability of the operating figures for the two years, it is regarded as a justifiably practical expedient.

[12] Sanders, Hatfield, and Moore, *A Statement of Accounting Principles* (New York, American Institute of Accountants, 1938), p. 41.

A similar practice is followed with respect to the non-operating section of the profit and loss statements; thus preserving the distinction between operating and non-operating. Opinion is divided, however, as to the treatment of extraordinary operating items of income or expense. Such unusual items may be considered extraordinary because of their size or because they are non-recurrent. In either event their treatment is more a matter of judgment than a matter of rule. The difficulty here is clearly set forth by Canning[13] in his question:

> But what is an extraordinary outlay? How large must it be or how infrequent in recurrence? Does the simultaneous occurrence, or the occurrence in any one period, of an unusually large number of small charges constitute an extraordinary item?

There are some who believe that extraordinary or non-recurring items of cost or income should be debited or credited to Surplus Account on the theory that they cannot be assigned to any particular accounting period. The modern viewpoint, however, is opposed to this treatment, it being regarded as better practice to assign such items to *some* profit and loss statement or statements even though they cannot be matched with corresponding items of income or cost.

13 John B. Canning, *The Economics of Accountancy* (New York, The Ronald Press Company, 1929), p. 286.

CHAPTER 11

ACCOUNTING CONVENTIONS AND THE CORPORATION

The accounting conventions may be said to apply without reference to any particular type of proprietorship. The entity convention, in particular, may refer to a single proprietor, to two or more proprietors in the form of a partnership, or to a group of proprietors as members of a club, citizens of a community, or stockholders in a corporation.[1] While the entity convention applies to all of these organization patterns, the rapid growth in the number and size of corporations has so profoundly affected accounting in general and the determination of accounting profits in particular as to justify special consideration. Such special consideration may not, according to Husband,[2] refer specifically to accounting:

> The theoretical approach to the accounting problems of the corporation should be the same as the theoretical approach to the accounting problems of the sole-proprietorship and the partnership; the entity concept need cause no variation in theory. In practice, however, the procedure followed in accounting for the transactions of the sole-proprietorship and the partnership must be modified to meet the requirements set up by law, the corporate contract with the state, and the various regulatory bodies. Acceptance of such an approach should eliminate much of the debate now found in accounting literature and place it where it belongs—in the fields of law, public policy, and finance.

As related by Littleton, the corporation had its roots in the medieval partnership and became popular in Italy during the

---

1 The same thought is expressed by Lewis A. Carman, "Primary Accounting Concepts," *The Journal of Accountancy,* May 1936, p. 353, as follows: "The possessions of a business entity and the amounts owed by it are attributes entirely independent of the ownership form. They are elemental facts of the business considered solely as an operating unit. A truck, for example, may be owned by a corporation, a partnership or a one-legged Chinaman without affecting in any manner its characteristics as an operating unit."
2 George R. Husband, "The Corporate-Entity Fiction and Accounting Theory," *The Accounting Review,* September 1938, p. 253.

twelfth and thirteenth centuries when there were prejudices against the taking of interest and also against the nobility's engaging in trade. These taboos were avoided by the formation of partnerships, forerunners of the modern corporation, in which the investor's liability against a third party was limited.

The resulting corporate form, because of its limited liability feature and its continuing existence regardless of changes in proprietorship, offered an ideal vehicle for raising capital, thus encouraging business operations on a much larger scale than would be possible with the limited resources of one or several individuals.

Because the corporation is a creature of the law and because of the large number of individuals affected in one way or another by corporations, these are regarded not as strictly private, personal enterprises but rather as types of economic activity directly relating to the public interest.

This is, obviously, a matter of special accounting significance. The original equation mechanism recorded the simple relationship between entity and proprietor in terms of investment and profit. Generally there was no distinction between ownership and management. The owner-proprietor could and did impose upon the entity such valuation symbols as he desired. Increased entity size, due to the corporate form, brought about a separation of the management and proprietorship functions. Because of the limited liability feature of the corporation, creditors were affected by the accounting methods employed. The adoption of income taxes introduced the government as a party at interest in corporation accounting. As a result of this increased public interest and the increase in the size of business units, there was noted an increased elaboration of accounting records. While this elaboration involved no basic change in the fundamental accounting equation or in its dependence upon the entity convention, it did introduce greater complexity into the recording mechanism.

As a collateral effect of these various changes, the original purpose of the valuation convention has been somewhat obscured. No longer is it a mere convenience for recording in homogeneous terms non-homogeneous assets and claims.

Rather, such valuation symbols are naturally, although erroneously, accepted by many outside interests as a reflection of values, often of realizable values. This misinterpretation of the valuation symbol has occasioned such developments as the doctrine of conservatism designed to prevent overvaluation, the balance sheet viewpoint which tended to subordinate earnings in favor of a static statement of so-called financial condition, and finally the practice of reporting accounting figures to large sections of the general public as distinguished from reporting to a single proprietor, which has resulted in the development of a body of rules, conventions, and doctrines of reporting separate from, although related to, the body of rules, conventions, and doctrines of accounting itself.

This distinction between accounting and reporting is not fully recognized. Rarely does a practical benefit result from making such a distinction. Occasionally, however, reasoning may be obscured unless reporting and accounting are recognized as two areas. That these functions really are separate may clearly be seen in connection with such a form as the consolidated statement which has no direct accounting basis.

Important Corporate Characteristics.—The problems of corporations and corporation accounting are so extensive that many substantial and important technical works have been written on these subjects only.

There are, however, a few obvious corporate characteristics which are particularly pertinent to this present discussion. These characteristics are: (1) legal entity, (2) continous life, (3) limited liability, and (4) delegated management.

LEGAL ENTITY. The corporation is one form of business organization which has been recognized legally as an entity. The entity convention still remains a fiction in the single proprietorship and partnership.

Legal recognition of the corporate entity does not include legal recognition of corporate proprietorship as a liability, nor is the legal entity concept always applied consistently, since it is somewhat contradicted by recognition of consolidated statements, by the utility aboriginal cost decision of the Supreme

Court, and, as Husband has shown, by income tax law and regulations which dispense with the entity in the principle of contructive ownership, the tax on improperly accumulated surplus, and the surtax on personal holding companies.

Husband[3] also advances the thought that there is a contradiction to be noted in connection with income, as follows:

> Consistent with the entity theory, it is usually contended that the income of a corporation does not constitute income to its stockholders; yet, when this same income is credited to surplus, it is added to the stockholders' interest as portrayed by the capital-stock account to secure the stockholders' total equity. But how can that which is not the stockholders' equity as income justly become the stockholders' equity as surplus?

This particular difficulty, however, does not arise if the entity convention is strictly interpreted as meaning that the entity never, as an entity, makes a profit or a loss but merely increases or decreases its debt to proprietorship.

The more or less complete recognition of the corporation as a legal entity results from the manner of its creation and control. Its creation is legal and its characteristics are predetermined by statute. Its operations are controlled by statute, and uncertainties with respect to the statutory significance of various corporate accounting problems are resolved by the courts. Nowhere in business accounting is the legal influence more powerful or more extensive than in the accounting for corporations.

CONTINUOUS LIFE.   The corporation is characterized also by continuous life regardless of shifting ownership.

This is not true of the common accounting entity the existence of which is dependent upon the existence of one or more proprietors. In the sole proprietorship or partnership, for example, when a proprietor dies the entity dies and when there is a substitution of proprietors there is a substitution of entities.

The corporate entity, on the other hand, may continue regardless of death, disaster, retirement, or bankruptcy of any one of its individual stockholders. One proprietor or stockholder may be substituted for another by the transfer of stock

3 George R. Husband, "The Corporate-Entity Fiction and Accounting Theory," *The Accounting Review*, September 1938, p. 243.

ownership without practically or theoretically affecting the entity. The result is permanence of investment, regardless of the number of changes among stockholders.

Conceivably as well as practically, it is possible for a corporate entity to continue unchanged with the same capital even when all of the original stockholders have been replaced by others.

LIMITED LIABILITY. Limited liability is a characteristic of the corporate form. Generally this means simply that the individual fully paid-up stockholder in a fully paid corporation may lose all of his original investment but that he is not liable to assessment for further capital contributions.

This is a most important characteristic from the creditors' viewpoint, since the creditor must look only to the corporate entity for a payment of his claim and cannot, as in the other two forms of organization, make up any deficiency direct from the proprietors.

This limited liability feature generally prevents the stockholder from withdrawing his investment and emphasizes the importance of distinguishing between capital which is not available for dividends and surplus which is available. Many legal accounting tangles result from this necessity.

Creditors must be protected against overoptimistic calculation of corporate profits and their distribution. The natural desire of corporation directors to be "on the safe side" in computing profits and declaring dividends has greatly emphasized the importance of the doctrine of conservatism and accordingly has profoundly influenced accounting practice.

DELEGATED MANAGEMENT. Another characteristic of the corporate form is delegation of management.

The simple combination of proprietorship and management is seldom found in the modern corporation. The stockholders, by vote as legally prescribed, elect directors who are their representatives for management purposes. These directors, in turn, elect corporate officers to operate the business.

In small, closely held corporations one majority stockholder may control the election of the board of directors, may be one of the directors and may also be the chief executive officer elected by the board of directors. In a large corporation it is probable that no one individual will hold more than a small proportion of the total capital stock and the relationship between the individual stockholders and the business itself may thus be distant and indirect.

To. regard the stockholders of a corporation as its proprietors is theoretically correct from the entity viewpoint. Practically, many stockholders never think of themselves as being proprietors. This is particularly noticeable in connection with corporations whose shares are actively traded on security markets.

The purchaser of corporate shares through the New York Stock Exchange usually thinks in terms of profit or loss based upon the increase or decrease in the market price of his shares. He regards his purchase of stock certificates in no different light from his purchase of corn or wheat on a commodity exchange. The consequent gulf between proprietorship and management emphasizes the importance of directors' responsibilities and is the direct cause of various legal safeguards which have been established for the purpose of protecting investors against their own directors.

Types of Corporate Ownership.—The sole proprietor's claim against the entity reflects a simple relationship. The corporate form, however, permits various types of ownership.

Since there may be outstanding at any one time various issues of preferred stocks bearing various dividend rates and carrying various distinctive provisions with respect to voting power, liquidation rights, and rights to be exercised only upon failure to pay dividends, some of the issues being convertible and others not, some having cumulative features and others not, it is clear that the proprietor-entity arrangement may no longer be simple and direct.

As a complicating feature, different classes of common stock may be outstanding. One class may have voting power and another not; one class may have a right to priority of dividends over the other.

Such complexities necessitate another accounting convention the convenience of which is obvious. By this convention one individual may be regarded as though he were two or more individuals. Thus, if one man owns a certain amount of Class A common stock, a block of Class B common stock, some shares of 6% cumulative preferred, some shares of 8% non-cumulative preferred, is an officer of the corporation, a holder of bonds in the corporation, and finally a customer of the corporation, this particular accounting convention treats him as though he were seven persons instead of one. In one form or another the corporation will maintain seven accounts with him which, in the normal course of business, are never consolidated. Each one of these seven separate personalities has certain, sometimes conflicting, claims upon or obligations to the corporate entity, all of which complicates the simple entity-proprietor relationship.

Corporate Profit Determination.—The most serious problem in corporate accounting is that of profit determination.

It is the directors' responsibility to guard against impairing the capital of their corporation by refusing to distribute more profits than are earned. Unfortunately, some of the statutes which restrict dividends to profits have not been entirely clear and it has been necessary for the courts to determine whether capital has in any given instance been impaired by the payment of a dividend. The courts have been forced to pass upon such technical accounting matters as the distinction between capital and revenue, depreciation, depletion, valuation of receivables or inventories, and similar matters. Considerable legal and accounting attention has accordingly been directed to surplus which in simple theory represents accumulated undistributed profits.

Certain types of surplus not composed of accumulated undistributed profits are frequently noted. Those amounts paid to corporations by stockholders in excess of the par or stated value of the stock must be credited to a special surplus account. In reality the total contribution by the stockholder is capital and, if such a fictitious surplus is considered available for dividends, such dividends may represent merely a return of part of the stockholder's investment.

Then, too, donations by stockholders are not unknown. Such contributions result in an accounting surplus. Clearly that surplus does not represent earned profit in the ordinarily understood sense of that term. Accordingly, accountants distinguish sharply between true earned surplus and those various forms of capital surplus which they regard as equivalent to capital contributions. It must, however, be noted that it is the courts rather than the accountants which have the controlling and often confusing voice in all phases of surplus and dividends.

The conservation of capital and the calculation of profits in many industries are dependent upon correct computation and allocation of depreciation. Hence, the courts interest themselves in this engineering-accounting problem. Occasionally their findings have indicated some confusion. The generally recognized purpose of depreciation is to recover the cost of the investment in fixed assets, and has no reference whatever to replacing that asset, but this distinction is not one which has always received legal recognition.

Control of the Corporation.—Referring again to the original entity convention, it will be remembered that a distinguishing characteristic of proprietorship is that of control over the entity.

Originally this control could be exercised in a number of ways, including the withdrawal at any time of previously invested capital or of accumulated profits. Proprietorship in a corporation carries with it no such freedom, not only because of legal restrictions but also because of the practical necessity for majority control which leaves the minority stockholder with few rights and little power. He may desire dividends but, if the majority of his fellow stockholders oppose him, he has no power to enforce his desires. He may wish to withdraw his capital but, even if the corporation has no creditors, he will not be permitted to do so save by agreement of the stockholders. Disgruntled at his inability to enforce the payment of dividends or to withdraw his investment, he has but one recourse, namely, that of selling his stock.

In large corporations the gulf separating the entity and the proprietorship is so great that it is not necessary to own more than 50% of the voting stock in order to control the corpora- tion. Often one man or a group of men holding perhaps no more than a small percentage of the total outstanding stock will be able to control the corporation.

Secret Reserves.—The rights and responsibilities of pro- prietors have been so greatly modified in many corporations that the stockholders' own representatives, namely, the directors, often feel it necessary to protect stockholders against themselves and actually to understate the financial condition of the cor- poration in order to prevent extravagant dividend demands by stockholders.

This particular form of understatement is often referred to as the creation of a "secret reserve." The phrase is unfortunately chosen, since it results generally from the understatement of assets often brought about by charging to expense those expendi- tures which properly should be shown as assets. Misrepresenta- tion of this type sometimes represents paternalism, having for its object the protection of the real owners of the business. Sometimes it is sanctified as conservatism. Occasionally it has been used as a means of defrauding stockholders, the insiders in a corporation using their secret knowledge of the true state of affairs for the purpose of trading in the company's stock and thus acquiring a private profit.

Disclosure to Stockholders.—In spite of the precedent set in 1902 by the U. S. Steel Corporation in recognizing stock- holders' rights to information, the management of a corporation often refuses to divulge certain kinds of facts to stockholders as being against the best interests of the corporation, just as though the interests of the corporate entity were of a separate order from the interests of its stockholders.

The argument generally advanced, and one which carries considerable weight, refers to the danger that a competitor may purchase a few shares of stock for the sole purpose of gaining inside information. In other instances, however, the entity seems to have changed its character from an artificial person and has taken unto itself some of the attributes of an actual living human being in the assertion of rights and viewpoints independent of and sometimes opposed to its owners.

Corporate Complexity.—One interesting effect of the corporate form is noted in the widened range of business activity engaged in by a single entity.

In the older, simpler forms of proprietorship one principal business activity was about all that could be handled. In the modern corporate form one entity may engage in a number of separate lines of business, including the manufacture of not only one but many different final products, coupled with the manufacture or production of raw materials, supplies, or parts required in making finished products. The entity may own railroads or other transportation systems; it may own real estate which it rents to its own employees.

This widened range of entity activity has had the effect of elaborating the account classification in such a way that the actual number of profit or loss accounts in a large corporation may run into the thousands.

AFFILIATED CORPORATIONS.   Sometimes these various activities are separately incorporated so that one corporate entity owns all or a large part of the stock of other corporate entities.

In large corporations such as General Motors, U. S. Steel Corporation, and some of the larger utility companies, such intercorporate relationships may become quite complicated.

The ownership of one entity by another entity presents some interesting accounting problems. Consider, for example, two business enterprises exactly identical, each with a dozen manufacturing plants. In the first instance but one entity is involved, the corporation owning all of its various plants and treating them as departments.

In the other instance thirteen different entities will be involved, the parent entity owning and controlling the twelve subsidiary entities. Each entity is by law a separate and distinct person. Each must maintain its own record of stockholders, must hold annual meetings, elect directors and officers, and carry through the elaborate ritual which characterizes corporation procedure. And yet in reality there is no fundamental difference between the two situations. The business man properly regards the two as alike, i.e., in both there are the same number of physical operating entities.

UNREALIZED PROFITS.   In the first situation, where but one entity is involved, a department or plant may produce raw materials which are then transferred to another department or plant.

It is a commonplace of accounting that no profit can be realized by transfers from one part of a business to another, from one department to another, or from one plant to another. Hence, all such transfers are made on the basis of cost.

There is, however, no such restriction when one corporation deals with another, even though they are commonly owned and controlled. Thus subsidiary corporation B may sell to subsidiary corporation C at a profit. From the viewpoint of the parent corporation A, corporations B and C are merely departments. Legally, however, they are separate entities and may profit by selling goods to one another.

CONSOLIDATED STATEMENTS.   This intercorporate buying and selling has introduced a series of difficult accounting problems involved in the preparation of consolidated statements, the purpose of which is to disregard the legal fiction of separate corporations and to bring together the reports of the different corporations into one composite report, at the same time eliminating intercompany profits and intercompany claims.

The purpose of a consolidated statement is to present a picture of the entire group as if it were one corporation. Here is a difficult technical problem of reporting which is in reality not an accounting problem at all, accounting itself being so intimately associated with the entity that it cannot be divorced without doing violence to the fundamental conventions. In the case of the departmentalized industry, therefore, there is one accounting entity and one accounting system. In the other instance there are thirteen accounting entities and thirteen accounting systems, and the thirteen entities are treated as one only for consolidated statement purposes.

Initial Valuation of Corporate Assets.—An important problem of corporation accounting refers to the valuation of assets acquired in exchange for stock.

While many corporations are organized on a cash basis, more often the corporation issues its stock in return for the property of an already existing business. Legally it has been generally held that in the absence of fraud the judgment of the directors of a corporation controls the valuation of the assets received. Often, however, the stockholders and the directors of a newly formed corporation are the same people who sell the assets to that corporation. Brushing aside legal technicalities, the situation somewhat resembles that of a man buying from and selling to himself.

While subject to criticism from other viewpoints, there is nothing in the basic convention of accounting to prevent such newly acquired assets from being recorded at any desired figure, if the capital stock issued in exchange therefor represents the same amount.

It is, however, necessary to consider the rights of subsequent stockholders who may, by excessive valuation, be induced to pay an extravagant price for the stock. If those who originally acquired the stock at the time of the corporation's birth continue to hold it in perpetuity and if creditors are not deceived, then the valuation of the assets so acquired is unimportant.

Frequently, however, inflated asset values are adopted by promoters as a preliminary to a widespread stock-selling campaign. The protection of such investors not part of an inside group is now regarded as a matter of public interest, and lawyers, courts, and regulatory bodies look suspiciously upon extravagant asset valuations originally imposed upon a corporate entity.

Admittedly, however, it is difficult to prove asset overvaluation without going back to the accounting records of the original owners of those assets—a procedure which is not always feasible. Were it not for the protection of creditors and for the constant buying and selling of shares and the consequent changes in individual ownership thereof, it would make no difference what values were assigned to assets at the inception of the corporation. The greater value assigned, the greater the amount of annual depreciation, the ultimate profit or loss upon termination being the same regardless of original asset valuation. From the strictly entity viewpoint there can be no such thing as overvaluation.

Treasury Stock.—Interesting and controversial accounting problems arise when a corporation deals in its own stock.

Generally, lacking an earned surplus, the corporation legally cannot purchase shares of its own stock, since that is equivalent to the retirement of one or more stockholder's investment to the neglect of the others. Accordingly, a fiction has been established that a reacquired share of stock, or treasury stock, is a deduction from earned surplus.

Instead of holding such reacquired stock, the corporation may sell it at any desired price. Accordingly, there may appear to be an element of profit or loss involved in the sale of treasury stock. Not even yet have authorities agreed whether such losses and gains are true losses and gains or whether they represent capital adjustments.

PROFIT AND LOSS ON SALE. Some authorities hold that there can be no element of true profit or loss when a corporation deals in its own stock. Still others insist that such losses and gains are similar to losses and gains made on the sale of merchandise. In this latter group there is no less an authority than Robert H. Montgomery. Sanders, Hatfield, and Moore[4] also agree, particularly "when such profits or losses occur in small amounts." Bacas, Madden, and Rosenkampff[5] say that the profit on treasury stock sold "should be stated as a separate item in the statement of income." This procedure is indicated as permissible only where the purchase and sale of a stock is made on the open market. If the treasury stock was donated to the corporation or if it was purchased for an arbitrary amount then "the excess of the sales price would not be considered as a profit but as capital surplus."

4 Sanders, Hatfield, and Moore, *A Statement of Accounting Principles* (New York, American Institute of Accountants, 1938), p. 90.
5 Bacas, Madden, and Rosenkampff, *Auditing Procedure* (New York, The Ronald Press Company, 1937), pp. 328, 329.

ANALYSIS BY ENTITY CONVENTION. Considering this problem strictly on the basis of the entity convention, a rather interesting line of argument results.

The entity convention recognizes no accounting distinction between the liability of an entity for borrowings and the liability of an entity for proprietorship investment. Both are liabilities. Accordingly, one method of exploring this problem is to assume the existence of a sole proprietorship which borrows $1,000 from each of three persons.

The liability side of the entity balance sheet might, therefore, appear somewhat as follows:

Owed to John Smith	$1,000
Owed to George Brown	1,000
Owed to William White	1,000
Owed to James Black	5,000
Total Liabilities	$8,000

In this illustration it is assumed that James Black is the proprietor. If the indebtedness to Smith, Brown, and White is evidenced by three ten-year promissory notes bearing an interest rate of 6%, then the entity will owe each of these creditors $60 a year for interest and at the end of a ten-year period will owe each of them $1,000.

Immediately after making his loan, John Smith changes his mind and sells his note to the entity for $1,000. Instead of cancelling the note, the entity resells it to Walter Jones for $1,100. At the time the money is received from Walter Jones, $1,000 of it is recorded as a liability to him, while $100 of it is treated as a deferred credit to be amortized against interest expense. In other words, from the entity viewpoint it is a deferred credit to the proprietor's account, an offset to the interest expense which will be debited annually to the proprietor's account. Such a premium is, of course, common in connection with bond issues but there is no reason for not using a similar account in connection with a note issue. The entity must pay Walter Jones $60 a year interest, which is credited to Cash and debited to Expense. Each year $10 must be transferred to Interest Expense from Premium on Notes Payable.

If it is assumed that these notes mature in 100 years instead of in ten years, the same original entries will be made but instead of amortizing the premium at $10 a year, it will be amortized at $1 a year. If the maturity of the notes is 1,000 instead of 100 years, then the premium on notes payable will be amortized at the rate of 10 cents per year. If the liability represented by this note is perpetual, then the premium on notes payable will never be amortized but will continue to stand as a perpetually deferred credit to the proprietor's account.

According to the entity convention the proprietor's investment is a liability of the entity. Accordingly, the investment by stockholders in a corporation must be considered a liability of the entity to those stockholders regardless of legal contradictions. The illustration, therefore, may be changed to show John Smith, George Brown, and William White each investing $1,000 in a corporation, a $5,000 interest in which is owned by James Black, the four of them being the only stockholders. Disregarding legal prohibitions, assume that John Smith sells his stock certificate to the entity for $1,000. This stock certificate then represents treasury stock and is resold to William Jones for $1,100. Of this $1,100, $1,000 represents a liability of the entity to William Jones. $100 may be considered a premium on capital stock, also a liability. This $100 credit item may be considered as a deferred credit applicable against dividends, but since the liability represented by the capital stock is a perpetual liability, this deferred credit item of $100 will stand forever on the accounting records and will not be amortized against William Jones' dividends.

Recognizing the dangers in analogy, nevertheless this particular one appears to have some analytical value to those who, having once adopted the entity convention, are prepared to use it in any kind of an accounting problem. This analogy and argument logically suggest that the "profit" resulting from the sale of treasury stock at an amount greater than its cost to the entity is in the nature of a perpetually deferred credit to income and hence to proprietorship, and is not an item of income which will ever come to fruition until the termination of the corporation itself. Christening such a perpetually deferred credit as "capital surplus" is merely a matter of terminology and its inclusion under that title as one of the proprietorship items seems entirely logical and correct.

If treasury stock is sold at a loss, the amount of that loss represents a perpetually deferred debit to income and hence to proprietorship.

OPINIONS OF AUTHORITIES. Based upon different reasoning the majority of authorities seem to have come to about the same conclusion.

Marple[6] says: "Where treasury shares are reissued for more than cost to the corporation, there arises an element of capital surplus." The *Accountants' Handbook*[7] asserts that in capital surplus should be included "gains from the favorable reacquisition or disposition of a company's own stock or obligation." The Committee on Definition of Earned Surplus of the American Institute of Accountants[8] says that: "Capital surplus comprises paid-in surplus and revaluation surplus." In describing items properly to be included in paid-in surplus, the committee mentions "profits on resales of treasury stock."

Hatfield[9] insists, "Where reacquired stock is sold at an advance over the purchase price, the excess should be credited to some account clearly showing the nature of the item. A descriptive title such as Premium on the Sale of Treasury Stock would be satisfactory. It should not be credited to current Profit and Loss or ordinary Surplus."

Kester[10] mentions among the more common sources of capital surplus "resale of treasury stock for more than its purchase price." Sanders, Hatfield, and Moore include surplus from the sale of reacquired stock as an item of capital surplus.

McKinsey[11] advises that profit or loss on the sale of treas-

---

6 Raymond P. Marple, *Capital Surplus and Corporate Net Worth* (New York, The Ronald Press Company, 1936), p. 74.

7 *Accountants' Handbook* (New York, The Ronald Press Company, 1934), p. 965.

8 *Accounting Terminology* (New York, American Institute Publishing Co., Inc., 1931), p. 119.

9 Henry Rand Hatfield, *Accounting* (New York, D. Appleton-Century Company, Inc., 1927), p. 183.

10 Roy B. Kester, *Advanced Accounting* (New York, The Ronald Press Company, 1933), p. 526.

11 James O. McKinsey, *Accounting Principles* (Cincinnati, Ohio, South-Western Publishing Co., 1931), p. 480.

ury stock should be transferred to "the surplus, or capital surplus account."

The Executive Committee of the American Accounting Association among their twenty postulates recognizes only two major subdivisions of corporate capital: paid-in surplus and earned surplus. Postulate 15 includes gains from the sale of reacquired shares as an item of paid-in capital. Postulate 18[12] says: "Earned surplus should include no credits from transactions in the company's own stock."

BALANCE SHEET CLASSIFICATION. The matter of gain or loss on the sale of reacquired shares by a corporation is closely related to another controversial accounting question: Are reacquired shares assets of the corporation until they are sold?

This question is not strictly pertinent to the subject matter of this volume, but in passing it may well be observed that the majority of authorities do not regard such reacquired shares as assets.

The Executive Committee of the American Accounting Association says that such shares should "be regarded as an unallocated reduction of capital and surplus rather than as an asset."

According to *A Statement of Accounting Principles*,[13] reacquired stock "is, strictly speaking, not an asset, but may indicate an instrument which may be used for obtaining assets." This same authority also mentions an investigation of balance sheets of which 45% showed treasury stock as an asset in 1933 and only 28% in 1936 thus indicating a trend.

Husband[14] asserts:

Few accountants would advocate that the withdrawal of a partner from a partnership should be exhibited as an asset no matter how short a period existing between the date of withdrawal and the date of investment by a new partner; yet many accountants contend that treasury stock should be so exhibited.

12 Executive Committee of the American Accounting Association, "A Tentative Statement of Accounting Principles Affecting Corporate Reports," *The Accounting Review*, June 1936, pp. 190, 191.
13 Sanders, Hatfield, and Moore, *A Statement of Accounting Principles* (New York, American Institute of Accountants, 1938), p. 90.
14 George R. Husband, "The Corporate-Entity Fiction and Accounting Theory," *The Accounting Review*, September 1938, p. 250.

DIVIDENDS ON TREASURY STOCK. The treatment of dividends on a corporation's stock held in its own treasury has caused similar controversies although the majority of authorities hold that they do not represent profit. This opinion is advanced in *A Statement of Accounting Principles*[13] as follows: "Dividends on reacquired stock should not be reported as income of the company."

The Executive Committee of the American Accounting Association, as part of Postulate 12, excludes such dividend payments from income.

In *Audits of Corporate Accounts*,[15] prepared by the American Institute of Accountants, it is said: "While it is perhaps in some circumstances permissible to show stock of a corporation held in its own treasury as an asset if adequately disclosed, the dividends on stock so held should not be treated as a credit to the income account of the company."

RETIRED STOCK. The question sometimes arises as to the status of the apparent profit or loss which results from the purchase and retirement of a corporation's own stock.

Such purchase and retirement constitutes a reduction of capital.

The entity convention considers a profit to be an increase in entity indebtedness to proprietorship. If, for example, the entity is a corporation with just $4,000 in cash and its proprietorship is represented by four $1,000 stockholders, by unanimous consent one stockholder may sell his shares to the corporation for $800, there being no creditors or legal restrictions.

After completion of this transaction the corporation will show $3,200 in cash, a capital stock liability of $3,000, and a gain, represented by surplus, of $200. That this is an actual gain by the test of increase in proprietorship from $3,000 to $3,200 can scarcely be disputed. It is, however, not an operating gain in any sense. Marple[16] says that it is "contributed capital left in the business," hence it is a credit to capital surplus.

The *Accountants' Handbook* says it is paid-in surplus.

[15] *Audits of Corporate Accounts* (New York, American Institute of Accountants, 1934), p. 24.
[16] Raymond P. Marple, *Capital Surplus and Corporate Net Worth* (New York, The Ronald Press Company, 1936), p. 105.

Husband[17] believes that "from the standpoint of the remaining stockholders such a transaction represents a definite gain since it actually increases their capital; from their viewpoint it may even be considered an earned surplus item subject to dividend charges. From the viewpoint of the corporation, however, it represents a saving, not a gain. The corporation's net worth is not increased but merely readjusted."

Broad[18] quotes from a release of the Securities and Exchange Commission dated May 10, 1938, as follows:

> It is recognized that, when capital stock is reacquired and retired, any surplus arising therefrom is capital and should be accounted for as such and that the full proceeds of any subsequent issue should also be treated as capital. Transactions of this nature do not result in corporate profits or in earned surplus.

The American Accounting Association, Postulate 15,[19] classifies as paid-in surplus "gains from the sale of reacquired shares and from the retirement of reacquired shares purchased at a discount." If a loss rather than a gain is made, the association specifies in Postulate 16 that it "should be charged to paid-in surplus up to an amount not in excess of the prorata portion of paid-in surplus applicable to the shares; any part of the cost which cannot be thus absorbed should be charged to earned surplus." In explanation the further statement is made that no portion of a stockholder's contribution should be credited to earned surplus but "that a repayment of a stockholder's equity may, in fact, be a distribution of earned surplus if the amount of the repayment exceeds his portion of paid-in capital."

Conclusion.—To summarize, the corporate influence upon accounting practice has become dominant in that it has modified the basic accounting convention. While the corporate form has legitimized the entity convention it has at the same time modified its practical application by: (1) limitation of proprie-

---

[17] George R. Husband, "Accounting Postulates: An Analysis of the Tentative Statement of Accounting Principles," *The Accounting Review*, December 1937, p. 398.
[18] Samuel J. Broad, "Cooperation with the Securities and Exchange Commission," *The Journal of Accountancy*, August 1938, p. 84.
[19] Executive Committee of the American Accounting Association, "A Tentative Statement of Accounting Principles Affecting Corporate Reports," *The Accounting Review*, June 1936, pp. 190, 191.

tary liability, (2) adding the concept of perpetual entity life regardless of shifting proprietorship, and (3) separating proprietorship from management.

Because the corporation affects the public interest, the valuation convention is no longer a simple expedient for symbolizing the proprietor-entity relation of charge and discharge. Rather, the valuations used are assumed to have some further significance, usually that of unamortized cost or current realizability.

The third convention, that of periodic income recognition, has become one of special importance in corporation accounting which emphasizes conservatism in the distributable profit computation of which the proper recognition of income is the first element.

The corporate form also has added new elements to the problem of income recognition. These new elements arise from a corporation's transactions in its own shares, which elements in the case of a relatively few companies have assumed importance far out of proportion to their general business significance.

It is through corporations that coercive legal influence upon accounting has been marked with a consequent modifying, broadening, or distorting effect upon the simple basic conventions.

CHAPTER 12

THE SEARCH FOR ACCOUNTING PRINCIPLES

Previous chapters have attempted to establish that the accounting structure rests upon certain conventions. Their origins and their relation to the growth and development of accounting have been considered in some detail. Important as these conventions have been in establishing the design of accounting, there are certain doctrines, rules, and principles which may be considered even more influential in determining what the accountant does and does not do in the calculation of accounting profits. Because of various developments in commerce and the increasing necessity for accounting submission to legal domination, it has been found necessary to elaborate the simple equation of entity accounting.

Elaboration of Accounting.—This elaboration was necessary for two important reasons: (1) to cope with the increasing complexity of business, its larger size, its more complex organization, and (2) to cope with the increasing number of problems caused by variations of business practice.

Increasing Complexity of Business. The first elaboration was one of detail. There was no inherent difficulty involved in the substitution of perhaps twenty accounts receivable ledgers for one such ledger. The problem of expanding one expense account into several hundred departmentalized expense accounts did not violate the simple mechanism of accounting. Such expansion was primarily a problem of classification.

Increasing Problems of Business. Elaboration of the accounting mechanism resulted from the increased popularity of the corporate form of organization and the increased domination of business by government. Accounting transactions formerly simple became difficult. Even the original problem introduced by the corporate form, namely, preservation of the integrity of invested capital, began to puzzle accountants and lawyers.

The allocation of accounting profits to fiscal periods, the administration of surplus, the treatment of non-operating or capital losses, fluctuations in the market value of investments, the recording of depreciation, the treatment of unamortized discount on obligations retired before maturity, all had to be considered from a variety of viewpoints.

The invention by financiers of new types of preferred and common stocks and of profit-sharing liabilities increased the difficulties of income determination. Since shares and securities had to be marketed to the public, special agreements and indentures of various types deemed to be attractive to prospective investors were devised, with the result that the accounting for invested capital was complicated not only by the increase in various types of investors but also by the increase in the number of clauses designed for their enticement or their protection.

Accounting Precedents.—Dominated on the one hand by the law, as represented by the statutes of the various states and of the national government, and the rules and regulations of numerous governmental agencies and bureaus, harried on the other hand by the insistence of business men for reports suitable for tax avoidance purposes or to furnish a financing background, the accountant, realizing the artificiality of his basic accounting mechanism, could hardly refrain from doubt as to its adaptability to meet modern conditions.

As a result the accountant has come more and more to rely upon precedent as the justification for his various practices.

There appears to be some similarity in this respect between law and accounting. The English common law consists of certain concepts, rules, theories, or principles based upon precedents. Similarly, there seems to have been developed a sort of common law in accounting. Like the English common law, it has not adequately been set forth in complete written form but has developed from practical experience. This body of opinion is the direct result neither of statute nor edict but was developed by the method of trial and error.

Principles of Accounting.—It has been customary to refer to this common law as the "principles of accounting."

Obviously, the use of "principles" in this connection is subject to criticism. Nevertheless, "principles of accounting" is firmly fixed upon the accounting profession and until 1933 caused little or no confusion either among students or practitioners.

With sublime disregard of lexicography, accountants speak of "principles," "tenets," "doctrines," "rules," and "conventions" as if they were synonymous. Generally, however, the word "principles"[1] is most commonly used to characterize the common law of accounting.

It has not seemed any more important to accountants than to lawyers that their "common law" was unwritten and undescribed. Consisting as it does of a heterogeneous combination of legal, economic, and statistical concepts, the entire body of precedent has been taken for granted.

It is as though each accountant felt that while he himself had never taken the time nor the trouble to make an actual list of accounting principles, he was comfortably certain that someone else had done so.

In spite of the fact that no actual code of such principles existed, the phrase "principles of accounting" or some variant thereof has always been a popular title for accounting texts. Its employment as a book title has, however, carried with it no obligation to present a list of such principles or in many instances even to isolate and describe one or more of them. Of at least eight different and fairly recent texts entitled "Principles of Accounting" or some variation thereof, not one includes even the word "principle" in its index.

New Form of Certificate.—During a period of about sixteen months in the years 1932, 1933, and 1934, important correspondence passed between the American Institute's special

---

[1] Repeating a previous caution, the use of this word does not indicate its approval and must be interpreted in the light of the discussion in Chapter 16.

committee on cooperation with stock exchanges and the committee on stock list of the New York Stock Exchange.

Undoubtedly the severe depression originating in 1929 and reaching its bottom in 1932 brought to light certain improper accounting practices which became matters of special concern not only to accountants but to the stock exchange authorities. As a result the accountants developed a new form of certificate, proposed a schedule of five "accounting principles," and emphasized certain accounting viewpoints or accounting policies which have long been recognized but which assumed new importance in the light of the revised certificate.

The new certificate was noteworthy in a number of respects. For the present it will be sufficient to comment on two aspects of the certificate.

First of all, the new form of certificate emphasized the examination of the income and surplus statements rather than the balance sheet.

The new form of certificate also introduced a phrase which is of special importance. The certificate voices the opinion that the balance sheet and related statement of income and surplus "fairly present, in accordance with accepted principles of accounting consistently maintained by the Company during the year under review," its position and the results of its operations for the year.

In this quotation there are two important elements—the emphasis on consistency, and the recognition of "accepted principles of accounting."

Probably the American Institute's committee never believed that the five principles enunciated by them represented a complete list of all principles. If they did hold this belief, however, the developments of the following months must have been disillusioning.

Disagreement as to Principles.—While the new form of certificate was adopted by nearly all of the larger accounting firms, its emphasis upon accepted principles of accounting has attracted widespread attention.

Many who had perhaps taken it for granted that such prin-

:iples, if necessary, could be codified and defined, now awoke to
he dismaying realization that such a task was one of major
lifficulty. Not only did accountants consider the first list of
ive principles inadequate but they have been unable to agree
among themselves as to what accounting principles are or even
vhether any principles actually exist. The Securities and Exchange Commission, through its chief accountant, seriously
juestioned the significance of the term "generally accepted
accounting principles."

Byrne[2] pointed out that accountants must agree as to recognized principles of accounting, for, as he said, "if there is not
his agreement, accountants have indeed stultified themselves."

His point was well taken since the accountants are in the
unenviable position of having committed themselves in their
certificates as to the existence of generally accepted accounting
principles while between themselves they are quarreling as to
whether there are any accounting principles and if there are how
many of them should be recognized and accepted.

Attempts to Formulate Principles.—Since they will be considered subsequently, only brief mention need be made here of
the more important attempts to enumerate the principles of
accounting. These attempts are as follows:

List of five accounting principles as shown on page 14 of the
booklet *Audits of Corporate Accounts,* published January
21, 1934 by the American Institute of Accountants, which
contained correspondence between the American Institute's
committee and the New York Stock Exchange committee.

Tentative statement of twenty principles of accounting affecting corporate reports, by the executive committee of the
American Accounting Association, published in the June
1936 issue of *The Accounting Review.*

List of nine accounting principles and conventions presented
by D. L. Trouant in his book, *Financial Audits,* published
January 1937 by the American Institute Publishing Co.,
Inc.

---

[2] Gilbert R. Byrne, "To What Extent Can the Practice of Accounting Be
Reduced to Rules and Standards?" *The Journal of Accountancy,* November 1937,
p. 367.

List of eight principles of accounting provided by Gilbert R. Byrne and published in the November 1937 issue of *The Journal of Accountancy* under the title, "To What Extent Can the Practice of Accounting Be Reduced to Rules and Standards?"

List of twenty-five principles of accounting summarized by Messrs. Sanders, Hatfield, and Moore in their book, *A Statement of Accounting Principles,* published early in 1938 by the American Institute of Accountants.

List of six accounting principles discussed by A. C. Littleton in "Tests for Principles," *The Accounting Review,* March 1938.

In addition to the list given here there have been numerous criticisms and suggestions in the form of technical articles, letters, and round-table discussions at conventions of the American Institute of Accountants, many of which will be given due consideration at a later point.

Even these attempts to state the principles of accounting are distinguished by lack of agreement as to the number of accounting principles involved, although in all fairness to the authors thereof it should be recorded that they have made no pretense of providing inclusive lists.

Also it is only fair to point out that theirs was pioneer work beset with important and unexpected difficulties.

Difficulties in Formulating Principles.—These difficulties are at least eight in number:

1. Difficulties due to the convention of the annual accounting period and the valuation convention.
2. Difficulties due to the necessary application of the simple entity mechanism to the diverse and complex relationships of modern business.
3. Difficulties due to the limitations of accounting.
4. Difficulties caused by the shift from the balance sheet to the profit and loss viewpoint.
5. Difficulties due to contradictions among principles.
6. Legal difficulties.
7. Difficulties due to self-interest.
8. Difficulties due to lack of proper definitions.

THE ACCOUNTING PERIOD CONVENTION. The arbitrary convention of annual accounting periods offers more serious problems than are apparent at first thought. The original mechanism of accounting as applied to single ventures was both simple and logical. As soon as accounting was treated from the going concern valuation basis, it became necessary to provide for interim accounting reports for which it was quite natural to select the calendar year as the fiscal period.

The problem of allocating income and expense as between periods was responsible for many difficulties in attempting to formulate specific principles of accounting.

ENTITY CONCEPT. Since accounting is founded upon a concept which is logical but inelastic, many of the difficulties in enunciating accounting principles are due to the fact that the accounting mechanism recognizes only obvious relationships between the entity, its capital, and the sources of its capital.

This has resulted in a body of rules, doctrines, and conventions of reporting which can be distinguished from accounting, i.e., accountants have found it necessary to adopt a general policy of parenthetical or footnote disclosure to supplement the mechanical limitations imposed by the entity concept.

Such artificial conventions as the entity concept, accounting periods, and dollar valuation cause corresponding artificiality in connection with principles borrowed from the fields of economics and statistics.

So impressed are some accountants by these difficulties that they seem to despair of ever reaching an agreement upon a code of principles. Thus, Greer[3] refers to the "difficulty of choice between equally defensible alternatives, the impossibility of exactness in measuring values and results, the inevitability of compromise and approximation."

Sanders,[4] commenting upon the manner in which capital and income intermingle, said that it "creates a situation where nobody can make positive assertions with complete assurance."

[3] Howard C. Greer, "To What Extent Can the Practice of Accounting Be Reduced to Rules and Standards?" *The Journal of Accountancy*, March 1938, p. 213.

[4] Thomas H. Sanders, "Is It Desirable to Distinguish between Various Kinds of Surplus?" *The Journal of Accountancy*, April 1938, p. 284.

Byerly[5] voiced the same thought when he said: "To ask for an income-tax law that is both equitable and simple is like asking for the moon, and it seems that the same is true of asking for a clear, concise and comprehensive statement of accounting principles."

The problem was well expressed in an editorial appearing in *The Canadian Chartered Accountant*[6] which observed in part that the "term 'accounting principles' has come to be a common one in the language of the public accountant but for him to explain its meaning or to give illustrations of accounting principles is not easy."

SHIFT OF VIEWPOINT.   The shift in emphasis from the balance sheet to the profit and loss viewpoint has also created various problems.

Principles that appeared acceptable from the balance sheet viewpoint must now be reexamined. Whether principles are subject to change merely because of a shift of viewpoint is an open question, but in any event this shift has been troublesome.

CONTRADICTORY PRINCIPLES.   Then, too, one cannot fail to note some contradiction among suggested principles. The principle of conservatism comes definitely into conflict with the principle of matching costs with income. The principle of consistency comes into conflict with the principle of cost or market valuation of inventories.

LEGAL DIFFICULTIES.   Many difficulties result from the relationship between law and accounting.

In this connection law is used in its broadest sense as applying not only to statutory law and judicial decisions, but also to releases and regulations of governmental, regulatory, and taxing bodies. It often seems impossible to reconcile the accounting concept with some of these legal viewpoints.

That entire branch of accounting activity commonly referred to as corporation accounting is controlled by various illogical and conflicting statutes and by legal decisions regarding ac-

5 F. P. Byerly, "Formulation of Accounting Principles or Conventions," *The Journal of Accountancy*, August 1937, p. 95.
6 Editorial, "Statement of Accounting Principles," *The Canadian Chartered Accountant*, May 1938, p. 325.

counting matters in which it is obvious that legislators and courts are unfamiliar with accounting.

Arthur[7] refers to the "lethargy of the government with respect to changes in tax rulings" and discusses "the complacency with which both our business-men and the government have come to accept the rules governing our accounting methods as an infallible guide to the measurement of true profits."

Kester[8] has already been quoted as referring to the influence of "Government bureaus and regulatory bodies and self-appointed bodies such as security exchanges." He indicated his opinion that their contributions "have been arbitrary assumptions or determinations of what such accepted principles are, or what they should be in order best to serve the purpose of the one formulating them."

The Securities and Exchange Commission[9] did little to clear the muddy waters in their statement of administrative policy dated April 25, 1938, wherein they referred to "accounting principles for which there is no substantial authoritative support."

Perhaps the most salty expression of opinion was that of Montgomery[10] wherein he said that in arriving at "what we fondly call good accounting principles we should not be guided in the slightest degree by the weird and sometimes naive and at times arbitrary definitions of income which we find in the tax laws."

SELF-INTEREST OF ACCOUNTANTS. Despite the fact that it was the practicing accountants who started this whole difficulty about principles, they have done little but criticize educators who have attempted to state and define accounting principles.

The two most complete attempts to prepare statements of accounting principles were the work of university professors rather than accounting practitioners. These attempts were the

---

7 Henry B. Arthur, "Inventory Profits in the Business Cycle," *The American Economic Review*, March 1938, p. 36.

8 Roy B. Kester, *The Journal of Accountancy*, March 1938, p. 265.

9 "Accounting and the S.E.C.," *The Certified Public Accountant*, May 1938, p. 12.

10 Robert H. Montgomery, "Dealings in Treasury Stock," *The Journal of Accountancy*, June 1938, p. 466.

one made in 1936 by the American Accounting Association and the other made in 1938 by Sanders, Hatfield, and Moore.

Superficially this critical viewpoint appears somewhat puzzling. It is to the obvious interest of professional accountants to adopt principles of accounting for the purpose of making good on the wording of their own certificates.

They have, however, been somewhat captious. Only too often practitioners condemn as "academic" and "theoretical" the constructive work done by university men.

There is, of course, an incurable difference of viewpoint between the man who makes his living by the practice of accounting and the one who does so by teaching accounting. It is the age-old conflict between the practical expedients of any man of affairs and the reasoned conclusions of the aloof research worker. While it is easy enough to understand the critical attitude of the professional accountant, it is not so easy to explain why, if he is dissatisfied with the efforts of his pedagogical brother, he does not do a better piece of work.

There is some indication that the professional attitude toward codification of accounting principles is somewhat tinged by self-interest. This is not necessarily the practitioner's own direct interest since, in some instances, he may champion a client who for one reason or another desires to adopt certain accounting procedures.

It is, of course, simpler and more effective to label a proposed accounting principle as academic or theoretical than to say, "I am against it because its adoption will cost my clients more in taxes." While this inquiry lies in the field of surmise, it seems to represent a logical explanation of the attitude shown by a few practicing accountants toward the codification of principles.

By and large, the practitioners' contribution to this difficult problem has been to suggest so many exceptions to the proposed principles as to rob them of any real value.

LACK OF DEFINITIONS. Among the more important difficulties of codifying principles is the difficulty of terminology. Until the accountants can agree as to the meanings of such commonly employed words as "principles," "conventions," "rules," "tenets," "policies," and "methods," it will be impossible to bring order out of this chaos of opinion. Examination of existing discussions of accounting principles shows a most unsatisfactory condition of terminology.

Practicability of Formulating Principles.—Perhaps the practical and theoretical difficulties are so serious as to offer slight hope of any early agreement as to accounting principles.

Obviously, any code of principles which is subject to numerous exceptions can possess but little value. Bell[11] probably reflected a common opinion when he said, "I dislike very much to have these ironclad principles that give no consideration to exceptional circumstances."

May[12] voiced about the same opinion in a lecture before the graduate school of business administration of Harvard when he said, "The field of financial accounting is not one in which guidance is to be found wholly in fixed principles." Elsewhere in the same address he intimated that "alternate methods of accounting which will produce materially different results may be equally permissible." Such comments as the foregoing were probably responsible for the pessimistic view of Dohr[13] when he said, "If accounting is merely a matter of convention and convenience, all rules might as well be scrapped."

That accounting is a matter of convention and convenience seems to be the belief of George C. Mathews[14] who suggested that one reason why accountancy has not more nearly fulfilled its possibilities is "the tendency to rely on precedent and authority rather than on the scientific method." He also asserted that "it is as if engineers had no agreement on the required strength of foundations, structural steel requirements for skyscrapers, or efficient design for power plants."

In the light of these various opinions it is quite possible

[11] William H. Bell, *Fiftieth Anniversary Celebration* (New York, American Institute of Accountants, 1938), p. 194.

[12] George O. May, "Improvement in Financial Accounts," *The Journal of Accountancy,* May 1937, p. 335.

[13] James L. Dohr, "Comments on 'A Statement of Accounting Principles,'" *The Journal of Accountancy,* April 1938, p. 317.

[14] George C. Mathews, in an address before the Milwaukee Chapter of the Wisconsin Society of Certified Public Accountants, January 8, 1937.

that any attempt to formulate a list of accounting principles may be described in Robert Murray Haig's[15] devastating comment on the 1913 income tax law, which he termed "a pious avowal of a vague ethical aspiration, replete with technical imperfections." Nevertheless, the accounting profession must agree upon a code of principles or must eliminate reference thereto in its audit certificate or must continue, in Byrne's words, to "stultify" itself.

[15] Robert Murray Haig, in the Foreword to *Taxable Income,* by Roswell Magill (New York, The Ronald Press Company, 1936).

CHAPTER 13

TERMINOLOGY REFERRING TO ACCOUNTING PRINCIPLES

The necessity for clear and adequate terminology is particularly evident in discussions of accounting principles.

While many accountants and teachers have called attention to the confused thinking which results from misusing technical words, by none has the situation with respect to accounting principles been set forth with greater clarity than by Byrne[1] who emphasizes that "there is no clear distinction, in the minds of many, between that body of fundamental truths underlying the philosophy of accounts which are properly thought of as *principles,* and the larger body of accounting rules, practices and conventions which derive from principles, but which of themselves are not principles."

Disagreement as to Principles.—Until accountants can agree on an accepted meaning for the word "principle" discussion and controversy cannot fail to be confused.

Byrne speaks of rules, practices and conventions as being *derived from* principles. Robert H. Montgomery, on page 478 of *The Journal of Accountancy* for June 1938, takes the opposite viewpoint, intimating that good accounting principles are *based on* conventions or expediency. Littleton[2] speaks of coordinating rules, conventions and principles "into a body of dependable doctrine" which he intimates will "make use of real principles resting upon recognized premises."

Broad[3] pleads "for a return to first principles" but in his

[1] Gilbert R. Byrne, "To What Extent Can the Practice of Accounting Be Reduced to Rules and Standards?" *The Journal of Accountancy,* November 1937, p. 368.
[2] A. C. Littleton, "Business Profits as a Legal Basis for Dividends," *Harvard Business Review,* Vol. XVI, No. 1, 1937, p. 57.
[3] Samuel J. Broad, "Is It Desirable to Distinguish Between Various Kinds of Surplus?" *The Journal of Accountancy,* April 1938, p. 282.

179

plea he refers to certain practices of corporate accounting which are based upon statutes or rules of law, thereby giving the impression that accounting principles may be derived from the law. Some writers use such phrases as "various accounting principles and conventions" with no attempt to distinguish between them. One author complains that accounting principles include "a conglomeration of accounting practices, procedures, policies, methods, and conventions." Other accountants have made various assumptions as to the relationship of principles to rules, conventions, and practices, indicating that they are not thinking from a common viewpoint.

This lack of agreement cannot fail to confuse the practitioner if he is called upon to explain his reference to principles in the standard form of audit certificate. It is confusing also to teachers of accounting. Referring to the list of five principles proposed by the American Institute Committee in Cooperation with Stock Exchanges, Littleton[4] asks, "Why are they principles? That is what teachers must face when they present the subject to their classes. They feel sure that some wide-awake members of their classes will ask: 'What makes this a principle? How do you judge, and on the basis of your answer, are there not more than five principles?'"

Some of the examples of unsatisfactory terminology probably indicate no more than hasty deviations from careful technical writing, but no such simple explanation will account for differences of opinion as to whether rules are derived from principles or vice versa. And yet the whole philosophy of accounting and the integrity of the present-day audit certificate may depend upon reaching agreement on this point.

Additional confusion is caused by lack of agreement as to whether the phrase "principles of accounting" includes the principles of reporting. Is report preparation an activity separate and distinct from accounting? Byrne[5] takes the definite stand that two separate sets of principles are here involved and that the title "accounting principles" should not be applied to "the

---

4 A. C. Littleton, *Fiftieth Anniversary Celebration* (New York, American Institute of Accountants, 1938), p. 261.

5 Gilbert R. Byrne, "To What Extent Can the Practice of Accounting Be Reduced to Rules and Standards?" *The Journal of Accountancy*, November 1937, p. 375.

manner of preparation of the statements, the classification of the data shown thereon, and the various methods of disclosure of pertinent information." He thinks that the rules for presenting financial statements are not to be confused with the principles of accounting. His seems to be a lone voice. Others who have attempted to enumerate principles of accounting have made little distinction between accounting and reporting.

Legal and Business Influences.—To what extent if any can principles of accounting be modified and changed by outside influences, particularly the influence of statutes, court decisions, and the rulings of governmental bodies or business practices?

Andersen[6] takes the position that principles are developed "as a composite of the best and most enlightened business experience." Canning, in his *The Economics of Accountancy*, intimates that the client and the accountant working together agree as to certain practices and rules commonly thought of as accounting principles. The Haskins and Sells Foundation,[7] in its letter of invitation to Sanders, Hatfield, and Moore, hopes that "there may be evolved a reasonable number of accounting principles, based on practical business concepts of capital and income."

This committee obviously believed that accounting principles are substantially influenced by legal rules and decisions, one member of the committee, Underhill Moore, being a lawyer rather than an accountant. In addition the committee[8] definitely put itself on record by saying, "It is the function of the liabilities side to show the amounts of the different classes of equities or interests in the assets listed on the other side of the balance-sheet. To this extent, therefore, the principles of accounting are dictated by legal considerations."

Number of Accounting Principles.—The inability of accountants to agree as to whether accounting principles are

[6] Arthur Andersen, "Present-day Problems Affecting the Presentation and Interpretation of Financial Statements," *The Journal of Accountancy*, November 1935, p. 332.

[7] Haskins and Sells Foundation, in *A Statement of Accounting Principles* (New York, American Institute of Accountants, 1938), p. xiv.

[8] Sanders, Hatfield, and Moore, *A Statement of Accounting Principles* (New York, American Institute of Accountants, 1938), p. 3.

derived from rules or vice versa, as to whether accounting principles also include the principles of reporting, and finally as to whether accounting principles are subject to modification and change because of business, economic, and legal influences, may represent one important cause of the present difficulty.

If agreement could be reached on these matters, accountants and groups of accountants might not be making contradictory estimates as to the number of accounting principles ranging all the way from one or two to as many as twenty-five.

Certain accountants believe that there are only a few actual accounting principles and that others so called are to be classified as rules.

Holding a different viewpoint are such groups as the Executive Committee of the American Accounting Association, which presented twenty principles, and the Sanders, Hatfield, and Moore committee, which presented a list of twenty-five.

Conjugate Principles.—One factor which thus far has received but slight recognition is the well-known phenomenon of conjugate principles.

Conjugate principles are conflicting principles. There are numerous examples of them in current writings. If one thinks of conservatism as a principle, then he must note its conflict with another principle—that one which calls for assigning costs and expenses of all kinds to the accounting periods receiving the benefit therefrom. If, on the other hand, he deems consistency to be a principle of accounting, he will find that it contradicts the principle referred to as "the cost or market rule." If he insists that there is a principle requiring income to be realized, he must observe a conflict with approved practices of valuing inventories at market price in farm accounting or the practice of apportioning income on long-term construction contracts.

To fulfill Littleton's[9] hope that accountants may achieve "real principles resting upon recognized premises and affording definite 'bench-marks' from which to measure the departures made necessary by the exigencies of practical affairs" requires solution of: (1) the problem of conjugate principles, (2) care-

---

[9] A. C. Littleton, "Business Profits as a Legal Basis for Dividends," *Harvard Business Review*, Vol. XVI, No. 1, 1937, p. 57.

ful differentiation between principles and rules, (3) common understanding as to whether rules are derived from principles or vice versa, and (4) a decision as to whether accounting principles can be affected and modified by the rules and practices of law, business, and banking.

Until these points are settled it seems evident that the problem of principles will continue to plague the accounting fraternity and that accounting will advance "by over-accentuation of one principle at a time, like a sailing vessel which can not head up in the eye of the wind, but first on one tack and then on the other is making to windward on both."[10]

Definitions.—Since some of the words under consideration are partially defined in terms of one another, it is necessary to give consideration not only to the literal dictionary meaning but also to connotations and popular usage.

Accordingly, the following discussion of definitions, synonyms, and connotations represents no more than a tentative attempt to establish reasonable meanings for the purpose of clarifying discussion.

From the various quotations already noted it seems that four words are often used interchangeably and with little discrimination. These words are "principle," "convention," "doctrine," and "rule." In addition, and selected by authors probably for the sake of variety, are such additional words as "tenet," "dogma," "usage," "practice," "method," and "policy." The first four words, however, deserve particular emphasis. Of the four, probably the word "principles" is most often used and is of the greatest importance. For that reason its analysis is left until the last.

DEFINITION OF CONVENTION. The word "convention" is frequently used in accounting writings and discussions. It is defined by *Webster's New International Dictionary* as follows:

5. A rule or usage based upon general agreement; a rule or practice generally adhered to; an arbitrary or inflexible rule, form, principle, etc., as in an art; a conventionalism.

10 Abbott Lawrence Lowell, *Conflicts of Principle* (Harvard University Press, 1932), p. 7.

The *Century Dictionary* emphasizes "general agreement," "tacit understanding," and "common consent." The *Oxford English Dictionary* mentions "general agreement or consent." The *Dictionary of Philosophy and Psychology* asserts that "uniform recognition" is a characteristic of a convention. All of the definitions which have been compared are consistent in pointing out that general agreement, tacit understanding, common or general consent are characteristic elements of a convention.

A second important phrase in the *Webster* definition is "arbitrary or inflexible." The *Century Dictionary* uses the words "arbitrarily established." The *Oxford English Dictionary* speaks of an "arbitrary rule or practice recognized as valid in any particular art or study."

Even more enlightening is the comment contained in the supplement to the *Oxford English Dictionary,* published in 1933, which illustrates the meaning of "convention" by its application to card games in such words as "the observance of the unwritten rules of play" and again "applied to any method of play which is not based on the principles of the game." The *Dictionary of Philosophy and Psychology* illustrates the meaning of the word "convention" as follows: "Thus two men pull the oars of a boat by common *convention* for common interest, without any promise or contract. Thus gold and silver are made the measures of exchange; thus speech and words and language are fixed by human *convention* and agreement."

In reasonable accord with the above meanings is the use of the word "convention" in accounting. The expression of physical quantities in terms of dollar valuation is obviously a convention. The treatment of a proprietor's investment as an entity liability is a convention. The annual accounting period is a convention. These and other common conventions are "based upon general agreement" and are "more or less arbitrarily established."

DEFINITION OF RULE.   Next certain definitions of the word "rule" may be examined. *Webster's New International Dictionary* provides the following:

1. A prescribed guide for conduct or action; a governing direction; as, the *rules* governing a school; a *rule* of etiquette or propriety; the *rules* of cricket. Syn.—Law, maxim, guide, canon, order, method; direction. See principle.

Of the four words under present consideration, this word "rule" seems to be used most accurately in technical writings and discussions. Whatever confusion exists seems to refer to the problem previously noted, i.e., whether rules are derived from principles or principles derived from rules.

Clarence W. Fackler, in a personal letter dated May 27, 1938, insists that a *"rule* is the practical application of a principle, describing a common, customary, regular, and uniform procedure." The *Oxford English Dictionary* defines "rule" in terms of the word "principle" as follows: "A principle regulating the procedure or method necessary to be observed in the pursuit or study of some art or science," but this reference to "procedure or method," together with *Webster's* phrase "a prescribed guide," indicates that a rule implies human decision and human authority. In other words, a rule must be devised and laid down rather than discovered.

In the comparative discussion which follows these four definitions, the differences commonly noted between rules and principles will be considered further.

DEFINITION OF DOCTRINE.   Rarely in accounting literature does one encounter the word "doctrine."

By strict interpretation the word may not be entirely appropriate for accounting use, since in all definitions there is insistence upon such words as "authoritative teaching." Thus, the definition provided by *Webster's New International Dictionary* is as follows:

2. That which is taught; what is held, put forth as true, and supported by a teacher, a school, or a sect; a principle or position, or the body of principles, in any branch of knowledge; tenet; dogma; principle of faith; as, the *doctrine* of atoms. "The *doctrine* of gravitation." Syn. —Principle, position, opinion, article, maxim, rule. In its general sense, *doctrine* applies to any speculative truth or working principle, esp. as taught to others or recommended to their acceptance.

The *Century Dictionary* also emphasizes that teaching is an essential characteristic of a doctrine by the use of such phrases as "whatever is taught; whatever is laid down as true by an instructor or master." Confirmation is found in the *Oxford English Dictionary,* which says that a doctrine is "That which is taught." In the general sense the word means "instruction, teaching; a body of instruction or teaching." Fackler insists that a doctrine is "defended or taught by some person or particular group of persons as true."

Thus through all the definitions are references to teaching, to teachers, and to schools.

It should, however, be noted that there are secondary meanings not so closely related to pedagogy. *Webster* refers to a doctrine as a "principle of faith" and also describes it as a "principle or position or a body of principles in any branch of knowledge." The *Century Dictionary* uses almost the same words in referring to a "principle or body of principles relating to or connected with religion, science, politics, or any department of knowledge." The *Oxford English Dictionary* speaks of "a body or system of principles or tenets."

Because certain broad accounting policies, such as those referring to conservatism, disclosure, consistency, and materiality, are of more general application than many of the propositions commonly termed "principles," it would be a matter of considerable convenience to call these four propositions "doctrines." Strictly such usage would not be entirely correct in view of the fact that they are not specifically taught nor is any relationship of student and instructor implied. The practical convenience of adopting such a nomenclature might well justify a certain amount of freedom from the severe limitations imposed by dictionaries.

Perhaps some justification for the proposed adoption of the word "doctrine" can be found in such a phrase as the "Monroe Doctrine," which in effect is a statement of policy and scarcely implies a pupil-instructor relationship. Only by considerable stretching of strict definition does the policy enunciated by President Monroe represent a doctrine.

If, therefore, it is legitimate to adopt "doctrine" as referring to a general statement of accounting or reporting policy as evidenced by the words "materiality," "disclosure," "conservatism," and "consistency," such legitimacy may be derived from such a usage as the "Monroe Doctrine." Fackler agrees with this, at least in part, since he asserts that the "term 'doctrine of conservatism' in accounting, can be used."

DEFINITION OF PRINCIPLE. Finally, consideration must be given to the most important of all of the four words.

The word "principle" is commonly used in a variety of different meanings. The particular definitions which seem to bear upon accounting are quoted here from *Webster's New International Dictionary:*

4. A fundamental truth; a comprehensive law or doctrine, from which others are derived, or on which others are founded; a general truth; an elementary proposition or fundamental assumption; a maxim; an axiom; a postulate.

5. A settled rule of action; a governing law of conduct; an opinion, attitude, or belief which exercises a directing influence on the life and behavior; a rule (usually, a right rule) of conduct consistently directing one's actions.

Syn.—*Principle, rule* are here compared in the sense of that which exercises governing or guiding influence. *Principle* emphasizes the idea of fundamental truth or general application; *Rule,* that of a more specific direction or regulation; as, to follow certain *principles* of administration, to lay down certain administrative *rules.*

In this definition are several significant words, the first being the word "fundamental." The Macmillan Company publication, *An Etymological Dictionary of the English Language,* refers to a principle as a "fundamental truth or law." The *Oxford English Dictionary* says that a principle is "a fundamental truth or proposition." While not using the word "fundamental," a somewhat similar meaning is noted in the *Dictionary of Philosophy and Psychology,* which says that "a principle is a proposition upon which conclusions depend for their validity."

This latter definition leads to another characteristic of a principle upon which authorities seem to agree, namely, the matter of derivation. *Webster's New International Dictionary* uses the phrase "from which others are derived, or on which others are founded." The *Century Dictionary* says that a principle is "a law on which others are founded, or from which others are derived." The *Oxford English Dictionary* uses the phraseology "a primary truth comprehending, or forming the basis of, various subordinate truths." The attitude of the dictionary makers toward the problem of whether principles are derived from rules or vice versa seems to be uniform.

Webster's word "comprehensive" is echoed by both the *Century* and the *Oxford* dictionaries with "comprehending." Accordingly, it seems a fairly safe assumption that a principle is "fundamental," "comprehensive," and that it represents a truth "from which others are derived."

Throughout the various definitions which have been quoted there runs a tendency to describe any one of the four words in terms of the others. Thus, a principle has been referred to as a law or doctrine; a doctrine has been referred to as a principle; a rule has been referred to as a principle; and a convention has been referred to as a rule or practice. Such intimation that these words are somewhat interchangeable is unfortunate since it provides a certain amount of authority for those who seek to justify narrow rather than broad terminology. It therefore seems desirable to consider these four words comparatively.

Distinctions.—Of particular interest because of the confusion noted in some accounting writings is the distinction between "principle" and "rule."

PRINCIPLE AND RULE.   This is well treated by the *Century Dictionary:*

There are no two words in the English language used so confusedly one for the other as the words *rule* and *principle.* You can make a *rule;* you cannot make a *principle;* you can lay down a *rule;* you cannot, properly speaking, lay down a *principle.* It is laid down for you. You can establish a *rule;* you cannot, properly speaking, establish a *principle.* You can only declare it. *Rules* are within your power, *principles* are not. A *principle* lies back of both *rules* and *precepts;* it is a general truth, needing interpretation and application to particular cases.

Here is full agreement with the quotation from *Webster's New International Dictionary* previously noted.

DOCTRINE, PRECEPT, AND PRINCIPLE. *Crabb's English Synonyms* provides an excellent comparison between the words "doctrine," "precept," and "principle" in the following:

A *doctrine* requires a teacher; a *precept* requires a superior with authority; a *principle* requires only a maintainer or holder. A *doctrine* is always framed by some one; a *precept* is enjoined or laid down by some one; a *principle* lies in the thing itself. A *doctrine* is composed of *principles;* a *precept* rests upon *principles* or *doctrines* .... *principles* are often admitted without examination and imbibed as frequently from observation and circumstances as from any direct personal efforts; children as well as men acquire *principles.*

PRINCIPLES, PROCEDURES, AND METHODS. Added to these non-accounting opinions are certain technical viewpoints expressed by well-known accountants.

John B. Canning holds the name "principles" properly applies to no more than a few elements of accounting. Stempf[11] thinks "that rules should be stated simply as *acceptable* applications of recognized principles and not as *mandatory* procedures." Simpson,[12] during a round-table discussion at the 1937 American Institute Convention, called attention to the fact that various acceptable methods may be found "within the framework of certain broad general principles of accounting."

Sanders, Hatfield, and Moore[13] attempt a definition in the following words: "The principles of accounting are, therefore, the more general propositions describing the procedure which should be followed in the making of records and the preparation of financial statements." But their definition is not entirely helpful since it does not distinguish between principles and rules, nor does it confirm the dictionaries by the use of such words as "fundamental" and "comprehensive," nor does it cover the important matter of derivation.

[11] Victor H. Stempf, "A Critique of the Tentative Statement of Accounting Principles," *The Accounting Review,* March 1938, p. 56.
[12] Harold Simpson, *Fiftieth Anniversary Celebration* (New York, American Institute of Accountants, 1938), p. 237.
[13] Sanders, Hatfield, and Moore, *A Statement of Accounting Principles* (New York, American Institute of Accountants, 1938), p. 5.

PRINCIPLES, RULES, PRACTICES, AND CONVENTIONS.   The contribution of Byrne,[14] published in the November 1937 issue of *The Journal of Accountancy,* contains so many excellent and quotable statements that it is difficult to select the better ones. He, too, attempts a definition which with one exception appears sound and defensible.

> Accounting principles, then, are the fundamental concepts on which accounting, as an organized body of knowledge, rests. Like the axioms of geometry, they are few in number and general in terms; they possess the distinguishing characteristic of a compelling and coercive nature, and they are the foundation upon which the superstructure of accounting rules, practices and conventions is built.

Considering this problem in terms of foundation and superstructure, is there not some basis for difference of opinion as to Byrne's inclusion of conventions as part of the superstructure of accounting? Surely the fundamental basis of accounting is conventional. In fact, it may be argued that accounting itself is a convention. Consequently, Byrne might well have pointed out that conventions underlie the foundation of principles to which he refers.

Of particular interest is Byrne's insistence that principles possess the distinguishing characteristic of a compelling and coercive nature. This is, perhaps, but another way of stating that principles are fundamental and comprehensive.

Byrne[14] emphasizes this point more than once. He asserts that engineering principles have a coercive and compelling character in the sense that they are self-enforcing and he argues that principles of accounting are similarly characterized. He insists that principles of accounting remain the same regardless of particular cases wherein they differ from "the body of accounting rules, practices and conventions." (Again his inclusion of conventions is subject to question.)

He touches upon derivation also, suggesting that the rules derived from principles "have validity only to the extent that they properly reflect the principle."

14 Gilbert R. Byrne, "To What Extent Can the Practice of Accounting Be Reduced to Rules and Standards?" *The Journal of Accountancy,* November 1937, pp. 372, 370, 368.

Alternative Meaning of Principles.—Following the publication of Byrne's article in *The Journal of Accountancy* in November 1937, certain comments were made by May, which appeared in the December issue of the same magazine.

May[15] attempted to explain the meaning of the word "principles" that had been adopted by the American Institute's Committee on Cooperation with Stock Exchanges, of which he was chairman. The following quotation is taken from his short article:

> The *Oxford Dictionary* divides its definitions of "principle" into three groups, one of which is headed: "Fundamental truth, law, or motive force." Within this group it gives three meanings, each sanctioned by centuries of usage; namely:
>
> > "A fundamental truth or proposition on which many others depend; a primary truth comprehending or forming the basis of various subordinate truths;
> >
> > A general law or rule adopted or professed as a guide to action; a settled ground or basis of conduct or practice;
> >
> > A general fact or law of nature by virtue of which a machine or instrument operates."
>
> Mr. Byrne seems to assume that in the certificate the word is used in the first of these three senses, but an examination of the history and development of the certificate will, I think, clearly show that it is used in the second.

He went on to say that "the second sense of the word 'principle' above quoted seemed, however, to fit the case perfectly. Examination of the report as a whole will make clear what the committee contemplated; namely, that *each corporation* should have a code of 'laws or rules, adopted or professed, as a guide to action,' and that the accountants should report, first, whether *this code* conformed to accepted usages, and, secondly, whether it had been consistently maintained and applied."

The italics have been added for clarity since the point at issue is not entirely obvious at first glance. It appears from this explanation that principles of accounting are represented by an individual code for each corporation. In other words, the author

---

[15] George O. May, "Principles of Accounting," *The Journal of Accountancy,* December 1937, pp. 423, 424.

infers that one code of accounting principles might be found in the United States Steel Corporation, another code of accounting principles in Swift and Company, and a third code of principles in General Motors, and that if one public accountant should audit these three large corporations, it would be necessary *in each separate case* to determine whether its individual code conformed to accepted usages and had been consistently maintained and applied.

It is quite clear, therefore, that as many codes of principles exist as there are separate corporations, although a general code of "accepted usages" is inferred.

This explanation appears somewhat lame in several particulars. In the first place May quotes three meanings of "principle" from the *Oxford Dictionary* and says that he recalls the "discussion and searching of dictionaries which took place before the perhaps rather magniloquent word 'principle' was adopted in preference to the humbler 'rule'."

The feeling that his viewpoint must be authoritative because of the "dictionary searching" is somewhat modified by the fact that the definition chosen appears to have more reference to personal conduct than to the fundamental truths of accounting. Does it not seem to refer to that use of the word "principle" commonly noted in such statements as, "It is against his principles to take a drink before lunch" or "It is against his principles to play golf on Sunday"?

This, however, is a matter of secondary importance. It may be assumed for the sake of argument that the dictionary searching and discussion referred to resulted in a conscious and deliberate decision to use the one particular meaning as contrasted with the one having to do with "fundamental truth" adopted by Byrne and generally agreed to by many others.

The Institute's Five Principles.—If the committee deliberately decided to adopt this specific meaning of the word "principle," it is a matter for wonder that they should have enunciated five principles of accounting labeling them as "statement of certain accounting principles" which are obviously generalized and not prepared for an individual corporation.

These five principles refer to corporations generally, but May says that each corporation should have its own code of laws or rules and that each such separate code is to be considered a code of principles of accounting for *that* corporation.

A careful reading of the five principles clearly confirms this contradiction, since principle No. 1 with reference to unrealized profit is first stated and then modified by the words "an exception to the general rule may be made in respect of inventories in industries (such as the packing-house industry)."

In addition to the contradiction between the committee's list of principles of accounting and its chairman's definition of the word "principles," it is still not clear why the committee adopted without explanation a definition which could hardly fail to cause misunderstanding, controversy, and confusion.

On the assumption that the viewpoint advanced by Byrne is one with which the majority of accountants would agree and one which stockholders, creditors, governmental agencies, and managers would consider the more logical and reasonable, there still remains the problem of devising tests to distinguish between the principles on the one hand, and rules, conventions, and doctrines of accounting on the other.

Tests for Principles.—It is suggested that tests for principles can be put in the form of three questions, as follows:

1. Are principles of accounting identically the same in Germany, for example, as in the United States?
2. Are principles of accounting identically the same in the automobile industry, for example, as in the meat packing business?
3. Are principles of accounting identically the same in a corporation, for example, as in a partnership or sole proprietorship?

The first may be thought of as the varying statutes test; the second as the varying industries test, and the third as the varying proprietorship test. All three are variations of the general "identical company test" described in Chapter 1.

An affirmative answer to the first question will solve the principal difficulty which has been encountered by those attempting to codify the principles of accounting. If accounting principles are identically the same in Germany as they are in the United States, then principles obviously are not modified or affected by statute laws.

Principles are fundamental, general, and comprehensive. Also, they are uniformly defined as truths.

Can a fundamental, comprehensive, general truth be different in one country from what it is in another country? Apparently not without flouting established dictionary authority.

If it be asserted that principles of accounting *are* different in Germany from what they are in the United States, then a narrower question presents itself. Are the principles of accounting the same in Michigan, for example, as they are in South Dakota? If the answer to this question be "yes," it ignores the fact that in certain respects the statutes of the two states differ. If, on the other hand, it is still maintained that differences in laws cause differences in accounting principles, the argument can be carried into smaller and smaller subdivisions of government so long as they have legal influence on corporation accounting.

The tentative position taken here assumes an affirmative answer to the "varying statutes test" as well as to the other two. The tentative position may be stated as follows: If there are any principles of accounting, then according to definition and common understanding those principles must be the same in Germany, Russia, the Sahara Desert, the South Pole and Kalamazoo, Michigan, in that they are not subject to modification by law, legal decisions, or the rulings of governmental bodies; that they are the same for a corner grocery, an air line, a lumber company, a bank, or a dance hall, in that they are not subject to modification by type of business activity; finally, that they are the same for a sole proprietorship, a partnership, a corporation, a social club, or a municipality in that they are not subject to modification by types of proprietorship.

After having given consideration to the composite list of suggested principles in Chapter 14, these tests will be reconsidered and the tentative position taken will be reexamined.

CHAPTER 14

COMPOSITE LIST OF PRINCIPLES

Mention has already been made in Chapter 12 of various attempts which have been made to list the principles of accounting.

It is doubtful whether any of these lists were intended to be complete. Their presentation has generally been prefaced by such comments as, "It is not the purpose of this article to attempt a formulation of the principles of accounting," or "Accounting principles and conventions are difficult to summarize, but a few examples may suffice to indicate their nature," or "Presumably the list would include some if not all of the following."

The American Accounting Association referred to its statement as "tentative" and specifically indicated that it was not attempting to "establish the postulates of all accounting theory and procedure."

Some of the lists include items which might properly have been termed conventions, rules, or doctrines. Others omitted some of the conventions upon which accounting is based.

It has seemed desirable to consolidate these various accounting principles into one composite list. The arrangement of this composite list closely follows the classification proposed by Sanders, Hatfield, and Moore. The adoption of this classification carries with it no implication of superiority. Rather, it is based entirely upon the fact that the Sanders, Hatfield, and Moore list contains more items grouped, perhaps, according to a somewhat better classification than the other lists or codes.

The Sanders, Hatfield, and Moore classification is based primarily upon Roman numerals as follows:

I. General Principles
II. Income Statement Principles

III. Balance Sheet Principles
IV. Consolidated Statements
V. Comments and Footnotes

Under each of these general heads is a subsidiary alphabetical classification the items of which are again subdivided, where necessary, either alphabetically or numerically.

In attempting to effect this consolidation occasional difficulties of classification were encountered, i.e., not always did the "principle" suggested by some other writer or group fit exactly into the stated scheme of classification. Accordingly, it has been necessary to expand the Sanders, Hatfield, and Moore classification slightly and in occasional instances to broaden the significance of some of their items. It is believed, however, that no substantial violence has been done to the basic scheme of classification.

To save tiresome repetition of references, the following abbreviations have been employed to indicate the sources of items:

Reference	Source
A.I.A. . . .	Special Committee on Cooperation with Stock Exchanges of American Institute of Accountants, *Audits of Corporate Accounts* (New York, American Institute of Accountants, 1934).
A.A.A. . . .	Executive Committee of the American Accounting Association, "A Tentative Statement of Accounting Principles Affecting Corporate Reports," *The Accounting Review,* June 1936.
S-H-M . . .	Sanders, Hatfield, and Moore, sponsored by the Haskins and Sells Foundation, *A Statement of Accounting Principles* (New York, American Institute of Accountants, 1938).
Byrne . . .	Gilbert R. Byrne, "To What Extent Can the Practice of Accounting Be Reduced to Rules and Standards?" *The Journal of Accountancy,* November 1937.
Trouant . .	D. L. Trouant, *Financial Audits* (New York, American Institute Publishing Co., Inc., 1937).
Littleton . .	A. C. Littleton, "Tests for Principles," *The Accounting Review,* March 1938. A. C. Littleton, "High Standards of Accounting," *The Journal of Accountancy,* August 1938.

Reference   *Source*

Mason . . .   Perry Mason, *Principles of Public-Utility Depreciation* (Chicago, American Accounting Association, 1937).

Paton . . .   W. A. Paton, "Comments on 'A Statement of Accounting Principles,'" *The Journal of Accountancy,* March 1938.
                W. A. Paton, *Accounting Theory* (New York, The Ronald Press Company, 1922).

Broad . . .   Samuel J. Broad, "Cooperation with the Securities and Exchange Commission," *The Journal of Accountancy,* August, 1938.
                Samuel J. Broad, *Fiftieth Anniversary Celebration* (New York, American Institute of Accountants, 1938).

Husband . .   George R. Husband, "Accounting Postulates: An Analysis of the Tentative Statement of Accounting Principles," *The Accounting Review,* December 1937.

Stempf   . .   Victor H. Stempf, "A Critique of the Tentative Statement of Accounting Principles," *The Accounting Review,* March 1938.

Montgomery .   Robert H. Montgomery, *Auditing Theory and Practice* (New York, The Ronald Press Company, 1912).

Hosmer   . .   W. A. Hosmer, "The Effect of Direct Charges to Surplus on the Measurement of Income," *The Accounting Review,* March 1938.

Rorem . . .   C. Rufus Rorem, "Accounting Theory: A Critique of the Tentative Statement of Accounting Principles," *The Accounting Review,* June 1937.

Because the Sanders, Hatfield, and Moore list is used as the basis of classification, the quotation from their list will in each instance appear first, to be followed by appropriate quotations from other sources. Again it should be noted that this order of listing implies no superiority.

Some of the quotations included in this composite list are critical rather than constructive. The list is intended to picture not only the suggested principles but also some of the conflicting opinions.

Based upon these preliminary explanations, the material which follows can be taken to represent a composite and reasonably complete list of those accounting principles, conventions, doctrines, and rules which have been suggested by various accounting writers, committees, and other groups to the completion date of this volume.

I. General Principles

I.A. "Accounting should make available all material information of a financial nature relating to (a) the financial condition or status of the business, (b) its progress in earning income." (S-H-M)

This statement was not made, in so many words, by other authorities. Is it a principle or is it a rule or doctrine? Inclusion of the word "material" hints at policy rather than fundamental truth, while the limitation implied in "financial nature" gives it an essential characteristic of a convention. Possibly this item expresses a moral, rather than a technical, principle.

The next three items are so closely related as to justify simultaneous consideration.

I.B. "Transactions which add to or subtract from capital must be distinguished from those which add to or subtract from revenue, and, where both kinds of change occur in one transaction, the extent of each must be shown." (S-H-M)

I.C. "A reliable historical record must be made of all transactions of the business; but this record must also be analytical, or susceptible to subsequent analysis, to preserve the necessary distinction between capital and income." (S-H-M)

I.D. "The use of long-term assets involves the apportionment of capital and income over the several accounting periods; the accuracy of the accounts depends in large measure upon the exercise of competent judgment in making these apportionments." (S-H-M)

"Recognition invariably should be given to depreciation, depletion, and all other diminutions or expirations of cost, even when the amounts thereof are not subject to precise measurement and must be estimated. Estimations of costs applicable to future periods must be based upon business judgments, seasoned experience, and expert opinion, rather than rigid formula. In each enterprise and each industry reasonably consistent practices should be developed for determining the portion of a past cost that properly may be carried forward to future periods." (Postulate 3, A.A.A.)

"The investment in an industrial plant should be charged against the operations over the useful life of the plant." (Principle 2, Byrne)

"It is a generally accepted principle, for example, that the investment in an industrial plant should be charged against operations over the useful life of the plant." (*Examination of Financial Statements by Independent Public Accountants,* New York, American Institute of Accountants, January 1936)

"It is an axiom of economics that the maintenance of invested capital is a prerequisite to the showing of profit, that a business enterprise must deduct from its gross income for any given period of time the amount of all assets consumed and all values expired in the earning of the income before a figure of net income or net loss for the period can be determined." (Mason)

Propositions B, C, and D refer to various aspects of distinguishing between capital and revenue. Proposition B has specific reference to transactions; proposition C, to the reliability of the historical record; and proposition D, to the application of judgment to the treatment of long-term assets. By treating the three propositions as one, quotations from other authorities can be grouped here more logically.

The American Accounting Association's committee provided seven postulates having to do with costs and values. Postulate 3 has been quoted above. But the report of this committee insists that each of the seven embodies a corollary of one fundamental axiom, namely, "accounting is thus not essentially a process of valuation, but the allocation of historical costs and revenues to the current and succeeding fiscal periods." It would seem that this comprehensive axiom might well have been substituted for propositions I.B., I.C., and I.D. in the Sanders, Hatfield, and Moore report.

Judging from the views of various writers, this axiom, when suitably modified by the various viewpoints expressed, comes about as close to representing a true principle of accounting as any. But one minor and perhaps unimportant contradiction exists. Implicit in this principle is the fiscal period convention. If one is prepared to admit that a principle can depend upon a convention, the convention in this instance being the annual accounting period, then this one broad general proposition referring to capital and revenue might be termed a principle of accounting.

At this point it is well to note that the American Accounting Association Postulate 5, of the seven just mentioned, is not fully quoted here or elsewhere in this composite list, since it is not a proposition which stands by itself but rather is explanatory of the first four postulates. It is, however, mentioned again as part of proposition III.C.2.

I.E. "The basis of the treatment applied to the several items should be adhered to consistently from period to period; when any change of treatment becomes necessary, due attention should be drawn to the change." (S-H-M)

"While it is not in many cases of great importance which of several alternative accounting rules is applied in a given situation, it is essential that, once having adopted a certain procedure, it be consistently adhered to in preparing the accounts over a period of time." (Principle 8, Byrne)

". . . if there has been any change as compared with the preceding period, either in accounting principles or in the manner of their application, which has had a material effect on the statements, the nature of the change should be indicated." (*Examination of Financial Statements by Independent Public Accountants,* New York, American Institute of Accountants, January 1936)

Numerous other quotations are available but there seems to be little or no dispute as to the necessity for consistency. Oddly enough, the twenty postulates of the American Accounting Association did not include this most important proposition but the desirability of consistency is mentioned more than once in the accompanying text.

No proposition referring to consistency was included as a principle by the American Institute's committee but repeated references to consistency are found in the accompanying letters and papers. In the committee's letter of September 22, 1932, to the Committee of the New York Stock Exchange,[1] this policy of consistency was endorsed several times in such words as, "The importance of method, and particularly of consistency of method from year to year, is by no means equally understood." And again the suggestion is made that corporations should disclose "methods employed and consistency in their application from year to year." The committee reiterated the point by saying, "Within quite wide limits, it is relatively unimportant to the

1 *Audits of Corporate Accounts* (New York, American Institute of Accountants, 1934), pp. 8, 9.

investor what precise rules or conventions are adopted by a corporation in reporting its earnings if he knows what method is being followed and is assured that it is followed consistently from year to year." Not only do these quotations emphasize the importance of consistency, but as a matter of collateral interest it may be noted that much of the correspondence which preceded the development of the standard certificate referred to consistency of methods, rules, or conventions rather than to consistency of principles. The use of the word "principles" in the standard certificate was evidently intended, originally at least, to cover methods, rules, and conventions.

Trouant, while not including a definite proposition referring to consistency in his list of nine principles and conventions, repeatedly acknowledges the importance of consistency as a fundamental proposition in accounting.

While practically all modern authors recognize the importance of consistency, it is far from clear that they all regard the practical application of this policy in the same manner. Nor does there seem to be any general agreement that consistency is a principle of accounting. The Byrne list includes it and the Sanders, Hatfield, and Moore list also includes it, but the American Accounting Association list, the American Institute committee's list, and Trouant exclude it.

It is difficult indeed to see how this policy properly could be characterized as a principle of accounting. Obviously, it is not a fundamental truth nor has it any exclusive application to accounting. It is also difficult to see how it can be considered an accounting convention, which leaves the alternative of christening it either as a rule or a doctrine. The latter seems more satisfactory.

I.F. "The possible extent of unforeseen contingencies of adverse character calls for a generally conservative treatment of items to which judgment must be applied." (S-H-M)

"Losses, if probable, even though not actually incurred, should be provided for in arriving at net income." (Principle 5, Byrne)

"The authors [Sanders, Hatfield, and Moore] support—not without some hesitation—the general doctrine that minimizing asset values in 'recognized' ways is conservative and hence sound. That this position is unjustified in theory or practice has been demonstrated again and again. Asset valuation is a two-edged process. From an immediate balance-sheet standpoint, the understatement of assets is reflected in a reduced net worth. This has a flavor of conservatism, although it does not follow that the resulting balance-sheet is a good report. From the standpoint of succeeding income statements, on the other hand, the understatement of assets (of the cost type) very definitely and literally brings about a decrease in reported operating expenses and a corresponding increase in net—a result to which no vestige of conventional conservatism attaches. Indeed, as every accountant knows, the favored method of padding the profits of future periods is that of the extraordinary write-off of inventories or plant costs—a fact which helps to explain the ready acceptance by many managements of the so-called conservative devices of the accountant." (Paton)

"Conservatism, or the discounting of future uncertainties, is a major principle, demanding recognition in any consideration of policy or procedure for a particular set of circumstances. In some cases it is the governing principle. In other cases it is of minor or no importance. It is in frequent conflict with other principles, such as that of matching costs and revenues if we are to obtain true net income, and explains some inconsistencies in our rules." (Comments of Wyman P. Fiske on Paton's "Comments on 'A Statement of Accounting Principles,'" *The Journal of Accountancy*, April 1938)

"The traditional 'conservatism' of accounting procedures produces by no means consistently conservative figures of profit (as was demonstrated many years ago by the late Sir Gilbert Garnsey) and is indeed calculated to depress profits unduly in times of recession and to exaggerate profits in times of advance." (Editorial in *The Canadian Chartered Accountant*, August 1938)

Neither the American Accounting Association's committee, the American Institute's committee, nor Trouant specifically lists conservatism as one of the principles of accounting, although Trouant's third proposition, which distinguishes between the treatment of profits and the treatment of costs, losses, and expenses, is clearly based upon conservatism. Recognition of the importance of conservatism is clearly indicated, however, by the American Institute's committee as it is by nearly all writers in accounting.

Failure by the American Accounting Association's committee to list conservatism among their postulates or to discuss it among their comments appears significant. Their Postulate 7, which reads: "If values other than unamortized costs are to be quoted they should be expressed in financial statements only as collateral notations for informative purposes," is indicative of this attitude. While Postulate 7 does not cover all possible applications of the policy of conservatism since an unduly large proportion of costs may previously have been amortized, nevertheless the committee's position seems to be definitely opposed to the policy of conservatism in the sense of understatement as it is usually understood.

Rorem[2] does not fully agree with this. He interprets Postulate 7 to mean "be accurate if you possibly can, but in case of doubt, be conservative." Despite all of this, Rorem labels the committee's arguments and discussion as "convincing and sophisticated."

Certainly it does not seem proper to say that conservatism is an accepted principle of accounting. Entirely too many accounting authorities are opposed to it. Montgomery[3] has said that "it is not courage which started the conservatism which accountants have, but fear."

Lorig[4] says that those who favor it "make of conservatism a god so domineering that the objective of accounting—providing useful financial information for intelligent guidance—is somewhat forgotten."

Peloubet[5] points out that: "You can always be conservative in a balance sheet; you can never be consistently conservative in income accounts. It is mathematically impossible."

These few quotations are echoed by others too numerous to quote.

If conservatism is a principle, it is not an *accepted* principle.

2 C. Rufus Rorem, "Accounting Theory: A Critique of the Tentative Statement of Accounting Principles," *The Accounting Review*, June 1937, p. 134.

3 Robert H. Montgomery, "Accountants' Limitations," *The Journal of Accountancy*, October 1927, p. 251.

4 Arthur M. Lorig, "Accounting Postulates: An Analysis of the Tentative Statement of Accounting Principles," *The Accounting Review*, December 1937, p. 401.

5 Maurice E. Peloubet, *Fiftieth Anniversary Celebration* (New York, American Institute of Accountants, 1938), p. 356.

There seems, however, to be a strong case against conservatism as a principle at all. Perhaps it is a stronger case than almost any of the others in view of the common definition of a principle as "a fundamental truth." Conservatism infers understatement and understatement infers falsity. Falsity cannot be characterized as fundamental truth.

Mention of the falsity of understatement is not intended to reflect any opinion as to the moral questions involved. There are many and highly reputable citizens who hold understatement to be a virtue and others who hold that understatement made for a "good purpose" is permissible. These are viewpoints to be given some consideration, but here is presented the question of whether conservatism is a principle, and since conservatism carries with it the suggestion of understatement and hence of misrepresentation, whether for good or bad motives, it cannot be classified as a principle.

It does not partake of the characteristics of convention. Shall it be referred to as a rule or as a doctrine? Since it is broad and general and is in the nature of an accounting policy there seems to be a certain amount of justification for preferring the word "doctrine" to the word "rule."

The following eight propositions were not included among the twenty-five specifically listed by Sanders, Hatfield, and Moore, but they have been coded in accordance with the Sanders, Hatfield, and Moore classification.

I.G. "The balance-sheet equation [is an accounting convention]." (Paton)

Is the accounting equation primarily a mathematical concept or does it partake of the arbitrary characteristic of a convention?

Accountants generally agree upon the phrase "the rule of debit and credit" and rarely is it discussed as a principle or convention. Certainly it is fundamental to all accounting work. This fact in itself does not justify terming it a principle. Mathematically the equation is a fundamental truth and by the mathematical standard it might be called a principle. The accounting equation also may be considered the expression of a conventionalized viewpoint, namely, that of the entity. As the mathematical expression of the entity convention, the equation itself may be regarded as a convention.

I.H. "The business entity." (Paton)

The business entity has been referred to heretofore as the accounting entity since it applied to any unit for which a double entry accounting record is maintained and is therefore not limited to business. No serious error would have been made by combining this convention with item I.G. having to do with the equation. The equation implies an accounting entity and vice versa, although the equation may be said to describe the system of double entry record while the entity refers to that unit for which the double entry record is maintained.

I.I. "The 'going concern.'" (Paton)

"Another important convention in accordance with which statements are prepared is that the business is a going concern which will continue to operate on a more or less normal course." (S-H-M)

While this convention was mentioned in the Sanders, Hatfield, and Moore report, it was not included among the twenty-five items. This convention is generally admitted by accountants and many other quotations recognizing it could be shown. The principal difference between these two quotations lies in the fact that Paton applies the convention to accounting, whereas Sanders, Hatfield, and Moore apply it to reporting. Unquestionably this particular proposition is a convention, since in any particular instance it may not be true but may still be maintained as the basis for record keeping until the entity to which it applies faces liquidation.

I.J. "The accountant finds it necessary to adopt certain premises with respect to sequences of data and relationships between series of facts. For example, he commonly takes it for granted that a loss in asset value falls upon or extinguishes the most recently accumulated proprietorship." (Paton)

There are other types of conventional sequences. Paton has pointed out another assumption of this type, namely, that inventory withdrawals are taken from the oldest in stock (or under another system the newest in stock). Such assumptions, while useful, are of course arbitrary. For convenience they may be grouped under the title "sequence conventions."

I.K. ". . . everyone knows the value of land does not remain constant, but this assumption is one of those conventions of accounting which are intended to make a complicated matter a little less complicated." (Spencer B. Meredith, in *Barron's,* April 4, 1938)

This convention is somewhat broader than Meredith intimates. There are, of course, different underlying assumptions with respect to the valuation of various types of assets. One assumption applies to land which does not apply to buildings upon the land, inventories are viewed in another manner, receivables in still another, intangible assets in another. Generally the practices involved are a matter of practical convenience and accepted usage, but they may be loosely grouped as a general convention of expired values. The Sanders, Hatfield, and Moore report intimates that "accounting conventions have come to require that the historical amounts be adjusted to something nearer to practical present-day conditions."

I.L. ". . . the balance-sheet and income statement are a resultant or composite of two very different classes of information." (S-H-M)

This proposition has been included because it is specifically mentioned in the text of the Sanders, Hatfield, and Moore monograph. Acceptance of the entity theory appears to eliminate this proposition as a convention of accounting.

I.M. Doctrine of disclosure.

Commonly accepted by accountants as a general proposition of financial reporting is the doctrine of adequate disclosure. It is in accordance with this doctrine that the accountant prepares balance sheets, profit and loss statements, and other accounting reports with properly descriptive headings, clear explanations, and explanatory footnotes. In harmony with this doctrine the accountant indicates bases of valuation, pledged assets, contingent liabilities, arrears in preferred dividends, the effect of price declines in relation to long-term contracts, and similar matters. This doctrine is normally considered applicable to reporting rather than to accounting, but it should be observed that its application is required by the complexity of present-day conditions in order to supplement the limitations of simple accounting mechanism which by its very nature can reflect only obvious relationships. When these relationships cease to be simple and obvious, application of the doctrine of disclosure is required.

I.N. Doctrine of materiality.

Materiality as a doctrine of reporting has been considerably publicized by the Securities and Exchange Commission because of the fact that the buyer of securities sold upon untrue statements or omission of material facts may sue those who have participated in their distribution either knowing of such untrue statements or having failed to take care in discovering them.

Former Commissioner Landis[6] of the Securities and Exchange Commission explained materiality from the Commission's viewpoint in the following words: "facts become material for the purpose of omissions and misstatements when, as a consequence of such omissions and misstatements, non-existent values are attributed to a security."

This, of course, is an explanation from the reporting viewpoint of the Commission, but the accounting doctrine of materiality is much older than the Securities and Exchange Commission. It has long been recognized that the relative size of amounts involved may be permitted to influence accounting procedures. Transactions involving relatively small amounts are often recorded in a manner which would not be permissible if the amounts were relatively large. Materiality conforms to this so-called "practical viewpoint" and underlies many accounting rules and also many accounting arguments. Different viewpoints as to the treatment of treasury stock are often based upon materiality. Small accounting corrections are often handled in one way whereas substantial ones are handled in another. Often it is contended that if amounts are small enough not to influence the comparability of periodic figures, they are immaterial.

Materiality is essentially a matter of judgment. Materiality cannot be dignified as a principle because it often results in a

[6] Lasser and Gerardi, "The Relation of Accountants to the Federal Securities Act." *N.A.C.A. Bulletin*, July 15, 1936, p. 1305.

showing which, in a minor way, is the opposite of "fundamental truth." It is hardly specific enough for a rule, nor is it sufficiently flavored with arbitrariness and general acceptance to be characterized as a convention. It may, therefore, be classified as one of the doctrines of accounting and reporting.

II. INCOME STATEMENT PRINCIPLES

II.A. "The income statement should show, for the period it covers, (a) income from all sources, (b) costs and expenses of all kinds, and (c) net income." (S-H-M)

"The income statement for any given period should reflect all revenues properly given accounting recognition and all costs written off during the period, regardless of whether or not they are the results of operations in that period: to the end that for any period of years in the history of the enterprise the assembled income statements will express completely all gains and losses." (Postulate 8, A.A.A.)

"The income statement for any given period should, where necessary, be divided into two sections, one showing particulars of operation for the period, measured as accurately as may be at the time, and the other showing realized capital gains and losses and extraordinary credits and charges resulting from income realization and cost amortization not connected with the operations of that period." (Postulate 9, A.A.A.)

"The operations section of the income statement should disclose the gross revenues from sales made and services rendered; the elements of operating cost and expense incurred, including the amount of depreciation and other amortization of assets applicable; the amount of interest incurred on borrowed money, including debt discount and expense properly amortized during the year; income and profits taxes accrued; and all other increases or decreases in the equity of stockholders resulting from transactions of the period which are of a normally recurring nature." (Postulate 10, A.A.A.)

"Amounts affecting profit and loss should be reflected in the profit-and-loss statement, either in the year to which the amount applies or in the year in which the amount is determined." (Trouant)

"... the authors [Sanders, Hatfield, and Moore] quote, with apparent approval, the following statement from Arthur Andersen: 'The practice of equalizing earnings is directly contrary to recognized accounting principles.' But on page 43 (and elsewhere) they go out of their way to support a European practice, the base-stock inventory method, which was strongly urged on the Treasury Department by three or four corporations in 1918-1919, and has been vigorously revived and sponsored in recent years under the 'last in, first out' label, which represents nothing more nor less than a major device for equalizing earnings, to avoid showing in the periodic reports the severe fluctuations which are inherent in certain business fields. Here is a truly serious matter. The very essence of the stand of the professional accountant is the maintenance of the integrity of the periodic statements." (Paton)

"I see nothing improper in the establishment of operating reserves to provide for liabilities emanating within a given period, out of the income of that period, although the amounts may be indeterminable at the time." (Stempf)

"It occurs to me that the 'cost hypothesis' which I have described, acting as a leveler of the peaks and valleys of industry's profits and losses, should recommend itself to the consideration of prudent management." (E. W. Graham, "Current Practices in Inventory Valuation," N.A.C.A. Bulletin, March 1, 1937)

"We might state as a fundamental principle, for example, that the income account for the year should include all the income and all the expenses which are deemed to be applicable to that year (or which are recognized in that year, as some prefer)." (Broad)

"Periodic costs and their related revenues are the most important data for accounts to produce." (Littleton)

The general proposition as advanced by Sanders, Hatfield, and Moore can hardly be disputed, but collateral to this proposition is another; the matter of operating reserves. As will be noted, the practice of equalizing earnings was condemned elsewhere in this report. This brings to a sharp focus operating reserves and other devices frequently employed to effect the equalization of earnings.

Is there in this proposition, or any variation thereof, an accounting principle which conforms to the specification of a general fundamental truth? This seems doubtful. The proposition in any of its variations, and surely in many of its applications, is so flavored by the doctrine of conservatism as to eliminate it as a principle of accounting. Nor does there appear to be general acceptance. If this proposition and its variations must be labelled, it can be done only by a process of elimination, which leads to the conclusion that it is a rule of accounting, a rule based primarily upon conservatism, and furthermore a rule which is not one of general agreement.

The American Accounting Association has taken a stand against the inclusion of "various types of operating or surplus reserves to which may be carried expense charges or income credits." Elsewhere, it has insisted that: "Income statements for a series of periods should not be distorted or artificially stabilized through the practice of creating large operating reserves in certain periods and charging to such reserves losses in succeeding periods which it is desired not to reflect in the current income statement." The position taken is a logical one and might well represent the basis for an accounting rule. Surely it is more specific and more logical than item II.A. of Sanders, Hatfield, and Moore.

II.B. "Only income realized by the sale of goods or rendering of service is to be shown in the income statement. Unrealized income should not be recorded, nor utilized to absorb proper charges against earnings." (S-H-M)

"The income account of a corporation should not include credits or charges resulting from profits or losses on transactions involving the issuance, purchase, or retirement of its own stock; from any adjustment of the capital accounts; or from dividend payments or stock-dividend distributions." (Postulate 12, A.A.A.)

"Revenue from actual sales marks the realization of profit (or loss)." (Littleton)

"Profits and income should be reflected in income and surplus accounts only when realized." (Trouant)

"The income shall include only realized profits in the period during which realized; profit is deemed to be realized when a sale in the ordinary course of business is effected, unless the circumstances are such that collection of the sale price is not reasonably assured." (Principle 4, Byrne)

"Unrealized profit should not be credited to income account of the corporation either directly or indirectly, through the medium of charging against such unrealized profits amounts which would ordinarily fail to be charged against income account. Profit is deemed to be realized when a sale in the ordinary course of business is effected, unless the circumstances are such that the collection of the sale price is not reasonably assured. An exception to the general rule may be made in respect of inventories in industries (such as the packing-house industry) in which owing to the impossibility of determining costs it is a trade custom to take inventories at net selling prices, which may exceed cost." (Principle 1, A.I.A.)

"Thus even though it may be established logically that income is earned with production and not with sale, except insofar as the sale is an act of production, it may be practical to accept the sale as the point of crystallization of income. Or again, while it may be logically and economically proven that appreciation is income, it may be impractical to concede its universal recognition because of its instability and because of the overly optimistic attitude of human nature." (Husband)

There appears to be substantial agreement among various authorities as to the desirability of applying the realization test to income. There are, however, three important exceptions to this general proposition. The first refers to so-called losses or gains resulting from the sale of reacquired capital stock. Since this will be given consideration later, no further comment is needed here save perhaps an intimation that some of the lack of agreement among accountants on this matter may be due to unconscious shifting of viewpoint.

In the analysis of any accounting proposition it seems essential to adopt one viewpoint and cling to it throughout the process, even though for further analysis a later step may require the assumption of a different viewpoint. In a problem such as that of profit or loss on reacquired shares, it is important to decide whether the entity viewpoint, the viewpoint of the stockholder, or the viewpoint of others shall be adopted. From the entity viewpoint the stockholder is nothing more than a creditor.

A second difficulty in the application of this proposition referring to realization is the one mentioned by the American Institute committee as an exception to the general rule. This refers to those cases where it is impossible to determine inventory costs and, as a result, inventories must be taken at net selling prices, a procedure which may involve unrealized income.

The third exception is found in connection with uncompleted long-term contracts where periodic profits or losses are assumed to depend upon the percentage of completion of contracts in progress.

These exceptions indicate that the proposition under discussion is not a principle that represents a fundamental truth.

A. C. Littleton, in a round-table discussion at the 1937 American Institute Convention, asked someone to tell him *why* income realization represented a principle. Paton says that the proposition under discussion is in conflict with the "principle" of inventory valuation later enunciated by Sanders, Hatfield, and Moore, and he goes further in his *Accounting Theory,*[7] clearly intimating that he considers realization as a convention because the accountant assumes that "expense accrues but that net revenue or profit suddenly appears, full-blown, on some specific occasion, commonly that of the sale."

Another argument in favor of christening this proposition as a convention is found by retracing the steps of its development. In the earlier, simpler days of accounting, the convention called for realization in actual cash, which was later modified by the assumption that legal transfer of title constituted realization, the resulting account receivable merely representing a deferred charge to cash, while still later the mere act of shipment and billing was assumed to be equivalent to the legal transfer of title. It accordingly appears that this proposition is a convention which has twice been reconventionalized!

II.C. "Income from sources other than the main operations of the business should be stated separately." (S-H-M)

This is derived from a well-recognized and thoroughly sound rule of classification which is generally accepted as proper in all of the sciences. It is not peculiarly a proposition referring to accounting, and it is difficult to see why it should be thought of as an accounting principle. It partakes somewhat of the nature of a rule.

7 W. A. Paton, *Accounting Theory* (New York, The Ronald Press Company, 1922), p. 493.

II.D. "Costs and expenses must include:

    (a) all current operating costs,

    (b) inventory losses of the period,

    (c) provision for losses on other current assets, which have become imminent in the period,

    (d) proper allocations for the depreciation, depletion, or amortization of all capital assets subject to those processes."
    (S-H-M)

"Accounting is essentially the allocation of historical costs and revenues to the current and succeeding fiscal periods." (Principle 1, Byrne)

"In computing the net income (available for dividends) for a period, all forms of expense incurred in the production of such net income must be provided for." (Principle 3, Byrne)

"Profits cannot be realized until the capital has been conserved; or, profits cannot be determined until provision has been made for all costs entering into the transactions from which the profits arose." (Trouant)

(At this point American Accounting Association Postulate 10, already quoted in connection with proposition II.A., should again be considered.)

"One of our fundamental tenets of accounting requires that expenses should be charged against the income in the production of which they have been incurred." (Stempf)

"Depreciation, depletion, and analogous phases of amortization are fixed expenses which must be borne by operations from year to year on some consistent basis, predicated upon some logical estimates by those qualified to form sound judgments thereon as the result of considered studies." (Stempf)

"It may be cited as a general principle of accounting that depreciable assets should be written off over a period of their expected use." (Kenneth W. Dalglish, *Fiftieth Anniversary Celebration*, New York, American Institute of Accountants, 1938)

". . . one fundamental and very broad principle is that the income account for a year should bear all the charges applicable to that year, and under this general principle we make provision for depreciation, we write off unrealized inventory losses, we amortize discount on bonds, and so forth." (Broad)

"My own opinion. which I am aware is not considered by all to be entirely orthodox, is that any adjustment of inventories for market fluctuations is a balance-sheet adjustment preferably made through surplus, or in any case, excluded from operating results and shown separately in the income account." (Maurice E. Peloubet, *Fiftieth Anniversary Celebration,* New York, American Institute of Accountants, 1938)

"By way of interjection, it may be well to ask the Committee [American Accounting Association] at this point where it would exhibit losses resulting from pricing the inventory at 'cost or market whichever is lower' (assuming that this method of pricing the inventory is permissible in spite of the question raised in connection with the discussion regarding Postulate No. 3)? Would the Committee exhibit such loss implicitly in the operating section of the income statement as an increase to the true cost of the goods sold or in the non-operating section as a capital loss?" (Husband)

This is not one proposition, but four. Little exception can be taken to items (a) and (d), but considerable opposition has been evidenced to the other two.

There is a general agreement as to the desirability of matching costs and expenses with revenues in so far as possible and practicable. The proposition as advanced by Sanders, Hatfield, and Moore is faulty in that it fails fully to distinguish between costs and expenses on the one hand and losses on the other hand. An important school of thought holds that an unrealized inventory loss, due solely to price change and not to decrease in physical quantity, deterioration, or obsolescence, represents no more than an application of the doctrine of conservatism, particularly unfortunate in the way that it causes distortion of comparative profits.

To proposition II.D.(c) similar opposition exists. The premature recognition of unrealized losses caused entirely by price fluctuations is based upon the balance sheet viewpoint and is inconsistent with the general convention of valuation.

Byrne,[8] whose views are generally sound, refers to "the principle that it is necessary to provide for probable losses" and goes even further, saying that the accountant has full liberty to

[8] Gilbert R. Byrne, "To What Extent Can the Practice of Accounting Be Reduced to Rules and Standards?" *The Journal of Accountancy,* November 1937, p. 373.

employ the most appropriate rule to this end in view of all the circumstances and "whichever one he selects, he should not be charged with violation of any accounting *principle*."

Those accountants who accept all four subdivisions of the proposition should, it appears, be willing to call it either a rule or a convention, with a definite preference for the former. Many believe that accounting is merely a specialized branch of statistics, but any good statistician would be horrified at the way accountants refuse to match up certain costs with income all in the name of conservatism.

II.E. "Nonrecurring items should be reported in terms which indicate their nature." (S-H-M)

"The operations section of the income statement should be followed by an appropriate listing in reasonable detail of capital gains and losses, extraordinary charges and credits to income, including substantial adjustments applicable to but not recognized in prior years, extraordinary gains, losses and amortization resulting from factors other than current operations, gain or loss from the discharge of liabilities at less or more than their recorded amount, and other comparable items." (Postulate 11, A.A.A.)

". . . it is unsound to credit extraordinary income to current profit and loss and to charge extraordinary losses directly to current surplus. Both should be handled consistently and both should be disclosed." (Stempf)

". . . the Committee [American Accounting Association] conceives of operating costs and operating income as those items which are of a more or less 'normally recurring nature.' Non-operating items are those items which are extraordinary, of a non-recurring nature. Are these the proper bases for distinguishing between the two? Does not the term 'operating' refer rather to the specific utilities which the owners conceive it to be their function to perform in contra-distinction to the phases which accompany operations more or less in the nature of side issues?" (Husband)

"It is proper to show deductions from gross income, but there should be no deductions from net income except extraordinary items of substantial amounts which have no relation to the current period. Every effort should be made to avoid this class of deductions." (Montgomery)

"In the treatment of large amounts of discount at which corporate bonds have sometimes been retired during periods of depression there is also diversity. Some companies credit such discount against the debit balance of unamortized discount; some credit it to surplus, and some to profit and loss. Arguments can be made for each of these three treatments. Personally, I think the first is the soundest." (F. P. Byerly, "Formulation of Accounting Principles or Conventions," *The Journal of Accountancy*, August 1937)

"It is not the normal function of the periodic profit and loss statement to reflect charges covering abnormal costs and losses which are beyond the control of management. These must find record and reflection elsewhere." (Roy B. Kester, *Advanced Accounting*, New York, The Ronald Press Company, 1933)

"The clear separation of capital gains and losses in all the variety of situations encountered in practice will always be a matter of extreme complexity; but in so far as practicable, such gains and losses should be clearly segregated in the financial statements. Investors and others would then be put on notice that such income or expense would probably not recur." (Hosmer)

"Would it not be constructive to give some indications of a basis for good business judgment in choosing between the alternatives of (a) writing off a so-called capital loss against current income, (b) carrying the amount as deferred, or (c) absorbing it into earned surplus?" (Littleton)

This proposition is rather definitely related to the one which follows (II.F.) and is of special importance in view of the differing viewpoints which have been expressed.

The proposition as advanced by Sanders, Hatfield, and Moore is obviously a rule of reporting rather than a principle of accounting.

II.F. "As far as possible net income should be so determined that it will need no subsequent correction. When, however, such correction becomes necessary, it may be made through current income only if it is not so large as to distort the statement of that income; otherwise it should be made through earned surplus." (S-H-M)

"Earned surplus should represent the accumulated earnings of the business from transactions with the public, less distributions of such earnings to the stockholders." (Principle 7, Byrne)

"Charges against capital surplus or against unrealized profits should not be made to relieve income accounts of charges properly applicable thereto. Similarly, charges should not be made against earned surplus if the result would be to distort the amounts of earnings for the current year or for a period of years." (Trouant)

(Postulate 8 of the American Accounting Association, already quoted, II.A., has a positive bearing on surplus adjustments since it insists that for any period of years the assembled income statements should "express completely all gains and losses.")

"When the income for any period or series of periods is found to have been inaccurately stated to such a degree that it is desirable completely to recast the accounts, at least one published report after such revision should include a corrected income statement for each prior period for which adjustments have been made." (Postulate 13, A.A.A.)

"Costs charged off in accordance with these principles [Postulates 1, 2 and 3] should not be reinstated as assets subject to reamortization, except as required corrections are reflected in revised income statements for each period affected." (Postulate 4, A.A.A.)

"Minor surplus adjustments affecting prior periods are preferably included under this caption [other charges] since it is impossible to close the accounts of any one period without continual overlapping of miscellaneous income and expense items." (*Examination of Financial Statements by Independent Public Accountants,* New York, American Institute of Accountants, January 1936)

"The total change in proprietorship during the life of the business should be equal to the sum of the partial changes during each fiscal period. To adjust the report of one period without presenting revised statements for other affected periods would obviously confuse or mislead interested parties." (Rorem)

"Certain of the inaccuracies which may be the cause for such a re-casting of statements, which is a very desirable procedure, surely have no place in a statement limited by the date line to the income and costs circumscribed by the beginning and end of a current fiscal period. Such costs when written off and such income when incorporated into the accounts are logically surplus corrections." (Husband)

"In point of conservatism it is far better to charge capital losses and deductions to income than it is to charge income deductions to capital. When there is no doubt about the items, good accounting

practice does not sanction the charging of capital items to income."
(Montgomery)

". . . in the ordinary course of business some items technically
applicable to the operations of one year will be entered in the accounts
during a later period. Overlapping items of this character which arise
in the ordinary course of business should be asborbed in the income
account of the period in which they are taken into the accounts and
should not, except in extraordinary circumstances, be treated as adjustments of earned surplus. Obviously where overlapping charges or
credits are substantial in amount they should be set forth as special
items in the income account so that their effect on the operating results
may be readily observed. The practice of making direct surplus adjustments for items of this character is in the nature of a bookkeeping
approach that may easily lead to serious misrepresentation. In good
practice the earned surplus account should be virtually closed except for
dividends and the balance of the net profit-and-loss account for the
year." (Arthur Andersen, "Present-day Problems Affecting the Presentation and Interpretation of Financial Statements," *The Journal of
Accountancy*, November 1935)

"The income statement for a year should reflect all determinable
items applicable to the year, whether recurring, non-recurring or
extraordinary, and minor items applicable to prior years which will not
distort the results of the current year.

On the other hand, charges and credits applicable to prior years
which would tend to distort current year's net results should be carried
to earned surplus." (Stempf)

"Direct charges to surplus, however, which arise out of a cataclysm
such as that through which business has passed in the last 10 years
are more readily justified than those which occur in more normal
periods." (Hosmer)

". . . in general all items should be carried through income unless
the circumstances of a particular case justify a different treatment.
Every direct entry of a loss or gain in surplus is an exception to the
normal procedure of carrying such items through income, and may be
justified only on the basis of unusual conditions." (Hosmer)

". . . the transfer from income account to surplus account marks a
conversion of profit into (accumulated) capital. A loss charged directly
to surplus, therefore, becomes a species of charge against one kind of
capital and tends to obscure the distinction between capital and income,

a distinction which the whole force of accounting theory is bent upon clarifying." (Littleton)

The selection of these quotations has been made with difficulty since the proposition has been widely discussed. Some confusion has been evident owing to lack of differentiation between actual correction of substantial past errors and extraordinary items of loss or increase.

The American Accounting Association took a bold and much criticized stand in its positive insistence against surplus adjustments in reports. Recognizing the occasional need for substantial correction, the American Accounting Association preached the desirability of recasting previous profit and loss statements in order to give effect to corrections of error.

Can the general proposition as stated by Sanders, Hatfield, and Moore be dignified as a principle? It offers alternatives which stamp it as a practical application of the doctrine of materiality. It approves the correction of error by making an offsetting error and, hence, cannot be classified as "a fundamental truth." The proposal of the American Accounting Association appears more fundamental, comprehensive, and general, but it still falls short of meeting the necessary tests of a principle.

Section III of the Sanders, Hatfield, and Moore statement which follows is concerned with balance sheet principles, a subject which is not of first importance in this book. Its inclusion here seems desirable, first, for completeness and, second, because there are profit and loss aspects to certain of the propositions.

III. BALANCE SHEET PRINCIPLES

III.A. "A balance-sheet should show (a) the nature and amounts of the assets, (b) the nature and amounts of the liabilities, (c) the nature and amounts of the invested capital, (d) the amounts of earned and of capital surplus." (S-H-M)

"The net worth section of the corporation balance sheet should clearly distinguish invested capital and undivided profits." (Littleton)

"All items in the net worth section of the corporation balance sheet other than earned surplus and earned surplus reserves are related to invested capital." (Littleton)

"Everything having a value has a claimant." (Trouant)

The lists of the American Institute committee, the American Accounting Association, and Gilbert R. Byrne do not contain propositions which match this one from Sanders, Hatfield, and Moore. Even the ones quoted from Trouant and Littleton are not entirely appropriate.

The proposition as given is in the nature of a general statement or explanation of a desirable practice. Preferably it may be referred to as a rule rather than a principle.

Paton, in his *Accounting Theory,* discusses many of the general assumptions or conventions upon which accounting is based. He refers to them as postulates and includes therein the balance sheet equation, which he follows by a further postulate or convention bearing upon financial condition in relation to the balance sheet. The fundamental assumption involved is that the statement of assets and liabilities in terms of money is complete representation of the financial condition of the enterprise, which Paton asserts is obviously untrue.

III.B. ". . . with reference to fixed or capital assets in the balance-sheet:

1. The amounts should be based upon the amounts invested in such assets.
2. Reserves for depreciation, depletion, and amortization should show the cumulative progress of prorating their cost over their useful lives.
3. Proper distinction should be made between: (1) tangible assets, (2) intangibles, and (3) investments." (S-H-M)

"The accountant's valuation of physical assets at any given point of time involves the determination of what part of original cost should be written off to reflect consumed, expired, or lost usefulness, and what part should be carried forward as reasonably applicable to future operations." (Postulate 1, A.A.A.)

"Where a substantial change in beneficial ownership has occurred, cost is measured by cash outlay or by the fair market value of property acquired in exchange for securities." (Postulate 2, A.A.A.)

"If values other than unamortized costs are to be quoted they should be expressed in financial statements only as collateral notations for informative purposes." (Postulate 7, A.A.A.)

"No attempt is made [by A.A.A.] to differentiate, in principle, between the evaluation of current and fixed assets. In the writer's opinion, this position is sound, and the accountant has in the past weakened his standing as a scientist by attempting to discover differences rather than recognize similarities." (Rorem)

"An economist may be disappointed that more attention was not given [by A.A.A.] to the discounted-values of future income. But, after all, future income is an estimated figure, and one must look for a reasonable basis for such an estimate." (Rorem)

"Whenever an item is purchased from another enterprise, the change in ownership is easily recognized, in point of fact as well as time. But the case is less clear when a reorganization involves an issue of new securities or a shift in the control of a corporation. Do such occasions justify a revaluation of physical assets, on the ground that ownership has changed? This question is one which must be dealt with when the principles are expanded." (Rorem)

"The only cost recognized in accounting for record purposes will be outlay-price (historical cost)." (Littleton)

"It seems to me that a statement of principle relative to accounting for fixed assets requires first and foremost a reavowal of the desirability of stating the amount of fixed assets on the basis of 'cost less accrued depreciation, depletion, and/or amortization.'" (Stempf)

"I am not ready to adopt without qualification the provision [Postulate 2, A.A.A.] that the fair market value of property acquired in exchange for securities measures the cost of the property. What of instances in which the securities issued have a readily ascertainable market price? May it be assumed that the market price of the securities is equivalent to the fair market value of the property?" (Stempf)

"Does writing up fixed assets actually increase the cost of using the assets, and does writing them down decrease the burden of owning assets that were bought at high price levels?" (Littleton)

It should be noted that Sanders, Hatfield, and Moore say that fixed asset values should be "based" upon the amount invested in them. This, of course, is not the same as saying that they should be shown at cost.

The American Accounting Association, on the other hand, emphasizes costs throughout, although they indicate the desirability of parenthetical disclosure if values other than costs are quoted.

The desirability of original cost as the basis for fixed asset valuation runs into difficulties, of course, when mixed aggregates of assets are acquired in exchange either for cash or securities. Appraisal often represents the only satisfactory expedient to adopt in such instances.

The general accounting practice of valuation at cost is sometimes referred to as a principle, often as a rule, but Hatfield[9] says it "clearly rests upon an assumption and is not an expression of a fundamental principle." From this viewpoint, therefore, cost valuation is a convention.

Paton also, in his *Accounting Theory,* intimates that this is a convention since he says that valuation at cost is based upon the assumption that business men are rational—that coercion, fraud, bad judgment, and carelessness are absent from business.

Still a third convention is involved in the valuation of fixed assets, namely, the going concern convention. The American Institute publication, *Examination of Financial Statements by Independent Public Accountants,* specifically labels this assumption as a convention, while Trouant refers to it in his list of "principles and conventions."

While the accounting profession generally frowns on the practice of writing up fixed assets and the consequent creation of unearned surplus, a different attitude is ordinarily taken in connection with writing down fixed asset values. It is held by many that there is little logical difference between that scaling down of asset values which occurs through a formal reorganization and a similar revaluation when fixed charges cannot be borne by normal operations. The proposition as set forth by Sanders, Hatfield, and Moore cannot be characterized as a principle, being little more than a mixture of conventions and rules having the merit of common acceptance.

III.C. "The proper showing of current assets requires:

    1. that inclusion or exclusion of particular items be determined on the same time basis as is applied to current liabilities;

9 Henry Rand Hatfield, *Accounting* (New York, D. Appleton-Century Co., Inc., 1927), p. 66.

2. that the values in general be the lowest of cost, replacement market, or realization, as may be applicable for the several items;

3. that reserves be plainly associated with the current assets to which they apply;

4. that separate mention be made of items not in the ordinary course of business." (S-H-M)

"The application of these principles should be broad enough to cover . . . reductions of inventory and investment costs to amounts allocable to succeeding periods." (Postulate 5, A.A.A.)

"Amounts due from stockholders, officers and employees and from affiliated companies should be separately shown and liabilities to such persons are preferably to be segregated." (Trouant)

"Assets realizable within one year and liabilities payable within one year are ordinarily shown as 'current.'" (Trouant)

"Notes or accounts receivable due from officers, employees, or affiliated companies must be shown separately and not included under a general heading such as Notes Receivable or Accounts Receivable." (Principle 5, A.I.A.)

". . . the fall in the market price for unsold merchandise represents an expiration of value just as much as sale of a fixed asset at a price lower than the 'cost less depreciation.'

"The accountant's task is to measure the original cost, and the portions which expire during each fiscal period. It makes no difference whether they expire through sale, depreciation, depletion, obsolescence, or fall in market-values." (Rorem)

Gilbert R. Byrne does not include inventory valuation among his eight propositions, although his Principle 5 probably applies. Principle 5, which reads "Losses, if probable, even though not actually incurred, should be provided for in arriving at net income," seems to apply to inventory valuation. The American Accounting Association's Postulate 7, which calls for parenthetical disclosure of all values other than unamortized costs, is probably not in conflict with that part of Postulate 5 above quoted. The American Accounting Association has apparently taken a definite stand in favor of the cost basis even with respect to inventories.

Nowhere do the difficulties of accounting terminology appear more evident than in connection with the practice of valuing inventories at the lower of either cost or market. Despite numerous references to it as a principle, it appears that the majority of accountants prefer calling it a rule.

Rorem, in his comments on the twenty postulates of the American Accounting Association, thinks that: "The rule of cost-less-depreciation for fixed assets is the same in principle as the rule of cost-or-market for current assets," but few accountants seem to agree with him. Paton takes a very definite stand on this cost or market rule, saying that it juggles income and is not conservative because the understatement of income in one period is balanced by an overstatement in the following period. George O. May thinks that the cost or market rule is based upon the viewpoint of the balance sheet audit and that some change of method or presentation may be necessary in view of the increasing importance of the profit and loss statement.

In the text of the Sanders, Hatfield, and Moore report, approval is given to such inventory methods as the last-in, first-out method and the base-stock method, all of which appears to be justified by the importance these authors attach to the doctrine of conservatism.

Theoretically, the convention of the going concern applies with just as much force to current assets as to fixed assets. In practice, particularly with such inventory methods as the base-stock method, resulting values may be so low as to be on a liquidation, rather than a going concern, basis. It is probably fair to say that the doctrine of conservatism and the balance sheet viewpoint have so influenced accounting practice that current asset valuation in many instances fails to give full weight to this particular convention.

This entire proposition referring to current assets represents such an intermingling of rule, convention, and doctrine as to render a specific labeling impossible.

III.D. "Particular care must be given in reporting deferred charges:
   1. to the distinction between charges inuring to the benefit of future periods and losses actually sustained;

2. to the basis of amortization, which in general should be the periods to be benefited by the deferred charges." (S-H-M)

Other lists of accounting principles have not included propositions which exactly match with this one but rather have treated deferred charges as an integral part of the whole problem of asset valuation.

The American Accounting Association, however, in its Postulate 6, made a suggestion which displeased a number of accountants. This postulate advocated that discount on bonds payable should be shown as a reduction of the face value of the indebtedness. This proposal aroused a considerable amount of criticism but since it refers to balance sheet arrangement only no discussion of the proposal seems justified here.

The proposition as advanced by Sanders, Hatfield, and Moore carries with it the concept of benefit to future periods which is generally considered to be an essential attribute of a deferred charge. The best accounting opinion seems to frown upon a deferred charge which is really in the nature of an unabsorbed loss. Montgomery advocates the rule that "deferred items must carry a benefit to future periods."

The logical application of this rule is often greatly modified by the doctrine of conservatism. Many expenditures which theoretically should be considered as deferred charges at the end of a period are currently absorbed, thus causing certain distortion in profit and loss statements.

III.E. "Contingent liabilities should be noted in the balance-sheet or in a footnote, if they are material, imminent, and of reasonably determinable amount." (S-H-M)

This is a specific application of the general doctrines of conservatism and disclosure to reporting. Practically all accounting authorities agree on the desirability of this proposition.

III.F. "Reacquired stock should be shown as a deduction from capital stock, unless exceptional circumstances justify showing it as an asset, when the reason should be given." (S-H-M)

This is a proposition to which most authorities would give full approval. The American Accounting Association made a

similar statement in its Postulate 16, and the American Insti
tute's committee in its Principle 4.

D. L. Trouant indicated that no profit or loss could be real
ized by a company on transactions in its own capital stock
There are three separate problems which really should be con
sidered in this proposition: (1) the method of showing re
acquired stock on the balance sheet, (2) the treatment of los
or gain on the sale of such reacquired stock, and (3) the treat
ment of dividends on such reacquired stock while held by th
corporation.

Whatever the common viewpoint toward treasury stock, i
can hardly be considered a principle in view of the fact that i
refers only to corporations and may be considered a legal
accounting rule rather than a principle of general accounting.

The next two propositions as shown by Sanders, Hatfield
and Moore have been combined since they both refer to capita
surplus.

III.G. "The restatement of capital assets at higher values results i
capital surplus. Restatement at lower values may result in a subtractio
from capital, capital surplus, or earned surplus, depending on circum
stances." (S-H-M)

III.H. "Capital surplus should not be utilized to relieve either earn
ings or earned surplus of charges which should be made against them.'
(S-H-M)

"Capital surplus, however created, should not be used to relieve th
income account of the current or future years of charges which woul
otherwise fall to be made there against. This rule might be subject t
the exception that where, upon reorganization, a reorganized compan
would be relieved of charges which would require to be made agains
income if the existing corporation were continued, it might be regarde
as permissible to accomplish the same result without reorganizatio
provided the facts were as fully revealed to and the action as formall
approved by the shareholders as in reorganization." (Principle 2
A.I.A.)

"Two major divisions of the capital of a corporation should b
recognized; paid-in capital and earned surplus. Subdivisions of eacl
section should appear as may be appropriate." (Postulate 14, A.A.A.)

"Paid-in capital consists of amounts received for shares issued: Capital stock, paid-in surplus, gains from the sale of reacquired shares and from the retirement of reacquired shares purchased at a discount, and transfers from earned surplus to capital-stock account by means of the stock dividends, recapitalizations, or otherwise. Reductions of paid-in capital accounts may arise from the redemption of outstanding shares, retirement of reacquired shares, or liquidating dividends." (Postulate 15, A.A.A.)

"Neither paid-in surplus nor surplus reserves should be availed of for the absorption of losses. Charges for all cost amortization, losses recognized, and other asset values expired should be by way of the income account to earned surplus." (Postulate 17, A.A.A.)

"Capital-stock and capital-surplus accounts, taken together, should represent the net contribution of the proprietors to the business enterprise." (Principle 6, Byrne)

"Surplus should be divided, where practicable, between 'earned surplus' and 'capital surplus.'" (Trouant)

Problems referring to capital surplus refer in part to accounting theory and in part to statutes. There is a growing feeling among accountants that statutory permission, expressed or implied, to do certain things should not be considered controlling by accountants. Logically, amounts contributed by stockholders should be considered as accounting capital, regardless of the form of the contribution, even though only a portion thereof may be legal capital.

As to the creation of capital surplus by writing up the value of assets, it is now well recognized that such a transaction is in the nature of a meaningless gesture. The temporary increase in apparent net worth is in the long run cancelled by higher depreciation.

Like other accounting propositions which are derived from statutes, decisions, or other law, its designation as a rule seems to be appropriate.

The next proposition, which has been classified as III.I., was not included in the list of twenty-five propositions of Sanders, Hatfield, and Moore, but seems to be required for completeness.

III.I. "Earned surplus should be credited or charged only with the following: the balance of the income account, as periodically reported;

distributions to stockholders; the excess of the cost over paid-in capital of shares purchased for redemption, or of reacquired shares retired; and reductions of surplus reserves, set aside for such purposes as the protection of working capital or the coverage of sinking funds. Earned surplus should include no credits from transactions in the company's own stock or transfers from paid-in capital or other capital accounts." (Postulate 18, A.A.A.)

"Where by proper corporate action a deficit has been absorbed through a reduction of par or stated value of capital stock or by transfer to paid-in surplus, earned surplus thereafter should be so labeled as to indicate that it dates from a point of time subsequent to the inception of the corporation." (Postulate 19, A.A.A.)

"Periodic reports should include analyses of capital stock and surplus accounts in sufficient detail to disclose the nature of the changes taking place during the accounting period, including increases and decreases in paid-in capital resulting from sales or purchases of shares." (Postulate 20, A.A.A.)

"Postulate No. 20 states that 'Periodic reports should include analyses of capital stock and surplus accounts in sufficient detail to disclose the nature of the changes taking place during the accounting period, including increases and decreases in paid-in capital from sales or purchases of shares.' The Committee might well add 'and increases to paid-in capital from stock dividends, properly dated, in order that a reader of the statements might be enabled to distinguish the capital amounts contributed by stockholders from those amounts which are provided out of the earnings of the corporation.'" (Husband)

"When companies are required to re-date their earned-surplus account after recapitalization proceedings involving extensive capital write-offs, even the average investor will have a new and valuable clue, on the face of the balance-sheet, as to what may have taken place in a company's past history." (Howard C. Greer, "Is It Desirable to Distinguish between Various Kinds of Surplus?" *The Journal of Accountancy,* April 1938)

"Dividend declarations should rest upon the existence of accumulated realized profits alone, that is, in accounting terminology, on earned surplus." (Littleton)

"Provision should be made each year through the income account not only for all known losses but also in reasonable amount for indeterminable losses, and such losses when definitely ascertained and liquidated may with propriety be charged against such provisions. Liabilities or reserves thus reared are, in my opinion, quite different from similar provisions made out of earned surplus for future possible losses." (Stempf)

The purpose of these propositions is to preserve the integrity of earned surplus. The provision for redating the earned surplus account is designed to take care of the occasional situation where such surplus is necessarily affected by substantial adjustments. Dependent as these propositions are upon law they properly may be indicated as rules.

IV.   CONSOLIDATED STATEMENTS

IV.A. "Consolidated statements should include only units which are effectively controlled by the parent company." (S-H-M)

IV. B. "The amount at which the stock of a subsidiary is carried in the parent company books constitutes in effect a revaluation of the subsidiary properties, either tangible or intangible, and is reflected as such in the consolidated balance-sheet." (S-H-M)

IV.C. "Surplus of subsidiaries existing at the time when control of them was acquired by a parent company should not be shown in the consolidated balance-sheet." (S-H-M)

IV.D. "Minority interests in subsidiaries may be shown in the consolidated balance-sheet at their net value in the subsidiary books." (S-H-M)

The above propositions have been included for the sole purpose of completing the Sanders, Hatfield, and Moore classification. Because they refer to consolidated statements, a phase of accounting which is not part of the subject matter of this book, it has been considered necessary to include the opinions of other authorities. Byrne and Trouant did not include any propositions in this category. Principle 3 of the American Institute of Accountants has intentionally been omitted and also all of the ten propositions prepared by Kohler[10] at the direction of the Executive Committee of the American Accounting Association.

10 E. L. Kohler, "Some Tentative Propositions Underlying Consolidated Reports." *The Accounting Review*, March 1938, p. 63.

V. Comments and Footnotes

V.A. "Comments, footnotes of reasonable length, and supplementary schedules may be used to elucidate items in the statements calling for explanation, or to supplement the statements." (S-H-M)

This is a general statement reflecting the doctrine of disclosure and refers only to reporting.

CHAPTER 15

ACCOUNTING DOCTRINES AND CONVENTIONS

Even a superficial survey indicates that the accounting propositions presented in the last chapter are not easily labeled.

Many of them consist of two or more elements. For example, one proposition suggested by Sanders, Hatfield, and Moore[1] reads: "Only income realized by the sale of goods or rendering of service is to be shown in the income statement. Unrealized income should not be recorded, nor utilized to absorb proper charges against earnings."

This particular proposition in some of its aspects is a convention since realization itself is a convention. There are also traces here of the doctrine of conservatism. And finally, the entire proposition might be considered a rule rather than a principle since it is definitely subject to exceptions, as in the case of substantial long-term uncompleted contracts or farm income.

This is only one example of the difficulties encountered in attempting to distinguish between rules, conventions, doctrines, and principles. In some few instances the accounting propositions were more simply stated. The Sanders, Hatfield, and Moore proposition, I.E., is the doctrine of consistency while I.F. is the doctrine of conservatism.

Complete agreement among accountants as to the usage of rule, principle, convention, and doctrine can hardly be expected in spite of the practical convenience which would result. Perhaps it will never be possible to make a clean-cut distinction between principles and rules. The task of distinguishing doctrines and conventions does not appear quite so formidable.

As previously indicated, this book assumes that there are four doctrines of accounting. Possibly some will think there are more, others less. The number to be included does not appear to

---

1 Sanders, Hatfield, and Moore, *A Statement of Accounting Principles* (New York, American Institute of Accountants, 1938), p. 114.

be important so long as conventions, rules, and any principles of narrow rather than broad application are omitted.

Doctrine of Conservatism.—Few outside of the accounting profession realize the overwhelming importance of the doctrine of conservatism and the extent to which that doctrine has understated balance sheet values and distorted profit and loss statements.

The doctrine of conservatism has been justified by analogy with the engineering "factor of safety" idea as an expression of the human desire to be "on the safe side."

Conservatism has often been urged for the protection of stockholders against their own rapacity for dividends. It protects directors against impairment of corporate capital. It has been mentioned as having a favorable effect upon labor relations. In part, this same doctrine may succeed in impressing tax assessors or political groups to whom a prosperous corporation is a bright and shining mark.

One potent reason for the present general acceptance of the doctrine of conservatism resulted from the threefold relationship between business man, banker, and accountant. The credit man is by nature somewhat suspicious of financial statements, in that he is inclined to look for overstated values. He has long been urging upon accountants the importance of conservatism.

Frequently repeated is the warning that conservatism should not be carried to the point of serious understatement of assets or earnings. This warning has been fully justified by past history, particularly in cases where conservatism has been used to depress values in order that insiders might profit.

Conservatism is one of those vague but sanctified concepts like honesty, morality, democracy, and Nordic supremacy, so much so that its critics generally consider it necessary to tread lightly as if on holy ground. Accordingly but little real effort has been made to measure the effects of conservatism.

The doctrine of conservatism is an old one—considerably older than consistency, disclosure, and materiality. References to the importance of "playing safe" and "erring on the safe side" are found in the accounting literature of many years ago.

MEANING OF CONSERVATISM. Oddly enough, the original meaning of conservatism was quite different from its present connotation. Formerly it referred to those attributes which characterized members of the Conservative Party in England.

The 1897 edition of the *Oxford English Dictionary* defines the adjective, conservative, as "characterized by a tendency to preserve or keep intact or unchanged." The 1911 edition of the *Century Dictionary* defined conservatism as "the disposition to maintain and adhere to the established order of things; opposition to innovation and change."

In neither of these definitions is there any reference to understatement. Strictly applied, either of these definitions would appear to be just as appropriate if applied to a consistent practice of overoptimistic reporting, i.e., it would be a change from overstatement to understatement which would be unconservative.

The implication of understatement now attaches to conservatism. This meaning was recognized by the *Oxford English Dictionary Supplement,* published in 1933, which added to its definitions the words: "Characterized by caution or moderation; (esp. of an estimate) purposely or deliberately low or 'on the right side.' " This dictionary adds that this particular meaning of the word originated in the United States.

As previously intimated, conservatism is more of a policy than a principle.

Policy is defined by the *Oxford English Dictionary* as "any course of action adopted as advantageous or expedient," and this definition is indicated as representing the chief living sense.

Conservatism is obviously not a principle,[2] since a principle is a fundamental truth whereas the essence of conservatism is understatement, and understatement "falls below the truth or fact."

APPLICATIONS OF CONSERVATISM. There are various methods of applying the doctrine of conservatism either in actual

2 That this depends upon the meaning attached to the word "conservative" is suggested by the following quotation from R. G. H. Smails in *The Canadian Chartered Accountant* (August 1938, p. 161): "It is possible that no word is more abused and no principle is more distorted than the word 'conservatism' and the principle which it represents."

bookkeeping or in the adjustments preliminary to the preparation of financial statements.

A common method is to charge capital expenditures to expense. The business which follows this practice will have in its possession a machine, a building, a right-of-way, or other material tangible asset which, in whole or in part, is not represented as an asset value in the records.

Another common method is overdepreciation, the effect of which is to amortize the cost of an asset over less than its useful life.

Still another method creates other unduly large reserves, particularly contingency reserves.

OBJECTIONS TO CONSERVATISM. There are serious objections to some applications of the doctrine of conservatism. The principal one and the most important is its effect upon comparative net profits. Thus, according to the *Accountants' Handbook*,[3] conservatism implies that "all charges of whatever nature are treated as attaching to current operation unless the nature of the transaction is such as to make such treatment clearly improper."

Any of the common methods of applying conservatism have a tendency to distort earnings so that during a period or several periods profits will appear unduly small, to be followed by a period or periods when the reverse effect is noticed. This is true in connection with the undervaluation of fixed assets which involves charges to costs or expenses which are unduly large.

The effect of such understatement of fixed asset values is to relieve future periods of part of their depreciation charges, with a consequent overstatement of income.

Nowhere is this effect more clearly demonstrated than in the case of inventories, and particularly in that application which has been referred to as the rule of cost or market. Since this will be fully analyzed in a later section, it is sufficient here to note that the weakness of the doctrine of conservatism lies in the fact that it must be followed sooner or later by overstatement of earnings.

---

3 *Accountants' Handbook* (New York, The Ronald Press Company, 1934), p. 1103.

Just as depressions are followed by booms, so is accounting understatement bound to be followed by accounting overstatement, and vice versa. Accordingly, there is only a temporary advantage to be gained from overstatement or understatement.

CONFLICTS AND CONTRADICTIONS. The matter of conjugate principles has already been mentioned.

Conservatism often conflicts with the convention of the "going concern." This occurs when values are so conservatively stated as to make them equivalent to liquidation values, as might happen in occasional applications of the base-stock method of inventory and which certainly happens when substantial non-current asset values are written down to nominal amounts such as $1.

Conservatism also may conflict with the doctrine of disclosure. The theory that stockholders should be protected against their own rapacity by telling them untruths about their corporation's condition is obviously opposed by the doctrine of disclosure. For some unexplained reason, the protection of the incoming investor has seemed to be a matter of greater importance than discouragement of one whose holdings have already been acquired.

Conservatism is opposed to consistency, this conflict being particularly evident in the effect of the cost or market rule on earnings. Conservatism also conflicts with that desirable but often unattainable accounting ideal of matching costs with income.

Even the most firm advocates of conservatism seldom attempt to justify it upon logical grounds. And this is indeed wise since it is simple enough to indicate its lack of logic. It is illogical to adopt a procedure which understates balance sheet values and at the same time cannot fail to overstate the earnings of some future period. It is illogical to disclose contingent liabilities without at the same time disclosing contingent assets. It is illogical to understate values and insist upon adequate disclosure.

Montgomery[4] summed it all up when he said, "The so-called

4 Robert H. Montgomery, "Accountants' Limitations," *The Journal of Accountancy*, October 1927. p. 251.

conservatism of the accountant hides understated values which it can never harm anyone to know or hides overstated values which it would be useful to know."

The insistence by nearly all authorities on the importance of conservatism insures its influence upon accounting and reporting for many years to come. Hence, conservatism is distinctly entitled to a ranking position among accounting doctrines.

Doctrine of Consistency.—The doctrine of consistency has been so greatly emphasized since the revised form of audit certificate was presented to the accounting fraternity in 1933, that it might easily appear to be a new accounting policy. On the contrary, competent accountants have long recognized the importance of consistency.

Arthur Lowes Dickinson talked about it in 1904. William R. McKenzie criticized the cost or market rule on the grounds of inconsistency in 1909. In 1918 the Bureau of Internal Revenue[5] issued a ruling which referred to consistent inventory practice in the following words:

> In order clearly to reflect income, the inventory practice of a taxpayer should be consistent from year to year, and greater weight is to be given to consistency than to any particular method of inventorying or basis of valuation so long as the method or basis used is substantially in accord with these regulations.

THE AUDIT CERTIFICATE. May,[6] who was chairman of the Special Committee of the American Institute which revised the audit certificate, intimated what the committee's attitude would be, in an address at the annual meeting of the American Institute of Accountants, October 1932, at which time he used the words, "a fair and consistent application of acceptable methods of accounting." This wording, incidentally, had a marked advantage over the one which the committee subsequently adopted, in which the word "methods" was unfortunately changed to "principles."

To what extent the Securities and Exchange Commission

5 George O. May, "Improvement in Financial Accounts," *The Journal of Accountancy,* May 1937, p. 353.
6 George O. May, "Influence of the Depression on the Practice of Accountancy," *The Journal of Accountancy,* November 1932, p. 345.

influenced the increased popularity of consistency is hard to say. The Commission has strenuously advocated the doctrine of consistency, without, however, making the error of referring to consistency of principles exclusively. Blough,[7] while chief accountant of the Commission, clarified the Commission's attitude in the following words:

> So far as the commission is concerned, it does not matter what the definition of the word "principle" may be. Its rules specify that the "accounting principles and procedures" followed by the registrant shall be commented upon. What is important to the reader of the financial statements in this respect is whether the company has been sufficiently consistent in the keeping of its accounts that the statements of one period are comparable with the statements of another, or whether they contain differences that may be misleading.

INCREASING IMPORTANCE OF CONSISTENCY. Probably not one, but several, causes were responsible for the increased recognition of consistency that was apparent during the years 1932-1934.

The country was just passing through a major depression which focussed attention upon the inadequacy of the balance sheet audit because of its comparative disregard of income verification.

Many accepted practices of accounting crystallized during the period when the balance sheet audit was popular. They were discovered to be somewhat inappropriate and misleading when emphasis was shifted to the profit and loss statement. Many of these accepted practices were fathered by the doctrine of conservatism. It is more than likely that official insistence upon consistency was intended as a sweeping correction of some of the methods used to produce conservatism in balance sheets. Instead of giving separate consideration to each accounting practice which needed correction, it was apparently believed that application of the doctrine of consistency would sufficiently correct all of them. Naturally, however, conservatism was in no degree abandoned with the result that these two doctrines often conflict.

---

7 Carman G. Blough, "Accountants' Certificates," *The Journal of Accountancy,* February 1938, p. 109.

MEANING OF CONSISTENCY. Formal definitions of the words "consistency" and "consistent" are only partly helpful in reflecting the meaning adopted by accountants.

The *Oxford English Dictionary* uses as synonyms "agreement, harmony, compatibility (*with* something, *of* things, or *of* one thing *with* another)."

It is also interesting to note the relationship between consistency and compatibility as explained by *Crabb's English Synonyms:*

> *Compatibility* has principally a reference to plans and measures *consistency,* to character, conduct and station. Everything is *compatible* with a plan which does not interrupt its prosecution; everything is *consistent* with a person's station by which it is neither degraded nor elevated. It is not *compatible* with the good discipline of a school to allow of foreign interference; it is not *consistent* with the elevated and dignified character of a clergyman to engage in the ordinary pursuits of other men.

These quotations are of no more than general interest. The accountant employs the word "consistent" with a limited meaning.

He does not believe that the doctrine of consistency is offended when he adopts a certain method for one client and a different method for another. Nor does he consider it inconsistent to adopt the valuation rule of cost or market and at the same time submit comparative profit and loss statements which have been distorted thereby. The accountant does not consider it inconsistent to apply the convention of realization to gains without applying it to costs, expenses, and losses.

The doctrine of consistency, so far as the accountant is concerned, refers to one particular accounting entity and its application is considered satisfactory when the entity's accounting methods, practices, or usages which have some background of general acceptance remain unchanged from period to period.

APPLICATIONS OF CONSISTENCY. This convenient interpretation has, of course, certain interesting advantages, since it permits the accountant to use his judgment as between clients without being accused of contradicting himself. Thus, one client may adopt the base-stock method of inventory, another the first-in, first-out method, a third the average cost method, a fourth the net selling price method. If each client keeps on using his selected method from period to period, then there is no offense against consistency.

It was perhaps this viewpoint which prompted George O. May to explain that each individual company was supposed to have its own special code of principles of accounting.

Even this limited significance of the doctrine of consistency has measurably improved accounting reports. There is reason to hope that the doctrine of consistency will become the dominating accounting policy and that its observance will do much to place accounting upon a logical rather than a pragmatic basis. The only real opposition ever expressed to this doctrine comes from those who misunderstand its meaning and who fear that it may lead to uniform accounting such as might be imposed by governmental or bureaucratic edict.

CONSISTENCY AND COMPARABILITY. The suggestion that consistency tends to remedy certain common and more or less arbitrary accounting practices, thus promoting historical comparability of financial statements, appears to have a sound statistical background.

Statistical respect for consistency is evidenced by such observations as those made by A. L. Bowley, the well-known English authority, reported in part by Cohen[8] and in part by the Webbs[9] as follows:

It is a well-known maxim of statistics that we can study changes even when the definition or the enumeration is faulty.

It is usually indifferent on which side of a line relatively small marginal quantities are placed; the rate of change is hardly affected. More important is the consideration that while very varying estimates may be made by different investigators for one date the change shown over a period is definite if the method and classifications are the same throughout.

8 Jerome B. Cohen, "The Misuse of Statistics," *Journal of the American Statistical Association*, December 1938, p. 662.
9 Sidney and Beatrice Webb, *Methods of Social Study* (London, Longmans. Green & Co., 1932), p. 205.

Superficially, Bowley's comments seem to refer to the same doctrine of consistency endorsed by accountants. There is, however, some reason to doubt whether this is strictly true.

Bowley is talking about independent enumerations of the "census type."

A count of the number of farms in the state of Illinois in 1930 will be greatly influenced by the statistical definition of a farm. Using different definitions, several enumerators might easily obtain widely different counts.

If the same enumerators, each using the same definition as before, made counts in 1940, their results would still be widely apart. But for each enumerator, based upon his own particular definition, the percentage of increase or decrease in the number of farms would closely correspond with the percentages computed by the other enumerators.

This is, however, not the same type of situation as is commonly noted in accounting where to the problems of enumeration and classification is added that of periodic allocation. In the farm census, no question arises whether a given farm should be included in the 1930 or the 1940 total. Such decisions regarding periodic allocation are, however, typical of accounting.

Errors in accounting allocation may or may not cause distortion in periodic profits, depending upon such factors as business stability, continuity of policies, price levels, and other significant characteristics. Consistency will not cure periodic profit distortion when instability, shifting policies, and fluctuating prices tend to emphasize in one period as compared with another the effects of deliberate or unintentional errors in allocating income, costs, expenses, and losses to accounting periods.

The accounting doctrine of consistency does, therefore, tend to remedy inaccuracies of enumeration in so far as consistency is applied to definition and classification. It must not, however, be relied upon to correct comparisons which are affected by periodic distortions such as often are caused by conservatism or its lack.

Doctrine of Disclosure.—The doctrine of disclosure refers primarily to reporting rather than accounting. For example, the accounting mechanism does not provide any means for indicating the amount of arrearage of preferred stock dividends. Application of the doctrine of disclosure requires the inclusion in accounting reports of information regarding such arrears.

It might be argued that the doctrine of disclosure is only collaterally related to accounting, since it is applicable to all reports including those of engineers, economists, statisticians, lawyers, as well as accountants.

Furthermore, even in its accounting aspect it is not limited to accounting facts and figures, but is in part designed to supplement the limitations of accounting by revealing information with which the accounting mechanism is inadequate to deal.

AUTHORSHIP OF DISCLOSURE. The doctrine of disclosure as it specifically applies to accountants' reports is subject to an assumption which is rapidly receiving that general acceptance which characterizes a convention.

Regardless of the actual facts, it is assumed that disclosure is always made by the company or other accounting entity, not by the professional accountants who have been employed to examine the accounts and statements.

Referring specifically to the footnote method of disclosure, the chief accountant of the Securities and Exchange Commission at a round-table discussion during the 1937 American Institute Convention said:[10]

Financial statements are the presentation of the company, and the related footnotes are the presentation of the company.

In my opinion, it is wholly improper for a balance-sheet or a profit-and-loss statement to make a statement and then in a footnote to say it is not so.

In some cases it is almost as if the company were to say in the face of the balance-sheet. "We have five hogs," and then in the footnote say, "It is not five hogs; it is four sheep." The footnotes are therefore explanation. They expand facts which are already in the financial statements, or explain what is there.

Some time later, a member[11] of the Commission asserted:

10 Carman G. Blough, *Fiftieth Anniversary Celebration* (New York, American Institute of Accountants, 1938), p. 203.
11 George C. Mathews, "Accounting in the Regulation of Security Sales,' *The Accounting Review,* September 1938, p. 231.

There have been many complaints originating in the accounting profession against the use of footnotes in financial statements to explain the use of improper accounting procedures or to correct the effect of items in the financial statements themselves.

The assumption involved here may partake of the nature of a convention. The public accountant usually applies the doctrine of disclosure, sometimes finding it necessary to force it down the throat of his client, but when he has been successful it is generally agreed that the client himself has done the disclosing, not the accountant.

APPLICATIONS OF DISCLOSURE. The common application of this doctrine to accounting statements is by means of descriptive captions, or footnotes.

Where disclosure refers to some matter unrelated to accounting or not directly affecting accounting figures, other devices may be employed. Thus, if a company has in the past been convicted of an income tax evasion, disclosure of this fact might be required. Since it has no direct relationship to the accounting statements, it properly would be handled by comment in the text of the report.

Broadly speaking, the doctrine of disclosure requires the revelation of information which, if withheld, might influence a prospective creditor's decision to loan funds or a prospective investor's decision to buy securities.

In its more limited application to accounting, the doctrine of disclosure is commonly held to refer to such matters as the basis of asset valuations, the existence of material contingent liabilities, arrears of preferred stock dividends, and probable price losses on future commitments. The fact that property is pledged to secure debts must be disclosed and information must be given with respect to assets or liabilities the status of which may readily be changed, such as assets acquired under terms of a hire-purchase agreement or liabilities (including various classes of stock) which have conversion privileges. The subdivision of surplus into such classifications as earned surplus, appreciation surplus, donated surplus, or other groupings represents the application of this doctrine. The redating of surplus after informal reorganizations or substantial write-offs represents another example of necessary disclosure.

ACCOUNTING JUDGMENT.   Application of the doctrine of disclosure often tests the accountant's judgment.

He has no obligation to insist that his client disclose trade secrets or other information which could be used harmfully by his competitors or other outsiders. Furthermore, there is always a danger that overdisclosure of a variety of minor matters may result in giving the reader of a report a false impression. Not knowing where the line should be drawn between material and immaterial disclosures, accountants have been tempted to play safe and as a result in many instances have presented profitable, well-managed corporations in such a poor light as to be actually misleading.

There was for some time a feeling of apprehension that this practice might result in frightening investors, although it was soon discovered that most of them had neither the patience nor the inclination to read elaborate prospectuses.

A particularly unfavorable picture might be presented, for example, in the case of a company guaranteeing its product in some unusual way or for some unusual term. Such guarantees might easily involve large contingent liabilities and yet as a practical matter might be relatively unimportant. Clearly the showing of such contingent liabilities is entirely a matter of good judgment. This same saving rule of common sense is also applicable to many other problems of disclosure.

Doctrine of Materiality.—The fourth and possibly the least important of the four accounting doctrines is that of materiality.

Materiality clearly implies relative importance. Mention has already been made of materiality of information as it applied to registration with the Securities and Exchange Commission.

More closely related to accounting is the problem of materiality of amounts. If a certain accounting procedure is regarded as generally accepted and entirely proper for a transaction amounting to $10,000, should it be applied in exactly the same way to a transaction amounting to only $1? To what extent will such decisions be influenced by the size of the company using the procedure? Clearly a $10,000 transaction for the United States Steel Corporation is no more important than a $100 transaction for a grocery store.

Accountants usually take the viewpoint that it is impractical to be too meticulous about trivial amounts. If an accounting decision is not sufficiently important to influence the comparability of financial statements, there may be some hint of immateriality.

Materiality is held to depend also upon the accounts affected. An error of $50 in a substantial inventory account might be held immaterial. An error of $50 in the cash account might be regarded as highly important.

The implication of materiality is obvious in most of the standard works on accounting. The pamphlet, *Examination of Financial Statements by Independent Public Accountants,* has various references direct or indirect to materiality. But this is not a matter of complete accounting agreement and, increasingly, voices are raised in protest against improper accounting short-cuts or entries tolerated merely because of the insignificance of the amounts involved.

Comparison of Doctrines.—This completes the present discussion of the four doctrines of accounting. Measured by their effects and measured also by the amount of discussion which they have caused, they seem to rank in importance in about the order given here.

The doctrine of conservatism has for many years been the most important. It is still important, but the doctrine of consistency is assuming greater and greater prominence. Where the two conflict, there is some reason to believe that the doctrine of consistency will influence many accounting decisions against the less logical, often arbitrary, dictates of conservatism.

The doctrine of disclosure is of first rank importance in connection with all investor relationships. Strictly as an accounting doctrine for use even in bread-and-butter audits, accountants are more and more inclining toward increased disclosure. It can scarcely be doubted that the doctrine of disclosure is essential to honest, adequate reporting.

Finally, the doctrine of materiality, of front rank importance as applied to registration with the Securities and Exchange Commission, is for general accounting work perhaps the least important of the four.

Accounting Conventions.—Accounting conventions conform substantially to the dictionary definition but in addition they often have certain special connotations. Perhaps this is true of most conventions; the theatrical convention of a three-sided room becomes an absurdity when divorced from the stage; the mathematical convention of plus and minus is meaningless when considered apart from mathematics; certain conventions of card games have no significance save in relation to actual card play.

NATURE OF CONVENTIONS. It has been suggested that conventions are the foundations upon which the superstructure of accounting doctrine, principle, and rule is raised. If this be true, then all accounting thought is influenced by the artificiality of these elemental accounting assumptions. In fact, many of the accounting errors that have been made by courts, lawyers, economists, and business men have been due to their failure to realize the fictional element inherent in accounting conventions.

Investigation fails to disclose any attempt to list and describe all of the conventions of accounting. Paton, in *Accounting Theory,* came close to such a list when he described a number of "postulates" of accounting referring to them from time to time as "assumptions." In other works, scattered references are made to accounting conventions but with little attempt to organize them into a definite related pattern. It is, in fact, doubtful whether anyone could feel certain of recognizing and listing all of them. There are, however, certain conventions which are well known and are generally admitted to represent fundamental assumptions.

ENTITY CONVENTION. Chief among accounting conventions is that of the entity.

Whether the entity convention originated in the manner described by some authors is a matter of slight importance. It exists regardless of origin and regardless of whether it is fully recognized by those who use it. This is evidenced by the accounting equation itself. It is evidenced by the titles given to accounting statements. It is evidenced by the types of records kept by individual proprietors who own two or more business units. The only legitimate quarrel anyone can have with this convention lies in the extent and consistency of its application.

Plainly, if it is fundamental to accounting, the entity convention cannot be dropped as soon as it becomes embarrassing. If the double entry accounting record implies an invisible artificial person having possession of certain assets and owing corresponding amounts to others, then obviously lawyers and economists cannot be permitted to rule out this concept merely because the proprietor's investment is not a *legal* liability of the business to him.

It is, furthermore, generally customary to speak of a corporation or other entity as if it made profits. Thus, a corporation is reported to have enjoyed certain profits for a year and taxes are levied against it accordingly. Also it is commonly said that a man owns "a profitable business" or that a company "shares its profits with its employees." Nearly all business thinking and business writing evidences the conviction that it is the entity which makes profits or suffers losses.

That this is strictly untrue is a matter of slight importance save in connection with any attempt to determine the nature and significance of profits. From such an exploratory viewpoint it must, of course, be recognized that the adoption of the entity convention leads irresistibly to the conclusion that the entity cannot possibly make a profit or a loss but can merely increase or decrease its debt to proprietorship.

Since the entity has no existence save as it explains the relationships involved in the accounting equation, the equation, as expressed by the balance sheet, is derived directly from the entity convention and inherits all of its faults and its virtues.

VALUATION CONVENTION. The second important accounting convention is that of valuation.

The accounting entity comes into possession of various types of assets—buildings, automobiles, merchandise, raw materials, and machinery. Conceivably it might be possible, although it would be impractical and inconvenient, to adopt the entity convention and at the same time reject the convention of valuation, but the problem of record keeping involved would be most difficult. It is, however, based upon this possibility that the convention of valuation is considered to be separate and distinct from the entity convention.

Derived from the valuation convention are such subordinate conventions as that of realization and also the assumption of the equality of dollars regardless of purchasing power. That this latter convention is implicit in the whole theory of accounting has not always been recognized by those who invest in enterprises when price levels are low and whose investments plus accumulated profits are recovered by them when price levels are high. In this situation the convention of valuation may provide the basis for reporting dollar profits, whereas from the investor's personal viewpoint of purchasing power he has suffered a loss.

Excluded from the valuation convention is the proposition, "that the historical amounts be adjusted to something nearer to practical present-day conditions," which Sanders, Hatfield, and Moore[12] called an accounting convention.

If it be conceded that dollar valuations are no more than symbols, then it follows, in theory at least, that consistency results from leaving the symbols unchanged. Thus, if the symbol $5 is used to represent one ton of fuel, as long as that ton of fuel remains intact, the symbol itself should theoretically remain unchanged. There is a relation here which is somewhat akin to symbols in algebra. Essentially all that the convention of valuation really accomplishes is substitution. Confusion results from the use of the monetary symbol coupled with a shifting viewpoint. Instead of calling a ton of coal $5, it might be called X. Just so long as the ton of coal remained, it would be symbolized as X, but as soon as half of it was consumed, it would be symbolized as $X/2$.

When the dollar is used as a symbol, however, it is entirely too easy to shift from the equation viewpoint to the trading viewpoint. As soon as the trading viewpoint is adopted, it is inevitable that consideration will be given to changes in the

12 Sanders, Hatfield, and Moore, *A Statement of Accounting Principles* (New York. American Institute of Accountants, 1938), p. 2.

market value of coal so that for the original symbol of $5 another symbol of perhaps $4 may be substituted, even though the physical thing represented by the symbol has not changed.

The dollar symbol which represents an asset in the accounting equation theoretically remains unchanged as long as the physical asset itself remains unchanged. Where the quantity of that asset, as in the case of coal, is actually reduced, then the financial symbol is proportionately altered. It is this type of adjustment which occurs when property is destroyed or disappears in such a manner that a lesser quantity of it remains.

By analogy this adjustment of symbols has been extended to cover depreciation, in spite of the fact that there is no lessening in the physical size or weight of the building, machine, etc., which is being depreciated. There is, however, a change of physical usefulness which the analogy recognizes. It may be maintained that depletion and depreciation are more closely related to one another than to changes in value due to lowered price levels.

Based upon this line of reasoning, it would appear that the suggestion of Sanders, Hatfield, and Moore represents a combination of the doctrines of conservatism and disclosure rather than a true convention of accounting. The discussion centering around this particular point does not represent any argument for or against the common practice of adjusting amounts "to something nearer to practical present-day conditions," but rather refers only to terminology and classification.

ACCOUNTING PERIOD CONVENTION. The third major convention of accounting is that of accounting periods which, by introducing an artificial and arbitrary feature into the simple mechanism of accounting, has sired numerous subsidiary conventions, including the convention of accruals and of deferments, of amortization and depreciation, of accounting adjustments, and finally the convention of the going business, which has no significance save in relation to accounting periods.

OTHER CONVENTIONS. There are, of course, other conventions which are commonly accepted and seldom questioned. One of them is the convention of debit and credit.

Mention has already been made of Paton's suggestion that there is a convention of sequences and also a convention of cost transferals. Finally, there is the convention by which one person is considered, for record keeping purposes, as if he were two or more persons.[13]

Conclusion.—The list need not be elaborated here in view of previous extended discussion of accounting conventions. It should, however, be reasserted that, at least, the three basic conventions, i.e., entity, valuation, and accounting period, together with their derivations are controlling in that they have predetermined the general design of the accounting mechanism.

---

[13] According to Peragallo, this convention was used as long ago as 1867 by Francesco Marchi who employed "the fiction of ascribing more personalities than one to the proprietor if he assumed duties usually delegated to his subordinates, maintaining separate accounts for each of these several personalities." (Edward Peragallo, *Origin and Evolution of Double Entry Bookkeeping,* New York, American Institute Publishing Co., Inc., 1938, p. 109.

CHAPTER 16

ACCOUNTING PRINCIPLES AND RULES

Assuming that certain doctrines and conventions of accounting are distinguishable from other propositions, it would appear simple to eliminate them from the composite list in Chapter 14 after which each remaining proposition could be identified as a rule or a principle. Unfortunately, this is not feasible.

The composite list is an assembly of separate lists prepared by various groups or individuals. Each of these separate lists represents a mixture of doctrines, conventions, rules, and principles. It is as though five different cooks were to combine ingredients varying in number and varying in kind, after which the five batches were mixed together. Thereafter it would be impossible for anyone to separate the eggs from the butter or the two of them from the flour.

Tests for Principles.—It is, of course, true that certain tests for principles have been suggested in Chapter 13, but it is doubtful whether such tests will be generally acceptable because their application indicates that there are few, if any, principles of accounting.

That this possibility has been recognized is clear from the writings of various authors who have doubted whether there are more than a few principles of accounting. May,[1] for example, reports that the Special Committee of the American Institute, of which he was chairman, found itself unable to suggest more than half a dozen principles of accounting and he followed this with the significant statement that "even those were rules rather than principles, and were, moreover, admittedly subject to exception." If this was the opinion of the committee which was responsible for starting the whole controversy, it is by no

---

[1] George O. May, "Improvement in Financial Accounts," *The Journal of Accountancy*, May 1937, p. 335.

means improbable that serious consideration of the tests, discussed in a preliminary way in Chapter 13, would lead to the unhappy conclusion that there are no principles of accounting.

VARYING STATUTES TEST. Among the tests which have been suggested is a legal test—are principles of accounting the same regardless of law and judicial decisions? Broad[2] phrased a similar question with reference to economic principles, thus:

Are we to assume that economic principle will produce one result in California and one directly contrary in other states just because the relative state laws differ? Or is economic principle to give precedence to the varying legal requirements of different states?

If such questions be answered affirmatively, then all accounting propositions which are related to or derived from statute, ukase, or decision are rules rather than principles. This applies to that entire field which is generally referred to as corporation accounting, since the corporation itself is a creature of the law and the typical corporation accounts are accounts which have been made necessary by law. It applies to all types of tax accounting. It applies to those semi-public enterprises like the railroads and utilities the accounting for which is shaped by decisions of governmental control bodies. Finally, it applies to the accounting for municipal and governmental units.

The general proposition that principles of accounting, as compared with methods and rules, cannot be influenced by law was somewhat supported by Staub[3] who advanced an opinion that accounting principles "are not necessarily controlled by the corporate statutes of a given state."

Sanders, Hatfield, and Moore[4] have already been quoted as thinking otherwise at least in relation to the liabilities or equities side of the balance sheet, asserting that "the principles of accounting are dictated by legal considerations."

VARYING PROPRIETORSHIP TEST. Another test is implied in the following question—are principles of accounting the same

[2] Samuel J. Broad, "Some Comments on Surplus Account," *The Journal of Accountancy*, October 1938, p. 218.

[3] Walter A. Staub, *Fiftieth Anniversary Celebration* (New York, American Institute of Accountants, 1938), p. 192.

[4] Sanders, Hatfield, and Moore, *A Statement of Accounting Principles* (New York, American Institute of Accountants, 1938), p. 3.

regardless of the form of proprietorship? If the answer to this is in the affirmative, propositions which apply solely to one rather than all forms of proprietorship must be eliminated as principles.

Sanders, Hatfield, and Moore answer "no" to this question. The American Accounting Association[5] was not quite so definite but did touch upon the matter by saying, "The application of satisfactory accounting principles to paid-in capital and surplus is handicapped in some degree by conflicting provisions of corporate laws."

VARYING INDUSTRIES TEST. The third test is represented by the question—do principles of accounting remain the same regardless of the type of activity recorded? If so, then all propositions which do not apply equally to banks, mining companies, manufacturers, governmental units, hospitals, and farms must be rules rather than principles.

The difficulty was referred to by the American Accounting Association[5] which observed that: "Business enterprises are so different in nature that the principles applied to any single corporation must make allowance for its individual characteristics and for the characteristics of the industry as well."

TEST OF LOGIC. Littleton[6] discussed tests for principles from a somewhat different approach.

Recognizing that the word "principles" has been extensively used "with little discrimination in the context between the truths of accountancy (the expressions of fundamental reality upon which right doing rests) and the practices of accountants (the customary ways of doing what needs to be done)" and recognizing that each discussion about principles "usually contains a mixture of axioms, conventions, generalizations, methods, rules, postulates, practices, procedures, principles, and standards," he proposes a test of principles which employs a syllogistic method of major and minor premises and conclusions.

Unfortunately, while he admits that "we need a test by

5 Executive Committee of the American Accounting Association, "A Tentative Statement of Accounting Principles Affecting Corporate Reports," *The Accounting Review*, June 1936, pp. 191, 188.
6 A. C. Littleton, "Tests for Principles," *The Accounting Review*, March 1938, p. 16.

which to recognize a proposition as a statement of accounting principle," he adopted Byrne's[7] idea of "a coercive or compelling force." Byrne adopted his words "coercive or compelling" because, as he says, "inherent in accounting principles are business laws which must be obeyed if in the long run the enterprise is to survive."

This attempt to tie up accounting with business is unfortunate. Are there then no accounting principles in social clubs or municipalities, in which survival is not necessarily dependent upon the observance of economic law?

It seems obvious that accounting principles, if there are any, must represent fundamental truths for all accounting, not merely for the commercial phases thereof. Littleton,[8] however, subscribes to a more limited viewpoint when he says, "Accounting principles, then, express fundamental truths about a business enterprise."

This primary assumption underlies his syllogistic tests with the result that his conclusions are tinged accordingly. Throughout his argument appear such words as "economic facts," "management," "managerial policies for a business," "economic enterprise," "selling prices," "bargain prices of services rendered," etc.

What conclusions might be reached by Littleton's method based upon other assumptions is an open question. It is not believed, however, that the tests proposed are valid for principles intended to represent "fundamental truths" applied to accounting for all types of enterprises or types of proprietorship and all types of legal restrictions and control.

Substitute Terminology.—Later Littleton[9] proposed that accountants adopt the word "standards" to replace "principles" or "rules."

He suggests that the real reason why some men say there are no principles, or so few principles that they constitute over-

7 Gilbert R. Byrne, "To What Extent Can the Practice of Accounting Be Reduced to Rules and Standards?" *The Journal of Accountancy*, November 1937, p. 371.

8 A. C. Littleton, "Tests for Principles," *The Accounting Review*, March 1938, p. 17.

9 A. C. Littleton, "High Standards of Accounting," *The Journal of Accountancy*, August 1938, pp. 99, 100.

generalizations, is because "the term 'principles' does not carry the necessary connotation of adequate flexibility." He adds that: "The word 'principle' will generally suggest a universality which obviously cannot exist in a service institution such as accounting." Accounting standards, in his opinion, should have a direct reference to managerial judgment and should be flexible in order to permit departures from the standards, although he adds that "the burden of proof falls upon the one who advocates a variation."

Littleton[10] summarizes by saying, "The use of the conception of 'standards' instead of 'principles' would carry with it the thought of stating standards as points of departure, while making plain the necessity for clear justification for any variations from the standard." The reverse of rigid codification of rules, this concept would emphasize the semi-judicial nature of public accounting. Unfortunately, it appears that accountants may be too deeply committed to the word "principles" to accept this desirable substitute.

Conjugate Principles.—The attempt to formulate principles of accounting has undoubtedly been discouraging because of the element of conflict, although workers in this field might well take heart from the excellent discussion of conjugate principles in Lowell's *Conflicts of Principle.*

Before accountants need to worry about conjugate principles, however, the primary question must first be solved—are there *any* accounting principles? The observations of such authors as F. P. Byerly, who points out a conflict of principles in connection with treasury stock, and W. A. Paton, who proves a conflict between realization and the proposition of cost or market valuation, are interesting, thoroughly logical, but perhaps of little practical benefit until the accountants have decided that the propositions referred to really are principles of accounting.

If at some future time accounting propositions of any type are proved to be principles, then the fact of their occasional conflict does not necessarily invalidate them.

10 A. C. Littleton, "High Standards of Accounting," *The Journal of Accountancy,* August 1938, p. 104.

Engineering Analogy.—Attempts have been made by analogy and otherwise to dispose of some of these vexing difficulties in distinguishing between principles and rules or reconciling conflicts between various accounting practices and usages.

One such attempt was made by Byrne[11] in his analogy between accounting and engineering.

He referred to the designing of the Manhattan and Williamsburg bridges, which were proposed to span the same stream. He said, "Presumably sound engineering principles were applied to the problem in each case. In the application of those principles the results, so far as appearance of the two structures are concerned, are quite different, yet no one accuses the engineers of having applied different principles to their respective problems merely because the results of such application have not been identical bridges."

The analogy appears to be questionable. In the first place it refers to engineering *design* as compared with accounting *operations*. If the comparison were between engineering design and accounting system design the illustration would be more appropriate.

Furthermore, it compares accounting and engineering, which may not be entirely fair since they refer to different types of professional activity.

Whether engineers have succeeded in formulating certain principles as fundamental truths cannot be affirmed, but if so they doubtless have reference to physical properties of materials, whereas in accounting they are concerned with such intangible matters as recording and reporting according to a specialized, highly conventionalized, and strictly limited mechanism. And it is more than possible that any principles involved pertain primarily to the subject matter of reporting rather than of recording.

Statistical Analogy.—In attempting to examine the possibility just mentioned, another type of analogy may be appropriate.

[11] Gilbert R. Byrne, "To What Extent Can the Practice of Accounting Be Reduced to Rules and Standards?" *The Journal of Accountancy*, November 1937, p. 369.

Accounting procedure is perhaps more closely related to statistics than to any other field. In fact, it is probably fair to say that accounting is basically a specialized and conventionalized branch of statistics.

Suppose the inquiry had to do with principles of statistics rather than principles of accounting. Statistics, like accounting, can be applied to numerous fields. Thus, statisticians may be concerned with problems of sociology, economics, biology, law, medicine, etc. Because, for example, a statistician specializes in sociology, do the principles of sociology thereby become principles of statistics? Because the statistician investigates phenomena having certain relationships to law, do principles of law thereby become principles of statistics? Similarly, do principles of economics become principles of statistics?

All of this appears to be most doubtful. The science of statistics has to do with the methods of collecting, recording, and interpreting numerical data and can be applied to any field without at the same time adopting as its own the particular principles of that field.

Similarly, does it not appear that accounting is a mechanism more conventionalized than general statistics but still a mechanism the purpose of which is to collect and record statistical data expressible in financial units? Are not the same general methods of collection classification and interpretation employed in both?

Accordingly, are not many or all of the principles of accounting mere borrowings?

There seems to be some merit to this general viewpoint, unacceptable as it may be to those who must support the theory that there are principles of accounting or otherwise, as Byrne has said, "stultify themselves."

The tests proposed, the analogies suggested and some, at least, of the opinions quoted seem to represent a fairly good case against the existence of accounting principles. Perhaps it was May's belief that principles of accounting are not the same in various localities, in various industries, or in situations involving various types of proprietorship that led to his conclusion that the accounting for each separate corporation was based upon an individual code of principles.

If the various tests proposed, particularly the "varying statutes test," are regarded as valid, then those who have attempted to codify principles of accounting should find it desirable to eliminate from their lists all so-called principles which are derived from or dependent upon corporate statutes, legal decisions, and those rulings handed down by governmental bodies which have in fact almost the same coercive power as statutory law.

If to these various lists the "varying proprietorship test" is applied, still more so-called principles would call for elimination, and finally, if application were made of the "varying industries test," it would result in a further weeding out, and there would be few if any propositions left in any of these lists which would not call clearly for relabelling as doctrines, conventions, rules, or mere statements of opinion.

The frank admission that there are no principles of accounting will leave the accounting profession in the more defensible position of being guided by general doctrines, specific conventions, and various rules, practices, methods, and standards derived from the relationship between accounting and other fields, which by the test of experience have been proved practical and acceptable.

By such admission the accountant will be relieved of that embarrassment and awkwardness which results from trying to justify a proposition as a principle of accounting because it is based upon a principle of mathematics, or because it is derived from a principle of economics, or because it is required by statute or edict.

A situation where accountant quarrels with accountant, no two agreeing as to the definitions of principles, the distinction between principles and rules, or even the number of principles in the one field in which accountants are deemed to be most expert, is intolerable and almost forces an affirmative answer to the question:[12] "If so wide a discretion has to be allowed to management in the application of accepted principles are we justified in using the word 'principle' and is not accountancy a business rather than a profession?"

[12] From an editorial in *The Canadian Chartered Accountant*, August 1938, p. 93.

CHAPTER 17

DEVELOPMENT OF ACCOUNT CLASSIFICATION

Having assembled and considered in the foregoing chapters the various conventions, doctrines, and rules of accounting, the ground work has now been laid for a discussion of account classification in relation to profit computation.

Despite the fact that modern accounting is largely a matter of estimate and judgment, despite lack of agreement as to doctrines, conventions, principles, and rules, despite certain conflicts and contradictions, accounting does have its scientific side in its constant employment of classification.

Classification is considered by many as *the* basic scientific method. This has been clearly set forth by Wolf[1] in his comment: "The method of classification is the first method employed in every science."

Account classification, as suggested in Chapter 5, has been greatly influenced by the natural groupings which characterized early accounting.

In applying the valuation convention the physical characteristics of assets naturally were selected for descriptive purposes. Thus, they were subdivided in some such obvious way as cash, wheat, corn, oil, ship, rope, etc.

The natural classification of liabilities was according to the names of creditors.

Since the primary purpose was to maintain a historical record of transactions as a basis for establishing entity charges and discharges, these types of classification were practical and adequate.

Current Assets and Liabilities.—The adoption of financial periods called imperatively for the preparation of periodic ac-

[1] A. Wolf, *Essentials of Scientific Method* (London, George Allen & Unwin, Ltd., 1928), p. 30.

counting reports but did not necessarily call for any change in the plan of classification in so far as proprietorship was concerned. Other creditors, however, having access to such reports, emphasized the important distinction between trading assets and those assets which were not owned for purposes of resale but rather to facilitate operations.

These outside creditors were naturally more interested in the trading assets than in the fixed assets. It was also natural to recognize the distinction between the liability owed by the entity to its proprietor and those other liabilities owed to creditors who have temporarily supplied goods or money.

CREDITOR VIEWPOINT. Money lending is an ancient institution and it is not hard to imagine the early discovery that it was safer to finance trading operations than to finance the purchase of fixed assets, the cycle from cash to merchandise to receivables to cash covering a much shorter period than the cycle from cash to fixed assets to cash.

Born of this financing viewpoint was the concept of current assets and current liabilities, the relation between which has long been regarded as a credit index. From this credit viewpoint has developed a custom of reporting assets in the order of their liquidity and in reporting liabilities in the order of their due dates.

Credit necessities are, therefore, largely responsible for the elements of present basic account classification, namely, current assets, fixed assets, and current liabilities, long-term liabilities, and proprietorship.

OWNERSHIP VIEWPOINT. Managers, owners, and stockholders also are interested in the liquidity of an enterprise.

The investor who fails to consider this factor omits the most important of all negative tests of a good investment. A prospective investment may appear most attractive because of an excellent product, an efficient plant, and a hopeful future. But all of these factors may be of secondary importance compared with the company's current position.

If current liabilities are large in proportion to current assets, there is the ever-present danger that some impatient creditor may demand immediate cash payment. No investor would buy stock in a company merely because it had a substantial excess of current assets over current liabilities, but he would do well to hesitate if the reverse were true.

That is why this comparison may be termed a negative test.

From the more positive viewpoint the typical investor is primarily interested not in the relationship between current assets and current liabilities but in earnings, costs, expenses, losses, and net profits, with reference not only to the past and to the present but, more important, to the future.

Recital of these factors is helpful in explaining some of the origins of classification; balance sheet classification having developed from the credit viewpoint while profit and loss classification developed from the management and ownership viewpoints.

Basic Account Classification.—Just as most human beings having two eyes, two ears, a nose, and a mouth do not resemble one another, so are account classifications both alike and unlike.

Since this is not a treatise on accounting systems and is not concerned with special kinds of accounts made necessary by individual variations in industrial types of organization or operation, it has seemed desirable to adopt as a vehicle for discussion the general classification used by the American Institute of Accountants in the bulletin, *Examination of Financial Statements by Independent Public Accountants.*

While there is, in accounting, no standard or ideal classification, the one presented in this bulletin is rather generally accepted as representing a composite of commonly accepted opinion. That this classification may have its faults cannot be denied. Usually, however, criticism refers to details of classification rather than to the general structure.

It has been criticized because it overemphasizes the credit grantor's viewpoint. It has been criticized because it has underemphasized the profit and loss elements. It is, indeed, subject to Canning's[2] general criticism: "In examining some thousands of annual income statements prepared by professional accountants,

2 John B. Canning, *The Economics of Accountancy* (New York, The Ronald Press Company, 1929), p. 140.

very few have been found by the writer to follow any one primary basis of classification."

The American Institute form, however, represents a good working standard adequate to serve most purposes of accounting discussion.

The bulletin emphasized the fact that the classification requires modification to meet the requirements of each particular situation, even though it is generally satisfactory for the average industrial company. It would, of course, be unsuitable for use in municipal accounting, governmental accounting, railroad accounting, or the accounting for non-profit institutions. Some of these industries, notably railroading, must follow accounting classifications prescribed by governmental authorities.

Asset Classification.—The simple distinction between current assets and fixed assets, while fundamental, is inadequate to meet modern accounting requirements. Certain kinds of assets cannot properly be classified as either current assets or fixed assets.

By common consent,[3] items to be classified as current assets "should be those presumably to be converted into cash in time to meet the liabilities classified as current." In general, the one-year rule is followed by many accountants. Montgomery[4] says, "Current assets are unrestricted cash and other assets which in the regular course of business will normally be converted into cash within one year. To this rule there are some exceptions." He also says that current liabilities comprise "all of a concern's obligations the maturity of which will not extend more than one year after the date of the balance sheet."

CURRENT VS. NON-CURRENT. Paton and other authorities regard the distinction between current and non-current assets as having been unduly emphasized and believe that the only fundamental difference is that of relative permanence. Paton suggests several general points of difference between current and non-current assets, such as normal length of life within the business,

---

[3] Sanders, Hatfield, and Moore, *A Statement of Accounting Principles* (New York, American Institute of Accountants, 1938), p. 71.

[4] Robert H. Montgomery, *Auditing Theory and Practice* (New York, The Ronald Press Company, 1934), pp. 83, 93.

liquidity, the method of consumption, and also the rapidity of consumption.

For example, an excess of one particular kind of inventory over what should be required over a year's period may not be considered a current asset but may be separately captioned.

An item of inventory which will be consumed by the business, like stationery, is frequently distinguished from an item of inventory held for manufacturing purposes or for sale, the former being excluded from the current asset classification.

Investments for which there is no active market, or which represent permanent holdings, deferred charges, and prepaid expense, and those intangible assets, such as patents, copyrights, or franchises, while fixed in nature, are so different from tangible assets as to warrant separate grouping in the non-current category.

Based upon these and other considerations, the following asset classification appears:

> Current assets group
> Non-current assets group
> > Investments
> > Property, plant, and equipment
> > Intangible assets
> > Deferred charges
> > Other assets

It should be noted that this method of grouping conflicts somewhat with the original natural grouping. Assets described by their obvious characteristics cannot always be assigned to any one division.

Under the primitive classification for a farm there might be an item of horses. Using the captions just developed, it might be necessary to assign some of the horses held for sale to current assets and some kept for operating purposes to fixed assets. An adding machine in the stock room of the Burroughs Adding Machine Company may be a current asset. An identical adding machine in the auditor's office of the Burroughs Adding Machine Company is a fixed asset.

While the captions "current assets" and "current" are popular, Fjeld having found them in 90% of the 587 balance sheets he examined, the other group caption "non-current" is practically unused, the major items of non-current assets simply being arrayed under a variety of titles. This inconsistency of classification is practically unimportant, the total of current assets being regarded as significant while the total of non-current assets has little meaning. It is, nevertheless, interesting to note that modern accounting tends to employ two basic asset classifications, current and non-current, and that the original natural classification has become subordinate thereto.

CURRENT SUBCLASSIFICATION. The subclassification of current assets in the American Institute bulletin is as follows:

> Cash in banks and on hand
> Marketable securities
> Notes and accounts receivable
>> Customers
>> Others
> Inventories
> Other current assets

VALUATION ACCOUNTS. For the notes and accounts receivable, reserve or valuation accounts are usually provided.

Such reserves are considered offsets to their corresponding asset accounts and measure the probability of losses through uncollectibility. There is nothing in accounting theory to prevent applying these estimated deductions directly to the asset accounts. There are, however, certain practical advantages in using these offsetting valuation accounts.

SPECIAL RECEIVABLES. Receivables from stockholders, directors, officers, and employees, unless they refer to normal purchases in the ordinary course of trade, are not included with other receivables but are separately set forth for the very good reason that such stockholders, directors, officers, and employees have a special relationship to the company which should not be abused. Accordingly, their indebtedness to the company should be separately scheduled in order that it may come to the attention of all concerned.

SUPPLIES. The American Institute classification includes supplies as an item of inventories.

Practically all accountants will agree with this treatment for manufacturing supplies, but in the case of office supplies which will ultimately be charged to expense rather than to cost of sales, some accountants prefer showing them as prepaid expense on the theory that they will not, in the normal course of events, be converted into cash available for meeting current liabilities.

NON-CURRENT SUBCLASSIFICATION. A distinction is commonly made between property which is used for operating purposes and property which is held for investment or for future expansion, non-operating property often being included under "other assets" or "investments."

The American Institute caption "property, plant, and equipment" covers the following items:

Land used for plant
Buildings used for plant
Machinery and equipment
Patterns and drawings
Office furniture and fixtures
Other items

As in the case of receivables, it is common to provide valuation accounts to which are credited periodic depreciation provisions. These valuation accounts are offsets to their corresponding asset accounts.

As before, it would not be contrary to accounting theory to credit such depreciation direct to the asset account, but this would result in disappearance of the original figures. Hence, such valuation accounts represent a practical expedient accepted almost uniformly by accountants.

LAND. Ordinarily land does not depreciate and accordingly no valuation account need be provided.

One objection which has been made to the American Institute classification refers to the deduction of the depreciation reserve from the total of the depreciable items plus non-depreciable land. Many authorities believe it is desirable to connect the depreciation reserve with the related assets only.

In his survey of 587 balance sheets, Fjeld noted that 77% of them included land with buildings or included all of the fixed assets as one item so that the depreciation was either deducted from the combined asset figure or, in some instances, shown on the liability side of the balance sheet. It therefore appears that common accounting practice confirms the form set forth by the American Institute.

DEFERRED CHARGES. The distinction between prepaid expenses and deferred charges previously quoted from the Sanders, Hatfield, and Moore book is not specifically recognized in the Institute classification, which uses the caption "deferred charges" to cover both. The distinction, however, is mentioned in the body of the bulletin.

Liability Classification.—The natural classification of liabilities is according to individual creditors.

Logically the primary grouping of such liabilities should consist of one group of non-proprietorial creditors and another group representing proprietorship liabilities. This natural grouping has become secondary because of the importance attached to the aggregate of current liabilities.

CURRENT LIABILITIES. Nearly always the primary grouping of the liability side is twofold: current liabilities and non-current liabilities. The non-current liabilities in turn are subdivided into: (1) liabilities to others, and (2) liability to proprietorship.

Corresponding to the current assets it is noted that current liabilities are often distinguished by the one-year rule. Whether this or some other rule is adopted is less important than consistency between the two groups. The test for inclusion or exclusion in either group should be consistent with the test adopted for the other since the totals are significant only when compared.

NON-CURRENT LIABILITIES. Non-current indebtedness to others than proprietors is so frequently secured by the pledge of specific assets that the group is often captioned "funded debt" or "mortgage debt."

The caption adopted from the American Institute bulletin is "funded debt." This includes bonded debt, mortgages, and other funded indebtedness but does not provide for unfunded long-term indebtedness, presumably because a corporation seldom incurs such indebtedness.

RESERVES. The problem of classifying reserves has always been difficult.

The word "reserve" has been badly misused by accountants since it applies to such valuation accounts as Reserve for Depreciation and Reserve for Doubtful Accounts, to current liabilities as in Reserve for Taxes, and to allocations of surplus as in Reserves for Contingencies.

Practically, it is often difficult to decide whether a reserve should be deducted from an asset account, appear as a current liability, or be included as one of the liabilities to proprietorship, due to the fact that the reserve may be a mixed account containing two or more different elements. In other instances reserves are created for operating or equalization purposes, the meaning or interpretation of which, according to Fjeld,[5] "remains one of the mysteries of financial statements."

The difficulty has been avoided in the American Institute classification by providing a general liability captioned "reserves" under which may be detailed the credit balances of reserve accounts which cannot be shown as deductions from assets, as current liabilities or as allocated surplus.

Theoretically, such general reserves are in the nature of general liabilities to persons unknown. This concept is made necessary by the mixed or uncertain character of such accounts and is derived from a practical rather than a scientific difficulty. Since the creation of such reserves often represents some general application of the doctrine of conservatism, it may be doubted whether the directors who authorize them are influenced by any other motive than the general desire to play safe.

DETAILS OF CURRENT LIABILITIES. Corresponding in a general way to the classification of current assets, it is noted that current liabilities are often divided into many subclasses.

5 E. I. Fjeld, *Balance Sheet Classification and Terminology* (New York, 1936), p. 181.

In the American Institute form of balance sheet the subclassification of current liabilities is somewhat elaborate:

Notes payable:
    Banks
    Brokers (commercial paper)
    Merchandise creditors (including notes given for machinery, equipment, etc., purchased)
    Acceptances (for merchandise and raw material purchased)
    Stockholders, directors, officers, and employees
Accounts payable and accrued expenses
Advances from stockholders, directors, officers, and employees
Accrued interest
Provision for federal and state taxes
Other current liabilities (describe)

This classification has been criticized on two general counts: first, because it does not provide for deferred income, and second, because it is not mutually exclusive with respect to accruals.

The caption "accounts payable and accrued expenses" conflicts with the caption "accrued interest" and also somewhat with the caption "provision for federal and state taxes." Clearly it is intended that some but not all accrued liabilities should be included in the caption "accounts payable and accrued expenses," although this must be inferred since the title does not so indicate.

The major division of liabilities into current and non-current tends to overemphasize payment dates. As in the case of the assets, this overemphasis is a credit necessity interfering with natural grouping.

NON-CURRENT SUBDIVISION. The division of non-current liabilities into those owing to proprietorship and those owing to others is always implied even if not specifically set forth.

The proprietorship liability is, of course, not a liability from any viewpoint save that of the entity convention. It should, however, be noted that the general caption of the right-hand side of the Institute form is the single word "liabilities." Fjeld reports that 86% of the balance sheets he studied used this caption alone, a little over 9% used the caption "liabilities and capital," 2% used the caption "liabilities and net worth." It appears, therefore, that companies commonly adopt the entity viewpoint in describing the right-hand side of their balance sheets in spite of legal and other objections.

PROPRIETORSHIP CLASSIFICATION. The primary classification of proprietorship liability reflects the important distinction between proprietorship investment and proprietorship profits.

In incorporated enterprises the distinction is reflected by the two captions, "capital stock," and "surplus." In unincorporated enterprises a similar distinction is permissible although seldom used.

The distinction between profits of prior periods and profits for the current period is seldom made in the balance sheet. The balance sheet is prepared as of midnight of the last day of the accounting period and accordingly all amounts reflecting profits refer to periods already past and gone. Accordingly, the surplus on a balance sheet dated December 31, 1938 includes undistributed profits held over from 1937 and prior years and also undistributed profits for 1938. This is consistent with the fiction that the books are closed and the net profit determined and transferred to Surplus at midnight on the last day of the fiscal period.

The asset and liability classification has been reviewed in this chapter in order to lay the foundation for detailed scrutiny of profit and loss subdivisions.

CHAPTER 18

PROPRIETORSHIP CLASSIFICATION

Consistency in maintaining the entity viewpoint forbids the use of that convenient phrase "net worth" for which no satisfactory substitute exists.

Commonly used are such other phrases as "capital and surplus," "capital stock and surplus," or "capital." Fjeld found that the title most frequently employed was "capital stock and surplus." Next in importance was the title "capital," and ranking third was "capital and surplus." Some one of these three captions appeared on 210 of the balance sheets he studied, while the caption "net worth" appeared on only 34. Considering only the 244 statements which bore one of these four captions, it may be observed that "net worth" occurred in but 14% of them.

In accounting writings and discussions, it has been found difficult to devise a satisfactory substitute for the term "net worth." This is particularly true because other titles usually refer to corporations only, whereas "net worth" can be applied to all proprietorship accounts.

"Capital" is sometimes used as a substitute for "net worth" but such usage is unfortunate, being at variance with the economic viewpoint which considers capital to be a fund or stock of wealth. Fisher[1] explains that "a dwelling house now existing is capital; the shelter it affords or the bringing in of a money-rent is its income. The railways of the country are capital; their services of transportation or the dividends from the sale of that transportation are the income they yield."

"Proprietorship," while far from ideal particularly in the case of corporations, seems to be about the only practical and convenient substitute for "net worth" in any discussion of

[1] Irving Fisher, *The Nature of Capital and Income* (New York, The Macmillan Company, 1930), pp. 52, 53.

accounting classification as distinguished from the classification itself.

Primary Classification of Proprietorship.—Reference has already been made to the primary classification of proprietorship into:

Investment
Surplus or undivided profits

The investment account is credited with the amount of funds invested, whether in the form of money or property, and is debited with the return of investment by the entity to the proprietor.

Surplus or undivided profits is credited with that net increase of entity indebtedness to the proprietor commonly referred to as profit, is debited with that net decrease in entity indebtedness to the proprietor commonly referred to as loss, and is debited with any distribution of profit to the proprietor.

"Profit and loss" is the general, somewhat academic, title of a large group of temporary accounts reflecting certain types of transactions or occurrences which during an accounting period affect the entity liability to the proprietor. At the end of the accounting period any net balance in this group of accounts, representing net profit if a credit and net loss if a debit, is transferred to surplus and the profit and loss accounts are reopened again at the beginning of the next following accounting period. Often the entire group of profit and loss accounts is referred to as if one account, a practice usually representing mere technical convenience although sometimes, under simple conditions, conforming to actuality. Thus, an early German author, Franz Hautschl, is quoted by Littleton[2] as explaining "the profit-and-loss account as a temporary resting place for the increases and decreases of capital which, if entered direct in the capital account, would overburden it with detail."

The simple primary classification of proprietorship is necessarily altered and expanded in the case of corporations, due not so much to true accounting necessities as to legal requirements

[2] A. C. Littleton, *Accounting Evolution to 1900* (American Institute Publishing Co., Inc., 1933), p. 178.

having to do with capital stock on the one hand and the determination of surplus profits available for dividends on the
other hand.

Corporate Proprietorship.—Various complications have
resulted from legal requirements affecting corporations. A
familiar difficulty is one which results from the issuance of capital stock with a par value. The total par value of the stock
issue is taken as the aggregate indebtedness of the corporate
entity to its stockholders for their investment.

The dollar amounts so described may be more or less than
actual values contributed by the stockholders. Reference has
already been made to the prevalent promotional practice of some
years ago whereby overvalued property was turned over for
capital stock at par, following which the subscribing stockholders donated some of the capital stock to the corporation.
Legally such stock could be resold by the corporation at any
desired price, whereas the original sale had to be at par value
or above.

In order to finance new enterprises it was sometimes necessary
to adopt this plan, which in turn required the adoption of
accounting expedients adequately to reflect the transaction and
to create such an account as donated surplus, which in reality
roughly measured the overvaluation of the property invested by
the original subscribers.

The adoption of no-par value stock by New York State in
1912 proved popular and was soon followed by amendments
in the corporation laws in nearly all states. These new statutes
overcame the difficulty imposed by those state laws which pro-
hibited the original sale of stock for less than par.

Unfortunately, the idea that some nominal value should
attach to each share of stock could not be forgotten. In the case
of no-par shares this nominal valuation was called "stated
value."

Marple[3] comments: "The general effect of the stated value
provisions has been to substitute for the rule that all amounts
paid in for shares represent capital, the wholly illogical rule that

---

[3] Raymond P. Marple, *Capital Surplus and Corporate Net Worth* (New York,
The Ronald Press Company, 1936), p. 35.

the consideration paid in may be divided between capital and surplus by corporate organizers and directors in almost any proportion they desire." Surplus thus created is a special kind of surplus in no sense representing accumulated undistributed profits but rather representing investment just as truly as the capital stock itself.

Types of Surplus.—There are, of course, other varieties of capital surplus which have resulted from legal-accounting necessities. The Executive Committee of the American Accounting Association recognizes only three classifications of surplus: paid-in surplus, earned surplus, and surplus reserves. The American Institute form of balance sheet recognizes an additional type, namely, revaluation surplus.

REVALUATION SURPLUS. There is a growing recognition of the impropriety of creating a surplus by revaluation of assets. Montgomery insists that revaluation surplus must be classified separately, although the American Institute[4] bulletin rather dodges the question by indicating that fixed assets are usually carried at cost but that "if any other basis is used it should be stated on the balance sheet as concisely as the material facts will permit."

The Executive Committee of the American Accounting Association,[5] on the other hand, took a definite stand against "periodic revaluation of assets, up or down, in accordance with current price levels and expected business developments," and made its recommendations in its Postulate 7: "If values other than unamortized costs are to be quoted they should be expressed in financial statements only as collateral notations for informative purposes."

THE PROBLEM OF SURPLUS ACCOUNTS. One of the more significant discussions of surplus is ascribed to Cranstoun[6] who, in the January 1938 issue of *The Journal of Accountancy,*

---

[4] *Examination of Financial Statements by Independent Public Accountants* (New York, American Institute of Accountants, January 1936), p. 21.

[5] Executive Committee of the American Accounting Association, "A Tentative Statement of Accounting Principles Affecting Corporate Reports," *The Accounting Review,* June 1936, p. 189.

[6] William D. Cranstoun, "The Commentator," *The Journal of Accountancy,* January 1938, p. 68.

speaks of the misspent time and energy "which have been expended in discussing the proper allocation of charges and credits between earned and capital surplus."

He suggests abolishing both of these terms on the theory that the average investor is concerned only with the availability of surplus for the payment of dividends. He suggests discontinuance of the words "capital" and "surplus" in the one term "capital surplus" and the adoption of each of these words to describe the separate elements of net worth.

His position is undoubtedly sound. Either capital is contributed, or it is not, and it is this distinction which is important. Nevertheless, in current use a number of special surplus accounts are commonly found. Fjeld reported 43 different titles or methods of describing various kinds of surplus.

EARNED SURPLUS. Practically all modern authorities who recognize more than one type of surplus are insistent upon employment of the title "earned surplus" for that account which reflects accumulated undistributed profits, although May[7] expresses a preference for the term "undivided profits." Surplus, he says, "often includes credits which cannot be said to have been earned in any legitimate sense of that word."

The common preference for the term "earned surplus" has been reflected by the American Institute's appointment of a special committee to define the phrase. Following several years of study the committee[8] reported the following definition: "Earned surplus is the balance of the net profits, net income, and gains of a corporation after deducting losses and after deducting distributions to stockholders and transfers to capital-stock accounts."

Whether surplus items other than earned surplus should be grouped under one caption of "capital surplus," or whether different captions should be employed, is still under discussion. The *Accountants' Handbook* lists the constituents of capital surplus as:

Paid-in surplus
Revaluation credits

7 George O. May, "Improvement in Financial Accounts," *The Journal of Accountancy*, May 1937, p. 365.
8 *Accountants' Handbook* (New York, The Ronald Press Company, 1934), p. 966.

Surplus from donations of stock and property assessments
Gains from favorable reacquisitions or disposition of a company's own stock or obligations

The *Handbook* also points out the desirability of separately
reporting the constituents of capital surplus according to the
sources from which they are derived.

AVAILABILITY FOR DIVIDENDS.   Despite arguments pro and
con, it appears that the credit balance of earned surplus account
can have only one significance. Obviously, it does not measure
earning power, because its balance may have been reduced by
prior dividend declarations and by various adjustments such as
downward revaluations. By a process of elimination, therefore,
the balance of this account can mean but one thing, availability
for dividends, even though many accountants would recoil from
the idea of so describing it in a financial statement, not only
because of the encouragement thus given to greedy stockholders, but also because the phrase "availability for dividends"
refers to the legal status of the accumulated profits and does not
imply that the corporation has sufficient cash on hand to make
the dividend disbursement.

The problems having to do with the different types of surplus
constitute a fascinating field but not one particularly interlocked
with the determination of periodic profits which is the main
theme of this volume.

Profit and Loss Classification.—Reference has been made
to the possibility of obtaining all of the materials necessary for
a profit and loss statement by analyzing the proprietor's account
in the entity ledger, abstracting from that account all items of
increase or decrease in entity liability referring to the current
period which did not represent investments or withdrawals by
the proprietor.

The inconvenience of profit determination by this means is
due to the large number of items usually involved. Of course,
an equivalent analysis actually is made in modern accounting
but it is made currently, not at the end of an accounting period;
at the time of recording, not subsequently.

All of this is a matter of operating convenience and efficiency having no relation to the fundamental accounting mechanism. The elements of the profit and loss classification would be the same regardless of the time or mode of analysis.

PRIMARY SUBDIVISION. The primary classification of profit and loss is twofold, requiring the segregation of items of income on the one hand, and items of cost, expense, and loss on the other hand.

It has, however, been long settled that the intelligent management of business requires a further classification of items according to whether they are operating or non-operating, with the result that the second step in the classification of profit and loss may appear as follows:

Profit and loss
  Income
    Operating
    Non-operating
  Costs, expenses, and losses
    Operating
    Non-operating

With respect to income, the classification above shown is commonly employed but with different titles in present-day classifications. In the American Institute bulletin, the captions corresponding to the ones shown are "net sales" and "other income."

The classification of costs, expenses, and losses is influenced by an additional consideration. The phrase "costs, expenses, and losses" indicates the threefold classification of income deductions.

It is regarded by most, but not all, accountants as important to distinguish between the actual cost of merchandise which is sold and those other expenses which, while of operating significance, are not specifically connected with the merchandise itself.

The reason for this distinction lies in the fact that the unprofitableness of operations may be due: (1) to insufficient margin between the cost and the selling price of merchandise, even though the expenses of selling and administration are reasonable, (2) to excessive expenses of administration and selling even though the margin between actual cost and selling price is sufficient, or (3) to both excessive costs and excessive expenses in relation to sales price.

The segregation of direct merchandise costs from selling, general, and administrative expense is deemed desirable for management control purposes.

The cost of merchandise which is sold generally consists of the purchase cost of the merchandise plus other outlays properly related thereto, such as the cost of incoming freight.

When merchandise is manufactured instead of being purchased, the fiction is adopted that the factory replaces the vendor and accordingly the factory cost of producing the merchandise replaces the purchase cost. In either event the same general course is followed, namely, the costs pertaining to the merchandise sold are separated from expenses of the office, and the costs of selling and administration.

Operating costs and expenses are, therefore, subdivided, with the result that the next step in the development of profit and loss classification appears thus:

> Profit and loss
> Income
>> Operating
>> Non-operating
> Costs, expenses, and losses
>> Operating
>>> Cost of merchandise sold
>>> Other operating expenses
>> Non-operating

This outline shows the constituents of profit and loss classification. The terminology of the details does not, however, conform to current usage. It may, therefore, be restated as given here:

> Income group:
> Net sales
> Other income

Costs, expenses, and losses group:
Operating group:
Cost of sales
Selling, general, and administrative expenses

Non-operating group:
Other charges

Regardless of terminology, the classification appears to be mutually exclusive, subject, of course, to legitimate differences of opinion as to the classification of certain kinds of items.

AMERICAN INSTITUTE CLASSIFICATION. Based upon the skeleton classification above, the American Institute form is:

Gross sales
Less outward freight, allowances, and returns
Net sales
Cost of sales
Gross profit on sales
Selling, general, and administrative expenses
Net profit before other income and charges

Other income:
Income from investments
Interest on notes receivable, etc.
Other non-operating or extraordinary income (separately shown)

Other charges:
Interest on funded debt (and amortization of bond discount)
Interest on notes payable
Other non-operating or extraordinary charges (separately shown)
Provisions for income taxes
Total deductions

Net profit (loss) for period carried to surplus

INCOME. The significant figure for operating income is indicated as "net sales." This item is derived from gross sales less certain applicable deductions which are assumed to be matched against gross sales, although in practice it is not uncommon to find that some of the deductions do not refer to the same accounting periods as do the gross sales. Nevertheless, these deductions purport to be extinguishments, corrections, or cancellations of sales properly to be offset against gross sales for the purpose of obtaining the significant net figure.

That income from sales should result from arm's-length transactions ordinarily with outsiders is fundamental.

COSTS AND EXPENSES. The first subdivision of operating cost is shown here as "cost of sales." Another commonly used title is "cost of goods sold," which has, however, been held too restrictive for general use where services instead of merchandise are involved. The title "cost of sales" has also been criticized since it might be confused with selling expense. It has therefore been suggested that "cost of goods sold" be employed in merchandising and "cost of services sold" be adopted in service organizations.

Since the difference between net sales on the one hand and cost of sales on the other, generally referred to as gross profit, is commonly regarded as a significant figure, it becomes necessary to distinguish sharply between items chargeable to cost of sales and other operating costs and expenses.

Even under simple conditions of merchandising certain problems of classification are noted, particularly with reference to the treatment of purchase discounts, inventory write-offs, and the booking of buying, receiving, and other costs.

Manufacturing industries present even more serious difficulties. It is easy enough to state the bare rule that cost of manufacturing shall consist of factory costs only, but it is not so easy in any given instance to decide just what a factory cost is.

Numerous different practices have been noted in the treatment of such items as general executive salaries, which are sometimes apportioned between factory costs and those of general administration. Other problems of cost allocation may be derived from fixed asset accounting with particular reference to depreciation, depletion, obsolescence, and inadequacy.

Since factory accounting is almost entirely a problem of inventory accounting, a host of troublesome inventory problems are directly related to cost of sales. Among these are problems of excessive cost due to operation at less than capacity and the disposition of unabsorbed manufacturing expense. It is often difficult to distinguish between temporary and permanent plant idleness, and cost specialists have not yet succeeded in evolving regarding this matter a philosophy which can be considered generally applicable.

It is generally stated that factory costs end when products are completed and put in the finished stock room, but in specific situations it is not always easy to interpret this rule. Some industries, for example, require expert field installation of product, giving rise to questions as to when factory expenses really end and when other operating expenses begin.

These other operating expenses not directly related to product or services sold are called "selling, general, and administrative expense" in the American Institute classification. A variety of alternative titles have been suggested, such as "operating expenses" and "commercial expenses."

The American Institute terminology is considered satisfactory despite its failure to emphasize the essential operating characteristic of this group.

The Institute form also fails to emphasize that the "other income" and "other charges" groups are non-operating although this failure is not deceptive to accountants and perhaps not to laymen. Good classification would, however, demand recognition of the primary distinction between operating and non-operating.

The Sanders, Hatfield, and Moore[9] report treats classification in a satisfying manner by flatly stating: "The income statement should be divided into at least two sections, an operating section and a non-operating section." The report distinguishes between these two sections as follows:

A somewhat liberal definition of what constitutes "operations" is permissible in the preparation of this [operating] section. It must include the operation of the main functions of the enterprise. It need not include incidental operations. It must exclude the interest cost on borrowed funds. . . . This [non-operating] section, if only two sections are used, should include such items as profit on sale of capital

9 Sanders, Hatfield, and Moore, *A Statement of Accounting Principles* (New York, American Institute of Accountants, 1938), pp. 27, 36, 37.

assets, interest, unrealized gain from appreciation (if shown at all as income), and gains and losses due to causes not connected with the immediate management of operations.

The same bulletin distinguishes between cost of sales and other operating expenses by explaining that the former, in a manufacturing company, "is usually the cost of making the goods; in a trading company it is usually the purchase invoice cost of the merchandise plus freight"; as to operating expenses, "As a general rule, no part of selling and general administrative expense becomes a part of the inventory value of merchandise on hand."

To this, proponents of the Clark plan of retail accounting would take exception. They assert:

> The purpose of shifting of certain expenses from the Selling, General, and Administrative classification into the Cost of Sales is to make the department store statement more comparable with that of manufacturing establishments. Department stores usually show a gross profit of around 35% whereas, manufacturing establishments show a gross profit of somewhere around 20%. Clark argues that for profit and loss purposes, the costs of buying, receiving, and marking, etc., should be included in cost of sales so as to arrive at what he calls "counter cost." He also maintains that "counter cost" should be the basis for fire insurance purposes.[10]

INCIDENTAL OPERATIONS.   Sanders, Hatfield, and Moore are somewhat indefinite in their reference to incidental operations, implying that personal choice may control the decision as to whether they are operating or non-operating.

The *Accountants' Handbook*[11] suggests that "gains or losses which are clearly extraordinary and only in the most incidental way connected with the avowed activities of the enterprise can be segregated; beyond this point it is hard to go."

Kester[12] uses the words operating and non-operating as approximately equivalent to major and minor. He says: "Non-operating profits are those which arise from the minor activities

---

10 Hugo Kuechenmeister, in a personal letter dated April 4, 1938.

11 *Accountants' Handbook* (New York, The Ronald Press Company, 1934), p. 1093.

12 Roy B. Kester, *Advanced Accounting* (New York, The Ronald Press Company, 1933), p. 493.

—those which are supplementary, auxiliary, or even incidental to the main operations." He expresses his poor opinion of the terms operating and non-operating and suggests that "the terms auxiliary and supplementary are more accurately descriptive."

Montgomery[13] refers to two sections, the first called "the trading or manufacturing account" and the second the "general profit and loss account."

Paton[14] asserts that profit and loss classification depends upon viewpoint and says: "If all accounts and accounting procedures and classifications are constructed and defined solely from the standpoint of proprietorship, a non-classified income statement is the natural result." He continues: "To the common shareholder Federal taxes, bond interest, losses, etc., are in exactly the same class as labor and material costs—deductions which must be recognized before his available profit is disclosed. Yet from the operating, managerial standpoint these charges are entirely incongruous and should be carefully divided into at least two main groups."

Elsewhere he insists that: "Net operating revenue measures the net increase (allowance being made for withdrawals and new investments) in *all the equities*. A rational cleavage is thus developed between *deductions* from *gross* revenue, and *distributions* of *net* revenue."

FUNCTIONAL CLASSIFICATION. It is a matter of common knowledge that functional or departmental classification is largely employed for administrative purposes in modern business. Usually it is a subordinate classification often referring to asset accounts as well as profit and loss accounts.

Asset accounts may be classified departmentally not only for enforcement of some charge and discharge relationship but also to obtain departmental depreciation.

Even where assets are not departmentally classified, it is customary to provide a functional or departmental classification for income and expense accounts. The operating significance of such subsidiary classification is obvious. Properly used and

13 Robert H. Montgomery, *Auditing Theory and Practice* (New York, The Ronald Press Company, 1934), p. 459.

14 W. A. Paton, *Accounting Theory* (New York, The Ronald Press Company, 1922), pp. 265, 88. (Also refer to discussion of interest cost in Chapter 7.)

interpreted the resulting figures provide organization control. Departmental classification refers, of course, to operating rather than non-operating income, costs, and expenses and is distinctly practical, the subsidiary accounts clustering around the personalities of certain employees, department heads, division heads, superintendents, and other key men.

From other viewpoints the status of interest earned, purchase discounts, interest expense, and similar items may be arguable, but the operating executive knows full well that if someone in his organization is responsible and accountable for interest, discounts, and various other so-called non-operating items, these items may have definite operating significance because they are used by management to evaluate employee performance.

From the viewpoint of a practical general manager much of the discussion about operating and non-operating classification seems unrealistic, simply because he thinks in terms of measurement and control with reference to employees and groups of employees.

Following Paton, who has pointed out that it is only the needs of management which justify distinguishing between operating and non-operating, it might be desirable to go a step further and permit the requirements of management to provide the real test. There seems to be but little merit in setting up categories for one specific purpose and then defeating that purpose, in part at least, by applying theoretical distinctions.

SIGNIFICANCE OF PROFIT AND LOSS DIVISIONS. Regardless of what specific theory is adopted in sectionalizing the profit and loss statement, it is generally noted that such statements are sectionalized and that the various classifications commonly employed do not differ greatly from one another.

The relationship between sales and cost of sales may be considered a natural one and the resulting figure of gross profit, while not a profit, does afford a valuable intermediate figure for control purposes.

Paton[15] does not agree with this viewpoint. He suggests

15 W. A. Paton, "Comments on 'A Statement of Accounting Principles'," *The Journal of Accountancy*, March 1938, pp. 198, 199.

hat all costs of production, including administration and depreciation charges, are "on substantially the same level in their relation to revenue, that no type or class of cost is in a preferential position with respect to recovery from customers or in any other vital connection. And it follows that it is poor reporting—no matter how common—to strike a balance and give it a prominent position with the term 'profit' attached, when only a limited portion of the total of the unquestioned costs applicable to revenues has been deducted." He refers to the "shadow-line" between cost of goods sold and other operating costs and says that its preservation "is one of the most unfortunate chores attempted by the accountant."

ALLOCATION. It has been contended that lack of uniformity in allocating losses or profits to sections of the profit and loss statement is one of the serious accounting problems. Greer[16] deems it unnecessary to deplore net profit inaccuracies which result from errors of valuation "as long as substantial items of loss or gain may be written off at the client's pleasure either to current income, to earned surplus, to capital surplus, or to a reserve."

This is regarded as the professional accountant's responsibility by Hoxsey,[17] who has asserted:

When non-recurring income, shown separately on the books, is merged with recurring income in the annual accounts, or when items properly chargeable against current income are charged against surplus or reserve, the facts are bound to come to the attention of the accountant who makes even the most cursory examination, and he should not certify without a clear qualification accounts in which anything of this kind has been done.

A somewhat opposing viewpoint has been expressed by Sanders, Hatfield, and Moore, who believe that some of these matters of allocation may be left to the judgment of the management. There does, however, seem to be a certain order of importance in this matter of allocation. In other words, an

16 Howard C. Greer, "To What Extent Can the Practice of Accounting Be Reduced to Rules and Standards?" *The Journal of Accountancy,* March 1938, p. 220.

17 *Audits of Corporate Accounts* (New York, American Institute of Accountants, 1934), p. 29.

error in the distribution of a loss or gain item as between (1) surplus and (2) profit and loss seems to be more important than an error of allocation between (1) cost of sales and (2) selling, general, and administrative expense. This decision in turn is more important than one between the several selling, general, and administrative expense accounts.

The first and most important decision is to determine whether a loss or gain has actually resulted. The next most important is the determination of what period is affected. Subsequent decisions in a descending order, while sufficiently important, become less and less so as the choices are narrowed and classifications become more limited.

The gift of 10 cents to a child is from his viewpoint the most important fact. The disposition of that coin in one or another pocket is of secondary importance.

DISTORTION AND CONSISTENCY.   Granting the importance of a mutually exclusive classification, it remains true that few such classifications are to be found in accounting.

It is doubtful whether the most painstaking care in the construction of a classification would greatly improve the quality of management information, simply because of the more far-reaching effects of various profit-distorting factors. Distortions which may result from inventory valuation or depreciation may be and often are so gross as to make it relatively impractical to strive for meticulous exactness in establishing mutually exclusive classifications of profit and loss.

In this connection considerable reliance is often placed upon the curative effects of consistency. There seems to be little doubt that the recent wholehearted adoption of this time-honored doctrine does in a rough practical way do more to promote comparability of financial statements than the adoption of some scientific or theoretically correct accounting. This is particularly true in a business which rides along from year to year on a fairly even keel.

As far as the erratic type of business is concerned, neither the doctrine of consistency nor any other factor is likely to prove helpful in obtaining comparability.

FINAL NET PROFIT. Practically all accountants seem to be in agreement that the item of "net profit before other income and charges" is a particularly significant figure and that special effort to preserve the integrity of this figure is justified.

It is only in the non-operating sections, such as "other income" and "other charges," that time incidence and comparability are less important. These groups are designed to collect items of an extraordinary, capital, or financial nature or items which represent the correction of prior-period errors. It is not intended to minimize the importance of these often substantial items. It is only their periodic incidence and hence their comparability which may be doubted.

Because of the introduction of non-comparable items into the profit and loss statement, it follows that the final figure of "net profit for the period carried to surplus" is in no sense net profit for the one period, since it has no periodic significance nor can it properly be compared with another item of net profit for a different period.

The informed investor, in his analysis of earning power and his surveys of trends, may be skeptical of such final net profit figures. This does not mean that he will neglect consideration of substantial non-operating items. They may greatly influence final results but they cannot be assumed to have periodic significance.

The Profit and Loss Statement.—Like accounting, and usually overlapping it, reporting has its conventions, its doctrines, and its rules.

There are generally considered to be either two or three principal financial statements. When there are only two, they are commonly known as (1) the balance sheet and (2) the statement of profit and loss and surplus. Where three principal statements are used, they are commonly known as (1) the balance sheet, (2) analysis of surplus or surplus reconciliation, and (3) profit and loss statement.

The profit and loss statement is, in fact, a report which furnishes the detailed analysis of one balance sheet item, usually surplus.[18] In Chapter 9, a form of balance sheet was presented which included on the liability side the elements of a complete profit and loss statement. This form emphasized the relation of profit and loss items to the entity liability. It would, in fact, be perfectly proper, even if not convenient or feasible, to prepare such a single statement.

Commonly the balance sheet and profit and loss statement are viewed as two major exhibits of equal rank. This view has been responsible for certain expressions of opinion that the two statements really reflect two different orders of information.

Numerous analogies have been presented, some of them unfortunately chosen, to support this view. The suggestion that a balance sheet resembles a still snapshot as of a given moment of time, while the profit and loss statement resembles a moving picture and accordingly refers to a period of time, has been somewhat popular.

Such suggestions and opinions are neither helpful nor illuminating. Greater clarity results from adopting Kester's concept, namely, that "the profit and loss statement is merely a balance sheet schedule."

Accountants are accustomed to making analyses of many different kinds of accounts. Such an analysis as shown by a practitioner's working papers often presents the balance of an account at the beginning of a year, followed by a classification of the various debits and credits made to that account during the year, and closing with the balance of the account at the end of the year. Such an analysis is merely a break-down of one account accompanied generally by a rearrangement and grouping of the items. It could be made of any liability account, such as an account with a trade creditor. When completed, the resulting schedule would show not only the beginning balance and the final balance, but also the various classifications of pur-

18 Again it should be noted that the profit and loss statement is not always a break-down of the surplus item on the balance sheet. Some accountants prefer that the profit and loss statement should end with the final item of net profit in which case it becomes necessary either (1) to provide a surplus reconciliation statement, or (2) to replace the single item of surplus on the balance sheet with at least three items, i.e., surplus beginning of period, net profit for the period, and surplus at the end of the period. The relationship adopted in this volume is logical from the viewpoint of developing profit and loss classification and as an additional advantage seems to be growing in popularity among accountants.

chases made from him and the various classifications of debits against him, i.e., whether in cash or by note or by price adjustment or by return of merchandise. Seldom if ever would such an analytical exhibit be of value in a report, but there is no reason why it could not be prepared if the resulting information justified. If the analysis was included in a report, it would be entirely clear to all concerned that it represented no more than a subsidiary schedule supporting and explaining one account payable.

There seems to be no difference, save in the kind of items involved, between an analysis of an account payable to an outside creditor and an analysis of an account representing the indebtedness of an entity to its proprietor for undistributed profits. The two analyses would be much the same in general structure. Both could be started with the opening credit balance followed by various classifications or groups of charges and credits during the year and ended by the credit balance in the account at the end of the year.

If such a schedule is prepared to explain earned surplus in the balance sheet, it should not be difficult to think of it as a supporting schedule. The profit and loss statement really represents such a schedule although it is not commonly so considered, not only because of its great importance but also because it is seldom presented in the usual form of an accountant's analysis.

Accounting History and Disclosure.—While accounting itself may be considered as history, it does not necessarily follow that accounting statements are histories, i.e., interpretation of the balance sheet would be considerably modified if its full historical background, particularly with respect to fixed assets, were taken into consideration. Where the historical background is of material importance, the doctrine of disclosure is applicable.

In so far as the balance sheet is concerned, disclosure requires stating the basis of asset valuation and furnishing information regarding contingencies which the accounting mechanism is not designed to reflect. In so far as the profit and loss statement is concerned, the doctrine of disclosure requires explanation, parenthetically or by footnote or by detailed listing, of items of extraordinary operating expense, correction of errors of prior periods, and capital gains and losses. Where substantial write-downs affecting surplus have occurred, the doctrine of disclosure requires that the new surplus be dated or the effect of the adjustment otherwise explained.

Where the profit and loss system relies upon cost accounting for essential information, certain significant totals must be reconstructed. The total figure for depreciation is extinguished by the cost accounting process of apportionment. As stockholders and others at interest are entitled to know whether a company is cheating on its depreciation, it is regarded as essential to disclose by footnote the total depreciation and depletion provisions for a fiscal year. Corporations are also beginning to realize the desirability, from a public relation viewpoint, of disclosing the total amounts of wages and taxes instead of permitting these items to remain merged with other figures.

It is considered of special importance that any disclosures, parenthetical or otherwise, must be considered the disclosures of the reporting company rather than the disclosures of its auditors, and the wording of footnotes and comments should be consistent with this view.

Accounting as a conventionalized mechanism is rather inelastic. Reporting, even though it is the reporting of accounts, is much more elastic. A broader application of the doctrine of disclosure to reports would silence some of the important criticisms which have been directed against traditional accounting.

CHAPTER 19

EXPENDITURES, ASSETS, AND INCOME

This and the following two chapters are of particular significance in their relation to accounting profit. Any understanding of the conventionalized accounting profit must necessarily be based in large part upon some reasonable concept of expenditures. It is from the relationship between expenditures and realized income that some of the more conventionalized aspects of profit are derived.

If, on a Tuesday, a child spends a nickel for a bag of candy which is immediately consumed, the situation is one of simultaneous expenditure and consumption. If, on a Tuesday, the child spends a nickel for a bag of candy which is not eaten until Wednesday, then the expenditure and the consumption do not coincide, nor do they coincide if the candy is eaten on Tuesday and paid for on Wednesday.

In business there are similar lags. An expenditure is generally considered to be the result of a cash disbursement or the incurrence of a liability, the effect of which is to increase assets or increase costs, expenses, or losses. It is not identical with expense in spite of the fact that such a misconception is sometimes noted. An expenditure may be made without an immediate cash disbursement, the expenditure arising from the increase of liabilities payable in cash.

Expenditures and Income.—Expenditures generally are made for the purpose of causing a favorable effect upon future income. This was emphasized in the American Institute bulletin, *Examination of Financial Statements by Independent Public Accountants*[1] as follows:

---

[1] *Examination of Financial Statements by Independent Public Accountants* (New York, American Institute of Accountants, January 1936), p. 1.

From an accounting viewpoint, the distinguishing characteristic of business today is the extent to which expenditures are made in one period with the definite purpose or expectation that they shall be the means of producing profits in the future.

Littleton[2] expressed about the same thought in different language when he said, *"income* is the earning flowing from the work done; it is the consequence of a prior *outlay* made with intent to generate income."

The relationship between expenditures and income is often so obvious as to justify but little comment. The man who repairs his house or his car is making an expenditure for future benefit. The man who purchases a boat does so in the expectation of its future utility. In a business the benefit which results from an expenditure is often related to future income, gain, or profit even though the exact nature of the resulting benefit cannot be measured or timed exactly.

The extent to which large sums of money are expended for the sake of future income is well illustrated by the following quotation :[3]

... it is often a long time before these dollars come home to roost, if ever. Witness a case related in the annual report of the duPont Company for 1937.

When the company went into the making of dyestuffs more than $22,000,000 was invested over a period of six years before a dollar of annual net profit was earned. Another $21,000,000 had been put into dyes through a further span of 12 years before enough profits had been earned to offset the accumulated previous losses. Into the manufacture of synthetic ammonia and related chemicals was poured an investment of $27,000,000 by gradual additions for ten years before cumulative results finally registered the first dollar of profit.

For accounting purposes reference to future, as in the phrases "future benefit" or "future income," is too indefinite, since it may have reference to no more than an instant of time or it may have reference to a period of years. If the benefit or income is expected to result prior to the end of the current fiscal year, then the expenditure is considered an expense. Such an

---

[2] A. C. Littleton, "Business Profits as a Legal Basis for Dividends," *Harvard Business Review*, Vol. XVI, No. 1, 1937, p. 58.
[3] Editorial in *Nation's Business*, September 1938, p. 7.

expenditure is often referred to as a revenue expenditure in contrast to the capital expenditure the future benefit or gain from which is not expected to materialize until after the end of the current fiscal year.

Herein lies the fundamental distinction between certain kinds of assets and expenses.

Littleton[4] says: "The only difference between asset and expense is one of time of appropriation or association with specific units of income," and he regards the differentiation between assets and expense as one of the two functions of accounting, the other being the matching of costs with income.

Canning[5] infers that: "An asset is any future service in money or any future service convertible into money." Sprague[6] referred to assets as "a storage of services to be received." Mason[7] suggests that: "If we can think of the investment in an asset, then, as the price paid for a series of future services, the asset account may well be thought of as a deferred charge to operations or a prepaid operating expense."

This is a most helpful concept and one which has been recognized by many authors in their discussions of capital and revenue. It promotes clear thinking and often helps to simplify complex accounting problems.

The relationship between expenditures and income must be considered not only from the viewpoint of time but also from the viewpoint of directness. The purchase of merchandise is directly related to an expected sale of that merchandise. Here the connection is simple and unmistakable. The purchase of a machine by a manufacturer is related to items of future income, but less directly. The purchase of insurance protection is related to items of future income, but the relation is even less direct.

Costs, Expenses, and Losses.—From the operating viewpoint it is commonly regarded as important to distinguish

4 A. C. Littleton, *Accounting Evolution to 1900* (New York, American Institute Publishing Co., Inc., 1933), p. 201.

5 John B. Canning, *The Economics of Accountancy* (New York, The Ronald Press Company, 1929), p. 22.

6 Charles E. Sprague, *The Philosophy of Accounts* (New York, The Ronald Press Company, 1913), p. 41.

7 Perry Mason, *Principles of Public-Utility Depreciation* (Chicago, American Accounting Association, 1937), p. 13.

between costs, other operating expenses, and losses, the last being without operating significance. A loss has been defined as "a disappearance of value without compensation."

A longer and more explanatory definition is provided by Paton:[8]

> From a strictly technical point of view a loss may be defined as *any deduction from equities (either capital or income) resulting from the expiration of some asset value for which no compensatory values are acquired.* Thus *loss* is in sharp contrast with *expense.* Expense is the cost of revenue; it measures the consumption of resources which is made good (at least in part) from the proceeds of sales. A loss measures an expiration for which there is no return.

Certainly, few would question the operating desirability of distinguishing between the three general types of income deductions. Proper distinction as a matter of classification does not mean that they should be differently treated in the calculation of final net profit. This point has been emphasized by Littleton,[9] who asks: "Is not the income statement the recognized means of conveying information to the reader about asset diminutions? Why should loss diminution have a status different from that given to expense diminution?"

As losses, costs, and expenses have elements in common, it appears that little practical advantage can result from the attempt to make hair-splitting distinctions.

COST VALUATION. That portion of an expenditure the beneficial effect of which is expected to be experienced measurably in future fiscal periods is commonly called an "asset." Not all assets originate in this way but those that do often introduce interesting problems of valuation to which some reference is now appropriate.

The difficulties inherent in the word "value" or "valuation" have been mentioned, but it is almost impossible to discuss accounting without them. By some, valuation is considered equivalent to appraisal. By others, valuation is considered an

8 W. A. Paton, *Essentials of Accounting* (New York, The Macmillan Company, 1938), pp. 105, 106.
9 A. C. Littleton, "High Standards of Accounting," *The Journal of Accountancy,* August 1938, p. 101.

ndex of the present worth of an asset's earning power at any
ime in the future.

Accountants who are not too greatly influenced by economic
theory ordinarily consider the original value of an asset and its
cost as synonymous. Allocation of portions of original cost to
the profit and loss of subsequent periods results in a reducing
balance which is often referred to as "book value." This process
of allocating is sometimes called "valuation" or "evaluation."

Greer[10] refers to the estimation of expired and unexpired
cost as "evaluation" and echoes the general accounting opinion
that this task of evaluation is a matter of "almost superhuman
insight, discrimination, and nicety of perception."

Over the long term, proprietorship can gain no advantage
from valuing assets initially at any figure other than actual cost.
This is so well recognized that practically all accounting authorities express their preference for cost valuation.

Hatfield[11] asserts that the valuation of assets at cost "clearly
rests upon an assumption," but says that cost in most cases is
"easiest of objective verification."

Canning[12] suggests that valuation at cost is founded upon
the presumption that the purchase thereof "was reasonably a
prudent act."

May[13] says that: "When the accountant records an asset
acquired at cost and retains it at that figure even though its value
is greater than cost, he does so because it is the cost that is
significant to him, not because he desires to value the asset and
accepts cost as the measure of value, in default of any better."

Husband[14] conceives of cost "from the viewpoint of what
the purchaser gives up and not from the viewpoint of what he
receives."

10 Howard C. Greer, "To What Extent Can the Practice of Accounting Be
Reduced to Rules and Standards?" *The Journal of Accountancy*, March 1938,
p. 218.
11 Henry Rand Hatfield, *Accounting* (New York, D. Appleton-Century Company, Inc., 1927), p. 66.
12 John B. Canning, *The Economics of Accountancy* (New York, The Ronald
Press Company, 1929), p. 231.
13 George O. May, *Twenty-Five Years of Accounting Responsibility 1911-1936*
(New York, American Institute Publishing Co., Inc., 1936), p. 402.
14 George R. Husband, "Accounting Postulates: An Analysis of the Tentative
Statement of Accounting Principles," *The Accounting Review*, December 1937.
p. 390.

Littleton[15] introduces the concept of arm's-length negotiation as follows:

Accounting principles are perhaps quite incapable of properly drawing distinctions between (1) a value tested by really independent bargaining, (2) a value legally established only by quasi-independent bargaining, and (3) a value not tested at all but resting at best upon some asserted analogy with certain collateral conditions outside of the enterprise.

ENTITY VALUATION. From the entity viewpoint, all of the arguments for and against the cost basis seem to have but little merit.

To the entity, valuation at cost is natural and obvious. When the expenditure of entity funds sooner or later becomes charged against the proprietor, the valuation of such an expenditure on any basis other than cost merely destroys the significance of that ultimate proprietorship deduction. This is in accordance with the opinion held by many that there is no difference between a capital expenditure and a revenue expenditure save that of time, hence there is no more reason for valuing an asset at more or less than cost than there is for booking an expense at more or less than cost.

ELEMENTS OF COST. Valuation of an asset at cost is generally accepted to mean its completed cost, not merely its bare purchase price.

Such items as incoming freight on the purchase of a machine or equipment, plus outlays for installation, are considered proper constituents of asset cost. The same rule holds true where the asset acquired is in bad condition, the expenditure necessary to make it usable being included as an element of acquisition cost.

In purchasing real estate for the purpose of erecting a new structure, it is often necessary to wreck an existing structure. The net cost of such wrecking is generally considered a proper element of the cost of the new building. Architects' fees, taxes, and interest during construction, cost of making surveys, preliminary legal expenses, and a great variety of similar expendi-

15 A. C. Littleton, "The Relation of Function to Principles," *The Accounting Review*, September 1938, p. 240.

ures may at times enter into asset cost. The opinion has been
xpressed that taxes on standing timber should be added to the
book value of that timber.

DIFFICULTIES OF COST VALUATION. To say that assets are
commonly valued at cost is not to state an invariable rule.
Under some circumstances valuation of specific assets at cost is
an impossibility if cost is assumed to mean cash outlay or its
equivalent.

Several common illustrations may be noted in this connection. The purchase of a manufacturing plant by the issuance
of capital stock represents a common transaction. The valuation
of that plant at the par value of the stock is almost an account-
ng necessity and, from the entity viewpoint, can be stated as
valuation at cost and yet the resulting values are often known
to be different from what they would have been had the transaction been consummated on a cash basis.

It may, in addition, be impossible to value specific assets on
a cost basis when they form part of a mixed purchase.

Also, when assets are donated to a company, they have no
true cost and any valuation assigned thereto can be considered
cost only by courtesy and for the purposes of record keeping.

In other instances, due to the limitations of the accounting
mechanism and its fundamental conventions, costs of assets
cannot be determined even though it is known that outlays have
been made. This rather common situation results when costs
are incurred in manufacturing a finished product and when that
finished product is reabsorbed in other costs. This is an accounting problem of considerable interest to which further reference
will be made in Chapter 26.

Occasionally, the cost basis of asset valuation is not adopted
because of the substantial expenditure of effort necessary to
determine costs. When the amount of error involved in valuation by estimate obviously is not material, as in the case of certain by-products, the cost basis of valuation may be abandoned
for purely practical reasons.

BARTER. Numerous interesting, even though generally
unimportant, accounting problems result from trade or barter.

In the country store a couple of dozen eggs may be traded by a customer for three gallons of kerosene.

One method of analyzing such transactions is based upon the artificial assumption that cash was realized by sale, immediately followed by a cash purchase. Thus, the proprietor of the country store may, if he so desires, consider that he has sold three gallons of kerosene at 14 cents a gallon, or 42 cents, and, with the money received, has immediately bought two dozen eggs at 21 cents a dozen, or 42 cents, thus establishing a cost value for the eggs.

This fiction may be helpful in establishing the cost value of the eggs, but it is a dangerous and highly improper fiction in its relation to the kerosene. Its adoption leads to the inevitable conclusion that the kerosene has been sold, resulting in realized income. If the convention of realization means anything, it must refer to the receipt of cash or cash equivalent in the form of a legal claim to cash. Regardless of how marketable the eggs may be, they represent neither cash nor a legal claim to cash and consequently there has been no sale and no realization of income.

A more acceptable theory of barter valuation recognizes that one deferred charge against future income, i.e., kerosene, has been exchanged for another deferred charge of the same type, i.e., eggs. The incoming asset takes the valuation of the outgoing asset. The eggs, therefore, are valued at 42 cents for just one reason, namely, that 42 cents was the cost of the kerosene. Such cases clearly represent substitution and value equivalence.

TRADE-INS. The amount named by an automobile dealer as representing the trade-in value of an old truck may be indicated as its sales price.

Assuming that the old truck cost $5,000, that its depreciated cost at the time of the transaction is $1,000, and that its trade-in value is $1,500, this method of viewing the transaction may indicate a "profit" of $500 on the sale of this capital asset. The purchase of the new truck at $6,000 is then imagined as a separate deal involving the disbursement of $6,000 in cash and the acquisition of a new fixed asset at a cost valuation of $6,000.

It is, however, well recognized that this method of splitting the transaction into two parts has an inflationary aspect. The

rade-in value of $1,500 for a $1,000 used truck may be unduly
igh because of the vendor's desire to sell the new truck.

The two aspects of the transaction are, therefore, not sepa-
ate and the apparent gain of $500 is not a true realized profit.
Nevertheless, there must be some recognition of the difference
between the $1,000 book value of the old truck and the $1,500
rade-in value. This $500 difference if not a profit must be con-
idered an offset to the cost of the new truck which will, there-
'ore, be shown not at $6,000 but at $5,500.

Bacas, Madden, and Rosenkampff,[16] in referring to a situa-
ion similar to the one just described, intimate that "there is a
profit from the viewpoint of good accounting practice. How-
ver, the U. S. Treasury Department does not consider such an
amount as a profit for the purpose of computing income taxes
but as a reduction of the purchase price of the new asset." The
Treasury Department views the so-called profit not as a gain but
as a saving. With this view most accountants would agree.

Some of the illustrations given help to explain why accountants cannot adhere uniformly to cost valuation. That they are
irmly inclined toward the cost basis whenever possible or prac-
icable is generally accepted, initial valuation at cost being the
only logical treatment from the entity viewpoint. The mere
act that original cost or depreciated cost may have but little
'elation to present conditions carries no weight with those who
accept the entity viewpoint, in which money valuation represents
10 more than a convenient symbol for describing a charge and
lischarge relationship.

Assets as Deferred Charges.—A most helpful accounting
concept, particularly in relation to profit determination, is the
one which considers non-cash assets as being equivalent to
leferred charges.

Its helpfulness lies in the fact that it eliminates the factors
of tangibility and intangibility and also the confusion between
economic values, resale values, and accounting values. Expendi-
ures are often made in the hope and expectation of a favorable
effect upon any future profits. Often such effects are meas-

---

16 Bacas, Madden, and Rosenkampff, *Auditing Procedure* (New York, The
Ronald Press Company, 1937), p. 327.

urable. On the logical ideal of matching costs and revenues the expenditures should then be considered as deductible from the future income for the encouragement of which they were made.

The purchase by a business of a factory, a machine, an item of office equipment, a supply of merchandise, or a carload of coal has some relation to future income. The relation may be reasonably direct, often it is remote.

THE DEFERRED CHARGE CONCEPT. While it is common to think of some assets as being deferred charges against future profits, it is not generally recognized that all assets except cash may be considered deferred charges, i.e., some of them are deferred charges against future income, others are deferred charges to cash.[17]

The most typical example of a deferred charge to cash is the ordinary account receivable. Other examples are notes receivable or such investments as bonds or other instruments payable on a due date. Strictly, cash in bank might also be included here, but this seems to be carrying the theory too far, justifying such an absurdity, for example, as considering cash in the custody of a cashier as being a receivable rather than cash on hand.

TESTS FOR CLASSIFICATION. When a corporation has a temporary fund of cash in excess of its needs, it may purchase stocks and bonds in the open market. On the other hand, the corporation may make a permanent investment in another corporation which produces an essential raw material.

Superficially it might appear that intent would determine whether the investment is a deferred charge to cash or a deferred charge to future income.

It is probably true that the treasurer making a short-term

[17] It is, of course, recognized that this theory is subject to misinterpretation. It is not advanced here as a practical suggestion for reconstructing balance sheets nor is it contended that some of its more extravagant applications introduced for explanatory purposes should be literally applied to the computation of profit. Neither the illustrations nor the reassembled balance sheet which follows is intended as anything more than an application of the exaggeration test referred to in Chapter 1. The differentiation which has been made in the following page between notes, bonds, mortgages, and receivables on the one hand and capital stock, inventories, and fixed assets on the other hand may be considered valuable in so far as it provides a basis for logical thinking about income and values. The resulting general concept is believed to be essential to an understanding of accounting profit.

nvestment for temporary employment of idle funds does, as a
matter of fact, think of such an investment as being related to
cash. He is also likely to think of the permanent investment
as being somewhat equivalent to a fixed asset.

A sounder basis of classification results from considering the
instruments which evidence the investment. If the instrument
shows a definite due date and is payable in cash on that date,
then the investment is properly to be classified as a deferred
charge to cash, no action of any kind, in theory at least, being
needed to obtain the cash upon maturity.

If, on the other hand, the instrument is one not carrying a
due date, then the only possible way that the investment can be
recovered is by a sale. Save for unusual coincidence, the sale
of the instrument will result in either a profit or a loss. An
investment without due date is, therefore, in the nature of a
deferred charge against future income, not a deferred charge
to cash.

The two typical forms of investment are, of course, bonds
and stocks. Because bonds have a due date, they represent
deferred charges to cash. Because stocks have no due date, they
represent deferred charges to future income.

This distinction is more significant than appears at first
glance, since it is related to the broader problem of income realization. It is, of course, true that the temporary investment of
excess funds may be evidenced by common stocks, it being the
intention to sell those stocks within a short period of time. The
stocks themselves may be listed and enjoy an active market.
Nevertheless, they cannot be classified as deferred charges to
cash since the intermediate step of selling is necessary in order
to effect their conversion.

Investment in bonds, on the other hand, may be a permanent
investment made with the expectation that the bonds will be
held for a decade or more. Nevertheless, because such bonds
have a definite due date, and will be converted into cash without
the intermediate step of selling, such an investment represents
not a deferred charge to future income but a legal claim to
future cash and must be considered a deferred charge to cash.

The bonds may have been acquired for the temporary invest-

ment of idle funds with the definite expectation that they wil
be sold within a few months. This, however, does not alte
their theoretical status as deferred charges to cash.

An ordinary account receivable may be and often is sold
The fact that an account receivable may be sold and a loss suf
fered upon the sale does not affect its classification as a deferred
charge to cash.

The distinction lies in the nature of the instrument or claim
not in intent or final outcome. It is not affected by such consid
erations as marketability or credit rating except in so far a
these factors may, for balance sheet purposes, be scrutinized
unfavorably by auditors.

Is non-depreciable land acquired for permanent holding to
be classified as a deferred charge against future income? The
analysis here has some elements of interest. Assuming that a
corporation has a perpetual life, and assuming that land pur
chased for business purposes has perpetual value in that it i
not exhausted, depleted, or depreciated, then the land represent
a deferred charge against all of the income of the future and
since the future in this case means perpetuity, at least theoreti
cally, the amount of the investment in such land to be charged
against income in any one period is practically zero.

REARRANGEMENT OF BALANCE SHEET. Adopting the con
cept that all assets except cash are deferred charges either to
cash or against future income, then one logical, even if theoreti
cal, scheme of asset classification may replace the familiar "cur
rent, non-current" basis. Since the substitute classification ha
some analytical value, it deserves fuller description.

The classification is based upon the assumption that any asse
of a business enterprise may fall logically into one of three
mutually exclusive groups:

    Cash
    Deferred charges to cash
    Deferred charges to future income

Applying this classification with a few necessary changes to
the American Institute form of balance sheet, the following
unorthodox but perhaps interesting rearrangement results:

Cash:
  Cash in banks and on hand . . . .

Deferred Charges to Cash:
  Bonds (marketable or otherwise) . . . .
  Notes and accounts receivable:
    Customers:
      Accounts receivable . . . .
      Notes receivable . . . .
    Others . . . .
    Less—
      Reserve for doubtful notes and accounts . . . .
      Reserve for discounts, freight, allowances, etc. . . . . . .
    Indebtedness of stockholders, directors, officers, and employees
    Indebtedness of affiliated companies . . . .

Deferred Charges to Future Income:
  Inventories:
    Raw materials and supplies . . . .
    Work in process . . . .
    Finished goods . . . .
  Investments:
    Stocks (marketable or otherwise) . . . .
  Property, Plant, and Equipment:
    Land used for plant . . . .
    Buildings used for plant . . . .
    Machinery and equipment . . . .
    Patterns and drawings . . . .
    Office furniture and fixtures . . . .
         Total property, plant, and equipment . . . .
    Less—
      Reserves for depreciation, depletion, amortization, etc. . .
  Intangible Assets:
    . . . .
  Deferred Charges:
    Prepaid expenses, interest, insurance, taxes, etc. . . . . . .
    Bond discount . . . .
         Total . . . .

Nature of Inventories.—Inventories are commonly shown as current assets. Inventories, however, are not of the same order as other current assets. The total of current assets is composed of unlike elements, i.e., cash, deferred charges to cash, and, in so far as inventories are concerned, deferred charges against future income.

This viewpoint should bring some comfort to those proponents of the base-stock method who insist base inventories are
equivalent to fixed assets since it appears that inventories and
fixed assets have much more in common than inventories
and accounts receivable.

INVENTORIES AND FIXED ASSETS. The differences between
inventories, particularly merchandise inventories, and fixed
assets are more obvious than significant. The disappearance of
merchandise value usually is accompanied by a diminishment
of quantities, whereas the disappearance of fixed asset values
usually is not.

The disappearance of specific items of merchandise often is
directly correlated with items of income, whereas the relation
between income and expired fixed asset value is usually less
direct. The deferring of the inventory charge against future
income generally involves a short period of time. The deferring
of the fixed asset charge against future income is often a matter of many years. These, however, are obvious rather than
basic distinctions.

Essentially, inventories and fixed assets are alike in that they
represent deferred charges against future income. Without
pressing the point unduly, it may be suggested that this view
has a certain practical value in that it tends to clarify some problems of inventory valuation which are obscure when inventories
are considered as part of a homogeneous group of deferred
charges to cash. Because in the normal course of events inventories are converted into cash, it is plausible to think of them in
their relation to cash rather than in relation to profits. But the
relation of the inventory to cash more nearly resembles the relation of fixed assets to cash than it does the relation of accounts
receivable to cash.

The sales transaction completely changes the character of
inventories, fixed assets, or other deferred charges against
future income. The sale is a process of transmutation the principal significance of which is fully recognized in all accounting
literature but which perhaps has not been considered fully in
some of its less obvious implications.

INVENTORY REVALUATION. Confusion is evidenced by various proposals and practices having to do with inventory valuation. Such a rule as that of cost or market is derived from the natural but improper assumption that inventories represent a deferred charge to cash and that accordingly they should be valued on some basis having a direct, indirect, or at least a plausible relation to cash.

The result of this assumption is unfortunate because of the consequent distortion of periodic profits.

Just as certain diseases leave in their train permanent weaknesses and impairments, so did the overemphasis of the balance sheet viewpoint leave accounting with a heritage of misconception and confusion. The balance sheet viewpoint, not by direct assertion but surely by implication, viewed inventories as deferred charges to cash and valued them accordingly. While accountants, credit men, and other financial experts certainly recognized the obvious differences between receivables on the one hand and inventories on the other, nevertheless the persistence of the balance sheet viewpoint resulted in such unsound derivatives as the current ratio so commonly used as a credit test of debt-paying ability.

That the transition from merchandise to cash may be rapid or long drawn out is a matter of no consequence. Where it is, or can be, rapid, as in the case of standard raw materials or finished products of ready salability, the use of the current ratio, while no more justifiable, is at least harmless. It is, however, based upon a false assumption which may prove deceptive and costly when the inventory consists of special materials, work in progress, or finished goods for which there is no natural or broad demand and the marketing of which represents a far more difficult technical task than its manufacture.

Recognition of the similarity of inventories and fixed assets is desirable from two viewpoints, that of valuation in the balance sheet and that of distortion in the profit and loss statement. From both viewpoints the matter is particularly significant because of the dominance of inventories and fixed assets. To say that the aggregate of these two items in the ordinary business will account for 80% or 90% of the total assets is obviously a mere guess, but surely the guess is reasonably well supported by observation and shows the importance of these assets.

INVENTORY CHARACTERISTICS. Those who hold that inventories are deferred charges to future income find that some statements regarding inventory valuation seem strange.

To say that an inventory valuation can have no significance except as an index of funds to be produced, is to adopt the balance sheet viewpoint with its unspoken but nevertheless inherent concept of inventories as deferred charges to cash. To say that customers pay for the mistakes and misfortunes of management when actual cost is used as the basis for valuing inventories, attaches improper significance to the inventory.

Of course, the customer may pay for the mistakes and misfortunes of management not only in connection with inventories but also in connection with the plant which was bought at too high a price, or the sales promotion campaign which proved to be abortive, or the unwise labor policy adopted. Such utterances assume a relationship which is generally discredited in so far as individual enterprises are concerned, namely, that costs instead of supply and demand predetermine selling price. Only under peculiar monopoly conditions does the cost theory present any appearance of reality.

Intent as a Test of Classification.—It is no contribution to accounting thought to assert on the one hand that inventory and machinery are both capital and then attempt to distinguish between them by saying that inventory is for sale while machinery is for use.

Such a comment is based upon superficial physical characteristics. Is there any impropriety in claiming that machinery is for sale in the sense that the amounts periodically deducted from its book value enter into inventory valuations under almost any plan of cost accounting and find their way to cost of sales just as truly as does purchased material or labor or any other classification of factory cost? If a fixed asset having a ten-year useful life is acquired and at the end of that life one profit and loss statement covering the entire ten years is prepared, it is indeed difficult to see why that machine has not been sold to the public.

By the deferred charge theory presented here, there is no essential difference between inventories, fixed assets, intangible assets, and prepaid expense. They are basically alike in so far as their relation to future income is concerned, regardless of the fact that different engineering, management, and accounting techniques may influence their periodic association with income. In fact, it is difficult to comprehend how a logical philosophy of accounting can evolve unless this concept is adopted as a fundamental article of faith.

Apportionments and Transfers.—One of the simplest accounting concepts is that of exchanging asset value for asset value. This is a type of value transference which is obvious. Not so direct is the transfer which results from the application of factory labor to material or application of manufacturing expense to material, yet these are only variants of the first. This convention of transferred values has already been referred to as the basis of modern cost accounting. It does not, however, belong exclusively to cost accounting.

In a retail store or an office the same phenomenon is noticed. The retailer who purchases a new counter or display shelf may have to call upon one of his employees to unpack it, paint it, and install it. During the time he is working on the showcase, this employee's wages may be transferred to the new equipment, with the result that the true cost of that new equipment to the retailer is its original purchase price plus the other costs necessary to put it into usable condition.

Professional men may not be meticulous about accounting matters but almost any doctor or lawyer purchasing a second-hand table for $15 and employing a carpenter to repair it for $5 more will consider the cost of the table to be $20.

CONVENTION OF TRANSFERRED VALUES. Illustrations could be multiplied to establish the declaration that the convention of transferred values naturally conforms to non-technical thinking. It is a convention which is elaborately used in certain phases of accounting, particularly in cost accounting. A simplified situation may be used here to illustrate the application of this convention.

A carpenter sets himself up as a builder of wooden rowboats. He purchases the lumber cut to size at a cost of $15 per boat. He employs a workman at $20 a week. If that workman takes two weeks to complete the boat, the carpenter, whether he is accounting trained or not, recognizes that there has been a transfer of value as the result of which the cost of the finished boat is $55. Because the carpenter's rent, light, heat, taxes, and similar items are not so directly connected with the construction of one particular hull, the carpenter may not realize that a transference of value also occurs in the case of these items. But even without accounting training he will learn to realize this fact when he has completed twenty boats, sold them all, and terminated the business to go into some other employment. At that time it is simple indeed for him to realize that 1/20 of his rent, 1/20 of his taxes, 1/20 of his heat and of his light were in reality transferred to and attached to the cost of each boat to be recovered, if possible, by selling. All of this is commonplace and is accepted not only by accountants but by laymen.

Application of this convention to a specific situation represents one of the most delicate and complex of all accounting operations. A discussion of cost accounting technique, with particular reference to expense apportionment and distribution, is not within the province of this volume, but a few fundamental questions which are derived directly from this convention are appropriate for present discussion.

Modification of Convention.   Of special interest is the cost accounting practice which attempts to distinguish in connection with any given item of factory outlay that portion which properly should be transferred and that remaining portion which should not.

Returning to the boat builder illustration, dullness of trade resulting in the lack of orders for boats might require that the boat builder's shop be closed for a week. Assuming that the $20 a week employee was laid off during that period, the question then arises whether the costs of rent, taxes, and similar items during the week of idleness are transferred to the cost of the boats fabricated in other weeks. From the long-term viewpoint, i.e., when the twenty boats are completed and the business terminated, the cost of constructing each boat includes its fair share of the expense which continued during the week of idleness. For a variety of plausible operating reasons this viewpoint is not maintained by the majority of cost accountants who attempt to distinguish between normal costs and total costs.

In the factory which operates at less than capacity, part of the expense is attached to the inventory of work in progress and part is withheld from that inventory, being considered a loss to be absorbed currently. Reference has already been made to the desire for cost comparability which has had a strong influence against the inclusion of extraordinary operating costs. Even in so-called old-fashioned systems of cost accounting which attempt the difficult task of accumulating "actual" costs, it is prevailing practice to use predetermined rates based upon some standard of normal operations, with the result that a substantial part of the total expense may not be transferred to work in progress when the factory is operating at much less than capacity.

This procedure is justified by the fact that many of the expenses of manufacturing are in the nature of fixed expenses which are reduced only slightly, if at all, by a decrease in manufacturing activity. Among such items are rent, taxes, insurance, and depreciation. When a factory is operating at full capacity, these costs are all transferred and become elements of inventory. When the factory is operating at less than capacity, the excess portion of these costs is considered an immediate loss. It is seen that the simple and logical convention of transferred values has been considerably modified by certain practical considerations.

An elaboration of this factory viewpoint finds expression in standard cost accounting, which operates to pare off still other costs during the process of transference. This naturally has its effect upon the resulting inventory values. Hence, it can also be maintained that standard cost procedure results in a distortion of comparative profits to the extent that inventories are held over from one period to another.

Some of these problems derived from the convention of transferred values are of dominant importance in accounting for manufacturing inventories. The relationship of these problems to periodic net profit is so influential as to justify further discussion in Chapters 22 to 27, inclusive.

Recovery of Deferred Charges.—From the long-term viewpoint of a single venture a profit cannot be made until all deferred costs have been recovered.

This has been illustrated by the venturer's ship which had to be sold before the net profit of the venture could be determined. It is considered improper to figure profit this way under modern business conditions, owing to the facts that because of their corporate organization enterprises often have perpetual life and that business ventures are so overlapping as to be practically continuous.

As a substitute for complete realization of assets, accountants distribute the deferred costs ratably and equitably against the incomes of the several accounting periods involved. Such distribution, which periodically converts part of an asset value into an expense, cost, or loss, is commonly known as amortization, depreciation, or depletion. When such transfers are not made according to a predetermined plan, they are commonly referred to as write-offs.

The transfers from inventories to various cost, expense, or loss classifications may not be referred to by any of these descriptive titles. Credits to inventory accounts for merchandise or other values which have been withdrawn are often referred to as "inventory withdrawals" or "inventory reliefs."

These various types of recovering deferred charges, while having the same fundamental purpose, are applied in different ways and with different effects under different conditions. The distribution in so far as practicable is according to the accounting periods benefited and in proportion to those benefits.

The amount of asset value yet to be distributed at the end of any accounting period has little significance save in relation to its future distribution. The cost of the asset at the time of its acquisition or determination is based upon a convention, and even at that time may have little or no relation to market value, realizable value, future service value, or any other kind of value. Rather it must be regarded as no more than a convenient symbolization for the purpose of establishing a charge against an accounting entity. If the original cost has only this significance, then any undistributed portion of that cost can have no more significance.

It is upon this theory that the current emphasis on the profit and loss viewpoint is firmly established. As Mason clearly indicated in *Principles of Public-Utility Depreciation* (p. 26), "Once the assets have been acquired the enterprise is committed to their use and their undepreciated balances are of little significance to anyone."

CHAPTER 20

PROBLEMS OF EXPENDITURE AND COST

That expenditures are not incurred without motive, that they often have some direct or indirect relation to future income, is essentially simple and convincing in connection with such major classifications as inventories and fixed assets. There are, however, certain common expenditures the relation of which to income is none too obvious. In this category are the various types of insurance and certain other costs, incurred for protective purposes, which may logically be grouped with insurance.

There are in addition certain deferred charges, such as organization expense, the practical treatment of which does not always coincide with accounting theory. Finally, there are problems of cost for the treatment of which the traditional accounting mechanism appears inadequate. Among such problems are those referring to imputed costs, joint costs, and reabsorbed costs, together with others having to do with time lags.

Expenditures of the Insurance Type.—Expenditures for insurance are usually related to future income. Clearly, however, the relationship is of a protective nature differing from expenditures of the sales promotion type which have for their direct objective the augmenting of future income.

KINDS OF INSURANCE. Various kinds of insurance protect future income against the possibility of violent diminutions due to non-operating loss.

Insurance protection is sought not only against loss by fire and dishonesty but also against a wide variety of business contingencies. Commonly available are such types of business insurance as liability insurance for injuries to employees and to the public, insurance against robbery, burglary, and hold-ups in connection with various types of assets, insurance available against specific accidents, such as boiler explosion, plate glass breakage, and fly-wheel explosion. Business life insurance is available in different types of policies both for groups and individuals. Insurance may protect against riots and civil commotion, against loss of profits, against some legal responsibility for malpractice or other alleged unprofessional conduct.

This partial list by no means exhausts the contingencies against which insurance protection can be purchased. Regardless of type or purpose, the expenditure for insurance is commonly made with a definite motive of safeguarding future profits. Occasionally, as a substitute for wage or salary increases, insurance protection for employees has the same relation to income as the wages or salaries themselves.

NATURE OF INSURANCE COSTS. Insurance payments may usually be considered a loss of the same general type as the contingency to which they refer. Periodic payments for fire insurance can be imagined as equivalent to small and regular fire losses accepted in lieu of the contingency of a large fire loss. In theory such expenditures should be accounted for in the same manner as an uninsured fire loss. The cost of fidelity bonds is the same kind of a loss as that which might otherwise be suffered because of dishonesty.

Payments made upon a policy protecting against loss by riot may be regarded as the costs of small regularly recurring riots.

Because insurance payments are made regularly, it is common to view them not as losses but as operating expenses or costs. The general viewpoint toward insurance has been clearly set forth by Mason[1] as follows:

. . . the risk of loss by fire is an inevitable accompaniment of business activity and the premium paid on a fire-insurance policy is therefore treated as a regular operating cost or expense. In certain localities tornadoes are so rare that tornado insurance is not carried and if property damage does result from such a cause, the amount of the loss is usually not considered as an operating cost or expense but is handled as an adjustment of net income or surplus.

[1] Perry Mason, *Principles of Public-Utility Depreciation* (Chicago, American Accounting Association, 1937), p. 6.

The logic of such treatment is not convincing. It is true that the risk of fire loss is an inevitable accompaniment of business activity. It is equally true that risk of tornado loss is also an inevitable accompaniment of business activity. The fact that one risk is greater than the other is a matter of no theoretical consequence.

It does not justify any difference in treatment of the two types of premiums nor, if uninsured loss should occur, of the two types of loss.

INSURANCE AND VALUATION.   Not all authorities look upon insurance in its relation to future income.

Canning[2] attempts to relate it to asset valuation by saying: "If a building burns, the loss, unless otherwise provided for, falls upon the owner. The building, freed of the risk of loss by fire, is worth more than if subject to that risk."

Unfortunately, the same type of reasoning cannot be applied to other insured contingencies. Cash on hand insured against embezzlement is not worth more than if no insurance was carried. It is difficult to see what, if any, business asset is worth more because of public liability insurance or group insurance the cost of which may be thought of as an increase in employees' salaries and wages.

The suggestion that an insurance premium represents a small certain loss of the same type as the contingent one to which it refers finds some support in the practice of self-insurance adopted by large corporations where properties are widely scattered. The theory of self-insurance is based on the belief that occasional losses by fire will average less per annum than the cost of the insurance. The occasional fire loss which does occur under these conditions is a direct substitute for insurance premium expense and may properly be so regarded in spite of the fact that the bookkeeping procedure generally employed involves the creation of insurance reserves by regular periodic deductions from income.

If formal insurance protection evidenced by contracts with established insurance companies was the only problem involved,

2 John B. Canning, *The Economics of Accountancy* (New York, The Ronald Press Company, 1929), p. 37.

the subject might not merit more than passing mention. It is, however, noted that the insurance concept helps to explain certain types of expenditures which are otherwise difficult to classify.

CHARITABLE DONATIONS.   Consider the contribution of a New York corporation to some local charity.

Assuming that the stockholders of that corporation are widely scattered throughout the various states of the union, it may appear that the corporation has no right to deduct from its profits a contribution to a New York charity. The stockholder in Iowa might well argue that this represents a forced levy upon his equity, that he has his own local charities to take care of, and that he has little or no interest in making a contribution to the unfortunate citizens of New York. One may, in fact, wonder whether such a charitable contribution by a corporation is not an *ultra vires* act.

The attempt to analyze a corporation's charitable contribution from any viewpoint other than that of insurance protection is likely to lead into difficulties. A corporation is presumed to be soulless and its charitable contribution is unthinkable save on two grounds.

It may be suggested that the corporation is soulless but that the officers and directors of the corporation are not. If this be accepted, then the stockholder in Iowa has a valid complaint against the officers and directors, either because they are substituting a corporate contribution in lieu of making their own personal donations, or because they are so weak or so ignorant that they approve an expenditure which has no business objective.

It may, however, be contended that a donation by a New York corporation to a New York charity has a business objective on the ground that such a donation is in the nature of insurance protection and is therefore directly related to future profits: that failure to make such a donation would, in fact, result in so much unfavorable publicity and ill-will as to cause profit shrinkage resulting in a loss comparable with other uninsured losses whether by fire, theft, or otherwise.

There may be ample reason why individuals should contribute substantially to political war chests, homecoming celebrations, and organized charities. There is no reason why a corporation should do so save that failure to make such contributions carries a threat against the future profits of the corporation.

TAXES.   Among the insurance type of costs, taxes of certain kinds may be included.

One may ask what business motive underlies a tax expenditure, particularly in those cases where the corporation received no measurable benefit therefrom. It has always been held that the justification for paying taxes is to be found in governmental preservation of law and order, in police protection, and various other services and safeguards. But it is also to be noted that many a corporation pays taxes in spite of the fact that its management does not regard the expenditure as well made or one which will bring in a proportionate return.

Paton[3] recognizes that: "Taxes are coerced; their amount is largely outside the control of the management; they do not follow price trends closely; they can hardly be said to measure the value of services received and utilized in production. Taxes, therefore, are not congruous with ordinary expenses and are not a cost of sales in any strict sense." This, however, seems to be an explanation which does not explain. Many payments made by business are coerced. The influential salesman by his threat to leave his employer, taking a number of good customers along with him, receives his increase in salary by coercion. Extortionate payments required by a poorly phrased contract may be coercive.

Expenditures are made either for some benefit or as a protection against some loss. The first motive is generally ruled out in connection with taxes, leaving the second as the only logical explanation.

If business expenditures are never made without motive, then the only possible motive for paying taxes for which no equivalent benefit is received is that of protection against some threat to future profits, the threat, of course, being governmental retribution both swift and certain. It is to avoid tax penalties

3 W. A. Paton, *Essentials of Accounting* (New York, The Macmillan Company, 1938), p. 101.

and to avoid serious troubles having a direct relationship to future profits that tax expenditures are made, and it is only as insurance that they can be explained logically from the individual business man's viewpoint.

LEGAL EXPENDITURES.   While expenditures for legal services are sometimes justified by profit making motives they more commonly refer to profit saving.

It is safe to say that the majority of consultations between business men and lawyers are for the purpose of avoiding or minimizing probable future business losses. Legal services in connection with damage suits, tax controversies, threatened legislation, and various property rights and contractual obligations somewhat resemble insurance.

GRAFT, BRIBERY, AND ESPIONAGE.   It is assumed by most business writers that no expenditures are ever made for such base and improper purposes as graft, bribery, or espionage. Montgomery is one of the few who have actually written about such matters as secret commissions and other forms of graft.

These practices not only exist but are often unavoidable. It is not always possible or advisable for the corporation manager to be too courageous when a crooked labor leader invites a secret and personal cash settlement. The management of a company must sometimes make the choice between having certain important work delayed or paying tribute to a building inspector.

Generally expenditures which have been made for such secret purposes have for their motive the protection of future profits and hence are explainable as being in the nature of insurance since they involve a small certain loss as contrasted with a larger contingent one.

Organization Expense.—In the formation of a corporation certain necessary costs are incurred. Lawyers must be compensated, underwriting costs must be paid, and stock certificates must be printed.

These and other items of organization expense are unavoidable in the formation of a corporation. If that corporation has a life limited, for example, to thirty years, then the aggregate of such preliminary costs represents a deferred charge to be written off one-thirtieth each year.

If the corporation has an unlimited life, then organization expense is a perpetually deferred charge none of which should be periodically amortized.

BALANCE SHEET VIEWPOINT. It is in relation to such an item as organization expense that the conflict between the balance sheet and the profit and loss viewpoints is clearly evident.

The balance sheet viewpoint, based as it is upon either an open or an implied concept of non-cash assets as having value in and of themselves and apart from their relation to future income, finds difficulty in recognizing organization expense as an asset. From the balance sheet viewpoint it apparently has no asset characteristics, being utterly intangible and having no realizable value. It has therefore been generally conceded by accountants that organization expense should be written off as promptly as possible in the early years of a corporation's life.

Montgomery[4] has stated the case for this treatment as follows: "they [organization expenses] have no realizable value in liquidation, and little or none specifically even when the corporation is sold as a going concern." He adds that "it is customary to write them off immediately against capital surplus or as rapidly as possible against current earnings or earned surplus after the business begins to accumulate profits." As to amortization of organization expense he suggests charging "directly against surplus, or as a deduction from current net income."

Canning[5] has noted certain difficulties in connection with this item: "Some accountants and writers on accounting assert that it is an asset; others treat it without comment as though it were an asset; still others rightly say it is not an asset at all, but no one unconditionally denies the item a place in the balance sheet." He attempts to justify asset classification for organization expense by intimating that "the assets remaining after the outlay may be more valuable to those beneficially interested in the proprietorship."

[4] Robert H. Montgomery, *Auditing Theory and Practice* (New York, The Ronald Press Company, 1934), p. 299.
[5] John B. Canning, *The Economics of Accountancy* (New York, The Ronald Press Company, 1929), p. 31.

Kester[6] takes a somewhat different view: "In the same way that the costs of installing machinery in position and ready for use are capitalized by being added to the value of the equipment, so may the organization expenses of a corporation be legitimately capitalized as being the measure of the amount of the greater value which these organized business elements have over the same elements unorganized." Recognizing the practical rather than the theoretical necessity rapidly to amortize organization expense indicates, in this instance, Kester's acceptance of the balance sheet viewpoint.

Kester also notes the Treasury Department's opposing contention "that legitimate organization expenses add elements of actual and continuing value to the business, value which does not depreciate but continues throughout its life."

Profit and Loss Viewpoint. The following scattered quotations from Paton[7] are suggestive and interesting.

He observes "that whether or not a particular outlay results in an addition to the value of a specific *tangible* asset is a point of little significance as far as its fundamental accounting character is concerned." He adds that: "Financiering is as essential as engineering." "Hence promotion and other preliminary costs may be considered quite as legitimate as the costs of surveying, grading, etc." Paton[8] also suggests that the balance sheet viewpoint calling for rapid amortization of organization expense is unreasonable and "is based upon a conception of organization costs as an uncertain, dubious item, a necessary evil, which should be eliminated as soon as possible."

Sound as the above observations are, Paton[8] nevertheless refused to take the extreme position that "organization costs are a bona fide value throughout the legal life of the enterprise, and should only be extinguished if the business is liquidated and its existence terminated," since he considers this practice "hopelessly unsound if carried to extremes."

6 Roy B. Kester, *Advanced Accounting* (New York, The Ronald Press Company, 1933), pp. 395, 396.

7 W. A. Paton, *Accounting Theory* (New York, The Ronald Press Company, 1922), p. 334.

8 W. A. Paton, *Accounting Theory* (New York, The Ronald Press Company, 1922), pp. 338, 339.

In lieu thereof he mentions with some favor the plan of amortizing organization expense (1) during the life of the principal physical properties for which the initial funds were expended, (2) during the life of a terminable security in connection with which the organization cost was incurred, and (3) to the extent that the total of other asset values is reduced through depletion, depreciation, etc.

In shifting from the balance sheet to the profit and loss viewpoint, it is difficult to attach importance to the asset character of organization expense. If its nature is properly disclosed it can deceive no one.

On the other hand, any of the various plans of amortization which have been suggested are deceptive from the viewpoint of profit distortion, this being particularly true of those suggestions for charging it to capital surplus or earned surplus or amortizing it against current earnings as rapidly as possible.

From the profit and loss viewpoint, the third treatment is much more deceptive than to continue showing the organization expense as an asset item. Organization expense is obviously a cost to be amortized over the corporation's life and if that life is perpetual then the periodic amortization is zero. If the corporation's life is prematurely terminated, organization expense will not be the only asset on the corporation's books which will be unrealizable.

Special Cost Problems.—Logically to be treated here in spite of their obvious relationship to manufacturing inventories are certain special cost problems. These problems are of four general types referring to: (1) imputed costs, (2) reabsorbed costs, (3) joint costs, and (4) situations involving excessive time lags.

Imputed Costs.—Imputed costs have an economic background and are conceived by economists as meaning costs not specifically incurred nor even fully defined and measurable which must be deducted from business profits in order to determine "pure profits."

ECONOMIC RECOGNITION OF IMPUTED COSTS. Applicable primarily to non-corporate forms of business enterprise business profits of an entrepreneur consist in part of interest on capital he has actually invested, rent for land which he has devoted to the use of the business, and a salary return for his own services.

In the common type of sole proprietorship, such as the small grocery store, the hamburger stand, or the neighborhood drug store, the owner makes no distinction between the business as an entity and himself as the owner. While he may withdraw funds from time to time, he does not specifically consider part of these funds as representing his salary and the remainder as representing profits. No part of his net income is thought of as interest or rent.

The profit shown on his books may consist of four separate and distinct returns: (1) rent, (2) interest, (3) wages, and (4) pure profit.

The economic view is well set forth by Kiekhofer[9] in the following question: "If we assume that the entrepreneur, be he farmer, merchant, or manufacturer, is able to supply all of his own capital and land, and thus pays neither loan interest nor contract rent, does the absence of such explicit payments mean a proportional increase in profits?" He adds that: "There is no convincing reason for thinking so," and suggests that: "If the entrepreneurs of a business enterprise are obliged to hire an outsider as manager, the manager's salary would unhesitatingly be entered as an expense of operation. Is it any less so when the entrepreneur functions as manager himself?"

ACCOUNTING FOR IMPUTED COSTS. Not always do the economists consider the relationship of these imputed costs to accounting. Ely and Hess[10] do so as follows: "By proper accounting, these derelict cost items [unpaid salaries of owner-managers, unpaid interest on their capital and unpaid rent on their land] may be separated or allocated and added to operating costs and fixed charges. The result will be a differentiated statement of *all costs* and a residual item of *pure profits*."

While intimating that these imputed costs should be estimated and entered as though they were actual costs, Ely and

9 William H. Kiekhofer, *Economic Principles, Problems and Policies* (New York, D. Appleton-Century Company, 1936), pp. 582, 583.
10 Ely and Hess, *Outlines of Economics* (New York, The Macmillan Company, 1937), pp. 490, 491.

Hess did not suggest the proper accounting treatment of the off-setting credits. It is in the treatment of the credit element of the imputed cost entry that a problem arises.

From the entity viewpoint an imputed cost has no significance, since it results simultaneously in a deduction from and an addition to the proprietor's account and is therefore an artificial inflation of both sides of that account. As a matter of sound business analysis it is, of course, important for the proprietor of a business to make certain calculations, outside of the bookkeeping scheme, for the purpose of giving effect to imputed costs. Commonly these calculations are informal and may involve no more than the comparison of a year's profit with the return that the proprietor believes he *could* have made if instead of operating his business he had done the following things: (1) invested his cash capital in bonds or some other form of investment requiring no direct supervision, (2) leased his land to others at a fair rental, and (3) hired himself out as an employee to some other business man.

These calculations are a familiar part of the mental arithmetic of shrewd business men. Whether or not they should be introduced into the double entry scheme of bookkeeping seems to be unimportant. If, as Ely and Hess have suggested, these "derelict cost items" should be added to operating costs, then by clear implication they must at the same time appear as a credit to some one of the proprietor's accounts in the entity record. The artificial loss reflected by one half of the entry must be balanced by an artificial gain due to the other half.

Superficially it may appear that this form of accounting manipulation cancels itself. If it did cancel itself during an accounting period, there would be no accounting problem involved.

IMPUTED COSTS IN MANUFACTURING. It is only when the imputed costs are credited to income and shown as income for an accounting period, and are reflected as a cost addition only part of which is actually written off during the period, that the fiction becomes highly improper.

In the case of the ordinary retail merchant, this problem seldom presents itself. If such an owner-manager so desires, he can value his services at $100,000 a year, charging that $100,000 to operating expense and crediting it to income, the two completely offsetting each other during the period. The profit for that period would be no different from what it would be had the imputed cost of $100,000 been omitted. If, on the contrary, the business under consideration is a manufacturing establishment, and if any of the imputed costs find their way, through processes of apportionment and reapportionment, into work in progress and finished goods, and if the amount of such imputed costs contained in these inventories is more or less at the end of the period than it was at the beginning, an entirely different situation prevails.

To the extent that imputed costs in inventory at the end of an accounting period exceed the imputed costs in inventory at the beginning of that period, the net profit for the period is overstated. If the opposite situation prevails and the imputed costs in the inventory at the end of the period are less than at the beginning, the net profit for the period will be correspondingly understated.

It may be contended that if the difference between the imputed costs in inventory at the beginning and end of the period is determined, and if the relationship between them is such that an artificial and unrealized profit has been shown, the amount thereof specifically can be disclosed or segregated on the profit and loss statement.

While this is, of course, true, it must be observed that it is not always an easy matter to analyze the constituents of inventories, particularly where the identity of the original components has been lost in the bookkeeping processes.

IMPUTED DEPRECIATION. If imputed costs were no more than an economic concept, they would scarcely deserve extended accounting discussion. Unfortunately, suggestions are sometimes made and sometimes adopted which result in an equivalent to imputed costs. Possibly economists would not so label some of them, particularly when they do not refer to rent, interest, or wages.

An example of something similar to imputed cost has been noted in connection with depreciation.

When an asset costing $1,000 is assumed to have a life of ten years with no residual value, $100 will be charged off each year and at the end of the tenth year no asset value will appear on the books. If, however, an error was made in estimating the future life and if it actually should have been twenty years instead of ten, the result of the error is twofold. First, a usable asset remains in existence although it has been fully depreciated, and, second, costs have been distorted since they have been charged with $100 a year for the first ten years when the correct charge should have been only $50, and will be charged with nothing during each of the next ten years instead of $50.

The American Accounting Association suggests that the asset may be reinstated and that the correction be reflected in revised profit and loss statements for the prior periods.

Others have seen no necessity for such reinstatement but rather have suggested that the depreciation be continued at the rate of $100 a year for each of the second ten years. The purpose is cost comparability. Any such depreciation provision for the second ten years is a clear equivalent to imputed cost.

IMPUTED INTEREST IN MANUFACTURING.   Another type of imputed cost formerly much argued over is interest as an element of manufacturing expense.

The late Clinton H. Scovell was an ardent proponent of the recognition of interest as an element of cost and during his lifetime the subject was much discussed. The argument in favor of including interest as an element of cost is twofold. From the viewpoint of the business as a whole, it helps to point out an important fact to the managers of any enterprise which persistently fails to return a normal current rate of interest on the investment. From the more detailed cost accounting viewpoint, it is said to make an important cost distinction between those manufacturing departments using costly machinery and those using inexpensive machinery or none at all.

Scovell[11] also insisted that "the inclusion of interest in detailed costs is essential to the process of making comparisons and formulating managerial judgments."

11 *Accountants' Handbook* (New York, The Ronald Press Company, 1937), p. 1114.

Since the majority of accountants and business men have lost interest in this controversy, it hardly seems to justify extensive consideration of arguments for and against. The most practical argument against the inclusion of interest in costs is the unfavorable attitude of the Treasury Department. The best theoretical argument is the possibility that the inclusion of this imputed cost in inventories may cause unrealized profits.

This may happen when the amount of interest in inventory at the end of an accounting period is greater than at the beginning. A simplified illustration based upon the "identical company test" follows:

COMPANY A

Sales		$100,000
Inventory, beginning	$10,000	
Cost of Goods Manufactured	70,000	
	$80,000	
Inventory, end	20,000	
Cost of Sales		60,000
		$ 40,000
Expenses		30,000
		$10,000
Other Income		
Net Profit		$ 10,000

COMPANY B

Sales		$100,000
Inventory, beginning (incl. int. $1,000)	$11,000	
Cost of Goods Manufactured (incl. int. $7,000)	77,000	
	$88,000	
Inventory, end (incl. int. $2,000)	22,000	
Cost of Sales		66,000
		$ 34,000
Expenses		30,000
		$ 4,000
Other income (imputed interest)		7,000
Net Profit		$ 11,000

The two companies are assumed to be identical in every way save that Company B charges $7,000 interest into manufacturing cost and credits $7,000 interest to other income. This company followed a somewhat similar practice the preceding period computed, for comparability, on a consistent percentage basis, hence the $1,000 difference in the opening inventories of the two companies. If this had not been done the profit discrepancy would, of course, have been $2,000 instead of $1,000.

Because of the assumption that the two companies are identical, the additional profit of Company B is, of course, due only to the imputed interest. This extra $1,000 cannot be considered a true realized profit since it resulted only from a "stroke of the pen," and became evident only because the amount of interest so created was greater in the final than in the opening inventory.

PREMIUM ON RETIRED BONDS. A corporation having bonds outstanding may desire to retire all or part of them prior to their maturity. Often this may be done by payment of a specified premium over the face value. This premium, according to the *Accountants' Handbook*,[12] "may be carried directly to surplus, or it may be included in the non-operating section of the income statement."

Montgomery,[13] however, advances a suggestion based not on actual retirement but on intent to retire: "When bonds are to be retired at a premium, good practice requires that the amount of the premium be accumulated by periodical pro-rata charges to expenses, in the nature of an interest equalization factor, thus creating a deferred credit sufficient to offset the premium when paid."

Regardless of intent to retire bonds, their actual retirement may not be accomplished due to changed conditions. Such a periodic pro-rata provision, therefore, somewhat resembles an imputed cost.

OTHER IMPUTED COSTS. Seldom do individual business men deliberately enter fictitious salaries for themselves as part

---

12 *Accountants' Handbook* (New York, The Ronald Press Company, 1934), p. 901.
13 Robert H. Montgomery, *Auditing Theory and Practice* (New York, The Ronald Press Company, 1934), p. 365.

of their operating costs, although such a procedure has from time to time been urged by those who are interested in promoting the welfare of small business enterprises. Sanders reports that the great majority of trade associations which have prepared uniform cost systems for their members have included interest on investment even if not imputed salaries among the costs of production.

There is, of course, good reason for calculation of interest on partnership investments when their investment accounts are not equal. This is, however, a somewhat different situation since it is handled as a preliminary distribution of net profit, not as an imputed cost having a possible inflationary effect.

Recognition of the relation of imputed costs to manufacturing inventories and the consequent effect upon net profits is sufficient to condemn their inclusion in the actual bookkeeping procedure. Where no question of manufacturing inventories is involved, no harm can result from the inclusion of imputed costs, although on the other hand calculations regarding such costs are preferably made outside of the double entry system.

Reabsorbed Costs.—The phenomenon of reabsorbed costs has received singularly little attention from accounting writers. In fact, it has not been christened officially in spite of its frequent recurrence, although such descriptive phrases as "revolving costs," "circular costs," or "back-lash costs" are noted.

Reabsorbed costs are not at all the same as apportioned or reclassified costs.

The latter refer to expense, usually factory expense, distribution ending with final transference to finished product ready for sale and intended to be sold.

Reabsorbed costs, on the other hand, refer to finished product which can be sold but which actually is used by the maker as part of a further cycle of manufacturing more of the same kind of finished product.

CoAL Mining.   One of the simplest and most obvious illustrations of reabsorbed costs is furnished by those coal mines in which part of the coal mined is consumed in the mine power plant for the purpose of aiding in the production of more coal.

Since part of the coal produced is consumed in the production of more coal, a vicious circle is created as a result of which it is impossible to determine actual costs; nor can actual costs of mining coal ever be known until the mining enterprise is terminated and liquidated.

The common expedient in a situation of this kind is to adopt some estimated basis of valuation and assign it to the coal consumed in the power plant. Often market prices are used to determine how much shall be charged to the power plant and credited to cost of coal production for that tonnage which is consumed instead of being sold.

FARMING. Similar cost situations occur in farming and represent, along with accretion, a convincing explanation of the inadequacy of farm accounting.

Of the salable products produced by the farmer a substantial portion is consumed on the farm, finding its way into the cost of the next year's crop. While there are many variations and complications, the reabsorption of farm costs can be most simply explained in connection with the cost of producing hay.

Of a farmer's total hay crop a small part may be sold and a substantial part may be used for feeding work horses, thus influencing to some indeterminate extent the cost of live power which in turn enters into the cost of production of another hay crop, thus causing a never-ending cycle of reabsorbed costs which makes it impossible ever to determine the true cost of producing a ton of hay.

An approximate cost may be established by an arbitrary valuation of hay consumed. Usually the market price basis is adopted but clearly such a basis has no cost accounting significance.

INSTITUTIONS. The phenomenon of reabsorbed costs is noted in restaurants, hotels, and institutions where part of employees' pay is represented by board and room.

A somewhat unusual and rather dramatic illustration of reabsorption occurs in connection with colleges which provide work for students in lieu of part of the cash cost of tuition, room, and board.

Berea College, located in central Kentucky, is partially supported by an endowment and partially by gifts and donations. It is an essential policy in this college to charge no tuition, but other costs per student, including room and board for the nine months of the school year, approximate $150. Each student is expected to work a minimum of ten hours per week, for which he is paid in labor credits which are applied against this amount.

The college engages in a variety of activities, operating a farm, a dairy, a creamery, a canning factory, its own boarding halls and rooming houses, a hotel, and a hospital.

In this situation is noted a most complex case of reabsorbed costs, the student body consuming a large proportion of the results of its own labor. Thus the student assigned to the dairy finds that his wages become part of the unit costs of producing milk and cream, which in turn become part of the unit cost of producing butter, which in turn is charged against the student boarding houses, the hotel, the hospital, and, as cost of sales, to butter which is marketed to the general public. The benefit of part of these costs then reverts to the student body, trickling back by one channel or another through the boarding halls, the free hospital, nursing and medical service, and other channels so that the benefits received by the student are in substantial part valued according to the cost of his own services.

Since the value of labor credits earned by students is necessarily arbitrary, the system of unit costs throughout the many departments of the college represents calculations upon an arbitrary base, having little or no reference to true costs. Such unit cost data, derived as they are from estimates in the constant process of reabsorption, can have no more than statistical significance and the so-called profits of the canning factory, the creamery, or the hotel, even though from transactions with outsiders, cannot be substantiated as true profits.

REABSORPTION AND ACCOUNTING THEORY. While the phenomenon of cost reabsorption is not common in institutions and enterprises in which refined and accurate profit calculations are sought, the importance of cost reabsorption is found in its relation to the basic conventions of accounting.

It seems clear that this phenomenon reflects a problem to

which the essential accounting mechanism is not adapted and in relation to which the common accounting conventions are inapplicable. It may be considered fortunate for the development of modern accounting that cost reabsorption in the average enterprise is an immaterial factor.

If cost reabsorption in the typical industrial corporation was as material a factor as it is in Berea College, the entire structure of doctrines, conventions, and rules forming the present basis of accounting practice would be radically different.

Joint Costs.—Unlike imputed and reabsorbed costs, less fantasy characterizes joint costs.

While the detailed figures which result from the common procedure of joint cost accounting are necessarily estimates arbitrarily based upon non-accounting factors, nevertheless joint costs are realistic in that the sum of joint cost valuations represents an aggregate having a true cost basis.

If 100 gallons of whole milk cost $40 and if the whole milk is separated into 20 gallons of cream and 80 gallons of skim milk, it can be no more than an estimate to assert that the 20 gallons of cream cost $35 and the 80 gallons of skim milk cost $5. Some other estimator might claim that the 20 gallons of cream cost $30 and the 80 gallons of skim milk cost $10. But these estimated valuations have one thing in common, i.e., the sum of $35 and $5, or of $30 and $10, represents actual cost.

Economic Recognition of Joint Costs. Economists have given adequate consideration to joint costs, finding therein a problem of special interest.

Mill[14] discussed the cost of two different commodities representing products of the same operation or set of operations and noted that : "The outlay is incurred for the sake of both together, not part for one and part for the other. The same outlay would have to be incurred for either of the two, if the other were not wanted or used at all."

Among the examples he cited were the production of coke and coal gas, mutton and wool, beef hides and tallow, calves

[14] John Stuart Mill, *Principles of Political Economy* (New York, The Colonial Press, 1900), p. 88.

and dairy produce, and chickens and eggs. With respect to all of these he asserted that the "cost of production can have nothing to do with deciding the value of the associated commodities relatively to each other. It only decides their joint value."

Referring to several joint products, Marshall[15] observed that "there is seldom any rule of nature to determine either the relative importance of these uses, or the proportions in which the total cost should be distributed among them."

Jevons,[16] in his criticism of John Stuart Mill's *Principles of Political Economy,* emphasized the large number of cases of joint production by insisting that: "All the great staple commodities at any rate are produced jointly with minor commodities." He supported this assertion as follows:

In the case of corn, for instance, there are the straw, the chaff, the bran, and the different qualities of flour or meal, which are products of the same operations. In the case of cotton, there are the seed, the oil, the cotton waste, the refuse, in addition to the cotton itself. When beer is brewed the grains regularly return a certain price. Trees felled for timber yield not only the timber, but the loppings, the bark, the outside cuts, the chips, etc.

Seligman[17] added further illustrations of joint costs including railway charges, distilling, the staterooms in a steamer, and the seats in a theatre. Like other economists he insists that: "It is the whole, not the parts, to which we can assign a cost; and this cost is the joint cost. The normal price of all the parts together adjusts itself to the joint cost, but the price of any particular part may be above or below the level."

How far the individual joint costs may be influenced by the market price basis of valuation is noted by Slichter[18] as follows:

When two goods are jointly produced, there is no assurance that the relative amounts of the two will be in proportion to the relative intensity of the demand for them. For example, at the same price per

15 Alfred Marshall, *Principles of Economics* (London, Macmillan & Co., Ltd., 1920), p. 390.

16 W. Stanley Jevons, *The Theory of Political Economy* (London, Macmillan & Co., Ltd., 1924), pp. 197-199.

17 Edwin R. A. Seligman, *Principles of Economics* (New York, Longmans, Green & Co., 1926), p. 253.

18 Sumner H. Slichter, *Modern Economic Society* (New York, Henry Holt & Company, 1928), pp. 314-317.

pound, the public might demand three times as much of A as of B. But the two goods might be produced in the proportion of two pounds of A for one of B. Obviously, in this case, the price of A would be higher than the price of B. The difference in the prices of several joint products is likely to be especially large when the less desired commodity happens to be produced in greater abundance.

He also notes how variations in demand affect the so-called "costs" of two joint products, asserting that "a rise in the demand for one—the demand for the second remaining unchanged—brings about an increase in the supply of both and a decrease, therefore, in the price of the second."

Other important economic authorities discussing joint costs are in agreement that individual joint costs have little or no actual cost significance. Referring to two products Curtis[19] insists that "no one can say exactly what it costs to produce either considered separately," while Frain[20] states that "there is no possible way in which the cost for the separate products can be determined."

ACCOUNTING RECOGNITION OF JOINT COSTS. If economists are puzzled over joint costs, accountants are no less so.

Generally they have not attempted to develop any original theory regarding such costs but rather have been forced to accept the economists' solution, namely, that the joint costs are determined by dividing the total cost among the various products in proportion to the market prices of those products as a result of which the aggregate of the product costs is equal to the actual cost of the original material.

Since market prices are not always obtainable for certain types of products, it has become a matter of practical necessity to introduce certain estimates into the calculation. Thus two products, A and B, are derived from one common material. If a unit of that common material costs $10 and if two pounds of product A and three pounds of product B are derived, it becomes necessary to determine the market price per pound for A and

---

19 Roy Emerson Curtis, *Economics, Principles and Interpretation* (Chicago, New York, A. W. Shaw Company, 1928), p. 91.

20 H. LaRue Frain, *An Introduction to Economics* (New York, Houghton Mifflin Company, 1937), p. 443.

B separately. In the simplest case where such market prices for both are available, the calculation might appear as follows:

2 lbs. of A at a market price of $2.50 per lb. = $ 5.00
3 lbs. of B at a market price of $5.00 per lb. = $15.00

The total value of two pounds of A and three pounds of B on a market price basis is $20. This must, however, be reduced to a cost basis, which is done by assigning 5/20 of the original cost of $10 to A and 15/20 of the original cost of $10 to B, with the result that the joint cost of A is $2.50 or $1.25 per pound and the joint cost of B is $7.50 or $2.50 per pound.

If it be assumed that the market price for A is determinable at $2.50 while there is no actual market for B, this elementary calculation is not feasible. If, however, by the application of $3 worth of labor B can be converted into C, which has a market value of $6 per pound, then the cost of B can be calculated. Three pounds of C at $6 per pound is $18. Deducting from $18 the $3 labor cost required to convert B into C provides a net amount of $15 which by courtesy can be called the selling price of B even though there is no actual market for B. Having deducted the expense of conversion amounting to $3, the computation is then made as before.

It should, however, be noted that this roundabout method introduces another element of uncertainty. The labor cost of $3 is an estimated, not an actual, cost. It is asserted that the cost of converting B into C will be $3, but when such conversion actually takes place conditions may have changed and the actual labor cost may be greater or less than $3. In a simple calculation of this type the resulting error might not be significant. Where the product B must go through a number of additional manufacturing steps, being first converted into C, then into D, again into E, F, G, etc., before a reliable market price is determinable, the errors involved in estimating costs between product B and product G may be large.

As an expedient to be adopted, this plan of deducting estimated future processing costs is the only one which can be employed. The possibility of profit distortion because of probable errors in estimating should, however, not be overlooked, particularly where the chain of operations between B and G may involve substantial costs.

JOINT COSTS AND PROFITS.   Clearly the general and, in fact, the only possible method of determining joint costs, namely, that of calculating them in proportion to market prices, is arbitrary and without true cost significance.

The problem is, therefore, one with which the basic accounting mechanism is not equipped to deal and the introduction of joint costs completely destroys the traditional basis of accounting for profits. Assume, in the illustration previously given, that while A and B are both produced during the accounting period, only B is sold, all of A being retained in inventory. If during that period 10,000 pounds of B are sold to customers at $3.25 per pound, the gross profit would appear to be determinable from the following calculation:

Sale of 10,000 lbs. of product B at $3.25 . . . . $32,500
Cost of 10,000 lbs. of product B at $2.50 25,000

Gross profit . . . . $ 7,500

Based upon the assumption made, namely, that the joint costs of A and B are determined in proportion to their market prices, and the further assumption that 6,666⅔ pounds of A are produced during the period but are not sold, while 10,000 pounds of B are produced and sold, it seems clear that the reported profit of $7,500 is a meaningless figure not supportable by accounting logic.

To assert that such a situation is not imaginable not only begs the issue but probably can be disproved, particularly in the case of joint costs in mining where several different metals result from one ore. One mine might produce both gold and silver. Since there is a fixed price on gold, there would be no good reason for refusing to dispose of it promptly. Since the market price of silver varies, it might be considered good judgment to hold the silver in inventory in the hope of a favorable market change in some subsequent period.

Usually, of course, the disparity between production and sales of two or more joint products would not be so great as in this illustration, but unless the amounts of each of such products held in inventory were approximately proportional to their production, reported profits would be more or less meaningless.

A variety of interesting situations involving periodic distortion can be imagined even with a very simple illustration using but two joint products. Where a disproportionate amount of one of them is sold during one accounting period followed by the disproportionate sale of the other during the following period, not only are the reported profits of each period unprovable but the relation of the profits of the two periods one to the other has no determinable meaning or significance.

Another cause of profit distortion is to be found in the methods used for determining selling prices as the preliminary basis for the proportional cost calculation. Should market quotations on the last day of each month be used? Should the daily quotations for the entire month be averaged? Should the averages for the past three months be used?

Under mercurial market conditions these questions become important. The purpose of the popular three months' average plan is, according to McKee,[21] "to eliminate temporary market fluctuations, and reflect costs by market trends instead." He adds that "even this must be taken with the proverbial grain of salt, else a one month price war might be permitted to affect a single month's profits unduly." He proves his point by a good variation of the "identical company test" in which the profits of three companies on equal quantities of crude oil were as follows:

> Example 1 . . $17.50 loss
> Example 2 . . 6.68 loss
> Example 3 . . 28.31 profit

In general, problems of joint cost have not been considered adequately in accounting literature. This may, of course, be due to their arbitrary nature or it may be due to a prevalent belief that joint cost problems are relatively uncommon, being confined to a few industries such as packing houses, oil refineries, and lumber mills. While it is true that these and similar

21 Raymond W. McKee, *Handbook of Petroleum Accounting* (New York, Harper & Brothers, 1938), pp. 334-336.

industries represent noteworthy examples of joint costs, it is
nevertheless true that joint cost problems are far more numerous
than modern accounting literature seems to intimate. It has
been suggested that joint cost is a typical phenomenon in many,
if not most, lines of business simply because the activities of
many concerns are so fused technically and economically that
cost classification on any but an arbitrary basis becomes almost
impracticable.

Expenditures and Time Lags.—The concept of matched
costs and income is somewhat artificial under any conditions.
In certain specific situations it becomes utterly impracticable.

SMALL ENTERPRISES.   The concept is perhaps most convincing in small simple enterprises, particularly those having no
substantial inventories.

In a small millinery store, a restaurant, a grocery, an ice
cream factory, or a cigar store, the relation between costs and
income is relatively simple and direct. This is also true in professional work. Items of outlay and income for a dentist, a
public accountant, a physician, or a lawyer can be closely associated. In all of these various examples, however, certain kinds
of expense cannot, except by arbitrary decision, be related
specifically to items of income.

The rent paid by the dentist cannot be associated specifically
with the $5 charged for filling John Smith's teeth. The cost of
spoiled vegetables in the grocery store is not assignable to the
$3 paid by Mrs. John Smith for eggs, butter, potatoes, and
spinach. The cost of repairs to a typewriter in the public accountant's office is not an item assignable against the $300 audit fee
paid by John Smith and Company.

Because many of these indirect costs refer to the same period
in which the sales are made, it is held that income and costs are
practically if not exactly matched. In such establishments some
principal costs actually do relate themselves to specific items of
income largely because of the fact that indirect expenses are
at a minimum and specific outlays for labor and merchandise are
readily accounted for in terms of corresponding income items.
The cost of a hat or a fur coat or a gallon of ice cream can

with little difficulty be set off against the sale of the hat, the coat, or the ice cream. The lawyer, or the public accountant, can by a process of simple time-keeping distribute the services of himself and his assistants to the various clients served.

LARGE ENTERPRISES. In larger and more complicated enterprises, the process of matching costs and income becomes more conventionalized.

This is particularly noted where materials are carried in inventory for long periods, where a substantial portion of outlays consists of indirect expenses, and where costly activities cannot be identified in terms of individual customers. Often matching of such costs with income is believed to be relatively obtainable if certain assumptions are accepted.

CONVENTION OF TRANSFERRED VALUES. Regardless of the known fact that one particular casting may have been bought by a manufacturer in May 1936, the inclusion of that casting in a finished product which is sold in May 1939 is not considered any violation of the concept of matched costs and income. The convention of transferred values takes care of this and the association of cost and income is believed to be just as direct, despite the three-year time lag indicated, as if the casting had been purchased in May 1939.

This convention of transferred values operates to extinguish a number of other time lags. The casting bought in May 1936 may have been machined in June of 1936, and the labor and expense transferred thereto at the time of the machining becomes an item of cost which is matchable against the income resulting from the sale made in 1939. Frozen in that cost for three years there may be such elements of outlay as light, heat, power, water, rent, insurance, and taxes, all expenditures of 1936 made with the definite objective of future income production.

Seldom are these time lags considered to have any real significance when costs have been added to inventories by the convention of transferred values. When this convention does not apply some interesting situations, carrying with them the threat of serious profit distortion, may be evident.

NON-MANUFACTURING TIME LAGS. In a non-manufacturing business, or in connection with the commercial functions of a manufacturing business, the convention of transferred values is not generally applicable, with the result that the relation between certain expenditures and income is attenuated and indirect.

The reverse of this situation is true when income is fully realized in one accounting period although, because of guarantees or for any other reason, costs truly relating to that income may be experienced in subsequent accounting periods.

Almost every income producing transaction involves expenditures of three types: (1) those made in advance and for the purpose of producing income, (2) those incurred simultaneously with the realization of the income, and (3) those following the realization of the income and directly or indirectly resulting therefrom.

Illustration. In the simplest possible way these three types may be illustrated by the sale of a dozen eggs in a grocery store.

On September 1, the grocer may insert an advertisement at a cost of $2 in his daily paper offering eggs at 30 cents per dozen. It should be noted that the expenditure was incurred for the direct purpose of selling eggs not on September 1 but on September 2. The $2 expenditure partook somewhat of the nature of a gamble, the grocer not knowing how many eggs he would sell as a result. The expenditure is in this respect typical of many of the speculative outlays of business.

On September 2, the grocer sells 50 dozen eggs at 30 cents a dozen, or $15. If the eggs cost him 25 cents a dozen, then the total cost of the eggs sold was $12.50. In so far as a specific purchase of one dozen eggs, made by Mrs. John Smith, is concerned, a definite and readily ascertainable gross profit of 5 cents is realized. Against this, however, must be applied part of the previous day's advertising cost of $2.

Here it is necessary to make an assumption. It is necessary to assume that all of the customers who took varying quantities of the 50 dozen eggs sold were influenced by the previous day's advertisement and that each sale of a dozen eggs carried with it an advertising cost of 4 cents. Accordingly, Mrs. John Smith's purchase of a dozen eggs, for which she paid 30 cents and which cost the grocer 25 cents, is additionally burdened by 4 cents of advertising cost carried over from the previous day.

As a result of this the grocer properly figures that he has not made 5 cents from Mrs. Smith but 1 cent, in spite of the fact that he has no possible way of directly relating the 4 cents of advertising cost to Mrs. Smith's purchase. On the one hand she may never have seen the advertisement and would have bought the eggs anyway. On the other hand she may have been directly influenced by the advertisement and have come into his particular store in order to buy a dozen eggs. While in the store she may have been attracted by other items with the result that she may have spent $15 on meats, canned goods, and various other commodities.

In so far as Mrs. John Smith is concerned, it is pure unrealistic fiction that her purchase should be penalized by a 4-cent advertising cost. More nearly true, but not entirely so, is the assumption that the entire sale of 50 dozen eggs, resulting in a gross profit of $2.50, should be charged with the total advertising cost of $2. Even this is not entirely correct, however, since the prospect of a 50-cent profit would not have induced the grocer to place the $2 advertisement for eggs.

It is only because of his firm belief that some of the egg buyers would purchase non-advertised merchandise also that he placed the advertisement at all.

On the third day of September and other days thereafter, additional costs are incurred which directly result from the egg sale. The display facilities provided for the egg sale may demand dismantling or moving. Bookkeeping entries must be made for the credit sales. Cash proceeds from the sale must be verified and deposited. At the end of the month statements must be prepared and postage purchased for their mailing, and even later collection letters may need to be prepared and mailed. These subsequent costs are the direct result of the egg sale even though it may not be possible to match them directly against the $15 of income produced. Some of these costs, particularly those referring to the cost of collecting credit sales, might be classified as deductions from income on the ground that they represent costs necessary to convert a legal claim to cash into cash itself and that they represent a correction of reported gross income in order to put it on a realized basis. From this arguable viewpoint collection costs partake somewhat of the nature of provisions for doubtful accounts. Other expenditures which follow the realization of income are contractually associated with it. Still others represent expenditures of a service nature not so much relating to a past sales transaction as to insuring customer satisfaction in the hope of future profitable relations.

On a small and simple scale this example serves to illustrate three types of costs which are commonly incurred in all business organizations: those which precede the realization of income and are often promotional in their nature, those which coincide with the realization of income, and those which follow the realization of income.

SALES PROMOTION COSTS. In a medium-sized or large corporation, costs which are incurred for the purpose of obtaining later income are substantial and varied.

The costs of hiring and training salesmen, of preparing catalogues, booklets, and other sales literature, of preparing and publishing advertising, of marketing research, of sales conventions, customer entertainment, the preparation of sales demonstrations, and the cost of samples and their distribution are only a few of the many items which can be grouped under the general title of sales promotion costs.

In some business organizations such costs may be equal to or even in excess of the true production costs which relate directly to the product.

Seldom can these sales promotion costs be matched with the income they are designed to obtain, either by specific items or in total. It is, of course, recognized that such an expense as advertising bought and paid for in December but not published until January represents a deferred charge to appear on the December 31 balance sheet, but few accountants would be willing to recognize the cost of a sales convention as a deferred charge to future income, nor would they be willing to approve similar treatment for such other costs as entertainment, traveling expense, circularization, or sales training programs.

Since the aggregate of such expenditures may be large and

since they are commonly not treated as deferred charges to be applied against future income, it is clear that the idealistic concept of matched costs and income is substantially modified.

In explanation of such modification accountants properly point out first, that it is practically impossible to relate some of these costs to specific increments of income, and second, that the activity of most business organizations is fairly comparable from year to year with the result that no serious profit distortion results merely because certain expenditures are absorbed in one period while in theory they relate to the following period. If the bookkeeping treatment is consistent from period to period, no important profit distortion threatens.

Both of these assertions are fairly convincing. The first one, referring to the impossibility of correlation, is particularly so. The second is perhaps more broadly applied than is justified under all circumstances. It is this opinion which is reflected by Montgomery's[22] assertion that: "Most concerns which sell ahead have a fairly constant and uniform business and no statistical problem arises when sales expenses are charged to one period while the following period reaps the benefit."

Too often it is taken for granted that a business organization operates at about the same rate of activity year after year. In some of the more stable enterprises this is true but it is in exactly those enterprises that sales promotion activities may be less important.

In the highly erratic type of business enterprise involving the manufacture and sale of specialties, sales volume and business activity may vary sharply from year to year. During a year of relatively low income the expenditures for sales promotion effort may be high, there being a direct cause and effect relationship between the inadequacy of the income and the need for its stimulation. In such a business income may be compared to a series of spurts rather than an evenly flowing stream, this spurting effect being accounted for by sporadic selling and advertising campaigns.

In some such specialized field as that of the office equipment

[22] Robert H. Montgomery, *Auditing Theory and Practice* (New York, The Ronald Press Company, 1934), p. 490.

manufacturer, for example, it is not uncommon for a year of reduced income to cause special activity in product redesign or in the adoption of new products. In order to get the best possible sales of these redesigned or new products, selling and advertising campaigns of a costly nature may be instituted. The absorption of such costs during the year of low income serves to reduce the net profit of that year to a figure even lower than would otherwise appear. The next following year which bears few of the sales promotion costs nevertheless experiences the favorable effect of the sales stimulation with the result that profits may be attractively large.

Because of the very nature of the problem it is obviously impossible to measure the extent of the distortion which results from absorbing in one accounting period promotional expenditures which are logically related to a subsequent period. It is, however, safe to infer, at least in many organizations, that this cause of periodic profit distortion is one of the most influential of all, ranking perhaps with the depreciation and inventory revaluation factors to be discussed in subsequent chapters.

FUTURE SERVICE AND GUARANTEE COSTS. Commonly, costs which follow income realization are of a routine nature relatively undistorting because relatively inconsequential as to amount.

This is, however, not always true, it being a matter of common knowledge that certain kinds of products are sold on the basis of service guarantees the fulfillment of which may be costly. It is, of course, true that attempts usually are made to estimate the amount of such future expenditures, such estimate being matched up with the income realized by the original sale, the offsetting credit being carried to a reserve.

In the case of new products or during periods of violent change in price levels and wage rates, accurate estimation of future service and guarantee costs may be impossible, with the result that the amount appearing as realized profit in any one year may, in fact, be substantially over- or understated.

Matching of costs or expenses and income may refer to specific items of both in the case of factory or direct costs, or to corresponding accounting periods in the case of other outlays,

In the latter type it is observed that a certain limited and approximate matching results from the accounting recognition of some but not all advance expenditures as prepaid items to be carried over to following accounting periods, and the recognition of some but not all expenditures to be made in the future by providing reserves.

These provisions do not, however, provide complete matching because of conservatism, the impossibility of allocation, or the inability accurately to foresee the future.

CHAPTER 21

PERIODIC DISTRIBUTION OF ASSET COST

The actual distribution or allocation of the cost of those assets which have already been classified as deferred charges to future income is accomplished by various accounting processes. These processes, while having common characteristics, may be differentiated by the:

1. Nature of the asset, i.e., tangible or intangible.
2. Basis used for allocation, i.e., time, use, sale, or consumption.
3. Debit accounts affected, i.e., operating cost or expense, non-operating expense or surplus.
4. Credit accounts affected, i.e., asset account or a valuation account.
5. Purpose of the allocation, i.e., actual cost recovery or replacement cost recovery.
6. Accounting periods affected by premature retirement, i.e., past, present, or future.

It is the purpose of this chapter to consider some of the more important general phases of the allocation problem, thus laying a foundation for more detailed consideration of inventories and fixed assets.

Terminology of Asset Distribution.—It is unfortunate that one word such as "amortization" cannot be applied to the common types of asset distributions. The report, *Accounting Terminology*,[1] while not now regarded as authoritative, comments interestingly on "amortization" as follows:

The basic idea suggested by this word is that of reducing, redeeming or liquidating the amount of an account already in existence. In finance and accounting this word means the gradual extinguishment of an asset,

[1] *Accounting Terminology* (New York, American Institute Publishing Co., Inc., 1931), p. 9.

a liability or a nominal account by prorating the amount of it over the period during which it will exist or its benefit will be realized.

Amortization is caused by and the computations are based upon effluxion of time or units of production.

The report mentions certain items to which the term properly is applicable, such as debt discount, bonuses paid for a lease, buildings or machinery on leasehold property, and the value of mine equipment whose useful life is known to exceed the life of the mine.

This and other definitions indicate the impropriety of using the word "amortization" to cover depreciation or depletion.

When tangible asset values are distributed the words "depreciation" or "depletion" are appropriate. Thus it is proper to speak of the depreciation of a building, the depreciation of a machine, the depreciation of equipment. It is not proper to speak of the depreciation of an oil well, of a tract of timber, or of a mine. In these connections the word "depletion" is used.

In depreciation there is no perceptible lessening of physical quantity but merely the disappearance of cost value. In depletion physical quantity and cost value are affected simultaneously. Of course, this is also true of a pile of coal held in the inventory of a manufacturing company, and it would not be improper to think of the lessening of this coal due to its use as depletion. This would not, however, be in accord with accepted terminology.

With reference to such intangible items as prepaid insurance, prepaid rent, or bond discount in which the expiration of asset value is distinctly a function of time, "amortization" is appropriate.

When the transfer from asset value to the cost, expense, or loss category is arbitrary, having little or no reference to use or lapse of time but rather to changes in general price levels, the term commonly used is "write-off."

Methods of Distribution.—Depreciation, depletion, and amortization refer to the periodic extinguishment of asset value, dependent upon forecasting of the asset's life. At the time of acquiring assets to which these terms may appropriately be applied, it is necessary to formulate a plan, program, or schedule of allocation to serve as the basis for periodic accounting entries.

The formulation of such a plan requires estimating the useful life of an asset.

In the case of prepaid insurance expense, prepaid rent, or (generally) bond discount, this forecasting is simple enough. In the case of tangible fixed assets, the estimate may at times be reasonably accurate, more often it may be shrewdly approximate, and still more often it may be so complicated by such indeterminate factors as obsolescence and inadequacy that no engineer, no appraiser, no accountant is clairvoyantly qualified to make an accurate depreciation plan.

Inventories do not expire in the ordinary time sense. They are specifically withdrawn for use or for sale, and such withdrawals provide the signal for adjusting entries. Write-offs, too, are relatively independent of the time factor.

It appears, therefore, that there are three bases for the discharge of the various kinds of assets which are part of that group hitherto referred to as deferred charges to future income —the time basis, the consumption or use basis, and the arbitrary basis.

THE TIME BASIS. When disappearance of asset value is considered a function of time, it is necessary to adopt one of several methods of distribution.

Such methods as the annuity method, the reducing balance method, the straight-line method, and others have their adherents and are much discussed. Despite such discussion the great majority of industrial organizations use the straight-line method, both in connection with depreciation of tangible fixed assets and the amortization of intangible items. The general use of this method reflects a common sense viewpoint toward depreciation and amortization.

The substantial element of error involved in all forecasts, when coupled with any scientific method of allocation, results in an incongruity which has been recognized by industrial accountants and their employers.

Straight-line depreciation or amortization distributes asset values in equal amounts over the number of accounting periods affected. Graphically charted this distribution would be represented by a straight line; hence the name of this method. Its adoption disregards known factors other than time which may be responsible for the disappearance of asset value. Rapidity and severity of use, maintenance, and repair policies may be important factors, and it is also observed that obsolescence and inadequacy may have but little relation to time. These and other considerations are disregarded by those industrialists who realize full well that inaccuracy of time forecasts cannot be cured by the adoption of refined methods of allocation.

Considered solely upon its own merits the straight-line method is so subject to criticism that many can see no virtue in it whatever. This viewpoint has been clearly expressed by Canning,[2] who asserts that "no modification of the straight line rule that stops short of eliminating the very essence of it can become a generally applicable method."

Use or Consumption Basis. When disappearance of asset value is accompanied by the measurable diminution of its physical quantity, as in the case of the depletion of mines, oil wells, and other natural resources, or in the case of inventories, the use or consumption method of allocation is adopted.

In general, it is an accurate method, since it assigns to the proper accounting periods those cost units used, sold, or consumed during such periods. This comment, of course, refers only to the basis of allocation, since inaccuracies may result from other factors—notably from the inability to measure the amount of ore or oil in the ground, or from the methods used in asset valuation in the case of inventories, or from unaccountable inventory losses.

When the use or consumption basis is adopted as a substitute for the time basis, other inaccuracies may be noted. While there is much to be said in favor of depreciating automobiles and trucks on a mileage basis, rather than by the number of years of use, and while a similar expedient may well be adopted in distributing the depreciation of other machinery and equipment, it

2 John B. Canning, *The Economics of Accountancy* (New York, The Ronald Press Company, 1929), p. 288.

must be observed that depreciation is seldom a sole function of use or time. Generally it is a combination of the two, and it is often desirable to check one method by applying the other.

COMBINATION BASIS. Both the use and time basis may be used simultaneously by predetermining, roughly at least, what part of depreciation can be attributed to the time element only. Included in the time element should be the deterioration not due to use, and the probabilities of obsolescence and inadequacy. If by careful study based on experience it is determined, for any substantial asset, that 70% of depreciation is a factor of time only, then 30% may be considered to come from wear and tear due to normal use. When production falls below or rises above what is considered normal, the depreciation may be decreased or increased accordingly. To illustrate simply, it may be assumed that production during one year is only one-half of normal. The depreciation then would be 70% for the time element and one-half of 30%, or 15%, for the use element. If, on the other hand, production during one year is 50% above normal, then the depreciation would be 70% for the time element and 45% for the use element.

DEBIT ACCOUNTS AFFECTED. Generally the debit accounts affected by amortization, depreciation, or depletion are obvious. Depreciation of factory assets becomes part of the factory overhead expense to be distributed to work in progress. The depreciation of other tangible operating assets is chargeable to selling, general, and administrative expense, while the depreciation of such other tangible assets as investment property may be treated as a non-operating charge.

In connection with inventory withdrawals or depletion, the physical movement of the items ordinarily determines the account to be charged.

The amortization of prepaid expense and other deferred charges may be reflected in factory costs, other operating expenses, or in the non-operating category, according to their nature and according to the purpose of the original expenditure.

Ordinarily the use to which an asset is put determines the account to be debited with its allocation.

When asset accounts are reduced in amount as the result of arbitrary write-offs representing financial revaluation, a variety of accounting practices are adopted, and the resulting problems have caused considerable disagreement among accountants. Some of these problems and viewpoints bearing thereon will be set forth in following chapters referring to inventories and fixed assets.

CREDIT ACCOUNTS AFFECTED.   In charging any part of an asset value to expense, cost, or loss, the corresponding credit logically should appear in the asset account itself.

Sometimes this is done, notably in the amortization of such assets as bond discount or in the relief of inventories. In the case of fixed assets, the credits are usually withheld from the asset account, thereby postponing the actual subtraction of the credits from the debit amounts representing the asset's cost.

The accounts employed for the purpose of storing these asset subtractions are commonly referred to as "valuation accounts," "allowance accounts," or "reserves."

There are three ways of viewing such an offset account. It may be considered:

1. An account subsidiary to the asset account, or
2. A deferred credit to its corresponding asset account, or
3. One of two equal divisions of the asset account.

The second and third viewpoints have some merit. The third in particular is often used in accounting instruction by establishing the fiction that the asset account is divided in two, thus converting one account into two. Of the two resulting accounts, one may be considered to have a debit aspect and the other a credit aspect. Viewing them as twin accounts clarifies the relationship between the two and justifies the commonly accepted balance sheet treatment.

It is conceded that valuation accounts should be displayed on balance sheets as deductions from the asset accounts to which they refer, and that seldom, if ever, should they appear among the liabilities or be combined with surplus reserves.

If depreciation credits were made direct to the asset account, significant information about costs might, over a period of years, be lost, particularly when the assets have been acquired at different times.

The separation of an asset account from its corresponding valuation account is not permanent. The deferred credit represented by the balance of the valuation account can be transferred to the asset account when the asset itself disappears as the result of sale, abandonment, destruction, or some other mode of ending. The combination of an asset account and its offsetting valuation account permits ready calculation of the depreciated cost value of the asset which must disappear when the asset is disposed of. When another asset replaces the first one, a new asset account will be provided.

The accounting distinction between depreciation and replacement forbids debiting the cost of the new asset direct to the valuation account, even though the cost of the new asset is identical with the cost of the one replaced.

Problems having to do with valuation accounts commonly occur in relation to receivables and fixed assets. Valuation accounts are sometimes employed as an offset to perpetual inventories. They are seldom employed to record the cumulative amortization of other assets.

Valuation accounts are found useful in certain cases where the corresponding asset account is a controlling account or where original charges often dating far in the past must be preserved for convenient reference.

Replacement Theory of Depreciation.—In so far as depreciation is concerned, some confused thinking has been observed. Failure to adopt strictly the viewpoint that the conversion of these asset values into deductions from income is simply a matter of cost distribution, has caused misunderstanding as to the purpose of such accounting. The purpose of recording depreciation may be stated as the recovery of an expenditure through its equitable apportionment to the accounting periods benefited. This should not be confused with the cost of replacing the asset. The problem as it might present itself may be outlined in simple terms.

In January 1939, a corporation purchases an automobile truck for $3,000. It estimates that the truck will last for six years. For simplicity it may be assumed that there will be no residual value. Briefly, therefore, $500 of the truck value is transferred to expense each year for six years, at which time the corporation has recovered $3,000. On December 31, 1944, the cost of the truck has been completely written off and the truck must be replaced. But on December 31, 1944, the price of an identical new truck is no longer $3,000; it is $4,500. This may be imagined as having resulted from changed business conditions, inflation, or other similar forces. At that time the company has recovered only $3,000 with which to purchase a $4,500 truck.

To some it appears that the cost of replacement should be taken into consideration at the time of making the original depreciation plan. They insist that the depreciation estimate should be modified and that the forecast of future life should also include the forecast of future price levels; that it is insufficient to depreciate at the rate of $500 a year—the proper rate, on the replacement theory, being $750 a year.

This argument was more plausible in the past than it is at present, the general public having received considerable education as to the purpose of recording depreciation through enforced study of, and compliance with, income tax requirements. From the simple illustration just cited, few would now hold that the depreciation rate should be $750 a year. Generally it is conceded that it is the purpose of recording depreciation to recover the original expenditure, the purchase of a new truck being a separate and distinct transaction having no possible connection with, or relation to, the recovery of the original investment.

It is simple to point out that the truck at the end of six years may be replaced at a higher price or a lower price, or at the same price, or by teams and wagons, or that no replacement will be made if the need for a truck has disappeared.

The above arguments seem sufficiently convincing to discredit this replacement theory in so far as it is related to fixed assets.

Replacement Theory of Inventories.—Unfortunately, the replacement theory still persists in other areas, notably in connection with inventories.

Disregarding selling, general, and administrative expense, it is held by many that when a business man sells for $1.25 an item of merchandise costing $1.00, and then finds that it will cost him $1.25 to replace the inventory, he has made no profit. This is a situation analogous to the one illustrated by the automobile truck and is controlled by the same general concept, namely, that the cost of the asset written off has no relation whatever to the cost of any new asset immediately or subsequently acquired, even though the two assets may be alike and may have been acquired for the same purpose.

It would be tedious and none too complimentary to quote from many writers who have adhered to this replacement cost theory of inventories.

One economist writing upon this topic illustrated his point in terms of real estate. A hypothetical, none too intelligent man mentioned in his illustration bought a home for $5,000, later selling it for $8,000 and replacing it with an identical home for $8,000. With rising price levels he finally sold the second home for $12,000, and through a bit of shrewd but rather unnatural trading replaced it with an identical one for $11,000, at which time it is claimed the home-owner might show a profit of $8,000. It is also claimed that this is not his profit, since $6,000 of the $8,000 merely represents the effect of the increased price level upon an identical house.

The plausibility of this argument is somewhat shaken if the man in this illustration failed to buy the third house, but instead put his $11,000 into U. S. Steel common which, it may be assumed, had also increased in price along with the real estate. The illustration also falls down if it is assumed that the man merely kept the $11,000 on hand in the bank and rented a home. The purchasing power of $11,000 in cash at that time is perhaps just the same as the purchasing power of $5,000 at the time the first house was bought, but it would hardly be argued that the man had not made an accounting profit.

Examples of this type do illustrate a serious problem. Anyone who has heard the often-told tales of inflation in Germany, when employees were paid daily and thereafter ran at top speed in order to spend their money for commodities, needs no argument as to the seriousness of rapidly jumping price levels.

That certain industries have been affected by the increased cost of replacing inventories cannot be denied. It may, however, be asserted that large inventories are usual in these industries.

It is often argued that inventories must be replaced or a company cannot continue in business. It can also be contended that competitive conditions are such that prices in such industries cannot be increased rapidly enough to compensate for the increased cost of inventory replacement. Is it not reasonable, however, to suppose that the problems involved are of a financial and business nature having no relation to the determination of accounting profits and that good financial and business judgment will give consideration to changing price levels in formulating buying and selling policies?

Artificially to inflate current inventory costs to estimated cost of replacement cannot in any way change the total net profit of an enterprise from the long-term viewpoint.

Depreciation Funds.—It should be obvious that cost recovery is not related to the obligation to accumulate funds for replacement.

The recovery of asset cost is not always reflected in the cash account entirely or permanently. The resulting funds generally find their way to the cash account but may subsequently be disbursed in many ways, the result of which may be to convert such cash receipts into fixed assets or other values not readily realizable.

When the time comes to replace a substantial asset there may not be sufficient cash on hand. This, however, may be considered the fault of financial planning, an area which is clearly distinct from accounting. It also has been said by Archibald Bowman (*The Journal of Accountancy,* May 1938) that some of the present financial embarrassment of railroads would have been greatly minimized had the railroads accumulated cash or securities in order to provide for replacements.

Each purchase of an asset, however, is a new and independent financial act and cannot be consummated, regardless of prior profits or losses, regardless of depreciation provisions, and regardless of every other factor, except from available cash. This remains true whether the new commitment is for a building, a machine, an item of inventory, or any other asset.

Book Values and Premature Retirement.—Premature retirement of an asset gives rise to certain problems having to do with the disposition of its book value.

It is commonly held that the disappearance of the asset itself must be accompanied by the extinguishment of the book value, which may be considered as a loss to be charged to earned surplus or against current income to be disclosed in one of a variety of ways.

This commonly accepted rule is not, however, unanimously endorsed, some authorities having indicated their willingness, for a variety of reasons, to distribute such a loss over future accounting periods, even though the corresponding asset is no longer in the possession of the accounting entity. In the case of an uninsured fire loss, for example, the net amount of such loss is at times shown as if it were an asset in the nature of a deferred charge to be absorbed by subsequent amortization.

Sanders, Hatfield, and Moore[3] have indicated that the apportionment of a capital loss "among the current and succeeding income statements is a matter to be determined by sound business judgment, made upon all the facts of the particular case, guided by the principle of conservatism."

Where the loss results from the premature retirement of a tangible fixed asset it is probable that most authorities would not agree with this statement. With other types of assets less unanimity is noted. Lack of agreement is particularly evident in connection with such an asset as discount on bonds when the bonds have been redeemed before maturity for interest-saving purposes.

Losses Carried Forward.—If a manufacturer had an item of machinery which was costing him too much to operate and

[3] Sanders, Hatfield, and Moore, *A Statement of Accounting Principles* (New York, American Institute of Accountants, 1938), pp. 38, 39.

which he could replace with a more efficient machine, he would probably retire the old one before the expiration of its useful life.

This retirement might involve a substantial book loss. Seldom, if ever, would that manufacturer argue that the loss should be deferred and be considered a part of the cost of the new equipment, although there might be considerable business logic underlying such a claim. The same logic is used to support the suggestion that unamortized bond discount applicable to a retired issue of bonds should be continued as a book asset with no change in the original amortization program.

Those who support this view observe that the first bond issue would not have been retired unless the refunding issue was on a more attractive interest basis. Therefore, they claim that part of the cost applicable to the new issue is unamortized discount referring to the old issue.

Andersen[4] supported this view, saying:

The unamortized bond discount and expense applicable to the issue retired and the premium paid in connection with such retirement should be amortized over the period of years ending with the maturity of the refunded bonds. The debt discount and expense applicable to the new issue should be amortized over the life thereof. This procedure would appear to be fundamentally sound as it limits the spread of the amortized discount and premium applicable to the refunded issue to those years which, as can be definitely determined in advance, will receive the benefit of the lower cost of money as a result of the refinancing.

A letter written by the American Institute Special Committee on Cooperation with the Securities and Exchange Commission, dated January 26, 1937, is quoted by Broad.[5] In part, the letter suggests that those holding the same view as that expressed by Andersen "believe that, although an immediate write-off against surplus may result in a more conservatively stated balance-sheet, the income account of succeeding years may be held to be less conservative." Discussing the opposing view, namely, that the bond discount should be charged to earned surplus just as soon

---

[4] Arthur Andersen, "Present-Day Problems Affecting the Presentation and Interpretation of Financial Statements," *The Journal of Accountancy,* November 1935, p. 343.
[5] Samuel J. Broad, "Cooperation with the Securities and Exchange Commission," *The Journal of Accountancy,* August 1938, p. 86.

as the corresponding bonds are retired, the committee observes that "if bond discount is to be considered as an asset, it should be treated in the same way as would be the remaining value of any other fixed asset when scrapped or abandoned." Paton's unpublished comment on this issue seems well worth preserving, namely: "The ghost of a preceding asset must not be charged to the cost of the asset in use."

In the report of the Sanders, Hatfield, and Moore[6] committee, three methods of dealing with bond discount on retired bonds are recognized as follows:

"1. To write off the entire unamortized balance at once out of earned surplus.

2. To continue to amortize the old balance at the same rate as hitherto, thus completing amortization by the maturity date of the bonds now retired.

3. To combine the unamortized discount on the retired bonds with the discount or premium on the new bonds, the total to be amortized over the life of the new issue."

In support of method 1 the committee observes, "that subsequent income statements will thus be charged with the effective interest rate incurred for those periods, and one in consonance with the then current market rates." The second and third methods are said to "have the advantage of continuing to charge all this expense through the income accounts, thus avoiding overstatement of earnings by its omission."

Here the Sanders, Hatfield, and Moore committee[7] seems to defer too greatly to managerial decision in saying: "It is a proper exercise of the functions of management to choose which of the three methods shall be followed."

If upon retirement of bonds the bond discount is transferred to earned surplus, the amount thereof will never appear on any profit and loss statement.

To such an entry the American Accounting Association[8]

---

6 Sanders, Hatfield, and Moore, *A Statement of Accounting Principles* (New York, American Institute of Accountants, 1938), p. 79.

7 Sanders, Hatfield, and Moore, *A Statement of Accounting Principles* (New York, American Institute of Accountants, 1938), p. 80.

8 Executive Committee of the American Accounting Association, "A Tentative Statement of Accounting Principles Affecting Corporate Reports," *The Accounting Review,* June 1936, p. 191.

objects and insists that the adjustment shall be "by way of the income account to earned surplus." This method has practical disadvantages in that it may introduce into the profit and loss statement of one period a loss so large as to dwarf many of the other items appearing thereon. Such a showing might be considered bad business policy unfavorably affecting the relations between a corporation and its stockholders and, as an alternative, corrected profit and loss statements for prior years might be prepared and presented to stockholders.

Theoretically, bond discount is so closely associated with the bonds themselves that when the bonds are retired the bond discount should be extinguished. Practically, any of the methods suggested for the extinguishment may be unacceptable.

As an abstract proposition the logic supporting immediate write-off of bond discount seems convincing. Logically there is no more relation between refunded bonds and refunding bonds than there is between a replaced fixed asset and a replacing asset.

The argument that bonds are refunded before maturity because of a desire to lower interest costs and that the discount on the old bonds is one of the factors considered at the time of deciding to refund does not, it seems, justify carrying forward the old discount balance. The same argument might also be applied when a corporation having substantial funds on hand decides to save values by retiring its own bonds before maturity without refunding them. Under such circumstances would anyone contend that the bond discount on the retired bonds should be carried forward to be amortized in future periods?

Whether bonds retired before maturity are refunded or not, it seems that the amount of bond discount referring thereto must be extinguished when the bonds are retired. Such discount ceases to have any significance from either the balance sheet viewpoint or the profit and loss viewpoint as soon as the bonds to which it is related no longer exist.

As to the methods of extinguishing the discount, by a process of elimination the earned surplus charge should be discarded.

When the amount is substantial it seems improper to show all of such bond discount on a profit and loss statement for any one period.

Despite certain admitted objections the third choice seems to be the best of the three, namely, to recast the profit and loss statements for prior periods and to distribute the bond discount to those periods which would have been affected if at the time of incurring the bonded indebtedness it had been known that the bonds would be retired before maturity.

The problem is not one of general importance. The luxury of issuing bonds is not available to the great majority of corporations nor are bonds a common type of liability for sole proprietorships or partnerships. The problem is stressed here only because of its relationship to the larger problem of allocating deferred charges to accounting periods, it being assumed that any practice of allocation which can be justified in this particular case might be extended to cover the allocation of other assets, thus modifying the conventional practices of accounting.

CHAPTER 22

INVENTORY CHARACTERISTICS

Having in the foregoing chapters assembled various conventions, doctrines, and rules of accounting, having considered some of the problems of accounting classification, and having developed a general theory of expenditures in relation to profit, it now remains to apply these materials to typical accounting problems. Two of these problems have been selected for examination because in the average business situation their effect upon the profit calculation is controlling.

The first problem is that of the inventory in relation to profit, consideration to which is given in this and the following five chapters. The second problem is that of fixed assets in relation to profit, which will be discussed in Chapters 28 through 31.

Inventories often represent a substantial percentage of total assets. In a trading enterprise occupying leased property and selling on a cash or short-term credit basis, the inventory alone may represent as much as half or three-quarters of the total assets.

In some kinds of manufacturing, particularly where materials must be aged as in the case of alcoholic liquors and tobacco, the accounting for inventories may be of dominant importance. In any business having for its principal activity the sale of merchandise or manufactured products, inventory bookkeeping and inventory valuation may greatly affect periodic profit and loss.

Canning[1] notes that, "any error in valuation, *no matter in which direction,* misleads the management to their harm," and asserts that, "improvement of inventory valuation offers a prospect for a greater gain in usefulness of accounting reports than does any other element of technique in accountancy."

[1] John B. Canning, *The Economics of Accountancy* (New York, The Ronald Press Company, 1929), pp. 259, 227.

Byerly[2] speaks of the "tremendous differences" in financial statements resulting from different inventory valuation policies. Hosmer[3] ranks inventory valuation with depreciation as representing areas of primary importance in income determination.

Differences of opinion as to proper accounting for inventories are based upon two viewpoints. From the balance sheet viewpoint, the inventory is considered somewhat equivalent to a fund of values convertible into cash.

Balance Sheet Viewpoint.—It is implied that this fund of merchandise may, if credit necessities require, be converted into cash by forced sale. It must be granted that this is only an implication, seldom stated directly. The implication is, however, affirmed by the inclusion of inventories in current assets, the matching of current assets with current liabilities, and the inventory rule of cost or market.

Arthur[4] says: "Although banks regard inventories as a most liquid asset upon which to extend credit, it will be found that the liquidity they offer is largely superficial." In 1915 Dicksee[5] referred to inventories as follows: "The element of immediate realisation is an important factor in their value." Canning[6] asserts that an inventory valuation "can have no significance except as an index of funds to be produced," although elsewhere he observes that certain materials, such as molten metal in the steel industry, have no value to anyone except the manufacturer. Nickerson[7] mentions the "firmly established principle that inventories should be valued at their debt-paying ability."

The doctrine of conservatism in inventory valuation furnishes similar evidence. Repeatedly it has been intimated that understatement of inventory values is desirable.

The only possible justification for such a view is to be found

---

2 F. P. Byerly, "Formulation of Accounting Principles or Conventions," *The Journal of Accountancy*, August 1937, p. 97.

3 W. A. Hosmer, "The Effect of Direct Charges to Surplus on the Measurement of Income," *The Accounting Review*, March 1938, p. 31.

4 Henry B. Arthur, "Inventory Profits in the Business Cycle," *The American Economic Review*, March 1938, p. 38.

5 Lawrence R. Dicksee, *Auditing: A Practical Manual for Auditors* (London, Gee and Company, 1915), p. 201.

6 John B. Canning, *The Economics of Accountancy* (New York, The Ronald Press Company, 1929), p. 227.

7 Clarence B. Nickerson, "Inventory Reserves as an Element of Inventory Policy," *The Accounting Review*, December 1937, p. 354.

in the credit man's viewpoint. To the credit man, understatement of inventory values may be desirable, bolstering as it does his confidence in the realizable value of current assets despite the possibility that it may confuse him as to actualities. Gross understatement of inventory values has been praised as a virtue by those who argue for such plans as the base-stock method.

In substantiation, Davis[8] asserts that auditors cannot object to a stabilized inventory valuation, "for at all times our total inventories are well below either cost or market no matter how these might be figured. The amounts by which our closing inventories at certain times are below the lower of cost or market is perhaps rather startling. A little thought, however, will show that in the last analysis these amounts really represent just how far from being really safe and truly conservative we would have been, if we had stuck to the traditional methods of accounting."

Gross understatement of inventory values may be referred to by one group as "conservative", others view such understatement as deceptive and harmful. Peloubet,[9] during a round-table discussion at the 1937 American Institute Convention, is reported as thinking that: "We are in at least as much danger of understating as we are of overstating—particularly, I would say, in regard to the S.E.C. I think it is quite possible that we may get court action where an investor says he has been induced to part with his securities because of an unduly conservative statement." This is no new idea. As long ago as 1920, Gower[10] discussed the serious abuses which might result through the understatement of inventory values and the corresponding understatement of profits.

Profit and Loss Viewpoint.—Contrasted with the traditional balance sheet viewpoint is the newer emphasis upon the profit and loss statement.

This shift, by implication at least, recognizes inventories not as deferred charges to cash but as deferred charges to future

[8] Albion R. Davis, "Inventory Valuation and Business Profits—The Case for a 'Stabilized Basis,'" *N.A.C.A. Bulletin,* December 1, 1937, p. 389.
[9] Maurice E. Peloubet, *Fiftieth Anniversary Celebration* (New York, American Institute of Accountants, 1937), p. 356.
[10] William B. Gower, "Unsold Goods and the Income Account," *The Journal of Accountancy,* March 1920, pp. 171-179.

income. The profit and loss viewpoint toward inventories emphasizes the doctrine of consistency as being more important than the doctrine of conservatism. As early as 1918, the Bureau of Internal Revenue required that: "The inventory practice of a taxpayer should be consistent from year to year."

Peloubet[9] in the round-table discussion previously mentioned observed that: "You can always be conservative in a balance sheet; you can never be consistently conservative in income accounts. It is mathematically impossible."

In manufacturing industries it has been found helpful to think of inventories as reservoirs connected with one another by streams. Operating men tend to visualize inventories in terms of their flow. Thus, Arthur[11] speaks of inventories as "analogous to the water in the pipes of the economic system." According to Nickerson,[12] an executive of a meat packing company expressed a similar idea as follows: "We have a river of meat flowing through our plant. At times it widens and then again it narrows, but we cannot stop it and still remain in business." This is the operating, as opposed to the financial, viewpoint toward inventories.

Comparison of Viewpoints.—These viewpoints often conflict with one another, particularly in relation to the numerous problems of inventory valuation.

Their reconciliation is not always successful. Hatfield[13] noted that the practice of inventory valuation "is curiously inconsistent and illogical."

FINANCIAL STATEMENTS. Some authorities have given up hope of satisfying both financial and operating interests and have seriously suggested that different types of financial statements be prepared for different groups, i.e., one report for operating men, one for bankers, and one for income tax purposes.

It has been suggested[14] that: "The difficulties into which we

11 Henry B. Arthur, "Inventory Profits in the Business Cycle," *The American Economic Review*, March 1938, p. 27.
12 Clarence B. Nickerson, "Inventory Reserves as an Element of Inventory Policy," *The Accounting Review*, December 1937, p. 347.
13 Henry Rand Hatfield, *Accounting* (New York, D. Appleton-Century Company, Inc., 1927), p. 99.
14 Max Rolnik, *Fiftieth Anniversary Celebration* (New York, American Institute of Accountants, 1938), p. 343.

are getting in this question of inventory valuation, the concept of what income is, and so forth, are due to the fact that we are trying to make one type of income statement meet all of our requirements." Referring to the separate requirements of owners, managers, creditors, and taxing and regulatory bodies, Sanders, Hatfield, and Moore[15] suggest that: "It sometimes becomes necessary to prepare separate statements to serve the several purposes."

CONSISTENCY. Other accountants have believed that the doctrine of consistency is not incompatible with the doctrine of conservatism, in spite of the fact that theirs represents a rather limited concept of consistency.

In 1904, Sir Arthur Lowes Dickinson intimated that consistency did not call for the same price basis at the beginning and end of a period but rather the same basis of valuation. More recently there was a somewhat similar expression in the American Institute bulletin, *Examination of Financial Statements by Independent Public Accountants*. The point is also emphasized in *A Statement of Accounting Principles*.

It is generally recognized that the doctrine of consistency is desirable in order to obtain comparable periodic statements for one company, although Montgomery[16] adopts the broader, but questionable, intercompany viewpoint that: "It is important that uniform methods be followed, else comparisons of the financial statements of one concern with those of another will be misleading."

PRODUCTS FROM NATURAL RESOURCES. Some writers discern a difference between manufacturing and trading inventories and those resulting from the exploitation of natural resources, and have proposed different methods of valuation for the two.

Justification for the separate classification of ore, oil, timber, and farm products is found in their ready marketability. It has been proposed that such products should be valued on a selling

15 Sanders, Hatfield, and Moore, *A Statement of Accounting Principles* (New York, American Institute of Accountants, 1938), p. 26.
16 Robert H. Montgomery, *Auditing Theory and Practice* (New York, The Ronald Press Company, 1934), p. 205.

price basis, i.e., selling price less costs of marketing. That this anticipates the realization of profit is, however, seldom denied.

Inventory Classifications.—Inventories may be classified in a number of different ways. The primary classification may be according to location or according to physical characteristics or otherwise.

In general, however, the balance sheet viewpoint so far prevails that the primary classification of inventories is twofold, current and non-current. Subsidiary to the current classification are such groups as raw materials and parts, manufacturing supplies, work in progress, and finished products or merchandise.

In the current category, but seldom specifically called inventories, are investments in stocks and bonds. When trading in such stocks and bonds is the principal business objective, as in investment banking, they represent inventory in a true sense. When trading in such stocks and bonds is incidental to the main operations of the business, the inventory characteristic of such items is not lost, but neither is it emphasized by a balance sheet caption or otherwise. While there are important accounting differences between inventories of securities and other inventories, they are not sufficiently important for the purpose of this volume to justify special consideration.

In the non-current category are found such groups as office expense supplies, including stationery, catalogues, letterheads, pens, pencils, ink, salesmen's samples, and similar items intended for use rather than for sale. Shipping containers are usually in this category since they are seldom considered current assets. Materials on hand acquired for construction or repair purposes are considered to be non-current.

When viewed in relation to profits, the distinction between current and non-current inventories is not significant. While certain types of inventories are directly related to specific sections of the profit and loss statement, nevertheless any attempt to survey inventory problems from the profit and loss viewpoint does not require primary distinction between inventories of raw material, inventories of expense supplies, or even inventories of investments.

In a larger sense they are all inventories and can be studied s a group in their relation to periodic profit distortion.

The Periodic Inventory.—In spite of numerous variations here are but two basic plans of inventory accounting—the eriodic inventory plan and the perpetual inventory plan.

The periodic inventory plan determines what part of an inentory at the beginning of an accounting period plus acquisiions during the period has been used or consumed, by counting p how much is left at the end of the period. This is the tradiional method inherited from an earlier and simpler accounting.

COST OR MARKET VALUATION. Valuation of an inventory t realizable market price when lower than cost was an inheriance from the early trading ventures, strongly encouraged in ater years by the doctrine of conservatism preached by credit nen and accountants under the influence of the balance sheet iewpoint.

It has persisted in modern accounting practice. As a result, he debit balance of cost of sales account generally consisted in part of the actual cost of merchandise sold, in part of losses of nerchandise, and in part of unrealized losses, representing the lifference between any high cost of merchandise remaining on and at the end of the period and its lower selling price.

MERCHANDISE RECORDS. This periodic inventory plan reults in a figure for cost of sales which is known to be made up of diverse elements not easily analyzed or interpreted. As a igure having specific management control value the balance of he account has little to recommend it.

It is, therefore, necessary to supplement the actual inventory iccounting with various statistical analyses, controls, or merhandise records. Such supplementary records are generally separate and apart from the accounting mechanism. Often they ire used to promote more effective buying. Generally they are naintained in quantities rather than dollar values to show the relative popularity of different sizes, as well as patterns, of nerchandise.

In their more elaborate forms such statistical records somewhat resemble perpetual inventories save that they are not subject to full accounting control.

The Perpetual Inventory.—With the increase in size of manufacturing establishments which accompanied the general adoption of the corporate form of organization, modern cost accounting was born.

In order to apply various types of costs and expenses to materials passing through a factory, it was necessary to adopt a different kind of inventory accounting generally referred to as the perpetual inventory plan.

ELEMENTARY PROCEDURE.   The perpetual inventory provides an account with each kind of inventory item. If ten different sizes of bolts are carried in stock, ten separate and distinct accounts may be required, one for each size.

To such an account is debited each receipt of the item, which thereafter cannot be released except upon written authority based upon which a credit is made to the inventory account. At all times, if all entries have been made, the inventory account shows the amount of that item which should be on hand. By the adoption of this plan it becomes unnecessary to take a complete physical inventory periodically.

The actual counting done in connection with perpetual inventories is for the purpose of checking the balance shown by the record against the quantities actually on hand to determine whether items have been issued without requisition or have been stolen, mislaid, or have otherwise disappeared. Such counting can be done as part of a regular program of verification throughout the accounting period, not as one burdensome task at the end

This plan contemplates an individual account for each individual classification of inventory.

CONTROLLING ACCOUNTS.   In a modern manufacturing plant with its great variety of inventory items in various sizes and grades, the number of perpetual inventory accounts may be large, running often into thousands. For simplification such accounts are treated as subsidiary accounts to general ledger controlling accounts. In a factory there may be one control account for raw materials and parts, another control account for manufacturing supplies, another for goods in process, and another for finished product.

PERPETUAL INVENTORY REVALUATION. Traditionally, the debits and credits to any perpetual inventory account should be at actual cost, the balance of the account showing the cost of the items still remaining in the inventory.

With the adoption of perpetual inventories a conflict between valuations at cost and at realizable market price was noted. The conflict had, of course, long existed but was seldom clearly realized by those who used the periodic inventory plan. The adoption of perpetual inventories automatically resulted in a balance sheet valuation of inventories at cost (or practically so, subject to considerations discussed later). To substitute lower market prices for any high cost prices reported by the perpetual inventory required deliberate action, and the question naturally arose as to why any such change should be made.

The perpetual inventory purports to show true costs of the inventory items which have been consumed or sold. Any downward adjustment of the balance is a loss of a different type from that represented by consumption or sale. This fact alone has awakened interest in problems of inventory valuation as related to net profit.

As a result there are two schools of accounting thought. One recognizes cost as the only basis for balance sheet valuation of inventory and the other favors the use of the lower of cost or market price for valuation. For convenience the first group may be thought of as the cost accountants and the second group as the auditors, although members of each group have argued on the other side.

DISSIMILAR ELEMENTS IN COST OF SALES. The cost accountant is interested in costs in their relation to efficiency and to profits. The auditor is interested among other things in realizable or semi-realizable valuation of current assets.

The periodic inventory with its periodic valuation tended to conceal rather than reveal the fact that cost of sales consisted of dissimilar elements: (1) actual cost of the merchandise parted with, and (2) the difference between the cost of the merchandise remaining on hand and the value assigned to it at the time the inventory count was made.

The perpetual inventory plan gives closer control over inventories, this being a feature of considerable value. Perpetual inventory records are subject to verification because the various debits and credits made to the detailed inventory accounts are supported by written evidence. The desirability of such verification is somewhat offset by the cost of clerical work in maintaining such inventory records, which cost may be prohibitive where it is necessary to account for a great variety of items of slight value.

Retail Inventory Methods.—Having some but not all the advantages of the perpetual inventory is a substitute plan commonly referred to as the retail inventory method.

By the retail inventory method it is possible to distinguish with reasonable accuracy between inventory items which have been sold or properly disposed of and inventory items which have been lost or stolen. But this difference can only be determined approximately by classified totals, seldom by items.

In its essence the retail inventory plan is simple. Purchases of merchandise are recorded at both cost and selling price. Withdrawal of inventory items is shown at selling price. It is a simple matter to determine, by broad classifications, the inventory remaining on hand at the end of the period at selling price. This total can be verified by actual count of the merchandise remaining on hand, assigning the proper selling prices to it, and comparing the total with the corresponding ledger account.

In its actual operation the retail system of inventory is somewhat complicated by selling price changes. At the time a dozen cans of corn, for example, are acquired it may be safe to assume that the selling price per can is 15 cents, but a week or two later competition may require the establishment of a new selling price of 25 cents for two cans. This makes it necessary to readjust the records. In any establishment such as a chain store where prices change rapidly this may prove to be a burdensome and complicated task.

At the end of any accounting period the amount of inventory reported by the books of a retail store will reflect selling prices rather than costs. As accountants with few exceptions wholeheartedly condemn the practice of valuing inventories at selling price, it becomes necessary to reverse the original calculation and return to the cost basis. This is accomplished in totals by applying percentages the correctness of which depends upon the accuracy in recording the original cost of merchandise acquired, the selling prices assigned to it, and subsequent changes therein.

The advantages of this method have been noted by Montgomery[17] as follows: "By use of the retail inventory method the laborious process of inventorying and costing thousands of small items to get an inventory for balance sheet purposes is eliminated."

Summary of Methods.—Several different inventory methods may be used in the same establishment. In a department store, for example, costly items such as coats, suits, and similar units may be controlled by perpetual inventories. Less important items may be recorded by the retail method. Other items may be handled according to the traditional plan of periodic inventory.

In certain merchandising situations it is possible to establish standard stocks. This is sometimes true in connection with branch stores where standard quantities of merchandise are established for each store. Each day or each week the manager of a store requisitions from a central warehouse enough of each item of merchandise to bring his stock back to standard. This method facilitates auditing.

It should, however, be noted that no substitute method possesses all of the advantages of the perpetual inventory with its running record of quantities and values and its written evidence supporting additions and withdrawals.

Occasionally perpetual inventories are kept in terms of quantities only, merely for control purposes. Such records may have no direct accounting significance unless the cost of acquiring materials is standardized. Granted a constant acquisition cost it

17 Robert H. Montgomery, *Auditing Theory and Practice* (New York, The Ronald Press Company, 1934), p. 215.

would be a clerical waste to compute money values for every entry, since the money value of the balance at any desired time can be determined by multiplying the quantity shown by the fixed price. Fixed prices of this kind are, of course, uncommon except in standard cost accounting, where they are arbitrarily fixed.

The actual technique of accounting control of inventories depends greatly upon the kind of materials involved, their value, their size or ·bulk, and upon operating procedure, class of help employed, and numerous other factors. The accounting for inventories of pig iron, ore, coal, or other bulk commodities may be quite different from the accounting for inventories of precious metals or precious stones. The adoption of mass production methods and the use of assembly lines may greatly modify inventory procedure. In one form or another, however, the perpetual inventory plan exists in practically all industrial organizations.

The Research Department of the National Association of Cost Accountants[18] reported a survey of 197 companies—157 or 79.7% of which controlled over 90% of their raw materials by perpetual inventory. Only 13 of the companies, or 6.6%, did not use perpetual inventories at all for controlling raw materials.

It may be conceded that problems of inventory valuation actually are the same regardless of whether periodic or perpetual inventory records are maintained. The periodic inventory, however, tends to conceal rather than reveal the essential factors which may be important in surveying periodic profit distortion. For that reason the discussion of inventories in subsequent chapters assumes perpetual inventory control.

[18] *N.A.C.A. Bulletin,* March 15, 1937.

CHAPTER 23

INVENTORY CHARGES

Consistent and sometimes substantial profit distortion may result from the methods adopted for making charges to inventory accounts. For a variety of practical operating reasons it may be unwise, inexpedient, or impossible to base such charges on actual cost.

An inventory charge may refer to the acquisition of an item of raw material or other commodity (including, of course, securities) as the result of a purchase transaction, or it may result from the transfer of an item from some other inventory account as where raw material, labor, and overhead are transferred to work in progress, or from work in progress to finished product, or where by-products or scrap are transferred from one department to another or from one account to another.

Invoice Cost of Purchases.—In so far as original purchases are concerned, it is common practice to enter them at invoice cost.

Of 197 manufacturing companies questioned by the Research and Service Department of the National Association of Cost Accountants,[1] 177 or about 90% charged purchases to raw materials account at invoice price, the remaining 20 companies using either standard costs or both actual and standard costs.

Actual cost and invoice cost are not necessarily the same. Freight, express, cartage, and other acquisition costs should often be included on the same general theory that costs of transportation and installation are added to the book value of fixed assets. The number of small items comprised in one purchase may be too great to justify accurate treatment of such items. The clerical work of allocating them to perpetual inventory

1 *N.A.C.A. Bulletin,* March 15, 1937.

cards may not be justified by resulting benefits. When these costs are not included among inventory charges they are often considered expenses, thus resulting in a slight but definite misstatement of inventory valuation.

In acquiring stocks and bonds, part of the legitimate cost thereof is the broker's commission. This is now well settled, the United States Supreme Court[2] having reversed a lower court decision, the lower court[2a] upon return of the case having held that while purchase commissions are part of the cost of the stock purchased, selling commissions are 100% deductible.

Purchase and Trade Discounts.—Purchase discounts are properly considered as deductions from the cost of purchases although there is no substantial agreement on this treatment, since by some they are also viewed as income.

The treatment of purchase discounts as non-operating income is endorsed by such authorities as MacFarland and Ayars,[3] and also Finney.[4] MacFarland and Ayars claim that: "Purchase Discount is additional income of the business resulting from allowances obtained from creditors by the payment for merchandise purchases within stated periods," while Finney unequivocally asserts that: "Cash discount on purchases is income earned by paying bills within a definite time."

Consistently, these writers consider sales discounts as expenses, MacFarland and Ayars characterizing them as "costs which arise from other than the major operating causes."

Canning[5] observes that "many accountants—and an increasing proportion of accountants—treat the neglected 'cash discount' on sales as an item of financial income." One who adopts this viewpoint would, if consistent, treat neglected purchase discounts as items of financial expense.

Husband and Thomas[6] argue soundly: "If purchases dis-

2 Helvering v. Robert C. Winmill (1938), 59 S.Ct. 45.

2a Alexander Tax News Letter, Vol. III, No. 31, February 17, 1939.

3 MacFarland and Ayars, *Accounting Fundamentals* (New York, McGraw-Hill Book Company, Inc., 1936), p. 38.

4 H. A. Finney, *Introduction to Principles of Accounting* (New York, Prentice-Hall, Inc., 1936), p. 96.

5 John B. Canning, *The Economics of Accountancy* (New York, The Ronald Press Company, 1929), p. 111.

6 Husband and Thomas, *Principles of Accounting* (New York, Houghton Mifflin Company, 1925), p. 248.

counts are an income, it follows that they may be earned by the simple expedient of buying goods and paying for them within the discount period. This is contrary to fundamental accounting principles. Income is not earned by the acquisition of merchandise but rather by its sale."

Trade discounts as distinguished from cash discounts are uniformly deducted in arriving at acquisition cost, but where such trade discounts are retroactive, based upon cumulative volume, it may be impractical to apply them to previously recorded purchases.

Advertising allowances sometimes made in connection with substantial transactions may in fact represent special discounts properly to be deducted from acquisition cost. Ordinarily, however, they are considered as a direct or indirect offset to the advertising expense account of the purchaser which may result in an overstatement of inventory.

Indeterminable Acquisition Costs.—In some industries it is an utter impossibility to determine the cost of materials charged to inventory. Crude oil, for example, in an integrated company is charged to the refinery division at current market price, thus carrying an unknown and unknowable interdivisional profit which cannot, except by sheer guess work, be eliminated for statement purposes. Not knowing, except in the most general way, how much crude oil remains underground effectively prevents the producing division from costing it on a unit basis in so far as the important element of depletion is concerned.

A similar difficulty is frequently noted in some mining enterprises.

Repossessed Merchandise.—Merchandise returned to a vendor by a customer is commonly treated in about the same way as a purchase.

If such returned merchandise is in good condition and requires no repairing, repainting, or other refinishing, it may be charged to inventory at the same cost as before. If the returned merchandise has deteriorated, it may be necessary to book it at a lower value, taking into consideration the cost of reconditioning.

OPINIONS OF AUTHORITIES. In this connection the *Accountants' Handbook*[7] asserts: "In general all repossessed merchandise should be valued at cost less proper estimate for damage, etc., unless this figure is above net selling price, in which case net selling value may be substituted for the other basis."

Montgomery[8] approaches this question of valuation in a different way by saying: "Repossessed merchandise is generally valued at estimated selling price, less an allowance for selling expenses and cost of reconditioning. The value thus arrived at should be used unless it exceeds replacement cost. Such stock should never be valued higher than cost to replace." There is little or no conflict between these two assertions, the difference in wording being due to differences in method of approach. From that same viewpoint which regards the cost or market rule as opposed to sound accounting, the first part of the *Accountants' Handbook* statement appears proper.

Somewhat unsatisfactory because of over-insistence upon conservatism is the assertion made by Taylor and Miller[9] that: "The valuation should be a conservative one, taking into consideration the loss due to depreciation and also the present market for used merchandise."

Eliminating from consideration any application of the cost or market rule, it would appear that there is no logical reason to apply any different standard to the valuation of repossessed merchandise than to the valuation of the same merchandise when first acquired, neither having any logical relationship in so far as valuation is concerned to a possible resale. This viewpoint is, however, not uniformly held, and most authorities follow the procedure which is acceptable to the Treasury Department.

THE TAX VIEWPOINT. The profit calculation for income tax purposes is given in Article 44-1 of Regulations 94 thus:

If for any reason the purchaser defaults in any of his payments, and the vendor returning income on the installment basis repossesses the property sold, whether title thereto had been retained by the vendor or

7 *Accountants' Handbook* (New York, The Ronald Press Company, 1934), p. 446.

8 Robert H. Montgomery, *Auditing Theory and Practice* (New York, The Ronald Press Company, 1934), p. 212.

9 Taylor and Miller, *Intermediate Accounting* (New York, McGraw-Hill Book Company, Inc., 1934), Vol. II, p. 28.

transferred to the purchaser, gain or loss for the year in which the repossession occurs is to be computed upon any installment obligations of the purchaser which are satisfied or discharged upon the repossession or are applied by the vendor to the purchase or bid price of the property. Such gain or loss is to be measured by the difference between the fair market value of the property repossessed and the basis in the hands of the vendor of the obligations of the purchaser which are so satisfied, discharged, or applied, with proper adjustment for any other amounts realized or costs incurred in connection with the repossession.

Merchandise Trade-Ins.—Accounting difficulties may result from sales transactions involving trade-ins. Such transactions are common in marketing automobiles, domestic appliances, and office equipment, the price established for the trade-in often being considerably in excess of cash value.

Occasionally the old equipment received by a vendor is worthless. In order to effect the sale of a new radio it is often necessary for the dealer to accept an obsolete radio in part payment. The dealer may establish a trade-in value on an old set of perhaps $5, although the set itself has no value for purposes of resale and usually does not repay disassembling for the sake of the parts. In other words, the amount allowed for the obsolete set is a complete loss and properly should be considered as an offset to the sales price of the new equipment.

Where traded-in equipment can be reconditioned and sold there results a problem of cost apportionment which may cause inventory inaccuracy and profit distortion. If a dealer sells a new car for $600 and accepts in trade an old one at $200, and if the old car after being reconditioned at a cost of $15 can be sold for no more than $170, and if the expense of selling such a reconditioned car at $170 is 20%, or $34, then it is evident that part of the $200 trade-in value represents actual asset acquisition and part represents expense of selling the new car. Using the figures just cited, the old car might be inventoried at $170 less $15 reconditioning cost and less $34 selling cost, or a total deduction of $49. The actual asset value of the old car, therefore, is not $200 but is $121, the difference of $79 being an item of selling expense or trade discount directly related not to the old car traded in but to the new car sold.

An alternative method of treatment would first reduce the value of the used car to the current market quotation, after which a reserve for selling expense would be set up. An important objection to this method is found in the position of the Treasury Department, which has been attempting to disallow such items if set up as a reserve, whereas if the estimated selling expense is actually deducted in establishing the inventory value of the used car no question has arisen.

Hedging Transactions.—The effect of hedging transactions upon inventory valuation and upon profit determination is variously stated. Altman[10] presented the problem in his questions:

As the flour merchant buys his grain, he hedges it. As that grain goes down in value, he is fully protected on the hedge. How would you present that in a financial statement? Would you present it at cost where he is protected, or would you present it at the lower price and offset it by the profit on the hedge?

These questions suggest two general viewpoints. One viewpoint considers that hedging operations merely insure the value of materials in process, thus closely relating the two; another, that separate and distinct transactions are indicated and that mere intent on the part of management to offset one against the other is not coercive upon accounting.

HEDGING RELATED TO OPERATIONS. In support of the first view the *Accountants' Handbook*[11] says:

If the management views the hedging operations as merely a device to insure the value of materials in process, and not as a separate speculative activity, the gain from hedging can reasonably be treated as an operating adjustment.

This view is supported in practice as evidenced by the following quotation from Harvey:[12]

10 Harry L. Altman, *Fiftieth Anniversary Celebration* (New York, American Institute of Accountants, 1938), p. 346.
11 *Accountants' Handbook* (New York, The Ronald Press Company, 1934), p. 1093.
12 John L. Harvey, "Some Observations on Accounting Practice with Special Reference to Inventory Valuation," *The Journal of Accountancy,* December 1937, p. 449.

Grain and cotton dealers, because of the difficulties in attempting to determine costs of grain and cotton on hand, usually inventory at market values which are equivalent in these cases to sales values. These companies, as a matter of protection, hedge against the actual "spot" or cash transactions and against future purchases or sales as the case may be, and these future transactions are included in the inventory.

A somewhat roundabout argument against this viewpoint may be gleaned from the following words of Arthur:[13]

Nevertheless, we find—somewhat ironically—that the Bureau of Internal Revenue has ruled that the unrealized capital gain or loss on a hedge contract may be regarded as an "income" item, in order that unrealized inventory losses or profits may continue to be regarded (erroneously) as income items, rather than as unrealized capital gains or losses.

The tax authorities have, in other words, insisted that inventory profits be regarded as income, even to the extent of being inconsistent in their handling of capital gains and losses.

HEDGING NOT RELATED TO OPERATIONS. While it is difficult to justify the term "inventory profits" in the sense in which Arthur used it, nevertheless the above quotation does help to support the view that greater accounting clarity might result from regarding the hedging operation as one entirely separate and distinct from the inventory problem. Aside from a superficial relationship represented by the similarity of the materials bought and sold, there seems to be no good accounting reason for considering the purchase and the hedge as offsetting transactions. Business men are constantly entering into transactions the purpose of which is to modify or cancel some prospective unfavorable development. Offsetting transactions are necessarily matched in the final figure of net profit but, for clarity, accountants have generally insisted that separate transactions should be kept separate and that the profits or losses thereon should, in so far as practicably possible, be separately computed and exhibited.

That a price loss on materials in process may be offset by a non-operating gain appearing in a different section of the profit

[13] Henry B. Arthur, "Inventory Profits in the Business Cycle," *The American Economic Review*, March 1938, p. 35.

and loss statement does not, it appears, offend good accounting and reporting practice. On the contrary, if properly disclosed such treatment appears to be informative. Few accountants would contend that $5,000 of interest earned on $100,000 worth of bonds should be merged with $3,500 of interest expense on the $70,000 unpaid balance of the purchase price of the same bonds, even though the two interest items represent parts of the same transaction. Nor would they contend that the mortgage interest on partially paid-for rental property should be merged with the rent receipts from that property. Does not this same general rule of accounting and reporting support the position that profits or losses on the speculative activity of hedging are separate and distinct from profits or losses due to changed price levels on inventories?

Burden and Normal Capacity.—Of special importance, not only because of their materiality but also because of their accounting interest, is the effect upon inventory of certain modern cost accounting procedures of burden allocation. This distinctly refers to inventories in view of the fact that cost accounting itself is inventory accounting. Since modern practice in accounting for burden results in withholding part of the burden charge from the inventory of work in progress, the discussion of burden allocation logically belongs in this present chapter.

Because many of the items composing manufacturing expense are fixed or practically fixed and hence do not fluctuate in proportion to operating activity, the practical application of manufacturing expense to work in progress is substantially different from pure theory.

The convention of transferred values requires that all costs of manufacturing be attached to the cost of materials going through a factory. Such transfers refer to the cost of direct labor and the costs of indirect labor, supplies, service department expenses, depreciation, light, heat, and water, and many others. In general, the cost of labor is roughly in proportion to manufacturing activity either because labor is paid upon a piece-work basis or because workmen are laid off during slack time and reemployed when active operations are resumed.

VARIABLE AND FIXED EXPENSE. Some of the items composing manufacturing expense are similarly variable. Many of them, however, are fixed or semi-fixed with the result that they remain at approximately the same level regardless of the rate of operating activity.

To require that all of such costs be transferred to and become a part of the cost of material in process simply means that the total cost per unit of product will be substantially greater in dull periods than in active ones. This phenomenon is unacceptable to those factory executives who believe that unit manufacturing costs should represent a rough index of efficiency.

Plant inactivity is often caused by lack of sales which lack may in turn be due to general economic conditions.

PREDETERMINED RATES. Any attempt to show unit costs which are excessive due to general economic conditions necessarily offends the factory executive. From this situation has developed the general practice of transferring manufacturing expense to work in progress at predetermined rates based upon some concept of normal operating capacity.

If, argue the cost accountants, a manufacturing establishment owns two plants one of which is entirely idle and the other working at full capacity, it would be improper to transfer the cost of depreciation and maintenance on the inactive plant to the product passing through the active plant. Such depreciation and maintenance, it is said, should be treated as a loss rather than as an element of cost attaching to materials in progress.

The analogy may be carried further. Instead of two manufacturing plants, only one such plant may be assumed. If that one plant is operating at 50% capacity it is argued that burden rates based upon 100% capacity should be used and the amount of burden not absorbed by these rates should be treated as a loss rather than as an element of manufacturing cost.

There may be serious question as to whether unit manufacturing costs are properly to be compared, historically, as indexes of operating efficiency. Assuming, however, that such is their purpose then the cost accounting argument for predetermined rates based upon normal capacity seems to be well founded.

NORMAL CAPACITY CONCEPT. The popularity of normal burden rates is traceable to the efficiency engineering movement during the early years of the present century.

Giving but secondary consideration to the balance sheet viewpoint or to general problems of financial accounting, cost accountants, engineers, and efficiency men approached accounting problems from the engineering side with the result that they looked upon accounting data as statistical measures of operating efficiency.

The engineering concept of normality was bounded by the walls of the factory, and as late as 1921 a committee of the National Association of Cost Accountants defined normal capacity as the capacity to make or manufacture and ruled out "any prospective future lack of orders" as a factor in the determination of normal rates.

Investigation shows no general acceptance of normal burden rates nor underabsorbed burden accounts before the turn of the century. This, of course, does not mean that this concept was unknown in the latter part of the nineteenth century. Goodwin[14] reports a visit he made in 1928 to the Atlas Works of John Brown and Co., Ltd., in Sheffield, England, where he was shown "accounting sheets, ledger size, on soft gray, fine-quality paper, with soft-colored machine-ruled lines and bearing a handwritten list of departments." He adds: "Of a number of columns, on the extreme right appeared one entitled: 'Unabsorbed Burden'—and the date—December 31, 1886."

It is, however, probable that this early recognition of unabsorbed burden was not general. In 1887 the first edition of Factory Accounts, by Garcke and Fells, appeared. In that volume the authors said: "When the indirect charges and depreciation are of a more or less fixed character, it is probably sufficient to know the cost of an article in wages and materials only, but if the indirect expenses and wear and tear of plant form a more direct element in the cost of production, it would be highly desirable to apportion such items among the various operations or departments." In 1903 an English authority, H. S. Garry,

14 J. Pryse Goodwin, Forum Section, *N.A.C.A. Bulletin*, November 1, 1938, p. 295.

advocated treating as a dead charge the cost of excess capacity. He suggested dividing up actual cost into standard cost, excess cost, and increase in cost due to excess capacity.

One of the early American pioneers in the use of normal burden rates and in the recognition of the problems associated with under- and overabsorbed burden was William J. Gunnell, who applied these concepts in practice as early as 1906. By 1908 C. E. Knoeppel, H. S. Gantt, and A. Hamilton Church were using and writing about normal burden and suggesting such expedients as supplemental burden rates or the allocation of unabsorbed burden direct to "loss and gain" accounts.

In 1911 Clinton H. Scovell was using normal burden rates and on October 22, 1913, discussed various aspects thereof in a paper presented to the National Association of Machine Tool Builders. His book, *Cost Accounting and Burden Application,* published in 1916 by D. Appleton & Company, mentioned the reserve method as well as the method of making a direct allocation to profit and loss for the disposition of under- or overabsorbed burden.

All of the early authorities seemed somewhat puzzled over the proper treatment of over- or underabsorbed burden. Some advocated its direct allocation to profit and loss, others suggested that it should be charged or credited to cost of sales, and still others advocated the establishment of reserves created by an appropriation from surplus.

This was the method that was used by the electrical manufacturing industry. The reserve method involving an account called Reserve for Indirect Manufacturing Expense, or some equivalent title, remained popular for many years, but has, by now, become almost completely discredited.

DETERMINATION OF NORMAL CAPACITY.   As has been noted in connection with other attempts to utilize the accounting mechanism in ways to which, by nature, it is ill adapted, numerous accounting difficulties have resulted from the general adoption of normal burden rates.

The principal difficulty refers to the determination of normal capacity. Simple examples of some of these problems are noted in connection with seasonal industries such as the canning business, in which actual activity is confined to a few weeks. The canning factory has an actual capacity far in excess of its practical capacity, the latter being strictly limited by the supply of vegetables and fruits and the shortness of the season. Shall the entire overhead of the canning factory be considered in establishing burden rates or shall the costs during those months when the factory is shut down be treated as a loss?

Instead of a canning factory which is actually closed during a large part of the year, consider an industry of highly seasonal nature in which, for example, operations are very active for three months and, while still continuing during the other nine months, are at a decidedly low rate. The application of actual expense to materials in progress would naturally result in excessive unit costs during the dull period.

It is somewhat difficult to make a distinction between alternating periods of activity occurring within one calendar year and alternating periods of activity in various phases of the business cycle. It is true that seasonal fluctuations, while no more certain than cyclical fluctuations, are more predictable. Possibly that fact offers sufficient excuse for a difference in treatment.

In the business cycle there are alternating periods of high and low activity but these cannot definitely be forecast, nor is it reasonable or acceptable to devise methods for equalized distribution of manufacturing expense over the different cyclical phases. And yet in all logic, in spite of its practical impossibility, it seems just as important to adopt the same theory of normal capacity for the cycle as for the year.

OVERCAPACITY.   There have been noted numerous cases of chronic overcapacity.

An unnecessarily large factory may be purchased at a bargain price with the full knowledge that it may never be utilized fully. In other instances a prosperous plant, because of some change in consumer preference or because of the passage of restrictive laws, may be operated at much less than capacity for a period of many years. Shall the total burden on either plant be divided in such a manner that part of it is treated as an immediate loss and part of it as a legitimate cost of manufacturing?

Peloubet[15] thinks that this is a question of intent:

If you are spending your money partly to maintain a factory because you hope to use your full facilities later on, I see no justification for putting part of that expense against your current production. If you never expect to have a greater production and if your expenses are directed to your current production, then I say it is cost.

COMPARISON OF BURDEN PRACTICES. An interesting research study entitled "Practice in Applying Overhead and Calculating Normal Capacity" was published in Section 3 of the *N.A.C.A. Bulletin,* dated April 1, 1938. This study was based upon questionnaires sent to 224 manufacturing companies.

Only eighteen of the number reported using actual rather than predetermined burden rates. Nearly half of the companies using predetermined rates revised them annually.

It was one of the purposes of the study to determine on what basis of reasoning rates were established. Of the number of replies adequately covering this matter, 35% reported that they computed burden rates by dividing the estimated overhead for the period by the estimated production for the period. If estimates are made accurately then all of the manufacturing expense for the period will be applied to the goods produced during the period. As a result any over- or underabsorbed burden is due to errors in the estimates.

It will be apparent that this is merely a convenient substitute for actual rates. In the absence of error, both methods apply all of the burden for the period to materials in progress for the period. It therefore appears that the 18 companies reporting the use of actual burden rates and the 67 companies calculating their predetermined rates according to the method above quoted should be grouped together for the purpose of measuring the relative popularity of actual burden rates as against those based upon normal capacity.

Using the base of 224 companies, it is apparent that 38% of them do not base their burden rates upon any estimate of normal capacity to produce. Of the 62% using predetermined rates on some sort of a normal capacity basis, it was noted that

15 Maurice E. Peloubet, *Fiftieth Anniversary Celebration* (New York, American Institute of Accountants, 1938), p. 353.

the minority gave consideration only to the ability of the plant to produce with no consideration to the ability of the sales department to utilize that productive capacity.

Almost three times as many formulated their rates by "taking into consideration both expected sales for the period and the capacity available."

BURDEN BALANCES. When burden rates are predetermined on the basis of normal productive capacity or on the basis of expected sales in their relation to capacity, it is apparent that there may be important discrepancies between the actual burden and the amount absorbed by the product. These discrepancies are referred to as overabsorbed and underabsorbed burden.

If the factory is operating at a low rate, only part of the burden will be transferred to the goods in progress and the remainder will be termed underabsorbed burden to be disposed of at the end of the accounting period. Occasionally a company will become intensely active without changing its burden rates, in which event the burden may be overabsorbed, i.e., the amount charged to work in progress is in excess of the actual expense. Such overabsorbed burden somewhat resembles an imputed cost, being in the nature of a fictitious profit offset by a fictitious debit made to work in progress.

To the extent that such overabsorbed burden is reflected in inventories at the end of a financial period the inventories are just as truly inflated as if they had been deliberately appraised and adjusted to a higher basis.

TREATMENT OF BURDEN BALANCES. Opinions seem to differ as to the proper treatment of underabsorbed or overabsorbed burden at the end of an accounting period. Because of the possibility of periodic profit distortion the question is not limited to proper or conservative inventory valuation for balance sheet purposes. Various opinions and contradictory practices have been noted.

The *Accountants' Handbook*,[16] while recognizing various viewpoints, says that over- or underabsorbed burden for the

16 *Accountants' Handbook* (New York, The Ronald Press Company, 1934), p. 1312.

year "should be added to or deducted from (depending on whether a debit or a credit balance) the manufacturing costs and in closing the books at the end of the period should be closed out to the account exhibiting the manufacturing costs."

This treatment is subject to criticism. To the extent that such over- or underabsorbed burden refers to inventory remaining on hand at the end of the period, the comparison of profits between that period and the subsequent one will be distorted.

Carl L. Seeber, in the *N.A.C.A. Bulletin* of June 15, 1937, says: "Over- or underabsorbed burden is charged direct to profit and loss." Lawrence[17] agrees in somewhat similar words, saying that "any balance for under- or overapplied expense is carried to the Profit and Loss account" as an "extraordinary loss or gain for the year." This treatment gives the same distorting effect as the one recommended by the *Accountants' Handbook*.

The research report in the *N.A.C.A. Bulletin* of April 1, 1938, to which full reference was made on a preceding page, comments on a curious difference in accounting practice as between those companies which eliminate idle equipment costs and fixed charges on idle plant and equipment from burden prior to distributing it to product, and those other companies which do not make such a preliminary segregation. In the first group it was found that the idle equipment costs were charged to profit and loss. In the second group the underabsorbed burden containing identical types of losses was charged against cost of goods sold.

Clarence B. Nickerson, in the *N.A.C.A. Bulletin* of October 31, 1931, presented pro forma profit and loss statements which are interesting in this connection. In these profit and loss statements underabsorbed burden was deducted from net operating profits (the same figure referred to as "net profit before other income and charges" in the American Institute bulletin, *Examination of Financial Statements by Independent Public Accountants*). When the burden was overabsorbed, the amount thereof was added to the operating net profit.

[17] W. B. Lawrence, *Cost Accounting* (New York, Prentice-Hall, Inc., 1937), p. 226. Also see page 226 for better method suggested by the same author.

The only treatment of over- and underabsorbed burden which will not result in distortion is one which determines what part of the production for the year (excluding the opening inventory) has been sold and what part is still retained at the end of the year, and then divides the debit or credit balance of the underabsorbed or overabsorbed burden in the same proportion, thus providing amounts which can be added to or subtracted from cost of sales. Lawrence,[18] previously quoted as discussing another treatment, also recognizes that: "If the difference is considerable the best treatment is to apportion it between Work in Process, Finished Parts, Finished Goods, and Cost of Goods Sold in order that the inventories as well as the cost of goods sold may be valued correctly."

Husband and Thomas[19] believe that under- or overabsorbed burden "should be distributed over (1) the cost of the work still in process, (2) the cost of the finished goods in the storeroom, and (3) the cost of the goods that have been sold." Regarding such treatment as not feasible in the majority of cases, however, they observe that: "The necessary correction is therefore either charged or credited to the Cost of Goods Sold account or to the Expense and Revenue Summary."

It must be noted that the correct treatment is seldom advocated. Rather, any treatment is preferred which provides the lowest inventory value, thus applying the doctrine of conservatism with full force and with utter disregard of profit and loss distortion.

PROFIT DISTORTION. If one can imagine two companies identical in every way save that one uses actual burden rates and the other burden rates based upon normal capacity, it will be apparent that any of the recommendations above noted might easily result in material differences in reported profits; differences which would be magnified if both companies experienced the same sharp variations in operating activity from year to year.

There is, to be sure, a certain amount of logic in predeter-

18 *Ibid.*, p. 226.
19 Husband and Thomas, *Principles of Accounting* (New York, Houghton Mifflin Company, 1925), p. 498.

mined burden rates based upon actual manufacturing capacity but any attempt to modify or adjust these rates by forecasting future sales volume introduces a type of untrustworthy clairvoyance which cannot fail to pervert the results.

To permit guessing about future sales to deform the historical record of profit and loss is difficult of justification. Not satisfied with estimating normal capacity and with guessing at future sales, some companies go even further and "to be on the safe side," as reported by Sanders,[20] set up an account entitled Reserve for Burden Adjustment.

To this account they will credit a small amount every month, the corresponding debit being into the Work in Process, where it is included with the actual burden expenses. The main object accomplished by this device is that it provides a margin of safety in the burden distribution.

Standard Costs.—There are two types of standard costs one of which, basic standard cost, requires carrying actual costs as well as standard costs in the general ledger accounts, thus permitting the application of ratios at the end of the year in order to convert the standard cost of inventories at that time into something approximating actual cost. This method is one of operating convenience and efficiency since it eliminates a substantial volume of detailed clerical work in the cost department. The method does not to any marked extent result in distortion of net profits and hence is excluded from the present discussion.

The other and the more popular "standard cost method" is based upon dissatisfaction with historical accounting comparisons. It is based upon the general idea of normality and of using accounts as indexes of efficiency.

ORIGINS OF STANDARD COSTS. It is probable that the application of cost standards to direct material and to direct labor is derived to some extent from the contracting practice of making estimates and to some extent from the engineering efficiency practice of preparing product specifications and standard instructions with respect to operations.

The use of material standards has long been prevalent in

20 T. H. Sanders, *Cost Accounting for Control* (New York, McGraw-Hill Book Company, Inc., 1934), p. 379.

those industries where a number of products are derived from a common raw material, the calculation of standard yields for such products having directed attention to the value of standards in other accounting applications.

The most plausible explanation, however, for the original development of standard costs was the recognition of their value for management control purposes. Comparisons of actual figures with standard figures are simpler, quicker, and often more reliable than historical comparison, particularly when the effect of changed conditions cannot be measured accurately.

In the realization that product costs figured under any plan could not properly be compared from period to period in such a manner as to furnish quick reliable operating controls, standard cost accounting was adopted to substitute the comparison of actual costs with standard costs for historical comparisons. Standard costs are predetermined on the basis of engineering observations and calculations.

The idea is not new. For many years companies in such lines of business as the manufacture of structural steel boilers and tanks, boats, and similar individualized products have been accustomed to making careful estimates as the basis for submitting bids. Such estimates were based upon standards involving not only the amount but the cost of labor; not only the amount but the cost of material. Other estimates were made with reference to overhead expense.

It was, therefore, natural for the accountant in such industries to compare actual costs with the estimates.

FACTORY STANDARDS. This plan of estimating was extended into factories which were engaging in mass instead of individualized production.

Standards were predetermined for material and labor prices. The material and labor content of each product was studied. Overhead expense was analyzed, classified, and standardized with the result that a complete standard cost, item by item and operation by operation, was established for each product of the plant.

As actual costs were incurred they were not only compared with the standard but were immediately modified to correspond with the standard. Simply, if the standard purchase price of a certain accessory or part was 32 cents and the actual price was 35 cents, the 3 cent difference was immediately disposed of by charging it to a price variance account and was considered a loss of the period in which the purchase was made. Similar variance accounts were established for material usage, the cost of labor, and the quantity of labor predetermined for a particular job. Variance accounts also were established for overhead expense.

In the practical operation of this plan actual costs entering into production were constantly being changed to conform to standards, the differences plus or minus being carried to different variance accounts.

This plan, like the first one, saved a large amount of clerical work. Since all prices for each material were arbitrarily made identical, it was no longer necessary to show both quantities and prices on perpetual inventory cards. Quantity only could at any time be multiplied by standard price in order to determine the corresponding dollar value. A similar simplification was noted throughout the accounting process.

ADVANTAGES AND DISADVANTAGES. It has been claimed that standard costs make possible much closer executive control over factory operations owing to the fact that variance reports reflecting operating efficiencies and inefficiencies can be prepared daily or weekly, there being no necessity to wait until the end of the month for operating information which might be both old and cold at that time.

Assuming that standards are correctly determined, and this assumption is of course most important, then the results claimed for standard costs can hardly be denied. It must, however, be observed that standard costs also have their deceptive aspects. As Canning[21] has so truly remarked: "The term 'standard cost' is a grievous misnomer. Whatever may be the true character of the things called by that name, they are certainly not 'costs.'"

Canning probably referred to the fact that many of the values which otherwise would adhere to materials in progress

[21] John B. Canning, *The Economics of Accountancy* (New York, The Ronald Press Company, 1929), p. 271.

by strict application of the convention of transferred values are, as a matter of fact, treated as immediate losses. Occasionally, of course, variance accounts may show credit balances at the end of the year, in which event such balances represent unearned income.

TREATMENT OF VARIANCES. So firmly are standard costs established in factory accounting that any quarrel with the method would be regarded as evidence of a nineteenth century viewpoint. And yet modern emphasis upon profit and loss statements and their comparability justifies consideration of standard costs in their relation to profit distortion.

Only too often this question is evaded by those who believe that accounting is an instrument for the primary purpose of serving management. To disregard the possibilities of profit distortion because of the value of standard costs to management is to disregard an important concept of modern accounting.

Among the few faults in that otherwise excellent treatise, *A Statement of Accounting Principles* by Sanders, Hatfield, and Moore,[22] is the one reflected by the following quotation: "The division of expenses into those to be included in cost of goods sold and those to be treated as subsequent income deductions may be left to the judgment of the management."

It is possible that profit distortion which may result can be regarded as immaterial and hence of slight accounting significance but if such distortion *is* material it certainly is a matter for technical accounting consideration rather than a management problem only.

VIEWPOINTS OF AUTHORITIES. No one method of treating variances has been adopted. As in the case of over- and underabsorbed burden, a variety of treatments has been suggested.

Reitell and Johnston[23] indicate that: "All manufacturing variance accounts are usually closed to the Profit and Loss account and the balances of these accounts shown as additions to or subtractions from the cost of goods sold (at standard rates)

---

22 Sanders, Hatfield, and Moore, *A Statement of Accounting Principles* (New York, American Institute of Accountants, 1938), p. 31.

23 Reitell and Johnston, *Cost Accounting, Principles and Methods* (Scranton, Pa., International Textbook Company, 1937), p. 294.

on the profit and loss statement." These same authors also mention a method of apportioning total manufacturing variances between the cost of goods sold during the year and the closing inventories. Sanders[24] reports that: "The usual view of auditors on this subject is that they [variances] should be closed into Cost of Goods Sold in order that a proper figure of gross profit or gross margin may be shown on an actual basis." If the variances are included merely as part of cost of goods sold without giving consideration to the inventory, then the inventory and the gross profit are understated. It is difficult to see how this could result in "a proper figure of gross profit or gross margin."

The following illustrative monthly operating statement, adapted from Sanders, has some bearing on the interpretation of his comment:

Net Sales	$56,842
Less: Cost of Goods Sold—	
Materials Used, Actual	20,887
Labor, Direct, Standard	9,583
Burden, Standard	10,739
Total Costs	$41,209
Gross Profits at Standard Costs	$15,633
Less: Variances—	
Labor Excess	524
Burden Excess	1,390
Gross Profit, Actual	$13,719

Sanders comments: "If an operating statement were prepared on the ordinary basis, with no reference whatever to standard costs, the gross profits for the respective periods would be the same as on the last line in the foregoing form."

Possibly this would be true if the inventories at the beginning and end of the period were identical not only as to total amounts but as to constituent elements and if the standard labor and burden rates had been unchanged. It should, however, be noted that the upper half of this statement seems to refer only to finished goods which have been sold, while the labor excess

24 T. H. Sanders, *Cost Accounting for Control* (New York, McGraw-Hill Book Company, Inc., 1934), pp. 372, 373.

of $524 and the burden excess of $1,390 seem to refer to the entire manufacturing operations for the period. A portion of each of these amounts logically applies to inventories of work in progress and of finished goods on hand at the end of the period, thus reducing the amount of excess burden and labor excess properly to be shown on this statement to somewhat smaller amounts.

MATERIALITY. From comments appearing elsewhere in Sanders' volume [25] it seems that the doctrine of materiality is to be considered. Referring to unabsorbed burden he suggests:

> ... this debit amount of burden adjustment should be divided between cost of goods sold and inventory of manufactured goods on hand, in proportion to their respective amounts. But if, as is usually the case, the amount sold greatly exceeds the inventory, it is common to charge the entire amount of the burden adjustment into the cost of goods sold for the period as stated above. On the other hand, where the inventory is large compared with cost of goods sold, it might be considered desirable to add a proportionate part of the unabsorbed burden to the value of the inventory.
> But this would raise another question. Under this method, the less work was turned out, the greater would be the value per unit of the inventory, because the burden would be spread on a smaller quantity of goods.

CAUSES OF ERROR. As a matter of theory it is somewhat difficult to distinguish between the treatment of unabsorbed burden and the debit balances of variance accounts. If the one should be divided between cost of goods sold and inventory, logically the other should be divided similarly.

Practically, the amounts involved in variance balances may be too trivial to justify hair-splitting procedure.

It is noted, however, that the adjustments necessarily following a change in standard rates may involve a fairly substantial amount of clerical work and it is seldom considered desirable to change standards more often than once a year, or perhaps once in six months, unless price variances become significantly large. During periods of rapid price change the temptation to continue established standards may result in substantial vari-

25 *Ibid.*, p. 183.

ance balances. If such balances are judged only by their operating significance and not in relation to comparability of profits, the resulting distortion may be material.

The common belief that debit balances of variance accounts represent inefficiencies to be treated as immediate losses is acceptable to the engineer and to the cost accountant. Because of conservatism, auditors are not likely to insist upon adjustments of inventories to a higher basis. As a result standard cost procedure necessarily implies some distortion, large or small, of comparative profits. Practically, such distortion is often unimportant in any business operating on a fairly even basis with no violent fluctuations in annual sales price levels, inventory quantities, wage rates, or general factory efficiency.

In so far as monthly reports are concerned, variance account balances may remain on the books unclosed and be treated as part of the inventory of work in progress or may be written off monthly. Monthly net profits are seldom regarded seriously even by the accountants reporting them. It is the monthly detailed operating figures included in the profit and loss statement which are indispensable.

Recognition of the possibility of profit distortion inherent in standard costs is the best insurance against deceptive annual reports. The undeniable value of standard cost accounting seems to justify the modification of academic rules, traditional viewpoints, and strict accounting theory. That standard cost accounting has suffered from the unrestrained and extravagant enthusiasm of its proponents cannot be denied. This may, in part, be due to their failure to accept and heed such wise counsel as that offered by Peloubet's[26] assertion:

As soon as any elements other than direct material and direct labor enter into the cost of a product or article, we leave the realm of fact and certainty and enter that of opinion.

[26] Maurice E. Peloubet, *Fiftieth Anniversary Celebration* (New York, American Institute of Accountants, 1938), p. 338.

CHAPTER 24

INVENTORY CREDITS

In cost accounting, particularly, a credit to one inventory account is often accompanied by a corresponding charge to another inventory account, with the result that some of the inventory charges discussed in Chapter 23 are commonly offset by credits to other inventory accounts. In spite of this offsetting, certain inventory credits justify separate treatment here because of their effect upon profit determination.

Types of Inventory Credits.—Inventory credits usually arise from the following causes:

1. Shortages
2. Damaged items
3. Obsolete items
4. Shrinkage
5. Scrap
6. Use or sale

Shortages and damaged or obsolete items are usually recorded on the basis of special requisitions. The offsetting debit in the case of shortage is made to an expense or cost account. The offsetting debits in the case of damaged or obsolete items represent in part transfers of such items to special inventory classifications at a reduced value and in part charges to expense or cost accounts.

To some indeterminate extent the decision as to the residual value of such items may have some slight distorting effect upon profit and loss, but such distortion is generally so unimportant as to justify little consideration.

The accounting treatment of shrinkage and scrap depends upon whether it is inevitable or accidental. If inevitable, the cost thereof may not be removed from the inventory accounts.

If accidental, it is properly to be deducted from inventory values and treated as a loss. Unless the amounts involved are substantial, the accounting treatment is relatively unimportant in so far as comparative profits are concerned.

It should, however, be noted that this comment applies to the effect upon annual profit and loss statements. From an operating viewpoint, the proper statistical reporting of scrap, shrinkage, and waste may be invaluable for control purposes.

More fundamental and more influential is the problem of pricing requisitions in the case of materials withdrawn for use, consumption, or sale.

Methods of Pricing Requisitions.—There are five general methods commonly employed for pricing requisitions. These are:

1. Average cost basis
2. First-in, first-out basis
3. Standard cost basis
4. Actual or identified cost basis
5. Last-in, first-out basis

It is of interest to note the relative popularity of these different methods.

The *N.A.C.A. Bulletin* of March 15, 1937, presented a research report entitled "Practice in Accounting for Raw Materials." The methods of pricing raw material requisitions used by 209 manufacturing companies were tabulated. Nearly half of those reporting, or 45.4%, used the average cost basis; more than a quarter, or 27.3%, used the first-in, first-out basis; while about 20% used a standard cost basis. In other words, 92.8% of all of these companies used one of the first three methods.

A more extensive survey involving 916 companies was reported by the National Industrial Conference Board, Inc., in a publication entitled "Prevailing Practice in Inventory Valuation," dated February 1938. From this investigation it was learned that 39% of the companies used the average cost method, 15% the first-in, first-out method, and 16% a standard cost method, giving these methods a percentage of 70% as compared with 92.8% shown by the *N.A.C.A. Bulletin*.

The most surprising difference between the two reports had to do with the popularity of the identified cost basis which was referred to by the National Industrial Conference Board as "actual cost of specific lots." The *N.A.C.A. Bulletin* showed only 4.3% of the companies using this basis while the National Industrial Conference Board showed 16%.

Both showed that the last-in, first-out method was in use by no more than approximately 3% of all of the reported companies. In comparison with the publicity given this method in recent accounting literature its actual popularity appears to be slight.

Actual Cost Method.—The actual or identified cost method can, for the purpose of this volume, be dismissed rather briefly. Where materials are purchased to be applied to one order and are not merged physically or otherwise with similar materials, or if each purchase of materials is separately stored or piled, then such materials can be accounted for by lots, each lot carrying its own true cost and being represented by its own perpetual inventory card. In relation to profit distortion, the actual cost method appears to be theoretically and practically accurate.

Average Cost Method.—This most popular of all methods for pricing requisitions may be applied in different ways.

The original method, from which some practical variations are noted, is known as the weighted-average cost method. It is applicable when separate purchases of similar materials at different prices are not kept separate. On the corresponding perpetual inventory card it is necessary to recalculate the unit price after each new purchase or acquisition of materials.

If a furniture store buys a dozen chairs for $48 and then later buys two dozen similar chairs at $120, and if the chairs purchased in these two lots are indistinguishable from one another so that it is impossible when selling a chair to tell whether it was acquired as part of the first purchase or the second purchase, it appears logical that the cost per chair should be determined on the basis of an average. This is obtained by dividing the total purchase of $168 by the total number of chairs, or 36 chairs, and results in a cost price per chair of approximately $4.67.

Those who favor this method believe that $4.67 represents a closer approximation to cost than would result if 12 of the chairs were considered as having cost $4 and 24 of them as having cost $5, in view of the obvious fact that the chairs are indistinguishable from one another.

Even less distinguishable would be separate purchases of coal unloaded on one pile or separate purchases of fuel oil stored in the same tank.

It is difficult not to agree with Montgomery's[1] opinion that "Whenever there is a mingling, or a possible mingling, of goods or materials, the cost prices are also mingled. It is quite easy to reason otherwise, but the line of reasoning is fallacious."

Hatfield[2] takes an opposite view when he says:

By taking the average price, the goods on hand are charged with part of the burden of earlier purchases with which they in fact have no connection. It is a current delusion frequently held by dabblers in speculative activities that a later purchase at a lower price brings down the cost of the earlier purchase.

The obvious objection to the average cost method is the amount of clerical work it entails in the calculation of new averages and in the adjustments of decimals. To overcome these objections certain substitute methods are sometimes employed. Thus Sanders reports that tire manufacturers commonly compute an average price for a three-month period. In other instances an arithmetical average of prices disregarding quantities is used.

While one may agree with the *Accountants' Handbook*[3] that: "None of these more or less careless and incomplete average methods are to be recommended," nevertheless they do not appear particularly objectionable in relation to comparable annual net profits. Overs and shorts caused by inaccuracy of estimation can be and usually are reasonably well absorbed over

1 Robert H. Montgomery, *Auditing Theory and Practice* (New York, The Ronald Press Company, 1934), p. 206.

2 Henry Rand Hatfield, *Accounting* (New York, D. Appleton-Century Company, Inc., 1927), pp. 106, 107.

3 *Accountants' Handbook* (New York, The Ronald Press Company, 1934), p. 425.

a year's time, and any resulting profit distortion is likely to be relatively trivial.

First-in, First-out Method.—Ranking second in popularity is the first-in, first-out method which assumes that items requisitioned from the inventory are always the oldest items in the inventory and bear the oldest price.

DESCRIPTION OF METHOD. In the chair illustration just used, the cost of chairs sold would be $4 until the original purchase of one dozen chairs was exhausted, after which the unit cost applicable to subsequent sales would be $5 per chair until the second lot was exhausted.

This method when applied to perpetual inventories necessitates cumulating the quantities sold from each of the lots purchased and may, upon occasion, require splitting one withdrawal into two or more prices. In the case of the chairs, eight of them might be sold to one purchaser at a cost of $4 each and six to another purchaser. Of the six sold, four would carry the $4 price and two, coming from the second lot purchased, would bear the $5 cost price.

This is, of course, an operating inconvenience but it has been noted that generally the method requires less clerical work than the weighted-average cost method and has the additional advantage of reducing the number of fractional unit costs.

PRICING PERIODIC INVENTORIES. This method is commonly employed in pricing periodic inventories where no perpetual inventory records are maintained, since it is not necessary to go over all of the invoices for the past year but only the more recent ones.

The procedure has been described in the *Accountants' Handbook*[4] as follows:

> . . . it is necessary merely to go back over the entries on the stock sheets, cards, or tags, as the case may be, and, beginning with the latest in each case, accumulate quantity and value totals until the quantity total equals the inventory total shown on the appropriate inventory sheet; the corresponding value total gives the desired inventory value.

4 *Accountants' Handbook* (New York, The Ronald Press Company, 1934) pp. 426, 427.

ADVANTAGES OF METHOD. That this method has advantages for periodic inventory purposes cannot be denied.

Similar advantages have been claimed for it under the perpetual inventory plan. The *Accountants' Handbook*[4] has summarized six important advantages of this method as follows:

1. It is based on cost, and hence raises no question of unrealized income or loss.
2. It is drawn from the actual records in a systematic manner, without the use of estimates.
3. It conforms to sound principles of economics and business in that the resulting inventory value is usually a fair representation of current commercial values.
4. It is based upon a clear-cut assumption as to the movement of goods through the concern which it is good business for the management to adhere to as closely as possible.
5. It is approved by the Bureau of Internal Revenue.
6. It is a very convenient method to use in pricing out of stock under any continuous inventory system.

The fact that the method is approved by the Bureau of Internal Revenue[5] which has frowned upon the weighted-average cost method is, of course, the strongest of all practical arguments, although it is one with which this volume is not particularly concerned.

PROFIT DISTORTION. If the weighted-average method is accepted as the standard, and there seems to be some basis for so accepting it, then the first-in, first-out method may result in measurable profit distortion.

In the case of the furniture store previously mentioned the difference in final inventory price between $4.67 per chair and $5 per chair, if multiplied by a much larger number of chairs, might easily have an important effect upon the annual profit. From the $4.67 weighted-average cost viewpoint the use of a $5 unit valuation of chairs amounts to a 7% inventory inflation

[5] Reference is made to Article 22(a)-8 of Regulations 94 which provides that when shares of stock are sold from lots purchased at different dates or at different prices and the identity of the lots cannot be determined, the stock sold shall be charged against the earliest purchases of such stock in spite of the complexities that result when securities have been acquired in many different transactions followed by split-ups, stock dividends, and reorganizations prior to any sale.

with an inflation of profits corresponding to the dollar difference between the inventory as figured by the two different unit costs.

Last-in, First-out Method.—While relatively not so popular, as indicated by the two studies previously mentioned, the last-in, first-out method has been greatly publicized by those who have observed the income tax inequity of other methods when used by such industries as petroleum, tanning, and mining.

PURPOSE OF METHOD. It is difficult to escape the conclusion that this and its companion, the base-stock method to be described in Chapter 25, are intended deliberately to stabilize, or in other words distort, profits, although their proponents usually describe the objective otherwise. It cannot be doubted, however, that the purpose of these methods is to stabilize profits for industries wherein profits are inherently unstable.

Those in favor of either of these plans probably consider that they result in less distorted profits than do the traditional methods.

In fact, this was asserted by Staub,[6] who suggested that the last-in, first-out method is "closer to reality" than some other methods.

This confirms Broad's[7] opinion that: "Results in certain lines of industry seemed to have demonstrated rather conclusively that this method more fairly reflected the results of their operations."

Clearly, however, this depends upon viewpoint. Distortion as used here refers to distortion from a traditional base founded upon original accounting conventions. From this viewpoint, therefore, it seems entirely proper to refer to the distorting effect of these two methods, since it is more or less openly admitted that it is their purpose to stabilize profits often in order to remedy income tax inequities.

6 Walter A. Staub, comments at the American Institute of Accountants convention, September 29, 1938.

7 Samuel J. Broad, "Cooperation with the Securities and Exchange Commission," *The Journal of Accountancy,* August 1938, p. 88.

DESCRIPTION OF METHOD. The last-in, first-out method properly belongs in this chapter, since it has direct relation to the pricing of inventory withdrawals in contrast to the base-stock method which has to do with the undervaluation of a so-called normal or constant stock.

On November 12, 1934, the Board of Directors of the American Petroleum Institute at Dallas, Texas, approved recommendations of their committee on uniform methods of oil accounting. The report is too lengthy for complete quotation but the name, last-in, first-out method, reasonably well describes the procedure. It is practically the reverse of the first-in, first-out method. The general characteristics of the method are well described in the following :[8]

Cost or Market: In starting the "last in, first out" inventory plan, the prices should be set at a conservative or reasonable figure. In the future, inventory prices should not be reduced to market prices, when lower than the regular inventory value. Where the market value of the inventory is less than that carried in the balance-sheet, such condition should be shown in parentheses or as a footnote in such manner that the approximate difference can be ascertained, either in dollars or percentage.

In an article appearing in the *N.A.C.A. Bulletin* of December 1, 1937, Davis[9] commented upon the procedure of this method in the following words :

In closing your books at any time you simply back up on your purchases, starting with the most recent, and when a quantity equivalent to sales has been reached, that is your cost of sales. However, it is not nearly so simple as that if the true result is to be obtained. You either have to take your opening inventory and use it forever after as a reservoir from which, at the unit values existing when you started, you borrow and to which you pay back differences in quantity between current sales and purchases; or you have to figure the first period, and then the first and second together as a single period, and then the first, second and third together, and so on interminably with the differences between these successive totals giving the results for individual periods.

---

8 Special Committee on Inventories of the American Institute of Accountants, "Valuation of Inventories," *The Journal of Accountancy,* August 1936, p. 124.
9 Albion R. Davis, "Inventory Valuation and Business Profits—The Case for a 'Stabilized Basis,'" *N.A.C.A. Bulletin,* December 1, 1937, p. 390.

COMMENTS OF AUTHORITIES. During periods of declining prices the continuance of the last-in, first-out method may, as John L. Harvey has suggested, result in inventory losses on the earlier purchases. This can be overcome by arbitrary valuation of the earlier purchases at a low safe figure but, as the Treasury Department once pointed out, this "results in offsetting an inventory gain of one year against an inventory loss of another."

Condemnation of this and related methods which promote profit distortion has carried but slight conviction even to those otherwise adhering to the profit and loss viewpoint, since the method was given approval by the important committee on Federal taxation of the American Institute of Accountants in May 1938 as follows:[10]

The "normal stock" and "last-in, first-out" or "replacement" methods clearly fall within "approved standard methods of accounting" and are "best suited to the needs of certain businesses." They should, accordingly, be granted recognition.

The same committee[11] in November 1938 insists that "the last-in, first-out method which confines income to the actual operations of a period and which eliminates arbitrary profits and losses, will produce a steadier stream of income and, therefore, a steadier flow of taxes than the first-in, first-out method which exaggerates both earnings and losses." The committee also made the definite statement that: "The weight of accounting authority sanctions the use of the last-in, first-out method in the industries to which it is appropriate."

The Sanders, Hatfield, and Moore monograph,[12] also an American Institute publication, put the stamp of its approval upon the last-in, first-out method referring to the "wide fluctuations of material prices resulting in losses of one period, followed by profits of another period, in which the latter were taxable without proper offset." This group decided that "such

10 Committee on Federal Taxation of the American Institute of Accountants, "Recommendations for Amendment of Federal Revenue Act," *The Journal of Accountancy*, May 1938, p. 392.

11 Committee on Federal Taxation of the American Institute of Accountants, "The Last-in, First-out Inventory Method," *The Journal of Accountancy*, November 1938, p. 313.

12 Sanders, Hatfield, and Moore, *A Statement of Accounting Principles* (New York, American Institute of Accountants, 1938), p. 74.

valuation methods as base-stock or last-in, first-out are intrinsically proper, as well as being proper from a business point of view."

CONFLICTS. It is, of course, difficult to reconcile the Sanders, Hatfield, and Moore approval and that of the committee on Federal taxation with the strong endorsement of the profit and loss viewpoint contained in *Examination of Financial Statements by Independent Public Accountants,* in which the undesirability of profit distortion is emphasized by such admonitions and statements as : "The first objective has been to secure a proper charge or credit to the income account for the year" or "Fair conclusions as to earning power cannot be drawn without comparison of the profits over a period of years."[13]

While the bulletin above mentioned asserts also that it may not be a matter of great importance whether the first-in, first-out rule or the last-in, first-out rule is adopted so long as it is adopted consistently, nevertheless none of those who excuse or justify this method has successfully overcome the former Treasury Department objection.

Apparently, therefore, approval of the last-in, first-out method appears to recognize that tax considerations outweigh the importance of undistorted comparative profits. To those who believe that accounting is no more than a servant to business, this position may be tenable, but the method requires either undervaluation of a substantial portion of the inventory or, during a period of declining prices, the recognition of inventory losses on earlier purchases. In either case comparative profits will be affected.

PRACTICAL JUSTIFICATION FOR METHOD. These comments are, of course, not intended as arguments against the use of the method. Its belated recognition by the Treasury Department[14] and the obvious tax inequities it may cure are decidedly convincing from the practical standpoint.

The present question refers to profit distortion, its existence

---

[13] *Examination of Financial Statements by Independent Public Accountants* (New York, American Institute of Accountants, January 1936), p. 4.

[14] See T.D. 4865, dated September 29, 1938, relative to election by tanners and producers and processors of certain non-ferrous metals in taking inventories of raw materials.

or non-existence, but it is recognized that distortion of profits may represent the lesser of two evils. To one who seeks to avoid paying confiscatory taxes the alternative of moderate profit distortion, particularly if adequately disclosed, may seem a small price to pay for a substantial benefit. Unfortunately, this weighing of practical advantages and disadvantages has not always been done openly and frankly nor have the inconsistencies always been appraised and disclosed realistically.

Since this method has not been widely adopted and since its general effect upon profit and loss closely resembles the base-stock method, further comments regarding it are deferred until Chapter 25.

Replacement Cost Method.—The replacement cost method must be distinguished from other methods in that it ignores actual purchase cost. This method may adopt an inventory price based upon market quotations of December 31, even though no goods have actually been added to inventory since July 1, at which time costs may have been much higher or lower.

Any replacement cost method utterly abandons the cost of acquisition concept. It does not necessarily represent what recent purchases have cost but may, on the other hand, represent what recent purchases *would* have cost had such purchases been made.

Objections to Method. While the *Accountants' Handbook*[15] does not take a positive stand against this method, it notes that:

. . . the use of this basis tends to result in the inclusion in the statements of profits not realized by sale, in the case of advancing prices, and losses not so realized in the case of falling prices. In the typical situation the trader has little if anything to gain in the direction of sound accounting by shifting to this basis.

Because it is not approved by the Bureau of Internal Revenue, because it may result in unrealized income, because it is not considered conservative, and because it abandons the time-honored concept of actual cost as evidenced by bona fide arm's-

15 *Accountants' Handbook* (New York, The Ronald Press Company, 1934), p. 418.

length transactions, it is not a method which is likely to prove popular. When applied merely to the valuation of a year-end inventory, it represents a type of adjustment more appropriately dealt with in Chapter 25 than here, but because it has somewhat influenced the pricing of inventory withdrawals it is included as a minor feature of this chapter.

FLUCTUATION ACCOUNTS. Nickerson[16] has illustrated the use of a "Finished Goods Price Fluctuation Account" to which the actual cost of goods sold is transferred from finished goods account.

At the same time a credit is made to the finished goods price fluctuation account, "at same price for labor and overhead as charged to this account but use *replacement cost* for material." The offsetting debit on the same basis obviously is made to cost of goods sold. It is suggested that the balance of this account be closed out to profit and loss.

Referring to this method, Nickerson[16] said that: "Gross Profit can then be computed with Cost of Goods Sold at replacement cost."

This same article made reference to a more complete recording of the differences between actual and replacement costs. By this plan price fluctuation accounts are inserted between raw material and work in process, between work in process and finished goods, and between finished goods and cost of goods sold.

These price fluctuation accounts are entitled "Raw Material Price Fluctuations," "Work in Process—Price Fluctuations," and "Finished Goods—Price Fluctuations Account."

The debit to the first account is made at average cost and the credit to that account is made at replacement cost, thus altering the valuation basis for work in process. The debit to Work in Process Price Fluctuations Account is made at the same price at which the corresponding credit was made to work in process, but the credit to this account is made at the replacement cost of material, labor, and overhead at the time the work

---

[16] Clarence B. Nickerson, "Inventory Valuation—The Use of Price Adjustment Accounts to Segregate Inventory Losses and Gains," *N.A.C.A. Bulletin*, October 1, 1937, p. 157.

is completed, and it is this same value that is debited to finished goods. When the merchandise is sold, Finished Goods Account is credited at this same modified price and the offsetting debit goes to Finished Goods Price Fluctuations Account, which again is credited with the replacement cost of material, labor, and overhead at the time of the sale, the offsetting debit being made to Cost of Goods Sold Account.

This is a scheme even more elaborate than the one first mentioned, since it introduces fresh replacement costs at different stages in the accounting process. Such plans seem to be backed by no substantial number of accountants and cannot be accepted as a serious threat to the integrity of traditional profit determination. Whether such methods have special value to business management cannot be judged or verified. Superficially, it appears that the introduction of such accounts into the accounting mechanism accomplishes results which could be more easily obtained by other methods of business calculation not requiring formal double entry control.

To say that replacement costs should not be taken into executive consideration would be foolish. To complicate the accounting structure, however, by the introduction of replacement cost valuations tends to make accounting reports so much a mixture of recorded fact and estimate as to handicap their interpretation.

CHAPTER 25

INVENTORY REVALUATION METHODS

The valuation of the inventory as it appears on a balance sheet results in part from routine bookkeeping methods used in charging and crediting inventory accounts. In part it may be due to special adjustments made for the express purpose of changing the value normally resulting from the bookkeeping routine.

Principal Revaluation Methods.—First and foremost in importance among such methods is the one commonly referred to as "the cost or market rule."

This rule has been so completely accepted in modern accounting practice that the great majority of all published balance sheets display inventories which have been so revalued. Out of 197 companies reported in the *N. A. C. A. Bulletin* of March 15, 1937, 172, or over 87%, valued raw material inventories at cost or market.

In the National Industrial Conference Board report, entitled "Prevailing Practice in Inventory Valuation," separate tables exhibited the popularity of this method in relation to raw materials, goods in process, and finished goods. Out of 833 companies, 525, or 63%, valued raw materials on this basis for balance sheet purposes. Out of 818 companies, 309, or 38%, valued goods in process at the lower of cost or market, while 335 out of 842, or 40%, valued finished goods at the lower of cost or market.

In addition certain other methods have been used which in one way or another require a deliberate adjustment for valuation purposes. These methods are the retail method, the net selling or market price method, and the base-stock method.

It should be observed that a mixture of methods is often employed. During a fiscal year requisitions may be priced on the first-in, first-out method, for example, thus resulting in a balance on hand at the end of the period which presumably represents cost. This figure, however, may not be the one actually appearing in the final balance sheet, since it may be subject to further modification by application of the cost or market rule.

Because final valuation of inventories may be the composite result of routine bookkeeping and of deliberate change in the trial balance figure at the end of the period, discussion might be clearer if a distinction was made between valuation and revaluation, the latter being somewhat akin to appraisal.

Factors Encouraging Revaluation.—Long recognized as a most important accounting problem, the determination of inventory values has been the subject of increased discussion based, it appears, upon three factors:

1. Possibility of inflation
2. Tax considerations
3. Shift from the balance sheet to the profit and loss viewpoint

INFLATION. Because of governmental policies a number of well-informed and intelligent people have begun to fear uncontrolled monetary inflation. Having in mind the experience of certain countries with printing press money, they have given serious consideration to the possible effects of inflation in the United States.

In Germany, particularly, it was noted that merchants engaged in many trading transactions each of which showed an accounting profit in spite of which they faced ruin because their costs of inventory replacement were not or could not be given full consideration in setting selling prices.

Knowledge of this experience has resulted in the development of a school of thought which attaches much importance to replacement cost rather than to actual cost of merchandise sold. It has been intimated that traditional accounting not only fails to help a business man during a period of uncontrolled inflation but actually deceives him. At various times it has been suggested that inventories should be valued at replacement cost regardless of original cost, in order that business men might not be misled by their own accounting systems into underpricing merchandise.

Reference has already been made to the confusion sometimes resulting from overemphasis of the replacement aspect of inventories in a rising market. Strictly there is no more reason why the process of withdrawing items from inventories should provide for replacement than there is why depreciation should provide for the replacement of the depreciating asset. Both refer to asset classifications which may be considered as deferred charges. Replacement cost, for both, is a matter for financial calculation, and a most important matter.

To sell for $10 an article of merchandise costing $8, and then to be required to replace the item with similar merchandise costing $12, cannot help but result in serious drain upon cash. The replacement of the merchandise at a higher price, however, has nothing whatever to do with the sales transaction immediately preceding it. Rather it is a preliminary step taken in anticipation of a subsequent sales transaction.

The replacement of merchandise sold is in the nature of a new venture. It is entered into only in the expectation that the higher cost of acquisition will be compensated by a higher subsequent income. Each purchase of merchandise, therefore, represents no more than an expenditure in the nature of a deferred charge to income and can have no relationship whatever to the extinguishment of prior deferred charges. This reasoning is often ignored, deliberately or unintentionally, with the result that the similarity between the merchandise parted with and the new merchandise purchased assumes such great importance that modifications of the accounting mechanism have been suggested and have been supported by such arguments as "you cannot make money by having an inventory this year at higher prices than you had last year."

There may be some legitimate doubt as to what is meant by the phrase "make money," but surely an entity can earn accounting profits year after year even though inventory values are on an ascending scale. Of course, earning profits and retaining the cash are two different things and it may be admitted that the cash account may suffer and the purchasing power of the proprietor's income may diminish. Nevertheless, profit is not money nor is money profit, and it is truly disconcerting that any accountant should fall into the same error of confusing proprietorship credits and asset debits which is so strongly condemned when made by lawyers in relation to surplus and funds.

TAXATION. The fact that taxing authorities necessarily consider each taxable year separately and not in relation to preceding or subsequent taxable years, and necessarily demand a share of the profits made in good years without contributing to the losses of poor years, has had a most unfortunate effect upon certain types of industries which are inherently unstable and alternately show substantial profits and substantial losses.

In many such industries large inventories have augmented the difficulty. Accounting writers have noted that this "has had the effect of turning a tax on income into a levy on capital," that "this situation is intolerable," and that the tax collector's demands can only be satisfied "by the liquidation of the business."

SHIFT IN VIEWPOINT. The third reason for increased scrutiny of inventory methods is to be found in the shift from the balance sheet to the profit and loss viewpoint.

Whether it be admitted or not, the balance sheet viewpoint toward current assets was based directly or indirectly upon their realizability. This is the money lender's or creditor's viewpoint.

The profit and loss viewpoint is not concerned with realizable values but rather with the proper allocation of costs to accounting periods. In so far as it relates to inventories, the profit and loss viewpoint necessarily regards them as deferred charges to future income to be allocated to those periods in which that income is recorded. The profit and loss viewpoint, therefore, can find no satisfying valuation save valuation at cost. This is based on the general theory that there is no more reason for undervaluing or overvaluing a deferred charge to future income than there is for undervaluing or overvaluing a current charge to current income.

As a result of these three important influences—inflation,

tax inequities, and the shift from the balance sheet to the profit and loss viewpoint—various and opposing methods of inventory revaluation have been suggested.

Some of them admittedly result in overvaluation. Others admittedly result in undervaluation. The extent of such over- or undervaluation is not always known or measurable but it is believed by many accountants that any possible ill effects which might result from the use of such methods can be cured by the observance of the two accounting doctrines of consistency and disclosure.

To a considerable extent this is true with but one exception, that exception referring to the rule of cost or market. Because of the general acceptance of this rule and because of the unique nature of its distorting effect upon profit and loss, its consideration will be deferred for more complete discussion in Chapter 26.

Three Inventory Methods.—Much less important either because more limited in their use or because they cause less profit distortion are the three methods commonly referred to as the retail method, the net selling or market price method, and the base-stock method.

Since it is necessary to establish a point of departure in viewing these methods, it may be assumed that the least profit distortion will result from the valuation of inventories at cost where cost is determinable. To echo Paton,[1] other methods shift "the emphasis from the records of actual cost—the recognized foundation of all accounts—to the field of estimate and conjecture."

Retail Method of Inventory.—The use of the retail method, as the name implies, is confined almost entirely to department stores and other retail establishments. It is widely used and has been approved by the Bureau of Internal Revenue.

Speaking in the most general terms, it may be repeated that this method occupies the middle position between the control offered by the perpetual inventory plan and the lack of control inherent in the periodic inventory plan. The method does not attempt to provide control over items of merchandise, nor does

[1] W. A. Paton, "Comments on 'A Statement of Accounting Principles,'" *The Journal of Accountancy*, March 1938, p. 204.

it require a great amount of clerical work in posting entries for the details of merchandise transactions. It resembles the perpetual inventory plan in that it provides an approximate controlling figure over the amount of inventory which *should* be on hand at the end of an accounting period. It also requires an actual inventory taking in order to determine the extent of discrepancy between that actual inventory and the controlling figure which purports to show what the inventory should be.

The *Accountants' Handbook*[2] considers it "essential that merchandise cost, selling values, and actual sales be fully classified and that the inventory be calculated in terms of the distinct groups."

The method has a certain superficial resemblance to the basic standard cost method which deliberately employs non-cost figures for the purpose of simplifying record keeping. These figures are later reconverted to a cost basis for statement purposes by the application of proper percentages. Similarly, the retail method starts on the basis of actual costs and ends on the basis of actual costs or a fairly close approximation thereto. All of the intermediate accounting, however, is done on the selling price basis.

Description of the method is included here only because it does require a deliberate revaluation in the form of an adjustment at the end of each accounting period. Any profit distortion resulting from this method is likely to be slight. It may be said that the retail price basis provides results which are reasonably comparable to perpetual inventory accounting on a cost basis. The subject, therefore, is not one requiring additional consideration.

Net Selling Price Methods.—Under some circumstances it is impossible to obtain actual inventory costs. This is particularly true in the accounting for by-products.

In other instances the inventory is so readily salable that, it is often contended, legal technicality of title transfer becomes practically meaningless. Such arguments are advanced in the case of natural products, or in the case of securities enjoying an

[2] *Accountants' Handbook* (New York, The Ronald Press Company, 1934), p. 438.

active trading market on some recognized exchange. In these instances it has been urged that market prices are much more significant than cost for inventory valuation.

DEDUCTION OF ESTIMATED COSTS. There is no one method uniformly suggested for valuation at market.

Commonly it is suggested that readily salable materials should be valued at selling price less the estimated costs and expenses normally to be incurred before that price can be realized. In other instances it has been suggested that the further deduction of the normal rate of profit results in a figure closer to but obviously not identical with actual cost.

The doctrine of materiality also may be given consideration. If, as may be true in the case of certain minor by-products or scrap, the amounts involved are comparatively trivial, unadjusted market quotations may be applied for purposes of inventory valuation.

FARM PRODUCTS. Consider the problem involved in valuing farm inventories.

In farming it is clearly impossible to determine actual costs because of the phenomena sometimes referred to as cost reabsorption and accretion. The impossibility of determining true costs coupled with the ready market for farm products seems to justify the market price method of inventory valuation. This method, which has been approved by the Treasury Department, permits the farmer to value at current selling price less estimated marketing cost his agricultural products unsold at the end of an accounting period.

Paton[3] comments upon the resulting profit distortion in the following words: "If a farmer adopts this rule it means, essentially, that he 'takes his profit' in the year in which his wheat, for example, is raised, rather than the year in which it happens to be marketed, provided the two are different."

MINERALS, TIMBER, AND SECURITIES. In the case of natural products of mines and forests, a somewhat similar method is often used. Reference has already been made to the proposal

3 W. A. Paton, *Accounting Theory* (New York, The Ronald Press Company, 1922), p. 436.

of William B. Gower that special inventory valuation procedure should be applied to "the natural products of the soil or natural resources extracted from mines, oil wells, timber lands, etc., produced in marketable form by owners engaged in operating on their own premises."

In this connection Gower[4] asserts that:

> . . . the marketing of the product is usually a secondary and incidental matter, and the primary consideration is volume of production. The predominant feature and main effort of their business is production; they think, act and operate in terms of units and measures produced; when production ceases their business is in liquidation; and they measure their costs, their profits and their losses in terms of production.

He suggests that the inventory of unsold product be calculated as "a reasonable estimate of its fair value, based upon good judgment of market conditions and with due allowance to cover the unpaid charges and the risks intervening before it will be marketed."

The editor of *The Journal of Accountancy* commented on this suggestion, saying: "The views expressed by Mr. Gower in this article do not conform to those of most accountants and we do not endorse the arguments which he presents."

In so far as the general valuation of securities is concerned, the Bureau of Internal Revenue recognizes valuation at cost. In the case of recognized dealers in securities, the Bureau will recognize any one of three consistent uniform bases of pricing:

1. Cost
2. Cost or market
3. Market value

SPECIFIC CONTRACTS. When the selling prices have been determined by specific contracts, Hatfield[5] believes that work in process may be inventoried at selling price

> . . . making due allowance for the unfinished work still to be done, the risks intervening, and the interest charges involved. Where the contract period extends beyond the current fiscal period such inventorying

---

4 William B. Gower, "Unsold Goods and the Income Account," *The Journal of Accountancy*, March 1920, pp. 171-179.
5 Henry Rand Hatfield, *Accounting* (New York, D. Appleton-Century Company, Inc., 1927), p. 109.

is not only permissible but is the only correct method. Otherwise the profits on the contract work would all appear in the year when goods are delivered, although the labor involved belonged almost entirely to a preceding year.

It is somewhat difficult to follow this reasoning. Is it not true that, specific contract or no specific contract, it often happens that labor expenditures of one year properly are carried over to apply against the income of a subsequent year? The logic here does not seem sufficiently convincing to justify abandonment of title transfer as the test of income realization.

In connection with this and similar arguments which attach importance to specific contracts, one is tempted to inquire as to the certainty of contract fulfillment. Can specific performance be enforced if cancellation is attempted because of declining prices, and if it can be enforced then what will be the legal cost of enforcing it? Will business men run the risk of alienating good customers by insisting upon such fulfillment? These and other similar questions cast some doubt upon the wisdom of relying upon even the firmest contracts.

PROFIT ANTICIPATION.   Harvey[6] mentions the anticipation of profit which results from valuing inventories at market price but believes that "if full disclosure is made and provided the practice is uniform from year to year, no great objection could be raised to this method."

There are various suggestions for valuing inventories on a market price basis and at the same time avoiding the anticipation of profits. Canning[7] proposes using a fixed constant to be multiplied into each unit selling price. He suggests determining that constant by calculating a ratio of loss on bad debts, collection expense, and selling and general expenses, plus profit to sales. He comments that: "The constant which is to be multiplied into each selling price then becomes one minus the sum of the rate allowances for subsequent expenses and for a normal profit on the inventory."

6 John L. Harvey, "Some Observations on Accounting Practice with Special Reference to Inventory Valuation," *The Journal of Accountancy*, December 1937, p. 448.
7 John B. Canning, *The Economics of Accountancy* (New York, The Ronald Press Company, 1929), pp. 221, 222.

Hatfield[8] recommends the use of special valuation accounts and suggests such titles as "Allowance for Decline in Inventory Value" or "Reserve Due to Marking Up Inventory," from which accounts transfers are to be made either to profit and loss account or to surplus when the goods are sold.

Accountants in general, and auditors in particular, commonly oppose any method of inventory valuation which results in anticipation of profit on the theory that such valuation sets a dangerous precedent. Possibly their objection has had more particular reference to inventory valuation from the balance sheet viewpoint than to profit and loss distortion. Regardless of their reasons, accountants believe that the burden of proof rests upon him who suggests including any element of profit in inventories. This opinion does not, however, conform to an observation by Canning[7] that:

It is no longer matter for surprise to find an unqualified certificate attached to a balance sheet in which the inventory has been valued at selling price less estimated expenses allocable to the volume of sales represented by the inventory.

INCOME DISTORTION.   It must be conceded that full disclosure of the method of valuation would go far toward curing the faults of such a method in so far as the balance sheet is concerned.

Regardless of disclosure or lack of disclosure of the basis of valuation, distortion of comparative profits cannot be cured so easily. It is from this viewpoint rather than that of a conservative current ratio that the procedure must be judged.

When no other basis of valuation can possibly be used, as in the case of farming, then the consequent profit distortion is a necessary evil which cannot be avoided. In other instances the adoption of valuation at market price, if so computed as to anticipate any material amount of profit, violates the fundamental rule of income determination. Referring to the fictitious profit involved in marking up inventories, Mimeograph 4703, issued by the Commissioner of Internal Revenue on December 4, 1937, says: "This increase is not the result of a sale, since the goods

8 Henry Rand Hatfield, *Accounting* (New York, D. Appleton-Century Company, Inc., 1927), p. 103.

are still on hand, and therefore, is clearly not income realized from operations or gain within the meaning of the Revenue Acts."

This quotation clearly sets forth the traditional accounting viewpoint toward income realization. It is, however, only fair to point out that contrary opinions have long been voiced by men of standing and authority.

OPINIONS OF AUTHORITIES. Kester[9] argues the matter from the balance sheet viewpoint, suggesting that that statement may present "an entirely inadequate and even misleading story as the basis for credit" when cost values are used, although such valuation does place "the profit or loss in the period when realized."

Canning[10] believes that the selling price method properly adjusted gives "more reliable valuations than are found by other methods."

Some authorities believe that the adoption of the market price basis results in less rather than more distortion of profit and loss. Sweeney,[11] for example, noting that merchandise may grow in value during a period, thinks that "that period should receive credit for such enhancement in economic power as income, even though sale at the enhanced value is deferred until the next period." He adds that "the income is earned but not realized in the earlier period, and realized but not earned in the later one." A somewhat similar observation was made by Hatfield[12] when he said: "An argument in favor of inventorying merchandise at its market value is that only by so doing can the operations of each year be properly judged."

These observations are interesting in that they suggest that distortion or lack of distortion is a matter of viewpoint depending upon what concept is adopted as a basing point. Just as the Californian thinks of Chicago as an eastern city while a New

9 Roy B. Kester, *Advanced Accounting* (New York, The Ronald Press Company, 1933), p. 152.
10 John B. Canning, *The Economics of Accountancy* (New York, The Ronald Press Company, 1929), p. 218.
11 Henry W. Sweeney, *Stabilized Accounting* (New York, Harper & Brothers, 1936), p. 21.
12 Henry Rand Hatfield, *Accounting* (New York, D. Appleton-Century Company, Inc., 1927), p. 102.

Yorker calls it western, so does this question of profit distortion depend upon one's fundamental philosophy of profits.

GOLD INVENTORIES. The proponents of market price valuation sometimes refer to the inventory problems of gold mining companies. If one imagines a mining company producing only gold and carrying it in its final refined form in inventory, then a strong, if somewhat imaginary, case apparently justifying market price valuation results. Surely, it is argued, an inventory of gold can be considered the equivalent of cash.

This argument has been used so often in support of market valuation of inventory that it deserves some consideration. The *Accountants' Handbook*[13] suggests that such an inventory "is clearly worth from every standpoint its net selling price, especially as this price is unchanging." This statement as to worth could, of course, be even stronger in view of the U. S. Government's obligation to buy gold in any offered amount.

If it be admitted that an inventory of pure gold should be valued at market price, then, from the accounting viewpoint only, by analogy inventories of other metals could be valued similarly. If all metals can be valued at market price, then by analogy other products resulting from the exploitation of natural resources could be valued similarly. It therefore appears that the case for and against market price valuation of a gold inventory justifies some discussion.

First of all, it seems necessary to note that the accounting for the production of metals usually involves problems of joint costs. Hoover[14] asserted that:

Where one metal predominates over the other to such an extent as to form the "back bone" of the value of the mine, the value of the metals is often deducted from the cost of the principal metal, in order to indicate more plainly the varying value of the mine with the fluctuating prices of the predominant metal.

This refers, of course, to joint costs. In some applications of joint costs, particularly in that phase commonly referred to as

[13] *Accountants' Handbook* (New York, The Ronald Press Company, 1934), p. 449.
[14] Herbert C. Hoover, *Principles of Mining* (New York, McGraw-Hill Book Company, Inc., 1909), p. 41.

by-product cost, market price valuation is common. It should, however, be observed that the usual argument for valuation of gold inventory on a market price basis is not derived from the common practice of by-product accounting but rather relates directly to the fact that gold is the fundamental basis of money. It is, therefore, necessary to consider the matter entirely apart from the practical problem of joint or by-product costs.

VALUATION SYMBOL. If the inventory valuation of gold is considered only from the balance sheet viewpoint, if the concept of realizable value is applied as a test, then the market valuation of a gold inventory may be justified. The argument against such market valuation must, therefore, be based upon the concept of valuation as a symbol.

In accounting by the entity convention, valuation symbols are applied to various assets for convenience in recording and without regard to the salability of the assets so symbolized. The use of valuation symbols is necessary to establish the charge and discharge relationship implied by the entity convention.

This relationship applies in exactly the same way to assets which are readily marketable as to those others which are not marketable at all. A valuation of $1,000 is properly just as applicable to a stretch of railroad track in a plant yard as it is to a pile of coal, utterly regardless of the fact that the coal could be sold immediately and with but little loss whereas the trackage might not be convertible into immediate cash save on a scrap metal basis.

REALIZABILITY. If it be conceded that accounting valuation is a symbol not related to ready realizability, than the mere fact that gold is readily realizable seems to have no bearing upon the method of its valuation.

To base methods of accounting valuation upon realizability opens the door to a host of problems. Realizability is a relative matter and the scale of realizability runs from zero in the case of certain prepaid expenses to 100% in the case of gold inventories. In between these two extremes are to be found the thousands of different kinds of assets owned by any large industrial corporation.

Any attempt to establish the doctrine that an accounting method may depend upon realizability opens the way to an argument as to the proper kind of method to be applied to any one of these thousands of different assets.

If, on the other hand, valuation is considered only as a symbol for the convenient recording of entity charge and discharge, then the realizability of an asset so symbolized is a matter of no importance, the entity being just as truly charged and accountable for a non-realizable right-of-way as for a gold bar. On this theory and by this test an inventory of gold dust should be valued on the same cost basis as any inventory of other finished product whether it be shoes, washing machines, automobiles, or fence posts. Since, from the entity viewpoint, there is no advantage to be gained by valuation at other than cost when cost is readily determinable, the cost basis for the gold inventory seems to be indicated.

PROPONENTS OF COST VALUATION. A few voices have been heard in defense of the cost basis. T. O. McGrath, in *The Mining Congress Journal* of August 1926, specified valuation at cost be used in connection with his chart of accounts for metal mines.

In answer to an inquiry regarding mine accounting, which appeared on pages 153-155 in *The Journal of Accountancy* of February 1936, two unnamed accountants replied in favor of the cost basis of valuation for metal inventories, one of them suggesting that while "the concentrates could be readily sold, the same would be true of many items in the finished-goods inventories of most companies, and it does not seem advisable in the circumstances mentioned to divert from the usual practice of carrying inventories at cost if cost is below market and stating income accordingly."

The *Accountants' Handbook*,[15] referring specifically to gold inventories, asserts that: "In practice valuations on a cost basis are in general favor, and the Bureau of Internal Revenue has not recognized the propriety of the consistent use of net realizable value."

15 *Accountants' Handbook* (New York, The Ronald Press Company, 1934), p. 449.

PRACTICE IN MARKET VALUATION. Investigation does not substantiate the claim that cost valuations are in general favor.

From an examination of reports submitted on Form 10K to the Securities and Exchange Commission by gold mining companies, from mining companies' annual reports, and from various engineering reports and prospectuses, it has been possible to check the inventory valuation practices of 23 corporations most of which produced gold as a principal product. These 23 companies divided themselves into groups in accordance with the following four inventory methods:

1. Cost method
2. Cost or market method
3. Cost for ore and estimated sales price for bullion
4. Market value or estimated sales price

The Walker Mining Company's balance sheet of December 31, 1937 used the cost basis for valuing ores and concentrates on hand (although it valued copper on hand at market price). The consolidated balance sheets as of December 31, 1935, 1936, and 1937 of South American Gold and Platinum Company showed that the cost method of valuing was employed.

Among those valuing metal inventories at the lower of cost or market was the Hecla Mining Company, although the same report also showed ore in transit at net realizable value. The December 31, 1937 balance sheet of Consolidated Mining and Smelting Company of Canada, Ltd., showed unsold products valued at cost or market, while products which were under sales contracts were valued at selling price less estimated expenses. On four balance sheets of St. Anthony Gold Mines, Ltd., dated December 31, 1930 to and including December 31, 1933, concentrates were shown at the lower of cost or market. The American Zinc, Lead and Smelting Company followed the same practice in its annual reports for the years 1936 and 1937.

Two corporations valued bullion at estimated sales price, at the same time valuing ore at cost. These companies were New York and Honduras Rosario Mining Company and Federal Mining and Smelting Company, the balance sheets in each case being dated December 31, 1937.

Of the 23 companies, fifteen, or more than half, showed inventories at market value or estimated sales price. Four of these companies were: Wright-Hargreaves Mines, Ltd., 1936; Kirkland Lake Gold Mining Company, Ltd., 1937; Teck-Hughes Gold Mines, and United Verde Extension Mining Company, 1936. In these four instances it is obvious that the market valuation was used but this fact was not specifically disclosed as part of the caption.

Nine other companies did disclose the market value basis parenthetically or by footnote. In this group were: Lucky Tiger-Combination Gold Mining Company, 1937; Pioneer Gold Mines of British Columbia, Ltd., 1938; Nipissing Mines Company, Ltd., 1937; Hollinger Consolidated Gold Mines, Ltd., 1936; Home Stake Mining Company, 1935-1936; Alaska Juneau Gold Mining Company, 1936; Callahan Lead-Zinc Company, 1937; Polaris Mining Company, 1937; and Compania Minera Cibala, S. A., 1937.

Two other mining companies, Dome Mines, Inc., and Sigma Quebec Mines, Ltd., showed no actual inventories of bullion but they did report bullion en route or bullion settlements outstanding which, obviously, they had valued on the market price basis.

Of the 23 companies, twenty used the market valuation basis for one or more classes of inventory, either on hand or en route. In several instances two different methods were used in the same balance sheet.

In general this sample of mining company reports, while not referring entirely to gold inventories, indicates a decided preference for the market valuation method. Evidently this method is regarded as logical by mine managers and their accountants, and this view has been confirmed by many who have written on the subject of mine accounting.

PROPONENTS OF MARKET VALUATION. Spurr and Wormser[16] have supported this viewpoint by the rather obvious comment that "of all the metals and minerals, gold is undoubtedly the easiest to sell."

16 Spurr and Wormser, *The Marketing of Metals and Minerals* (New York, McGraw-Hill Book Company, Inc., 1925).

Paton[17] suggests that: "An industry in which pricing at realizable market value is peculiarly justifiable is gold mining."

Referring to the imaginary case of a mining property producing but not selling, Gower[18] asserts that "it would involve curious economic ideas" to conceive that such lucrative production "might continue indefinitely without resulting in any earnings to the enterprise."

In an unpublished opinion, dated July 27, 1938, Peloubet,[19] an authority on mine accounting, asserts:

The number of mining companies which produce nothing but gold is quite small and their published reports, while not entirely clear, indicate that refined bullion on hand or in transit is carried at the price which will be received from the mint, which is of course the market value less a small mint deduction.

He adds that "refined gold in the form of bullion is invariably carried at market where it is the principal product, the co-product or by-product."

IMPORTANCE OF GOLD PROBLEM. Undoubtedly gold mine accounting is a highly specialized and limited field and would hardly justify detailed consideration were it not for the fact that selling price valuation of gold inventories is common which, by analogy, has been used as a precedent for the valuation of other inventories, metallic or otherwise, on the same basis.

From the practical viewpoint it cannot be a matter of great importance how a small handful of gold mining companies value their products. From an equally practical, as well as theoretical, viewpoint, it may be a matter of special importance to determine whether the market basis of valuing gold inventories is or is not fundamentally proper.

This importance lies in the fact that gold inventory valuation, unimportant as it may be in the entire field of business, is most important as representing a severe and logical test of the whole theory of inventory valuation. If, upon analysis, market valua-

17 W. A. Paton, *Essentials of Accounting*, Part II (Ann Arbor, Michigan, Edwards Brothers, Inc., 1937).
18 William B. Gower, "Unsold Goods and the Income Account," *The Journal of Accountancy*, March 1920, pp. 171-179.
19 Maurice E. Peloubet, unpublished opinion dated July 27, 1938.

tion can be justified in the case of refined gold, then the fundamental conventions of accounting are affected and realization
as a test for profits in other areas of business is dethroned.

For that reason the problem has been considered at some
length and the fundamental conventions of accounting have
been reiterated in the belief that it is from the entity viewpoint
with its implied charge and discharge concept, that reasonable
justification may be found for the valuation of all inventories,
gold or otherwise, on the basis of cost or cost equivalent.

Base-Stock Method.—The base-stock method has been selected for discussion since its distorting effect upon profit and
loss is similar to that of other related methods the result of
which is substantial undervaluation.

The method is founded upon an assumption that a substantial part of the inventory, particularly in certain industries,
partakes of the character of a fixed asset. While items composing the inventory are constantly changing, it is held that the
basic fund of the inventory remains undisturbed.

This analogy is carried still further. In the past understatement of fixed asset values has been tolerated, if not actively
urged, by many accountants. Such undervaluation has been
deemed a proper application of the doctrine of conservatism.
Once having asserted that part of an inventory is in the nature
of a fixed asset and having noted that fixed assets have been
substantially undervalued, it is natural to adopt a similar undervaluation for the inventory of base stock.

Profit Stabilization. The avowed purpose of the base-
stock and similar plans is profit stabilization. Often the avoidance of inequitable income taxes has been indicated as the principal argument in favor of such stabilization, although some
authors attempt to justify the method on other and less convincing grounds.

Sweet[20] has advanced the most logical reason for sudden
growth of interest in the base-stock and equivalent methods as
follows:

[20] Homer N. Sweet, "The Case for a 'Cost or Market' Basis," *N.A.C.A.
Bulletin*, December 1, 1937, p. 401.

Pricing the inventory as low as the probable lowest cost likely to be experienced has been in use for years to some extent. Of late the scheme has gained impetus because of income taxes and particularly the vicious surtax on undistributed profits.

It is somewhat surprising to note the slight use of this method as compared with the voluminous discussion of its merits and demerits. The report of the National Industrial Conference Board, entitled "Prevailing Practices in Inventory Valuation," discloses only 3% of the companies transferring raw materials into work in progress on the last-in, first-out method which belongs to the same general family as the base-stock method. This same report shows that 4% or less of the large number of companies studied use the basic or normal stock method for valuing inventories of raw materials, work in progress, and finished goods on the balance sheet. Actual usage of this and related methods is, therefore, slight.

UNDERVALUATION. The adoption of the method requires that the normal inventory be reduced to a permanent base price.

It has been suggested that this should be a low price, thus insuring understatement of the total inventory in order that it may not be criticized from the credit viewpoint. Nickerson[21] has suggested that the "upper limit of the base stock should be an average of the low points for inventory quantities (seasonal lows), computed over a period of years," while Arthur[22] insists that "the method of valuing inventories must be changed so that price fluctuations do not affect the book value of the basic inventories needed to run the business."

When starting the base-stock plan or any equivalent method calling for similar undervaluation, a substantial adjustment is necessary. Davis[23] believes that: "The loss resulting from reducing the normal inventory to a permanent base price, is a capital adjustment and should be charged to surplus in the same way that any other capital inflation would be handled."

21 Clarence B. Nickerson, "Inventory Reserves as an Element of Inventory Policy," The Accounting Review, December 1937, p. 346.
22 Henry B. Arthur, "Inventory Profits in the Business Cycle," The American Economic Review, March 1938, p. 32.
23 Albion R. Davis, "Inventory Valuation and Business Profits—The Case for a 'Stabilized Basis,'" N.A.C.A. Bulletin, December 1, 1937, p. 386.

After the plan has been put in operation, some change in business methods or manufacturing processes may call for a reduction of the base stock. Any profit made by selling a portion of the base stock is, according to Peloubet,[24] "the same kind of a profit that you would make by selling scrap machinery or by selling an unnecessary piece of real estate. It is not an operating profit; it is a capital profit."

The actual application of the base-stock method is clearly illustrated on pages 434, 435, and 436 of the *Accountants' Handbook,* second edition, to which reference is made. The discussion here is not concerned with the actual technique of inventory computation, although it may be noted that a common method of applying the base-stock method is described by Montgomery[25] as "valuing inventories at cost or market and creating a special account to record variations between that valuation and the fixed base price." Davis[26] suggests that: "There is not the same need for discounting possible losses in connection with speculative inventories [inventories in excess of or less than normal] that there is for normal inventories which have to be maintained at all times regardless of price fluctuations."

Obviously, the method is especially adapted to industries having substantial inventories of basic and homogeneous raw materials involving a long processing period.

ARGUMENT AS TO STABILIZATION.   Any arguments in favor of the base-stock or related methods frankly presented as a practical cure for tax inequities are difficult to criticize. An acute business necessity necessarily outranks accounting traditionalism, particularly when the understatement of values and distortion of profits are adequately disclosed.

For some reason, however, less convincing arguments have been proposed in favor of these methods, with the natural result that they have been criticized in various ways. It has been said, for example, that if certain kinds of business are highly seasonal, they must accept the penalty of their own characteristics

24 Maurice E. Peloubet, *Fiftieth Anniversary Celebration* (New York, American Institute of Accountants, 1938), p. 349.
25 Robert H. Montgomery, *Auditing Theory and Practice* (New York, The Ronald Press Company, 1934), p. 217.
26 Albion R. Davis, "Inventory Valuation and Business Profits—The Case for a 'Stabilized Basis,'" *N.A.C.A. Bulletin,* December 1, 1937, p. 385.

nd not try to change accounting fundamentals in order to pre-
ent the appearance of stability.

Sweet[27] thinks it "against the interests of industrial com-
•anies to operate on the base-stock method" because of the
naterial understatement involved and says further that he is
'unable to accept the theory that some section of the inventory,
alled a normal stock, is a thing apart, a fixed asset."

Paton,[28] admitting that in some situations the year may be
oo short a period, believes that "the solution lies not in doctor-
ng the annual report, but in lengthening the period." He adds
hat: "It is not good accounting to issue reports for a copper
ompany, for example, which make it appear that the concern
ias the comparative stability of earning power of the American-
Telephone and Telegraph Co."

One explanation offered to justify the substantial capital
adjustment resulting from pricing the normal inventory is that
t "represents profits which have been reported but which are
iot real because they are not permanently owned, since they
nust be given up in the form of losses on the next price decline."[29] Such an argument as this cannot fail to arouse criticism, based as it is upon assumptions which do not underlie the
accounting mechanism.

APPROVAL OF METHOD IMPLIES DISCLOSURE. Regardless
of criticism or approval, the base-stock and equivalent methods
iave been approved at least for some industries by eminent
authority, including the American Institute bulletin, *Examination of Financial Statements by Independent Public Account-
ints,* the American Institute Committee on Inventories, and the
Sanders, Hatfield, and Moore monograph, *A Statement of
Accounting Principles.*

Such approval is, of course, coupled with the requirement of
proper disclosure. Disclosure is an absolute necessity in view of
the substantial understatement of asset values.

27 Homer N. Sweet, "The Case for a 'Cost or Market' Basis," *N.A.C.A. Bulletin,* December 1, 1937, pp. 403, 405.
28 W. A. Paton, "Comments on 'A Statement of Accounting Principles,'" *The
Journal of Accountancy,* March 1938, p. 200.
29 Albion R. Davis, "Inventory Valuation and Business Profits—The Case for a
Stabilized Basis,'" *N.A.C.A. Bulletin,* December 1, 1937, p. 386.

Harvey[30] advises "suitable notation on the balance-sheet as to the actual market value." Sanders[31] asserts that undervaluation should be "clearly announced and explained."

Fearing that stockholders may be deceived by undervalued inventories, Montgomery[32] suggests that "the balance sheet should contain enough information about inventory values to guide those who may be thinking of disposing of their interests."

DISTORTION. Some proponents of the base-stock method, notably Walker, have regarded arguments against the base-stock method as being unconvincing. Walker[33] feels that the problem "deserves something more from its opponents than the characteristic vague charge that it is not good accounting," and he refers to authoritative opposition as being "little more than a condescending frown of disapproval."

If this is correct, it may be explainable since much of the opposition to the plan has been presented from the balance sheet viewpoint. From the balance sheet viewpoint, substantial under valuation of an asset, if adequately disclosed and explained, can not be regarded as unduly serious. It appears that the real objection to this or similar plans is the effect upon comparative profit and loss statements, the distortion of which, as has been noted, appears to give the copper company the same appearance of earning stability as American Telephone and Telegraph Company.

To say, as Nickerson[34] has done, that under the base-stock method "the balance sheet is made subservient to the profit and loss statement" cannot be interpreted as meaning that the method does not cause profit distortion. Profit distortion or more euphemistically, rationalization or stabilization, is in fact the announced purpose of the method. This is evidenced by

30 John L. Harvey, "Some Observations on Accounting Practice with Special Reference to Inventory Valuation," *The Journal of Accountancy*, December 1937, p. 446.
31 T. H. Sanders, "Reports to Stockholders," *The Accounting Review*, September 1934, p. 210.
32 Robert H. Montgomery, *Auditing Theory and Practice* (New York, The Ronald Press Company, 1934), p. 216.
33 Ross G. Walker, "Income Accounting and the Base-Stock Inventory," *Credit and Financial Management*, June 1938, p. 16.
34 Clarence B. Nickerson, "Inventory Reserves as an Element of Inventory Policy," *The Accounting Review*, December 1937, p. 350.

Purpose No. 1 mentioned in a monograph of the Boston Advisory Committee on Accounting of the Tanners' Council[35] in the following words:

> To rationalize the profit curves of individual tanning companies by offsetting, in so far as average operations are concerned, the excessive profits from sales over costs on a rising price market with the inevitable inventory losses sustained on succeeding declining price markets.

This admission that rationalization, stabilization, or, as it is referred to here, distortion, is the primary purpose of the method must be given considerable weight and might be regarded as an objection of greater significance than a mere "condescending frown of disapproval."

Whether approval of such stabilization is consistent with that modern viewpoint which asserts that "the first objective has been to secure a proper charge or credit to the income account for the year,"[36] is a matter for considerable doubt. It is only the admitted necessity of tax relief which could justify such a noteworthy exception to the statement of an objective the recognition of which has too long been delayed.

CONCLUSION. The unusual amount of professional attention which has been given to some of these plans hardly seems proportionate to their relative importance. Only in a few industries is the base-stock method a necessity. Replacement costs are not a cause of worry in approximately half of the business organizations studied by the National Industrial Conference Board, and even in those instances where product is priced for sale on the general basis of replacement or market cost, it has not been intimated that the accounting mechanism itself requires much change, since only 20% of the reporting companies find it necessary to keep separate statistical records to determine profit and loss on current business and to fix selling prices.

By and large, this entire matter of pricing in relation to cost is dependent upon financial rather than accounting calculations. Furthermore, relatively few accountants still believe that pro-

---

[35] Tanners' Council of America, "Standard Accounting Method for the Tanning Industry."

[36] *Examination of Financial Statements by Independent Public Accountants* (New York, American Institute of Accountants, January 1936), p. 4.

duction costs as reported by the accountant are of primary sig
nificance in price setting. It therefore seems fair to conclud
that, aside from the taxation angle, the distorting methods o
inventory revaluation do not possess sufficient merit to justify
alteration in basic accounting methods, accounting conventions
or the traditional accounting mechanism.

CHAPTER 26

INVENTORY REVALUATION AT COST OR MARKET

The inventory rule of revaluation commonly referred to as the "cost or market rule," or as the "rule of valuation at the lower of cost or market," has become firmly fastened upon modern accounting. Statistics indicating its wide acceptance have already been cited in Chapter 25. Nearly all authorities on auditing recommend the rule. Accounting writers, even those opposing it, recognize its general use. It has been approved by such bodies as the American Institute of Accountants, the Securities and Exchange Commission, and the Treasury Department. It is regarded as highly important by credit men and investors.

Despite its universal acceptance and despite the fact that it has even been dignified as a principle of accounting, there is a substantial body of opinion opposing the rule on the ground that it refers not to one but to two methods and hence violates the doctrine of consistency. The rule has been persistently arraigned as an important cause of profit and loss distortion, a defect which has been admitted by many of those who favor it.

The effect of applying this rule to inventories is sometimes startling. Meredith[1] mentions a company showing 1937 profits of $6.97 per share of common based on an inventory at cost of $84,329,759. The adjustment of this inventory to the lower of cost or market changed the inventory to $73,987,017, a reduction of more than $10,000,000, or more than 12%. This 12% adjustment changed the per share earnings from $6.97 to $1.95, a reduction of 72%. These figures, while perhaps somewhat more dramatic than usual, illustrate the magnified effect of inventory revaluation upon profits.

[1] Spencer B. Meredith, in *Barron's,* April 18, 1938, p. 9.

Conflict of Viewpoints.—The cost or market rule emphasizes the constant conflict between the balance sheet viewpoint and the profit and loss viewpoint.

By those who think in terms of realizable value, the inventory is considered in relation to the possible cash proceeds from selling that inventory. While seldom taking the indefensible stand that an inventory is in any way equivalent to a deferred charge to cash and is therefore of the same order as receivables, some who seek to report realizable current asset values do revalue inventories on the same general theory that they value receivables, namely, as an adjustment of a deferred charge to cash, in order that it may represent the approximate equivalent of cash.

This is the view expressed as long ago as 1915 by Dicksee who made the following statement regarding current assets or as he called them, floating assets: "The whole aim of the undertaking is to convert—or be able to convert—them into cash at the earliest possible opportunity." He therefore concludes that "The element of immediate realisation is an important factor in their value."

The profit and loss viewpoint, consciously or unconsciously considers inventories as deferred charges to future income and hence is interested in allocating the cost of such inventories to the correct accounting periods. From this viewpoint valuation at any figure other than cost merely represents an unnecessary and befogging complication. This viewpoint was emphasized by Husband,[3] who said: "The whole of the cost of the inventory is really applicable to, or a cost of, future operations."

Since May[4] was chairman of the American Institute Committee on Cooperation with Stock Exchanges, it is interesting to note that, less than two months after that committee instituted correspondence with the New York Stock Exchange, he published in *The Journal of Accountancy* a paper in which he emphasized the profit and loss viewpoint in these words:

[2] Lawrence R. Dicksee, *Auditing: A Practical Manual for Auditors* (London: Gee & Company, 1915), pp. 200, 201.

[3] George R. Husband, "Accounting Postulates: An Analysis of the Tentative Statement of Accounting Principles," *The Accounting Review*, December 1937, p. 390.

[4] George O. May, "Influence of the Depression on the Practice of Accountancy," *The Journal of Accountancy*, November 1932, p. 341.

I think it must be admitted that the cost or market basis is designed primarily to afford a sound balance-sheet value, and that some change of method, or some change in the form of presentation of results, may be called for at this time, when the income account is becoming recognized as potentially at least more significant than the balance-sheet.

Price Levels and Realization.—Not all of those who have discussed this inventory rule have appreciated the fundamental characteristic which distinguishes it from other types of revaluation. No accountant could possibly quarrel with the idea of inventory valuation if it referred to obsolete items found in the inventory or items which were damaged or otherwise unsuitable for use. Deterioration of inventory is always recognized as a loss to be written off in the period when it is recognized.

The rule of cost or market, however, does not refer to deterioration or diminution of physical quantity. It specifically refers to materials, supplies, or goods which may be in perfect condition for sale or use but which, it is claimed, must be revalued merely because of a decrease in price levels. Those who attempt to defend the cost or market rule by using depreciation of fixed assets as an analogy apparently fail to take this distinction into consideration.

Since the rule refers to a price adjustment only of otherwise acceptable and useful inventory items, its purpose is self-evident. Like the provision for doubtful accounts, the inventory is adjusted in order to bring its value closer to a realizable basis, disregarding the fact that receivables result from the sales operation and are usually no more than slightly overstated deferred charges to cash, whereas inventories are prerequisite to the sales operation and are deferred charges to future income.

Derivation of Rule.—Some searching of accounting literature fails to confirm the natural assumption that the rule of cost or market was derived from the method of valuation used at the termination of a trading venture.

In times past, in order to make a settlement with the venturers, it was necessary either to realize upon all the assets or determine profits by the equivalent of realization, namely, by valuing the assets at the price they would bring if they were put on the market. It does, however, seem reasonable that this practice may have had some influence upon the adoption of the market price basis for inventory valuation. Clearly market price is a much more logical basis than cost from the viewpoint of termination of a single venture.

It should, however, be observed that inventory valuation at market price is not at all the same kind of valuation as is implied by the phrase "cost or market." Valuation at market price may result in an inventory figure which is either higher or lower than cost. From the viewpoint of those few who have favored it, valuation at market has at least the merit of consistency.

The "heads I win, tails you lose" cost or market rule appears to have evolved as the result of credit insistence[5] and tax necessities. Its continued acceptance and enthusiastic application bear testimony to the powerful influence of conservatism which has so long been a controlling doctrine in auditing.

Not satisfied to demand reduced inventory values according to the lower of cost or market on the date of the balance sheet, some accountants have carried the doctrine of conservatism even further and have provided for additional reductions based upon market declines during the period between the date of the balance sheet and the termination of the audit. Not always is such a provision actually reflected in the profit and loss statement for the year under review. Generally the subsequent decline in market prices is a matter for footnote disclosure.

Occasionally, however, such subsequent declines are actually reflected in a balance sheet prepared as of a date when declines could not have been foretold and have been included in the profit and loss statement for the year ended that date. The published report of Eitingon-Schild Company, Inc., for year ended November 30, 1937, showed in the profit and loss statement an item under the heading of special charges which read in part as follows: "Decline, subsequent to November 30, 1937, in market value of inventory and joint venture merchandise from market value at that date . . . $272,230.52." This debit item was based upon events occurring in December, 1937 and January, 1938,

---

[5] This is also Paton's view as indicated by his reference to "the somewhat unintelligent attitude of commercial bankers." See W. A. Paton, *Essentials of Accounting* (New York, The Macmillan Company, 1938), p. 486.

and the credit side of the entry was to an account entitled "Reserve for decline subsequent to November 30, 1937, in market value of inventory, etc." This item was then shown on the balance sheet as a liability.

It is not usual, however, to carry the theory of revaluation this far, parenthetical comments or explanatory footnotes usually being considered sufficient. The objection to the Eitingon-Schild treatment does not, of course, refer so much to the balance sheet as to the inclusion of this heavy loss in the profit and loss statement. It could under no circumstances be considered a loss of that fiscal year.

This particular report, otherwise not important, is mentioned to indicate the extremes to which the balance sheet viewpoint may lead and the utter disregard of profit and loss distortion.

Influence of the Current Ratio.—The desire of any accountant to proceed to such extremes can indicate but one thing, a desire to show current assets on a realizable basis of valuation. It is difficult to see any motive for such drastic treatment other than a credit motive. The occasional insistence by bankers upon a conservative statement of current assets may lead to excesses of this kind.

Fortunately, it appears that credit men no longer make a fetish of the so-called current ratio. Credit administration has been greatly modified during recent years and credit men have learned that factors other than current position may have an important bearing upon the propriety of credit granting. Leaders among bank and commercial credit men realize full well that sound financial position does not, when coupled with unprofitable operation, afford a good credit basis for continued credit dealings, and these men have learned to regard profitable operation as assurance for the future and as an index of management.

It is now being recognized that the current ratio has long been overemphasized, that it is only one of several important credit tests, and that its forecasting value is slight.[6]

It is a matter of common knowledge that strong credit in-

[6] Bulletin 51, July 16, 1935, of Bureau of Business Research, College of Commerce and Business Administration, University of Illinois, Urbana, Ill.

sistence upon the current ratio has been responsible for many exaggerated cases of window-dressing.

Probably in no other phase of accounting has the doctrine of conservatism been more universally and more narrowly applied than in the revaluation of inventories, in utter disregard of the fact that such so-called conservatism is generally admitted to be unconservative in so far as future period earnings are concerned. This, however, has been a matter of slight consequence to proponents of the balance sheet viewpoint.

It is in connection with inventory revaluation that the most serious conflict has arisen between the balance sheet viewpoint which is now waning and the profit and loss viewpoint which is now waxing. That the distorting and unconservative effects of cost or market revaluation will in due time be recognized seems almost a foregone conclusion, unless by some mischance accounting should retrace its own steps of development and reaffirm its former allegiance.

Application of Cost or Market.—The actual application of the cost or market rule is simple in theory although not always so simple in practice.

Periodic Inventories. Considered first in relation to the periodic inventory the quantities involved are inspected and enumerated on inventory sheets, after which the inspection of the most recent invoices or other evidence permits valuation of the inventory on a cost basis.

The next step determines current market prices (or replacement costs). Each item on the inventory sheet is extended at cost and at market values, and the lower of the two values is then extended into a third column where it becomes one of the constituents of the complete inventory which is a factor in the computation of cost of goods sold. This is the simple essence of the method in so far as the periodic inventory is concerned.

Because the periodic inventory requires no adjustment for prices separate and distinct from the adjustment for quantity, there has in the past been a tendency to lose sight of the fact that the one adjusting entry may in reality represent two separate and distinct adjustments. It is this fact which is so clearly noted in connection with perpetual inventories. It is, of course, true that some quantity adjustments are nearly always necessary in order to reconcile the perpetual inventory record with the quantities on hand, but such adjustments may be considered of minor importance, particularly when inventory has been carefully administered and recorded.

PERPETUAL INVENTORIES. Under the perpetual inventory plan there is no previous balance representing inventory on hand at the first of the year still remaining unchanged in the trial balance as of the end of the year.

The continuous program of posting receipts and issuances results in a trial balance figure at the end of the year which, barring error, may be taken as a correct reflection of the actual quantities and their costs as of the closing date. The application of the cost or market rule, therefore, requires an adjusting entry which is substantially a price adjustment, having little or no reference to quantities or condition such as might be caused by deterioration or obsolescence. Since the adjusting entry at the end of the year reflects a price adjustment, and since it must deliberately be made in order to alter the presumably correct book figures, the legitimacy of the adjustment and its effect upon earnings is brought into sharper focus.

The adjustment may be made to the hundreds or thousands of separate inventory cards or ledger sheets, or it may be set up in the form of a reserve or valuation account directly against the balance of the controlling account as it has been transcribed on the trial balance.

A question constantly arises as to the disposition of the debit element of the adjusting entry. With the periodic inventory plan no such question arises, both the quantity adjustment and the price adjustment being intermingled elements of cost of goods sold. When the perpetual inventory focuses attention upon this question of price adjustment only, the question arises as to whether such an adjustment is a proper element of cost of goods sold. As a result it has been proposed to eliminate it as a factor influencing gross profit and to show it in the profit and loss statement under one of the captions following the gross profit figure.

Historical Review of Cost or Market Rule.—To a visiting accountant from some other planet the cost or market rule might well appear so arbitrary and so illogical as to defy his understanding. Only by retracing steps in the development of this accounting practice would its endorsement by otherwise logical experts become understandable.

The development of this valuation rule has been so profoundly influenced by medieval trading practices, by banking and credit requirements, by the aftermath of war, and by inequitable taxation that it seems desirable briefly to consider and discuss certain significant occurrences and significant dates which may be considered milestones in the history of inventory accounting.

SIGNIFICANT DATES.   The significant dates include at least the ones listed in the following table:

1857   A conference was called to draft a uniform commercial code for the then independent German states.

1873   A German court decision interpreted the word "value" in the 1857 code as meaning "market value."

1897   The German commercial law provided rules for inventory valuation.

1904   A Congress of Accountants was held in St. Louis under the auspices of the Federation of Societies of Public Accountants, at which time Arthur Lowes Dickinson endorsed the cost or market rule.

1917   A British group known as the Association of Controlled Owners demanded of the Board of Inland Revenue a modification of the cost or market rule. The Inland Revenue, based upon recommendations of a committee of accountants, affirmed the general correctness of cost or market although not adopting all of the recommendations of the committee of accountants.

In this same year T.D. 2609 recognizing the cost or market rule was issued by the United States Treasury Department.

1932   A letter dated September 22, 1932 was written to the Committee on Stock List of the New York Stock Exchange by the American Institute of Accountants' Special Committee on Cooperation with Stock Exchanges, officially emphasizing that "the income account is usually far more important than the balance-sheet" and referring to the cost or market rule as the principal exception to the primary accounting objective of securing "a proper charge or credit to the income account for the year."

1936   In January the American Institute of Accountants prepared and published the bulletin, *Examination of Financial Statements by Independent Public Accountants,* officially approving various points developed by the interchange of correspondence between the American Institute Committee and the New York Stock Exchange Committee during the years 1932-1934. In June the Executive Committee of the American Accounting Association published *A Tentative Statement of Accounting Principles Affecting Corporate Reports.*

1937   Principles of inventory valuation were incorporated in the German special corporation code, No. 3 of Section 133 of which requires in stringent terms the so-called lower value, principally with respect to current assets. If the cost of production or the purchase price was higher than the market quotation at the date of the balance sheet, no higher value than the market price of that date can be chosen.

1938   Thomas Henry Sanders, Henry Rand Hatfield, and Underhill Moore prepared a monograph entitled *A Statement of Accounting Principles* which was published by the American Institute of Accountants. This monograph, while recognizing "some equalizing of profits over periods of prosperity and depression" accepted the base-stock method, accepted the rule "that the lower of cost or market is the primary guide," recognized the last-in, first-out method as representing "cost" and defined the word "market" as "the cost of reproduction or replacement, unless the realization prices are lower," as related to work in process and finished goods.

It is interesting to observe the relationship of some of these dates to wars, panics, and taxes. The year 1873, for example, saw the beginning of an abrupt business depression which was accompanied by legal approval of the rule of cost or market.

The year 1917, when the cost or market rule was approved, affirmed or recognized by the British Board of Trade and the United States Bureau of Internal Revenue, was a year of war and high taxes. The year 1932 which marked the beginning of the new emphasis upon the profit and loss viewpoint represented a low point in the depression which had started in the fall of 1929.

The dates above scheduled provide no more than a skeletonized summary which may be somewhat enriched by reference to written and spoken accounting opinion. While admitting that commercial and governmental necessities strongly influenced the development of inventory revaluation, it was also true that accountants and accounting writers were giving thoughtful consideration to inventory problems. Some selected samples reveal the trend of accounting thought over the past two centuries.

EIGHTEENTH CENTURY. In the year 1712, Jacques Savary[7] suggested that merchandise which could be replaced at 5% less should be reduced to the replacement price. In 1797 John Harries Wickes, in his *Book-keeping Reformed,* suggested inventory valuation "at prime cost." In the same year Edward Thomas Jones, author of *Jones' English System of Book-keeping,* subscribed to the prime cost rule for valuation.

NINETEENTH CENTURY. In 1813 James Morrison, in *Elements of Book-keeping by Single and Double Entry,* suggested estimating inventory "at prime cost, or at the current prices." This statement is, of course, ambiguous. It may mean that the inventory should be valued either at prime cost or at current prices or at the lower of cost or market price. In any event, Morrison's book marks one of the earliest disagreements with the straightforward prime cost rule.

In 1819 another English writer, Clerk Morrison, endorsed the market price view in his *Introduction to Book-keeping and Business,* in which he stated that it was fallacious to value at cost if the present price of an article is less than cost. He suggested that "the gain is in reality obtained as soon as the prices rise, or the loss suffered as soon as they fall."

Seventeen years later, in 1836, an English publication entitled *New Check Journal upon the Principle of Double Entry,* written by George Jackson, strongly advocated valuation at

---

7 A. C. Littleton, *Accounting Evolution to 1900* (New York, American Institute Publishing Co., Inc., 1933), p. 152.

cost. He insisted that at inventory time price increases or price decreases should not be taken into account since the gain or the loss is not realized or "has not actually yet been suffered."

Thus in the first half of the nineteenth century, British writers were noting the conflict between the balance sheet viewpoint as expressed by Clerk Morrison and the profit and loss viewpoint expressed by George Jackson.

As already noted, in 1857 a conference was called for the purpose of drafting a uniform commercial code for the German independent states. This draft specified valuation at the lower of cost or market but was not approved in that form, the statute being made to read that goods and materials should be shown at the "value which ought to be ascribed." German lawyers interpreted this as exchange value and in 1873 a court decision interpreted the word "value" as market value. This court, like so many other courts, was not unwilling to express technical accounting opinions. In part the court stated that "the idea of a fictitious instantaneous general realization of all assets and liabilities is the concept underlying the balance sheet; but at the same time the viewpoint is that in reality the continuation and not the liquidation of the business is intended."

The depression which began in Germany during 1873 prompted a legislative investigation from which it appeared that part of the previous prosperity was due to the interpretation of values as being equivalent to sales prices and a new corporation law was developed which approved the rule of cost or market.

In 1885 C. R. Trevor, F.C.A., addressed the Manchester Accountants Students' Society, endorsing the cost or market rule. His paper was of slight significance save for the discussion which followed its delivery. One member of the Society commented that it was "so thoroughly orthodox from beginning to end that it is very difficult to find any fault with the views of Mr. Trevor." This remark leaves little room for doubt that the cost or market rule had been generally accepted for a considerable length of time.

In 1897 the German Commercial Law, to which previous reference has been made, was passed. Section 261 of that law said in part:

(1) Securities and merchandise that have an exchange or market quotation may not be valued higher than at the price at which they were carried at the date of the balance sheet. Or if such price exceeds the price at which they were acquired or produced, then at the last mentioned price.

In 1897 two American authors, Broaker and Chapman,[8] insisted that "it is a sound principle to carry the stock at its actual cost, and let the profits or losses be determined upon final sale or disposition." These authors did qualify this instruction somewhat but it is interesting to notice their insistence upon the profit and loss viewpoint.

TWENTIETH CENTURY. In 1904 John A. Walbank, an English writer, in the *Encyclopedia of Accounting,* endorsed revaluation at cost or market. The same year at the St. Louis World's Fair in conjunction with which a Congress of Accountants was held under the auspices of the Federation of Societies of Public Accountants, Arthur Lowes Dickinson,[9] an outstanding English-trained accounting authority, read a paper which was significant in many respects. Of special interest, however, was his statement that "the general rule for valuation of Stocks on hand, namely, 'cost or market, whichever is the lower,' has been evolved and is adopted by the most conservative commercial institutions."

The significance of this is threefold. First of all, Dickinson was an undoubted authority, second, he refers to the rule as a "general rule," and third, by inference, he justifies the rule by the doctrine of conservatism. A dissenting voice, however, was heard at this meeting: another English accountant, John Hyde,[10] suggested that no "great harm would be done if we would simply continue to put this in at the cost price." In general, however, dissent was feeble.

In 1906 Lisle, in his *Accounting in Theory and Practice,*

[8] Broaker and Chapman, *The American Accountants' Manual* (New York, 1897), p. 60.

[9] Arthur Lowes Dickinson, Congress of Accountants, Official Record, 1904, World's Fair, St. Louis, under the auspices of the Federation of Societies of Public Accountants in the United States of America, p. 182.

[10] John Hyde, Congress of Accountants, Official Record, 1904, World's Fair, St. Louis, under the auspices of the Federation of Societies of Public Accountants in the United States of America.

endorsed the cost or market rule. In the same year William M. Lybrand[11] announced that the rule "has everything to commend it from a conservative viewpoint" although he confessed that it was not entirely logical.

In 1909 McKenzie[12] thought the cost or market rule "a safe guide to follow." His opinion was the general opinion of his time and for that reason his paper was not noteworthy. Of greater importance was his endorsement of consistency when he affirmed that once adopted the cost or market rule "should be strictly adhered to, as one year at cost and another at market, regardless of market being lower, will never produce any degree of dependability. Like depreciation, it is only the regular pursuit of the principle adopted that will give satisfactory comparative results."

In 1910 a courageous attack on the cost or market rule was made by Greendlinger.[13] Far in advance of his time, Greendlinger clearly saw the mischievous effect of this rule upon comparative profit and loss and his words deserve complete quotation:

It is wrong in principle to value it [inventory] at market price as it interferes with the correct showing of the profit and loss account. If we take the inventory for any reason, not for the purpose of rendering a correct profit and loss account for any given period, we are at liberty to use either form, cost or market value, but when we take inventory for the purpose of ascertaining the cost of sales, for the purpose of showing a correct profit and loss account, we must figure it at cost price only.

This bold statement by Leo Greendlinger seems to mark the beginning of a new school of accounting thought which has become increasingly heard during the years following. Among its leaders were such thoughtful students as Harry C. Bentley, Roy B. Kester, and most insistent of all, W. A. Paton. During those years voices raised in favor of the cost or market rule

11 William M. Lybrand, *Accounting in Theory and Practice* (Federation of Societies of Public Accountants in the United States of America), p. 195.

12 William R. McKenzie, "The Verification and Treatment of Inventories in Audits and Examinations of Manufacturing and Trading Concerns," *The Journal of Accountancy*, December 1909, p. 115.

13 Leo Greendlinger, *Accountancy Problems with Solutions, Vol.* 1 (New York, Business Book Bureau, 1910), pp. 192, 193.

were not quite so dogmatic as before. Lisle and Middleton,[14] in *Account-Keeping in Principle and Practice*, recommended the rule "so as to err on the safe side."

An editorial in *The Journal of Accountancy*, July 1921, while endorsing the method, admitted that it was "not strictly in accordance with the basic theory," a comment typical of many accountancy writings during the past two decades.

Practically, 1917 was a most important year in the history of the cost or market rule. This was the year of its recognition by the U. S. Treasury Department and by the British Board of Inland Revenue, although the Inland Revenue was not willing to go as far as its advisory committee of accountants recommended in eliminating the base-stock method for those companies which had been accustomed to apply it in the past.

The Association of Controlled Owners consisted principally of concerns engaged in the manufacture of munitions who were badly affected by the excess profits duty which in 1917 had reached 80% of the excess war profits. This association demanded relief, the whole problem arising out of the monetary inflation which was then gathering momentum in England. The Association of Controlled Owners had been using a method of inventorying based upon 1914 prices which, of course, involved an increasing undervaluation of stock. For the obvious purpose of increasing tax revenues, the Inland Revenue was demanding that such undervaluation be discontinued. To replace such undervaluation by strict application of the rule of cost or market would have resulted in a heavy increase in taxation to the controlled owners.

The advisory committee of accountants made two recommendations, one of which was accepted by the Board of Inland Revenue and the other of which was rejected. The rejected part of the report proposed that those concerns which have been using the base price method be put on a cost or market price basis. While this was rejected by the Board of Inland Revenue, the Board accepted the important general principle advocated by the accountants which read in part as follows:

14 Lisle and Middleton, *Account-Keeping in Principle and Practice* (London, Wm. Green & Sons, 1911), p. 10.

... all stocks of every sort or kind should be valued at the end of each accounting period on the basis of cost price or market value, whichever is the lower.

In the United States, prior to 1917, the Bureau of Internal Revenue had recognized the cost basis.

Paton,[15] in March 1938, reviewed the events of 1917, stating that originally the rule of cost or market "was not officially recognized as a sound practice by the United States Treasury Department." He asserted that in 1917 this rule was "an immediate method of reducing taxable income (and some concerns paid heavily for making the shift just before a higher level of tax rates appeared)." In other words, the wide use of the rule in the United States is not as time-honored as many think, and it waxed on account of considerations far removed from the development of sound accounting.

In 1922 Paton took a strong stand against the cost or market rule, labelling it as thoroughly unreasonable. He reiterated this opinion in his book *Accounting* in 1924, and stressed the importance of consistency.

Esquerré,[16] in 1921, opposed the rule, saying, "There is, however, a good reason why market value should not be used at all."

In 1925 Greer[17] then with Ohio State University, told the American Association of University Instructors in Accounting that he would like to "hear someone get up and say, for example, that the valuation of inventories at 'cost or market, whichever is lower,' is not the proper method of valuation; that such a theory is nothing but a time-honored piece of hocum."

At the annual meeting of the American Institute of Accountants held in September 1927, at Del Monte, California, Hatfield[18] (later a member of the Sanders, Hatfield, and Moore committee) inferred that accountants were permitting their

15 W. A. Paton, "Comments on 'A Statement of Accounting Principles,'" *The Journal of Accountancy*, March 1938, p. 202.
16 Paul-Joseph Esquerré, *The Applied Theory of Accounts* (New York, The Ronald Press Company, 1921), p. 171.
17 Howard C. Greer, in a discussion before the 9th Annual Meeting of the American Association of University Instructors in Accounting, Chicago, February 1925.
18 Henry Rand Hatfield, at the annual meeting of the American Institute of Accountants, September 1927.

clients to influence accounting thought and labelled arguments in favor of the cost or market rule as "so brilliant an instance of flabby thinking as to deserve some further attention."

Two years later Howard[19] showed that the rule tended to "underestimate both net revenues and net worth."

THE TREND SINCE 1930. In 1930 Sanders[20] advocated the cost or market rule but admitted that "there is very high business and accounting authority for modifications under certain conditions."

The American Institute correspondence with the Stock Exchange in 1932, the American Institute bulletin of January 1936, and the Sanders, Hatfield, and Moore monograph in 1938, have all been mentioned and discussed. These publications appearing at intervals between 1932 and 1938 have resulted in increased accounting discussion. Many of these discussions are too voluminous and of too recent dates to justify quotation here.

It appears that these various comments, arguments, and observations for and against arbitrary revaluation of inventory have awakened considerable interest and have in fact had a tendency to reopen the entire question, which so many believed was settled in 1917.

The period from 1932 to 1938 marks the real change from the former balance sheet viewpoint to the current profit and loss viewpoint with its insistence upon the dominance of the profit and loss statement and the necessity for proper allocation of cost or income items to accounting periods.

Such phrases as "the income account is usually far more important than the balance sheet," or "the cardinal importance of the income account," or "expenditures are made in one period with the definite purpose and expectation that they shall be the means of producing profits in the future," are all derived from that first letter dated September 22, 1932 from the American Institute Committee to the New York Stock Exchange, a letter which in future years will doubtless be considered as marking the turning point in accounting philosophy despite the com-

---

[19] Stanley Edwin Howard, *The A B C of Accounting* (Princeton, N. J., Princeton University Press, 1929), p. 88.

[20] T. H. Sanders, *Problems in Industrial Accounting* (New York, McGraw-Hill Book Company, Inc., 1930), p. 367.

mittee's willingness to make an exception in favor of the rule of cost or market, a willingness which may be considered the most serious flaw in this important accounting document.

Nature of Market Price.—In the process of adapting the traditional accounting mechanism to modern conditions, the meaning of the word "market" has become so changed that it frequently has little or no relation to realization.

BID PRICES. The definition provided by the Treasury Department in Article 144 of Regulation 77, approved by Montgomery as being "almost ideal," reflects the meaning which business men commonly attach to the word. This definition reads as follows: "Under ordinary circumstances and for normal goods in an inventory 'market' means the current bid price prevailing at the date of the inventory for the particular merchandise in the volume in which usually purchased by the taxpayer."

It is obvious that such phrases as "ordinary circumstances," "normal goods," and "in the volume in which usually purchased" must be given special consideration. When the circumstances are not ordinary and the goods are not normal, and where bid prices are nominal rather than applying to particular quantities, this definition may not be particularly helpful, and any calculation of market price may not provide a figure equivalent to realizable value.

It is reliably reported that the machine-tool industry became so inactive during the depression that its inventories could not be wholly disposed of at any price. Where inventories consist of specialty items such as electrical appliances, fountain pens, musical instruments, or clothing, it is doubtful whether there is any actual market referring to such inventories. Referring to such items Peloubet[21] said: "If prices such as these do constitute a market, the practical question of building up a hypothetical finished price and applying parts of that price to different stages of manufacture arises and should be discussed."

Even where applicable market prices are available, many

21 Maurice E. Peloubet, *Fiftieth Anniversary Celebration* (New York, American Institute of Accountants, 1938), p. 338.

would doubtless agree with Canning[22] that "both 'market' pricings in inventory sheets and their verification by auditors are much less reliable than the corresponding 'cost' pricings."

REPLACEMENT COSTS.   Because of various difficulties in the determination of true market prices, a substitute has been found in replacement or reproductive cost. The question propounds itself as to whether balance sheet readers are generally aware of this special technical interpretation which gives the word "market" a conventionalized meaning. Does the banker in scanning a creditor's statements always understand that the important item of inventory, in so far as it relates to goods in process or finished goods, may appear not at market value but at the cost of replacement?

As long ago as 1923, an English[23] writer in *The Accountant* asked the sensible question : " 'Market value' must have only one meaning and if that be held to be 'cost of replacement' why should the well-known but misleading phrase not be altered to read 'at cost of acquisition or cost of replacement whichever is the lower?' " Recognizing, however, that even this phrase would not cover all contingencies, the author arrived at the conclusion that "the only formula to cover adequately the proper method for valuing stock on hand at any time is 'at actual cost of acquisition, current cost of replacement, or current selling price whichever is the lowest.' "

Of what value to a credit grantor is knowledge of inventory replacement cost, which refers primarily to the buying or manufacturing function, as compared with market, which has to do primarily with the selling function? In those cases where specialized or style goods of uncertain salability are carried in stock, the history of business is replete with examples of costly merchandise which, due to lack of public acceptance, cannot be marketed at any price.

To value the inventories of such non-salable products at replacement cost and to call that replacement cost "market" is to pervert the commonly accepted meaning of "market."

[22] John B. Canning, *The Economics of Accountancy* (New York, The Ronald Press Company, 1929), p. 226.
[23] *The Accountant,* Vol. LXVIII, No. 2531, June 9, 1923.

The auditing viewpoint has been stated by Montgomery[24] in the following quotation: "Finished goods on hand, generally, should be valued on the basis of the market value of the component materials, if the market values are lower than cost." This quotation clearly reflects the buying rather than the selling interpretation of the word "market" and completely disregards the obvious fact that the process of manufacturing may, due to lack of business foresight, actually reduce rather than increase the value of the component materials.

REPLACEMENT COSTS IN MANUFACTURING.   Paper stock, for example, may have a definite market value, but if it is converted into a printed book which no one wants to buy, its market value has in reality become nil.

The creditor of a small manufacturing plant making concrete garden furniture might be interested in knowing whether the inventory of cement was stated upon a realizable basis. Cement is a standard commodity for which a ready market can be found. The creditor, therefore, has a feeling of assurance that if necessary he can take over the inventory of cement and apply the proceeds of its sale to the indebtedness. If, however, the manufacturer of garden furniture in an ill-advised moment undertakes to make concrete benches and tables in imitation of natural wood, for which the sales prospects appear somewhat limited, it is difficult to believe that the credit man would be interested in having the inventory of such finished or partly finished chairs and benches recalculated on the basis of the replacement price.

The same reasoning applies, of course, to work in progress. The moment that the manufacturer converts good salable cement into poorly designed garden furniture of doubtful sales possibilities, he may, from his viewpoint, have added value to the raw material by applying manufacturing labor and manufacturing expense to it. Certainly the astute credit man would hardly believe in such added value and, having his choice as to which asset would furnish him the greatest protection, would unfailingly prefer the bagged cement to the completed product.

[24] Robert H. Montgomery, *Auditing Theory and Practice* (New York, The Ronald Press Company, 1934), p. 210.

This type of situation exists in many industries. The confidence of management that a product can be manufactured and sold at a profit is perhaps derived from valuable experience in previous manufacturing and selling operations, but the credit man cannot expect to be an expert as to the marketing possibilities of all of his various customers' products. If there is any hint that such manufacturing and marketing requires expert talent or costly effort, the credit man simply disregards inventories of work in progress or finished goods, or at best marks them down to a fraction of their reported value. He knows full well that in order to realize upon such reported inventories he must be prepared to go into the business of completing and selling a specialty product, a task for which he may be singularly unequipped.

Further definitions from Montgomery[25] throw additional light upon the modern auditing viewpoint. "The term 'market price should be used synonymously with 'replacement price' whenever inventory valuations of finished goods are under consideration." He adds that replacement cost is "the cost of replacing property at the lowest obtainable prices, and comprehends buying in the open market; therefore the elements of salability, desirability, quantities, etc., are considered."

From these various references it seems apparent that accounting necessity has, by a technical change of meaning, altered the significance of the word "market."

INCREASE IN MARKET PRICES. It is further noted that the application of the rule of cost or market results in some illogical situations, as where inventories are written down to conform to market quotations which later have increased. At the end of a fiscal period the actual cost of a given item may have been $10. If at that time the market is determined as being $8, then the $8 valuation is carried over in the beginning inventory of the following period. If the same article is retained in stock all during the following period and at the end thereof the market value has increased from $8 to $9, the question arises as to whether the inventory value at the end of the second period

---

25 Robert H. Montgomery, *Auditing Theory and Practice* (New York, The Ronald Press Company, 1934), pp. 218, 219.

should be written up to $9. Montgomery[26] says, "no," and quotes a Treasury Department regulation, supporting his contention that the item should "be carried at the same value in the closing inventory as in the opening inventory," although he recognizes justification for departure from this rule when there is no question as to the salability or usability of the article.

Revaluation Adjustments.—The actual readjustment of costs of work in progress and finished goods to a replacement basis may be somewhat complicated, particularly with respect to the element of overhead, because of the many diverse elements which compose it. It is, of course, possible to recalculate all of the cost sheets on a replacement basis, but if the amount of clerical labor involved is excessive, approximate readjustments may be made on a percentage basis.

Montgomery[26] insists that: "When selling values decline and costs decline, the downward trend cannot be attributed solely to lower replacement costs of materials. The lower costs of labor and other elements must not be forgotten." Sweeney,[27] on the other hand, believes that this requires an enormous amount of work which he says "obviously explains why the labor and overhead costs in partly and wholly finished inventories are practically always valued at cost, regardless of how the raw materials throughout the inventories are valued."

When the perpetual inventory plan, as distinguished from the periodic inventory, is in use, revaluation of inventories necessarily requires specific bookkeeping adjustments. Both the debit and credit portions of such adjusting entries deserve consideration and discussion.

ALLOCATION OF LOSS. The natural and obvious method of handling the loss due to inventory valuation is to include it as an element of cost of goods sold.

This traditional disposition of the loss is derived from periodic inventory procedure which employs but one adjustment to correct inventory quantities and at the same time assigns

---

[26] Robert H. Montgomery, *Auditing Theory and Practice* (New York, The Ronald Press Company, 1934), pp. 213, 210.

[27] Henry W. Sweeney, *Stabilized Accounting* (New York, Harper & Brothers, 1936), p. 112.

valuation to the inventory on hand with an offsetting debit to cost of sales. This inherited practice was retained following the increased use of perpetual inventories.

As applied to perpetual inventories, however, the adjustment represented a price adjustment only, rather than a price and quantity adjustment, with the result that the correctness of this procedure was seriously questioned.

Is the correction for unrealized price decline a proper element of cost of sales in view of the fact that it has no direct reference to the accounting period in which the offsetting sales were made, and in view of the fact that it is a loss rather than a cost or expense and hence may be thought of as having slight operating significance? Consideration of this question has induced some accountants to favor other methods of treatment, some preferring to show such a revaluation loss as one of the items in "other charges" or in some equivalent non-operating category, others having been willing to give consideration to treatment of such a loss as a surplus adjustment, still others having been satisfied to show the loss statistically, i.e., modifying balance sheet without affecting the profit and loss statement.

Out of 648 companies investigated by the National Industrial Conference Board, 507, or 78%, absorbed in Cost of Goods Sold the revaluation loss caused by conforming to the rule of cost or market; 16% charged this loss against some other section of the profit and loss statement, while the remaining 6% followed some other method.

It may seem rather strange that accountants and business men after years of experience in revaluing inventories have not yet reached agreement as to whether the revaluation loss should be treated as an operating cost, and hence included as part of cost of goods sold, or should be treated as a non-operating loss. The explanation is, perhaps, a simple one. Almost universal in accounting literature and accounting practice there has been insistent and almost exclusive concentration on the balance sheet. Until recently the profit and loss aspect of the adjustment has seemed relatively unimportant. The current concentration of interest upon the profit and loss statement has directed technical attention to this hitherto neglected problem.

To say that it has been neglected completely would be erroneous. A few serious thinkers have long been disturbed by profit and loss distortion and by inaccuracies of profit and loss classification. The neglect of these matters by the majority has, it is logical to believe, been due to balance sheet emphasis induced primarily by the adoption of the financial rather than the operating viewpoint.

Among those who favor including inventory write-downs as part of cost of sales is the American Institute of Accountants.[28] The quotation is in part as follows:

Cost of sales includes all the costs in connection with buying and producing goods sold. Write-downs of inventory to market prices at the end of the period may have a material effect on the percentage of gross profit to sales, and where such write-downs result from general business conditions rather than from the buying or production policies of the company, it may be desirable to show them separately.

This quotation is not entirely clear, since the reference to separate showing may refer to special disclosure in the cost of sales section of the profit and loss statement, or it may refer to reflection of the loss in some section of the profit and loss statement other than cost of sales. The two sentences in conjunction furnish strong intimation that the inventory loss belongs in cost of sales but that if the loss is a large one it should be specially disclosed within that section.

In an article by Sweet[29] the following assertion is made: "If the market value of any materials on hand at the close of the accounting period is below cost, the difference should also be charged as a cost of operation for the period."

While this selected sentence refers to "a cost of operation" instead of "cost of sales," the use of the word "also" ties this sentence with the preceding one in which it is said that "the cost of materials used should be charged into the cost of sales."

In view of the 78% preference for this treatment of revaluation loss, as reported by the National Industrial Conference

[28] *Examination of Financial Statements by Independent Public Accountants* (New York, American Institute of Accountants, January 1936), pp. 31, 32.
[29] Homer N. Sweet, "The Case for a 'Cost or Market' Basis," *N.A.C.A. Bulletin,* December 1, 1937, p. 403.

Board, it hardly seems necessary to include additional quotations. There is, however, a substantial body of authoritative opinion favoring the inclusion of inventory valuation loss in the non-operating category. Canning[30] asserts that "the cost valuation is obviously the figure to employ in establishing the figure for 'cost of goods sold.' The difference between cost and carrying value should be given effect as an independent item of gain (or loss)." In the report of the American Institute Committee on Accounting Terminology,[31] of 1931, it is pointed out that the word cost is sometimes a misnomer and it is asserted that: "This misuse of the word may, however, be offset by stating inventories at cost and the . . . decrease in value in a subsequent section of the profit-and-loss statement." The committee further notes that: "This method is seldom employed, but it produces a clear statement of facts."

Sanders, Hatfield, and Moore[32] suggest that "unequalized declines in the value of current assets should be reflected in [the non-operating section of] the income statement."

The *Accountants' Handbook*[33] says that inventory valuation loss is "non-operating," while Kester[34] thinks it should be shown "separate and apart from the operating results." Elsewhere Kester has favored the idea of parenthetical balance sheet disclosure in lieu of making any balance sheet adjustment.

The reflection of inventory revaluation losses in surplus was mentioned in one of the above quotations. Others have favored this same treatment. Peloubet,[35] for example, has said: "I feel that, if you cannot maintain your inventory on a cost basis, an adjustment from that is no part of the operating account, and that such an adjustment should be examined very carefully to decide whether it may not in fact be a surplus adjustment."

30 John B. Canning, *The Economics of Accountancy* (New York, The Ronald Press Company, 1929), p. 226.
31 *Accounting Terminology* (New York, American Institute Publishing Co., Inc., 1931), p. 90.
32 Sanders, Hatfield, and Moore, *A Statement of Accounting Principles* (New York, American Institute of Accountants, 1938), p. 40.
33 *Accountants' Handbook* (New York, The Ronald Press Company, 1934), p. 40.
34 Roy B. Kester, *Advanced Accounting* (New York, The Ronald Press Company, 1933), p. 149.
35 Maurice E. Peloubet, *Fiftieth Anniversary Celebration* (New York, American Institute of Accountants, 1938), p. 362.

Crandell,[36] while insisting that: "Lower of Cost or Market is the proper basis for inventory valuation ('market' in this phrase being interpreted as the lower of replacement cost and net realizable value)," also maintains that the profit and loss statement should exhibit "the excess of proceeds from sales made in that period over the nearest practicable approach to the actual cost of the goods sold in that period."

To reconcile these two objectives he proposes the following treatment:

1. Do not change the book value of goods on hand because the replacement or the net realizable value has decreased since the goods were purchased or manufactured; on the contrary, leave them on the books at cost.

2. Provide a reserve for the difference between cost and the lower of replacement or net realizable value; and show Cost, Reserve, and Net Value of the inventory on the balance sheet.

3. On the profit and loss statement, determine the net realized income for the period by contrasting the proceeds from goods sold in that period with the cost of such goods, ignoring all intermediate net valuations based on market values.

4. At the very end of the profit and loss statement, apply to the Net Realized Income the adjustment of the Reserve to Reduce Inventory to Market, determining the Portion of Net Realized Income transferred to Surplus.

Judged from any viewpoint, there seems little justification for treating inventory revaluation losses as an element of cost of sales. It is difficult to see how such a loss has operating significance. If accountants believe that an actual adjustment affecting current profit and loss must be made, then such a loss obviously belongs, as Crandell insists, in the non-operating section. This treatment seems preferable to any kind of surplus adjustment. Surplus adjustments may be somewhat logical if they refer to correction of prior period errors. An inventory

36 J. Chester Crandell, "Principles Related to Inventory Valuation," a mimeograph outline of an address to the American Institute of Accountants, Cincinnati, Ohio, September 29, 1938.

revaluation loss, however, can hardly be considered the correction of a prior period error. It can seriously be doubted whether it is a loss at all.

It is a fictitious loss of the same general type as that which is sometimes recognized when fixed assets are written down not because of inadequate prior depreciation but merely for purposes of conservatism or to reduce future period costs.

TREATMENT OF ADJUSTMENT CREDIT. When the rule of cost or market is applied to perpetual inventories involving hundreds or perhaps thousands of individual card records, it would be a burdensome clerical task to adjust each separate card record. For this practical reason, some authorities favor the creation of a reserve the purpose of which is to adjust the inventory controlling accounts without affecting the subsidiary records.

The problem is somewhat similar to that noted in the provision for doubtful accounts where the balance of the controlling account in its relation to subsidiary ledgers is not affected, the provision being taken care of by a valuation reserve. It is not uncommon practice to maintain a standing valuation reserve against inventories to be increased or decreased by annual adjustment. This expedient takes care of the valuation problem from the balance sheet viewpoint but has an additional distorting effect upon profit and loss statements.

The point at issue was given consideration in an article, "The Valuation of Inventory," prepared by the American Institute Special Committee on Inventories and published in *The Journal of Accountancy* of January 1938. The discussion is too lengthy for full quotation but it refers to this reserve method "where, instead of actually writing down items from cost to market, in the inventories of such items, the market differential is carried, or treated, as a reserve (the balance-sheet effect being identical for both, at the beginning)."

The committee observes that these two methods have divergent effects when there is a partial or complete market recovery. The committee notes that "under the 'reserve' method the amount of the differential would be adjusted (through current profit and loss) to whatever the amount of the new differential at the subsequent date would be." This is contrasted with the method of actually scaling down the items in which "there would be no recoupment of any such market recovery until, of course, the items in question were sold."

Subsequently the same committee[37] reported upon replies received in answer to a questionnaire having to do with certain moot inventory considerations. While admitting that the number of replies received was disappointingly small, the committee believed that the careful consideration given to the questions made the replies "a gratifying body of opinion as to the points involved." In addition to "a definite preponderance of thought that 'market' should be construed as including the concept of 'reproductive cost,'" and that this construction should also apply to sundry supplies and repair parts if such items are included in current assets, the replies commented on the adjustable reserve method as against direct write-down of the inventoried items. The following excerpt from the committee's report indicates the viewpoint of those replying.

(a) It was the definite consensus of the replies that the occurrence of the reserve method in actual commercial practice was decidedly the exception rather than the rule; that it did exist as a practice, however, was clearly shown.

(b) Notwithstanding the condition shown in (a), of the replies taking a definite position either pro or con (that is, aside from two replies expressing either no preference or restricting the reserve to special instances only), the majority apparently evinced a favorable attitude toward the reserve method, from the viewpoint of sound theory. Expression was given in several replies to the desirability of specific recognition, as a separate item, of the market adjustment in the profit-and-loss statement.

It is interesting to note from this that the reserve method is not generally popular but that it is favored "from the viewpoint of sound theory."

The use of the inventory reserve by Crandell's method, fed as it is through profit and loss, i.e., the non-operating section of the profit and loss statement, permits cost of sales to be computed

[37] "Report of the Special Committee on Inventories," *The Certified Public Accountant,* October 1938, pp. 11, 12.

on a true cost basis. The alternative of actual adjustment of the inventory items erases true cost, with the result that the apparent cost at the beginning of any period is not cost at all but rather is the lower of cost or market at the end of the preceding period. Under the reserve method, gross profit remains a significant figure based upon actual cost, the distorting effect of the adjustment being noted only in the net profit. In contrast, when the individual items are actually adjusted, both gross profit and net profit are distorted.

The American Institute committee, however, comments that "this divergence in practice relates only to those industries in which substantial amounts of certain inventory items are carried in inventory over a prolonged period."

The reserve method was condemned by Harvey,[38] who took vigorous exception "to the practice which still appears to be existent of valuing the inventory on a disclosed basis and then deducting a reserve. This alters the original basis of valuation and leaves the reader of the statement in doubt as to the basis for the final valuation."

Arguments Favoring Inventory Revaluation.—The subject of inventory revaluation has been so greatly discussed pro and con that the number of quotable opinions is large. A few particularly interesting or particularly authoritative views as noted here may be considered little more than a sample of a much larger body of opinion.

Dicksee,[39] in 1904, included inventories among those assets "which it is the object of the undertaking to convert with all convenient speed into cash." Again, in 1905 Dicksee[40] said that any shrinkage in inventory in intrinsic inventory value "must consequently be regarded as a realised loss."

Montgomery,[41] in the fourth edition of *Auditing Theory and Practice,* thought that the substitution of market for cost because

38 John L. Harvey, "Some Observations on Accounting Practice with Special Reference to Inventory Valuation," *The Journal of Accountancy,* December 1937, p. 450.
39 Lawrence R. Dicksee, *Auditing: A Practical Manual for Auditors* (London, Gee & Company, 1904), p. 311.
40 Lawrence R. Dicksee, *Advanced Accounting* (London, Gee & Company, 1905), p. 5.
41 Robert H. Montgomery, *Auditing Theory and Practice* (New York, The Ronald Press Company, 1934), p. 182.

market is lower than cost "marks the approach to a more scientific and accurate statement."

Sanders,[42] in *The Accounting Review* of September 1934, indicated his belief that the cost or market rule "is a salutary and practicable one, its primary intent being that no inventory shall in any case be valued at more than the probable realized price." This quotation is interesting in its disregard for the common interpretation of market, with particular reference to manufactured goods, as replacement cost. In his book, *Cost Accounting for Control,* Sanders[43] says that the practice has been "attacked as being inconsistent, but it has in practice proved itself to be a pretty sound and reliable procedure."

Bell,[44] in his *Retail Merchandise Accounting,* reaches the somewhat surprising conclusion that: "Consistent use of the basis of cost or market, whichever is lower, should result in correct statement of income."

This quotation confirms the suggestion previously made that distortion or lack of distortion depends upon what viewpoint is adopted. This is somewhat confirmed by Judge Gibson's[45] decision in the case of Aluminum Company of America *v.* United States, which was tried during May 1937. In part the findings read thus: "Such inventories, carried at cost or market, whichever was lower, correctly reflected their net income for that year." While the case in question referred not to merchandise but to certain articles which were not part of Aluminum Company's finished products, the legal viewpoint as to the cost or market rule in relation to income is significant.

Rorem[46] considers the cost or market rule "an attempt to adjust the values to *such amounts as may reasonably be expected to be recoverable in the course of future operations.*" His analogy between depreciation of fixed assets and the rule of cost or market for current assets suggests that both are "attempts

[42] T. H. Sanders, "Reports to Stockholders," *The Accounting Review,* September 1934, p. 210.

[43] T. H. Sanders, *Cost Accounting for Control* (New York, McGraw-Hill Book Company, Inc., 1934), p. 102.

[44] Hermon F. Bell, *Retail Merchandise Accounting* (New York, The Ronald Press Company, 1936), p. 255.

[45] Judge Robert M. Gibson, WD.Pa.

[46] C. Rufus Rorem, "Accounting Theory: A Critique of the Tentative Statement of Accounting Principles," *The Accounting Review,* June 1937, p. 134.

to measure expired values," a thesis which appears indefensible, the former having no reference to market prices but being based upon life expectancy of the fixed assets themselves.

Arguing not so much against the cost or market rule as against strict adoption of the cost basis, Peloubet[47] approaches the problem from the customer's viewpoint, suggesting that the cost method of inventory required the customer to "pay for the mistakes and misfortunes of management and until he did so, the costs of these mistakes and misfortunes should be carried in inventories."

With few exceptions, those who have argued in favor of the rule did so from the balance sheet viewpoint of realizable value with but little concern for the distorting effects upon profit and loss statements. A different method of approach is noted among objectors to the cost or market rule.

Arguments Against Revaluation.—As early as 1904, a Chartered Accountant, John Hyde of Canada, previously quoted, faintly protested against inventory revaluation.

Leo Greendlinger's comment in 1910 has also been quoted.

Esquerré[48] was another early opponent of the cost or market rule. In *The Applied Theory of Accounts,* he stated the case as clearly and convincingly as any who followed him. He summarized his opinion by saying:

To reduce the inventory to a value lower than cost, is to add to the cost of the goods sold during the period; and to raise the inventory to a value greater than cost, is to reduce the cost of the goods during the period. In either case, the result is contrary to the truth.

At the same time that Esquerré was opposing the cost or market rule, Paton[49] was contending that those who argued for the rule were "throwing reason to the winds."

Canning[50] distinguished between the acquisition of more goods and the treatment of goods already acquired. About the

47 Maurice E. Peloubet, "Problems of Present-Day Inventory Valuation," *N.A.C.A. Bulletin,* March 1, 1937, p. 744.
48 Paul-Joseph Esquerré, *The Applied Theory of Accounts* (New York, The Ronald Press Company, 1921), p. 171.
49 W. A. Paton, *Accounting Theory* (New York, The Ronald Press Company, 1922), p. 453.
50 John B. Canning, *The Economics of Accountancy* (New York, The Ronald Press Company, 1929), pp. 219, 225.

atter, he said, nothing could be done. The costs are history. And he adds: "Nor, with respect to the inventory actually held, can anything be done about market. Market has to do with operating cycles not yet begun. Inventory valuation has to do with the finished business." Elsewhere he refers to market decline as "purely a fictitious adverse event," and observes that the rule "is least conservative when conservatism is most needed" and "is most conservative when conservatism is least important."

In *The Accounting Review* for December 1937, Husband[51] said: "the loss resulting from a decline in market values can scarcely be said to be the result of consumption, expiration, or lost usefulness of cost."

Paton,[52] who was opposed to the cost or market rule in his early writings, remained as much opposed in 1938. In his comments on the Sanders, Hatfield, and Moore monograph, he suggests that: "No writer has ever been able to find a single definite point supporting the proposition that 'cost or market, whichever is the lower' is a sound accounting rule." He also suggests that the cost or market rule is "the very antithesis of sound accounting."

Edwin S. Reno, during the 1938 American Institute Convention, made the point that if in connection with the valuation of securities or of inventories one makes downward adjustments to market for purposes of quarterly reports, and independently thereof makes similar adjustments for purposes of annual reports, the sum of the profit for the four quarters will probably not equal the profits for the year.

Summarized, the viewpoints of those who oppose cost or market revaluation generally do so from the profit and loss viewpoint. Many of them refer specifically to its distorting effect. Such distortion is clearly the most obvious objection to the rule in view of the shifted emphasis from the balance sheet to the profit and loss statement.

51 George R. Husband, "Accounting Postulates: An Analysis of the Tentative Statement of Accounting Principles," *The Accounting Review*, December 1937, 390.

52 W. A. Paton, "Comments on 'A Statement of Accounting Principles,'" *The Journal of Accountancy*, March 1938, pp. 202, 203.

Distortion of Profit and Loss.—Dickinson,[53] in his 190
paper, while approving cost or market, observed that an errc
neous basis of valuation, even if conservative and below true
cost, "may result in large and unexpected discrepancies betwee
the Profits shown in different periods."

H. A. Finney, also approving the cost or market rule, mer
tioned its effect upon cost of goods manufactured and cost o
goods sold.

Peloubet[54] showed that the effect of inventory revaluation o
income was "to reduce arbitrarily the profits of the year i
which the operation was performed in an amount equalling th
overstatement of profits in previous years."

References to "an improper picture," "question raised abou
the next period's earnings," and "inflation of earnings" wer
heard at the round-table discussion of inventories at the 193
American Institute Convention.

Bowman[55] asserts that "the effect on the annual profits of th
adjustments from the basis of cost to that of market should b
indicated if practicable."

Substitute for Cost or Market Adjustment.—The doctrin
of disclosure requires the use of parenthetical comments or foo
notes in financial statements for the purpose of supplementin
the limited information supplied by the accounting mechanism
It has repeatedly been suggested and may be suggested agai
that such parenthetical or footnote disclosure be employed t
exhibit alternative inventory values.

The adoption of this plan requires no adjustments of th
accounting records, nor does it distort the comparability c
profit and loss statements, and yet it gives to credit men, inves
ors, or others more information than they otherwise woul
obtain from the balance sheet. The credit man, for exampl
can use either the cost or the revalued inventory figure in deter
mining his current ratio.

53 Arthur Lowes Dickinson, Congress of Accountants, Official Record, 190
World's Fair, St. Louis, under the auspices of the Federation of Societies
Public Accountants in the United States of America, p. 181.
54 Maurice E. Peloubet, "Problems of Present-Day Inventory Valuation
N.A.C.A. Bulletin, March 1, 1937, p. 744.
55 Archibald Bowman, "Reporting upon the Corporate Investment," T.
Journal of Accountancy, May 1938, p. 404.

This is no new or radical suggestion. In fact, it has been well and authoritatively sponsored. In 1929 Canning inferred this possibility.

In 1933 Kester[56] suggested that the accountant

carry as the significant figure, in both the balance sheet and the profit and loss statement, the cost value of the merchandise inventory. To give the additional information desired, the net cash realizable value may be carried parenthetically in an inner column on the face of the balance sheet or in a footnote to it. By this means, the net cash realizable value is not brought into the books, being carried as a memorandum on the balance sheet, and no reference is made to it in the profit and loss statement.

In the 1934 edition of Montgomery's[57] *Auditing Theory and Practice,* he comments: "there has never been any objection to making note of market values in balance sheets when they were greater or less than balance sheet or book values."

In the June 1936 issue of *The Accounting Review,* the Executive Committee of the American Accounting Association[58] published its twenty postulates, of which number 7 is particularly pertinent to this discussion: "If values other than unamortized costs are to be quoted they should be expressed in financial statements only as collateral notations for informative purposes."

In the August 1936 issue of *The Journal of Accountancy,* the American Institute Special Committee on Inventories[59] suggested "a parenthetical disclosure in the balance-sheet of the current replacement value of the inventory, whether such value were greater or less than the stated inventory value."

In the December 1937 issue of *The Journal of Accountancy,* Harvey[60] noted that: "Published statements indicate a growing

[56] Roy B. Kester, *Advanced Accounting* (New York, The Ronald Press Company, 1933), p. 150.

[57] Robert H. Montgomery, *Auditing Theory and Practice* (New York, The Ronald Press Company, 1934), p. 203.

[58] Executive Committee of the American Accounting Association, "A Tentative Statement of Accounting Principles Affecting Corporate Reports," *The Accounting Review,* June 1936, p. 189.

[59] Special Committee on Inventories of the American Institute of Accountants, "Valuation of Inventories," *The Journal of Accountancy,* August 1936, p. 130.

[60] John L. Harvey, "Some Observations on Accounting Practice with Special Reference to Inventory Valuation," *The Journal of Accountancy,* December 1937, p. 447.

practice of showing parenthetically the value of the inventory at an alternative method of valuation."

During 1936 and 1938 other voices were raised in favor of this or equivalent procedure. Such writers as Samuel J. Broad, Arthur N. Lorig, and Edward A. Kracke discussed it. A bulletin of the National Association of Cost Accountants intimated its desirability, while the American Petroleum Institute's Committee on Uniform Methods of Oil Accounting directly recommended parenthetical disclosure "where the market value of the inventory is less than that carried in the balance-sheet."

This seems to be a practical and acceptable substitute, and since it is authoritatively supported, it is quite possible that inertia may be overcome and that not too long a time will elapse before the cost or market rule is abandoned. As has been pointed out, there are numerous accounting practices which have some distorting effect upon profit and loss statements but there seems to be no accounting practice as thoroughly illogical and unnecessary, practically or theoretically, as this practice of revaluing inventories at the lower of cost or market.

There is some reason to believe that the new emphasis upon the importance of consistency may stamp further use of this device as improper. Clearly, accountants would be on firmer ground in combating other unsound accounting practices if they took a definite stand against this rule.

CHAPTER 27

COMPARISON OF INVENTORY METHODS

Various attempts, some formal and others informal, have been made to compare methods of inventory valuation and their effects.

Some of these attempts are illuminating and the comparisons they offer indicate that inventory methods may affect profits in different ways. Generally the comparisons have no further significance, due to the necessity for assumptions with respect to price levels, sales volumes, and inventory quantities.

By adopting one set of assumptions in the comparison of the last-in, first-out method with the first-in, first-out method, for example, a different conclusion may be reached from that which would result had a different set of assumptions been made. For this reason these comparative studies should be interpreted broadly. By reviewing them, however, it should be possible to gain a general idea as to the characteristics of the inventory methods.

Some of the comparisons which have been offered by accounting writers do not even include assumed figures. Rather they may be taken as mere expressions of opinion based, it is hoped, upon actual comparisons and studies.

Opinion Type of Comparisons.—A good example of the opinion type of comparison is that emanating from the American Institute Special Committee on Inventories,[1] in which the cost of sales resulting from the last-in, first-out method is compared with current costs of the fiscal period. The quotation reads:

... let us assume sales to have exceeded the purchases for the period; to the extent of such excess, the aggregate cost of sales will be influenced

1 Special Committee on Inventories of the American Institute of Accountants, "Valuation of Inventories," *The Journal of Accountancy*, August 1938, pp. 130, 131.

by the amount thereof representing the amount regarded as taken out of the initial inventory, charged to cost of sales at the prices in such inventory, which might vary considerably from the current costs of the fiscal period. Initial inventories, either small or large, relatively, in point of quantities, and low priced or high priced, relatively, in point of valuation, would thus exert an influence on such comparative operating results.

Based upon the assumption stated, disagreement is noted with another Institute publication, *Examination of Financial Statements by Independent Public Accountants,*[2] which sets forth that:

. . . it may not be a matter of great importance whether cost of goods on hand is determined on the theory that the first goods in are the first goods to go out, or that the last goods in are the first goods to go out.

In a round-table discussion at the 1937 American Institute Convention, Peloubet[3] made a general comparison between the last-in, first-out method and the base-stock method. Granting the first "a little sounder theoretical basis," Peloubet concluded that "in essence, they are the same."

In some instances a comparison is offered without indicating exactly what methods are being compared. Thus, Paton[4] refers to the last-in, first-out method as one which "represents nothing more nor less than a major device for equalizing earnings, to avoid showing in the periodic reports the severe fluctuations which are inherent in certain business fields." That method which would show the severe fluctuations is not specifically named in this quotation.

There is, therefore, a comparison between a named method and some unnamed method which may be assumed, however, to be the actual cost method, the first-in, first-out method, or the weighted-average cost method.

2 *Examination of Financial Statements by Independent Public Accountants* (New York, American Institute of Accountants, January 1936), p. 3.

3 Maurice E. Peloubet, *Fiftieth Anniversary Celebration* (New York, American Institute of Accountants, 1938), p. 348.

4 W. A. Paton, "Comments on 'A Statement of Accounting Principles,'" *The Journal of Accountancy,* March 1938, p. 199.

Data Type of Comparisons.—Arthur[5] provides a comparison of the "identical company" type which offers some interesting possibilities.

In one column he shows reported profits of a large group of business organizations and in an adjoining column shows those same profits adjusted to exclude what he refers to as "inventory gains or losses," but which appear to represent the differences plus or minus in the cost of replacing inventories.

The figures (in millions of dollars) which have been adapted from his article are as follows:

Year	Business Profits or Losses Unadjusted	Business Profits or Losses Excluding Inventory Gains or Losses
1929	+8,552	+9,264
1930	+ 912	+5,243
1931	−3,718	− 410
1932	−6,193	−4,673
1933	− 881	−3,321
1934	+1,257	− 874
1935	+3,382	+2,597

This represents a more legitimate type of comparison than that commonly used since it relates to a group of actual business figures.

COST, COST OR MARKET, AND BASIC STOCK. Commonly comparisons are of the fully assumed type which are used by May.[6]

His method assumes the simple case of an apple vendor purchasing apples by the crate and selling them singly, using certain assumed prices and price changes. By calculating inventories according to three different methods, he was able to show a schedule of profits for each of four days—profits which varied considerably from one another in spite of the fact that the aggregate profit for all of the four days was the same.

His tabulation of the three methods and the profits for the four days is shown here:

5 Henry B. Arthur, "Inventory Profits in the Business Cycle," *The American Economic Review*, March 1938, p. 36.
6 George O. May, "Influence of the Depression on the Practice of Accountancy," *The Journal of Accountancy*, November 1932, p. 339.

	First day	Second day	Third day	Fourth day	Total
On the basis of stating the inventory at latest cost, the profit was	$3.00	$3.50	$2.25	$2.00	$10.75
On the basis of inventorying at cost or market, whichever was lower	3.00	3.50	2.00	2.25	10.75
On the basic stock method (that is, valuing stock at a uniform price)	3.00	3.25	2.50	2.00	10.75

FIRST-IN, FIRST-OUT; LAST-IN, FIRST-OUT; COST OR MARKET. Barr[7] attempted by a simple hypothetical case to show three methods of inventory valuation and their effect on profits.

He assumed that a company bought 120 units in the first year at $1 per unit. The second year 100 units were purchased at $2 each, the third year 100 units were purchased at $3 each, the fourth year 100 units were purchased at $2, and the fifth year 100 units were purchased at $1. Each year 100 units were sold at a 50% mark-up on the purchase price of that year.

Using these assumptions Barr compared the first-in, first-out method, the last-in, first-out method, and the cost or market method. Based upon his assumptions he obtained the following results (rearranged from his table):

	First Year	Second Year	Third Year	Fourth Year	Fifth Year	Total
Inventory, December 31:						
First-in, First-out . . .	$ 20	$ 40	$ 60	$ 40	$ 20	
Cost* or Market	20	40	40	20	20	
Last-in, First-out	20	20	20	20	20	
Cost of Sales:						
First-in, First-out . . .	100	180	280	220	120	$ 900
Cost* or Market	100	180	300	220	100	900
Last-in, First-out	100	200	300	200	100	900
Sales	150	300	450	300	150	1,350
Profit:						
First-in, First-out . . .	50	120	170	80	30	450
Cost* or Market	50	120	150	80	50	450
Last-in, First-out	50	100	150	100	50	450

* In the "cost or market" classification, cost is defined as "first-in, first-out."

7 Andrew Barr, in his comments on "A Statement of Accounting Principles," *The Journal of Accountancy*, April 1938, p. 321.

First-In, First-Out, and Cost or Market. Davis[8] compared the effect of three different inventory methods, using the same assumed figures for eight accounting periods.

The following table of closing inventory values is adapted from his more elaborate one:

CLOSING INVENTORY VALUES

Period	Cost First-in, First-out	Lower of Cost or Market Merchandise Account	Double Entry
1	$189.50	$189.50	$160.50
2	180.00	180.00	165.00
3	167.00	167.00	159.50
4	140.00	140.00	140.00
5	131.00	131.00	131.00
6	142.00	127.50	127.50
7	161.50	139.75	139.75
8	196.00	150.00	150.00

Some interest attaches to the figures in the last two columns, reflecting as they do the difference between a periodic and a perpetual inventory.

In the next to the last column Davis has used the "merchandise account method," which implies the use of a periodic inventory. In the last column he has applied the "double entry cost method" in which the inventory, once adjusted, is carried at the adjusted value until it has been worked out on the first-in, first-out basis regardless of subsequent market price increases.

COMPARISON OF NET PROFIT AND LOSS ACCOUNTS
UNDER CERTAIN VARIOUS ACCOUNTING METHODS
(Losses are shown in italics)

	PERIODS							
	1	2	3	4	5	6	7	8
Cost or Market—Double Entry Method . . .	$11.25	$18.75	$26.25	$33.75	$26.25	$ *3.75*	$15.50	$37.00
Cost or Market—Merchan- dise Account Method .	40.25	4.75	18.75	26.25	26.25	3.75	*15.50*	37.00
Cost—First-in, First-out Method	*5.75*	4.75	18.75	26.25	26.25	10.75	10.75	12.75
Last-in, First-out Method (starting with market) .	3.75	5.25	7.25	10.75	5.25	3.75	3.75	3.75

8 Albion R. Davis, "Inventory Valuation and Business Profits—The Case for a 'Stabilized Basis,'" *N.A.C.A. Bulletin,* December 1, 1937, p. 394.

FIRST-IN, FIRST-OUT; LAST-IN, FIRST-OUT; COST OR MAR-
KET.   The same author provides an elaborate table showing the
effects of different inventory methods upon net profits. Some
of the more significant figures are summarized on page 467.

COST AND COST OR MARKET.   Based on certain assumed
data, Paton[9] presented tables of differences in operating income
between the cost basis and the cost or market basis. These have
been adapted as follows:

	Sales	Net Income on Basis of Cost	Cost or Market	Deviation from Cost Basis
1st period . . .	$ 80,000	$40,000	$20,000	—50%
2nd period . .	60,000	30,000	50,000	+66
3rd period . . .	100,000	50,000	35,000	—30

FIRST-IN, FIRST-OUT; LAST-IN, FIRST-OUT; NORMAL
STOCK; AND AVERAGE COST.   In a bulletin entitled "Prevailing
Practices in Inventory Valuation," published by the National
Industrial Conference Board, February 1938, four common
methods of inventory valuation were compared first during
a year of rising prices and then during a year of decreasing
prices.

During the year of rising prices the cost of sales provided
by these four methods—based, of course, upon the assumptions
made—were as follows:

First-in, First-out Method $20,900
Cumulative Average Cost Method   23,352
Normal Stock Method   25,900
Last-in, First-out Method   26,300

During the subsequent period of declining prices, costs of
sales based upon each of these four methods were as follows:

First-in, First-out Method $29,100
Cumulative Average Cost Method   25,032
Normal Stock Method   26,100
Last-in, First-out Method   25,700

If the inventories during this period of declining prices had
been adjusted to conform to the cost or market rule, cost of sales
for the first two methods listed would have been increased some-

9 W. A. Paton, "Comments on 'A Statement of Accounting Principles,' " *The
Journal of Accountancy*, March 1938, p. 204.

what, although no such increase would have been observed for the last two methods.

The method adopted by the National Industrial Conference Board of separating the analysis into two tables, one for rising prices and the other for declining prices, is excellent, i.e., it is from the viewpoint of changing prices that inventory valuation methods should be examined.

It is interesting to observe that, during the period of rising prices, the cost of sales was lowest and the net profit accordingly highest where the first-in, first-out method was used. This, of course, is exactly the complaint which has always been registered against this method. The method which showed the highest cost of sales and hence the lowest profit was the last-in, first-out method, although the normal stock method ran it a close second.

During the period of declining prices, the method which produced the smallest cost of sales and hence the largest profit was the cumulative average stock method, although the last-in, first-out method gave nearly the same result. The first-in, first-out method showed the largest cost of sales and hence the smallest net profit.

To those who believe in profit stabilization, these figures must be convincing. To those who disbelieve in stabilization of enterprises which are inherently unstable, these figures offer evidence of net profit distortion.

If average cost is adopted as a standard from which to measure deviations, then cost of sales as reported by the last-in, first-out method is incorrect by nearly $3,000, or approximately 13%, during the period of rising prices. During the period of declining prices, and still using the average cost method as a standard, no great difference is noted between it and the last-in, first-out method. The greatest deviation is noted in the case of the first-in, first-out method which is indicated as $4,068, or approximately 16%.

Such studies are valuable even though based upon arbitrary assumptions. It must be admitted that the adoption of average cost as the standard for comparison is also arbitrary and would not receive the endorsement of those who believe in other methods.

The preference for average cost as compared to the first-in, first-out method is, of course, based upon the viewpoint expressed by Montgomery and previously quoted to the effect that: "Whenever there is a mingling, or a possible mingling, of goods or materials, the cost prices also are mingled."

REPRODUCTION COST AND FIRST-IN, FIRST-OUT. Not as elaborate as the analysis made by the National Industrial Conference Board, but nevertheless interesting because of its simplicity and clarity, is the comparison set forth in *The Journal of Accountancy* of August 1936, by the American Institute Special Committee on Inventories.

The illustration is based upon certain assumptions, namely, that a wagon-maker has one wagon in stock costing him $50, the selling price of which is indicated to be $65, in order to yield a profit of $15. Prior to making the sale, the wagon-maker learns of a material price increase which will add $10 to the replacement cost of the wagon. As a result, the wagon-maker changes his selling price from $65 to $75. He sells the wagon and builds a new one costing $60. According to the American Institute Committee,[10] the advocate of "reproduction cost of sales" would say to the wagon-maker:

> The profit you made is $15.00; and the proper inventory price for the present wagon you have in stock is $50.00. That is the number of dollars of your capital invested in your stock in trade; the only change that you have effectively realized in that investment is the substitution for one wagon of another wagon exactly like it—the same wagon in fact except only as regards physical identity.

On the other hand, according to the committee, the advocate of the first-in, first-out would say to the wagon-maker:

> Your profit is $25.00, although you may have only $15.00 more in cash to show for it. The other $10.00 is contained in the increased cost and value of the new wagon, $60.00 as against the old one at $50.00. You must not fail to recognize and to give effect to the price level change.

Continuing the illustration, the committee assumed that the price level had dropped back to the original status and that the

10 Special Committee on Inventories of the American Institute of Accountants, "Valuation of Inventories," *The Journal of Accountancy*, August 1938, p. 127.

wagon which had cost $60 was sold for $65 and replaced by one which cost $50. Based upon this assumption the committee asserts that "under either procedure, the latest wagon will be inventoried at $50.00. The profit on the second transaction, however, will have been $15.00, according to the 'reproduction cost of sales' advocate, or $5.00 according to the 'first in, first out' advocate. The aggregate profits on the two transactions, of course, will be the same in either case, but the periodic distribution will differ."

Conclusions as to Inventory Valuation.—Continuing the reference to the committee's illustration, the point at issue between the two schools of thought, as is so often the case, depends upon the viewpoint. It is plausible to argue that if a wagon is sold and immediately is replaced with another wagon, and if the two wagons are identical, the valuation symbols used should also be identical.

Those who oppose this view think that the analogy is a false one. Believing strongly that the first wagon on hand is merely a deferred charge against future income, they regard the first wagon episode as closed when the sale is made. They are not able to see that this transaction has any relation to the acquisition of a new wagon at any price, whether lower or higher, since they hold that the acquisition of a new wagon is the first step in a new transaction, i.e., that it is deliberately entered into in the expectation of a future profit and that the increased cost thereof is taken into consideration at the time the decision is made to acquire it.

They contend that the new wagon would not be acquired at the higher cost without some assurance or expectation that it too could be sold for a profit at some future time.

REPLACEMENT VS. SEPARATE VENTURES. One school of thought thinks in terms of replacement, the other in terms of separate ventures, and it is perhaps for this reason that the two are unreconcilable.

One thing seems theoretically, if not practically, certain, namely, that the sale of the first wagon is not necessarily followed by the acquisition of the second one. It may be argued that unless this occurs the wagon manufacturer will go out of business or that he may have to shift from manufacturing wagons to manufacturing chairs.

These possibilities are matters for business judgment to be decided by business men on the basis of all the facts at their command, and have little or nothing to do with accounting.

INFLUENCE OF EXPERIENCE.   One difficulty in connection with differences of opinion of this kind may be due to variations in the industrial experience of the accountants arguing. Long contact with certain types of industries and thorough familiarity with their characteristics may unconsciously sway an accountant toward one viewpoint or the other.

The accountant familiar with the petroleum industry, in which it is necessary to carry constant stocks of identical products, cannot be expected to view inventory valuation in the same way as another familiar perhaps with the retail book business or with style merchandise in department stores, where every purchase is often the beginning of a new business venture and where the decision to buy or not to buy any particular item of materials or products requires conscious recognition of the fact that inventory is indeed a deferred charge to future income.

VARIATIONS IN PERIODIC PROFITS.   In view of the great variation in periodic net profits which results from the employment of different valuation methods it is difficult to take the middle ground that any of the methods consistently employed is proper. Rather it seems better frankly to recognize that certain types of business enterprises are naturally handicapped by their inventory characteristics and that no change in the method of figuring can in reality change the amount of profit made.

Admitting for purposes of argument that the cumulative profit reported by the constant use of any of the various methods over a period of years may be the same, nevertheless in modern economy periodic profits have assumed greater importance than aggregate profits for the entire stretch between the inception and the final termination of an enterprise.

INVENTORIES AS DEFERRED CHARGES.   Those who favor viewing inventory as a deferred charge to future income can see no more reason for departure from the cost basis for that deferred charge than for changing the figures for labor or any other item of expense or cost which is immediately absorbed.

The only difference they recognize between a deferred charge to future income and an immediate charge to income is the element of periodic allocation.

It must be concluded, therefore, that actual cost, as nearly as actual cost can be determined, represents the proper basis for recording all deferred charges to future income, including inventories, and that any plan which departs from the actual cost basis has deception, usually innocent, as its intention regardless of whether the stabilization is rationalized as "good business policy," "a measure for tax relief," "a method of smoothing the business cycle," or "a device for helping management to avoid errors of judgment caused by alternating periods of heavy profits or losses."

CHAPTER 28

ACQUIREMENT AND VALUATION OF FIXED ASSETS

Often equal in importance to inventories in relation to profit and loss, the item of fixed plant assets, usually the most important of non-current assets, requires special consideration. This chapter provides a general survey of fixed asset problems, while Chapters 29, 30, and 31 offer a more detailed treatment of the more important topics.

In business entities, as contrasted with some governmental and charitable organizations, the cost of fixed assets must be allocated to those accounting periods benefiting from their use. This view has been so often advanced by eminent authorities that it hardly seems necessary to support it at any great length.

Referring specifically to depreciation of buildings, Canning[1] says:

By the end of the tenure of the building it makes no statistical difference in the balance sheet whether the outlay was treated as a single deduction from gross income when the outlay occurred or as a series of annual deduction items the summation of which is equal to outlay.

Mason,[2] whose *Principles of Public-Utility Depreciation* is generally regarded as authoritative, says: "the asset account may well be thought of as a deferred charge to operations or a prepaid operating expense, similar in a great many respects to prepaid rent or insurance—charged to the operations of the period in which the service is rendered."

Sanders, Hatfield, and Moore[3] assert that fixed assets "are

1 John B. Canning, *The Economics of Accountancy* (New York, The Ronald Press Company, 1929), p. 129.
2 Perry Mason, *Principles of Public-Utility Depreciation* (Chicago, American Accounting Association, 1937), p. 13.
3 Sanders, Hatfield, and Moore, *A Statement of Accounting Principles* (New York, American Institute of Accountants, 1938), p. 59.

really in the nature of a deferred charge against the future income they will help to produce."

Valuation of Fixed Assets.—The concept of fixed asset cost as equivalent to a deferred charge is helpful in that it tends to simplify problems of valuation. Obviously, no practical advantage can be gained by valuing a deferred charge at any figure other than actual cost, if such cost is practicably obtainable.

All of the arguments as to writing up or writing down fixed asset values appear unrealistic when the values are no longer regarded as important from the balance sheet viewpoint but rather as prepayments the benefit of which is chargeable to future periods. Certain exceptions, to be discussed later, have been urged by some writers but these exceptions are based upon legal rather than economic considerations.

Attempts have been made to exclude land from this deferred charge concept. It is commonly held that land does not depreciate. Generally this is true, nevertheless for consistency it is well to think of land as representing a deferred charge over an indeterminate or perpetual term. It is, of course, true that land is ordinarily not subject to wear and tear or that type of depreciation which results solely from the passage of time.

Other Non-current Assets.—Fixed plant assets represent only one classification in the larger group of non-current assets, all of which are in the nature of deferred charges to future income.

This larger group includes intangible assets such as patents, copyrights, organization expense, franchises and goodwill, and various items of prepaid expense. The cost allocation of these items has been referred to as depreciation, amortization, depletion, exhaustion, etc. Fundamentally all these terms refer to the same general phenomenon. Practically, each has reference to a particular kind of non-current asset.

Amortization is a term generally reserved for use with intangible assets. Depletion and exhaustion are often used interchangeably, depletion having specific reference to mines and oil wells, exhaustion being sometimes used in connection with overcropped agricultural lands.

Depreciation generally refers to tangible fixed assets.

There is considerable difference in the accuracy of forecasting as between amortization, depreciation, and depletion. Amortization can often be determined with considerable accuracy, i.e., the number of periods over which the charge is deferable is often known. Depreciation provisions are generally less accurate, while the determination of a proper provision for depletion of oil wells and mines is, as Sanders[4] has pointed out, "more difficult than the provision for depreciation, since the physical facts are more indeterminate."

Depreciation an Operating Cost.—Prior to the time when income taxation became a serious business factor, depreciation was often treated in an erratic manner. During prosperous years substantial depreciation was often provided and during unprofitable years the depreciation schedule was adjusted downward.

In some instances there is reason to believe that depreciation provisions were juggled for the purpose of misinforming stockholders and prospective investors. No doubt a certain amount of this still goes on, but the Treasury Department, for obvious reasons, has been insistent upon reasonable and consistent depreciation plans. Accounting literature of twenty years ago was filled with arguments supporting the contention that depreciation is an operating cost, a fact which few deny today.[5]

Hill[6] has advanced a reason in support of depreciation as a cost in his assertion that it "takes the place of some labor cost, which would have to be incurred in the absence of the plant units." He carries this analogy further, saying:

4 T. H. Sanders, "Reports to Stockholders," *The Accounting Review,* September 1934, p. 215.

5 A current exposition of the opposite view is noted in the following quotation: "As previously stated, the problem of whether to include depreciation among costs and operating expenses, where it unquestionably belongs, is one of expediency. If it is more conservative *not* to include it as an element of cost, of course, as inventories are thus placed on a lower cost basis. The disposition of financial analysts to point to the depletion and depreciation provision in a company's published report with fingers trembling with emotion has caused most large companies to lump the entire provision as an income deduction. Any attempt to include it in costs initially, throughout all the operating divisions, will result in considerable confusion when the time comes to eliminate it from cost of goods sold and inventories, in order to state it as a separate item on the income statement." Raymond Walter McKee, *Handbook of Petroleum Accounting* (New York, Harper & Brothers, 1938), p. 311.

6 Horace Hill, *Practical Aspects of Depreciation and Obsolescence* (New York, American Management Association, 1938), p. 27.

... the detail depreciation system permits the allocation of each plant unit to the particular operation which it serves, in much the same way as an employee's time card is marked with the work in which he is engaged, so that the payroll may be correctly distributed among the various cost accounts.

Methods of Asset Acquisition.—Adopting the convention that fixed asset value is in the nature of a deferred charge, and that such a deferred charge should be established at cost whenever cost practicably can be determined, represents the simple theory underlying valuation and depreciation.

In practice this simple concept may be greatly modified by various complicating factors. Substantial fixed assets are not always acquired by actual cash purchase. Important problems of fixed asset valuation arise when purchases are made with securities, when one asset is exchanged for another asset, when assets must be reconstructed or renovated, or when for one reason or another fixed assets are donated.

When fixed assets are acquired in exchange for the purchaser's own securities, the initial value of such assets is measured by the offsetting liability created by the issuance of such securities. From the entity viewpoint, no other basis of fixed asset valuation is logical despite the fact that the property for which a million dollars par value of common stock is exchanged could have been bought for $600,000 cash. Such knowledge has caused qualms to those whose interest centers on balance sheet values. To the entity, however, the creation of a million dollars in liabilities, even though it be a capital stock liability, is equivalent for record purposes to the disbursement of a million dollars in cash. The million-dollar valuation of the fixed assets is not only logical but, from this viewpoint, imperative. The fact that the practical conservative accountant would disagree violently with this concept is, of course, important from all viewpoints save that of developing a logical pattern of accounting theory.

The exchange of one asset for another involves a problem which is substantially the same as the valuation problem of trade-ins so often noted in the purchase of office equipment, automobiles, agricultural machinery, or household devices.

From the general income-tax viewpoint, subject to certain

exceptions, no profit or loss arises from exchanges of like for like. From the accounting point of view, authorities are not in agreement. Bacas, Madden, and Rosenkampff intimate, in *Auditing Procedure,* that an accounting profit or loss is made and this view is somewhat confirmed by the *Accountants' Handbook*[7] in the following words:

> An exchange of a farm for an apartment building, for example, is equivalent to the sale of the farm and the purchase of the city property with the proceeds. From a commercial point of view the book value of the farm in such a case should be closed out and the fair market value of the other property (what it would have cost on a cash or equivalent basis) substituted, the difference being gain or loss.

As a practical matter, however, the *Accountants' Handbook*[7] adds that "it is advisable for the taxpayer in general to keep his books on a basis conforming to the income tax regulations in this connection."

Kester[8] takes the definite stand that: "The trading of a fixed asset for another fixed asset is not ordinarily to be considered a profit-making exchange."

He[8] explains the common practice of applying the "profit" resulting from an exchange as a credit against the newly acquired fixed asset on the theory that the item is of the nature of a "discount from the stated price." He adds, however, that if a newly acquired fixed asset has a definite list price or if the price would not have been lower on a cash or other outright purchase basis, an accounting profit has been made. Illustrating his point by the exchange of an old truck for a new one, the profit, he asserts, "is explainable either as the result of a good bargain or because the old truck had been depreciated too rapidly, some portion of its reserve account being really a reserve of profits at the time of trade-in."

Problems arise when a fixed asset is partially or entirely constructed by the employees of a company. The actual direct labor and material costs are, of course, transferred to and become a part of the fixed asset valuation. The difficulty of valuation,

---

[7] *Accountants' Handbook* (New York, The Ronald Press Company, 1934), p. 489.
[8] Roy B. Kester, *Advanced Accounting* (New York, The Ronald Press Company, 1933), pp. 493, 335.

discussed later in this chapter, has to do with the allocation of overhead expense to the construction work.

Occasionally fixed assets are donated to an enterprise. Often such a donation is made by a group of business men seeking to attract new industries to a town. Sometimes the donation is conditional, but if an outright donation is made, it is common practice to have the property appraised, the offsetting credit not being considered a profit but rather as a type of capital surplus. This is the view expressed by Kester and by other authorities.

The amount of profit actually made is not determinable and will not be determinable except through depreciation or until the donated property is sold. The valuation established for such donated property is, therefore, only a symbol for record keeping purposes and the offsetting credit representing an indeterminate amount of unrealized income is correspondingly a symbol.

A similar problem referring to the donation of cash would result in a true accounting profit, albeit of an extraordinary and non-recurring type. The real differences between the donation of cash and the donation of a fixed asset are to be found in the definiteness of valuation and in realization.

When the donation is conditional there is no value in it, title not having passed. It may, however, be desirable to assign a value to the property, always to be offset for balance sheet purposes by a valuation account the effect of which is complete cancellation.

The problem of accretions has already been discussed in Chapter 8. In so far as fixed assets are concerned, accretion is seldom noted except in the case of growing timber. Theoretically it also exists in the case of growing crops, but as these are usually harvested and realized upon annually, the accounting problem is thereby simplified. From the strict accounting viewpoint, accretion represents an increase in fixed asset value which on the charge and discharge entity theory should be reflected in the accounting equation. Indefiniteness of valuation and lack of realization forbid treating the offsetting credit as an accounting profit. Tax considerations are also important, accretion not being considered taxable income except indirectly under the so-called "farm price" method of inventorying.

Hire-Purchase Contracts.—Among the more puzzling problems referring to asset acquisition is that which is derived from hire-purchase agreements. This particular type of contract is often used in order to simplify the sale of products which the purchaser may be somewhat reluctant to buy outright. Dwellings are sometimes contracted for on this basis and the hire-purchase agreement is a favorite device to aid in the marketing of new equipment. The manufacturer of a typesetting machine for which a sales price of $1,500 has been established may overcome sales resistance by providing that the customer may have the machine installed and may use it for a few months at a rental of perhaps $30 a month. At the expiration of this trial period, the customer may make one of two choices—(1) he may turn the machine back to the seller and consider the monthly rental payments as expense; or (2) he may decide to buy the machine, in which event all of the monthly payments already made apply against the purchase price of $1,500.

If the hire-purchase transaction takes place shortly before the end of a fiscal year and the trial period does not end until some time during the next following fiscal year, an interesting accounting question presents itself. Shall the machine be shown as an asset at $1,500, together with an offsetting liability of the same amount less the monthly rentals paid to December 31, or shall the machine not appear at all on the balance sheet, the monthly rentals being treated as expense?

Is this influenced by the fact that the legal title to the machine rests with the selling company? Canning[9] thinks not. Using a truck acquired under a hire-purchase contract for his illustration, he says that: "The situs of legal title is not determining," and he continues: "no public accountant will hesitate to list the truck as an asset of the vendee nor to list the notes (or other form of promise to pay) as the vendor's asset."

Canning has, however, assumed that notes are given in payment for the truck, a condition which does not exist in a strict hire-purchase transaction. Fackler's[10] criticism of this is quoted in part:

9 John B. Canning, *The Economics of Accountancy* (New York, The Ronald Press Company, 1929), pp. 14, 15.
10 Clarence W. Fackler, personal letter of May 27, 1938.

It seems that Professor Canning in his illustration of a hire-purchase contract assumes that the vendee signs promissory notes or incurs a liability on open account. This is an assumption which is questionable if title does not pass to the vendee. If title does pass, the point of the illustration is lost . . . usually hire-purchase contracts do not require an enforceable claim against the vendee in the form of a promissory note or an open book account. And, inasmuch as the title does not pass, such contracts contain an agreement that the object must be returned if the rent payments are defaulted. The object, which is purchased under such a hire-purchase agreement, is not an asset until the agreement is fulfilled. In my opinion, the careful accountant would not show it as an asset.

Fackler's view seems to be sound. While on December 31 the vendee may intend to acquire the asset, there is no commitment that he will do so. He may in fact have such unpleasant experiences in the use of that asset during the following January and February that he may change his mind. Assets cannot, it appears, be created merely by intent. It is probable that this same opinion is held by the Securities and Exchange Commission[11] as indicated by the following quotation: "We have previously held that it is not in accord with accepted accounting practice to set up as an asset the full value of property upon which the registrant has an option, even though payments may have been made under the option."

While not strictly pertinent to the subject matter of this chapter, the treatment of a hire-purchase transaction from the vendor's viewpoint may hold some interest. How should the rentals paid by a vendee to the vendor be treated on the vendor's books, assuming that the vendee's option has not yet been exercised? This may be in part a matter of intent or probability, according to a special supplement of the Alexander Tax News Letter of February 18, 1938, which reads as follows: "The rule is now well settled that if it is *highly probable* that the rent will be ultimately applied as *purchase price* then it is not reportable as income but as recovery of capital."

One may well ask how the vendor shall ascertain what is highly probable. Regardless of the degree of probability, it hardly seems possible that any criticism could attach to the pro-

11 Securities and Exchange Commission, Release 1665.

cedure followed by Automatic Voting Machine Corporation, which has been explained by Cranstoun[12] as follows:

> Among the liabilities an item, machine rentals, appears with the explanation following, "Applicable against selling price at option of lessees." The auditors' certificate includes this explanation: "Lessees of voting machines under rental agreements have options to purchase the machines and apply the rentals paid against the company's selling price. Rentals received and receivable under these agreements are carried in machine-rentals account in the balance-sheet until the lessees indicate their election either to purchase or to return the machines."

Methods of Fixed Asset Valuation.—Valuation of fixed assets at cost may be said to include costs established on other than a cash outlay basis, thus including those cases where one asset is exchanged for another asset or where an asset is acquired for buyer's own securities.

The valuation thus established has a definite significance as a symbol of chargeability and as a deferred charge to future income but otherwise has little or no meaning.

PURCHASE OF MIXED ASSETS. The problem involved in a purchase of mixed assets has already been noted as a variation of joint-cost. Such a situation calls imperatively for appraisal in order to establish the proportional values of the components of the purchase. These appraisal values may be used as the basis for calculations by which the separate assets may be booked at actual cost. More often, however, the appraisal figures themselves are used. When, as generally happens, the appraisal figures are in excess of cost, a credit to appreciation surplus is indicated.

APPRAISALS. The use of appraisals is not limited to mixed-asset purchases. Some years ago it was rather common for companies with assets which appeared to be undervalued to engage appraisers to establish new values based upon cost of reproducing the fixed assets at the time of the appraisal, less depreciation calculated from the date of actual acquisition to the date of the appraisal. Overly optimistic appraisals were not

---

[12] William D. Cranstoun in "The Commentator," *The Journal of Accountancy,* March 1938, p. 248.

uncommon and the resulting write-ups of value were sometimes rather extravagant. Such write-ups are no longer popular owing to increased realization of the fact that they carry with them increased depreciation requirements, the effect upon ultimate profit or loss being nil.

Where original records of asset acquisition are missing or are obscure, or where it is desirable to establish insurance data, appraisal services are often necessary. In general, however, accountants are apt to hold about the same opinion as that of Canning,[13] who expressed his skepticism of most appraisals and asserted that the appraisal formula "may be a good working rule in damage suits; it is absurd as a sole rule of going-concern valuation."

ABORIGINAL COST. Mention should be made of the public utility concept which is sometimes referred to as that of aboriginal cost. May[14] discussed "the requirement recently sustained by the Supreme Court that utilities shall record property on the basis of cost to the first owner employing it in the public service." He explained that this requirement was based on the idea that "the rights of the public are not affected by any changes of ownership that may have occurred." From the rate-making viewpoint, aboriginal cost may have its proponents. As an accounting concept, particularly in its relation to the entity convention, it is meaningless.

SELF-CONSTRUCTED ASSETS. The valuation of fixed assets constructed by a company's own workmen is sufficiently important to justify additional analysis. As previously intimated, the problem of valuing such fixed assets relates almost entirely to overhead or manufacturing expense. Direct labor costs can be assigned to the construction work upon the basis of time tickets. Materials can be assigned to it on the basis of written authorization. Amounts so charged do not improperly reduce regular manufacturing costs.

The problem of equitable overhead distribution is a difficult

13 John B. Canning, *The Economics of Accountancy* (New York, The Ronald Press Company, 1929), p. 255.
14 George O. May, "Improvement in Financial Accounts," *The Journal of Accountancy*, May 1937, p. 346.

one. Too great a proportion of overhead transferred to the construction work may reduce the balance assignable to regular manufacturing so greatly as to affect manufacturing costs and hence affect inventory values and both gross and net profits. Many authorities contend that no overhead expense should be applied to construction work unless there has been an actual increase in the overhead expense due directly to the work.

Referring to this problem Montgomery[15] thinks that: "It is a safe procedure to add to such asset accounts only the overhead that can be attributed directly to the work done on the plant or equipment." Sanders, Hatfield, and Moore[16] say:

> When plant assets are constructed by the company itself, the more conservative procedure is to charge to such assets only the direct costs of materials and labor, and actual supervision devoted to that work. It is permissible also to allocate to it a reasonable amount of general company overhead, but this should not be done to the extent of relieving the income account of charges which would normally be made against it.

These and other authorities emphasize the possibility of distorting profit and loss statements either at the time that the construction work is in progress or later because of the extra depreciation required to take care of any overvaluation.

The accepted method of treating overhead in relation to construction work is practically justified. It is, however, better practice than it is theory. Based on this latter viewpoint, it is entirely clear that if two or more results are achieved by a single effort, it is deceptive to fail to allocate the appropriate part of the cost of the effort to each of the results. More concretely, if an officer of a corporation devotes part of his time to construction and part to operations during any particular accounting period, the amount of his salary should be divided between the two. The practical objections to this are at least twofold. First of all, few executives would be willing to keep the records necessary to make this allocation, and second, the recognition of this practice might easily open the door to various undetectible schemes of manipulating profit and loss statements.

15 Robert H. Montgomery, *Auditing Theory and Practice* (New York, The Ronald Press Company, 1934), p. 274.
16 Sanders, Hatfield, and Moore, *A Statement of Accounting Principles* (New York, American Institute of Accountants, 1938), p. 60.

RECONSTRUCTION, ALTERATION, AND REHABILITATION. When a purchased asset is in bad condition, it is considered permissible to include as an item of its cost the expense of repairing it.

This rule is generally accepted but it cannot always be applied to reconstruction and alteration in rearrangements of buildings, changing doors, partitions and windows, moving machinery, and similar improvements. When the expenditure is made with the expectation of increasing the efficiency or the earning power of the asset, it may properly be shown as an addition to fixed asset cost but it appears that the burden of proof rests upon him who advances this view in any particular case.[17]

When it is known that the effect of any such expenditure will be short lived, as where alterations are made to suit a tenant and it is not known whether subsequent tenants will be willing to pay the carrying cost of such improvements, the expenditure may be charged to a prepaid expense account to be distributed over the rental period. As the *Accountants' Handbook*[18] observes, "the lease may be renewed, or a new tenant secured who will require no changes, but these conditions cannot be depended upon."

OVERDEPRECIATION. An interesting problem of imputed costs is noted in connection with fixed asset values which have been depreciated over too short a term.

Occasionally it happens that an asset is depreciated so rapidly that its entire book value disappears while the asset is still in use. The American Accounting Association,[19] in its Postulate 4, says that such costs should not be reinstated as assets subject to reamortization "except as required corrections are reflected in revised income statements for each period affected."

Assuming that such costs have been reinstated and such corrected statements have been prepared, the depreciation schedule

---

[17] A broader view is taken in the following quotation: "It is not even necessary that revenues be improved or expenses reduced, as compared with the past—all that is required is satisfactory evidence that conditions would be less favorable if the expenditures were not made." *Accountants' Handbook* (New York, The Ronald Press Company, 1934), p. 1102.

[18] *Accountants' Handbook* (New York, The Ronald Press Company, 1934), p. 544.

[19] Executive Committee of the American Accounting Association, "A Tentative Statement of Accounting Principles Affecting Corporate Reports," *The Accounting Review*, June 1936, p. 188.

can be recalculated and the reinstated costs charged off over th
remaining number of years of life.

It is, however, not common to reinstate such written-of
costs. In practice such assets may be owned and operated for
number of years in spite of the fact that no accounting value
are assigned to them.

It is in this connection that a problem somewhat similar t
that of imputed costs arises, since the suggestion is sometime
made that depreciation on such assets should be continued at th
same rate as in the past in order to obtain comparability of costs
The debit portion of such a depreciation entry may be treate
as an operating cost. The credit portion, however, is not an iten
of realized income until the manufactured articles which includ
such fictitious depreciation have actually been sold.

DISTORTION.   Fixed asset valuation, save upon an actua
cost basis, may have some distorting effect upon profit and loss
particularly in the case of assets constructed by a company's ow
force of workmen.

Distortion is also noted in connection with donated assets an
in connection with imputed costs. If appreciation based upo
appraisal is properly handled by the creation of an appreciatio
surplus account, and if the total depreciation of the inflated asse
is so divided that only the amount referring to the original asse
cost is charged to profit and loss, no distortion of profit and los
should result.

In the case of assets purchased for considerations other tha
cash, whereby extravagant valuations result, the effect upo
profit and loss may be consistently unfavorable owing to exces
sive annual costs, but this represents a definite bias rather tha
a distortion.

Of far greater interest in any discussion of accounting profit
are the problems which arise in connection with the allocation o
fixed asset costs to periodic profit and loss statements.

Allocation of Fixed Asset Costs.—Allocation of fixed asse
costs to the periods benefiting from the use of such assets i
complicated not only by tax considerations but by a variety o
difficulties relating to the estimates of useful life, forecasting

of residual or scrap value, choice of mathematical methods properly to be employed in determining the allocation, and a variety of conceptions referring to depreciation in its relation to income, to operating efficiency, and to asset replacement. Still another group of problems refers to over- or underdepreciation resulting from inaccuracies of estimation.

Examination of existing literature and the various arguments and special viewpoints expressed therein might easily present a false picture of current practices in depreciation accounting.

COMMON DEPRECIATION PRACTICES. It may be helpful to note common depreciation practices as described by R. P. Marple in the *N.A.C.A. Bulletin* of May 1, 1936. His study was based upon 28 selected manufacturing companies and his findings were as follows:

If your company is a typical American manufacturing concern, you follow the practice of depreciating fixed assets on the basis of original cost, you include depreciation on idle and excess facilities in production cost, you use the straight-line method for calculating depreciation, and you are likely not to follow the practice of capitalizing research developmental and experimental costs. It is your practice to charge all repair costs as expenses, and to record asset replacements as a charge to the asset account after relieving this account of the original cost of the asset retired and relieving the depreciation reserve of the depreciation applying against the replaced asset.

The same issue of the *N.A.C.A. Bulletin* reported a similar survey made by the Machinery and Allied Products Institute covering 150 companies engaged in the manufacture of machinery. Over 90% of the reporting companies calculated depreciation on the basis of original cost; 84% used the straight-line method; 86% charged all repairs to expense; 90% charged the cost of replacements to the asset account after that account and its corresponding reserve had been cleared with respect to the old asset.

EARLY VIEWPOINTS TOWARD DEPRECIATION. Littleton reports that the first book on the subject of depreciation was one by Ewing Matheson, published in London in 1884.

From that time the various problems referring to depreciation have been receiving more and more attention from auditors, cost accountants, lawyers, economists, and taxing authorities.

There is little reason to doubt that depreciation was originally calculated on the basis of appraisals. The appraisal, it may be conjectured, was originally on a market price basis in order to obtain a figure roughly equivalent to what would have been realized at the date of the appraisal had the asset actually been sold. This appraisal viewpoint persisted for many years and in fact has not yet entirely disappeared.

Reference has already been made to an old practice of combining, in one account, asset value together with the costs, expenses, and income relating to that asset. This method of bookkeeping almost necessitated taking an inventory of the asset in order to determine what part of the balance of such an account should be transferred to profit and loss.

Littleton[20] is authority for the statement that up to the middle of the nineteenth century depreciation appeared "simply as a variation in an inventoriable item." He also said,

> The treatment accorded a depreciating property in the accounts was to enter it at the end of a period on the credit side "as if sold." The method was a strict analogy to the goods account of the oldest texts. Depreciation apparently was not regarded as expense or cost but as loss, as "decay from use." The depreciation of a ship was therefore no different in principle from the loss of a ship in a storm.

In the early days such an appraisal or inventory probably was made whenever it was desired to calculate profits. After general adoption of the accounting period convention, such appraisals were probably made at the end of each accounting period. It must, however, soon have been obvious that such periodic appraisals gave erratic results depending, of course, upon who made them, how they were made and the general state of business at the time they were made. Conceivably a fixed asset could show a value at the end of one period larger than the value established at the end of the previous period in spite of intervening deterioration.

20 A. C. Littleton, *Accounting Evolution to 1900* (New York, American Institute Publishing Co., Inc., 1933), p. 237.

This must inevitably have led to the realization that fixed assets were in the nature of deferred charges against future income; that fixed assets, like human beings, do not have an infinite life; that life expectancy could be estimated and the cost of the fixed asset absorbed over the number of periods so estimated.

MODERN VIEWPOINT TOWARD DEPRECIATION. The present-day viewpoint toward depreciation has been set forth and explained so often by example and by definition that it is now almost a matter of general understanding.

An excellent but not widely distributed report entitled "Depreciation—A Review of Legal and Accounting Problems," prepared by the staff of the Public Service Commission of Wisconsin, defined depreciation as

the consumption of investment in property, or the loss in the service capacity of property, due to use, wear and tear, physical deterioration, the current action of the elements, obsolescence, inadequacy, or the demands of public authority.

Mason,[21] in his *Principles of Public-Utility Depreciation,* describes depreciation

by conceiving the amount of the investment in an asset with a terminable life as a capitalization of the value of the future services to be rendered by the asset, and depreciation as the amortization or expiration of the investment as the services are realized.

It hardly seems appropriate in this volume to engage in lengthy discussion of special problems of public utility depreciation, of depreciation in charitable or other institutions relying for their income upon donations, or of depreciation in governmental and municipal accounting. These are special fields in which depreciation problems are considered from special viewpoints.

From the general business viewpoint, the estimate of asset life has great significance in relation to accounting profits. Such an estimate, particularly in past years, has been little more than

21 Perry Mason, *Principles of Public-Utility Depreciation* (Chicago, American Accounting Association, 1937), p. 2.

a guess. Thus, Littleton[22] reports that a work, *Bookkeeping,* published in 1861 by W. Inglish, suggested that "a yearly deduction of 5 and 10 per cent requires to be made from original cost, to allow for deterioration, or wear and tear." Obviously, such figures could not have been based upon scientific estimation nor upon consideration of such special forces as inadequacy or obsolescence which may affect the rate for an individual item.

DEPRECIATION TABLES. Arbitrary figures of the Inglish type have often been suggested. The *Accountants' Handbook* contains 56 pages of depreciation rate tables obtained from 137 different sources suggesting, among other items, a 5% depreciation rate on mirrors in soda fountains; a 10% depreciation rate on pianos and organs in theatres and motion picture houses; a 5% rate on pipe organs in mortuarial services; a 10% rate on microscopes in hospitals; a 3⅓% rate on brick or concrete hangars in aviation fields; and a 20% rate on mine mules.

Obviously, many of these rates can have no sound foundation or are not applicable to specific situations. Most of them must disregard such factors as inadequacy, obsolescence, or accelerated use.

What possible basis, for example, can there be for an arbitrary decision that a mirror in a soda fountain will last twenty years? Have adequate statistical studies been made of such mirrors? Have the causes of mirror depreciation been surveyed? Is the 5% rate sheer guesswork?

Equally a guess, but probably a safer one, would be the assertion that few, if any, soda fountain mirrors now in use are twenty years old. Undoubtedly mirrors installed twenty years ago have been discarded not because they were worn out, but for the simple reason that they went out of style.

Why should the depreciation rate on a pipe organ in a movie theatre be 10% and in a mortuary 5%? Is the organ played twice as often in the theatre? Is it serviced more often in the mortuary? Are mortuary organs less subject to style changes than theatre organs? These and dozens of other questions suggest themselves in reading over depreciation rate tables.

[22] A. C. Littleton, *Accounting Evolution to 1900* (New York, American Institute Publishing Co., Inc., 1933), p. 226.

INCOME TAX INFLUENCE. The Bureau of Internal Revenue has always shown a lively interest in depreciation and has often objected to depreciation rates regarded as necessary by some business managers.

As an unfortunate result of such differences of opinion, it has been found necessary by some industrial companies to maintain different records of depreciation for cost accounting and for tax purposes. Nearly 40% of the companies studied by R. P. Marple, whose report was previously noted, maintain such separate records.

A somewhat similar situation was noted in the Machinery and Allied Products Institute survey. For example, 126 companies used the straight-line method of depreciation for cost accounting but only 112 of them used it for tax accounting; 129 companies charged all repairs to expense for cost accounting but only 112 did so for tax purposes. Similar variations were noted throughout the report.

DEPRECIATION AND PROFITS. Certain delusions regarding depreciation have long persisted. The first assumes that depreciation is a function of profits and that more depreciation should be taken during a profitable year than during an unprofitable year.

Mason,[23] in his *Principles of Public-Utility Depreciation,* refers to the following from a letter written by the president of a utility company:

I propose to follow the rule which was good business when Joseph was grain controller to old Rameses—namely, to make the good years contribute to reserves or to betterments which will maintain value, and to let the lean years travel into the past without marking them as defaulters.

Porter and Fiske[24] attempt to explain such viewpoints as follows:

The feeling of the business man that depreciation should be higher in good years than in bad is based on an intuitive understanding of the

23 Perry Mason, *Principles of Public-Utility Depreciation* (Chicago, American Accounting Association, 1937), p. 21.
24 Porter and Fiske, *Accounting* (New York, Henry Holt & Company, 1935), p. 419.

fact that depreciation is more nearly a function of use of equipment, that is, of production, than of time.

DEPRECIATION AND EFFICIENCY. Another delusion which has long persisted confuses depreciation with efficiency. Factory and plant managers sometimes assert their opinion that a given fixed asset has not depreciated, regardless of its age, because it is operating efficiently.

There is, of course, no inherent relationship between efficiency and life termination, whether it refers to natural life or the life of a physical asset. Depreciation of a machine, for example, is based upon a forecast as to how long that machine will be retained in use. If the estimate is correctly made, it is conceivable that that machine may operate efficiently until the day it is discarded. In fact, the depreciation rate on that machine may be determined on the assumption that it will be maintained in good operating condition. Noted here is the age-old confusion between accounting life and accounting valuation on the one hand, and physical efficiency and resale value on the other hand.

Nowhere in business are these discrepancies more clearly evident that in connection with the mules used in mining. A two-year-old mule may be acquired for $100. By the time that mule becomes five years old it may be worth $175, simply because it is more mature, more efficient, stronger, and better trained.

No mine manager would be foolish enough to claim that this increased value and increased efficiency had any bearing upon the mule's life tenure. Inevitably that mule must die and it is mandatory that its original cost be allocated to the number of accounting periods representing its normal life expectancy, the calculation of which cannot be affected by intermediate variations in efficiency.

Efficiency in relation to depreciation was discussed in the report of the Public Service Commission of Wisconsin[25] previously cited. The report mentioned the confusion "in identifying efficiency, serviceability and usefulness at a given time

[25] Staff of the Public Service Commission of Wisconsin, *Depreciation* (New York, The State Law Reporting Company, 1933), pp. 12, 13.

with depreciation." It also asserted that if efficiency and serviceability measured depreciation, "many, if not most, classes of plant would suffer little, if any, depreciation until retirement."

DEPRECIATION AND REPLACEMENTS. Of a different order from the two mentioned, a third delusion confuses financial policy with accounting procedure.

This delusion is founded upon a chain of reasoning which runs somewhat as follows. A soda fountain mirror is purchased January 1, 1938 for $200. Depreciation tables are consulted and it is learned that such a mirror should be depreciated 5% annually, thus giving the mirror an estimated life of twenty years. At the end of that time it is expected that the mirror will be useless and valueless. On January 1, 1959, it will therefore be necessary to dispose of the old mirror and buy another one.

The question arises as to what the new mirror will cost on January 1, 1959. Someone's good judgment informs him that mirrors are becoming more and more expensive. Accordingly, he estimates that the cost of replacing the mirror in 1959 will be $300. He therefore insists that $300 must be available on that date, and to make it available he suggests that $300 be divided by 20 and that the annual depreciation resulting should be $15 (instead of $10).

There are, of course, numerous fallacies in such a method of reasoning. No one is sufficiently clairvoyant to foretell the replacement cost of a mirror or any other asset twenty years hence. Even more serious is the probability that no identical mirror will be purchased January 1, 1959. By that time it may no longer be popular to have mirrors in soda fountains, or if mirrors are then popular they may be metal mirrors invented between 1939 and 1959, which can be acquired in 1959 at a mere fraction of the $200 cost of the glass mirror. Perhaps by 1959 soda fountains may be banned by law, in which event it may be necessary to buy the new mirror through underworld channels at an exorbitant cost.

There is, of course, no accounting relation between the amortization of an existing asset and its ultimate replacement.

Such replacement, if, as, and when it occurs, is a new, separate, and distinct undertaking.

The availability of money for replacement may offer serious financial problems. The problem of financing replacements may be sufficiently difficult to tax the resourcefulness and foresight of business men but it is in no sense whatever an accounting problem. The originally acquired asset was a deferred charge and its cost is recovered by the depreciation program. The replacement, whether it be an identical item or not, is a fresh transaction resulting in the creation of a new deferred charge the cost of which in turn must, from the accounting viewpoint, be recovered over the years which follow its acquisition.

Revived interest in making accounting provision for replacements has been due in part to business men's fear of inflation, as a result of which the replacement of one asset by an identical asset might involve double, triple, or quadruple the price. This possibility and the dangers inherent in it are evident.

The replacement theory has also been favorably viewed by those wise and cautious business men who have noted that the recovery of cost through depreciation does not always augment the cash account, the money being used for other purposes and the cupboard being bare when the asset must be replaced. Wisely, in many instances, they establish funds for replacement purposes. The segregation and earmarking of funds for asset replacement is an important function of finance. Illogically, they may attempt to relate those funds to the depreciation reserve and as a result they create confusion between depreciation and replacement.

Learoyd[26] shows the danger inherent in lack of foresight when a new type of equipment is developed making it possible to manufacture at a lower cost. He observed:

One company does not have funds available to buy the new equipment, but it is forced to meet the lower prices of its competitors. Profits dwindle, and there is no chance to accumulate enough funds to replace the obsolete, marginal machinery. As a result a vicious spiral has developed; the company is ultimately forced out of business.

26 John S. Learoyd, Jr., "Obsolescence in the Electric Lamp Industry," *N.A.C.A. Bulletin,* April 15, 1938, p. 954.

Woodbridge[27] has pointed out that "many instances of insolvency would surely be avoided if accountants could cause their clients to think in terms of funds (definitely segregated liquid assets) as well as reserves."

While recognizing the wisdom of this financing viewpoint, accounting authorities generally agree with the report of the Public Service Commission of Wisconsin[28] in its suggestion that "it would be just as absurd to say, if coal consumed in an electric power plant is replaced at a higher or lower price, the cost of energy generated to-day is fixed by the price of the fresh supply of fuel."

Mason[29] flatly asserts that: "Whether the asset is replaced or not has nothing to do with the amount or treatment of its depreciation." His statement is reinforced by the following from an important committee[30] report: "With actual cost as a base, accounting at least approximates fact and is not converted into a system of weird guesswork."

REPAIRS AND RENEWALS. An adequate and consistent program of repairs and renewals is generally contemplated in the preparation of depreciation schedules.

Repairs, while in theory representing the creation of a new deferred charge against future income, are generally treated as immediate charges to expense. Twenty-five out of 28 companies, or 89%, investigated by R. P. Marple followed this practice, while 129 out of 150 companies, or 86%, investigated by the Machinery and Allied Products Institute charged all repairs to expense.

There are some who believe that such repairs should be charged against the reserve for depreciation on the theory that the life of the asset has been increased, a theory which holds water only if such treatment was contemplated in the original establishment of the depreciation program. Substantial renew-

27 Frederick W. Woodbridge, "Reserves," *The Journal of Accountancy,* August 1938, p. 106.
28 Staff of the Public Service Commission of Wisconsin, *Depreciation* (New York, The State Law Reporting Company, 1933), p. 38.
29 Perry Mason, *Principles of Public-Utility Depreciation* (Chicago, American Accounting Association, 1937), p. 5.
30 National Association of Railroad and Utilities Commissioners, *Report of Special Committee on Depreciation* (New York, The State Law Reporting Company, 1938), p. 28.

als are commonly treated as replacements of assets, 26 out of 28 companies reported by Marple charging them to the asset account after that account had been relieved of the original cost and the reserve had been relieved of the accumulated depreciation. Ordinary renewals involving immaterial sums not sufficient in size or importance to justify consideration as replacements are commonly charged to expense.

Following this preliminary survey, consideration must next be given to that most important of all elements of depreciation, namely, the estimate or forecast of future life. Such life expectancy forecasts may have the most important and far-reaching effects upon the determination of accounting profits.

CHAPTER 29

USEFUL LIFE OF FIXED ASSETS

The general adoption of the accounting period convention has made it necessary to estimate the useful life of fixed assets in order to allocate to each accounting period its equitable share of asset cost.

Time and Usage Factors.—Two different estimating factors are often present. An asset's life is determined in part by severity of use and in part by passage of time.

In recognition of these factors, two common methods of depreciation have been proposed. By one method the cost of the asset is distributed on the basis of time. By the other such cost is distributed on the basis of usage. It is apparent that either method alone often must be inaccurate.

A simple example will illustrate the point. The purchaser of a new Ford automobile costing $600 may estimate that the car will be replaced after having been operated for 100,000 miles, at which time its estimated trade-in value will be $100. The depreciation rate will then be determined as ½ cent per mile.

The purchaser may, however, decide that the useful life of his car will be five years, at which time its residual value will be $100. If this basis is adopted, then the depreciation rate will be $100 per year.

The purchaser who calculates depreciation on his car at the rate of ½ cent per mile may, because of some unforeseen circumstance, fail to operate the car as he had planned. If, for example, his actual operation averages no more than 5,000 miles per year, it will take twenty years for depreciation at the rate of ½ cent per mile to recover the cost of the car. Such a car probably will not have a useful life of twenty years no matter how little it is run. Even if the car is not operated at all, it will still be considerably deteriorated at the end of twenty years, even disregarding obsolescence.

The reverse situation is noted where the annual depreciation rate of $100 is planned. The purchaser, because of unforeseen circumstances, may be required to operate his car at a rate of activity such as 50,000 miles per year, for example. In two years the car may be ready for retirement, but in two years only 2/5 of the cost will have been recovered through depreciation. It will be seen that either the time basis or the usage basis of forecasting may be substantially erroneous when the alternative factor is not taken into account.

Inadequacy.—There are other factors which may affect forecasting.

If the buyer of the Ford car selects the roadster type, an increase in the size of his family may make it necessary for him to dispose of the car before the expiration of the five-year period or the 100,000 miles of operation. This premature retirement of the car is due, not to its wear and tear, but to its inadequacy. Inadequacy is an important cause of fixed asset retirement, particularly in connection with buildings which are too small or machines the capacity of which is less than manufacturing pressure demands.

Obsolescence.—The buyer of the new Ford car may, after having operated it for 20,000 miles or for two years, discard it because the Ford Motor Company has produced a newer model the gasoline consumption of which is less or the design of which is particularly attractive to the public. Because of whim based upon style appeal, or for reasons of economy, or for a variety of other reasons, the car owner may discard his car long before its useful physical life has expired.

Substitution.—Finally, the owner of the automobile may reside 15 miles from his place of business. His principal reason for purchasing the car may have been its utility in transportation to and from his work.

If an interurban bus line is then established and if the fares, the schedules, and the accommodations are sufficiently attractive, the automobile owner may decide to give up his car. This represents an unexpected event not in the same category as the others but one which may operate to change the original forecast of useful life.

Not intended as an exhaustive catalogue, the illustrations indicate common causes tending to influence the life of fixed assets. None of them can be forecast accurately. Some cannot be forecast at all.

Physical and Functional Depreciation.—The majority of accounting authors have suggested a dual classification of depreciation, i.e., physical and functional.

The physical causes are said by Mason[1] to "include such things as wear and tear from use, chemical or physiochemical action such as rust, decay, and electrolysis, and the effects of wind and rain." In his description of non-physical causes, which he says are sometimes called functional or social, he includes

obsolescence or progress in the arts and inventions which reduce unit costs of production so far that they make the continued operation of the old asset uneconomical, changed conditions of operation which make certain assets inadequate as when a railroad has to lay heavier rail or purchase more powerful locomotives to meet the requirements of increased traffic, and conditions which require contraction of operations such as depopulation of a territory or the completion of a construction project.

Kurtz[2] speaks of "two forces, one the probability of removal by chance, inadequacy, or obsolescence; and the other, gradual deterioration, due to wear, or use, and the elements."

Not all authorities conceive of obsolescence as being a part of depreciation. An English magazine, *The Accountant*,[3] discussed this editorially as follows:

Depreciation is a direct and measurable charge against profits, capable of being deducted before net profit is ascertained; obsolescence, on

1 Perry Mason, *Principles of Public-Utility Depreciation* (Chicago, American Accounting Association, 1937), pp. 2, 3.
2 Edwin B. Kurtz, *The Science of Valuation and Depreciation* (New York, The Ronald Press Company, 1937), p. 38.
3 *Accountants Digest*, September 1938, p. 16.

the other hand, is a sacrifice voluntarily or involuntarily incurred in an effort to maximise profits in the future. The consequence of this distinction is that provision for the possibility of obsolescence ought to be made by withholding from distribution profits which have already been measured after the deduction of depreciation.

The staff of the Public Service Commission of Wisconsin uses the words "physical" and "functional."

An excellent discussion of depreciation factors, much too long for quotation, is provided in the *Accountants' Handbook,* second edition, pages 579 to 584.

For many years the attention of accountants was directed to the physical rather than the functional causes of depreciation. The latter, while recognized, were often regarded as impossible to forecast. Various applications of the doctrine of conservatism which resulted in asset undervaluation and in the setting aside of large contingency reserves, were often regarded from the balance sheet viewpoint as adequate protection against loss from functional depreciation. The increased emphasis upon the profit and loss viewpoint has directed accounting attention to such causes of depreciation as inadequacy and obsolescence. Obsolescence in particular has been much discussed. This is due in large part to the increased importance of redesign as a potent force in marketing.

Redesign and Obsolescence.—The favorable sales results obtained by manufacturers of household devices and equipment, such as electric refrigerators, washing machines, vacuum cleaners, and kitchen utensils, due merely to their redesign by artist-engineers, the influence of design in automobile merchandising, and the experiences of those who have experimented with modern packaging, have convinced many business men that applied art has a definite commercial value.

This increased recognition of design as a sales factor has increased the rate of obsolescence not only of products in the hands of users but also products unsold on the shelves and in the warehouses of retailers, wholesalers, and manufacturers. Because much of the efficacy of redesigning depends upon the use of new materials, new finishes, new shapes, and other factors, a demand has been created for new manufacturing equipment adapted to such new materials and capable of producing the new finishes and new shapes, with the result that obsolescence has crept into the heavier industries.

Redesign is not, of course, solely concerned with the creation of sales appeal through beauty. It also has direct reference to increased utility, convenience, strength, and other desirable factors. Much of the modern development in the chemistry of alloys is due to the search by manufacturers for lighter, stronger and more suitable metals. As a result of these and other forces, the problem of obsolescence has been assuming greater and greater importance.

Learoyd[4] believes that there are three principal types of obsolescence:

first, industry obsolescence in which a product is developed using entirely new principles for satisfying a need, thus rendering the old product and the old methods obsolete; second, product obsolescence arising from changes in the product within the same industry due to engineering advances; third, obsolescence arising from improved methods of manufacturing.

Wheeler[5] is responsible for the statement that "the Treasury Department does not limit obsolescence to one brand, but considers that there are two different species of that animal— both allowable as deductions from taxable income, but in different ways." The two classes he mentions are normal obsolescence and extraordinary obsolescence. The distinction is based upon ability to forecast.

Foster[6] makes a significant distinction as follows: "Obsolescence, inadequacy, and supersession, being speculative and prospective, play no part in . . . depreciation," while Montgomery[7] suggests that "extraordinary obsolescence cannot be foreseen, and therefore any attempt to reduce the contingency

4 John S. Learoyd, Jr., "Obsolescence in the Electric Lamp Industry," *N.A.C.A. Bulletin,* April 15, 1938, p. 950.

5 Bleecker T. Wheeler, *Practical Aspects of Depreciation and Obsolescence* (New York, American Management Association, 1938), p. 12.

6 H. A. Foster, quoted in the *Handbook of Business Administration* (New York, McGraw-Hill Book Company, Inc., 1931), p. 504.

7 Robert H. Montgomery, *Auditing Theory and Practice* (New York, The Ronald Press Company, 1934), p. 520.

to a definite allowance to form part of current operating costs defeats its own purpose."

Unit, Group, and Composite Depreciation.—Logically each separate identifiable item of fixed assets is the proper unit to use for depreciation purposes. Examples of such items are milling machines, lathes, electric motors, delivery trucks, and other types of tools, machines, and equipment. When such separate units are separately depreciated, the plan is sometimes referred to as the "unit" or "unitary" plan of depreciation.

GROUP RATE BASIS. Often a substantial item of fixed assets will be found to consist of many identical smaller items, the value of each being relatively slight. Telephone poles, piling, railroad ties, fleets of trucks, and railroad gondolas are all of this type. On the assumption that they are identical and will pass through similar physical and functional experiences, such assets may for depreciation purposes be grouped.

As has been explained by Wheeler,[8] "Depreciation on the group rate basis applies to assets of relatively similar type and character within the same group or classification in the plant account."

These remarks apply to homogeneous groups, but the group rate basis also is applied to non-homogeneous groups having the same estimated service lives.

COMPOSITE RATE BASIS. The depreciable unit may consist of an entire plant the various elements of which vary considerably in their depreciation characteristics.

Such composite depreciation is often condemned. The *Accountants' Handbook*[9] labels it as "seldom if ever satisfactory." Others have joined in this view. Nevertheless, it is not wise to indict this method under all conditions. To those who think of a factory, for example, as one mechanism equivalent perhaps to a single mammoth machine made up of numerous articulated parts and who think of the valuation of that plant as being directly related to its earning power, the idea of treating

---

[8] Bleecker T. Wheeler, *Practical Aspects of Depreciation and Obsolescence* (New York, American Management Association, 1938), p. 16.
[9] *Accountants' Handbook* (New York, The Ronald Press Company, 1934), p. 589.

it as a single unit for depreciation purposes is not regarded as absurd.

Those who give consideration to this viewpoint can hardly fail to recognize the analogy between (1) an entire plant and the items which compose it, and (2) a single machine and the parts which compose that machine. If the plant as a whole should not be taken as a depreciable unit, then it is argued that the machine as a whole should not be taken as a depreciable unit and that a separate record should be kept for each cog, gear, lever, and wheel of which that machine is composed.

The objection to composite rates is, of course, the fact that the components of a plant change. As parts thereof are retired they are not always replaced with exactly the same parts. An old machine, for example, may be replaced by a newer one having twice the life expectancy. The composite rate plan has a tendency to obscure the effect of such changes in the plant components. After the expiration of some years, the operation of the plan may result in accounting totals for assets and reserves which have little relation to actuality.

There is one type of situation where the composite rate may properly be applied. Such a situation is noted in connection with construction projects or logging camps where activity may terminate long before actual life of the fixed assets has expired. Buildings which house restaurants, hotels, and stores in the neighborhood of mining enterprises may last for years after the mines are exhausted.

Learoyd[10] believes that:

In situations where obsolescence is a large and dominant factor in the depreciation charge, all the equipment is apt to have the same economic life regardless of the varying physical lives of the separate pieces; hence, by lumping it all into one depreciable unit, satisfactory results may be obtained.

There is little doubt that the most popular of all plans of depreciation accounting are based upon some variation of the group method where the items within the groups have approximately the same useful life.

10 John S. Learoyd, Jr., "Obsolescence in the Electric Lamp Industry," *N.A.C.A. Bulletin,* April 15, 1938, p. 957.

Comparison of Unit and Group Methods.—Under the unit method, when a fixed asset is discarded an item of "profit" or "loss" is usually determined then and there and the asset account and its corresponding valuation account are adjusted. The group method, on the other hand, is based upon averages, and until the last unit in the group is discarded, the inaccuracy of the original forecast of depreciation cannot be measured. In a group of ten identical items, for example, eight of them may turn out to have lasted less than the forecast life but the remaining two may be so long lived as to offset the shortened lives of the first eight. If separate depreciation records were kept, a loss would have to be shown for each of the first eight as it was retired, whereas under the group plan these losses would not be absorbed currently but would be held over to be offset to some extent by the longer service lives of the remaining items.

The different effects of these two plans upon periodic profit and loss statements is, of course, self-evident and may represent an influential cause of periodic profit distortion.

Components of Asset Units.—Logical though the unit plan may be, its practical application leads into some puzzling situations since parts of the unit itself may have shorter lives than other parts.

Stempf[11] has illustrated this by "certain types of furnaces, ovens, boilers, etc., which may require periodic relining every two, three, four or five years." He suggests that:

Such linings should be separately classified, and should be amortized over the brief period, creating a reserve against which replacements may be charged when made, rather than using a composite rate, and distorting operations by charges for extraordinary maintenance at irregular intervals.

McKee[12] calls attention to similar problems in connection with refinery equipment, i.e., the lead linings of agitators and the various parts of acid recovery systems, and asserts that "a

11 Victor H. Stempf, "Accounting for Fixed Assets," *N.A.C.A. Bulletin*, April 15, 1938, p. 944.
12 Raymond Walter McKee, *Handbook of Petroleum Accounting* (New York, Harper & Brothers, 1938), p. 313.

number of companies do estimate the periodical cost of relining agitators and similar equipment, and accrue a special reserve for it, in order to equalize the charges; the actual cost of each relining job is then charged against this reserve."

Similar difficulties are noted where equipment is motor-driven, the motor being semi-permanently attached. Should the motor and the machine be considered one unit or should separate depreciation records be kept for each? Often the latter view is adopted but if carried too far there is some danger of useless multiplication of clerical work and of accounting records.

As the entire subject of depreciable units is one of importance in relation to periodic profits, it seems rather unfortunate that many accountants have been willing to rely upon engineering decisions. The engineers, due to common lack of accounting knowledge, are not properly equipped to think in terms of periodic profit distortion.

Residual and Scrap Values.—Older accounting texts were much concerned with forecasting the selling values of fixed assets at the time of their retirement.

In discussing the determination of service lives and depreciation rates, it was always suggested that the residual value be estimated and deducted from the original cost of the asset in order to determine the amount to be charged off during the asset's useful life.

Such estimates of future selling prices or scrap value of used equipment were generally no more than guesses. Seldom did such estimates give consideration to the costs of removing or dismantling the retired assets—costs which often amounted to more than the residual value.

The staff of the Public Service Commission of Wisconsin[13] asserts that for certain classes of plant "the cost of removal is often in excess of the gross salvage value," while Sanders[14] suggests that since the "residual value is usually small, however, and the whole computation is largely an estimate, this remainder is in practice often ignored." This advice appears quite sound in

13 Staff of the Public Service Commission of Wisconsin, *Depreciation* (New York, The State Law Reporting Company, 1933), p. 36.
14 T. H. Sanders, *Cost Accounting for Control* (New York, McGraw-Hill Book Company, Inc., 1934), p. 194.

view of the reasonable contention by Stempf[15] "that provisions for depreciation, generally speaking, have been far too low for many years, with the far-reaching economic effect commonly overlooked."

The suggestion to ignore the residual value is perfectly sound for some types of assets, particularly when the amounts involved are not material. When they are material and when the removal costs or demolition costs are also material, the net rather than the gross salvage value is the one to be used in calculating the periodic depreciation.

If this is done, Kester[16] points out, "the depreciable value—and therefore the depreciation expense written off over the life of the asset—contains the amount of the removal cost, not yet incurred nor paid for, as well as the written off value of the asset."

Forecasting Service Life of Fixed Assets.—The one factor deserving emphasis over and above all others, in so far as profit distortion is concerned, is that which refers to the forecasting of service life.

The estimate of an asset's future life may be made in terms of its productivity or on the basis of elapsed time.

Reference has already been made to the fact that either method may be inadequate. There is no logical reason why physical wear and tear are necessarily correlated with calendar months or years. Nor, on the other hand, is there any reason why a given number of units of production should represent a proper index of inadequacy, obsolescence, or the deteriorating effects of temperature and climate. For these reasons, as explained in Chapter 21, the two methods are sometimes combined. For clarity, however, they will be considered separately here.

From several viewpoints the production unit method is preferable to the elapsed time method. First, an asset is acquired for use and it is through its usefulness that the cost logically is recoverable. Second, the depreciation charge to profit and

15 Victor H. Stempf, "Accounting for Fixed Assets," *N.A.C.A. Bulletin,* April 15, 1938, p. 940.
16 Roy B. Kester, *Advanced Accounting* (New York, The Ronald Press Company, 1933), p. 305.

loss varies with operating activity, with the result that slack years are not so greatly burdened with these charges as years of intense business activity.

PRODUCTION AND TIME METHODS. There is some reason to believe, despite the admitted inaccuracy of both methods, that forecasting in terms of time is somewhat more reliable than forecasting in terms of production. For many types of fixed assets whose utility is indirectly rather than directly related to production, the time basis is the only feasible one. It would appear somewhat absurd, for example, to propose a depreciation forecast for a railroad bridge based upon the number of trains crossing that bridge or to predetermine the depreciation of a hotel building at so much per guest. There is such a thing as physical deterioration during idleness and, as Stempf[17] has asserted, "Even when physical equipment is subjected to the tests of observed depreciation, the matter of obsolescence remains an enigma."

Mason[18] considers the unit of product method "a very appropriate basis for a depreciation allocation," and it is probable that most accountants would agree with him were it not for the difficulty of forecasting in terms of such units.

When the useful life of a fixed asset is controlled by some factor which is susceptible of accurate measurement, such as the terms of a lease, the problem of forecasting is greatly simplified. Under some conditions depreciation of some fixed assets may be controlled by the depletion of others, as can be illustrated by logging camps or mine structures, and when such depletion can accurately be measured, the depreciation may be equally accurate. These are, however, special cases.

MAINTENANCE POLICIES. In general, the predetermination of useful life must be based upon certain repair and maintenance policies, and when these policies are changed, the effect thereof upon the depreciation rates may be substantial.

This is a point which is always emphasized by writers on this

[17] Victor H. Stempf, "Accounting for Fixed Assets," *N.A.C.A. Bulletin,* April 15, 1938, p. 945.
[18] Perry Mason, *Principles of Public-Utility Depreciation* (Chicago, American Accounting Association, 1937), p. 14.

subject. While observing that: "Maintenance will certainly not prevent the functional causes of depreciation and plant retirements," the staff of the Public Service Commission of Wisconsin[19] emphasizes the importance of a proper repair and maintenance program separate and distinct from and yet correlated with the depreciation plan.

Mason[20] observes that when

there is no essential difference between the physical aspects of depreciation and repairs—the smaller the unit used for calculating depreciation, the smaller will be the number of items in the repairs category—and the same principles of equitable and reasonable allocation to the accounting periods should be used as far as it is possible to do so.

Elsewhere,[20] with reference to maintenance, he asserts that a change in the maintenance policy "may require a change in the depreciation plan."

That the repair and maintenance policy should be explicit in its relation to depreciation is necessarily fundamental to any discussion of forecasting service life. The *Accountants' Handbook*[21] has pointed out the effect of carelessness in these words: "if a unit replacement is viewed as maintenance, and the cost in dollars is greater or less than that of the old unit, the effect is that the property account will not show the cost of property actually in use."

The *Accountants' Handbook*[22] again emphasizes the point by reference to the treatment of a large building or ship or airplane as a single accounting unit, ignoring the fact that certain parts thereof may be subject to replacement long before the entire unit is eliminated. This reference then asserts:

Such changes should be treated as adjustments of cost rather than current maintenance. This need not mean the use of a number of accounts for the single unit, . . . but it means a recognition of the fact that the total cost represents a number of elements, not all of which are subject to adjustment or retirement at the same time.

19 Staff of the Public Service Commission of Wisconsin, *Depreciation* (New York, The State Law Reporting Company, 1933), p. 52.
20 Perry Mason, *Principles of Public-Utility Depreciation* (Chicago, American Accounting Association, 1937), pp. 25, 23.
21 *Accountants' Handbook* (New York, The Ronald Press Company, 1934), p. 526.
22 *Ibid.*, p. 527.

This may, of course, call for the adjustment of the asset's cost "either up or down on account of the replacement of a part at a price either above or below cost."

Assuming, however, that a repair and maintenance policy is adopted, the next question refers to that actual forecasting of the asset's future life, which is commonly considered an engineering function. There is some reason to wonder whether engineers are fully aware of the faith that accountants have in the engineers' prophetic powers.

ACCOUNTING RELIANCE UPON ENGINEERING. As an indication of the accounting viewpoint toward depreciation and toward the engineer's part in the preparation of depreciation schedules, a few quotations from standard accounting authorities may be of some interest.

Montgomery[23] advises that the accountant "may base his opinion largely upon the opinions of engineers or other experts." Kester[24] thinks it is apparent that the determination of rates "is essentially an engineering problem." Sanders, Hatfield, and Moore[25] recognize that the question is "largely a technical and engineering one." Andersen[26] regards the accountant as "not qualified to determine plant values, adequacy of depreciation." The *Accountants' Handbook*[27] says that the estimate of service life "is primarily a matter of engineering and business experience" and that such an estimate must be based on "the opinions of engineers and operating men and on tabulations covering histories of similar units in similar service."

An editorial in *The Canadian Chartered Accountant*[28] asserts that the determination of provision for depreciation "is more a matter of engineering than of accounting."

It is natural to inquire whether the engineers themselves

[23] Robert H. Montgomery, *Auditing Theory and Practice* (New York, The Ronald Press Company, 1934), p. 534.
[24] Roy B. Kester, *Advanced Accounting* (New York, The Ronald Press Company, 1933), p. 253.
[25] Sanders, Hatfield, and Moore, *A Statement of Accounting Principles* (New York, American Institute of Accountants, 1938), p. 35.
[26] Arthur Andersen, "Present-Day Problems Affecting the Presentation and Interpretation of Financial Statements," *The Journal of Accountancy*, November 1935, p. 338.
[27] *Accountants' Handbook* (New York, The Ronald Press Company, 1934), p. 584.
[28] *The Canadian Chartered Accountant*, October 1938, p. 248.

realize the extent of their responsibility in this important matter. In certain types of industries depreciation is so material
an element of cost that errors in the predetermination of service
life may have far-reaching effects. Do engineers as a matter of
fact actually understand this? To what extent do they really
accept full responsibility? Just what is the training they receive
which qualifies them to undertake this form of clairvoyance?
Are all engineers equally competent to peer into the future?
What are the methods which they have been trained to use?

In searching for the answers to such questions certain authorities were consulted. In a letter dated April 27, 1938, regarding
this matter, Dexter S. Kimball, formerly Dean of the College
of Engineering at Cornell University, indicated that the engineer doubtless has superior knowledge when it comes to a visual
appraisal of an engineering or industrial property, but where
non-industrial properties are concerned he may not be so accurate, nor is he necessarily fully acquainted with all of the
theory of depreciation. With reference to the education of
engineers to become depreciation experts, Dean Kimball said
that the schools of civil engineering teach their students fairly
simple depreciation methods as applied to railroad equipment,
bridges, and structures and that the schools of electrical engineering have gone much further, particularly in those depreciation problems involved in public utility rate making. The
mechanical engineer, on the other hand, is provided with less
training in depreciation.

In a letter dated May 11, 1938, Professor William B. Cornell,
Chairman of the Department of Business Management of New
York University, set forth his belief that the engineer properly
qualified for the job is the one best equipped to arrive at an
accurate determination of what allowance to make for depreciation but in this he should be aided by accurate and detailed
records kept by management and by standard tables of depreciation rates, although such tables are likely to be rather old
and may show considerable variation in the rates suggested by
different authorities for the same item. Professor Cornell
believes that no one person is fully equipped to determine accurate depreciation rates and that there should be a meeting

of the minds of the accountant, the engineer, and the management, who should take into consideration company policies, plans for consolidation or abandonment of plant, possible need for retrenchment, and plans for using existing facilities for a longer than normal period of years. He suggests that plant records should be reviewed periodically to note any changes in the expected life of the various plant units.

ENGINEERING LIMITATIONS. It is clear from reviewing these opinions and from the survey of engineering literature having to do with depreciation, that the average engineer does not set himself forth as an expert on all phases of forecasting future asset life.

When it comes to a question of physical characteristics involving materials or engineering design, it seems clear that the engineer is best qualified to pass expert judgment. When it comes to a question of constructing mortality tables based upon observed experience, the problem becomes one of statistics rather than engineering and is accordingly more nearly related to accounting.

It is gravely to be doubted whether the engineer who is not a specialist on depreciation or valuation would be willing to accept more than limited responsibility for any forecast of an asset's life. If the accountant passes the entire burden over to the engineer, as is intimated by some of the quotations noted above, and if the engineer limits himself to certain physical aspects of depreciation, who is it that can be held responsible for looking into the future for the purpose of forecasting functional depreciation?

The importance of functional depreciation may in some instances be controlling, and it is quite possible that a competent marketing expert or advertising man might be better equipped to forecast some kinds of obsolescence than any other expert. It is a matter of common knowledge that the most carefully prepared engineering, statistical, and accounting computations may turn out to be worthless because of some sudden and unexpected shift in the opinions, tastes, or whims of the public.

Only too often a few major executives may possess secret knowledge of certain far-reaching changes in prospect for their corporation. Such contemplated changes may refer to expansion programs, attacks upon new markets, or the abandonment or relocation of plants in order to avoid labor troubles. Furthermore, such executives may, through secret sources, learn of developmental work done by some competitor which will cause general obsolescence in an entire industry.

Often this secret knowledge cannot be divulged to the accountants and engineers, who must be permitted to cover sheet after sheet with elaborate calculations which the executive himself, even at the time they are made, knows to be worthless.

TWO METHODS OF FORECASTING.   There are two standard methods used by engineers and accountants in forecasting the service life of fixed assets. One method which is often used in connection with new products is that of inspection of the asset itself from the viewpoint of its design, the materials of which it is composed, and the probable use to which it will be put.

The other method commonly used in connection with standard items for which adequate records have been kept corresponds roughly to the method used by actuaries for life insurance companies.

INSPECTION METHOD.   The first method is the only one which can possibly be employed with new devices or even with old devices put to new uses.

The manufacturer who has an entirely new machine tool manufactured for his exclusive use must adopt this method. After similar machine tools have been in use for a number of years and under a number of different conditions, then the second method may be employed. That the first method requires engineering knowledge is fairly obvious. Neither the accountant, the statistician, nor the sales expert is equipped to examine a new device and foretell how long it will last in active service.

This method of inspection depends, of course, on expert judgment. Essentially, however, it can be no more than a reasonable estimate which, despite great care, may be seriously in error. With less care it may be no more than a guess.

ACTUARIAL METHOD. The actuarial method, on the other hand, is a scientific method. If a thousand identical telegraph poles have had an average life of eight years, then it is safe to estimate that another thousand similar telegraph poles subject to similar conditions will have an average life of eight years.

This is the statistical method and its accuracy or its inaccuracy depends upon statistical safeguards and the quantity of available data. If records are available for only ten telegraph poles instead of a thousand, the average life estimate will be less accurate. This method, therefore, is one which can be applied only to certain types of assets such as telephone switch boards, cables, electric lamps, freight cars, agricultural machinery, and automobiles.

OLD FIGURES APPLIED TO NEW PROBLEMS. Two serious faults may be found with the actuarial method if it is improperly used. The first fault may be illustrated by life tables referring to automobiles.

It may accurately be determined, for example, that a thousand Ford cars have had an average life of six years, but such statistics must refer to Ford cars of some past model. It would not be safe to say that a thousand new cars just off the Ford assembly line would also have an average life of six years.

True enough, in each instance the figures refer to Ford cars but the Ford car of a decade ago bears little resemblance to the modern Ford car. A thousand new Ford cars, regardless of prior statistics, may last five years, eight years, or ten years, a fact which no one can determine from examining statistics of old Ford cars.

DISPERSION OF DATA. The second weakness of the actuarial method is noted when the deviations from average are great and when it is desired to use the statistics for forecasting the future life of just one unit.

A thousand cars have had an average life of six years but that is far from the same thing as saying that each of the thousand cars lasted for exactly six years. Some had a life of only one year, others a life of two or three years, while some of them lasted nine, ten, eleven, or twelve years.

Actuarial tables based upon a thousand cars may be helpful in forecasting the future life of another thousand cars and yet be of little value in forecasting the future life of one car.

This is a serious difficulty where the asset under consideration is of substantial value and where only one is acquired. Actuarial tables reporting the average life of brick buildings, paper making machines, high speed printing presses, or locomotives may be of little value to the corporation which acquires only one building, paper making machine, printing press, or locomotive instead of a hundred or a thousand.

To the statistician the deviations from average may be much more significant than the average itself. He often uses the average as no more than a convenient basis from which to measure deviations. Actuarial depreciation tables, on the other hand, emphasize the average rather than the deviations from average. The greater the deviations from average, the less reliable the average will be as a guide to be used in case of any one particular asset.

OPINIONS AS TO FORECASTING. These various causes of forecasting error have been well recognized by various important authorities.

The *Accountants' Handbook*[29] asserts that: "The determination of the service life of a property unit presents the most difficult problem in the application of depreciation accounting theory."

The staff of the Public Service Commission of Wisconsin[30] observes that "mortality studies are based upon the happenings in the past, and may not be representative of the future." They also suggest its limitation "to those classes of plant and equipment which consist of a fairly large number of units that can be studied independently." This same authority also refers to the cases where there are such "a small number of these units in any one company as to render valueless the mortality data for the purpose of an estimate of service life for the future," and more specifically it asserts that: "The life of a single pole

29 *Accountants' Handbook* (New York, The Ronald Press Company, 1934), p. 655.
30 Staff of the Public Service Commission of Wisconsin, *Depreciation* (New York, The State Law Reporting Company, 1933), pp. 185, 179, 180, 62.

cannot be forecast, but statistics with respect to the lives of many poles will be a reliable guide."

A committee on depreciation of National Association of Railroad and Utilities Commissioners[31] says:

The actuarial method of estimating service life consists of an actuarial analysis of property retirements to secure a life indication based upon the relationship of property previously retired to that exposed to the risk of retirement at corresponding ages. The method is particularly apt for classes of plant comprised of a large number of like units, such as poles, ties, cable, conductor, automobiles, meters, etc. It is ordinarily not used for structures and large equipment units because there are usually insufficient of these in the plant of any one utility to make mortality data particularly valuable. Furthermore, the experience of previous structures and equipment may not be representative of the life of present property.

Riggs[32] claims that there are no dependable life tables covering "hundreds of kinds of items which will be found on a large property," and that practically all of the so-called life tables "are made up by some group of engineers and represent the experience or judgment of the members of the group. They are not based on the average experience with hundreds of items. The figures in the tables may represent actual experience in only a few cases."

Kurtz[33] quotes a statement made by J. E. Allison to the effect that:

... estimates of average life admittedly represent only the opinions of certain men as to the probable average period of usefulness of different items of equipment. The fact that they coincide within certain limits only goes to show that the later guessers did not differ very greatly from their predecessors on a subject concerning which there was very little to be found to support an argument one way or another.

Kurtz, himself a proponent of the actuarial method, admits that: "The service lives of individual units of the same class

[31] National Association of Railroad and Utilities Commissioners, *Report of Special Committee on Depreciation* (New York, The State Law Reporting Company, 1938), p. 69.
[32] H. E. Riggs, *Depreciation of Public Utility Properties* (New York, McGraw-Hill Book Company, Inc., 1922), p. 99.
[33] Edwin B. Kurtz, *The Science of Valuation and Depreciation* (New York, The Ronald Press Company, 1937), pp. 19, 20.

of property are not the same. . . . Some units of a given group are replaced soon after being put into service, while others remain in service many years." This statement is confirmed by the numerous life characteristic charts appended to his book.

Such comments as the foregoing could be multiplied. In fact, nearly all authors writing on the subject of depreciation take care to protect themselves against charges of being overly credulous about forecasting methods. It is, however, noted that many of these same authors then continue their discussions just as though they really believed that forecasting future asset life is an exact science.

As a result, practically all discussions of depreciation seem unrealistic in their detailed descriptions of refined methods and formulae, all of which are of slight importance as compared with the substantial error which may so easily result from applying the actuarial method to one or a few asset units.

DEPRECIATION AND PERIODIC PROFITS. Is there not somewhere in this threefold relationship between accountants, engineers, and business men an area of slight knowledge the effect of which may practically nullify much of the careful computation of periodic profits?

Can the accountants, who are most concerned with profit determination, surrender to engineers and appraisers that function of forecasting when those same engineers and appraisers are willing to assume responsibility for only part of the task?

The errors which may result from blind adoption of engineering forecasts or implicit faith in inadequate mortality tables can be devastatingly large. Those who would assert otherwise are referred to the contribution of W. A. Hosmer in the March 1938 issue of *The Accounting Review,* some quotations from which will be found in Chapter 31. If large corporations having at their command the best of engineering and accounting talent do, as a matter of fact, make serious errors in the determination of depreciation rates, so serious in many instances as completely to pervert annual profit and loss reports, how much more serious is this problem for other manufacturing companies large and small.

OPINIONS AS TO OBSOLESCENCE. There is, of course, no way to keep ingenious men from making inventions.

Learoyd[34] has pointed out that: "Revolutionary, original ideas, such as would cause industry obsolescence, usually spring from inspiration, and there is no way of foretelling when they will appear or who will be affected by them."

Meredith[35] asserts that how long a building will last is "anybody's guess" and observes that "during a depression the actual rate of obsolescence is apt to increase as new technical developments are spurred by the necessity of greater operating efficiency."

The *Handbook of Business Administration*[36] likens obsolescence to a fire which occurs without warning and quotes the Illinois Manufacturers' Cost Association as follows: "past history teaches us that obsolescence has discarded more fixed assets than wear and tear."

Montgomery[37] thinks: "In view of the rapid strides in all the mechanical sciences, extraordinary obsolescence is likely to continue to be a serious factor in the ultimate cost of producing manufactured goods."

Hill[38] states that any engineer or accountant who has tried to provide for obsolescence "soon finds that he is faced with endless problems involving very arbitrary decisions."

A committee[39] report previously cited says that: "The technicians entrusted with the determination of depreciation rates are not imbued with prophetic vision as to events which lie in the future."

Justice Brandeis[40] of the United States Supreme Court

[34] John S. Learoyd, Jr., "Obsolescence in the Electric Lamp Industry," *N.A.C.A. Bulletin*, April 15, 1938, p. 953.

[35] Spencer B. Meredith, "Depreciation—A Guessing Game," *Barron's, April 4,* 1938, p. 8.

[36] *Handbook of Business Administration* (New York, McGraw-Hill Book Company, Inc., 1931), pp. 506, 507.

[37] Robert H. Montgomery, *Auditing Theory and Practice* (New York, The Ronald Press Company, 1934), p. 550.

[38] Horace Hill, *Practical Aspects of Depreciation and Obsolescence* (New York, American Management Association, 1938), p. 21.

[39] National Association of Railroad and Utilities Commissioners, *Report of Special Committee on Depreciation* (New York, The State Law Reporting Company, 1938), p. 17.

[40] Justice Brandeis, quoted by the Staff of the Public Service Commission of Wisconsin, *Depreciation* (New York, The State Law Reporting Company, 1933), p. 59.

(United Railways and Electric Company of Baltimore *v*. West, 280 U. S. 234) believed that "there is nothing in business experience, or in the training of experts, which enables men to say to what extent service life will be impaired by the operations of a single year, or of a series of years less than the service life."

Calling attention to the fact that a variety and diversity of forces usually contribute to depreciation, Kurtz[41] concludes that "predeterminable quantitative analysis is likewise impossible." The Public Service Commission of Wisconsin[42] says that depreciation inherently is "a matter of estimates and conjecture."

Believing that depreciation charges cannot be determined with precision, Backman[43] asserts that "the necessity for including them in costs leads to an element of uncertainty and instability." Fabricant[44] suggests that the computation of depreciation "must necessarily be more or less of a guess." Paton[45] says: "Here there is little opportunity for precise calculations; reasonable estimating, in the light of past experience and scrutiny of current developments, is all that can be hoped for. In general the very uncertainty justifies a conservative position. A rough-and-ready method followed by some industrial concerns is to set effective service life at about half the term which might be expected if it were only necessary to consider physical character and internal operating conditions."

CONCLUSION. The inability of engineers to forecast service life save from a limited viewpoint, the great deviations shown by depreciation mortality tables and the consequent unsuitability of average life figures for use with isolated assets, the startling increase in the rate of obsolescence noted in some industries, and last but by no means least, the necessary concealment by

41 Edwin B. Kurtz, *The Science of Valuation and Depreciation* (New York, The Ronald Press Company, 1937), p. 9.

42 Staff of the Public Service Commission of Wisconsin, *Depreciation* (New York, The State Law Reporting Company, 1933), p. 161.

43 Jules Backman, "Cost of Production as a Basis for Price Fixing," *The Journal of Accountancy*, September 1938, p. 153.

44 Spahr and Others, *Economic Principles and Problems* (New York, Farrar & Rinehart, Inc., 1936), p. 260.

45 W. A. Paton, *Essentials of Accounting* (New York, The Macmillan Company, 1938), p. 532.

executives of secret business plans, which, if divulged to engineers and accountants, would undoubtedly change their estimates materially, are serious influences toward substantial inaccuracy in profit determination.

Probably more often than is generally assumed, such inaccuracies are derived directly from inaccurate forecasting and are of sufficient magnitude to introduce a wide margin of error or distortion in profit and loss statements.

CHAPTER 30

DEPRECIATION METHODS

In industrial organizations the straight-line method of depreciation is so uniformly popular as to bar extensive discussion of other methods save perhaps those referring to volume of production or rate of activity. This comment does not, of course, apply to special problems of depreciation accounting for transportation and public utility corporations. Such problems have become so specialized and legalistic as to constitute a separate subdivision of accounting.

A broad treatment of industrial depreciation should include the related topics of depletion and amortization which are somewhat similar from the profit and loss viewpoint. There are, of course, differences because of the kinds of assets to which depreciation, amortization, and depletion are respectively applied. As a rather loose generalization it may be said that the estimate of depletion, save in the case of standing timber, is more often tinged with inaccuracy than the other two. Amortization may be and frequently is subject to accurate determination because the time element is predeterminable. Depreciation may be said to occupy the middle position.

In so far as the methods of depreciation are concerned, the distortion or bias resulting from the use of one method as opposed to others, while sometimes significant, is often slight in comparison with distortion resulting from inaccurate forecasting of service life. On any accepted theory of the relative precision of measurements, the selection of one depreciation method in preference to another often represents a decision of slight importance. It seems rather strange that the literature on depreciation accounting is so replete with animated and sometimes argumentative discussion of depreciation methods and has little discussion of the more important problem of forecasting service life. Possibly this is because accountants consider depreciation methods as being particularly within their province while regarding forecasting as an engineering function.

This is, perhaps, as it should be, although when a large surplus adjustment to correct erroneous depreciation is required, it is probable that the accountant rather than the engineer will have to bear the burden of criticism.[1]

The Depreciation Charge.—Any of the standard methods of depreciation will result in a charge to some cost, expense, or loss account and a credit either direct to the depreciated asset or to a valuation account offsetting the asset.

In a manufacturing establishment depreciation of factory property is usually treated as an element of departmental or general overhead expense which through processes of distribution and redistribution is finally attached to the inventory cost of work in progress.

Where one building, for example, houses both the factory and the office, a problem of joint cost must be solved in order that proper allocation of the building depreciation may be made. Welfare facilities used in common by both office and factory employees offer the same problem.

IDLE PLANT. When a manufacturing plant is idle or is operating at less than normal capacity, a question regarding the accounting treatment of depreciation is presented.

[1] This shift of blame is not as unlikely as it may sound. The book, *Two Cycles of Corporation Profits*, written by Laurence H. Sloan and Associates, commented (page 243) upon the drastic write-downs of the property accounts of oil companies, indicating that they provide "eloquent evidence that the overstatement of past earnings has been common." Responsibility for this is plausibly, if not fairly, charged to accounting in the conclusion that "it is only too clear that oil company accounting is at fault." Another confirmation occurred in England and was reported editorially by *The Canadian Chartered Accountant* of October 1938, page 248. At the annual meeting of his company the chairman thereof placed the problem of depreciation directly before the accountants when he said: "I feel that the Institute of Chartered Accountants and the Society of Incorporated Accountants and Auditors should form a committee in order to strengthen their position in reporting on how depreciation has been dealt with in a company's accounts, and so avoid what has happened in so many cases in the past, namely, writing down of capital because the assets have not been properly depreciated."
At the American Institute Convention in Cincinnati, 1938, Carman G. Blough, formerly chief accountant of Securities and Exchange Commission, was probably reflecting the S.E.C. viewpoint when he said that it was distressing to him to read published financial statements in which the certifying accountant makes the positive assertion that he has no basis on which to express opinion with respect to depreciation. At the same convention Edwin S. Reno said that the accountant should report, competently, on the adequacy of depreciation.

Some accountants hold that the depreciation on the unused portion of factory property should never find its way into the costs. Others merge such depreciation with the general burden but allocate a certain portion of that burden to some special cost or expense account instead of permitting it to become part of the cost of finished product.

The depreciation on non-operating property is properly chargeable to some account which will be matched with the income from that same property.

DONATED PROPERTY. Where depreciable property has been acquired by donation, any one of three plans may be followed. If the donated property is put on the books at its fair market value at the time of acquisition, there should have been established at the same time an item of donated surplus. Depreciation on such property may be said to represent a gradual realization of that donated surplus. If the donated property is not recorded save in memorandum form, or is valued on some nominal basis, the depreciation thereof may either be ignored or, if it is demanded for cost accounting purposes, a problem of imputed cost arises.

DISCLOSURE OF DEPRECIATION. In the manufacturing establishment depreciation of manufacturing properties is usually recorded functionally and departmentally. In other business establishments it is believed that the cost of depreciation has no departmental significance in that it is not a controllable cost for which a department head may be held responsible.

In such establishments no difficulty is encountered in following the suggestion appended to the form of profit and loss statement in *Examination of Financial Statements by Independent Public Accountants,*[2] namely, "It is desirable to indicate the amount of provision for depreciation, depletion, etc., for the period."

In factory accounting, on the other hand, this suggestion may offer some analytical difficulties since the amount of depreciation provided during the year may not be the same as the

2 *Examination of Financial Statements by Independent Public Accountants* (New York, American Institute of Accountants, January 1936), p. 40.

amount of depreciation intermingled with all of the various other costs comprised in cost of sales.

If the inventories at the beginning and end of a financial period are about the same, if depreciation has been treated consistently both as regards methods and rates, the discrepancy will not be serious and can best be ignored. It should, however, be recognized that a footnote showing the total depreciation provision for a fiscal year appended to a manufacturing profit and loss statement is not harmonious with the basis upon which such a profit and loss statement is prepared, and in any given instance it may be a question of accounting judgment as to whether the depreciation element of cost of sales should be closely estimated or whether disclosure should be made of the discrepancy.

Often it is a difficult task to determine the amount of depreciation included in work in progress and finished goods at the beginning and end of the period.

The Depreciation Credit.—In theory, the offset to the depreciation charge is shown by a credit direct to the asset account.

As a matter of practice, however, such direct credits in the case of fixed assets are seldom made. Rather they are made to valuation accounts. Such an account is often referred to as a "reserve for depreciation," although the term "allowance for depreciation" seems preferable. Such accounts may be considered as deferred credits to the asset accounts themselves and their use is justified by the practical convenience which results.

Because of the long life of many fixed assets, it seems desirable to maintain the original cost figures intact. The use of valuation accounts permits this, whereas the direct credit of depreciation to the asset account itself would result in a constantly reducing balance, thus obscuring the original valuation and possibly necessitating the search of old records for its determination.

The fact that a reserve or an allowance for depreciation has a credit balance may seem superficially to classify it as a liability. Occasionally it is so classified. Fjeld reported 62 out of 641 companies, or 9.7%, as classifying depreciation reserves on the liability side.

Despite its credit balance the reserve or allowance for depreciation has none of the characteristics of a liability. As a matter of practical accounting, each asset account and its corresponding valuation account must be considered as inseparable. In fact, they must be regarded as separate halves of but one account and the various adjustments which are required from time to time must conform to this theory. The retirement of a depreciated asset is, therefore, represented not only by a credit to the asset account but by a debit to the valuation account in the amount of the accrued depreciation.

Types of Depreciation Methods.—Depreciation methods are of three general types: (1) replacement or retirement methods, (2) production methods, and (3) time methods.

REPLACEMENT METHODS. The replacement, retirement, or renewal methods are in actual fact not depreciation methods at all. They have no features in common with the typical depreciation plan in that they involve no forecasting of service life and no provision for recording accrued reduction in asset values.

When a fixed asset consists of a great variety of relatively small units, it is often assumed that approximately the same number of such units will have to be retired each year. Under these circumstances some authorities believe that the replacement of such units should be considered an expense of the accounting period in which replacement took place. The original asset value remains constant on the books and the expense of replacement each year is, in theory at least, fairly uniform. When the asset items retired are exactly replaced, the method cannot be condemned, but when 100 units are retired and 150 new units purchased, it is clear that 50 of them should be capitalized and that unless this is done there is danger that asset undervaluation and profit and loss distortion will result. Overvaluation will be inevitable if the reverse of this situation obtains, i.e., if more units are retired in any year, or series of years, than are replaced.

A somewhat similar method, popular in some enterprises, involves capitalizing of all additions and improvements, making no annual provision for depreciation but charging to expense all units of property as they are retired. If the rate of retirement is reasonably uniform, and if the items retired have approximately uniform incidence upon profit and loss, the distorting effect of this method may not be more noticeable than that caused by errors in the forecasting of service life.

These methods are applicable to large organizations operating at a fairly steady rate. They are less suitable for the erratic type of business in which the management during a year of depression might find it expedient to postpone making replacements, in which event a substantial distortion of profits might result.

PRODUCTION METHODS. The production method of depreciation has the merit of allowing depreciation to fluctuate as the volume of production fluctuates, the rates being expressed in terms of units of product, i.e., per pound, per yard, per mile, or per gallon. It is this method which is used in accounting for depletion.

Just as it is difficult to foretell how many tons of ore still remain to be mined, so is it difficult to forecast the number of units of product to be adopted as the basis for forecasting an asset's future life.

Stempf,[3] commenting on the element of clairvoyance in the forecast of life in terms of productive units, thinks that "the production method of depreciation needs to be checked by straight line calculations or observed depreciation to assure the adequacy of the accumulated reserve."

Mason[4] suggests:

There is much to be said for allowing depreciation to vary with the volume of production. The important thing is to make sure that the total amount to be allocated to operations is all absorbed over the useful life of the asset in some systematic, conservative manner.

A variant of the production method, but one having substantially the same advantages, is the working hours method. This method forecasts the life of an asset not in terms of months or

[3] Victor H. Stempf, "Accounting for Fixed Assets," *N.A.C.A. Bulletin,* April 15, 1938, p. 945.
[4] Perry Mason, *Principles of Public-Utility Depreciation* (Chicago, American Accounting Association, 1937), p. 16.

years but in terms of estimated working hours. When the number of hours that a machine has been operated during a fiscal period is known, the depreciation can be calculated accordingly, with the result that the depreciation actually varies with activity.

TIME METHODS. Of the methods based upon time, the straight-line method is the simplest and most popular. Canning[5] disliked this method and criticized it in the following words:

> The straight line rule in all its forms seems to be merely a special case of the popular fallacy that the arithmetic mean, by divine or natural ordinance, is *the* average and that any other average is an evil to be avoided if possible.

His opinion is, however, not shared by the majority of accountants.

Such methods as the percentage of reducing balance method, the annuity method, and the compound interest method have their adherents but their practical business adoption is almost negligible. There is, perhaps, some merit in using a mathematical method of allocating depreciation to successive periods in such a manner that the earlier periods bear the heavier burden, since it is the later periods which must carry the burden of greater repair and maintenance charges. The point is, however, of doubtful importance under usual industrial conditions.

Where but one important and costly asset is involved, such as a hotel or apartment building or some very costly special-purpose machine, the use of some of these interest methods to replace the straight-line method may be justified, although the Special Committee on Depreciation,[6] previously quoted, argues otherwise: "The loss in service value caused by deterioration, inadequacy, obsolescence and other causes is not influenced by the cost of money. To reason so results in holding that depreciation on property accumulates more rapidly when money costs 2 per cent than when it costs 6 per cent."

On the whole, however, the accountant's or business man's

5 John B. Canning, *The Economics of Accountancy* (New York, The Ronald Press Company, 1929), p. 288.
6 National Association of Railroad and Utilities Commissioners, *Report of Special Committee on Depreciation* (New York, The State Law Reporting Company, 1938), p. 19.

sense of proportion causes him to reject ultra-refined methods in the treatment of estimates which ordinarily involve a wide margin of error. One can hardly fail to enjoy Canning's[7] boredom with "The interminable argument that has been carried on by the text writers and others about the relative merits of the many formulas for measuring depreciation."

Rechecking Depreciation.—If the forecast of an asset's service life and the resulting depreciation rates were never reviewed and adjusted, all of the loss or gain due to inaccuracy of estimate would have to be taken care of at the time the asset was retired.

Usually, however, it is not desirable to wait for retirement in order to correct depreciation errors. It is generally regarded as good practice to make a periodic examination of fixed assets and, if necessary, revise the estimates of life expectancy. Such a regular program will often justify changes in depreciation rates, with the result that the loss or gain upon asset retirement may not be shockingly large. It should be noted, however, that such inspection and such changing in rates may result in considerable distortion of periodic profits.

A periodic survey helps to forecast obsolescence. Obsolescence is sometimes sudden. More often it is fairly slow and can be foreseen some months or years ahead. To check machinery, equipment, structures, and various other fixed assets not only for wear and tear or inadequacy, but also for obsolescence, is unquestionably an enlightened policy. It permits the establishment of obsolescence rates upon something at least a little better than a guesswork basis.

Learoyd[8] has described such a program in the electric lamp industry in the following words:

At the beginning of every year, there is a thorough and detailed examination of all equipment, and present estimates of life are checked with the most recent developments. This investigation involves a careful study of all sources of obsolescence . . . engineers report not only on their own developments, but on everything which they have been

[7] John B. Canning, *The Economics of Accountancy* (New York, The Ronald Press Company, 1929), p. 204.
[8] John S. Learoyd, Jr., "Obsolescence in the Electric Lamp Industry," *N.A.C.A. Bulletin,* April 15, 1938, p. 959.

able to find out through their memberships in technical societies, technical publications, or from any other sources.

It seems that the lamp industry may be leading in a movement which has too long been delayed, as intimated by Stempf's[9] observation that: "Appraisal engineers repeatedly make the statement that there are entirely too many companies in which no attempt is made to check the physical existence of plant and equipment from time to time."

To replace the impossible ideal of absolute accuracy in forecasting, such a periodic inspection program, even though it has a distorting effect upon profit and loss, appears to provide the only acceptable substitute. Had it been a matter of common business policy for the past two decades, many heavy surplus adjustments would have been unnecessary.

9 Victor H. Stempf, "Accounting for Fixed Assets," *N.A.C.A. Bulletin*, April 15, 1938, p. 943.

CHAPTER 31

FIXED ASSET READJUSTMENTS

From time to time in the life of a business enterprise there may be developed a need, real or imaginary, for a substantial correction or restatement of fixed asset valuation. This need may result from inaccurate depreciation plans. It may develop because of the belief that the fixed assets as a whole are substantially overvalued or undervalued in relation to current phases of the business cycle.

Accounting adjustments referring to these various matters may result in a real or apparent profit or loss. Discussion of the loss or gain aspects of the sale, retirement, or revaluation of fixed assets leads inevitably into a morass of conflicting opinion.

Long recognizing that realized capital gains and losses, while non-recurring and non-operating in nature, may by their size greatly distort profit and loss comparisons, accountants are not yet in agreement as to the proper methods of recording and reporting them. Such capital gains and losses, if actually realized, must be recognized from the viewpoints of both accounting and law. Because they are abnormal or non-recurring, because they are not related to the principal operating activities of business, because they result from a variety of different causes, and because of their distorting effect on periodic profits, the resulting accounting problems are often troublesome.

Losses or gains recognizable only upon the termination of asset life may in general be classed as realized, regardless of whether the accounting adjustments are required to correct prior period errors, uninsured loss, abandonment, or the effect of an actual sale.

In a different category are asset revaluations which involve no retirement. Abandonment of the original cost basis of valuation is observed when assets are appraised and the result of that appraisal is reflected in the accounting records regardless of whether it represents an inflation or deflation of the book values. Such a revaluation may result in a bookkeeping loss or gain generally regarded as fictitious when it is not related to the termination of asset life nor to the correction of prior period errors.

While the possible causes underlying accounting adjustments of fixed assets are many, it appears that most of them can be classified in one of the following two groups:

1. Loss or gain resulting from actual retirement of assets:
    (a) Loss or gain representing the correction of prior period errors which has resulted in over- or under-depreciation.
    (b) Loss resulting from abandonment or uninsured destruction.
    (c) Gain resulting from overinsured destruction.
    (d) Loss or gain resulting from sale.

2. Loss or gain resulting from asset revaluation not accompanied by retirement:
    (a) Loss or gain resulting from correction of over- or underdepreciation due to prior period error.
    (b) Loss or gain resulting from asset revaluation for the purpose of correcting an obvious over- or undervaluation of assets which was not foreseeable but is due to changes in price levels or to the apparent, or real, necessity of relieving future accounting periods of burdensome depreciation charges.

Accounting Viewpoint Toward Actual Retirements.— Property may be retired when it is sold, destroyed, abandoned, or scrapped.

The *Accountants' Handbook*[1] indicates that the test of retirement is represented by the following question: "has the property ceased functioning and is there little or no likelihood of its

---

[1] *Accountants' Handbook* (New York, The Ronald Press Company, 1934), pp. 554, 555.

effective use later?" By this test, abandonment represents a retirement. Retirement being considered equivalent to realization, the same general accounting treatment is applicable to all forms. The asset account must be credited, the accompanying valuation account must be debited, the loss or gain upon the retirement must be computed and reflected in (1) a loss or gain account, usually non-operating, or (2) a surplus account, generally earned surplus, or (3) if a loss, an account representing a deferred charge against future income.

The fact that there is a possible choice among these three treatments has been responsible for much controversy.

LOSSES AS DEFERRED CHARGES. The proposal to show certain types of capital losses as deferred charges is by now fairly well discredited. Arguments in favor of this procedure were of two general types. Saliers was quoted in the *Accountants' Handbook*[1] as saying that "in a going concern there can be no such thing as a capital loss." This viewpoint is explained in the *Handbook*[1] as being based upon the position

that retirement losses arising in the case of premature elimination of structures and equipment on account of technological changes are actually assets, in the form of additional costs of the new type of structures and equipment, and must therefore be capitalized and absorbed against future revenues.

The second argument favoring the treatment of capital losses as deferred charges is based upon managerial intent. When an item of equipment, for example, is replaced by a more efficient unit, it is argued that the loss upon retirement of the old asset has been taken into consideration by the management in its decision to purchase the new asset and that the new asset would not have been acquired had it not promised such large cost reductions as fully to absorb the retirement loss. Like many accounting arguments based upon intent, this opens the door to a variety of undesirable inflationary practices.

To those who can see no relation between the retirement of an asset and its replacement, these arguments seem unreal. From the entity viewpoint the retirement of an asset discharges the entity from responsibility and accountability and results in the extinguishment of part of the entity's indebtedness to proprietorship. The acquisition of a replacing asset is another, a separate and a distinct transaction involving no increase or decrease in the proprietorship account. From the entity viewpoint, the profit or loss upon retirement of an asset merely modifies the charge and discharge relationship inherent in the accounting formula, this modification being the same whether the asset is replaced or not replaced.

Apart from theoretical considerations, capital losses are sometimes shown as deferred charges in order to present a more attractive looking balance sheet. Often, perhaps, this is the primary purpose, the arguments supporting it representing mere rationalization.

The choice between showing capital gains and losses in current profit and loss or as surplus adjustments cannot be disposed of so easily.

SURPLUS ADJUSTMENTS. When the loss represents an obvious correction of errors made in prior periods, it is thoroughly logical to make adjustment through the surplus account on the ground that the prior period errors have already affected previous profit and loss statements and that such errors at the time of their correction are reflected by the surplus account. If such prior period errors have actually resulted in an understatement of surplus, the surplus adjustment seems to be the only logical remedy.

The opponents of surplus adjustments, however, have an equally strong case since they are able to point out that this procedure keeps certain legitimate profit elements from ever being shown in any profit and loss statement. During a general session at the American Institute Convention, held on September 29, 1938, Henry T. Chamberlain referred to the "shaky arguments" in favor of surplus adjustments and intimated that such surplus adjustments were a direct invitation to management to understate depreciation.

Directly or indirectly, opponents of surplus adjustments infer that stockholders and others who receive annual reports do not study them but merely glance at them, giving particular attention to the final figure on the profit and loss statement. By inference at least it is claimed that those receiving annual reports either cannot or will not analyze a separate surplus statement. It would probably be admitted by any opponent of such surplus adjustments that less harm would result if those who receive annual reports would show as much interest in the surplus reconciliation as they do in the profit and loss statement. The point at issue between the two schools of thought is, therefore, not so much an accounting problem as it is a problem of reporting and of reader's psychology.

Admitting that profit and loss distortion results from either method, the question then boils down to this: Should the logical treatment of prior period errors through surplus account be adopted even though this eliminates certain profit and loss items from ever appearing on any profit and loss statement, or should the public be protected against its own carelessness by the inclusion in *some* profit and loss statement of all items of gain or loss even though they may have no reference whatever to the particular accounting period covered by the statement?

Since most of the arguments pro and con have already been quoted in Chapter 14, it seems unnecessary to repeat them here.

CORRECTED STATEMENTS. Reference has already been made to the fact that the American Accounting Association's Postulate 13 represents a procedure for the correction of substantial prior period errors which, subject to certain objections already noted, meets both arguments. This postulate, it will be remembered, calls for the preparation of corrected income statements for each of the prior periods affected by the error.

DEPRECIATION CORRECTION UPON RETIREMENT. Recognizing merits in both sides of the controversy about surplus adjustments and recognizing that Postulate 13 offers a possible solution, the accountant is nevertheless faced with the necessity of making certain practical decisions at the time of asset retirement.

Save as the result of some strange coincidence, it is inevitable that some loss or gain must be recorded upon retirement of a fixed asset. Whether such loss or gain will be recognized immediately depends upon whether such assets have been accounted for by units or have been grouped. Under the unit plan, the loss or gain must be recognized upon retirement of the asset.

Since the date of retirement probably will not fall upon the first or last day of a fiscal period, depreciation for a fraction of a period must be entered as an element of the profit and loss for that period. Such depreciation is properly to be included in the operating section of the profit and loss statement even though the capital loss or gain upon retirement is reflected in the non-operating section of the profit and loss statement or in the surplus account. This is the general rule. It is, however, affected by the doctrine of materiality and when numerous minor retirements occur throughout an accounting period it may, as intimated by the *Accountants' Handbook,*[2] be assumed "that all additions and all retirements occurred simultaneously at the middle of the period under consideration."

When the depreciation accounting is based upon groups of assets rather than single assets, no loss or gain adjustment is permissible until the entire group has been retired. Prior to that time the entire difference between the book value of any one of the retired items and its salvage value is charged to the valuation account.

The argument on this procedure has been well presented by Wheeler[3] as follows:

Certainly, if an average life of 15 years is the correct estimate for a group of similar machines, it is clearly to be anticipated that some individual machines may last only 12 or 13 years and that the loss which then results will later be offset by the fact that certain other machines will presumably remain in service for 17 or 18 years. Consequently, the Revenue Bureau insists in such cases that the entire cost be charged against the depreciation reserve when an item is thus discarded, and that no separate loss is allowable under those conditions.

That this treatment, as compared with the unit method, will affect the comparability of the profit and loss statements cannot be denied. As a practical expedient the final loss or gain determinable when the last asset in the group has been retired may be

2 *Accountants' Handbook* (New York, The Ronald Press Company, 1934), p. 648.
3 Bleecker L. Wheeler, *Practical Aspects of Depreciation and Obsolescence* (New York, American Management Association, 1938), p. 17.

appreciably reduced by interim changes in depreciation rates. This method also results in a recognizable, if not always material, distortion.

The retirement reserve method used by many public utilities is in reality an equalization device. The practice of equalization has been condemned by many authorities. If, however, the retirement method be adopted, then an equalizing retirement reserve may assist in curing its more obvious defects. To adopt one arbitrary method and then to attempt curing its defects by adoption of another may, in some instances, result in a fairly reasonable, fairly equitable showing. There is in reality no more reason to fear profit and loss distortion from the retirement method as modified by the proper use of an equalization reserve than there is from the more standard depreciation plans, based as they are upon dubious forecasts of life expectancy.

The Special Committee on Depreciation of the National Association of Railroad and Utilities Commissioners[4] disagrees with this viewpoint, however, in the following words:

> The old method of retirement reserve accounting was seriously abused in many cases. The method itself was unsound because it resulted in income statements which generally showed less than the cost of operation and balance sheets which did not reflect adequate provision for the loss in service value of plant.

DESTRUCTION. In any situation where an asset is prematurely retired and a capital loss is suffered the problem is always a mixed one, i.e., part of the loss may be due to erroneous depreciation in prior periods, the remainder being directly related to the premature retirement.

Seldom is it possible or practical to give effect to this distinction, although failure to do so admittedly results in profit distortion. If, upon accidental uninsured destruction a total loss of $1,000 is suffered, and if $400 of that loss could be said to represent inadequate depreciation of prior periods, some might argue that the $400 should receive different accounting treatment from the remaining $600.

[4] National Association of Railroad and Utilities Commissioners, *Report of Special Committee on Depreciation* (New York, The State Law Reporting Company, 1938), p. 24.

The recognition that any such forced retirement may involve profit and loss distortion does not justify hair-splitting procedure and the practical accountant must inevitably treat the entire $1,000 loss as a loss due entirely to destruction.

Forced abandonment is for all practical purposes equivalent to destruction in so far as the need for such abandonment could not have been foreseen. Often a capital loss due to destruction is partially offset by insurance. Generally such gain from insurance is applied against the total loss resulting in a net capital loss, although a fairly convincing argument could be presented in favor of showing the two items separately in the non-operating section of the profit and loss statement.

Regardless of the opinion held by some that a capital loss due to destruction or abandonment of a fixed asset is not properly assignable to any one accounting period, it is nevertheless common practice[5] to include it in the non-operating section of the profit and loss statement.

This practice has been endorsed by the Executive Committee of the American Accounting Association, and by *Examination of Financial Statements by Independent Public Accountants.* It is approved by Littleton,[6] who asserts that "it is difficult to see how one kind of fixed-asset diminution (loss) has more justification as a charge against capital or surplus than another kind of fixed-asset diminution (depreciation)."

A somewhat different stand is taken in *A Statement of Accounting Principles,*[7] as disclosed by the following quotation:

There is some opinion in favor of passing all capital losses and gains through the income statement, on the ground that resort to surplus account may be misused to relieve the income statement of proper charges, and to the end that the income statements may cumulatively

---

[5] That this is far from universal practice is indicated by the following from the annual report of American Water Works & Electric Company, Inc., for the year 1937, quoted by William D. Cranstoun in *The Journal of Accountancy* of November 1938: "Losses in asset value on account of certain abandonments of street railway operations have been charged on the books of certain subsidiary companies against surplus or special reserves arising from reappraisal of assets. Neither the practice of the companies nor general accounting practice calls for provisions for such losses out of income or out of reserves created out of income."

[6] A. C. Littleton, "High Standards of Accounting," *The Journal of Accountancy,* August 1938, p. 102.

[7] Sanders, Hatfield, and Moore, *A Statement of Accounting Principles* (New York, American Institute of Accountants, 1938), p. 39.

show all changes in net worth. Some capital gains and losses are, however, sufficiently abnormal to have no direct relation to current income, and sufficiently large to distort current income, even when clearly shown as separate items. In such cases charges or credits to surplus are justifiable. In cases of doubt the tendency should be to include such items in the income statement.

Husband[8] agrees with the viewpoint that a loss from property destruction "appears to be a capital or surplus deduction, an item which, had the facts been known earlier, would have been charged pro rata against the income of all of the periods which benefited through the asset's existence."

Kester[9] refers to "Hatfield's almost classic illustration" which he quotes as follows:

An individual's entire income is derived from ten houses each worth $10,000 and each yielding 10% net income. If two of these houses burn down, uninsured, the common sense view is that the proprietor's income is thereby cut down from $10,000 to $8,000 per annum, and that coincidentally, there is a loss of capital of $20,000. It never occurs to him that he must consider his income as entirely cut off for two years until the principal can be restored.

Broad[10] employs a similar illustration substituting two steamships for Hatfield's ten houses and reaches a similar conclusion, namely, that "while losses on working assets are income items, major and abnormal losses on permanent investments or fixed assets are losses of the company's capital."

That the surplus adjustment method has an appeal to the practical accountant is suggested by the treatment of depletion on stolen coal by the Lehigh Valley Coal Company. In 1934 the company charged $71,000 of such depletion direct to surplus.

Strictly from the entity viewpoint it makes no difference whether capital gain or loss is reflected in the current profit and loss statement or in surplus account. By either method the

8 George R. Husband, "Accounting Postulates: An Analysis of the Tentative Statement of Accounting Principles," *The Accounting Review,* December 1937, p. 393.

9 Roy B. Kester, *Advanced Accounting* (New York, The Ronald Press Company, 1933), p. 513.

10 Samuel J. Broad, "Some Comments on Surplus Account," *The Journal of Accountancy,* October 1938, pp. 222, 223.

proprietor's account is modified and the charge and discharge relationship is properly readjusted. The problem referred to by Sanders, Hatfield, and Moore is, therefore, a problem of periodic reporting. It is, however, an important problem and the intimation that any kind of a true gain or loss can be shunted directly into surplus account seems to represent a backward step in accounting thought.

Admitting the abnormal showing which must result from including such a loss or gain in a current profit and loss statement, it is nevertheless a material reportable item. If, as some maintain, those who read annual reports are too careless to analyze the surplus statement, it is all the more important that significant items should not be buried therein. The argument which supports showing corrections of prior period errors in surplus account is not, it seems, a blanket covering all extraordinary items.

GAIN FROM INSURANCE. Occasionally destruction of property results in a profit when the amount received from the insurance company is in excess of the book loss. This results in a realized capital gain properly to be reflected in the profit and loss statement for the period when the claim against the insurance company becomes legal and enforceable.

RECONSTRUCTION BY INSURANCE COMPANY. An interesting accounting problem is presented when an insurance company chooses to restore the destroyed property, the restoration involving some actual improvement in the property itself.

With reference to this problem the *Accountants' Handbook*[11] comments: "Under these conditions the most convenient treatment would be to credit buildings account and charge suspense (or insurance company) with the estimated loss, the same amount being closed back to the building account when the restorations were complete."

This procedure would not, of course, give any consideration to the fact that the restored property, having a longer service life, would be more valuable than the destroyed property. Recognizing this, the *Accountants' Handbook*[11] continued:

11 *Accountants' Handbook* (New York, The Ronald Press Company, 1934), p. 558.

A more accurate treatment would be to handle the matter as a reconstruction job, the funds, however, being provided from the outside. This would involve a careful estimate of the damage done in terms of book value, which amount would then be eliminated, and a charging in of the cost of the new work, less the part representing removal costs or excessive installation cost. As a result of such a treatment a net change in book value, and an equivalent profit or loss, as the case might be, would probably emerge.

To consider that such a profit or loss would be a realized one necessitates the adoption of the fiction that the insurance company actually turns over to the insured the amount of cash representing the reconstruction cost. It is from the relationship between that amount of cash and the depreciated book value of the old asset that the element of profit or loss must be determined.

The actual reconstruction, however, is a separate and distinct transaction and, like any other replacement, has no bearing whatsoever upon profit or loss resulting from the destruction of its predecessor asset.

ABANDONMENT. Abandonment of assets is usually the direct result of some unforeseen calamity having all the effect of property destruction without actually causing any physical damage, as in the case of the roadside restaurant which must be abandoned when the main highway is changed, or mining property which must be abandoned when a vein runs out, an underground fire occurs, or the mine is hopelessly flooded. Sudden obsolescence of the more violent and unforeseeable type may also result in abandonment.

With reference to such obsolescence Sanders[12] asserts: "If it is large enough to affect the results materially, it is better first to show the Net Profits before this charge and then to deduct the unusual charge from Profit and Loss as a special item or, better still, to charge it to Surplus." This surplus viewpoint, appearing in his book published in 1934, seems to foreshadow some of the viewpoints expressed by the Sanders, Hatfield, and Moore committee, of which he was chairman.

12 T. H. Sanders, *Cost Accounting for Control* (New York, McGraw-Hill Book Company, Inc., 1934), p. 200.

SALE OF PROPERTY. When fixed assets not acquired for purpose of resale are sold prior to the termination of their useful life, a loss or gain results. Such a loss or gain, even though non-operating and non-recurring, is fully realized and should appear in a profit and loss statement rather than in surplus account. By every test the gain resulting from any such sale is a true profit subject to dividend distribution. Whether it should be distributed is not an accounting question but refers rather to sound business and financial policy. That any material capital gain or loss arising from the sale of property should specifically be disclosed in the profit and loss statement is generally urged by accounting authorities.

Revaluation Without Retirement.—When a fixed asset has been substantially overdepreciated, a fair proportion of the cost thereof may be reinstated.

This constitutes a revaluation prior to retirement and is the situation to which reference was made in Postulate 4 of the American Accounting Association. It was the suggestion of this association that revised income statements be prepared for each period affected. The adoption of this suggestion represents one means of adjusting the revaluation credit which results.

CORRECTION OF OVERDEPRECIATION. On the older theory that prior period errors should be corrected through the surplus account, it would seem that such a reinstated cost should be offset by a contra-credit to surplus account.

There is good ground for arguing that such a credit represents a realized gain if the theory be adopted that the overdepreciation has been recovered by sales to customers in the regular course of business. Overdepreciation on that theory simply means that customers have paid more for the fixed asset than they should have. Any objection to overemphasis of this point is practical rather than theoretical and is due to the uncertainty as to the amount involved in such a readjustment; an uncertainty that continues until the actual retirement of the asset.

While interesting, the point is not one of great importance when the amounts involved are not material. As already observed, it is generally considered good practice to check depreciation periodically and to revise the depreciation rates. The staff of the Public Service Commission of Wisconsin,[13] in commenting upon this practice, asserted that "the legal doctrine apparently is at least that where excessive reserves have been accumulating through depreciation charges in the past, the annual depreciation allowances for the future may be adjusted to avoid a continuance of these excess accumulations."

APPRECIATION. Superficially, somewhat similar to reinstatement of costs is the practice of writing up asset values based upon appraisal. The former, however, can be justified as a correction of prior error. The latter departs entirely from the cost basis and hence involves no realization of profit.

The former popularity[14] of upward revaluation has greatly declined since 1929, but even so the problem has been given adequate accounting attention with the result that nearly all authorities insist either that such write-ups should not be permitted at all or, if they are permitted, the apparent gain which results must be registered in a special surplus account clearly labeled to indicate its nature and unsuitability as a basis for dividends.

That no distributable profit can result from any bookkeeping tricks is axiomatic. If pen and ink entries were the basis of making money, the poorest beggar could be a millionaire.

It would appear that those who condemn revaluations upward should, in all consistency, condemn downward revaluations. With some exceptions such consistency is not observed. The American Accounting Association[15] has, however, taken a strong stand in this matter, as will be seen from the following quotations:

[13] Staff of the Public Service Commission of Wisconsin, *Depreciation* (New York, The State Law Reporting Company, 1933), p. 158.

[14] As recently as December 31, 1937, according to William D. Cranstoun in the November 1938 issue of *The Journal of Accountancy*, E. I. duPont de Nemours & Company revalued their investment in 10,000,000 shares of General Motors common stock from $17.60 a share to $18.45 a share, involving a surplus credit of about $8,500,000. While this investment did not represent a fixed asset in the ordinary sense, nor did it represent control over General Motors Corporation, the revaluation was of the same general type as though it had referred to fixed assets.

[15] Executive Committee of the American Accounting Association, "A Tentative Statement of Accounting Principles Affecting Corporate Reports," *The Accounting Review*, June 1936, p. 189.

. . . there seems to be no sound reason for repeated adjustments of asset values for the ordinary changes in price levels commonly experienced from one generation to another.

Occasional uncoordinated "appraisals" produce in the average financial statement a hodgepodge of unrelated values.

A history of cost and cost amortization is a consistent record of actual occurrences measured according to an intelligible formula, and constitutes an essential starting point in financial interpretation.

In a significant article on capital and surplus, Cranstoun[16] suggests: "The confusion which has arisen because of the revaluation of assets can be avoided most easily by discontinuing the practice." He then comments on the valuation convention and points out the ultimate futility of rewriting the valuation symbols.

CORRECTION OF UNDERDEPRECIATION.   Underdepreciation is, for one reason or another, more common than overdepreciation. Underdepreciation may result from managerial optimism, from the desire to make a good operating showing or, more often, from inability to foresee all of the value-destroying factors which constitute entreprenurial risk.

Overvaluation of assets due to underdepreciation should, of course, be corrected when recognized. The comparative merits of the different methods of correction, i.e., through surplus or current profit and loss or recasting of prior period reports, require no repetition here.

Of special importance, however, is recognition of the prevalence of underdepreciation and the effects thereof on profits.

Based upon depreciation rates determined in good faith a steel corporation reports to its stockholders and to the public annual net profits which for ten years averaged $50,000,000 per year. During the ten years investors bought and sold large amounts of stock in that corporation based upon its reported profits.

At the end of the tenth year the corporation made a surplus adjustment of $270,000,000 to correct underdepreciation, ex-

16 William D. Cranstoun in "The Commentator," *The Journal of Accountancy,* January 1938, p. 70.

plaining the adjustment as follows: "Broadly, these adjustments are attributable to the developments in the art and mechanics of steel making which have operated to reduce the normally expected life of such facilities, and to changes in plant location based upon shifting markets and transportation facilities."

Assuming that this extra depreciation of $270,000,000 occurred during the ten-year period, then recasting the ten profit and loss statements would have reduced the average annual profit from $50,000,000 per year to less than $24,000,000 per year. In other words, each dollar of reported profits should, in reality, have been only 50 cents.

It was on the dollar profit basis that investors bought and sold during the ten years. Would they have made the same transactions had they known that the profits were, in reality, only half as much as reported?

It would be cold comfort to the investor who bought this stock heavily during the first nine years to be furnished with "a corrected income statement for each prior period for which adjustments have been made."[17]

This is no imagined illustration. It is what actually happened in the case of the United States Steel Corporation, the years involved being 1926-1935 inclusive, as reported by Hosmer.[18]

Hosmer's article is startling in its revelation of the extent of surplus adjustments, many of them correcting underdepreciation, and the effect of such adjustments on reported profits. Since his analysis deserves full reading, only a few of his other examples need be noted.

The United Carbide and Carbon Corporation's average annual report of net income for the same ten years was over $23,000,000 with an average net surplus debit of about $6,500,000. In other words, the reported average income was $23,000,000 when the average should apparently have been $16,000,000.

[17] Executive Committee of the American Accounting Association, "A Tentative Statement of Accounting Principles Affecting Corporate Reports," *The Accounting Review*, June 1936, p. 190.
[18] W. A. Hosmer, "The Effect of Direct Charges to Surplus on the Measurement of Income," *The Accounting Review*, March 1938, pp. 34, 35.

The American Smelting and Refining Corporation showed average net income of nearly $11,000,000 when, by Hosmer's analysis, it should have been $7,000,000.

Radio Corporation of America showed the most startling figures of all, since they reported average annual income of nearly $7,000,000 which, after giving effect to surplus adjustments, would have been only $750,000.

Hosmer's analysis of other well-known corporations indicated that surplus adjustments were relatively small in relation to net income. Nevertheless, where direct surplus charges can be permitted to modify reported income by as much as 50%, 60%, or in the case of the Radio Corporation nearly 90%, it seems clear that the investors would do well to avoid placing unquestioning reliance on reported earnings.

REVALUATION TO BENEFIT FUTURE EARNINGS. Hosmer[19] also suggested that it is possible to distinguish "between surplus charges which are in substance a substitute for past expenses and those which reduce future expenses."

Canning[20] said: "A grossly overvalued consideration received if booked at that value, requires adjustment as soon as the erroneous valuation is discovered." As an overvaluation he intimates that it "will mislead innocent persons to their harm" and "will have the effect of falsifying all future net incomes and all earning rates, unit costs, and all other statistical data in any way depending upon book valuations."

Stempf[21] comments on "many industries burdened with excess facilities and plants acquired at the peak of price levels," and asks:

Should management remain impotent in the face of these conditions and sink deeper and deeper into the mire of mounting losses? Or should management and stockholders face the facts squarely, take the loss on fixed assets, and adjust book amounts to a basis which may permit profitable operation on the remaining capital?

19 W. A. Hosmer, "The Effect of Direct Charges to Surplus on the Measurement of Income," *The Accounting Review*, March 1938, p. 39.

20 John B. Canning, *The Economics of Accountancy* (New York, The Ronald Press Company, 1929), p. 249.

21 Victor H. Stempf, "Accounting for Fixed Assets," *N.A.C.A. Bulletin*, April 15, 1938, p. 948.

Stempf thinks the answer is obvious, that: "The only hope of revival lies in an adjustment of fixed assets to a basis commensurate with potential operations."

Broad,[22] discussing a similar problem, suggested: "There is something to be said for reducing the value of the stock when such conditions are discovered, creating a capital surplus, and reducing the values of the properties by a charge against such capital surplus without disturbing the earned surplus of the company."

Is it proper to make such a revaluation without disturbing the earned surplus? May[23] thinks not, saying:

I have never been able to feel any sympathy with those who have sought to get the benefit of reduced depreciation charges, as if the corporation were a new one, and also to retain an earned surplus on the ground that, actually, it is still the old one.

The Executive Committee of the American Accounting Association[24] refers to the same general problem but not with reference to a corporation with a surplus, saying:

It may be, however, that corporations which have accumulated a deficit in earned surplus should be permitted, through a recapitalization approved by stockholders, to eliminate the deficit, with the understanding that future statements of undivided profits will designate the point of time from which the new surplus dates.

Kester[25] expresses his opinion in favor of revaluation of overvalued assets during periods of declining prices when the depreciation on such assets places a heavy burden on operating costs. Talking in terms of dollar purchasing power he asserts:

These depreciation expense dollars are cheap dollars; it took a lot of them to purchase the plant in the high price era. Current cash expense dollars, in a period of low prices, are dear dollars; their purchasing power is high. Thus, in the operating statement, dollars of different purchasing power are combined and the result is misleading.

---

[22] Samuel J. Broad, "Cooperation with the Securities and Exchange Commission," *The Journal of Accountancy*, August 1938, p. 80.

[23] George O. May, "Improvement in Financial Accounts," *The Journal of Accountancy*, May 1937, p. 351.

[24] Executive Committee of the American Accounting Association, "A Tentative Statement of Accounting Principles Affecting Corporate Reports," *The Accounting Review*, June 1936, p. 191.

[25] Roy B. Kester, *Advanced Accounting* (New York, The Ronald Press Company, 1933), pp. 540, 541.

He thinks that the only way this can be cured is "by devaluing plant account and basing depreciation on such deflated value."

May[26] also favors devaluation when a company is carrying depreciable assets "at a figure clearly and substantially in excess of the fair value which such assets possess today and seem likely to possess in the near future." It seems to him desirable to treat such excess book value as a capital loss "and by formal action to reduce the book value of the assets to a fair figure and thereafter compute depreciation on the basis of the reduced value."

Strictly as an accounting matter asset revaluation is meaningless. Considered over a long enough term it cannot possibly affect profit or loss. It is this viewpoint which is inherent in the entity convention, and which probably was responsible for the attitude of the American Accounting Association. It prompted Littleton's[27] question, "Does writing up fixed assets actually increase the cost of using the assets, and does writing them down decrease the burden of owning assets that were bought at high price levels?

Unhappily the problem is a legal rather than an accounting one and is serious only in connection with corporations, never in sole proprietorship or partnerships. It refers primarily to the legality of declaring dividends. If overstated values remain on the books of a corporation and the depreciation thereon is so high that no profits can be made, then the corporation cannot legally declare dividends. If, on the other hand, creditors consenting (if legally required) and stockholders authorizing, a capital readjustment can be made, the corporation can then legally declare dividends to its stockholders. Generally this is a consummation most devoutly wished for, and rightly so.

Without in any way denying the sound and thoroughly defensible viewpoint that fixed assets are no more or less than deferred charges to future income and that revaluation of such assets is a meaningless gesture, nevertheless this viewpoint expresses an ideal which must yield in a conflict with law. With

26 George O. May, "Influence of the Depression on the Practice of Accountancy," *The Journal of Accountancy,* November 1932, p. 347.

27 A. C. Littleton, "High Standards of Accounting," *The Journal of Accountancy,* August 1938, p. 101.

the best of intentions legislators have spoken freely regarding accounting matters but sometimes their statutes are contrary to good accounting theory, thus making it necessary to wink at expedients. Purely as an expedient when injustice would otherwise result, capital reorganizations may properly be approved by accountants even though they cannot be justified by accounting theory. The expedient harms no one and helps many stockholders to receive incomes where they would otherwise be denied. Whether Broad's opinion that the earned surplus of the company may remain undisturbed, or May's that it should not, or Andersen's[28] that revaluation losses "should be charged first against earned surplus, and only after earned surplus has been consumed should they be charged against capital surplus" should be adopted is, of course, arguable.

On Paton's convention of sequences May and Andersen are correct. As a matter of conservatism also, they are correct and one is inclined to agree with Andersen's[29] view that: "Earned surplus should be the cumulative result of all income, losses and distributions."

That the surplus earned after any such major devaluation should be dated and fully disclosed is accepted as fundamental.

Both May and Andersen in addresses delivered at the American Institute Convention, the one in 1932 and the other in 1935, have given serious warning against obvious understatement of values. May[30] suggests that the decreased charge for depreciation may result in "overstating the earnings of the company. Experience shows this point to be one of very considerable importance; the attempt is sometimes made to pave the way for the future inflation of earnings by deliberate understatement of present assets." Andersen[29] intimates that the immediate effect of drastic understatements is "an overstatement of future earnings, and dividends paid out of such earnings may in part represent a return of capital rather than a return on capital."

[28] Arthur Andersen, "Present-day Problems Affecting the Presentation and Interpretation of Financial Statements," *The Journal of Accountancy*, November 1935, p. 342.
[29] *Ibid.*, pp. 342, 334.
[30] George O. May, "Influence of the Depression on the Practice of Accountancy," *The Journal of Accountancy*, November 1932, p. 348.

Revaluations and Profit Distortion.—It is from the viewpoint of profit distortion that revaluations are significant.

While there is nothing inherent in the entity convention forbidding any kind of original or subsequent valuation, the whole procedure of valuation being no more than a process of symbolizing, nevertheless the convention of accounting periods and the doctrine of consistency both emphasize the importance of comparability. Comparability and distortion clearly contradict one another. With the possible exception of inventory revaluation, there is no phase of accounting so likely to produce profit distortion as that having to do with the accounting for fixed assets.

Every aspect of fixed asset accounting from initial acquisition to final retirement, including interim revaluations and periodic depreciation provisions based upon estimates, carries with it possibilities of serious profit distortion. In some instances the practices of fixed asset accounting result in such great distortions as to rob the report of periodic net profits of all significance.

Byerly[31] had this in mind when he said, "We are inclined to speak blithely of net profits realized within the year, forgetting that such a statement is based in large part upon the unprovable premise that the amount of depreciation charged to the income account for the period is adequate." This is also what Canning[32] referred to when he said he had never examined a set of accounts "in which the internal statistical evidence did not create a strong presumption of an indeterminate error, asset by asset, much greater than any proposed rate could be counted on to correct even if we knew the direction of the error." Elsewhere he observed that a depreciation write-off might result in a gross misstatement of profits which he believed to be "the most important matter that the accountant has to deal with in a year's reports."

Until the service life of fixed assets can be estimated on some more accurate basis than has yet been discovered, until

31 F. P. Byerly, "Formulation of Accounting Principles or Conventions," *The Journal of Accountancy*, August 1937, p. 96.

32 John B. Canning, *The Economics of Accountancy* (New York, The Ronald Press Company, 1929), pp. 297, 259.

obsolescence, destruction, and abandonment can be prophesied, the reported net profits of corporations having large property accounts will be subject to large error. There are no procedures, rules, doctrines, or conventions which can eliminate such distortion entirely.

Distortion can, however, be substantially reduced, first, by adopting the convention that fixed assets are in the nature of deferred charges and therefore should be recorded on a cost basis where that is possible, and second, by adopting the desirable policy of conducting an annual or semi-annual survey of fixed assets in order to check depreciation rates against observed conditions and against developments tending to hasten obsolescence.

CHAPTER 32

GROSS PROFIT ON SALES

The materials upon which the discussion of accounting profit thus far has been based are the conventions, doctrines, and rules of accounting, the account classification, and the theory of expenditures in relation to income. These materials have been applied first to inventories and second to fixed assets, both in their relation to profit. It is now necessary to review, consolidate, reclassify, and evaluate these numerous elements from the union of which the concept of accounting profit results.

Form of Profit and Loss Statement.—As a vehicle for the present discussion, the form of profit and loss statement contained in the American Institute bulletin, *Examination of Financial Statements by Independent Public Accountants,* has been adopted.

This adoption should not be accepted as being entirely uncritical. Not a few practitioners have taken the occasion to point out flaws in this form. Nevertheless, it is probably true that no other form of profit and loss statement has received wider acceptance.

The American Institute form is, of course, specifically arranged for the average industrial company. It hardly seems necessary to comment at length upon the changes which would be made necessary in order to adapt it to trading organizations or to those engaged in rendering service rather than in marketing goods.

Primary Classification. A profit and loss statement might consist of no more than a mere list of various items of income and outgo.

Such a profit and loss statement as that shown in the Institute bulletin represents, of course, a rearrangement and assembly of data conforming substantially to recognized standards of classification.

The primary classification is twofold, i.e., operating and non-operating. The operating section is divided into two sections, i.e., one which sets forth the elements entering into the computation of gross profit on sales, and the other which sets forth the elements entering into the computation of net profit before other income and charges.

In a broad and rather general way it may be said that all operating data appear on the statement above the intermediate item of net profit before other income and charges, while the non-operating data are added thereto or deducted therefrom in order to obtain the final figure of net profit for the period. This is, of course, not entirely true, it being difficult to make fine distinctions between operating and non-operating items.

SIGNIFICANCE OF OPERATIONS. The mere suggestion of an operating classification implies that it has some particular value or significance to operating executives or that it has special managerial value for control purposes.

Management, being more in the nature of an art than a science, is definitely individualistic. It might be relatively simple to list the various items of expense and income representing a composite opinion of perhaps a thousand business executives. It would, with respect to certain enterprises, be difficult to do the same thing for any one management. Management being so largely concerned with the control of organization, and organizations being composed of highly individualistic human beings, it is clear that certain items of costs or expenses may fall into either the operating or the non-operating category, as far as management is concerned, depending upon whether they are subject to strict organization control.

To the economist rent, interest, insurance, and profits represent concepts with certain specialized meanings. These concepts cannot uniformly be translated into the operating and non-operating categories.

Such items of expense as cost of maintenance, and watchman service for the idle factory building, such items of gain as income on rental property owned by a manufacturing corporation, such classifications as purchase discounts or sales discounts, all have operating significance to any manager who has definitely charged one of his subordinates with responsibility therefor. As Williams[1] has said, it would "be a mistake to sacrifice obtainable reliable information in terms of the persons responsible for expense for the sake of a minor difference in over-all cost which, however determined, must still be open to question."

Furthermore, in almost any form of profit and loss statement certain elements must necessarily be indicated as operating when as a matter of fact their actual operating significance may be slight or non-existent. The item of depreciation is illustrative, depreciation being inevitable, constant, uncontrollable, and not chargeable to any one of the Smiths, Joneses, or Browns within the operating organization. It is commonly conceded to be an operating cost but it has little direct operating significance to a general manager.

The distinction, therefore, between the operating and non-operating categories on any such form of profit and loss statement as the one used here is by no means coercive. In any given instance it may be accepted by business men as a sort of convention. The same observations, to a lesser extent, also apply to the two major subdivisions of the operating classification as evidenced by the two intermediate "profits," gross profit on sales and net profit before other income and charges. Some authorities, foremost among them being Paton,[2] find little significance in this twofold subclassification.

SIGNIFICANCE OF GROSS PROFIT. To many a merchant (although not to those who have adopted the Clark plan)[3] gross profit indicates the spread between (1) the actual, or revalued, purchase cost of merchandise which has been sold, and (2) the realized income therefrom, thus providing a figure which establishes the top limit to other expenditures and hence is believed to possess control and administrative value. In the case of the

[1] John H. Williams, *The Flexible Budget* (McGraw-Hill Book Company, Inc., 1934), p. 69.
[2] W. A. Paton, "Comments on 'A Statement of Accounting Principles,'" *The Journal of Accountancy*, March 1938, p. 198.
[3] See Chapter 18.

manufacturer, as contrasted with the merchant, it seems that the gross profit figure may have less significance being based more or less upon a convention that the office "buys" goods from the factory instead of buying them from some outside vendor.

This fiction may not always be as helpful as it has been imagined. Nor is it always possible to establish a clean-cut demarcation between manufacturing items and those referring to the selling, administrative, and other activities.

The constituents of gross profit, according to the American Institute bulletin, are net sales and cost of sales, the former figure being computed by deducting from the gross sales certain pertinent items such as outward freight, allowances, and returns. Not included is the important deduction for estimated credit losses necessary to establish net sales as the equivalent of estimated realized income. There is, therefore, no one figure on the Institute profit and loss statement representing the effect of that convention of realization which nearly all accountants accept as sanctified.

Gross and Net Sales.—Realization as the test of accounting income has been, it appears, sufficiently discussed in previous chapters and needs little repetition here.

Originally realization was cash realization. Subsequently a legal concept of realization was added thereto, the essentials being a transfer of title and the creation of a legally enforceable claim to cash. For a variety of reasons realization as the equivalent of cash made certain adjustments necessary.

The deduction of billed but not paid outward freight from gross sales is, of course, no more than a correction, the outward freight having originally been included in gross sales as a matter of convenience. The other two deductions shown in the American Institute profit and loss statement are allowances and returns.

ALLOWANCES AND RETURNS. A return is, of course, a cancelled sale. Hence, the deduction is a correction of a sale which was believed to have been made but which in fact was not made. That is, it was not made from the practical viewpoint of the business man despite the fact that title to the merchandise may have passed, delivery may have been made, and a legally collectible receivable set up.

Business men are not likely to be overly concerned with technicalities in their dealings with customers, being much more interested in keeping a customer satisfied than in enforcing certain strict legal rights. As a result, particularly when standard merchandise is dealt in, it is not uncommon to find that dissatisfied customers are permitted to return merchandise which they have bought.

Business men, particularly those in certain types of retail establishments, actually encourage customers to buy in excess of their needs with the full understanding that some of the merchandise may be returned. A woman intending to buy one dress may be invited by a merchant to take home three of them and then keep the one which she wants. The sales entry for two dresses is fictitious and must be reversed if the customer returns them.

Allowances are deductions in selling price made when a customer retains unsatisfactory goods. Here again the theory that the customer is always right seems to apply. It is regarded as wise to make a reduction in the price of some article already sold to a complaining customer, particularly if it appears that the complaint is justified or if it is believed that by making such an allowance the customer may continue to trade with the vendor.

INCIDENCE OF ALLOWANCES AND RETURNS. While returns and allowances represent a correction of gross sales, it must be noted that they do not necessarily refer to the same accounting periods unless they have been estimated and recognized therein.

Merchandise sold in December may appear as an item of gross sales for one fiscal year. The return of that same merchandise in January may be recorded as a deduction from the gross sales of the succeeding accounting period. Accordingly, there may be a lack of incidence between the gross sales and the deductions therefrom.

Ordinarily such lack of incidence is not regarded as a cause of serious distortion. The business man places a considerable reliance on his favorite "law of averages" and believes that transactions of this sort tend to even out from period to period. When some marked abnormality is evident, as where the pre-Christmas sales of a merchant are abnormally large in one year as compared with any other, the failure to deduct the January returns and allowances from that abnormal sales volume may have a rather marked distorting effect upon the profits of the two touching years.

PROVISION FOR DOUBTFUL ACCOUNTS. Acceptance of the realization convention necessarily carries with it acceptance of the propriety of deducting the provision for doubtful accounts from gross sales.[4] The two are so related that it seems inconsistent to accept the one and to reject the other.

It is difficult to see how any accountant can consider that net sales on a profit and loss statement represent realized income if he knows in advance that some certain part thereof never will be realized.

Nor does it appear that this modifies, except immaterially, the legal test of realization, i.e., passing of title and creation of a legally enforceable claim. The legally enforceable claim has a definitive or descriptive significance only, unless its acceptance carries with it the implication of future payment. Without that implication of future payment, it becomes meaningless. To the accountant income is realized by the passing of title and by the creation of a legal claim against someone who has, or reasonably appears to have, sufficient resources so that later enforcement of the claim may be fruitful.

Possibly because the provision for doubtful accounts is so much of an estimate, many deem it undesirable to introduce the deduction at the very beginning of the profit and loss computa-

4 See Robert H. Montgomery, *Auditing Theory and Practice* (New York, The Ronald Press Company, 1934), pp. 488, 489. He suggests that maintaining or not maintaining a credit department will influence the size of the provision for doubtful accounts and that "the cost of maintaining its credit department must be grouped with its bad debt losses if an intelligent comparison with the other concern is desired." Disregarding strong evidence indicating the general futility of such comparisons, the argument might also justify the inclusion of credit department expense as an additional deduction from gross sales! This whole argument seems misdirected. The objective is the estimation of realized income, not intelligent intercompany comparisons. There is a distinct difference between (1) adjusting gross sales for uncollectible, and hence unrealized, *income,* and (2) deducting therefrom, as a correction, an actual expense or cost representing an *expenditure.*

tion. Here again the law of averages and the doctrine of materiality should probably be given due consideration. Nevertheless, it is far from impossible to imagine situations where failure to deduct the provision for doubtful accounts from the gross sales might be truly deceptive.

This situation could result in any of the more unstable types of industries; those in which credit losses were variable being significantly affected by rapid changes in consumer purchasing power. It is well known that there are certain communities which are so dependent upon one industry that the purchasing power of their inhabitants shows wide variations from time to time. A city like Detroit, dependent upon automobile manufacturing and greatly affected by strikes and other industrial troubles, a one-crop agricultural community, dependent upon the success or failure of cotton, corn, or tobacco, or a mill town where tariff changes may mean all the difference between prosperity and ruination, are fair examples. The credit situation is aggravated, of course, when long-term datings are given.

It cannot, therefore, be accepted that the law of averages will take care of such situations. It seems desirable, as a matter of good accounting policy, to deduct the provision for bad debts from the sales volume to which that provision refers in order to obtain a figure of estimated realized net sales.

ERRONEOUS PROVISIONS. It is obvious that any provision for doubtful accounts may be in error and that actual realized income may be more or less than estimated realized income.

Past collection experience is by no means an infallible guide to future collectibility and the mere fact that accounts receivable which are taken as representing deferred charges to cash have realized 95% in the past does not mean that they will realize 95% in the future. Abnormal collection losses may from time to time have to be recognized. Being unexpected and unforeseeable, they somewhat resemble losses due to sudden obsolescence. Such abnormal losses often cannot be deducted from gross sales of the period to which they refer, not being recognized until after the books are closed and the statements published. They then represent adjustments of the non-operating or surplus type.

This appears to be the reasonable viewpoint to take, although it will be noted that the effect of such treatment is distorting.

PRICE AND VOLUME IN SALES. Little has been said here with respect to price as a factor in profit making. This may appear to be an unfortunate omission, since it is probable that most business men would be tempted to enthrone price as the dominant profit factor.

Sloan[5] has asserted that: "There are three major determinants of the size and trend of industrial profits: (a) commodity prices; (b) the volume of production; (c) cost of production and distribution." He emphasized the importance of price:

In 1931, for example, when our group of 21 major companies experienced a deficit of 81 million dollars, the receipt of an additional penny per gallon on their proportion of the 16,994 million gallons of gasoline marketed that year would have changed these results to a net profit of probably 20 million dollars or more.

It should be noted that problems referring to prices are economic rather than accounting in nature. Within recent years it has been fairly well recognized that from the individualistic viewpoint there is no inherent relationship between selling prices and costs. From that viewpoint the price structure in an industry is a practically uncontrollable factor. Accounting may and does record the history of prices in their effect upon accounting profits and should for interpretive purposes fully recognize the twofold relationship between prices and quantities in their relation to profits.

The item of gross sales on the profit and loss statement is the resultant of price and volume. It is probable that one of the most deceptive of all analytical errors is to conceive of gross sales of a business enterprise as having some significance entirely apart from these two important components.

SEASONAL FLUCTUATIONS. In the item of gross sales is to be found one explanation[6] of the deceptiveness of quarterly or

5 Laurence H. Sloan and Associates, *Two Cycles of Corporation Profits* (New York, Harper & Brothers, 1936), pp. 29, 241.
6 Another explanation previously ascribed to Edwin S. Reno is to be found in inventory revaluation. Such adjustments for quarterly reports when followed by a similar adjustment for the annual report result in a discrepancy between the profit for the year and the sum of the quarterly profits.

monthly reports. Such deceptiveness is caused by the seasonal nature of many business enterprises, the seasonal characteristics of which are reflected by sales.

It is the present or anticipated sales volume which sets the pace for many of the other activities of business. Because of the normal seasonal fluctuations of sales volume, a distinguishing individual characteristic of many enterprises, profit and loss statements covering a period of less than one year are apt to be deceptive. Such deceptiveness can, of course, be cured by adequate disclosure and by appropriate comparisons.

Inventories.—Of special importance in the computation of gross profits are those elements of cost which are stored in inventories. One of these important elements of inventory cost is depreciation.

In manufacturing plants where elaborate and costly machinery has substantially replaced labor, the item of depreciation is frequently one of the important constituents of cost and hence of inventories. If such fixed assets are regarded as stored costs somewhat equivalent to deferred charges, then the forecasting of periodic depreciation may represent an important source of error.

Errors of Bias. Unlike some other accounting errors, those due to inaccurate forecasting of asset life are often biased rather than compensating, this bias effect being particularly noticeable when the fixed assets consist of a few costly components. When the fixed assets consist of a large number of different kinds of items, forecasting errors may tend to compensate one another.

When management is overly conservative, estimates of asset life tend to be too short and annual depreciation provisions tend to be too large, as a result of which net profits may be understated for a series of years. Such understatement must inevitably be followed by a series of overstated profits or by substantial lump sum readjustments having an equivalent effect.

When the management tends to be overoptimistic an opposite bias is created, the profits for a series of periods being overstated with the reverse effect noted in the second series of accounting periods which follow. Underdepreciation which results in such overstatement of periodic profits is usually corrected by lump sum adjustment.

ERRORS OF COMPENSATION.   As contrasted with the biased error often introduced by inaccurate depreciation is the periodic distortion resulting from inventory revaluation, particularly that common type which results from application of the cost or market rule. Such revaluation tends to cause compensating errors of overstatement and understatement of profits from period to period.

Unnatural equalization, on the other hand, is the direct result of the base-stock method or the last-in, first-out method.

Often of minor importance, in those industries operating on a fairly even keel and controlled by the doctrine of consistency, are those distorting factors previously discussed which have to do with the disposition of under- and overabsorbed burden, or the balances of variance accounts, the phenomena relating to joint costs, by-product costs, and the special difficulties introduced rather rarely by cost reabsorption.

Without lengthy repetition of the pros and cons of asset valuation, it may be reasserted that the entity convention, coupled with the concept that inventories and fixed assets are in the nature of deferred charges to future income, represents potent and convincing arguments in favor of some sort of a cost basis. Which base may be accepted as standard is far from settled.

THE COST BASIS.   To the advocate of the first-in, first-out method, the average cost method is a cause of profit distortion. To him who advocates the last-in, first-out method, other cost methods result in profit distortion.

Expediency aside, and considering the problem as one detached from such considerations as income taxes or economy of bookkeeping, it is difficult to avoid the conclusion that average cost, by which of course is meant a weighted average which is changed whenever items are added to inventory, actually does represent the true cost properly to be used as a basing point for evaluating deviations which result from the application of other valuation methods.

It is, of course, recognized that under many conditions the amount of clerical work required for the determination of average costs is a practical obstacle to their use and that other methods not only may but should be employed. Such other methods may include the first-in, first-out method, the actual cost of specific lots, or some of the standard cost methods.

While common sense will not insist upon sound accounting theory when some practical compromise introducing but slight distortion is more expedient, the adoption of practical compromises should not be accompanied by rationalizing. No accountant can afford to close his eyes to the possibility of serious distortion under unusual conditions.

The argument, therefore, is first for an average cost basis of inventory valuation. As a practical substitute some other cost basis may be adopted, but this leeway does not extend to recognition or approval of any plan of replacement costs, nor does it justify revaluation at cost or market.

Cost of Sales.—The serious problems referring to cost of sales are those already discussed under the heading of inventories. Many inventory problems refer primarily to manufacturing situations and may require less consideration in the merchandising enterprise. Of more general interest is the concept of matching cost with income.

MATCHING COST AND INCOME. Repeatedly accountants and accounting writers have referred to such matching as a desirable, even if often unattainable, ideal.

Where merchandise or products can separately be identified costs can actually be matched with the sales price and the gross profit or loss on an individual sales transaction can be determined.

Where like merchandise or products are intermingled, the matching of cost and income is less direct because the costs themselves are averaged, whereas the sales prices of individual units of merchandise or product are separately determinable. This may, therefore, be considered a conventionalized rather than an actual matching.

The third situation occurs when costs are computed on an

average basis and sales are not separately identified. This might be true, for example, in a drug store or variety store offering a large number of different kinds of merchandise. Under such conditions it would, of course, require an extravagant amount of detailed record keeping to identify each individual unit sold.

Under such conditions, matching of costs with income can consist of no more than assigning them to the same financial period.

MATCHING AND DOLLAR VALUATION. Some voices have been heard in protest against the concept of matching as ordinarily practiced by accountants, the point at issue being dissimilarity of the dollar valuations represented by cost and by income.

In connection with the sale of an electric refrigerator, for example, it is not difficult to match the dollar income from its sale with the dollar cost of the refrigerator itself. It is, however, contended that the sales dollar involved is a current dollar, whereas the cost dollar may have its roots far in the past, particularly that portion of it representing depreciation. If the factory manufacturing the refrigerator was built ten years earlier, it is claimed with a considerable amount of logic that part of the cost of the refrigerator was based upon price levels existing ten years previously and hence cannot logically be matched with the current sales dollar.

Depreciation is, of course, the extreme example. Less extreme are labor and material costs which may actually have been incurred several months prior to the sale under different conditions of price level.

HISTORICAL LIMITATIONS OF ACCOUNTING. This argument is perhaps a sound one except as it attempts to saddle upon accounting a function which is not inherently a part of accounting.

Essentially accounting is a financial mechanism being founded upon and limited by the convention of money valuation. Just as the electric refrigerator is a device designed for the sole purpose of refrigerating and cannot be criticized because it will not heat the home, clean the rugs, or bring in foreign radio stations, so does the accounting mechanism function effectively within its limitations and derives its real effectiveness from the fact that it has such limitations.

The skilled historian, for example, attempts to relate the Treaty of Versailles with the breaking up of Czechoslovakia. He does not demand that the history of 1918 be rewritten in the light of modern conditions. He does not attempt to project the present characters of Hitler, Mussolini, Chamberlain, and Benes back into history in order to determine what might have or could have happened. He is interested in what did happen. If it is admitted that accounting is history, then the most that can be demanded of it is that it shall be as accurate as practicably possible. It is, therefore, no weakness of the accounting mechanism that it is not well adapted to restatement or modification in so far as shifting dollar valuation is concerned.

FIXED AND VARIABLE COSTS.   Of particular interest to managers, investors, and creditors is the distinction between fixed and variable costs and their relation to income. While this is a topic more logically to be treated in Chapter 33, it may be noted that the phenomenon of fixed costs establishes and predetermines the gross profit-making characteristics of the manufacturing business.

The choice between employing labor and buying machinery is one which the business man must constantly make. His decision in any given instance should not be based on comparative unit costs under assumed conditions of stability. Rather, serious consideration must always be given to the effect of his decision upon profit-making characteristics. It is not enough to realize that the purchase of a machine will replace two workmen and will therefore result in an assumed saving under assumed conditions. The purchase of that machine represents a commitment having a definite effect upon future profits. The fact that the machine cannot be furloughed during depressed conditions may have a permanent influence upon the profit pattern of the enterprise.

Gross Profit on Sales.—In a trading enterprise it may be said that the figure representing gross profit on sales has real significance in that it establishes a "ceiling" for profit control.

In a manufacturing organization it is rather doubtful whether this figure of gross profit has equivalent value, the line of demarcation between the factory and the office often being more imaginary than real.

DEPARTMENTAL GROSS PROFITS. This general statement requires modification where the manufacturer maintains separate selling departments for separate and distinct lines of products. Every accountant is familiar with cases in his own experience where the failure to compute gross profits for separate lines of product had an unfortunate effect on profits.

In commenting upon this type of situation, the Committee on Ethics and Professional Standing of the Controller's Institute of America[7] reported a company doing a national business of about $100,000,000 per year in several different types of markets and through several different sales divisions. This particular company kept no records of profit or loss by sales divisions and a subsequent analysis showed that more than half of the sales divisions were operating at a loss.

Properly interpreted the computation of separate gross profits classified according to natural selling divisions of the manufacturing enterprise cannot fail to have managerial value.

DEPARTMENTAL PROFIT INTERPRETATION. Insistence upon intelligent interpretation of such so-called profit figures seems to be justified.

The mere fact that some division appears to be showing losses is not adequate evidence justifying its discontinuance. Often the elimination of an apparent loss factor merely results in shifting substantial fixed costs to other divisions of activity, with the result that they too become unprofitable.

Furthermore, it is well known that in certain types of manufacture some products or by-products are necessarily produced and cannot be eliminated even though the figures indicate that their sale is unprofitable. The point involved here is well illustrated by what purports to be a true story of an accountant's audit of a coal company. The accountant's report contained a recommendation which read as follows:

[7] *The Controller*, August 1938.

A close examination of the company's business has revealed the fact that lump coal, egg coal, nut coal and mine-run are for the most part sold at prices which yield a profit. However, slack is invariably sold at prices below the cost of production. We, therefore, strongly recommend that the mining of slack be immediately discontinued.[8]

COMPARABILITY OF GROSS PROFITS. It is commonly believed that periodic gross profit figures are fairly comparable because they are not influenced by abnormal or extraordinary losses or gains. This is substantially, if not wholly, correct.

If errors of prior periods were reflected in the gross profits of those prior periods and were subsequently corrected either by surplus adjustment or in the non-operating section of a later profit and loss statement, then the aggregate of the gross profits as shown on, perhaps, ten profit and loss statements would differ from the gross profit on one profit and loss statement covering the entire ten-year period.

Also there is authority for including operating costs as an element of gross profits even when those operating costs are abnormal and hence distort comparison.

Finally, there is some authority for showing the correction of operating errors of prior periods in the operating rather than the non-operating section of the profit and loss statement for the period in which the errors are discovered. When the errors refer to items properly to be included as elements of gross profit, it is clear that a distortion of periodic gross profits results, the profits for one period being understated and the profits for a subsequent period being overstated, or vice versa.

It cannot, therefore, be taken for granted that the periodic totals of gross profit on sales are necessarily comparable. That they are more nearly comparable than net operating profits or final profits is generally conceded.

Any periodic distortion of gross profit is serious in that it carries all the way through the remainder of the profit and loss statement. Since two of the most important sources of distortion, depreciation, and inventory revaluation, are common elements in the computation of manufacturing gross profits, it is apparent that the distortion of the final figure in the profit and

8 In "General Notes," *The Canadian Chartered Accountant*, May 1938, pp. 399, 400.

loss statement may have had its origin in the first few lines thereof. This is, of course, true also of the profit and loss statements of merchandising establishments which adhere to the rule of cost or market.

In the computation of gross profit there is a combination of known fact with estimate and conjecture which tends to give a fictitious appearance of accuracy to the gross profit figure. Precision of measurement in the case of labor costs is, for example, much more exact than in the case of depreciation provisions. The combining of such different measures furnishes a result which can be no more accurate than the least precise of its components. The double entry bookkeeping rule of balancing to the penny requires exhibiting a gross profit figure of $85,234.16, for example, when as a matter of fact the most that could be known about gross profit might be that it lay somewhere between $80,000 and $90,000. Even this might be considered unduly definite.

ACCOUNTING DOCTRINES AND GROSS PROFIT. Because of the controlling influence of the four doctrines of accounting—conservatism, consistency, disclosure, and materiality—it seems desirable briefly to consider the effect of each upon the computation of gross profit.

The effect of conservatism is marked, since it is conservatism which is responsible for the inventory rule of cost or market. Nor, as is true in some other accounting situations, does the doctrine of consistency tend to iron out the distorting effects of this conservatism.

The doctrine of materiality is applicable here in relation to the continual overlapping of income and expense items. If the effect of such overlapping upon profit is not material and does not tend to cause noticeable distortion, meticulous correction thereof may not be justified.

Finally, the doctrine of disclosure is as important here as in other areas of reporting. This doctrine requires that any important disclosable information referring to sales or cost of sales, of which the accountant himself would wish to be informed if he were a stockholder or creditor, should be set forth either parenthetically or by footnote. At least the amount of depreciation should be separately set forth. Many are coming to believe that the aggregates of wages and taxes should also be disclosed. If sales volume or cost of sales is abnormally high or low due to some non-recurring factor, the facts should be set forth and commented upon.

SIGNIFICANCE OF GROSS PROFIT COMPONENTS. The analysis and interpretation of gross profits for business, credit, or investment purposes necessarily involves an examination of gross profit components. Some of these components have real significance, others have little.

SALES VOLUME. Sales volume measured in terms of dollars represents perhaps the most important factor in any accounting analysis. When the sales figure is broken down into its components of price and volume, analytical comparisons may be even more enlightening, particularly when such comparisons refer to a series of related accounting periods. Under certain circumstances and with proper safeguards, the comparison of sales trends for several competitors may prove most illuminating.

From such a comparison the relative market efficiency of one company in relation to its industry can be diagnosed, thus helping to provide the answer to a question which is often foremost in the minds of business executives, namely, whether a decreased profit caused by decreasing sales should be remedied by (1) changing the sales program, or (2) instituting a more rigid program of expense control.

APPORTIONMENTS. In a manufacturing establishment the analysis of cost of sales is rendered difficult by the common cost accounting procedure of apportionment and reapportionment of expenses. To the external analyst—the credit man or investor —comparisons, historical or otherwise, involving cost of sales may have only a general value. In the field of internal analysis final cost figures, because of the tortuous channels through which they have been accumulated, may have but little control value. The internal analyst is, therefore, not so much interested in final costs as he is in their inception and in the analysis and control of costs at their points of origin.

FINAL COSTS. Of particular analytical value to all who receive accounting reports is the distinction between fixed and variable cost elements.

The need for such information is not always recognized, as a result of which fact an essential item of information, namely, the rate of activity at which a given enterprise makes neither a profit nor a loss, is undisclosed. Granting the difficulty in many industries of determining this break-even point or pay point, it can often reasonably be approximated.

In many industrial situations such information regarding the effect upon gross profits of such varying volumes may be the most important that the accountant can furnish to managers, creditors, or investors.

CHAPTER 33

NET INCOME BEFORE OTHER INCOME AND CHARGES

The figure captioned "net profit before other income and charges" is commonly considered to have special operating significance. For that reason it is often referred to as "net operating profit." It is known also as "net profit on sales."[1] As between "net operating profit" and "net profit on sales," the first seems preferable since it emphasizes operation as the important characteristic of the item. Also it is a more general title since many enterprises receive income not from sales but from fees, rentals, or interest.

By whatever name the figure is known, it is computed by deducting from gross profit on sales all of the non-manufacturing costs and expenses which have operating significance.

This deduction is referred to in the American Institute bulletin as "selling, general and administrative expense."

Selling, General, and Administrative Expense.—The total of selling, general, and administrative expense consists of a variety of costs which can be classified in different ways.

For example, they may be classified as departmental and non-departmental. This is a classification for executive control purposes permitting the determination of costs in relation to various operating employees who can be held responsible for them. In the non-departmental group are to be found expenditures for services of different kinds, particularly those incurred for the general welfare of the business and not assignable to departmental units.

---

[1] This phrase is used on page 32 of *Examination of Financial Statements by Independent Public Accountants,* although the form of profit and loss statement on page 40 shows the longer caption, "net profit before other income and charges."

Another method of classifying these expenses is according to whether they are fixed, semi-fixed, or variable.

A third method of classification divides the expenses according to their time relationship with sales, i.e., those which are incurred prior to selling for the primary purpose of promoting sales and those others which are the result directly or indirectly of sales transactions already consummated.

The first of the three classifications is the one commonly employed. The division of selling, general, and administrative expense into those which have departmental significance and those which do not is effective for management purposes. Theoretically, this is somewhat illogical in that it combines a departmental grouping with a classification by objects of expenditure.

Attempts have been made to departmentalize all selling, general, and administrative expenses. To do this may require many arbitrary decisions and it is more than doubtful whether departmental apportionments of such expenditures as postage, electricity, telephone calls, legal and auditing fees, water expense, taxes, or rent are justifiable.

The fact that such apportionments must be more or less arbitrary often robs the results of real significance to management.

The Break-Even Point.—Never a primary classification, the division of selling, general, and administrative expense into fixed, semi-fixed, and variable may furnish enlightening information to managers.

Brief reference has already been made to this classification in Chapter 32. A more extended discussion seems appropriate here in view of the fact that the determination of the break-even point, or pay point, is just as important to the merchant as it is to the manufacturer. To the merchant, however, the relationships involved refer to gross profit rather than income. Furthermore, it is seldom necessary or desirable, even in a manufacturing establishment, to distinguish between factory expenses and selling, general, and administrative expenses in so far as the break-even calculation is concerned.

Various authors[2] have written extensively on numerous ramifications of this subject hence detailed discussion here seems unnecessary.

FIXED, SEMI-FIXED, AND VARIABLE. The theory of the break-even point is comparatively simple. Some of the costs and expenses in almost any business are fixed, i.e., they remain the same or about the same month after month regardless of the volume of sales or other index of activity. Fixed contractual salaries represent expenses of this kind, as do rent, interest, depreciation, and property taxes.

In contrast to these fixed items are variable costs and expenses which fluctuate more or less in proportion to business activity, and which are often measurable in terms of sales activity although for factory purposes measurable in terms of production. Direct labor paid for upon a piece-work basis represents a variable cost. Supplies and materials used are a variable cost. Telegraph expense, salesmen's commissions, and outgoing freight and express are apt to be variable expenses.

There are, of course, other costs and expenses which are neither fixed nor variable. The cost of operating a bookkeeping department, a credit department, and other office departments is ordinarily considered semi-fixed in that there is a certain element of such cost which, theoretically at least, cannot be eliminated even though sales volume temporarily falls to zero during any one month. Such semi-fixed costs do, however, have a variable aspect or element which tends to increase or decrease in proportion to business activity.

Because any business enterprise must bear a certain definite load of fixed cost and expense regardless of the rate of business activity, and because on top of this fixed base there are additional increments of variable expense which can be related to variations in business activity, it follows that there is some point below which sales cannot fall without resulting in a net loss rather than a net profit. That particular volume of income

2 Knoeppel and Seybold, *Managing for Profit* (New York, McGraw-Hill Book Company, Inc., 1937). Walter Rautenstrauch, *The Successful Control of Profits* (New York, B. C. Forbes Publishing Company, 1930). Paul W. Pinkerton, "A Step-by-Step Approach to the Predetermination of Profit at Varying Volumes," *N.A.C.A. Bulletin,* March 1, 1935. Stephen Gilman, *Analyzing Financial Statements* (New York, The Ronald Press Company, 1934).

which is equal to the total of the fixed expenses plus the total of the variable expenses for that particular volume is known as the break-even point, or pay point. Greater amount of income results in a net profit, a lesser amount of income results in a net loss.

There are two methods commonly used for determining the break-even point, i.e., it may be determined on the basis of past experience, or it may be determined more or less arbitrarily from a survey of current costs as modified by the judgment of management with respect to current and future conditions.

HISTORICAL METHOD. The first method requires intelligent discrimination of past experience in order to avoid misleading results.

Briefly, one variation of the method may be described as follows. In a business having well-marked seasonal characteristics, the monthly profit and loss statements for a series of perhaps twenty-four or thirty-six months may be rearranged in the order of sales volume. From these rearranged statements a graphic chart may be constructed, one line thereon representing sales volume and the other representing total costs and expenses at varying sales volumes.

The line representing sales volume will, of course, be a straight one running from the lower left-hand corner of the chart toward the upper right-hand corner. The line for costs and expenses will be jagged since it is necessarily influenced by accidental factors. The jagged line, however, can often be smoothed into a straight line and when this is done it will be found to show a lesser slant than the first line and hence will actually cross the first line at some point, or would cross it if extended.

The point of crossing is taken to represent the break-even point, or the pay point.

The second line, representing total of costs and expenses at varying volumes of business, can be extended to cut the left-hand margin of the chart, the point at which it intersects that margin being taken to represent the total of the fixed costs and expenses.

WEAKNESSES OF HISTORICAL METHOD. This method is a useful one if the statements themselves are properly comparable. Generally they are not, change, often violent change, being characteristic of business enterprises.

The chart will, therefore, tend to show deceptive results if selling prices have been changed during the months included in the calculation, or if wage and salary rates have changed, or if noticeable changes have occurred in commodity price levels, or if machinery has to any noticeable extent been substituted for human labor. The results will also be deceptive if there has been any general failure to match costs and expenses with income.

Where there are noticeable expense lags, i.e., where expenses are reflected in one period when in all propriety they belong to a preceding or following period, the break-even chart prepared according to this method may be so greatly distorted as to be meaningless.

To assert that the prior period statements can be recast giving effect to present conditions is, under some conditions, reasonable. Generally, however, the task of readjusting such statements is arduous and unsatisfactory because of the lack of proper statistical data. As a result of these difficulties another method is sometimes adopted.

CURRENT ANALYSIS METHOD. Essentially this second method consists of inspection of the existing business situation and of current costs, together with making certain assumptions based in part upon past experience as to what changes in costs and expenses are likely to take place at certain assumed variations of business activity.

A related but somewhat different procedure attempts to determine the irreducible minimum of cost and expense under current conditions. That irreducible minimum is presumed to represent the fixed cost element. The difference between the fixed element thus determined and the total of all costs and expenses is taken to represent the variable element. The percentage of that variable element to current sales volume is assumed to be applicable to higher or lower volumes.

Intelligently used by an experienced and careful executive,

the second method will often give more reliable results than the first with all of its calculations and adjustments.

Neither method can be relied upon for exactness. Nor is exactness required; an approximate knowledge of the break-even point either in round figures or in even percentages is sufficient for practical business purposes.

USE BY FINANCIAL ANALYSTS. The information resulting from such calculations is often used by financial analysts. Thus, the Cleveland Trust Company[3] refers to the break-even point in the following quotation: "Under present conditions of wages and prices the iron and steel industry must produce at about 60 percent of capacity to meet expenses and have anything left over for profit."

Barron's[4] is the source of several quotations bearing upon the pay point of certain steel corporations in the late spring of 1938, as follows:

In the case of United States Steel Corp., it was generally believed that, as a result of higher costs, the pay point had risen to between 55% and 60%.

Inland Steel Co. officially estimated its pay point at 40%.

The deficit reported by Republic Steel Corp. would indicate that its break-even point is probably higher than that of any other of the "Big Five," although it is impossible to estimate the exact figure. The chairman of the board, in answer to a stockholder's question, said that the pay point was definitely under 50%, although he did not say by what amount.

Although Bethlehem Steel Corp. showed a profit with operations at a rate of 34.6% of capacity, the president estimated that the pay-point is between 35% and 40%.

The following figures and comments provided by Sloan[5] are also interesting. Naturally, the break-even point will differ from one period of time to another, and even more sharply from one company to another. But the following table, comparing total automobile production in the United States with the aggre-

3 Cleveland Trust Company Business Bulletin, Vol. 19, No. 9, September 15, 1938.
4 Barron's, May 2, 1938.
5 Laurence H. Sloan and Associates, Two Cycles of Corporation Profits (New York, Harper & Brothers, 1936), p. 68.

gate amount earned for the common stock by 19 automobile parts and accessories producers, is suggestive.

Year	U. S. Automobile Production (Passenger Cars and Trucks)	Net for Common Stock of 19 Companies
1929	5,358,420	$80,500,000
1930	3,355,986	36,300,000
1931	2,389,738	9,700,000
1932	1,370,678	Def. 21,600,000
1933	1,920,057	Def. 300,000
1934	2,753,111	20,000,000
1935	3,946,936	44,600,000

Def. = deficit.

This indicates that the pay point for the parts and accessories industry is approximately 2,000,000 new cars per year.

These quotations and illustrations have been included for the purpose of indicating how highly information of this type is regarded by the financial analyst. The value of similar information to management should not, however, be overlooked.

USE BY MANAGEMENT. Important decisions relating to sales tactics, pricing, the opening of new territories, and the construction or acquirement of new plants or other fixed assets, may depend upon understanding the profit pattern of a business as portrayed by a break-even chart.

Various writers have directed attention to the importance of such information in business planning for advertising and similar sales promotion expenses. Once it is fully appreciated that a 10% increase in business may result in a 15% or 20% increase in net profits, it becomes self-evident that an additional volume of business may be well worth fighting for and well worth spending an extra amount of money to obtain. That business men generally have long been aware of this is evidenced by the various past experiments in dumping goods, selling marginal production at low prices, and other plans.

That the pattern portrayed by a break-even chart may justify investing unusually large sums of money in advertising and other sales promotion expenses in order to obtain an extra volume of business is perhaps not so well recognized.

Harrison,[6] referring to this possibility, suggests:

[6] G. Charter Harrison, *New Wine in Old Bottles* (published by the author in 1937), p. 24.

... the job of sales manager, however, is not to secure a certain definite volume of sales at a certain cost but to so operate his department as to obtain that combination of sales volume and selling expense which will produce the greatest net profits for his company. He derives little or no assistance from the usual accounting statements in determining what this winning combination is.

He adds that the "figure of the profit value of a dollar of sales, or in other words the maximum amount which can be spent in sales effort to secure an additional dollar of sales volume without loss ... is the most important figure by far which a company can secure."

He presents a strong case against the common practice of insisting that the sales department keep selling costs to a predetermined percentage.

Given certain assumptions, it is undoubtedly true that an enterprise enjoying a volume of a million dollars a year at 20% selling cost might find it profitable to spend $15,000 more, or $35,000 altogether, in order to obtain an additional $100,000 of sales.

The assumptions underlying such a proposal are, of course, important. It must be assumed, for example, that the additional volume can be obtained without acquiring any additional machinery or other plant facilities; that it can be obtained without disturbing the normal sales and distribution relationships; that the selling tactics involved are not those which would cause difficulties under the Robinson-Patman Act. These and other assumptions may be very important in any individual case.

Kohl[7] approves Harrison's suggestions and also makes some interesting comments relative to the influence of fixed charges on the granting of credit. Observing that the typical credit man measures his accomplishment by the annual percentage of losses to sales, Kohl relates the experience of his company, Gates Rubber Company of Denver, in using a flexible credit policy which permits the credit man to accept doubtful orders. This involves the creation of "a special insurance reserve for marginal receivables." While following a fixed and conservative credit policy

[7] Clem N. Kohl, "What is Wrong with Most Profit and Loss Statements?" *N.A.C.A. Bulletin,* July 1, 1937.

in connection with routine transactions, each doubtful risk is specially analyzed in order to see whether it may not prove profitable according to Harrison's method of figuring even if an abnormally large reserve is specially provided for it. In other words, a computation is made in connection with each doubtful credit to compare the effects upon final profit of (1) refusing to accept the order, or (2) accepting it with perhaps a 40% or 45% special reserve.

That this philosophy of profit-making has been promoted largely by engineers rather than accountants is somewhat of an anomaly, since it is the accountant who is presumed to be the authority on accounting profits and the factors tending to increase or decrease them. Seldom do accounting reports touch upon this question of pay points even though such information would be of special interest and value to clients, their bankers, and investors.

Percentage Analyses.—Greatly affected by the phenomenon of fixed and variable cost are certain percentage statements commonly used by business men and accountants. Because they have been misused so often and are subject to such gross misinterpretation, it seems to be within the scope of the present chapter to discuss them briefly. Many practicing accountants include percentage statements in audit reports. There is some reason to believe that such percentage statements improperly used may be not only unhelpful but actually deceptive.

COMMON REPORT PRACTICE.   Perhaps the foremost authority recommending percentage statements is the American Institute of Accountants[8] in the following quotation: "Net profit after deducting expenses but before other income and other charges is usually a significant figure, and determination of percentage to sales and comparison with previous years is desirable." This sentence is not entirely clear as to whether the comparison with previous years is to be a comparison of actual amounts or of the percentages to sales. Other authorities have, however, left little doubt on this point.

[8] *Examination of Financial Statements by Independent Public Accountants* (New York, American Institute of Accountants, January 1936), p. 32.

Himmelblau[9] suggests: "To facilitate comparison as between years in the case of a single company . . . it is advisable to prepare a similar tabulation in which each item is stated as a ratio to net sales."

Kohler and Pettengill[10] support the same view as follows:

A comparative summary, bringing out in totals the principal classes of income and expense, precedes the detailed discussion. A recapitulation of the summary in terms of percentages to net sales is usually of value and may be of more interest to the management than income and expense stated in dollars.

Trouant[11] asserts that: "The early preparation of working statements of profit and loss in comparative form, with ratios of expenses to sales or with amounts per unit of sales, will facilitate the accountant's examination."

COMPARATIVE STATEMENTS. The calculation of percentages of cost, gross profit, selling, general, and administrative expenses, and operating profit to net sales is entirely appropriate, even if none too illuminating, when applied to *one* profit and loss statement. When applied to two or more statements and shown comparatively, the results are very often apt to be deceptive.

Selected from numerous available examples, the following profit and loss statement taken from the *Cost and Production Handbook*[12] is typical.

The asterisks did not appear on the original statement but have been added for ease in reference. The first item so marked refers to cost of goods sold, which in the first year amounted to $5,185,000 and in the second year to $4,185,000, a decrease of $1,000,000 or about 19%. But the percentages shown appear to contradict this decrease since the percentage for the first year was 70%, and for the second year was 70.9%.

9 David Himmelblau, *Investigations for Financing* (New York, The Ronald Press Company, 1936), p. 209.

10 Kohler and Pettengill, *Principles of Auditing* (New York, McGraw-Hill Book Company, Inc., 1932), p. 173.

11 D. L. Trouant, *Financial Audits* (New York, American Institute Publishing Co., Inc., 1937), p. 139.

12 *Cost and Production Handbook* (New York, The Ronald Press Company, 1934), p. 19.

THE BLANK MANUFACTURING COMPANY

COMPARATIVE PROFIT AND LOSS STATEMENT

	Year Ended Dec. 31, 19–	% of Net Sales	Previous Year	% of Net Sales
Gross Sales	$6,000,000		$7,500,000	
Less Returns and Allowances . .	100,000		80,000	
Net Sales	5,900,000	100.0	7,420,000	100.0
Cost of Goods Sold	4,185,000*	70.9	5,185,000	70.0
Gross Profit	1,715,000	29.1	2,235,000	30.0
Selling Expenses	450,000*	7.6	530,000	7.1
General and Administrative . .	340,000*	5.8	360,000	4.8
Operating Profit	925,000	15.5	1,345,000	18.1
Other Charges:				
Interest Expense	3,000*	0.05	3,500	0.04
Cash Discounts on Sales . . .	50,000	0.8	63,000	0.8
Loss on Fixed Assets disposed of	4,000	0.07		
Net Profit before provision for Federal Tax	868,000	14.7	1,278,500	17.2
Provision for Federal Income Tax	100,000	1.7	150,000	2.0
Net Profit	$ 768,000	12.0	$1,128,500	15.2

The selling expense of the first year was $530,000; the second year it was $450,000, a decrease of $80,000 or 15%. It should, however, be observed that the percentages shown on the above statement are 7.1% for the first year and 7.6% for the second year, giving the superficial impression of an increase.

General and administrative expense decreased from $360,000 to $340,000 but the percentages shown for the first year are 4.8% and for the second year 5.8%.

Interest expense decreased from $3,500 to $3,000 but the percentages shown were .04% for the first year and .05% for the second year. The apparent contradictions between the actual amounts and the percentages shown by these comparative statements are far from unusual.

OTHER EXAMPLES. A profit and loss schedule presented by Finney[13] contains among other items one referring to purchase discounts which increased from $15,280 in 1935 to $17,005 in 1936, an increase of 11.3%, although the percentages of these amounts to net sales were 2.16% in 1935 and 1.77% in 1936.

Himmelblau[14] presented a statement in which the cost of sales in 1934 was $150,000 and in 1935 was $180,000, an increase of $30,000, in contradiction to which the percentages to net sales were 75% in the first year and 72% in the second year.

Bell[15] displayed figures showing an increase in cost of goods sold from $56,000 in 1932 to $63,250 in 1933, although the percentage to net sales dropped from 70% to 63¼%. Elsewhere, in a somewhat similar table, cost of goods sold increased from $16,127,308.19 to $18,955,332.87 but the percentages to net sales did not confirm this increase of 18% since they dropped from 85.96% to 82.01%.

DECEPTIVE COMPARISONS. It may, and probably will, be asserted that percentages of net sales are not intended to be compared historically. If that be true, it is difficult to explain why they are included with comparative statements. It may well be asked whether such inclusion may not in fact confuse or even deceive the reader of a report. Reverting to the figures taken from the *Cost and Production Handbook,* it does not seem unreasonable to imagine confusion or even deception resulting in those cases where the percentages appear to show an increase while the actual amounts indicate a decrease.

As a matter of fact, the percentages of profit and loss components to net sales are not historically comparable on two related counts, (1) because of fixed cost elements there is no reason why percentages based on varying rates of activity should be comparable, and (2) the percentage comparison is

13 H. A. Finney, *Introduction to Principles of Accounting* (New York, Prentice-Hall, Inc., 1936), p. 459.
14 David Himmelblau, *Investigations for Financing* (New York, The Ronald Press Company, 1936), p. 211.
15 William H. Bell, *Accountants' Reports* (New York, The Ronald Press Company, 1934), pp. 146, 239.

based upon an assumption of equal bases which becomes pure
fiction when historically viewed.

Distortion.—That section of the profit and loss statement
lying between gross profit from sales and net profit before other
income and charges is subject to distortion from various causes.
It is, of course, subject to the distortions resulting from the
correction of prior period errors.

If such prior period errors affected selling, general, and
administrative expense in prior periods but are corrected subsequently in the final section of the profit and loss statement or
through a surplus adjustment, it is clear that the sum of all of
the selling, general, and administrative expenses appearing on
ten profit and loss statements, for example, would not be the
same as the total appearing upon one profit and loss statement
covering the entire ten-year period.

LACK OF MATCHING. A more serious distortion results
from application of the doctrine of conservatism to this section
of the profit and loss statement.

In factory accounting close matching of costs and income is
attempted. In the accounting for selling, general, and administrative expense a definite lack of matching is often noticed,
with the result that many of the items may have no real relationship to the net sales of the same period.

This is particularly true in connection with sales promotion
expenses. When advertising, for example, is actually paid for
in advance and the advertising does not appear in print until a
subsequent period, accountants may show it as a prepaid expense. But other sales promotion charges are seldom deferred.

In how many reports does one find the cost of catalogue
preparation, for example, properly distributed over the subsequent periods benefited by that catalogue?

How often does one find the expense of conducting a costly
sales convention properly apportioned to those periods benefiting therefrom?

How often are special items of expense incurred for the purpose of entertaining customers, training salesmen, and preparing sales campaigns set up as a prepaid expense?

When these and dozens of other similar questions are asked, about the only answer that the accountant properly can give is to affirm that the incidence of such items upon future periods is not measurable nor determinable; that accordingly he must treat them as expenses of the period during which they were incurred. In other words, conservatism dictates that the accountant shall not set up operating expense items as prepaid expenses unless he has some reasonable basis for determining their subsequent incidence.

This accounting viewpoint is, of course, perfectly proper. The fact still remains, however, that it may result in substantial profit distortion, particularly where heavy expenditures occur as the result of changes in policy.

CHANGED BUSINESS POLICIES. If a corporation has for years been conducting sales conventions at an average cost of perhaps $20,000 per convention, then a consistent method of treating this expense is all that seems necessary. Each year bears a burden of approximately $20,000 which in reality applies to the following year, which in turn will bear an expense of approximately $20,000 which applies to the third year, and so on.

On the other hand, a company which has never held sales conventions may, in the latter part of 1938, hold its first sales convention at a cost of $20,000. If that company shows the cost as an element of selling, general, and administrative expense in 1938, distortion is caused. Such a convention, generally speaking, is held for the purpose of increasing future sales and it may be assumed that a major part of the cost thereof is properly applicable not to 1938 sales but to 1939 sales.

The cost of executive time and that of various technical experts in preparing plans for a new sales campaign or for the opening of new sales territories may amount to a substantial sum which is clearly incurred for but one purpose, namely, the promotion of future sales. Conservatism, however, and the inability to measure the influence of such an expenditure, may require that it be deducted from the net sales of a period which has experienced no benefit whatever.

PROFITS AND SALARIES.   In the small or closely controlled corporation, a further distorting element is sometimes introduced in that salaries paid to officers may in some part be equivalent to profit.

Whenever there is a possibility for a tax saving by the adjustment of salaries of a few principal stockholders, it is only natural that such adjustments may take place, with the result that such stockholders may withdraw funds, in the guise of salaries chargeable to selling, general, and administrative expenses, which are to some unmeasurable extent actual profits.

This is a matter which has been of some concern to economists. Backman,[16] for example, has said: "This question of wages and salaries is especially important in smaller organizations. In many cases, these companies include in wages a return on investment and an element of profit. This is frequently done to avoid paying taxes on excess profits."

Fabricant[17] considers this matter from the accountant's viewpoint of comparability, saying:

> The simple comparison based upon profits alone may understate the true profitability in the case of small companies. A way out of this difficulty is to combine profits with compensation of officers and relate this total to invested capital. This measure may overstate the true profitability; for a large part of officers' compensation represents labor cost proper.

Elsewhere[17] he refers to "the tendency in closely held companies to pay out profits in the form of officers' salaries."

Significance of Net Operating Profit.—Net operating profit has, of course, less significance than gross profit since it is affected by all of the factors which distort gross profits plus additional distortions originating in selling, general, and administrative expense.

That these various distortions are often ironed out by application of the doctrine of consistency cannot be denied. Where overdepreciation on one kind of fixed asset is substantially offset

16 Jules Backman, "Cost of Production as a Basis for Price Fixing," *The Journal of Accountancy,* September 1938, p. 148.

17 Spahr and others, *Economic Principles and Problems* (New York, Farrar & Rinehart, Inc., 1936), pp. 264, 261.

by underdepreciation on another, where the distortion resulting from the application of the cost or market rule to inventories is slight, where expenditures applicable to future periods but included as expenses of a current period run to about the same amount year after year, and finally where sales volumes, whether expressed in terms of physical volume or prices, do not vary too violently as between period and period, then the net profit before other income and charges is significant to the investor, creditor, and to the management. Under such circumstances the relation of profit to the average capital invested may furnish information of value.

Fabricant[18] has commented upon this as follows: "The first measure—profits for a given period as a percentage of the average capital invested during the same period—has an advantage in that it makes possible comparison with current rates of interest. This comparison provides one criterion of profitability." The same author has, however, noted that:

For some purposes, however, it is often convenient to combine all types of capital, no matter what kind of division of rights prevails among the participants, and to measure the rate of return on the total capital invested. In this case the measure of profitability that is used is the total of profits plus interest payments as a percentage of owned and borrowed capital combined.

In those instances where the distorting factors are more potent, such comparisons may be less valuable or even worthless.

In conclusion, it appears that the significance of net profit before other income and charges varies as between industry and industry and as between enterprise and enterprise, depending upon various factors some of an accounting nature and some not. It is to be noted that the general characteristics of a business, the violence of its sales fluctuations, the consistency of its policies, the nature of its product, its labor relations, the nature of its raw materials, and other factors may be of special importance in determining the significance or lack of significance of its net operating profit.

18 *Ibid.,* p. 263.

CHAPTER 34

NET PROFIT FOR PERIOD CARRIED TO SURPLUS

That area which lies between (1) net profit before other income and charges, and (2) net profit for period carried to surplus, has clearly been noted as the perennial battle ground of accounting. Disagreement as to what kinds of items should or should not be included therein results from certain divergent viewpoints which may never be reconciled.

In general, the issue seems to be drawn between those who emphasize comparability of net profits and those who insist upon the complete showing of net profits. The former group favors surplus entries for certain losses, gains, or adjustments which the other group considers to be essential elements in the computation of periodic net profit.

Components of Other Income.—For the purpose of disclosing some of the issues involved, a composite list of "other income" items is submitted.

This composite list is drawn from but three sources: (1) *Examination of Financial Statements by Independent Public Accountants,* symbolized below by the initials A.I.A., (2) *A Tentative Statement of Accounting Principles Affecting Corporate Reports,* symbolized below by the initials A.A.A., and (3) *A Statement of Accounting Principles,* symbolized by the initials S-H-M. No more than these three sources are used since it does not seem necessary at this point to repeat the detail from Chapter 14.

Since the American Institute captions "other income" and "other charges" have already been used, they are still retained here, although the American Accounting Association labels this group of loss and gain accounts, by inference at least, as "non-operating," while Sanders, Hatfield, and Moore refer specifically to "the non-operating section."

The abbreviated composite list based upon these three sources is as follows:

Components of Other Income

1. Income from investments. (A.I.A. and S-H-M)
2. Interest on notes receivable, etc. (A.I.A. and S-H-M)
3. Discounts. (A.I.A.)
4. Stock dividends received (if disclosed). (A.I.A.)
5. Capital gains:
   In case of doubt. (S-H-M)
   Always. (A.A.A.)
6. Substantial prior year adjustments, unless statements are recast. (A.A.A.)
7. Gain from the discharge of liabilities. (A.A.A.)
8. Other non-operating or extraordinary income. (A.I.A., A.A.A., and S-H-M)

It is, of course, obvious that this list and the one which follows are intended merely as summaries and do not pretend to reflect various qualifications and shades of opinion already discussed in Chapters 10, 14, and 31.

Components of Other Charges.—Somewhat similar to the foregoing table is another one showing the constituents of other charges.

Components of Other Charges

1. Interest on funded debt (and amortization of bond discount). (A.I.A. and S-H-M)
2. Interest on notes payable. (A.I.A. and S-H-M)
3. Losses on securities sold. (A.I.A. and A.A.A. based on item No. 9)
4. Provision for income, capital stock, and excess profits taxes (optional). (A.I.A.)
5. Adjustments affecting prior periods:
   If minor. (A.I.A. and S-H-M)
   If of any size unless statements are recast. (A.A.A.)
6. Capital losses:
   In case of doubt. (S-H-M)
   Always. (A.A.A.)

7. Unrealized declines in current assets. (S-H-M)
8. Certain reserves for future losses and contingencies (if imminent). (S-H-M)
9. Extraordinary losses and amortizatiou resulting from factors other than current operations. (A.A.A.)
10. Loss from the discharge of liabilities. (A.A.A.)
11. Other non-operating or extraordinary charges. (A.I.A., A.A.A. and S-H-M)

Summary of Viewpoints.—To summarize, it appears that the American Accounting Association takes a definite stand against surplus adjustments. If the inclusion in the profit and loss statement of items which otherwise might be considered surplus adjustments is too distorting, the only remedy suggested by the American Accounting Association is to recast the accounts and publish corrected income statements for the prior periods affected.

This solution is not advocated by the American Institute bulletin or by Sanders, Hatfield, and Moore. Both of these authorities give consideration to materiality. Both seem to favor adjustments through the surplus account if the amounts are large.

If small, the American Institute bulletin favors correction through other charges (although it does not specifically indicate a recommendation if the adjustment was a credit instead of a debit, but it is presumed that such an adjustment would be through other income).

Sanders, Hatfield, and Moore are willing to consider small corrections as non-operating items only if the original error affected a non-operating item. Otherwise, by inference, a small correction should be combined with the operating item to which it properly applies.

It seems, therefore, that a clean-cut issue is presented. The American Accounting Association[1] insists that the profit and loss statement must include all costs and income "regardless of whether or not they are the results of operations in that period:

[1] Executive Committee of the American Accounting Association, "A Tentative Statement of Accounting Principles Affecting Corporate Reports," *The Accounting Review*, June 1936, p. 189.

to the end that for any period of years in the history of the enterprise the assembled income statements will express completely all gains and losses." This is clear enough and definite enough to suit anyone. It is, therefore, evident that the American Accounting Association has abandoned the concept of comparability as applied to final net profits. The other two authorities are unwilling to go this far, apparently not believing that it is so important that "the assembled income statements will express completely all gains and losses" as it is that the final net profits from year to year shall be roughly comparable.

A *logical* compromise between these two opposing viewpoints is the correction of prior period profit and loss statements.

While this compromise is logical, there are, as previously suggested, certain objections to it. These objections are at least three in number: (1) the preparation of the corrected income statements may require an unjustifiably large expenditure of effort, (2) corporation managers may not care to have their past errors so signally emphasized, and (3) no suggestion has been made as to the circumstances which justify this procedure, i.e., no acceptable test of materiality has been proposed.

As a substitute measure representing a compromise perhaps not so logical but at the same time more practical, the surplus reconciliation may be appended to the profit and loss statement itself. It seems reasonable that if stockholders and others interested in reports would give as much consideration to the surplus reconciliation as they do to the profit and loss statement, it would not make much difference whether a given item appeared in one or in the other. If this be true, it appears that a practical compromise between the surplus and the profit and loss viewpoints might result from merging the profit and loss statement and the surplus reconciliation into one combined statement.

If this were generally done, stockholders and others could not help but notice the surplus reconciliation, simply because they have been accustomed to glance first at the bottom of the profit and loss statement. Thus their attention will inevitably be directed first of all to the surplus reconciliation and to those important items which represent correction of prior period errors, capital gains or losses, or other abnormal figures.

Surplus and Reserves.—While surplus and reserves do not properly form part of the subject matter of this present volume, the mere fact that they may be charged or credited with items having profit and loss significance justifies brief discussion.

It is rather important to foster a more intelligent public understanding of the nature of surplus. One expedient which should be helpful toward this end is to abandon the term "earned surplus" and substitute therefor the term "undivided profits," as suggested by May.

SURPLUS AS A LIABILITY. Another suggestion is almost bound to meet with some opposition.

Accountants generally avoid any reference to surplus or undivided profits which would indicate that they represent liabilities to the stockholders. Whether this reluctance is due entirely to legal influence, or whether it is due to some fear that stockholders might demand increases in dividends, is of no importance. It should be noted, however, that accountants actually do refer to capital stock and to surplus as liabilities in every balance sheet they prepare when they use the general caption "liabilities" for the right-hand side of the statement.

To label an entire list of items as "liabilities" and then to cavil at calling one of them a "liability" seems somewhat inconsistent.

Those legislators, lawyers, courts, and others[2] who, judging by their own utterances, firmly believe that surplus is some kind of a strong box or fund or bank account out of which actual monies can be disbursed would, it seems reasonable to believe, be somewhat enlightened if the accountant could feel justified in asserting that surplus is a special kind of a liability of the corporation to its stockholders.

This flat assertion, when coupled with the question, "How can you purchase treasury stock with a liability?" or, "How can you distribute a liability?" or, "How can you take cash out of a liability?" might assist greatly in overcoming a prevalent

2 Even so well informed a publication as *Time* (May 16, 1938, p. 61) said that Myron Taylor wiped out a substantial part of the U. S. Steel Corporation's funded debt "with money taken from surplus." A sister publication (*Fortune*, December 1938, p. 170) made a similar error quoted in part as follows: "But when Mr. Sloan asked his Board of Directors for the money—it came out of surplus."

misunderstanding which has been the cause of considerable irritation and confusion. Of the critic who insists that surplus cannot be a liability because it has no due date and therefore cannot become legally due and payable, one might well ask as to the status of such a security as the perpetual 6% certificates of Public Service Corporation of New Jersey secured by the preferred stocks of certain other corporations.

CONTINGENCY RESERVES. With brief reference to reserves, particularly reserves for contingencies, it is indeed difficult to convince business men that such a reserve having once been established should not be charged with the loss which is suffered when the contingency actually occurs.

If one is willing to grant that direct charges for capital losses properly may be made to surplus account, in all consistency it must be admitted that the cost of a loss by flood may in all propriety be charged to the reserve for flood loss when that reserve has been created from surplus.

In short, surplus reserves and surplus itself are part and parcel of the same thing. It is, however, observable that there is some confusion in this matter and that the man who might argue against making a direct charge to surplus would be entirely willing to divert that charge to a reserve account.

Regardless of opinions on surplus adjustments, charging a loss to a contingency reserve account is justified only if that contingency reserve was created by charges to profit and loss. The name of the reserve is not a matter of importance in this connection. The manner of its creation, i.e., whether by a charge to profit and loss or by a charge to surplus, may be considered the controlling factor.

Is it proper to create a contingency reserve by charges to profit and loss when there is only a remote possibility that such a contingency may occur? There are so many different kinds of contingencies, some of which are uncertain as to occurrence, some as to time, and some to amount, that it would be most injudicious to set forth any rule. Consider, for example, the contingency involved in the guarantee of a new product, particularly when that guarantee covers not only a few months but perhaps four or five years. Compared with this contingency consider that of flood damage on one of the lower streets of Cincinnati and then compare that with the contingency of flood damage on some of the higher Cincinnati streets in the neighborhood of the Gibson or Netherland-Plaza Hotels.

A convincing argument might be made for feeding a reserve from profit and loss in the case of the guarantee of new product. Less convincing, but still plausible, is the argument in favor of using profit and loss as the source of a flood reserve in those lower reaches of Cincinnati which are flooded almost every year. It would, however, be much less logical to require the establishment of a reserve for flood damage from profit and loss in the case of some business enterprise on a higher street.

DISPOSITION OF RESERVE BALANCES.   A problem of some difficulty may present itself when it is desired to dispose of a reserve balance. As an example, a reserve may be created in 1938 as the result of a judgment found by a lower court. The provision for that reserve appears as an item of loss in the 1938 profit and loss statement. In 1939 a higher court reverses the judgment and the reserve is no longer needed. The question then arises whether the credit balance of the reserve should be transferred to surplus or should appear as an extraordinary gain in the 1939 profit and loss statement.

As would be expected, there are two opposing schools of thought. One argues that the credit should go to surplus since, if it is permitted to swell 1939 profits, similar procedures could be used by management to equalize earnings by setting up unnecessary reserves in profitable years and reversing them in unprofitable years.

On the other hand, it is argued, and, it seems, properly argued, that it is the auditor's duty to see that the creation of such a reserve in 1938 is justified. If later and unforeseeable events indicate that the reserve is no longer needed, it should appear adequately disclosed as income of 1939 and not be shunted into surplus and therefore never appear on any profit and loss statement.

Just as in the case of debit surplus adjustments, it appears that opponents and proponents approach this problem from irreconcilable viewpoints. Since the same general arguments are involved, further elaborate discussion appears unnecessary.

INTENT IN THE CREATION OF RESERVE. As a general proposition, however, one may question the real purpose in creating a reserve in 1938. Was it created for the purpose of presenting a conservative balance sheet at December 31 of that year, or was it created in an attempt to assign to 1938 a cost properly to be included in the computation of 1938 profit?

The balance sheet motive may be suspected. Under some circumstances the events leading up to the lawsuit and the judgment of a reserve for flood damage from profit and loss in the often the legal controversy may have had its roots in 1937 or some prior year. If so, there is no particular reason for burdening 1938 with the estimated loss. To do so and then to follow in 1939 with a profit and loss correction might well be considered a double distortion. Unless the cost reflected in the creation of the 1938 reserve actually had 1938 incidence, the motive for creating the reserve must have been one of balance sheet conservatism, and, if so, a preferable procedure from the profit and loss viewpoint would be to set up the reserve as an allocation of surplus. In 1939 when the reserve is no longer necessary, the entry could be reversed.

By following this procedure, neither the 1938 nor the 1939 profit and loss statement would be distorted by the attempt to achieve balance sheet conservatism. If in 1939 the higher court upheld the lower court, then the amount of the judgment could be absorbed as an item of 1939 cost and in the same period the reserve could be transferred back to surplus. This procedure would result in a single instead of a double distortion. This, it appears, should be a treatment preferred by those who agree with the Executive Committee of the American Accounting Association.

DISCLOSURE OF RESERVE CHANGES. It is in connection with contingencies, their probability and measurability in terms of dollars, that the accounting mechanism appears somewhat inadequate as a means of measuring net profit.

About the only remedy is the present-day insistence upon

adequate disclosure. In this respect the requirement of the Securities and Exchange Commission is helpful, the Commission having, in its regulations, added to other required financial statements a report of the changes in reserves. It is probable that few would disagree with May's[3] comment as follows: "Such a statement throws a valuable light on the income account and is, I think, an addition to the sum of financial information which is of great importance and upon which the commission is to be warmly congratulated."

Net Profit and the Investor.—The objection to showing surplus adjustments in a separate surplus reconciliation statement has been from the investor's viewpoint. Other objections from the investor's viewpoint have been made to the proposal that assembled income statements should completely express all gains and losses.

Both of these plans are unacceptable because of the unfortunate overconcentration upon earnings per share. Littleton[4] touched upon this in the following statement: "Recurring earnings or earnings per share are not dependable bases for dividends if there are non-operating losses and gains that have to be considered along with operating earnings."

During the general session of the American Institute Convention in Cincinnati in 1938, this matter of earnings per share was somewhat discussed. Henry B. Fernald expressed his feeling "that a great deal of evil has come from undue emphasis on earnings per share." He suggested that it represented no real service to an investor for a company to report a heavy net loss per share when all of that net loss and more too was due to the correction of prior year depreciation errors, and where on a surplus adjustment basis a profit per share would have been reported.

Another speaker, A. Carl Fischer, referred to an incident in the financial history of the United States Steel Corporation occurring some years ago when the reported earnings per share were so greatly reduced by a heavy abnormal charge to current

3 George O. May, "Improvement in Financial Accounts," *The Journal of Accountancy,* May 1937, p. 363.
4 A. C. Littleton, "The Relation of Function to Principles," *The Accounting Review,* September 1938, p. 241.

income that the market value of steel stock took a severe drop, thus penalizing many stockholders who sold under misunderstanding of the facts.

Walter A. Staub also commented upon the same incident, saying that if his firm had been auditors of the company, they would not have suggested the inclusion of such a large abnormal loss in a current profit and loss statement. Rather, he suggested that this should have been shown as a surplus adjustment and adequately disclosed. It appears, however, that adequate disclosure is of little value unless the disclosure meets the eye of him who scans the report.

Added to this is the difficulty, as suggested by Andersen,[5] "for the accountant to state the actual monetary effect on the financial statement of a qualification or to state all material facts in terms of figures."

May[6] believes that "preoccupation with the importance of not misleading investors has obscured the desirability of enlightening them."

Running through much published accounting literature there is an apparent overemphasis of the investor viewpoint as compared with some other viewpoints. The question may well be raised as to how much real attention even the well-informed investor pays to accountants' reports. Some believe that individual investors are much less interested in profit and loss statements than in other factors. With specific reference to the elaborate prospectuses required by the Securities and Exchange Commission, it has been asserted that few non-institutional investors read them with any degree of thoroughness. Stewart[7] intimates that this may not be of any great importance, for, as he says, "even a registration statement under the securities act, with all its detail, gives no indication of the trends in an industry, which may be entirely contrary to that shown in the past experience of the particular registrant."

5 Arthur Andersen, "Present-Day Problems Affecting the Presentation and Interpretation of Financial Statements," *The Journal of Accountancy*, November 1935, p. 335.

6 George O. May, "Improvement in Financial Accounts," *The Journal of Accountancy*, May 1937, p. 359.

7 Andrew Stewart, "Accountancy and Regulatory Bodies in the United States," *The Journal of Accountancy*, January 1938, p. 39.

Finally, it has been intimated that individual investors tend to attach more importance to non-accounting facts bearing on future possibilities of an enterprise, and that their attention is directed not so much to past earnings records as to future earnings possibilities.

Perhaps in all of this discussion of accounting and reporting procedures relating to the investor, there is some lack of a realistic appraisal of the factors which influence an investor. It is, of course, as unwise to generalize about investors as any other classification of human beings, but there is room for considerable doubt as to whether all of the arguments for and against surplus adjustments are really as important to investors as their proponents seem to believe.

Net Profit and Business Management.—To the practical management of a business, inclusion or exclusion of certain items from other income and other charges is generally unimportant save for their effect upon stockholders and creditors.

To the management, a loss is a loss regardless of where it is shown. Since the losses under discussion are generally uncontrollable, they are commonly not greatly considered by the business man. Often he is unaware that such losses have occurred until his auditor points them out to him and insists upon their recognition.

While an executive may be greatly elated by an attractive report of net profit or downcast if a net loss is suffered, his real interest and concentrated attention are directed not so much to the end result of net profit or loss as to certain of the factors which are responsible for the final figure. He is interested in measurable items of daily, weekly, or monthly incidence and generally in those over which he has some control. Sales, wages, purchases, taxes, the costs of research, of planning and preparing for future sales campaigns, the statistics of production and of efficiency, the allocation of operating responsibilities, and the measurement of results excite his greatest interest.

Almost any auditor is familiar with the frustrated look so often appearing on his client's face when the conversation turns to matters of readjusting values or the correction of prior period errors. These things are of accounting significance but are uncontrollable annoyances or tragedies to the operations-minded business man to whom the significant profit figure on the profit and loss statement is apt to be "net profit before other income and charges" rather than "net profit for period carried to surplus."

CHAPTER 35

SIGNIFICANCE OF ACCOUNTING PROFIT

The suggestion that the conventions, doctrines, and rules of accounting constitute a body of propositions somewhat comparable to the English common law seems particularly significant when an attempt is made to summarize and evaluate the various elements from which the modern concept of accounting profit is derived.

To assert that accounting profit is the logical result of certain basic accounting conventions, while substantially correct, oversimplifies the problem. Such a statement disregards the more or less arbitrary or accidental effects of precedent, legal coercion, and practical economic influences.

Discussion of the meaning and significance of accounting profit is particularly difficult since the term "profit" itself may have a variety of different meanings and different significances. There is probably no one concept of profit which would be acceptable at the same time to the lawyer, the economist, the business man, and the accountant. There is probably no one concept of accounting profit which would be acceptable to all of the individuals in any one of these groups.

Any attempt, therefore, to define accounting profit by description, as has been the purpose of the preceding chapters, must necessarily resemble a composite photograph which is a good individual portrait of no one and yet emphasizes what may be termed the modal features of a group.

The Ingredients of Accounting.—It has been suggested that modern accounting may be thought of as a mixture of three ingredients: law, economics, and statistics. It has further been intimated that the proportions of these ingredients may vary, dependent, of course, upon such factors as types of industrial enterprises, the nature of local statutes, the extent of governmental control, the form of proprietary organization, and various trade customs. Whether it is more helpful to think of these ingredients as being combined mechanically or as being partially or entirely fused as by some chemical reaction, is perhaps an unnecessary refinement of an analogy which at best is only suggestive.

Specialized Profit Concepts.—A more promising approach might give consideration to the lawyer's concept of profit, to the economist's concept of profit, or even to the statistician's concept of profit, although it seems rather doubtful whether statisticians generally are much concerned one way or another with this particular problem. The attempt to establish legal and economic profit concepts, study them comparatively, and measure the influence of each upon the accounting concept of profit, would appear to be a task well worth while were it not for the fact that neither lawyers nor economists seem to have agreed among themselves. If a reader accepts as correct what any one lawyer or any one economist says about profits, he is likely to be somewhat puzzled when he reads another contribution by a second lawyer or a second economist.

It does appear, however, that lawyers as a class do seem to hold certain class opinions toward profits. Speaking generally, the same thing seems to be true about economists. Some of these class viewpoints deserve brief discussion in order that their general effect upon the mixture of law, economics, and statistics may be considered.

Accounting Profit and Accounting Conventions.—At the risk of overrepetition, it is necessary to reaffirm that the accounting system of historical record rests squarely and firmly upon three fundamental assumptions or conventions, namely, the entity convention, the valuation convention, and the convention of accounting periods. These conventions have predetermined the design of the accounting superstructure.

Derived from them are such helpful concepts as that of entity charge and discharge, valuation as a substitution symbol for record purposes—certainly not as an indication of salable or realizable values—and finally that of accounting profit as a liability of entity to proprietor. These assumptions and their derivatives provide, it is believed, a logical and reasonable description of traditional accounting profit unaffected by incidental or arbitrary influences.

It is, however, impossible to describe the modern concept of accounting profit without giving consideration to an alternative method of approach.

Entity vs. Proprietary Viewpoint.—Earlier it was suggested that either the entity or the proprietary viewpoint provides a satisfying explanation of accounting profit if adopted consistently; but that confusion and misinterpretation can fail to result from shifting first to one viewpoint and then to the other.

It is believed that much present-day altercation and disagreement with respect to income, costs, expenses, losses, and surplus are traceable to an unconscious swaying between these viewpoints. Thus, it is noted that lawyers as a class seem to be fairly well committed to the idea that a corporation is an entity, i.e., an artificial person. It is somewhat ironic that the lawyers, who have probably done more than anyone else to publicize and popularize the entity convention, do not themselves apply it consistently to all forms of proprietorship, nor in fact are they always consistent in applying it to the corporation.[1]

Even assuming consistency as to corporations, however, it is obviously difficult for the lawyer logically to conceive of profit when he applies the entity assumption to a corporation and the proprietary assumption to the partnership or sole proprietorship. While this shifting of viewpoint may be considered good law, it surely must provide the most logical of all explanations, if one may be permitted to generalize, why lawyers as a class have such difficulty in understanding the essentials of accounting theory and practice.

Viewpoints Toward Asset Values.—The entity convention asserts that an artificial person, even in the case of the sole pro-

---

[1] George R. Husband, "The Corporate-Entity Fiction and Accounting Theory," *The Accounting Review*, September 1938, p. 241.

prietorship or partnership, is the possessor of certain assets with which it is charged and for which it must account.

The proprietary assumption, on the other hand, conceives of the sole proprietor or the partners as being the custodians of those assets. The effect of adopting the proprietary theory can be simply illustrated by the practice of some frugal housewife who, having perhaps $25 in hand, sets aside $5 in an envelope marked for the butcher, $8 in another envelope marked for the grocer, $6 in another envelope marked for the landlord, and then says to herself, "This $6 is what I have left over; this is my surplus."

The adoption of this same mode of thinking in business results in a balance sheet somewhat as follows:

Total Assets	$100,000
Liabilities to Others	30,000
Proprietorship Interest	$ 70,000
Investment	60,000
Surplus	$ 10,000

This method of deducting from assets represents an approach to the determination of surplus directly from the asset side of the accounting equation. When surplus is calculated in this manner, the final figure obviously represents residual assets, that extra amount of assets which is left over after "providing" for the claims of all parties. Is it any wonder that those who use this approach think of surplus as if it were an asset?

DISTRIBUTIONS TO STOCKHOLDERS. It is this same method of figuring which often characterizes the legal mind in connection with such matters as dividend declarations. Thus Grange,[2] after discussing various aspects of the dividend problem, summarized the legal viewpoint in the following words: "It is a fixed principle of law that the directors of a corporation are charged with the duty of *setting aside a definite amount of assets, over and above the amount of the corporation's liabilities,* before they are free to make any distribution to stockholders."

[2] William J. Grange, *Corporation Law for Officers and Directors* (New York, The Ronald Press Company, 1935), p. 242.

The italics in the above quotation have been added for emphasis.

The lawyer is interested in knowing how much of the assets remain after having deducted from the total assets all of the liabilities and the capital stock. This general statement of a viewpoint is, of course, subject to various modifications, since corporation accounting cannot be so easily simplified. Nevertheless, it probably reflects the typical legal method of thinking about surplus available for dividends. This asset approach seems to be based upon the unconscious and, of course, indispensable assumption that asset values appearing on the books of a company have some meaning all of their own. It would be unfair to suggest that anyone would defend the proposition that such asset values are realizable. Nevertheless, there is some reason to believe that this particular approach has inherited, from some remote ancestry, a stain of that illegitimacy which looks upon asset valuations as realizable values apart from their utility to the owning entity.

It is probably true that the legal "trust fund" theory is somewhat discredited. Even in its heyday it was hardly more than a convention or a figure of speech, the assets of a solvent corporation not being subject to limitations of the trust type. But whether or not the trust fund theory has been rejected, it undoubtedly has had a strong influence upon legal thinking and has been more or less responsible for some of the statutory provisions referring to corporations.

INCOME AND PROFITS.   To define income as an increase in wealth not resulting from gift, appreciation, or investment immediately prompts the question, "Whose wealth?" Hanging upon such a definition and such a question are some interesting problems referring to viewpoint. Does a corporation make a profit or does it increase the amount of its liability to its stockholders?

Dohr,[3] in a scholarly treatment of income in relation to taxation, has made it entirely clear that income from the tax viewpoint means gross income and that deductions from gross in-

---

[3] James L. Dohr, "Income Divorced from Reality, *The Journal of Accountancy,* December 1938, p. 366.

come required for the computation of net income "are a matter of Congressional grace, and that if Congress does not specifically authorize a deduction, net income must be computed without allowance for the item in question." To those business men and others who are concerned because their accounting records and their tax reports do not agree, Dohr's article should be of considerable interest.

The economist's viewpoint toward income and profits has been well set forth by Fabricant[4] as follows:

The accounting definition of profits is simple and adequate for use in business records. But economists are interested in discovering in what way profits constitute a type of income distinct from other incomes. They are interested in "pure" profits, after deducting all rent, interest, and wages, whether paid out to others or whether allowed by the enterpriser for his own land, buildings, machinery, capital funds, and his own labor. The economists' problem is to discover the factors determining the size of profits in relation to other economic shares. The fact that profits are a residual in income accounts constitutes no explanation. Although the enterpriser must take as his share whatever is left at the end of the year, he is by no means completely helpless. By readjusting future contracts and investments he exerts a definite influence upon his own and others' shares. The economic problem consists of determining in just what way this influence is exerted, what limitations are upon it, and how it compares with influences originating with wage earners, capitalists, and those who rent buildings, equipment, and natural resources.

There seems to be a well-marked tendency among accountants to think of accounting profits in terms of historical costs. To the economist, on the other hand, it is present and future costs which are significant. Present-day accounting insistence upon the profit and loss viewpoint as contrasted with the balance sheet viewpoint narrows somewhat the gap between these two opposed concepts. In other words, accountants and economists find the profit and loss statement somewhat common ground. The balance sheet with its cost expressions which often date far into the past is not a document which appeals to the economic mind. Economic incidence upon accounting may be considered

4 Spahr and others, *Economic Principles and Problems* (New York, Farrar & Rinehart, Inc., 1936), p. 254.

partially responsible for such a concept as that of depreciation on the basis of replacement cost or such an inventory method as last-in, first-out.

REALIZATION. Income realization is by no means a concept which is common to law, economics, or accounting. Realization as a test for recognition of income was, of course, fastened upon accounting by law. It is not an economic concept. Magill[5] has said that the major difference between the tax and the economic concepts of income "lies in the legal requirement that the gain must be severed from capital; or . . . that the income must be realized."

This does not, however, seem to be strictly correct since an economist, E. R. A. Seligman,[6] has asserted: "Income in the true sense of net income is that which is separated from the capital, while leaving the capital intact." There is, however, some reason to believe that Seligman is not reflecting the consensus of economic opinion in this respect.

On the other hand, the legal concept of realization as applied in taxation differs somewhat from the concept usually adopted by accountants. To the accountant, realization means (1) passing of title and, usually, (2) the creation of a claim to cash. In other words, realization, narrowly but logically, requires two things: parting with one asset and the substitution of another asset, the substitution usually being limited, however, to a particular kind of an asset, namely, a claim to cash.[7] The tax viewpoint, however, recognizes the first half of this requirement but considerably broadens the second half, with the result that it is possible for taxable income to be realized by an exchange of asset for asset in which the substituted asset is not a legally enforceable claim to cash and may not even be a current asset. This makes it necessary to value the incoming asset on a "fair

[5] Roswell Magill, *Taxable Income* (New York, The Ronald Press Company, 1936), p. 21.

[6] Paul H. Wueller, "Concepts of Taxable Income," *Political Science Quarterly,* December 1938, p. 561.

[7] It is this theory which has been adopted here for consistency although some accountants would add that the new asset be a current asset, while others are willing to broaden the test by including exchanges as the result of which the new asset may be other than a claim to cash and hence subject to valuation on a market price basis. Thus, Sanders, Hatfield, and Moore assert (p. 29): "With few exceptions only sales which convey title to another in exchange for cash, a legal claim, or *other valuable consideration are properly included.*" (Italics supplied.)

market price" basis. The legal viewpoint in this matter has been well set forth by Magill[8] in his discussion of the Eisner *v.* Macomber decision.

Neither in the *Macomber* definition nor in the economist's is there any express requirement that income can only be realized in money. The *Macomber* definition stresses the necessity of severance from capital, but does not in terms place any restrictions upon the *form* which income may take. In an exchange, the gain is only extracted or severed from the capital in the sense that the *res* has been changed; the original cash investment plus any increment or increase in value now stand represented in another form, but the increment is not physically distinct. Neither the taxpayer nor the Treasury can say definitely that so much of the new *res* is income and so much capital.

OTHER INFLUENCES. Among other influences which have helped to shape the modern concept of accounting profit are: the credit viewpoint toward inventories as current assets, the economic concepts of imputed costs and true profits, and the various theories that have been advanced to the effect that production rather than sale marks the recognition of income or that unrealized appreciation of capital assets constitutes income.

The economist is not in entire harmony with the lawyer and accountant with respect to capital gains and losses. Carl C. Plehn[9] is quoted by Wueller as saying that "income is essentially wealth available for recurrent consumption, recurrently (or periodically) received. Its three essential characteristics are: *receipt, recurrence, and expendability.*" He explains recurrence by adding "if a wage-earner's house burns down or his automobile is wrecked, he does not consider that his income has thereby been reduced."

This viewpoint must, of course, be contrasted with certain accounting viewpoints previously noted, such as that of Sanders, Hatfield, and Moore,[10] to the effect that decision as to the inclusion or exclusion of capital gains and losses from any income statement is a matter to be determined by sound business judg-

8 Roswell Magill, *Taxable Income* (New York, The Ronald Press Company, 1936), p. 105.
9 Paul H. Wueller, "Concepts of Taxable Income," *Political Science Quarterly*, December 1938, pp. 565, 568.
10 Sanders, Hatfield, and Moore, *A Statement of Accounting Principles* (New York, American Institute of Accountants, 1938), pp. 38, 39.

ment, or Postulate 11 of the Executive Committee of the American Accounting Association[11] which calls imperatively for the inclusion of capital gains and losses in the non-operating section of the profit and loss statement.

As the result of a variety of influences, certain somewhat arbitrary modifications of the logical traditional structure of accounting have been made, with the result that accountants themselves are by no means of one mind as to whether asset values are to be considered significant in relation to the future as suggested by the deferred charge theory in Chapter 19, or in relation to the present as suggested by the balance sheet viewpoint, the current and non-current classification of assets and liabilities, and the various auditing adjustments that are made to change asset values without regard to the effect upon comparative profits.

A Concept of Accounting Profit.—Subject, of course, to a variety of exceptions and qualifications, the following outline may perhaps have some descriptive if not definitive value:

1. Accounting is conventionalized written statistical history expressed in terms of money of an artificial person or entity with reference to property, tangible or intangible, in the possession of that entity and with reference to various liabilities owed by that entity to those who have supplied it with goods, money, or services or who, by virtue of their power, can exact tribute from it.

2. At its simplest, accounting profit is the increase in entity indebtedness to proprietorship (disregarding additional proprietorship investments or withdrawals) during the life of the entity, the expiration of which implies termination and realization.

3. Periodic accounting profit represents an interim profit computation based upon estimates which are accurate only (1) when the sum of the periodic profits so computed is equal to the profit computable for the entire life of the entity from inception to termination, and (2) when the

11 Executive Committee of the American Accounting Association, "A Tentative Statement of Accounting Principles Affecting Corporate Reports," *The Accounting Review*, June 1936, pp. 189, 190.

items of income, cost, expense, or loss employed in the computation of profit for any one period are not properly assignable to another period.

4. The methods of estimating periodic accounting profit have been formalized by a variety of conventions, doctrines, rules, and practices based in part upon logic and in part upon expediency.

5. The significance of periodic accounting profit is, therefore, the algebraic sum of the separate significances of the various conventions, doctrines, rules, and practices which at any particular time constitute the common law of accounting.

Opinions of Authorities.—Without attempting to formulate a definition of accounting profits, it seems desirable to present certain definitions, descriptions, and concepts suggested by various accounting authorities.

There is considerable lack of agreement as to the terminology of profits. The words "income," "earnings," "revenue," "profits," and "gains" are not always used with discrimination. It seems to be a general practice to differentiate between income, revenue, and earnings on the one hand, and profits and gains on the other, the former group carrying no implication of a net increase in entity indebtedness.

By some accountants "income" would be applied to such an item as gross or net sales. By others it would be applied to such an item as gross profit on the theory that net sales cannot be considered income, since in part the sales total is a return of capital represented by the cost of the goods parted with.

The word "profit" is variously used and misused, being applied to such an interim figure as the difference between the net sales and cost of sales or to the figure representing net results from operations only. Net income is sometimes used interchangeably with net profit.

The terminology of the entire subject is, therefore, in a state of some confusion. While it is difficult not to agree in some respects with those who hold that income is equivalent to gross profit because of the capital return argument, it is believed that Paton's concept of income is the one which has the outstanding merit of common acceptance by non-technical people. He asserts :[12]

> The most conservative criterion of income is the receipt of cash. Cash—meaning thereby any generally recognized medium of exchange —can be used to purchase any desired commodity or service whatsoever, provided the same is available on the market, to retire obligations, to pay taxes, to pay dividends, to liquidate terminable proprietary invest- ment, etc. Cash is the asset *excellent*. The receipt of cash for product, consequently, furnishes the ultimate test of revenue realization. From this standpoint the cash sale and the collection of cash following the so-called credit sale constitute the principal income transactions, the important occasions for entries in the revenue account.

This concept and its companion concept of constructive real- ization, taken together, clearly indicate the desirability of apply- ing the word "income" to gross sales less appropriate deductions therefrom.

The word "profit" also is one which is commonly accepted by non-technical people, an advantage which seems particularly important.

Baker and Howell[13] say, in *The Preparation of Reports,* that profits were defined at the International Cooperative Congress in Delft, Holland, in 1897, as "the actual net balance of gain realized by the financial operations of the undertaking in rela- tion to which the scheme exists."

An American Institute's committee on the definition of earned surplus[14] defined net profits as follows:

> Net profits, net income, and gains include profits from the disposi- tion of any corporate asset (other than the corporation's own capital stock), and arise from transactions resulting in the acquisition of cash or of property which at the time of its receipt may ordinarily be classi- fied as, or converted into, a current asset; or from transactions in which the consideration received includes the complete or partial dis- charge of a liability.

12 W. A. Paton, *Accounting Theory* (New York, The Ronald Press Company, 1922), p. 444.

13 Baker and Howell, *The Preparation of Reports* (New York, The Ronald Press Company, 1938), p. 443.

14 *Accounting Terminology* (New York, American Institute Publishing Co., Inc., 1931), p. 119.

Kester,[15] in his *Advanced Accounting,* presented this definition:

... the term profit has been applied to those increments of value arising from whatever source, which flow from completed transactions with outsiders, as distinguished from the corporation's dealings with itself or its stockholders.

He comments that the occasional instance where profits are recognized before the completion of transactions does not "disprove the general thesis that completion of the transaction is necessary to accurate determination and measurement of profits."

Montgomery[16] says, in the fifth edition of his *Auditing Theory and Practice:* "If a public accountant were asked to define the term 'net income,' he would probably reply: 'The net income of a business is the surplus remaining from the earnings after providing for all costs, expenses and allowances for accrued or probable losses.' "

Elsewhere he presents another definition much the same save for specific inclusion of "losses arising from the sale of capital assets." In an article in the June 1938 issue of *The Journal of Accountancy,*[17] he seems to approve the statement that "every receipt is income which is not a contribution of capital or an even exchange for a capital asset."

In the *Accountants' Handbook*[18] is found not a definition but a suggestion as to tests of income realization:

... there are two fundamental tests or evidences of the realization of typical business income. First, income arises primarily as a result of business activity, production. Income, that is, must be recognized and measured in terms of the essential characteristics of business operation. Second, income must be evidenced and supported by genuine asset values, preferably in liquid form.

---

[15] Roy B. Kester, *Advanced Accounting* (New York, The Ronald Press Company, 1933), p. 492.

[16] Robert H. Montgomery, *Auditing Theory and Practice* (New York, The Ronald Press Company, 1934), p. 472.

[17] Robert H. Montgomery, "Dealings in Treasury Stock," *The Journal of Accountancy,* June 1938, p. 473.

[18] *Accountants' Handbook* (New York, The Ronald Press Company, 1934), p. 1079.

Hatfield[19] asserts that after the sale has been effected, the profit "does not depend merely upon the opinion of the proprietor as to the value of his own assets, but the opinion has been corroborated by an outsider and has been manifested by the giving or receipt of cash, or by the making of an enforceable contract."

Kohler and Morrison[20] offer the following: "Profit, as used by the accountant, is the increase in the owners' investment resulting from the operation of a business over a period of time, and he ordinarily does not distinguish between the portions attributable to capital invested and services performed by the owners."

MacFarland and Ayars[21] observe that: "Many accounting writers consider the actual amount of sales as income. As the figure for sales includes a return of capital it seems better to view as income only the profit arising from sales."

Paton[22] says: "Net business income or net revenue may be defined as the *amount by which the equities of the proprietors and all others entitled to participate in income are enhanced as a result of successful operation.*"

Not a definition, but a vivid description, was offered by Littleton[23] in the *Harvard Business Review:*

Net income then is shaped, as it were, by the interaction of the blades of a pair of shears—revenue as one, cost as the other. It is obvious that both blades are necessary to produce the result, but their action is not necessarily equal. One blade may rest passively on the table while the other blade moves actively up and down under the power of the operator's fingers. The passive blade represents revenue —the element under little direct managerial control; the active blade represents costs—the element under considerable managerial control in the process of producing net income.

In various explanations, certain elements are usually present.

19 Henry Rand Hatfield, *Accounting* (New York, D. Appleton-Century Company, Inc., 1927), p. 255.
20 Kohler and Morrison, *Principles of Accounting* (New York, McGraw-Hill Book Company, Inc., 1931), p. 8.
21 MacFarland and Ayars, *Accounting Fundamentals* (New York, McGraw-Hill Book Company, Inc., 1936), p. 31.
22 W. A. Paton, *Essentials of Accounting* (New York, The Macmillan Company, 1938), p. 82.
23 A. C. Littleton, "Business Profits as a Legal Basis for Dividends," *Harvard Business Review,* Vol. XVI, No. 1, 1937, p. 58.

First is the general insistence that income should be *realized* before it properly can be recognized by the accountant. With few exceptions, it should be the result of *completed* transactions with *outsiders*.

With respect to costs, expenses, and losses, realization is not a necessary element, i.e., included among the deductions from sales income or earnings are provisions for accrued or probable losses.

These appear to be the essential elements of an accounting definition. It is the insistence upon these elements which distinguishes the accounting concepts of income and profit.

Accountants favor the test of completion and practical realization to income but not to costs, losses, and expense, because it is otherwise impossible to match expenditures incurred for the purpose of obtaining subsequent income with such income or, in other instances, because of their firm adherence to the accounting doctrine of conservatism.

Distortion and Inconsistency.—The accounting viewpoint has caused some difficulty to those who use accounting figures.

The inclusion of various estimates among the deductions makes "true earnings and reported earnings very different figures," according to Woodward.[24]

The opinion is frequently voiced that there is little basis for comparison between the periodical profits of one company. In 1929 Canning[25] commented:

> The deviations of annually computed net income figures from figures that might, conceivably, be ultimately agreed upon, are, in general, much greater relatively than the corresponding errors of estimate in gross income; for as we shall see, certain of the common deduction items are much more difficult to measure with a given degree of reliability than are any of the gross income items.

Evidence bearing on this matter has been offered by Greer[26] in the March 1938 issue of *The Accounting Review*, where he

24 Donald B. Woodward, "Changes in Capital Financing," *Journal of the American Statistical Association*, March 1938, p. 13.
25 John B. Canning, *The Economics of Accountancy* (New York, The Ronald Press Company, 1929), p. 127.
26 Howard C. Greer, "What Are Accepted Principles of Accounting?" *The Accounting Review*, March 1938, p. 27.

tells of an investigation of 150 statements referring to 20 industrial enterprises, all of which had been audited by firms of Certified Public Accountants. He says:

> The examination of these statements discloses a considerable lack of uniformity in the treatment of items and transactions of identical character. These variations have been sufficient to convert losses into profits, to alter materially the values assigned to important assets, and to render the several statements wholly noncomparable except with the substantial revisions in the interests of consistency.

First he made a restrictive and then a liberal application of one of the tentative codes of accounting principles. The restrictive application showed an aggregate net profit for all of the companies combined of about $125,000,000, while the more liberal application would have produced a profit of $275,000,000.

In commenting upon this investigation, he said it was noteworthy that "none of the differences result from the difficulties of measurement of values (in which accounting judgment is considered so important) ; they arise exclusively from differing opinions as to what constitutes a profit."[27] Is it any wonder, then, that those who attempt to interpret accounting reports should find themselves so thoroughly handicapped by the basic nature of the materials offered for their study?

Conclusion.—Perhaps the best of all technical assertions as to the significance of accounting profit was Canning's.[28] His statement which follows must surely express the opinion of all accountants who have given serious thought to the problem: "what is set out as a measure of net income can never be supposed to be a fact in any sense at all except that it is the figure that results when the accountant has finished applying the procedure which he adopts."

Any suggestion that such a comment is destructive rather than constructive should be stoutly resisted. Accounting does not require an apologist even though it often requires an interpreter. It is in his rôle of interpreter that the accountant excels.

27 Howard C. Greer, "What Are Accepted Principles of Accounting?" *The Accounting Review,* March 1938, p. 29.

28 John B. Canning, *The Economics of Accountancy* (New York, The Ronald Press Company, 1929), p. 98.

Admitting that accounting has certain limitations, it may well be argued that these limitations are inherent in its functional design and that they are sources of strength rather than weakness. If it be granted that accounting is primarily a device or mechanism for the purpose of providing a historical financial record of charge and discharge relationships, the accounting mechanism is admirably adapted to that primary purpose.

That accounting requires interpretation is clearly evident when one considers the various interests affected thereby. Those who insist that the accounting facts should be separately reported and interpreted for specific classes of readers stand on firm ground. Surely the report which is ideally adapted for the creditor must fall short of an effective presentation to the investor, to the tax collector, or to management. Certain profit distortions of great significance to the investor may be of slight importance to the tax authority. Certain adjustments and revaluations of primary importance to the creditor may be no more than confusing annoyances to the business man.

Understanding of conventionalized and often arbitrary accounting figures requires not so much a knowledge of the technical procedures used in preparing accounting records as it does a knowledge and an evaluation of the various factors which have made accounting what it is. It is in the understanding of these influences and their effects that the roots of accounting interpretation are found.

INDEX